D0218516

Britain and the European Union

This engaging and concise text offers the student and the general reader a compact, readable treatment of British membership of the European Union from 1973 to the present day. It provides a highly distilled and accessible analysis and overview of some of the parameters and recurring features of Britain's membership of the European Union, touching on all of the major facets of membership.

Key features:

- examines the constant and changing character of British membership of the European Union (EU);
- discusses the problematical and often paradoxical features of membership;
- familiarizes the reader with both academic and public debates about the subject;
- offers thematic treatment of all aspects of policy and attitudes towards the EU;
- provides an overview of the main landmarks in the history of the EU since 1973;
- presents the most comprehensive and up-to-date text on the course and result of the EU referendum campaign.

This book will be of key interest to scholars, students and the generally interested reader in the areas of European Studies, British Politics, EU Studies, Area Studies and International Relations.

David Gowland was Director of the School of Contemporary European Studies and also Head of the History Department at the University of Dundee. He is the author of numerous successful books and articles including Longman's *The European Mosaic* series and *Britain and European Integration since 1945* (Routledge).

Britain and the European Union

David Gowland

Routledge
Taylor & Francis Group

LONDON AND NEW YORK

First published 2017
by Routledge
2 Park Square, Milton Park, Abingdon, Oxon OX14 4RN

and by Routledge
711 Third Avenue, New York, NY 10017

Routledge is an imprint of the Taylor & Francis Group, an informa business

© 2017 David Gowland

British Library Cataloguing in Publication Data
A catalogue record for this book is available from the British Library

Library of Congress Cataloguing in Publication Data
Names: Gowland, David.
Title: Britain and the European Union / David Gowland.
Description: Abingdon, Oxon; New York, NY: Routledge, 2017. |
Includes bibliographical references and index.
Identifiers: LCCN 2016017217| ISBN 9781138825093 (hardback) |
ISBN 9781138825109 (pbk.) | ISBN 9781315463537 (ebook)
Subjects: LCSH: European Union–Great Britain.
Classification: LCC HC240.25.G7 G683 2017 | DDC 341.242/20941–dc23
LC record available at https://lccn.loc.gov/2016017217

ISBN: 978-1-138-82509-3 (hbk)
ISBN: 978-1-138-82510-9 (pbk)
ISBN: 978-1-315-46353-7 (ebk)

Typeset in Times New Roman
by Out of House Publishing

For Flynn, Effie, Diane and Dudley –
and in memory of Isabelle

Contents

List of tables and boxes   xi
Preface   xiii
List of abbreviations   xiv

Introduction   1

1 Europe and the European Union   20

2 Back to the future   46

3 Belonging without believing   80

4 Leading from behind: opt-outs, opt-ins and red lines   111

5 Party games and politics   144

6 Devolution and European Union membership   177

7 The press and the European Union   199

8 The 'Bloody British Question'   219

9 Brief encounters and quick exits: the pound and
   Europe 1970–1992   237

10 The pound, the euro and the City   251

11 Britain, the European Union and the wider world   273

12 Still leading from behind: the Conservatives and the
    European Union since 2010   303

Conclusion: journey to an unknown destination   327

Appendix: how the European Union works   364
Chronological table   369
Bibliography   377
Index   393

List of tables and boxes

Tables

1.1	European Union: population and gross domestic product (GDP) data for 2014	31
1.2	The share of the European Union and four individual EU states in world trade in goods and services in 2004 and 2012	32
1.3	General government deficit/surplus of the EU states, 2010–2013	40
2.1	Relative values of British trade with the Commonwealth, the sterling area and Western Europe, 1952–1954	57
2.2	Coal and steel production 1938 and 1949	58
2.3	Britain: 'The sick man of Europe'	63
3.1	UK balance of trade with the EC, 1970–1977	88
3.2	Eurobarometer opinion poll (Spring 1983)	92
3.3	The turnout for the first directly elected European Parliament in 1979	93
3.4	Knowledge of European Union institutions in Britain compared with the EU average	109
3.5	Trust in European Union institutions compared with EU average	109
4.1	Estimate of the resident population of the UK (by non-British nationality) 2004–2012	126
5.1	European Parliament election results May 2014: British representation	170
5.2	European Parliament election turnout percentage for the United Kingdom and the average EU turnout 1979–2014	173
5.3	Social background of 'inners', 'outers' and 'undecided' voters	174
5.4	Attitudes towards Britain's continuing membership of the EU, 1983–2014	175
6.1	Views on Britain's long term EU strategy by country	194
7.1	Circulation figures of a selection of British newspapers: 1987, 2000, 2014	217
8.1	Britain's EU contributions, rebates and receipts	222
9.1	The value of the intra-European Community trade of each EC member state expressed as a percentage of each state's total exports in 1958 and 1980	242
9.2	The UK's annual import and export trade statistics (2012)	242
10.1	MORI public opinion polls November 1997–July 1998	253
10.2	International market share by country (2013)	264
C.1	Overview of economic aspects of alternative relationships	339

C.2   Annual impact of leaving the EU on the UK after 15 years
      (difference from being in the EU)   341
C.3   How party voters divided in the EU referendum of 23 June 2016   355
C.4   Britain and the EU referendum of 23 June 2016: final result
      and results by country   356
C.5   How the regions voted in the Britain and EU referendum of
      23 June 2016   357
C.6   Survey of 12,369 people by gender, age and socio-economic
      classification after they had voted in the Britain and EU
      referendum 23 June 2016   358

Boxes

12.1   What's the EU ever done for us?   324
12.2   Arguments for Britain leaving the EU   325

Preface

This book provides thematic treatment of Britain's relationship with the process of European integration associated with the European Union (EU) over the past 70 years. This study covers the period down to the referendum of June 2016 on British membership of the EU. It should be emphasized, however, that the bulk of the book was written prior to the referendum campaign and result that feature in the concluding section.

The book deals with key features of the subject in a distilled manner with an introductory overview of some of the complexities surrounding the topic. The book also considers the most recent, problematical aspects of Britain's fraught relationship with the EU and in particular with the Eurozone, while recognizing that judgements about contemporary developments are hazardous and are like trying to hit a moving target.

Throughout the text, I have used the expressions Britain and British rather than United Kingdom, but only as a matter of convenience and not in all cases. The title 'United Kingdom of Great Britain and Northern Ireland' is, of course, the accurate description of the multinational state currently comprising England, Northern Ireland, Scotland and Wales. The expression United Kingdom acquired widespread use as Britain and Britishness became increasingly contested expressions during and after the 1970s, especially in Northern Ireland and Scotland.

I should like to express my deep gratitude to the editorial team at Routledge, most especially Craig Fowlie (Global Editorial Director) and Andrew Taylor (Senior Editor). Their encouragement and assistance have proved invaluable throughout the writing period. I am particularly grateful for their willingness to give me more time than originally scheduled to prepare the text. Special thanks are also due to two of my former colleagues, Dr Arthur Turner and Dr Alex Wright, for sharing their views about the subject in the course of many discussions.

I should also like to thank my wife, Helen. She has patiently tolerated my long absences in the study and my occasional preoccupied appearance, while rightly reminding me that there are more important things in life than writing books.

List of abbreviations

AfD	Alternative für Deutschland
ALDE	Alliance of Liberals and Democrats for Europe
BDOHP	British Diplomatic Oral History Programme
BSE	Bovine Spongiform Encephalopathy
BTO	Brussels Treaty Organization
CAP	Common Agricultural Policy
CBI	Confederation of British Industry
CCP	Common Commercial Policy
CEAS	Common European Asylum System
CERN	European Council for Nuclear Research
CETA	Comprehensive Economic and Trade Agreement
CFP	Common Fisheries Policy
CFSP	Common Foreign and Security Policy
CJD	Creutzfeldt-Jakob disease
CoR	Committee of the Regions
COREPER	Committee of Permanent Representatives
CSCE	Conference on Security and Cooperation in Europe
CSDP	Common Security and Defence Policy
DUP	Democratic Unionist Party
EAEC	European Atomic Energy Community
EAGF	European Agricultural Guarantee Fund
EaP	The Eastern Partnership
EBA	European Banking Authority
EC	European Community/ies
ECB	European Central Bank
ECHR	European Convention on Human Rights
ECJ	European Court of Justice
ECOFIN	European Council of Finance Ministers
ECR	European Conservatives and Reformists
ECSC	European Coal and Steel Community
ECU	European Currency Unit
EDC	European Defence Community
EEA	European Economic Area
EEAS	European External Action Service
EEC	European Economic Community
EFDD	Europe of Freedom and Direct Democracy
EFTA	European Free Trade Association
EMS	European Monetary System
EMU	Economic and Monetary Union

EP	European Parliament
EPC	European Political Cooperation
EPP	European People's Party (Christian Democrats)
ERC	European Research Council
ERDF	European Regional Development Fund
ERM	Exchange Rate Mechanism
ERP	European Recovery Programme
ERRF	European Rapid Reaction Force
ESCB	European System of Central Banks
ESDP	European Security and Defence Policy
EU	European Union
EUL/NGL	European United Left – Nordic Green Left
FCO	Foreign and Commonwealth Office
FDI	Foreign Direct Investment
FTA	Free Trade Area
FTT	Financial Transactions Tax
GATT	General Agreement on Tariffs and Trade
GCHQ	Government Communications Headquarters
GDP	Gross domestic product
GNI	Gross national income
GNP	Gross national product
Greens/EFA	Greens/European Free Alliance
IGC	Intergovernmental Conference
IMF	International Monetary Fund
JHA	Justice and Home Affairs
MEP	Member of the European Parliament
MFF	Multiannual Financial Framework
NATO	North Atlantic Treaty Organization
NEC	National Executive Committee
NFU	National Farmers Union
NI	Non-attached MEPs
NIESR	National Institute of Economic and Social Research
NRC	National Referendum Campaign
NSA	National Security Agency
OECD	Organization for Economic Cooperation and Development
OEEC	Organization for European Economic Cooperation
ONS	Office for National Statistics
OPEC	Organization of Petroleum Exporting Countries
OSCE	Organisation for Security and Cooperation in Europe
PASD	Progressive Alliance of Socialists and Democrats
PCJ	Police and Judicial Cooperation
PLP	Parliamentary Labour Party
PR	Proportional Representation
PSBR	Public Sector Borrowing Requirement
QE	Quantitative easing
QMV	Qualified majority voting
RBS	Royal Bank of Scotland
S&D	Progressive Alliance of Socialists and Democrats
SDI	Strategic Defence Initiative
SDLP	Social Democratic Labour Party
SDP	Social Democratic Party

SEA	Single European Act
SGP	Stability and Growth Pact
SHAPE	Supreme Headquarters Allied Powers Europe
SIS	Schengen Information System
SNP	Scottish National Party
STV	Single Transferable Vote
TEU	Treaty on European Union
TFEU	Treaty on the Functioning of the European Union
TSCG	Treaty on Stability, Coordination and Governance
TTIP	Transatlantic Trade and Investment Partnership
TUC	Trades Union Congress
UKRep	United Kingdom Permanent Representation
UKIP	UK Independence Party
UKSA	UK Statistics Authority
UN	United Nations
UNCTAD	United Nations Conference on Trade and Development
UUP	Ulster Unionist Party
VAT	Value Added Tax
WEU	Western European Union
WTO	World Trade Organisation

Introduction

The signatories of the Treaty are determined to lay the foundations of an ever closer union among the peoples of Europe.

(Treaty of Rome, 1957)

On 23 January 2013, David Cameron, prime minister of the Conservative–Liberal Democrat Coalition government, announced that a Conservative government, if elected after the next general election (May 2015), would arrange a referendum on Britain's membership of the European Union (EU). The referendum would be held by the end of 2017 and after a renegotiation of the country's relationship with the EU. On this occasion Cameron identified what he later described as the most important change that he wanted to achieve in the process of renegotiation: an opt-out for Britain from the EU's founding principle and first item in the preamble to the 1957 Treaty of Rome – 'ever closer union among the peoples of Europe'. That opt-out was agreed as part of the final, renegotiated settlement of Britain's relationship with the EU at the European Council meeting of 17/18 February 2016.

Whether the 'ever closer union' phrase is anything more than tokenistic or a symbol is a matter of debate, especially in the field of EU law. In the British case, the idea of the opt-out as a permanent road block to deeper integration may perhaps be viewed with the same scepticism as one historian's description of the collapse of the Soviet Union and the triumph of liberal democracy as 'the end of history'. In any event, whether temporary or permanent, the opt-out joins a number of other distinctive and highly conditional features of Britain's 43-year history of EU membership.

The decision to hold a referendum on EU membership on 23 June 2016 puts Britain in a league of its own with two referendums on EU membership (the first on 5 June 1975). None of the other 27 EU states has ever held a referendum on its EU membership. Ironically, a referendum was long regarded in Britain as an unwanted continental European device that undermined the very essence of British parliamentary government based on elected politicians taking decisions. Its use on two occasions is indicative of a highly problematical subject.

The subject matter of the book

This book deals with the single most controversial subject in British politics during the past 70 years. It focuses on the relationship between Britain and the process of European integration associated with the European Union (EU), formerly European

Communities (EC). The book serves as an introductory text that examines the substance and implications of British membership of the EU. Coverage includes some of the constant and changing features of membership together with the problematical and often paradoxical aspects of the subject. Both academic and public debates also receive attention. It should be emphasized that the subject is tackled with a view to providing an historical understanding of the nature, scope and significance of British policy and attitudes towards European integration.

Such an approach offers an analytical framework for understanding the evolution of policy and attitudes. It also allows for exploration of how and why the mental maps of policymakers and the public at large have developed with an array of powerful narratives, widespread myths and prejudices. Historical treatment may not be sufficient in itself to illuminate contemporary problems, but it certainly helps to trace the longevity of ideas about Britain's role and self-image in the European context. An understanding of long-term trends and developments and an awareness of the haunting of the present by the past can shed light on how and why the past informs the present and may shape the future. Furthermore, the historical arena comprises contested interpretations of the past that are of vital importance in shaping perceptions of the current state of affairs; it is also the site of the ideas, interests and institutions that have governed the options available to policymakers.

The analysis is principally focused on the nature and significance of national government and party politics in determining the nature and extent of British involvement in the EU. The influence and interplay of principles, policies and personalities figure prominently in this context. This approach, admittedly one among many, pays particular attention to the role and interaction of internal and external factors in accounting for the stance of successive governments. Some of the main themes in this context are the interrelationship between domestic and foreign policy, the changing mixture of real or perceived constraints, opportunities and threats that faced and continue to face policymakers, and the British contribution to the EU. The book also considers the impact of European integration on British politics and economic performance, and in particular the 'Europeanization' of policymaking previously under exclusively national control and jurisdiction.

The book has several particular objects in mind. In covering the often multidimensional character of British policy and attitudes towards the EU, much attention is given to the problems, preoccupations, choices and dilemmas confronting policymakers, together with the substance and significance of the debate between political parties. Such matters are considered in the context of the changing character of the international system and of responses to the dynamics of European integration. In addition, the treatment deals with several themes that are closely linked to the question of Britain and European integration: the loss of great power status, the management of relative economic decline, elitist and popular attitudes towards European integration, the strains in Britain's relationship with the EU, the tensions between the territorial components of Britain concerning EU membership, and the significance of Britain–USA relations. Finally in this respect, the book examines the degree of continuity and change in British policy and attitudes towards European integration over the past 70 years.

The lengthy history of British handling of EU membership often involves an unpredictable trajectory full of policy twists and turns. It is a history studded with unexpected decisions, unintended consequences, and exchanges in public debate occasionally bordering on the farcical and invariably highlighting an intensely awkward relationship and set of circumstances. The issue has accounted for a massive expenditure of political energy. It has also given rise to a frenzied debate – a tinnitus of endless sound – seemingly going round in circles amidst a cacophony about threats, red lines and opt-outs and replete with hysterical rhetoric and sensationalist press headlines, touching on if not always amounting to a consequential debate about the country's national and European identity, its role in the world, and its past and future.

Among academics and commentators, there is a profusion of explanations for the making and significance of past and present British policy and attitudes towards the EU. Accounts of the original British decision to join the EU have variously explained this move as reflecting a conspiracy of silence by a political elite wanting to dupe the public, as the actions of a defeatist set of politicians scared of arousing the passions of the electorate and knowingly or unknowingly deceiving themselves about the consequences of EU membership, as a substitute for the loss of Empire, as a quest for economic modernization, and as a battleground involving inter- and intra-party rivalries and conflicts – to name but a few examples.

In recent years, very different views of informed opinion have either portrayed the EU as an 'empire of lies' with Britain embarking on 'a voyage with the damned' (Bernard Connolly, *The Sunday Times*, 27 January 2013) or have despaired at the 'surreal', quite 'barmy' European debate in Britain (Philip Stephens, *Financial Times*, 17 January 2013). A Conservative commentator described the Eurosceptic elements in the party as comparable to quasi-religious fanaticism in viewing the EU as 'the Great Satan of their political lives' (Matthew Parris, *The Times*, 18 January 2014). Meanwhile, Tony Blair, a former prime minister, likened the EU policy of his successor, David Cameron, to that of the sheriff in the Mel Brooks comedy *Blazing Saddles* who holds a gun to his own head and says 'If you don't do what I want, I'll blow my brains out'. It was hardly necessary for Blair to add much later that a decision to exit the EU 'would say a lot about us, and none of it good' (*The Guardian*, 7 April 2015). By January 2016, the preliminary political skirmishes in the referendum campaign suggested to another commentator that 'the dispute over EU membership is beginning to resemble a game of paintball played by executives on an awayday' (Matthew d'Ancona, *The Guardian*, 18 January 2016).

There is little doubt, then, that the colourful and intense debate about British membership of the EU occasionally reflects all the ingredients of a pyscho-drama and a political soap opera. EU membership throughout much of continental Europe may be a routinized part of daily life, even in the worst of times since 2010 with the euro area crisis, the massive influx of migrants and the rising tide of Eurosceptic opinion, suggesting a shaking of the foundations. The question of EU membership in Britain, however, has long figured as a highly inflamed varicose vein in British politics.

A heavily conflicted story

In the circumstances, it is scarcely surprising that the public at large is variously amused, bemused and confused by the political theatre attending the debate about Britain and the EU. In that respect, there is much substance to the view, expressed in one of the most cogent critiques of the EU, that when looking for material to come to a view about EU membership 'many people find only the ravings of extremists on both sides of the debate, wads of incomprehensible statistics, or oodles of impenetrable Euro-speak' (Bootle, 2014: 3). Public debate about the matter is all the more problematical because the subject at its most partisan is full of questionable assumptions, hypothetical figures and creative accountancy. It is also a subject that attracts economic forecasting which can be an unreliable aid to understanding; 'The only function of economic forecasting is to make astrology look respectable' commented Ezra Solomon, a leading American economist.

Beneath the flotsam and jetsam of daily political life, however, there are strong currents of opinion indicative of a heavily conflicted story about Britain's European role, interests and identity. This condition is reflected in the choice of language often used to characterize British policy and attitudes towards the EU: ambivalent, reluctant, hesitant, awkward, prevaricating, vacillating, procrastinating. It is evident too in the well-known comment by Winston Churchill with its telling, qualifying clauses reflecting a Janus-faced outlook: 'We are with Europe, but not of it. We are linked, but not compromised. We are interested and associated, but not absorbed' (*Saturday Post*, 15 February 1930).

The mixture of opposing voices and tendencies has attended all sides of this question since 1945. In some respects EU membership has raised in an acute form substantive questions about national identity and independence and demonstrated longer-term, deep-seated tensions in British strategy towards the external world, especially involving the key concepts of limited liability and continental commitment (see Chapter 2). Particular aspects of such a condition usually take such forms as balancing a European heritage against a global outlook or insisting on being 'in' Europe but not 'run' by it.

Time and again, this position has resulted in descriptions of the relationship between Britain and the process of European integration that are puzzling and mystifying to politicians and public alike. In the 1950s, at the time of the emergence of the EC, a seemingly incomprehensible variety of terms was used by politicians to describe the relationship between Britain and the emerging EC, ranging from more or less benevolent neutrality, association and close association to closest association and near identification. Even Churchill was hard-pressed to characterize the relationship between Britain and Europe at this time, making do with convoluted, ambiguous phraseology: 'a separate closely – and specially – related ally and friend' (National Archives [hereafter NA.], CAB 129/48, C. (51) 32, 29 November 1951). This language was in keeping with the idea of Churchill as the 'Great Equivocator' and the 'grandiloquent map maker' who wanted to dissolve divisions between warring continental countries but cast Britain as a facilitator, even a mere spectator, of the process (Young, 1998: 17).

The exercise of summing up British policy and attitudes towards the EU as a member state has proved no easier. It is clearly hard to obtain a purchase on firmly established attitudes and warring impulses that often wish at one and the same time to preserve and to sever Britain's ties with the EU, or as one French politician characterized the attitude of a British political leader towards the EU: 'I love you very much and I will marry you as long as I remain single' (*Financial Times*, 23 January 2013). The mixed and divided character of such opinion suggests a long-standing and bewildering capacity to be unhappy fully inside the EU while also being unhappy to be completely outside.

It is certainly the case that no other issue in British domestic politics since 1945 has so dramatically and repeatedly exposed major faultlines within governments or so vividly revealed profound divisions whether within and between the major political parties or among interest groups and the public at large. Unsurprisingly, any attempt to manufacture a 'national' consensus in favour of closer union with continental Europe has met numerous obstacles ranging from a largely hostile press and weak political leadership to ignorance and lack of appeal among the public at large.

A particular difficulty is that public debate about the subject invariably exposes fundamental divisions of opinion over more general questions touching on national identity, independence and sovereignty. Such matters have become all the more complicated and contested in recent times in a State that is subject to centrifugal forces at the extremes: from Scotland divided by tribal passions and seemingly on the cusp of national independence at one end to the 'city-state' pretensions and global, cosmopolitan character of London at the other. In that respect, this subject also ranks high in the class of issues that reveals much about the country's political culture. Furthermore, no other field of government policy has so persistently and devastatingly damaged the authority of prime ministers and the careers of Cabinet ministers in arguably the longest and most brutal saga of British politics since 1945.

Some problems and warnings

One way of approaching the seemingly interminable British debate about EU membership is to acknowledge some of the problems involved in tackling the subject. The subject can be framed in myriad ways when attempting to determine the weighting and influence of the factors shaping policy and attitudes. Treatment takes in a wide spectrum of protracted processes from the insular and European to the Atlantic and global. Coverage can also involve a variety of perspectives extending from high principle, strategic overview and grand designs about Britain's role and status in the wider world to low tactics and calculations of party or personal advantage.

It is also the case that studies of the subject have reflected the particular interests and expertise of the scholar. In the case of the political scientist, the focus of attention is often on theories of integration and comparative politics. In the case of the historian, detailed study draws on a number of different branches of historical scholarship such as international, diplomatic, economic, political, cultural and financial history. Unsurprisingly, therefore, this multifaceted subject can be approached and understood through a number of different pathways and perspectives.

A further problem in studying this subject concerns the availability of evidence. Part of the period covered in this book draws on publicly accessible and voluminous primary source material under the operation of the 30-year rule applying to British government papers. Any study of the more recent period, however, still has to rely mainly on secondary source material including the autobiographies of some of the principals involved in EU affairs.

Recollections in the form of political memoirs, however, are written with hindsight and, when not taking the form of self-serving mythology distorted by a private or partisan agenda, sometimes amount to what Alan Taylor once described as 'a form of oral history set down to mislead historians'. They may differ significantly from what the subject thought was happening at the time. At worst they may amount to unilluminating examples of 'old men drooling' or autobiographies motivated by a 'duty to history' and giving expression to the saying that history is the abused and forgotten orphan of politics. 'I gave up reading fiction long ago', commented Aneurin Bevan, one of the leading political figures of mid-twentieth-century British politics, when asked for his opinion about the memoirs of one of his Cabinet colleagues. No doubt he would have said the same about Churchill's history of the Second World War in the light of Churchill's view that 'History will judge us kindly because I shall write the history' (Churchill to Roosevelt and Stalin at the Tehran Conference in 1943).

This is not to say that primary source material should have privileged status or that historical studies cannot be undertaken while waiting for the documents to appear. Some questionable assumptions underlie what is described as document fetishism, not least of these being that the documents will yield major revelations and that they will provide evidence unavailable from other sources.

It is also the case that a selection process occurs before documents see the light of day, and numerous files are unavailable for public scrutiny. In July 2013, the Foreign and Commonwealth Office (hereafter FCO) admitted that it had withheld 1.2 million files that should have been sent to the National Archives. The files shed fresh light among other things on human rights abuses in the later stages of British colonial administration. These revelations outraged several leading historians who are not only concerned that major works about contemporary British and imperial history may need to be rewritten but also fear that the FCO has been attempting to manipulate favourable impressions of Britain's imperial past (*The Guardian*, 14 January 2014).

Any book on Britain and the EU is part of recent history which is by definition incomplete and runs the risk of lacking comprehensiveness and perspective. There is the particular difficulty of making sense of recent developments at a time of considerable flux and uncertainty. The major, problematical impact of the global financial crash of 2007–2008 and of the ensuing recession on the EU, on the euro area and on Britain continue to leave problems of analysis and meaning. Generalizations abound and are soon overtaken by events. In 2012, most of the British press predicted the collapse of the euro area was in the offing, while in 2013 it held that the end of British membership of the EU was imminent. Neither event has come to pass at the time of writing. In fact, as compared with the constant stream of British predictions regarding the break-up of the EC/EU over the past 60 years, Britain has come much closer than the euro area to a near-death experience in the Scotland independence referendum of September 2014. It is still unclear whether the Union of 1707 is on a life support system and in the throes of terminal decline or is about to morph into a federal system, disjointed or otherwise.

Lies, damned lies and statistics

Some further warnings about the handling of the subject matter should be noted, particularly relating to the statistical quagmire surrounding the subject, the character of the public debate, the use of language, and the dangers of headline or soundbite history.

A key element in the debate about Britain and the EU is the use and abuse of statistics in seeking to demonstrate the gross and net cost and impact of membership. Several aspects of EU membership are measurable, most notably financial contributions to and receipts from the EU budget, though even in this field the accounting system can be a mystery (see Chapter 8). It is also possible to put a figure on such matters as the value of British exports to the rest of the EU; the EU accounted for 50.5 per cent of total British exports in 2012 (HMRC overseas trade statistics, www.hmrc.gov.uk/statistics/trade-statistics.htm). Yet even that figure can be challenged with reference to the so-called Rotterdam-Antwerp effect, meaning that British trade with the Netherlands and Belgium, and therefore with the EU as a whole, is significantly over-inflated because many British exports to the Netherlands and Belgium are destined for the ports of Rotterdam and Antwerp for onward supply to countries outside the EU. Similarly, imports from the Netherlands may also simply be goods from outside the EU that arrived in Rotterdam from other non-EU countries on their way to the UK (for further details see HM Government, 'Review of the Balance of Competences between the

United Kingdom and the European Union Single Market: Free Movement of Goods', February 2014).

Public confidence in national statistics has also been undermined by parliamentary criticism of the Office for National Statistics (ONS), the country's largest independent producer of official statistics. Andrew Tyrie, the chairman of the parliamentary Treasury Select Committee, criticized the ONS for falling behind its international peers and jeopardizing policy decisions with poor quality data. In sum, according to Tyrie, the ONS had fallen 'a long way short, lacking intellectual curiosity, prone to silly mistakes', while its watchdog, the UK Statistics Authority (UKSA), set up to safeguard the quality of official statistics, had been 'asleep on the job' (*The Guardian*, 8 January 2016).

A further complicating feature concerns the extent to which competing claims about the impact of EU membership are based on questionable statistics that become entrenched in the public consciousness. A case in point involves the relationship between Britain's EU membership and employment figures. In October 2011, Nick Clegg, deputy prime minister in the Coalition government, claimed that the jobs of three million British citizens relied solely on Britain's current participation in the EU. This popular pro-EU argument entered the public domain following two reports on the subject in 2000 by the South Bank University and by the National Institute of Economic and Social Research (NIESR). Use of the three million figure, however, is questionable on several grounds. The figures are dated and neither report made Clegg's claim. Indeed, the NIESR report concluded that there was no reason to suppose that many, if any jobs, would be lost if Britain left the EU. Furthermore, it is argued that any statistics based purely on trade with the EU do not offer a fair cost–benefit analysis of the impact of EU membership on the labour market (Full Fact, 2 November 2011).

In some cases there is a limited availability of robust statistical data. This feature can give rise to untested or untestable general statements that stoke further controversy on particularly sensitive matters. The issue of welfare benefits for migrants entering Britain from the rest of the EU is a case in point (see Chapter 12). The Cameron government highlighted the subject in its renegotiation of the terms of EU membership programme. However, as one detailed government report on the free movement of persons within the EU conceded, only limited data is currently available concerning the numbers of EU migrants claiming benefits in Britain and the numbers of British citizens claiming benefits in other EU countries (HM Government, 'Review of the Balance of Competences between the United Kingdom and the European Union Single Market: Free Movement of Persons', Summer 2014: 7).

Very different constructions can be placed on the same set of figures, or as the old adage puts it: 'Torture a statistic long enough and it will tell you anything'. Statistical data can also leave the impression of spurious precision by quantification (as in the case of the three million figure noted above) and of being mistaken for indisputable facts. This practice is all the more the case in public debates about EU membership as figures are cherry-picked to support predetermined positions. Needless to say, all statistics in this book come with the warning that they are at best indicative, always contestable and never definitive.

The 'EU effect'

There is also the major problem of distinguishing between the 'EU effect' and the influence of other factors on economic performance and trading patterns. During the

1950s, when the EC came into being (see below), the six founding member states of the organization experienced economic growth and trade expansion before the EEC Treaty of Rome took effect (January 1959). Contrary to opinion in some quarters at the time, the EC thus reinforced rather than caused economic growth and trade expansion, but by how much has been and still is a matter of debate. A further disputed feature concerns the difficulty of determining the relative importance of two types of trade associated with the workings of a customs union: trade creation and trade diversion. Academic debate about the subject centres on the extent to which a customs union creates trade within the union but also diverts trade from countries outside the union.

The EC's Single Market initiative of 1986 is a further example of the difficulties involved in determining the impact of one measure. The initiative was accompanied by some extravagant claims about its positive impact including promises of economic efficiency gains. The precise effects, however, are not easily measurable or detected. The Single Market belongs to the class of continuous creation rather than 'big bang' acts, a process with a 1992 deadline but actually stretching down to the present day and beyond in terms of detailed legislation, especially in the increasingly important services sector such as banking, insurance and health care.

Whose interest?

There are also problems involved in determining who exactly gains and who loses in the process. Assessing the pros and cons of EU membership becomes all the more complicated when taking stock of the diverse economic interests involved in the matter. Determining what is in the British interest will reflect a balance of competing concerns, which may not always align. Competing producers may have different views on whether competitors should be allowed to enter the EU and British market, consumers may desire a different outcome in terms of access to imports than domestic producers, and taxpayer interest may be different again.

Understandably, it can be argued that there has been no convincing or comprehensive estimate of the welfare effects of British membership of the EU. Thus, for example, while it is possible to maintain that British entry to the EC in the 1970s worsened the UK's trade balance in manufactures (see Chapter 3), the greater availability of manufactured goods from elsewhere in the EU contributed to economic welfare, making an overall judgment of the economic pros and cons of EC membership problematical (HM Government, 'Review of the Balance of Competences between the United Kingdom and the European Union Trade and Investment', February 2014: 53).

Any assessment of the value or benefits of EU membership is also dependent on the criteria to be used in judging the balance sheet. Whether it is considered important that Britain should have a world role or not makes a considerable difference to any judgement (Ash, 2009: 121). In effect, a set of criteria that privileges Britain's external role and standing in the world in assessing the value of EU membership may be altogether different from a set of criteria that prioritize exclusively domestic controls over national borders or welfare matters.

The counterfactual

It is also the case that the debate about EU membership often enters the realms of the counterfactual or what might happen/have happened in the event of an alternative course of action. At that point an analytical fog can easily descend on some murky data. This condition often leaves a trail of unanswerable questions full of opposing conjectures and guesstimates whether speculating about the past – Britain joining the EC in the 1950s rather than in the 1970s – or the future – Britain exiting the EU (commonly referred to as 'Brexit'). There are of course even more general counterfactuals about the EC/EU and whether, for example, the economic growth and trade expansion of the founder members of the EC that was evident before the formation of the EC would have been significantly different in the absence of the EC.

The answers are unknowable, and yet the case for and against EC/EU membership is often based on such unknowables and counterfactuals. Supporters of EU membership invariably cite the EU's role in the emergence of a peaceful, democratic Europe while opponents argue for an alternative to membership. In both cases, however, we are being invited to enter the realms of the counterfactual. One authoritative study about the possibility of Brexit concluded with a wide range of calculations covering several percentage points depending on pessimistic or optimistic calculations (Ottaviano *et al.*, 2014). Another such study on the effects of Brexit varied in its estimate of the likely impact between a best case scenario that Britain's GDP would be 1.6 per cent higher by 2030 and a worst-case scenario of GDP being 2.2 per cent lower by the same date (Open Europe and Ciuriak Consulting, March 2015). Such statistics suggest that the economic case either for or against EU membership is far from conclusive.

Much is open to conjecture in this respect, as such studies may deal with so many values, imponderables and difficulties such as foreseeing how the government of the day would fill the gaps, and at what cost, left by withdrawal from the EU. In short, the argument that Britain stands a better chance of growth outside the EU is a claim about the future based on trading relations that do not yet exist. It is equally the case that an argument in favour of EU membership may amount to a claim about the future that is inherently unknowable.

The fact of the matter is that the pros and cons of EU membership are not susceptible to a strict cost–benefit analysis. There is no definitive, detached and widely accepted study of either the economic impact of EU membership or of the costs and benefits of withdrawing from the EU. One study of the subject concluded that 'Framing the aggregate impact in terms of a single number, or even irrefutably demonstrating that the net effects are positive or negative, is a formidably difficult exercise' (cited in Bootle, 2014: 243).

It is also important to note that numerous studies often arrive at different conclusions due to methodological variations and diverse assumptions. To take a case in point, it is possible to draw a distinction between a static and dynamic approach to the cost of Britain's EU membership. Most studies that find a significant net cost to membership take a static approach, calculating the various impacts – fiscal, regulatory, trade-related – and summing them to produce an overall cost. Against that position, however, studies that find a net benefit tend to look at the long-term effects of EU membership (as against some more restrictive trading arrangement) with gains accruing each year in the form of higher trade flows and foreign direct investment serving to offset the clear fiscal cost (House of Commons Library, 1 July 2013).

Apart from the problems of calculating the precise significance of economic factors, there are non-economic factors and considerations that enter into the question of EC/EU membership. Such aspects are even less measurable or quantifiable than economic factors. Yet they may be equally if not more important in any assessment of the advantages and disadvantages of EU membership, as we will see later.

'An incoming tide': the European Union in Britain

What is indisputable is that controversy about EU membership has become all the more intense over the years as a result of the changing boundary lines between foreign and domestic policy in the conduct of Britain's relations with continental Europe. At the beginning of the period covered by this book, continental Europe was widely perceived in British circles as belonging to the foreign policy sphere. Europe had long figured as the object of British policies of intervention and non-intervention. It was not perceived as the source of institutions and measures penetrating domestic affairs. EC/EU membership, however, has transformed this relationship. It has made for a much more fragmented, untidy process of policymaking across government departments and at different levels. EC/EU legislation has gradually impinged on numerous areas of national life to the point where domestic law on many issues is a product of negotiations and decisions reached in Brussels.

Shortly after delivering his judgment on the first case in the British courts concerning the application of EC law (22 November 1974), Lord Denning commented on the immediate and longer-term significance of the EEC Treaty of Rome: 'the Treaty is like an incoming tide. It flows into the estuaries and up the rivers. It cannot be held back' (*The Times*, 29 April 1978). Therein lay a measure of what the public failed to grasp and what its political leadership rarely explained about EC/EU membership, namely that it was not a case of signing up to a clear, finite set of arrangements but rather a matter of participating in a never-ending process. Thus, Denning later (1990) concluded that EU law was no longer like an incoming tide but 'like a tidal wave bringing down our sea walls and flowing inland over our fields and houses' (quoted in Charter, 2012: 40–1).

What Denning did not say but might have added is that the 'incoming tide' brought imprints of a constitutional and legal culture markedly different from the unwritten constitution and common law emphases that had for so long characterized English political life. It should be noted, however, that there is a marked difference between the common law systems of England, Northern Ireland and Wales, and Scotland's legal system that incorporates elements from both common and civil law traditions.

By contrast, the six founder member states of the EC (see below) were the possessors of newly minted post-war constitutions which, together with a Roman law tradition and Continental style civil codes, specifically detailed the rights, duties and obligations of their citizens. In 2014, David Neuberger, president of the UK's Supreme Court, observed that because of their written constitutions, other European countries were used to judges acting as a check on politicians while Britain is not, and therefore the overruling of decisions by the EU's Court of Justice 'is little short of offensive to our notions of constitutional propriety' (*The Daily Telegraph*, 14 February 2014).

The precise amount of legislation that arises from EU membership poses another virtually impossible problem of exact measurement. Steve Hilton, David Cameron's former director of strategy and no supporter of the EU's endless rules and regulations, once calculated that some 40 per cent of government business was about implementing EU regulations. A House of Commons Library research paper, however, concluded that 'there is no totally accurate, rational or useful way of calculating the percentage of national laws based on or influenced by the EU'. The same paper maintained that it is possible to justify any measure between 15 per cent and 50 per cent or thereabouts (House of Commons Library Research Paper, 'How much legislation comes from

Europe?' 10/62, 13 October 2010). Much depends among other things on the definition of 'UK law'. A definition comprising the following (acts put in place by the UK parliament, rules and regulations drawn up by ministers, and regulations produced by the EU which apply in the UK) results in the following estimates:

- Acts put in place by UK parliament with EU influence – account for 10–14 per cent.
- Regulations influenced by or related to the EU – account for 9–14 per cent.
- EU regulations and regulations influenced by or related to the EU – account for 53 per cent (https:fullfact.org/wp-content/uploads/2014/03/UK).

All studies agree that the influence of the EU is significant, and understandably so in view of its wide-ranging remit, including:

agriculture, fisheries and foods
border check, asylum and immigration policy
business
citizens' rights
civil and criminal and police matters
climate action
commercial policy and finance
culture, education and youth
economic, monetary and tax policy
employment and social policy
energy and natural resources
environment, consumer protection and public health
external relations, foreign affairs, defence and security policy
justice and home affairs (JHA)
regions and local development
science and technology
single market
transport and travel.

This extensive list testifies to the extensive degree of what has been called 'quiet Europeanization' that has penetrated the British political and economic system at primary and secondary order levels.

Sampling Britain's European dilemma

Divisions of opinion about British membership of the EU are also related to some of the major predicaments affecting policymakers and also of the extent to which a particular view may have a degree of substance. Two illustrations from the early period of Britain's engagement with the process of European integration demonstrate how the issue has been framed as a policy dilemma of the highest order.

First, in 1956 British policymakers believed that they were impaled on the horns of an acute dilemma in the wake of the decision by the six founder member states of the EC/EU – Belgium, France, Italy, Luxembourg, the Netherlands and West Germany (known as the Six in the literature) – to forge ahead with the common market idea. Peter Thorneycroft, president of the Board of Trade at the time, succinctly described the predicament: 'On any analysis it seems clear that we cannot afford that the Common Market should either succeed, or fail, without us' (NA., FO 371/122034).

In short, a common market without Britain would immediately have damaging effects on Britain's trading ties with the Six. In the longer run, such a prospect also presented the threat of a narrow, regional, German-dominated power bloc in Europe. Furthermore, a common market without Britain would seriously undermine the country's traditional, if self-styled, role and influence in Europe whether in maintaining a balance of power or in mediating in Franco-German conflicts. Such a project would also jeopardize Britain's standing in Washington and in the western system at large.

That said, however, it was also the case, warned Thorneycroft, that the collapse of the common market project would have dire consequences. It would weaken west European unity, resulting in an isolationist France and German revanchiste adventures in eastern Europe. It would divide the western alliance and possibly realize the worst security fears of the British government in the form of the withdrawal of the United States from Europe, while also leaving Britain exposed to European and US criticism for jeopardizing the project. And for historians who see parallels between now and then and who have noted the continuity as much as the change in British policy towards European integration since 1945, similar issues resonate down the years with due recognition of changing circumstances in the form of Britain coming to terms with the euro area and in relation to the debate about Britain's withdrawal from the EU. One challenge for British governments down to the present day was expressed by Prime Minister Harold Macmillan in 1959: 'The question is how to live with the Common Market economically and turn its political effects into channels harmless to us' (NA., PREM 11/2985).

The second illustration goes to the heart of the interminable argument about Europe in Britain. It reflects a kaleidoscope of different views rather than the often absolutist, all-or-nothing representations of the debate. In the summer of 1964, Con O'Neill, the British ambassador to the EC in Brussels, sent a despatch to the Foreign Office in which he observed that at one extreme the EC could be regarded as the most hopeful experiment in international relations embarked on for generations and one that Britain should be proud to join for both idealistic and interested reasons. At the other extreme, however, the EC could be regarded as constituting potentially, and already to some extent in fact, the kind of European structure against which Britain has repeatedly throughout its history gone to war. For those who take this view, O'Neill added, the EC has almost succeeded, by stealth, in achieving what Napoleon and Hitler failed to achieve by force: a Europe united without Britain and therefore against her. The problem, as O'Neill concluded, was that there was some truth in both extremes and also in all possible views in between (quoted in Wall, 2013: 80).

It is precisely this problem that makes for finely balanced judgments about the advantages and value of EU membership. Unlike the original member states of the EC, Britain had no overriding, fundamental or compelling reason for making European integration its top foreign policy priority. At least the case for making it such over the past 60 years was never entirely clear and convincing. The seeming absence of a definitive, unanswerable case for EU membership has fuelled an endless debate about the subject. Peter Mandelson, a former member of the EU Commission and keen supporter of EU membership, conceded that 'there was never a knockdown argument as to why Britain had to take the bold and uncertain leap of joining [the EC]' (*The Guardian*, 18 January 2007). Neither is there likely to be a 'knockdown' argument for leaving the EU any time soon (Open Europe, 2 February 2015), thus providing ample space for further controversy over the subject.

Word games and the European issue

The often frenzied debate about EU membership is also shot through with loose, emotive language that obscures as much as it reveals, often debasing language and meaning alike. In his essay – *Politics and the English Language* (1946) – George Orwell observed that political language has to consist largely of euphemism, question-begging and sheer cloudy vagueness. The manipulation of words by politicians to control the way people think meant, as he put it, the invasion of one's mind by ready-made phrases, each of which 'anaesthetises a portion of one's brain'. The essay is worthy of study by anyone seeking to get to grips with the way in which presentations and understandings of Britain's membership of the EU have developed over time.

Words like sovereignty, threat, fear, invasion, menace, identity and 'Brussels' are used liberally and in ill-defined ways to trigger a certain reaction. 'Brussels' alone conjures up a large number of connotations in the British discourse about the EU: remote, unaccountable, costly, wasteful. Similarly, shorthand expressions such as Europhile and Eurosceptic can have many meanings and mistakenly suggest a clear-cut division between two rival camps (see Chapter 5). Given the very limited knowledge of the EU among the public at large as testified by numerous opinion polls, it is not difficult for demonizing narratives as well as ingrained stereotypes to creep into British media representations of the EU, unhesitatingly stoking up hysteria and disseminating a shoal of myths (see Chapter 7).

It is equally easy for evidence-free assertions and concepts to seep into the popular consciousness. One such case concerns the use of the term 'benefit tourism' in connection with EU membership. The expression could be understood as referring to all manner of things. Some might see it as an appropriate description of Members of the European Parliament (MEPs) belonging to the United Kingdom Independence Party (UKIP) that is opposed to EU membership. According to the UKIP leader, Nigel Farage, the party's MEPs do little or no work in Strasbourg and Brussels but take as much public money as possible in the form of salaries and expenses while raging against 'welfare cheats' from eastern Europe (*The Guardian*, 27 May 2014). In other quarters the expression might be seen as referring to the benefits reaped by the owners of capital from the free movement of capital – one of the cornerstones of the EU. In still other quarters, it might be taken to mean either British nationals in nine of the other EU states who are banking unemployment cheques almost three times as high as the nationals of those countries receiving parallel British benefits or the cost to other states of medical treatment for British tourists in the EU that is five times higher than that of treating visitors from other EU states to Britain (*The Guardian*, 20 January 2015, 8 April 2015). In fact, the expression 'benefit tourism' is more commonly used in British political discourse either ostensibly to seek to curb the free movement of EU citizens within the EU (which is another of the EU's cornerstones) or as a scapegoat that panders to insecurities and prejudices.

The concept of sovereignty is a further example of a much used term with very different meanings and applications. A dictionary definition (*Oxford English Dictionary*) is at once concise and problematical: 'supremacy in respect of power or rank; supreme authority'. Parliamentary sovereignty is commonly regarded as the defining principle of the British constitution and one to which opponents of EU membership return time and again on the grounds that membership is inconsistent with this fundamental British tradition.

This meaning, however, becomes clouded whether in understanding the relationship between the executive and the legislature or in terms of the impact of European and devolution processes on parliamentary sovereignty. Furthermore, the European Communities Act (1972) – the foundation stone of Britain's EU membership – does not allow any EU institution to touch or qualify the conditions of parliament's supremacy in the UK. In short, although EU treaties and judgments of the EU courts provide that certain provisions of the treaties, legal instruments made under them, and judgments of the EU courts have direct application or effect in the domestic law of all member states, such EU law is enforceable in the UK only because domestic legislation, in particular the European Communities Act, makes express provisions for this. Nevertheless, the relationship between the EU and parliamentary sovereignty has remained a matter of debate down to the present day, arising at the time of the Cameron government's renegotiation of Britain's terms of EU membership (see Chapter 12).

National sovereignty is another problematical expression as the United Kingdom comprises four nations. Parliamentary sovereignty is an equally contested concept, as in Scotland where it is widely viewed as a distinctively English principle, classically expounded by A. V. Dicey, the jurist and constitutional theorist, in his major work *Introduction to the Study of the Law of the Constitution* (1885). The concept has no counterpart in Scots constitutional law. The indigenous Scottish tradition and doctrine of popular sovereignty is held to date back to the Declaration of Arbroath (1320). Before the 1707 Act of Union, sovereignty resided in the Scottish people and still does, as acknowledged by later events. The 1953 case of *MacCormick* v. *Lord Advocate* in the Court of Session clearly upheld the view that sovereignty rests with the people. So, too, did the Claim of Right for Scotland (1989) signed by the great majority of Scotland's MPs and many leaders of Scottish civil society.

Other very diverse views of sovereignty have had an enduring bearing on the question of EU membership. Theoretical sovereignty as formal or symbolic control signifying little if any substance exists at one end of a spectrum of opinion. At the other end of this spectrum there lies the idea of what is termed real or actual sovereignty, meaning the degree of control a country can exercise. Between these two positions there lies the controversial subject of losing or pooling sovereignty in the international sphere in such an organization as the EC/EU. There is also ample scope for differences of view about the relationship between power and sovereignty and the validity of the view at one extreme that 'A man in the desert is sovereign. He is also powerless' (*Financial Times*, 20 October 2004).

Further out in this field, there are also different views as to what counts as a loss of sovereignty in a wider meaning of that term whether, for example, any of the following relate to or challenge the idea of sovereignty: foreign ownership of one-third of the British infrastructure, foreign ownership of more than half of the market value of British listed firms, and the proposed Transatlantic Trade and Investment Partnership between the EU and the United States reportedly making provision for a secretive panel of corporate lawyers to overrule the will of parliament and destroy legal protections.

Popular understandings of Britain's EU membership are often derived from a simplified, two-dimensional pantomime routine of foot-stamping, finger-wagging and name-calling. The heroes and villains are clearly identified in the binary terms of all the black-and-white certainties of a triumphalist or defeatist story. There is little scope for acknowledging messy, complicated, contradictory and multilayered elements in this type of narrative or for recognizing the value of a nuanced, historical account. A mishmash of ignorance, prejudice and myth is easily entrenched in the simplifications of popular memory and consciousness that are often shaped and perpetuated by sound-bite or headline history.

It is often the case that assertions and perceptions that were shaped by the propaganda of the time harden into fixed narratives and acquire the status of seemingly immutable historical truths. In fact, highly questionable press versions of 'the first draft of history' with the emphasis on gladiatorial debate and kneejerk reactions often make the distorting mirror of some sections of the British press the least useful vantage point from which to view the EU at large. Scare stories about the EU, in particular, play to a nexus of easy media sensationalism that is aimed at sections of the public ready to believe the worst in the form of anti-immigration views and xenophobic tendencies.

Varieties of history

Among historians much of the detailed, monographic work on Britain and the EC/EU has so far concentrated on the period 1945–1980, making extensive use of government papers in the National Archives under the 30-year rule. According to some of the early studies of the subject, British governments failed to assume the leadership of the process of European integration in the 1950s and thus left a legacy of 'missed or lost opportunities'. Governments missed the European bus/train/boat according to the overworked metaphors of such literature. Whether taking the form of a powerful polemic as in Anthony Nutting's book *Europe Will Not Wait* (1960) or the more measured historical scholarship of Miriam Camps's book *Britain and the European Community 1955–1963* (1964), the basic criticism was to the effect that British policymakers of the time lacked vision and failed to recognize the value of the Community method of European integration.

Later accounts based on primary source material echoed some of these criticisms. They did so, however, while seeking only to explain Britain's absence from the origins of the EC and without making any unhistorical comments or judgements based on hindsight about whether any British government could or should have acted differently in this period. The 'missed opportunities' account, however, long remained a potent force, at least in political circles. During his premiership, Tony Blair regularly subscribed to this version of events in some of his major pro-EU speeches.

The 'missed opportunities' explanation was increasingly challenged as government papers for the 1950s were released in the 1980s. Historians were now more inclined to view Britain's European policy in a more positive and constructive light. They cited the willingness of British governments to participate in intergovernmental organizations and to support the origins of the EC by guarantees and forms of association while resisting, at least overtly, any attempt to sabotage the project. The earlier view that Britain in the 1950s could have had the leadership of Europe on its own terms was now dismissed, particularly on the grounds that, unlike the founders of the EC, Britain saw no need to abandon its sovereignty to common institutions.

More recent work on the subject suggests the makings of a new school of thought, at least according to one historiographical work that discerns the familiar model of traditional, revisionist and post-revisionist accounts in studies of the subject (Daddow, 2004). Such studies reject the name, blame and shame accounts of the 'missed opportunities' explanation. They are equally dismissive of other neat and tidy explanations. What is offered in their place is a more nuanced, sophisticated analysis that emphasizes the complex interplay of events and the contradictions, ambiguities, divided opinions and unintended consequences at the heart of policymaking.

The absence of underlying patterns, the emphasis on the contingent and the accidental, and the concentration on numerous, intricate interactions in multilayered organizations and negotiations imply a much messier and untidy account. In some cases British policy appears as an improvised process of muddling through or navigating a random series of events, this accounting for what is occasionally viewed as the incoherence and disorganization in the making of Britain's European policy. Such a condition may suggest elements of chaos theory combined with a view of history – 'one damned thing after another' (Fisher, 1935: 2) – that tests the compulsive pattern making of the historian. Certainly there are accidental occurrences and chance happenings in this story that colour, if not influence, the subsequent course of events.

The problems of generalization run up against the range and diversity of factors involved in the making and implementation of policy. In addition, contributions to the debate about Britain's relations with the EC/EU are often influenced by diverse considerations unrelated to the matter in dispute. Understandably, therefore, one recent study of British policy towards the EC in the period 1963–1975 dismisses the idea of offering a basic thesis or central argument underlying the analysis. Instead, this approach emphasizes the wide and changing mixture of influences at work and also the prevailing sense of uncertainty in the making of British policy over a period of time (Wall, 2013). That view chimes in with the experience of a former British ambassador to the EC, recalling that most of the decisions that influenced foreign policy were made 'in response to unexpected events and to actions by players over whom we had no, or little, influence or control' (Hannay, 2013: 277).

Much recent work has focused attention on the ways in which politicians, interest groups, campaigning organizations, the press and other agencies have drawn upon particular narratives as organizing frames for their handling of the subject. The importance of discourse analysis is evident at every point in the debate about EU membership and in any study of the evolution and changing character of opposing forces. Two examples at opposite ends of the period with which this book deals illustrate the point.

In 1960, Foreign Office officials made the then novel suggestion that a keynote speech by the foreign secretary, Selwyn Lloyd, should be entitled 'British policy in Europe' rather than the customary 'British policy towards Europe' (NA., FO 371/154503). This particular change in the framing of the issue – from an 'outsider' to an 'insider' perspective – significantly occurred at an important tipping point in British policy towards the EC, just as policymakers were persuading themselves that there were few, if any, viable alternatives to seeking EC membership terms. At the same time, Selwyn Lloyd paraded Britain's European credentials without qualification: 'By history, by tradition, by civilization, by sentiment, by geography, we are part of Europe' (*House of Commons Debates* [hereafter *H.C. Deb.*], 25 July 1960).

At the other end of the period in March 2015, Gordon Brown, the former prime minister, provided an object lesson in how the subject can be framed and reframed in diverse ways. He drew on his experience of how the referendum campaign on Scotland's independence started off as a contest between two patriotic visions of Scotland's future but descended into a choice – are you for Scotland or against Scotland? Brown maintained that the opponents of British membership of the EU were pulling off the same trick by framing the issue of EU membership in such a way that what should be a choice between two patriotic futures for Britain – one as part of the EU and one outside it – was already descending into a more basic emotional choice – are you for Britain, or are you for the EU? He selected one framing of the question of Britain's EU membership – the so-called Hong Kong option – 'leaving Europe to join the world', and reframed this representation in accordance with the familiar Europhile picture of Britain out of the EU and 'alone in the world', or as he put it: 'the North Korean option, out in the cold with few friends, no influence, little new trade and even less investment' (*The Guardian*, 9 March 2015).

The unexpected turn of events

There are certain patterns or tendencies that have persisted over time in the story of Britain's engagement with the EU, as we shall see. However, it is as well to recognize that in this field as in others politicians have often reacted to the course of events in a much more contradictory, wrong-footed, apprehensive and uncertain way than is allowed for in some historical accounts or political theories. Few political leaders over the past 60 years have escaped from the unanticipated turn of events presented by EU developments (see Chapter 5). British policy towards the process of European integration has rarely lost its capacity to surprise. It has often validated Macmillan's celebrated answer to a journalist's question about what can most easily steer a government off course: 'Events, dear boy, events'. As often as not, political leaders have encountered an unforeseen turn of events and also shown an uncertain sense of direction in 'the fog of war' or in the din of battle of round-the-clock media. Indeed, this area of British political life, like others, has been viewed as reflecting some of the weaknesses, blunders and incompetence of British governments at large in recent decades, in a study that subscribes to cock-up theory rather than conspiracy theory (King and Crewe, 2013).

I have endeavoured to stick to the always impossible undertaking of avoiding the benefit of hindsight and of reading history backwards. To do otherwise is to ignore the observation that 'This may be the most important proposition revealed by history: "At the time, no one knew what was coming"' (Murakami, 2012). In that respect it is worth noting the sometimes mocked comment of Donald Rumsfeld, the former US Secretary of State: 'There are known knowns. These are things we know that we know. There are known unknowns. That is to say, there are things that we know we don't know. But there are also unknown unknowns. These are things we don't know we don't know' (Rumsfeld, 2011). If that all seems far-fetched and remote from a study of Britain and the European Union, the recollections of a British diplomat intimately involved in the negotiations surrounding Britain's entry to the EC speak volumes for such problems; he referred to the particular issue of Britain's likely contribution to the EU budget and the way in which the principal negotiators were arguing about 'the impact of a budget of unknown and unknowable size an unknown number of years ahead' (Hannay, 2013: 50).

The organization of the book

The rationale for the structure of the book and the thematic treatment are here briefly explained. The treatment is thematic throughout but with a decidedly historical approach in each case.

Chapter 1 explores the historical conditioning that has affected and continues to influence British policy and attitudes towards the EU. It deals with the occasionally overlooked distinction between Europe and the European Union, and discusses the long-term or distant factors that have shaped British policy and attitudes towards Europe at large and the EU in particular. The chapter also provides a short overview of some of the key features, driving forces, and landmarks in the history of the EU.

Chapters 2 and 3 are scene-setters covering the period since 1945. Chapter 2 focuses on the period 1945–1973 when British aloofness from the origins and early evolution of the EU in the 1950s was followed by a reappraisal of British policy resulting in three attempts to secure EU membership. The chapter considers how far treatment of EU membership was influenced by a historically minded, backward-looking perspective involving a network of long-standing emotional ties rather than a forward-looking positive interest in a new project. It also discusses how and why the experience of seeking membership in the 1960s and 1970s influenced subsequent perspectives, policies and attitudes.

Chapter 3 considers British membership of the EC/EU since 1973 with reference to the theme of belonging without believing. It examines the distancing and contrast between some of the original ideas and inspiration underlying the EC and British interests and perspectives. The chapter discusses the particular factors that affected the transition to membership and that influenced the character of British membership down to the present day.

Chapter 4 deals with the strategy and tactics of successive governments in the EU policymaking arena. Among other topics, it examines how far governments have demonstrated a reluctance to accept further integration in the EU and have adopted tactics to resist this process. The chapter highlights enduring preferences such as EU enlargement, intergovernmental co-operation and 'negative' integration as well as entrenched opposition to such matters as federalism and 'positive' integration.

Chapter 5 focuses on EU membership in the context of British political culture and domestic politics. It deals with European integration as a persistent source of conflict in the field of inter- and intra-party divisions and also as indicative of personal, party, ideological and other aspects of British politics. The chapter discusses the emergence of Euroscepticism, and also considers the latent functions served by EU membership in party politics.

Chapter 6 discusses devolution and European Union membership. It covers the politics and interests of Northern Ireland, Scotland and Wales in this sphere. The chapter briefly explains the evolution of EC/EU policies towards regions and stateless nations. The analysis considers the devolution settlement of 1998 and the role and limitations of the devolved administrations in EU affairs. Finally, the chapter examines the policies and attitudes of nationalist parties, especially in Scotland and Wales, and concludes with a section on public attitudes towards the EU.

Chapter 7 takes up the subject of the influence of the press and public opinion on British politics and the EU. This section explores the process whereby European integration is projected as an alien, external force that gives rise to an 'us and them' discourse and imagery among the public at large and the press in particular. Several aspects are considered in this context including the construction of negative stereotypes, popular opposition to elitist politics, ignorance of the dynamics of European integration, growing disenchantment with the EU, and the rise of Euroscepticism.

Chapter 8 deals with the British contribution to the EU budget. This issue has loomed large in British press reporting of EU affairs, often attracting negative coverage and invariably occupying a large amount of government time and attention. The chapter explores the roots of the problem and the accompanying controversy surrounding the issue ever since the accession negotiations for EC membership. The chapter offers a case study of this long-standing, contentious and still topical issue. Management of the subject is also indicative of some of the distinctive features of British standing in the EU.

Chapters 9 and 10 focus on a much larger issue than the budget rebate. They concentrate on the process of monetary integration within the EU since the 1970s, and examine British responses to key developments along the way. Chapter 9 traces the early history of monetary integration in the period 1970–1992, and the fitful, eventually failed attempt to include the pound in this project. Chapter 10 deals with the emergence of the euro area as the third major stage in the evolution of the EU after the formation of the EC in the 1950s and the Single Market initiative of 1986. Particular attention is paid to the course and impact of the economic, monetary and financial crisis of 2007–2008 on the EU at large and on the euro area in particular, the effects of which continue to reverberate across the EU. The chapter explains why Britain has remained out of the euro area and also considers the role and interests of the City of London as a global financial centre in this context.

Chapter 11 develops the global theme on a wider canvas. It focuses on the relationship between EU membership and the changing nature of Britain's global role, power and interests. Part of the analysis features the long-standing but increasingly outmoded Churchillian 'three circles' model of British foreign policy and the dwindling options available to policymakers. In particular, the chapter discusses the relationship between Britain's EU membership and the country's extra-European ties and interests.

Chapter 12 covers the period since 2010. It offers detailed treatment of the Cameron Coalition government and necessarily more brief coverage of the Cameron Conservative government following the general election of May 2015. The chapter traces the emergence of the idea of a referendum on Britain's EU membership, the process of renegotiation, and the accompanying debate within the Conservative Party and among the public at large.

The Conclusion takes as its starting point the title of the BBC Reith lectures of 1972 delivered by Andrew Shonfield on the eve of Britain's entry into the EC. It covers the course and outcome of the referendum campaign of 2016 on Britain's membership of the EU. The Conclusion also considers alternatives to EU membership and aspects of continuity and change in the history of British membership of the EU.

1 Europe and the European Union

I remember being much amused last year, when landing at Calais, at the answer made by an old traveller to a novice who was making his first voyage. 'What a dreadful smell!' said the uninitiated stranger, enveloping his nose in his pocket handkerchief. 'It is the smell of the continent, sir,' replied the man of experience. And so it was.

(Trollope, 1836)

Introduction

In the period 1950–1955 the six original member states of the EC laid its foundations. The British Conservative government of the time wished them well, rated their chances of success poor and made clear that this venture was not for it. Britain, in short, stood on the sidelines. More than 50 years later, in 2010, the Conservative–Liberal Democrat Coalition government came to power with a programme including the promise that the UK would not join the euro area that then comprised a large majority of the EU states and represented the latest stage in the process of European integration. This declaration, together with earlier aspects of British policy, confirmed yet again that Britain was seemingly still content to stand on the sidelines, though on this occasion as a member of the European Union but one that had long since exhibited signs of semi-detachment.

This chapter considers how far this positioning towards the European mainland was invariably viewed through the prism of retrospective views and historical influences. We deal with the distinction between Europe and the European Union with a view to identifying some of the long-term or distant factors that have shaped British policy and attitudes towards Europe at large and the EU in particular. The chapter also examines some of the key features and landmarks in the history of the EU.

Britain as the 'outsider': 'island of the mind'

There are some fundamental parameters of history, geography and culture that have had a deep-seated, if imprecise and variable, impact on policy and attitudes towards the EU. Each has contributed to the profound uncertainty as to whether Britain is part of Europe, and each has also influenced the often contrasting renditions of the 'island story': insular, European, imperial, Atlantic, global. It is, however, difficult to gauge the precise relationship between British policy and attitudes towards the EU as such and British attitudes towards Europe beyond the exclusive confines of the EU. There are similar problems in determining how far geographical separation from mainland

Europe has contributed to psychological distancing in terms of Britain's relationship with the EC/EU.

Europe is a protean, highly contested concept comprising a large variety of definitions, images, representations and explanations. There are, in effect, many Europes ranging from the Europe of the EU and the Council of Europe (whose European Convention on Human Rights is commonly mistaken by the British press and public as an EU matter) to the Europe of Champions League football and the European Council for Nuclear Research (CERN).

The common expression 'Britain and Europe' and the different meanings attached to the concept of 'Europe' in British political discourse are indicative of considerable doubts about Britain's European credentials, status and identity. Such doubts find expression in the long-standing 'outsider' tradition of thinking about 'Europe' in British foreign policy (Daddow, 2015). There are of course shorthand expressions like the newspaper headline 'Britain and Europe' where Europe actually means the 'European Union'.

It is, however, necessary to make a distinction between 'European' and 'European Union', between European culture and civilization on the one hand and a particular set of political, economic and commercial arrangements known as the European Union on the other hand. This distinction is all the more crucial because of the familiar claim made in some quarters of being European but not 'European Unionists'. This features in UKIP's presentation of itself as avowedly anti-EU, but not anti-European. The party refuses to be labeled as 'Europhobe' as it denies being anti-European and claims that UKIP members are the only true Europeans as they want not only Britain but every country to leave the EU (Tournier-Sol, 2015).

It is equally possible for people to be disinclined to view themselves as 'European' and yet to support continued British membership of the EU. The widely respected British Social Attitudes annual survey (2014) yielded some noteworthy results in this respect. Only 15 per cent of respondents described themselves as 'European' when asked to choose as many identities as they liked from a list of every identity associated with Great Britain and Ireland. Similarly, the European Commission's Eurobarometer (conducted in May 2015) showed that 64 per cent of people in Britain saw themselves as 'British only', rejecting any sense of European identity (http//ec.europa.eu/ COMMFFrontOffice/PublicOpinion/). A further interesting aspect of the British Social Attitudes survey was that among those respondents who did not feel European as many as 51 per cent preferred Britain to continue in the EU, suggesting that this had little to do with how European or otherwise they felt (www.bsa.natcen.ac.uk/), and possibly pointing towards the country's unresolved identity as a European nation.

From an insular perspective, the idea of 'Europe' as a parallel universe or separate entity finds expression in the view that Britain is alongside Europe only as a result of geographical accident and not because of any deep-seated affinity with mainland Europe. At root, the British historical experience in this frame is altogether different from that of continental Europe, notably in escaping foreign occupation for some 950 years and with borders settled for a longer period of time than any of its major continental neighbours.

The expressions 'joining Europe' or 'going to Europe' are commonplace in Britain. It would be considered illogical to use such expressions as 'joining Europe' in France, Germany or other continental European states. Unsurprisingly, most people across Europe identify more with their national identity than with a 'European' one.

Nevertheless, in most other countries there is a much greater willingness than in Britain to express this national identity *alongside* feeling European, as in the case of France where just 36 per cent say they feel 'French only' with the rest feeling either 'French and European', 'European and French' or, more unusually, 'European only'. According to the same study and survey, Britain sits within a small group of EU countries, including Cyprus and Greece, in which a majority of the population appear not to consider themselves to be 'European' at all (Ormston, 2015).

The sense of apartness or 'island of the mind' reaches far back into history. It is possible to discern in attitudes towards the idea of European integration a strong and especially English suspicion born out of historic ruptures between England and the continent. The condition can be traced back as far as the Reformation and in its opposition to Roman Catholicism reaches into the early decades after the Second World War. The British public was judged to be so ignorant about the EC and so steeped in antipathies that a Conservative Party publication of 1962 included reassuring advice. According to this source, the Common Market was set up by the Treaty of Rome, but 'This has nothing to do with the Pope or the Vatican; the Treaty just happened to be signed in Rome and has nothing to do with religion' (Conservative Party Central Office Publication, 1962). The Protestant Association was unconvinced and insisted that 'The Common Market in Churches and States is a league with the World, the Flesh and the Devil' – one of the more unusual conspiracy theories concerning the meaning and significance of the EC/EU.

Few political leaders better enshrined the powerful myth of separateness from mainland Europe than Hugh Gaitskell, leader of the Labour Party, when he opposed the first British application for EC membership, maintaining that 'It means the end of a thousand years of history'. On one reading of this well-known quotation and speech, at least, Gaitskell was expressing a view comparable to that of John Maynard Keynes at the end of the First World War: 'England still stands outside Europe ... Europe is apart and England is not of her flesh and blood' (Williams, 1979; Keynes, 1920: 1).

Europe as the hostile 'Other'

A further, longer term and related feature of such a narrative has found expression in the projection of 'Europe' as the hostile 'Other'. There are, to be sure, many aspects to such imagery and also numerous functions served by such a presentation that touch on the evolution of Britain and the construct of Britishness.

'Europe' as the hostile 'Other' is often accompanied by definitions of Britishness that contrast what are represented as the outstanding features of British identity as outsider with the enduring, strongly unattractive characteristics of mainland Europe; 'If I shut my eyes and say the word Europe to myself', wrote the poet W. H. Auden, 'the various images which it conjures up have one thing in common, they could not be conjured up by the word England' (Auden, 1963: 53). George Orwell had earlier struck a similar note in his celebrated essay written during the Blitz of 1940. He argued that the crowds in the big English towns 'with their mild knobby faces, their bad teeth and gentle manners, are different from a European crowd' (Orwell, 1941).

The mental baggage of a generation or more of post-1945 policymakers contained a strong emphasis on the contrast between Britain and mainland Europe and on such projections of Britishness. The 'strange island, anchored off the continent' (Trevelyan, 1946: 11) had for a long time enjoyed a high degree of stability and continuity, though several historians have noted that the British have a genius for the appearance of continuity and for creating a semblance of continuity where little really exists (Ash, 2009: 63; Colley, 2014: 51). In addition, Britishness suggested a unique flexibility in the slow, incremental growth of institutions and of the concept of sovereignty. These features were combined with a suspicion of utopian schemes and written constitutions emanating from continental Europe, and a marked preference for operating on the basis of practical experience. There was also a weighty liberal tradition that asserted individual rights against state dominance, altogether unknown to the *étatiste* French or the *Volk*-centred Germans (Schnapper, 2014).

Fairness, tolerance, liberty, the rule of law, unbroken tradition and parliamentary democracy have greatly featured as characteristically British qualities. Such representations are usually accompanied by self-deprecation and self-congratulation in more or less equal measure. They are also associated with the remnants of a semi-feudal order most obviously reflected a generation ago in British passports explaining that the holder was 'a subject of Her Britannic Majesty'. Current British passports with European Union stamped on the front cover and the reference to 'British Citizen' inside are anathema to Eurosceptics who are equally ill at ease with the idea of European Union citizenship (introduced in 1993 as result of the Maastricht Treaty): 'I am not a citizen of the bloody European Union', wrote Simon Heffer, the *Daily Telegraph* columnist, in 2007, 'except on a technicality. I am an Englishman and a subject of Her Majesty the Queen' (*The Daily Telegraph*, 12 September 2007). The word 'citizen' in some quarters still evoked disagreeable memories of revolutionary France in the 1790s.

From a purely English perspective at least and according to one recent history of the English, 'England over the centuries has been among the richest, safest and best governed places on earth' (Tombs, 2014: 890). By contrast, English, if not British, perceptions of mainland Europe in recent times have often included centralized government, notwithstanding strong British traditions in that respect and the persistent failure to distinguish between federalism and centralization. In addition, political instability, undemocratic politics and military weakness have frequently figured in the English telling of the continental story. On a longer timescale, militarism, absolutism and Catholicism have featured as major, unattractive features of continental life and history. Furthermore, according to one view at least, Britain had only found its true destiny when it turned away from mainland Europe with its war-torn history, constantly turbulent politics, and changing political systems and borders. Through such portrayals Britain was often presented as not only different from but superior to continental Europe, all the more so with a dominant narrative of a liberal tradition and the assertion of the rights of the individual against state control.

'Damn foreigners'

A strong vein of xenophobia extending to all 'damn foreigners' but with mainland Europeans as a particular target has also underpinned the notion of Europe as the hostile other. Sometimes, the subject has taken the form of crude, lighthearted stereotyping in the tabloid press; 'Achtung Surrender. For you Fritz, ze Euro 96 Championship is over' the *Daily Mirror* emblazoned across its front page on the eve of the Euro 96 semi-final football match between England and Germany – England lost. Or else stereotyping has taken the form of satirized British images of other leading peoples, as in the case of schoolboy verdicts: 'a) the Russians are roters [*sic*] b) Americans are swank pots c) the

French are slack d) the Germans are unspeakable e) the rest are as bad if not worse than the above' (Willans and Searle, 1973).

In other cases a distaste for continental Europeans has found expression in the preferences of British prime ministers since 1945. Clement Attlee was unable to trust the continental Europeans because they did not play cricket. Harold Wilson disliked the continental style of life and rich food, generally preferring meat and two veg with HP sauce. John Major preferred Commonwealth meetings because all participants spoke English. In a characteristically less good-humoured manner, Margaret Thatcher claimed that her EC colleagues were 'unBritish'. She further complained that the trouble with Chancellor Kohl was that 'He's a German', that the European Commissioners were 'tiresomely foreign', and that while she liked the Danes 'the Germans are big but they feel so guilty ... you can't trust the French, the Italians are only good for clothes, the Dutch are most like us but too close to the Germans'. There was little evidence here to substantiate Thatcher's observation that one of the faults of British politicians was that they looked at foreign politicians 'through slightly rose-tinted spectacles thinking they are as we are' (Moore, 2014: 19, 488; Campbell, 2012: 60).

Such comments tapped into certain long-standing fears about individual European states, most obviously in the form of Francophobia that was especially virulent in the eighteenth and nineteenth centuries, Germanophobia that was most marked in the twentieth century, and outbreaks of Russophobia across the entire period. There is therefore much ammunition here for the bogeyman approach to European international politics that is espoused especially by English nationalist strands of opinion utilizing the language of fear, threat and invasion: 'nationalist rhetoric sung to the catchy tune of criticism of Europe' as one leading German politician put it (*The Guardian*, 28 January 2014).

On the eve of Britain's first application to join the EC in 1961, David Eccles, a government minister and one of the more pro-European members of the Cabinet, warned Prime Minister Macmillan that there was no sure hope of carrying the British people into the EC on the back of the advice of pro-EC economic pundits and enthusiasts who 'would be no match for the ghosts of Louis XIV and Napoleon, the Kaiser and Hitler' (NA., PREM 11/3554). In similar vein, Queen Elizabeth, the Queen Mother, expressed a widespread prejudice of her generation when she reportedly commented on the EU in the early 1990s: 'It will never work with all those Huns, wops and dagos' (*The Guardian*, 10 November 2008).

Britishness and Europe

Europe as the hostile other has also long figured as an important element in definitions of British identity and in the construction and unity of Britain. The referendum on the independence of Scotland in September 2014 was a vivid reminder that the political unity of Britain has never been a constant or a given. In the seventh century, England and Scotland were not even geographical expressions at a time when the Scots were centred in Argyle, the English realm of Bernicia extended into Lothian, and the Welsh ruled Strathclyde and Cumbria. Judged on this timescale, Britain is historically a relatively recent construct. Moreover, as often as not, today's Britain was forged as a result of war or the threat of invasion springing from continental Europe. The so-called Act of Union between England and Wales in 1536, the Act of Union linking these two countries with Scotland in 1707, and the Act of Union between Great Britain and

Ireland in 1800–1801, were all implemented either against the background of major European warfare as in the case of the Union of 1800–1801 or at a time of acute fear of war and of a perceived threat to the so-called Protestant ascendancy as in the case of the Union of 1707 (Colley, 2014: 148–9).

There is a further dimension to the notion of British identity that has a bearing on more recent attitudes towards the EU. 'Europe' as the hostile other has emerged as an even more important element in view of the diminishing appeal of the concept of British identity in recent decades and the limited attempts to imagine a new rationale for the Union. Some of the long-standing symbols of that identity, most notably monarchy, empire, Protestantism and two world wars, no longer occupy centre-stage. Meanwhile, in the case of Scotland at least, 18 years of Conservative government (1979–1997) with its neo-liberal view of the state and the free market society was not only at odds with predominant opinion in Scotland but contributed to the loosening of the Union. Furthermore, deliberate efforts to promote Britishness, as attempted by Gordon Brown when in office in the period 1997–2010, not only proved unsuccessful but coincided with an enhanced sense of English identity in England and of Scottishness in Scotland (Kenny, 2015).

The outcome of the referendum on the independence of Scotland (September 2014), however, serves as something of a warning about rushing to judgement on the declining appeal of Britishness. The most detailed academic study of this event to date undermines partisan accounts of the reasons for the majority 'No' vote of 55.3 per cent. It concludes that the principal motivation underlying the 'No' vote at least was 'feeling British/believe in Union' and was not due to the promise of more powers ('The Vow') or the impact of a biased media ('Why Scots Voted No', *The Herald*, 28 March 2015). Some 90 per cent of the 'No' voters surveyed viewed their national identity as 'British not Scottish' (Henderson and Mitchell, 2015). For the most part the Scottish electorate – pro- and anti-independence – was largely unmoved by a trainload of Westminster MPs descending on Glasgow a week before the referendum vote, and was in both cases unimpressed by Cameron's speech on the morning after the vote that sounded like undiluted English nationalism.

Particular attitudes towards the EC/EU at any given time have reflected changes, especially in the manufacture of British identity. 'Europe' as associated with the EC/EU has arguably accounted for many of the demons in British mythology about the outside world in the past 70 years and has certainly carried a load of negative connotations. In some political quarters and increasingly so in recent decades, projections of the EU as the hostile other are regarded as a principal means of buttressing the British state. At the same time, however, this state, so it is claimed, can achieve more in the external environment than its constituent parts or nations can on their own. This major argument in the campaign against an independent Scotland in the referendum of September 2014 was made all the more forcefully by key figures like Gordon Brown on the grounds that none of the ancient institutions of the Union were strong or popular enough in themselves to maintain the Union. There is thus a close relationship between the survival of the Union and that of British membership of the EU (see Chapter 6).

Britain: apart from or a part of Europe

Exclusive emphasis on the idea of Europe as a separate entity, however, fails to capture the extent to which Britain has long been intimately and inescapably linked to the geo-political history of mainland Europe. 'Splendid isolation' or masterly inaction do not reflect long-standing aspects of British policy towards the politics and international relations of mainland Europe. Whether of necessity or by choice, Britain has long featured as a leading actor on the European stage.

Current debates about whether Britain should primarily engage militarily, politically and financially with Europe or concentrate on the world beyond Europe have a long ancestry. Questions about whether the country is politically and psychologically part of Europe or is in more than the physical sense an island apart are scarcely novel. One historian of the rise and fall of the first British empire observed that these were precisely the sort of questions at the heart of eighteenth-century British politics, so much so that the British debate about European integration since 1945 'would have struck an informed eighteenth-century observer as remarkably familiar' (Simms, 2007: 2).

There is no shortage of narratives about Britain and European integration since 1945 that feed into and influence views of the controversy of the moment. Much of the debate about Britain's EU membership has involved irreconcilable opinions about current and future developments. Such opinions in turn have arisen out of fiercely contested and very different versions of the relationship between Britain and continental Europe over centuries.

In recent years, sharp divisions between historians have emerged about Britain's historical relationship with continental Europe and about the extent to which, if at all, the country has a unique history that sets it apart from the rest of Europe. 'Historians for Britain', a group of historians asserting their belief that Britain's unique history distinguishes it from the rest of Europe, is an offshoot of the Eurosceptic pressure group Business for Britain. It claims not to be hostile to Europe but maintains that in an ideal world Britain would remain within a radically reformed EU. It further declares that Europe has always been a part of the British identity but that it has never been an integral part of the nation's political identity (http://historiansforbritain.org/). This body of opinion acknowledges contacts and connections between Britain and continental Europe over centuries – from the wool trade in the Middle Ages and English conquests that reached as far as Gascony to Mediterranean acquisitions and involvement in two world wars. It nonetheless insists that Britain has always been a partner of Europe without being a full participant in it.

This position often underlies the portrayal of Britain as a singular or special case in the European context and that is translated into an exceptionalist political mentality demanding exclusions or opt-outs from general rules, as in the case of EU membership (see Chapter 4). The idea of British exceptionalism had its roots in the distinctive baggage of a global power with extra-European interests and powerful insular perspectives and history, the latter emphasizing continuity, unbroken traditions, and ideas of common law and parliamentary sovereignty different from continental history.

Other historians have rejected this view on the grounds that Britain's past is neither so exalted nor so unique. They emphasize that distinctive features and forms of exceptionalism are not confined to Britain but are characteristic features of other European states, whether in Germany with its *Sonderweg* ('special path') or in the case of France and the meaning attached to *grandeur* in French history. This viewpoint also emphasizes the Europeanness of British history at every juncture whether in terms of an imperial past (imperialism being a general European rather than an exclusively British phenomenon) or the common experience of two world wars. Furthermore, it rejects the idea that British institutions have experienced a degree of continuity unparalleled in continental European history. Besides, Britain as a state is a relatively recent invention and comprises nations with their own individual histories.

Another view of the matter plots a course between these exceptionalist and Europeanist accounts. This is to the effect that British history has been defined by the 'duality of ocean and continent', by which is meant that Britain is a European country but not just a European country (quoted in Ash, 2009: 116). That view, as we shall see, has been repeated on numerous occasions by British political leaders since 1945 whether in addressing American or continental European audiences.

Conflicts over the general importance of European history and particularly coverage of the EU also entered the school classroom in 2013 in a controversy over the new history curriculum for school pupils in England between the ages of five and 14. The first draft of this curriculum was criticized for its emphasis on local, British and world history to the neglect of continental Europe. The latter featured only as the scene of British triumphs over evil foreigners (*The Guardian*, 15 February and 13 July 2013). Coincidentally or otherwise, Michael Gove, the Conservative education secretary at the time, was the first senior Cabinet minister in the Coalition government to express support for Britain's withdrawal from the EU if a referendum was held at the time (May 2013). Meanwhile, a group of MPs with an opposing viewpoint criticized an A-level history textbook as too Eurosceptic. They did so on the grounds that the book devoted five lines to the advantages of EU membership and 26 lines to the disadvantages (*The Guardian*, 13 February 2013). The press also entered the controversy with much on the singular 'island story' as told by H. E. Marshall – *Our Island Story* (1905). The Eurosceptic *Daily Telegraph* backed a campaign to ensure that copies of the book were available in all 20,000 primary schools in Britain (Brocklehurst, 2015).

Widely differing assessments surround general treatment of why Britain became a member of the EC in the first place. At one end of the spectrum of views there is the argument that Britain joined the EC reluctantly in order to shore up its declining position as a world power while at the same time seeking to maintain delusions of grandeur and, either by inability or unwillingness, failing to come to terms with the past. The idea of EC membership as an historic necessity found eloquent expression in Hugo Young's opening sentence to his study of Britain and Europe since 1945: 'This is the story of fifty years in which Britain struggled to reconcile the past she could not forget with the future she could not avoid' (Young, 1998: 1).

At the other end of the spectrum, and far removed from Young's unavoidable future, the opponents of EC membership present a very different reading of the recent past. In short, EC membership was inflicted on the country by the defeatist politicians and policies of the 1960s and 1970s who departed from the potent narrative of the 'open sea' tradition and close Commonwealth ties. The accompanying prescription for reinstating the 'Great' in Great Britain, as various shades of Eurosceptic opinion put it, has remained consistent with one of the anti-marketeer slogans of the 1970s: 'Out of Europe and into the World', or what certain currents of contemporary Eurosceptic opinion call the 'Anglosphere' (see Chapter 11).

Possibly Margaret Thatcher best summed up the often two-sided face of Britain towards continental Europe. She never doubted that in her lifetime 'all our problems have come from mainland Europe', and observed that the ideas, traditions and history of continental European countries were fundamentally different from Britain's. She was, however, equally convinced that no enterprise could 'properly lay claim to the proud name of Europe that did not include Britain' (*The Times*, 6 October 1999). To be sure, there was here a distinction between Europe at large and the European Union in particular.

Whether Thatcher would have voted to remain in the EU in a referendum several years after her death is in itself an example of how the deceased can be pressed into a matter of speculation and historical controversy spilling over into contemporary politics. Thatcher's powerful legacy in terms of Conservative Party politics and factionalism about Europe was evident in February 2016 shortly before the completion of the renegotiation of Britain's EU terms of membership. Charles Powell, her foreign affairs private secretary, maintained that she would have voted to remain in the EU on the basis of the terms negotiated by the Cameron government. However, Charles Moore, her official biographer, recalled that in retirement Thatcher declared that it would be best to leave the EU, but she was persuaded not to say this in public (*The Guardian*, 7 February 2016). Others quickly joined in this writing or re-writing of history of what a dead person may or may not have said about a current issue; John Redwood, a veteran opponent of EU membership, found it disappointing that Powell should presume to be able to communicate with the dead, Bill Cash, another such veteran, referred to a letter from Thatcher dated 1993 claiming that she would not have signed the Maastricht Treaty and by implication would now vote to leave the EU, while Norman Tebbit, a former member of Thatcher's government, dismissed Powell's comment as the conjecture of an 'apparatchik' (*The Guardian*, 13 and 16 February 2016).

In any event, Thatcher's essentially English view of the commonality of British and continental European history is arguably all the more valid if the individual histories of Ireland, Scotland and Wales are considered in this context. At the same time, however, she went so far as to declare that 'God separated Britain from mainland Europe, and it was for a purpose' (Wellings and Baxendale, 2014). In saying as much, she evidently overlooked the extent to which Methodism, that figured large in her upbringing, actually had its roots in central Europe and was thus one small example of the long and varied interchange between Britain and continental Europe – the Renaissance, the Protestant religion, the eighteenth-century Englightenment, and much else besides being evidence of the country's European status and connections.

Balance of power politics

Balance of power politics has figured as a major driving force in accounting for British engagement in continental European affairs, especially in the face of continental threats and adversaries. Certainly, any form of engagement was invariably viewed as strictly limited and primarily designed to maintain a balance of power, while Britain pursued its more important imperial conquests and interests beyond Europe. Britain did not participate in European affairs, asserted Disraeli (the nineteenth-century British prime minister), but merely interfered when its position required it. What had to be resisted at all costs was the domination of the continent by a single power whether in what used to be referred to as a 'universal monarch' and in the shape of Charles V of Spain and Louis XIV of France or in the later form of Napoleonic France, Hitler's Germany and Stalin's Soviet Union. English preoccupation with continental hegemony can be traced back to at least the sixteenth century. It laid the basis for the increasingly consistent policy of opposing any power that threatened to dominate western Europe, to control the ports of the Low Countries, and to challenge English, and later British, trade and naval supremacy (Smith, 2005).

Political leaders like Attlee, Bevin and Churchill accepted balance of power considerations in the European context as a matter of course. They were also very much
in the mind of Prime Minister Harold Macmillan as he embarked on the faltering
steps towards making the first British application for EC membership. Macmillan's
approach to foreign policy was informed by his considerable knowledge of history,
though perhaps his knowledge of Greek tragedy 'made him inclined to exaggerate disaster' (Bennett, 2013: 57). As the EC looked to become an established reality in 1960,
he feared that its existence was comparable to the Napoleonic Continental System, a
blockade designed to destroy British commerce with the continent. He further maintained that the division between the EC and non-EC states in western Europe was
reminiscent of the Napoleonic period when Britain had allied with Russia to break
French ambitions. Another dimension in this respect, at least according to Macmillan,
was that Britain had to join the EC in order to strengthen western European unity in
the face of the Soviet presence in eastern Europe, a balance of power consideration on
the larger European stage.

In some respects, and more recently still, the EC/EU has featured as the latest version
of the single power dominating the European continent or an overbearing superstate-
in-the-making. Thatcher referred to Brussels and the EU bureaucracy as the 'Belgian
empire'. Furthermore, other British politicians besides Macmillan and also large sections of the British media over the years have frequently viewed the EC/EU as either a
tool for creating a France-dominated Europe or more often as a useful disguise for the
revival of German power in Europe.

Large-scale British participation in the two world wars of the twentieth century
amounted to more than interference in the execution of British balance of power politics. Nevertheless, the experience, aftermath and legacy of war resulted in contrasting
conditions between Britain and continental Europe that had enduring effects in shaping
later British ambivalence about the EC/EU. After the First World War, political instability and economic depression on the continent contributed to the rise of fascism in
Germany, in Italy and also in parts of eastern Europe. Such factors also accounted for
the outbreak of civil war in Spain, and for profound weaknesses in France resulting in
defeat at the hands of Nazi Germany in 1940.

Against all that, the British experience of political stability in the inter-war period
together with the sharp but relatively short-lived impact of economic depression in the
1930s made for a very different set of conditions from those on the continent. The
Second World War highlighted an even greater contrast between Britain and much of
continental Europe than had been the case in the First World War, at least during and
immediately after the war.

The origins and evolution of the European Union

The aims, activities and institutional character of the EU are dealt with as and where
appropriate in the text. Here it is sufficient to highlight a few key features of its history
and dynamics and to indicate the degree of continuity and change in two of the major and
sometimes conflicting processes associated with the EU – integration and enlargement.
The origins of the EU title first require some explanation. To avoid any confusion,
it should be noted that for the period 1957–1972 the literature on the subject often
employs the title European Economic Community (EEC) or Common Market as it was
popularly and significantly called in Britain until the late 1970s. The legally correct title

throughout this period and until 1992 was the European Communities (EC), comprising the European Coal and Steel Community (ECSC), based on the Treaty of Paris (1951), and the European Economic Community (EEC) and the European Atomic Energy Community (EAEC), founded on the Treaties of Rome (1957). The Treaty on European Union in 1992 (commonly known as the Maastricht Treaty) formally established the EU title and created a new political order.

The main landmarks in the sphere of European integration under the EC/EU umbrella are fourfold to date. First, the supranational principle and the idea of sector integration found expression in the ECSC Treaty of Paris, the only EU treaty to use the term 'supranational'. Second, the Treaty of Rome establishing the EEC was designed to create a common market for the free movement of goods, capital, labour and services. Third, the Single European Act (SEA) of 1986 committed the EC states to the creation of a single market by 1992. Finally, the Maastricht Treaty introduced institutional changes and established a programme for economic and monetary union including a single currency and a European Central Bank (ECB). Eleven of the then 15 EU member states eventually adopted the euro as their single currency (the euro area) in January 1999 with euro notes and coins in circulation as from January 2002.

For these and other reasons, the Maastricht Treaty marked an important turning-point in the history of the EC/EU. The divisions between European and domestic policy across a wide range of political, economic, legal and other policy areas became far less sharply defined than was previously the case. Debates surrounding ratification of the treaty gave rise to a greater degree of criticism of the organization, most evidently so when Denmark rejected the treaty and France narrowly voted in favour, all of which represented the emergence of a greater degree of scepticism about the EC/EU and the increasing use of referendums in EU affairs. Indeed, the expression 'Euroscepticism' emerged in the immediate aftermath of the lengthy and rancorous debates over the Maastricht Treaty, though the expression takes a variety of forms (see Chapter 5).

Maastricht also saw the formal beginnings of a differential approach to integration with 'opt-outs' from certain sections of the treaty for Britain and Denmark. Some member states were hereby allowed to press ahead with further integration either in the expectation that other member states would follow them in due course ('two-speed' Europe) or that other member states had no intention of following them, this being known as 'variable geometry' Europe (see Chapter 4). The Maastricht Treaty also contained the important principle of subsidiarity which aims at determining the level of intervention that is most relevant in the areas of competences shared between the EU and the member states. This principle may concern action at the European, national or local levels, and in all cases the EU may only intervene if it is able to act more effectively than the member states.

The enlargement of the EU represents one of the outstanding changes in its history over the past 40 years. It has proved a historic success for the EU with a positive transformational impact on incoming member states and on the EU itself (HM Government, 'Review of the Balance of Competences between the United Kingdom and the European Union EU Enlargement', December 2014: 6). The original membership of six states with a population of 233.9 million (Belgium, France, Italy, Luxembourg, the Netherlands and West Germany) has increased to 28 states, comprising a population of 504.4 million (Eurostat, 2014). The EU accounted for almost 25 per cent of total world production and around 20 per cent of total world trade in 2012 (see below and see also Tables 1.1 and 1.2).

Facts and figures on the position of the European Union in global markets (2013)
The European Union is:

- the largest economy in the world with a GDP per head of 25,000 euros;
- the world's largest trading block and the world's largest trader of manufactured goods and services;
- first in the world in both inbound and outbound investments;
- the top trading partner for 80 countries as compared with the United States which is the top trading partner for a little over 20 countries, and the top trading partner for China, Russia and the United States;
- the most open to developing countries and (fuels excluded) imports more from developing countries than Canada, China, Japan and the United States put together (http://ec.europa.eu/trade/policy/eu-position-in-world-trade/).

Enlargement has occurred in four major waves, the first involving Britain, Denmark and Ireland (1973), the next taking in the former military dictatorships of Greece (1981), Portugal and Spain (1986), the third extending to Austria, Finland and Sweden (1995),

Table 1.1 European Union: population and gross domestic product (GDP) data for 2014

	Population	*GDP per capita (euros)*	*GDP growth rate*
Belgium	11,161,642	35,999	0.9
Bulgaria	7,284,552	5,732	1.2
Czech Republic	10,516,125	14,704	2.5
Denmark	5,602,628	45,893	0.8
Germany	82,020,578	35,210	1.3
Estonia	1,320,174	14,754	1.9
Ireland	4,591,087	39,783	4.6
Greece	11,062,508	16,343	0.6
Spain	46,727,890	23,115	1.2
France	65,578,819	32,229	0.3
Croatia	4,262,140	10,170	−0.4
Italy	59,685,227	26,418	−0.7
Cyprus	865,878	20,013	−2.8
Latvia	2,023,825	12,120	2.6
Lithuania	2,971,905	12,338	2.7
Luxembourg	537,039	85,183	3.0
Hungary	9,908,798	10,279	3.2
Malta	421,364	18,404	3.0
Netherlands	16,779,575	38,505	0.9
Austria	8,451,860	38,612	0.7
Poland	38,533,299	10,668	3.0
Portugal	10,487,289	16,809	0.9
Romania	20,020,074	7,581	2.0
Slovenia	2,058,821	17,943	2.4
Slovakia	5,410,836	13,898	2.4
Finland	5,426,674	37,181	−0.4
Sweden	9,555,893	44,397	2.0
United Kingdom	63,896,071	34,579	3.1

Sources: European Commission, Eurostat.

Table 1.2 The share of the European Union and four individual EU
states in world trade in goods and services (%) in 2004 and 2012

	2004	*2012*
European Union	19.5	16.3
France	2.3	1.7
Germany	4.2	3.5
Italy	1.9	1.5
United Kingdom	3.2	2.4

The figures exclude intra-EU trade.
Source: Eurostat (Comext, Statistical regime 4).

and the fourth incorporating many of the former eastern Europe communist states: the
Czech Republic, Estonia, Hungary, Latvia, Lithuania, Poland, Slovakia and Slovenia –
known as the A8 states (2004). Bulgaria and Romania, known as the A2 states, joined in
2007. In addition, East Germany joined the EU as part of a united Germany (1990), the
island states of Cyprus and Malta secured membership in 2004, and Croatia, the most
recent new member state, joined in July 2013.

To date only Algeria (on securing independence from France in 1962) and Greenland,
currently a self-governing administrative division of Denmark and part of the EU in
the period 1973–1985, have left the organization. Some countries decided not to join.
Iceland's accession negotiations opened in 2010 but it chose to suspend them in 2013
following the election of a new government. Norway withdrew its applications for EC/
EU membership in 1972 and again in 1994. After a referendum, Switzerland suspended
its application in 1992.

The EU's next enlargement is expected sometime in the 2020s. Eight countries are
recognized by the EU as having the potential to become members.

Countries awarded candidate status:

*   Montenegro (2012), Serbia (2014), Turkey (2005) – in accession negotiations.
*   Albania (2014), Macedonia (2005) – not yet in accession negotiations.
*   Iceland (2010) – accession negotiations suspended.

Potential candidate countries:

*   Bosnia-Herzegovina and Kosovo.

Turkey's path to accession negotiations has been particularly long. It signed an
association agreement (the Ankara Agreement) with the EC in 1963, which allowed for
the possibility of its eventual accession to the EC. However, the European Council did
not award Turkey candidate status until 1999. Fresh efforts to re-start talks on Turkey's
application to join the EU were undertaken in November 2015 in exchange for Turkey's
co-operation in stemming the flow of refugees from the Middle East to Europe.

If all current candidate and potential candidate countries joined the EU, it would
comprise 36 member states with a total population of around 590 million. Where the
EU's borders should eventually lie is a matter of some debate which is why in many
respects the issue of Turkey's EU membership represents something of an identity crisis

for the EU. The EU has never attempted to define its borders. The Maastricht Treaty simply states that any European state may apply to become a member of the EU but it does not define the meaning of 'European state'. The Copenhagen criteria (agreed by the European Council in 1993 and strengthened by the Madrid European Council in 1995) established that a state wishing to join the EU should:

- have stability of institutions guaranteeing democracy, the rule of law, human rights and respect for and protection of minorities;
- have a functioning market economy and the ability to cope with competitive pressure and market forces within the EU;
- have the ability to take on the obligations of membership, including the capacity to effectively implement the rules, standards and policies that make up the body of EU law (the 'acquis'), and adherence to the aims of political, economic and monetary union.

(EUR-Lex)

There is little disagreement that enlargement should continue to the western Balkans (i.e. Albania, Bosnia-Herzegovina, Kosovo, Macedonia, Montenegro and Serbia) and, if they wish to join, the EFTA countries (i.e. Iceland, Liechtenstein, Norway and Switzerland). The possibility of EU membership for the Eastern Partnership countries, however, is more problematical; the Eastern Partnership was launched in 2009 as a joint initiative of the EU and the following states: Armenia, Azerbaijan, Belarus, Georgia, Republic of Moldova and Ukraine. The prospects for the latter receded when its government withdrew from signing a trade deal with the EU (November 2013) as a result of pressure from Russia that subsequently offered Ukraine substantial economic aid. This outcome led to considerable unrest in the country, so much so that Kiev saw the largest pro-EU public demonstration in the history of the EC/EU (December 2013).

Through enlargement, the EU has sought to extend peace, stability and democracy across the European continent. In its origins, the EC aimed to bring reconciliation between its members, notably France and West Germany. In the 1980s, EC membership was viewed as one of the most effective ways of entrenching democracy in post-authoritarian Greece, Portugal and Spain. After the end of the Cold War, the EU took the initiative in extending membership to the former communist bloc countries of central and eastern Europe, thereby reuniting much of the European continent. A further feature of enlargement has centred on the emergence of the market economy across Europe. This process was most marked in the transformation of previously centrally planned economies in central and eastern Europe into market-based economies. The prospect of EU membership helped to drive through painful political and economic reforms.

While the EU has not increased its membership since the accession of Croatia in 2013, the euro area has expanded from 11 to 19 states since the introduction of the euro currency in 1999. Greece joined in 2001, just one year before the cash changeover to the euro, followed by Slovenia (2007), Cyprus and Malta (2008), Slovakia (2009), Estonia (2011), Latvia (2014) and Lithuania (2015). Of the remaining EU states, Britain and Denmark negotiated 'opt-out' provisions in the negotiations resulting in the Maastricht Treaty, while Sweden has not yet qualified to be part of the euro area. The remaining EU states outside the euro area are among those which acceded to the EU in 2004 and 2007 after the launch of the euro. At the time of their accession, they did not meet the necessary conditions for entry to the euro area, but are committed to join as and when they meet them; they are thus member states with a 'derogation'.

Since its origins, the EU has displayed a fluctuating balance between supranationalism and intergovernmentalism. This feature has had a bearing on its changing standing between confederal and federal forms of government, resulting in a hybrid form of governance and a decision-making system often regarded as slow, cumbersome and bureaucratic. Support for supranationalism in the first decade or so after the Second World War was severely checked by Gaullist France in the 1960s. By the 1970s the EC resembled a traditional international organization as it demonstrated a strong emphasis on intergovernmental co-operation and a form of decision-making based on the lowest common denominator in which each state possessed a veto on any decisions. During the 1980s and 1990s, however, the relationship between the EU and its constituent states changed yet again. The Single European Act of 1986 greatly undermined the exercise of a national veto by a single member state in the EC's decision-making system through the introduction of qualified majority voting (QMV). The Maastricht Treaty subsequently shifted the balance even further in the direction of a supranational Europe, especially in its provision for economic and monetary union and for a European Central Bank.

The relationship between enlargement and integration in the EU's history has varied over time and in different cases. In the 1970s the implications of the first enlargement generally overshadowed the process of integration. In the 1980s, however, the EU expanded at the same time as it embarked upon the Single Market programme, and in the 1990s the decision to form the euro area preceded the enlargement of 1995. During the first decade of the twentieth century, enlargement acted as a spur to institutional reform, most obviously through the Treaty of Nice (2000) that prepared the way for the enlargement of the EU in 2004 and 2007.

A prolonged attempt to secure an EU Constitutional Treaty (2001–2004) ended in failure with France and The Netherlands voting against this measure. The Treaty of Lisbon, that took effect in December 2009, incorporated many of the features of the failed Constitutional Treaty but stripped away much of its objectionable language including the idea of a constitution, and arguably killed off post-Maastricht Treaty ideas of a European superstate. The Treaty amended the EU's two core treaties, the Treaty on European Union ('Maastricht Treaty') and the Treaty establishing the European Community. The latter was renamed the Treaty on the Functioning of the European Union (TFEU).

The Lisbon Treaty also indicated three different types of competence: exclusive, shared and supporting. Exclusive competence means that the power to take action is vested solely in the EU institutions, as in the case of the customs union. Shared competence makes provision for the EU institutions and member states to enact legislation, though the laws passed by member states in areas of shared competence may not conflict with EU laws enacted in that policy area (examples of such areas being energy, environment and transport). Supporting competence, as in the case of industry and tourism, allows for both the EU institutions and the member states to take action.

Theorizing European integration

European integration in the form of the EU and as a process or as a means has attracted a wide variety of theories, explanations and aspirations concerning its nature, course and direction. The underlying purpose of the EU, as specified in the EEC Treaty of

Rome and endorsed by the Maastricht Treaty, was 'to create an ever closer union among the peoples of Europe'. This declaration proved sufficiently imprecise to accommodate very different visions of the EU's potential in terms of federal and confederal systems of government or supranational and intergovernmental forms of decision-making. This reaches to the heart of the uniqueness of the EU as a political system in that it defies classification either as a conventional international organization or as a sovereign state.

Two of the classical theories of European integration – neo-functionalism and inter-governmentalism – were born out of the early history of the EU in the 1950s and 1960s. While a host of other theories developed in their wake, traces of their explanatory power and reach remain in evidence and reflect the difficulties of obtaining a purchase on the identity and the unique characteristics of the EU. Indeed, the debate amongst theorists of European integration studies was once likened to the fate of blind men discovering an elephant: each blind man touched a different part of the large animal, and each concluded that the elephant had the appearance of the part that he touched. While no man arrived at a very accurate description of the elephant, a lively debate ensued about the nature of the beast because each man disbelieved his fellows.

Neo-functionalism, a pioneering theory of regional integration, first developed in the 1950s. It was defined by its founding father as 'the process whereby political actors in several distinct national settings are persuaded to shift their loyalties, expectations and political activities towards a new and larger centre, whose institutions demand jurisdiction over the pre-existing states' (Haas, 1958: 366–7). A central theme of this theory is the idea that a limited degree of integration, as in the case of the ECSC, sets in motion a logic of change or 'spillover effect' as limited integration inevitably creates pressures for further integration in the economic sphere and ultimately leads to some form of supranational political community.

There is a wide range of potential contributors to this process including national governments, transnational interest groups and supranational institutions. Jean Monnet, the architect of the ECSC, was very much a key exponent of this 'chain reaction theory' that moving some policy functions to the supranational level will create pressure for more integration. To advance this cause and to overcome the resistance of local politicians to the idea of giving up their power, the role of pro-European technocrats like Monnet was to force the politicians' hands, taking advantage of any opportunity, especially moments of crisis: 'Europe will be forged in crises', observed Monnet, 'and will be the sum of the solutions adopted for those crises' (Monnet, 1978).

By way of contrast and as a challenge to neo-functionalism, the theory of intergovernmentalism emerged in the 1960s. It reflected the crises that the EC experienced in the 1960s and most especially the evolution of French policy under the presidency of General de Gaulle. Gaullist emphasis on national independence involved intransigent opposition to supranationalism. France particularly objected to plans for automatic funding of the EC. It boycotted all EC institutions in July 1965 until January 1966 and the making of the Luxembourg Agreement. This agreement amounted to an agreement to disagree between France and the other EC member states about the right to exercise a national veto in the Council of Ministers, the EC's decision-taking body. It was against this background that the theory of intergovernmentalism emerged. As applied to the EC, this theory insisted that only the central governments of the member states pursuing a form of national interest were the key actors. The emphasis is so much on relations between the governments of the member that this is often referred to as a state-centric approach.

Among more recent theoretical approaches, of which there have been many (see Gowland *et al.*, 2006: 343–62 for an overview), 'Europeanisation' is one such and has a variety of meanings according to one summary of its substance:

- Europeanization as changes in external territorial boundaries (such as in the case of enlargement);
- Europeanization as the development of institutions of governance at the European level;
- Europeanization as the export of European forms of political organization and governance beyond Europe;
- Europeanization as a political project in support of the construction of a unified and politically strong Europe;
- Europeanization as the penetration of European-level institutions into national and subnational systems of governance.

(Cini, 2007)

One further theory is worth mentioning here as it has a bearing on the discussion of devolution and the EU in Chapter 6. Some theorists of European integration seeking to understand and to explain the workings of the EU as a political system developed a theory of multi-level governance. According to this theory, EU policymaking basically involves the regions or sub-state actors playing an important role alongside states and supranational institutions.

The institutions of the European Union

The mixed character of the EU is also evident in institutional terms. EU institutions are normally classified as either supranational or intergovernmental. Neither of these terms was precisely defined in the original treaties, but they have emerged to indicate differences in the membership and representative functions of the EU institutions. Two of the five main institutions, the European Council and the Council of the European Union (hereafter Council of Ministers), are intergovernmental and comprise official representatives of the member states. They represent the interests of the individual member states in the EU decision-making process.

The terms 'intergovernmental' and 'supranational' also describe different decision-making procedures in the European Council and the Council of Ministers. Intergovernmental procedures mean that the government of a member state can exercise the right to veto unwanted decisions. Supranational decision rules, such as qualified majority voting (QMV), are procedures by which member states accept surrendering their veto.

The other institutions are supranational and consist of personnel either appointed or elected to serve and represent the collective 'European' interest. The European Commission and the European Court of Justice play an important role, initiating and overseeing policies in the former case and settling disputes between member states or between parties in the member states in the latter case. The European Parliament is a directly elected body and is involved in a system of co-decision-making with the Council of Ministers. There are also several other institutions like the European Central Bank (ECB) that play specialized roles.

- The European Council comprises the heads of state or governments of the member states, and became a formal EU institution as a result of the Lisbon Treaty. Its role is to provide the EU with the necessary impetus for its development and to define the general political guidelines. It does not exercise any legislative function. It elects its president for a period of two-and-a-half years. Incidentally, there is no short-age of presidents in the EU. Besides the president of the European Council, the Commission, the European Parliament and the European Central Bank are each headed by a president.
- The Council of Ministers is the EU's decision-making body. It consists of govern-ment ministers of the member states (varying in composition depending on the sub-ject under discussion). Its headquarters are in Brussels. In most cases, the Council's decisions, based on proposals from the Commission, are taken jointly with the European Parliament.
- The European Commission has its headquarters in Brussels. It comprises 28 Commissioners and acts in the general interest of the EU with complete independ-ence of national governments. Its main function is to propose and implement poli-cies adopted by the Council and the Parliament. As guardian of the Treaties, the Commission oversees the application of EU law under the control of the EU Court of Justice. The Commission is appointed for a five-year term by the Council.
- The Court of Justice is based in Luxembourg. It ensures compliance with the law in interpreting and applying the treaties. It comprises one judge per member state. Its two main functions are: to check whether instruments of the EU institutions and of governments are compatible with the treaties, and to give rulings, at the request of a national court, on the interpretation or the validity of provisions contained in EU law.
- The European Parliament comprises 751 members (MEPs) elected by direct uni-versal suffrage since 1979. The Parliament meets once a month in Strasbourg but is otherwise based in Brussels, an arrangement that has attracted criticism for being an expensive travelling circus. The Parliament shares legislative and budget-ary power with the Council. It also has power of control over the Commission in particular and among other things has the power to dismiss the Commission as a body.

(See the Appendix for further details about the EU's institutions and decision-making system.)

The history and functions of these institutions serve as a reminder that the original EC treaties were the products of a top-down, elitist, technocratic culture. Significantly, the Schuman Plan initially made no provision for a European Assembly. Furthermore, if the EC foundation treaties had been put to a popular vote with a built-in national veto they may not have left the drawing board. This history has given rise to the view of a 'democratic deficit' at the very heart of the EU, an organization that according to its critics does not satisfactorily answer some of the questions that Tony Benn, the former Labour government minister, claimed should be asked of anyone in a position of power:

What power have you got?
Where did you get it from?
In whose interests do you exercise it?

To whom are you accountable?
How do we get rid of you?

Some of the conflicts within the EC/EU and between Britain and the EU arise out of responses to such questions, most notably centring on tensions:

*   between the treaty and law-based character of the EU and democratic politics;
*   between the workings of an international organization and a federation;
*   involving the growing gap between elites and peoples;
*   between the traditional ways and means of politics and politically unaccountable bureaucracies or agencies.

(Mény, 2012)

The state of the union since 2000

Before the financial crisis of 2007–2008 and the subsequent lengthy slump posed a major challenge, it was increasingly apparent that the EU lacked a contemporary and compelling narrative and rationale comparable in vision, strength and impact to that of the founding fathers of the EC in the 1950s. On the fiftieth anniversary of the EC, it seemed that Europe had 'lost the plot' and 'no longer knows what story it wants to tell' (Ash, 2009: 125). One of the EU's grand designs for the first decade of the new century failed to take shape. The so-called Lisbon strategy, agreed by the European Council meeting in Lisbon in March 2000, aimed to make the EU by 2010 'the most competitive and dynamic-based economy in the world, capable of sustainable economic growth with more and better jobs and greater social cohesion' (European Council, 2000). It soon became clear, however, that particular targets, especially in the employment field, were being missed, and the crisis of 2007–2008 sounded the death-knell of such a strategy.

Meanwhile, there was an evident ebbing away of public support for the EU, again before the impact of events in the second decade of the twenty-first century. According to Eurobarometer (a series of public opinion surveys covering the EU member states and conducted regularly on behalf of the European Commission since 1973), in the period 1973–1991 the views of Europeans about the current benefits of EU membership improved considerably. Thereafter, however, support for the EU fell away, most markedly at the time of the Maastricht Treaty of 1992, again on the occasion of the abortive Constitutional Treaty and the enlargement of the EU to eastern Europe (2004), and with the onset of the euro area crisis.

The hardening of opinion against the further advance of the EU was first evident when Denmark initially rejected the Maastricht Treaty in a plebiscite, while the vote in France narrowly went in favour of the Treaty (the '*petit oui*'). Denmark and France both voted against the Constitutional Treaty and thus put an end to this project, while other member states including Britain would almost certainly have done the same if they had held referendums on the issue. The declining turnout at European Parliament elections from 61.99 per cent (1979) to 42.61 per cent (2014) may also count at the very least as evidence of growing disenchantment with the organization (www.europarl.europa.eu).

Design faults in the euro area were also evident before the post-2007 crisis highlighted them to even greater effect. In its origins, the euro area was born out of political rather than economic imperatives involving Germany's reluctant agreement to monetary union in return for French support for the idea of a united Germany. In laying the foundations for economic and monetary union, the Maastricht Treaty had included a set of rules to achieve that goal: low inflation, low interest rates, and controlled public debt and spending. Apart from political considerations the case for a monetary union was driven by several factors and claims:

- the elimination of transaction costs involved in changing currencies;
- the elimination of exchange rate uncertainty;
- the promotion of investment;
- reduced borrowing costs for countries with a history of high inflation and currency devaluation;
- increased scope for the comparison of prices and associated competition benefits;
- increased mobility of capital and integration of financial markets.

> (HM Government, 'Review of the Balance of Competences between the United Kingdom and the European Union Economic and Monetary Policy', December 2014: 35–6)

The Stability and Growth Pact (1997) established that the Maastricht Treaty rules should apply once the euro was launched. The pact applied to all EU member states, but some like Britain that refrained from adopting the euro were not bound by the penalties. All euro area states were required to keep their annual budget deficit below 3 per cent of GDP and to maintain total public debt below 60 per cent of GDP.

From the outset, a fundamental problem of these rules was that they were more honoured in the breach than in the observance. Indeed, the questionable qualifications of some of the original or early members of the euro area were initially overlooked and stored up trouble for the future. Strict adherence to the rules would almost certainly have excluded Belgium, Greece, Italy and Portugal. Several euro area states including France and Germany, the principal authors of the pact, subsequently broke the rules without any penalty. Furthermore, making the rules more flexible (2005) failed to solve the problem. The more general question and seemingly basic design fault of the euro area came to the fore with the crisis of 2007–2008, this being how to manage a monetary union at a time of crisis without a common banking, fiscal and political union.

The impact of the financial crisis of 2007–2008

The financial crisis of 2007–2008 with the accompanying credit crunch and the subsequently lengthy slump presented one of the greatest existential challenges in the history of the EU. The response to the crisis reflected the mixed, hybrid character of the EU, and the awkward, unique fit between its national and supranational dimensions. From the beginning of the crisis, the euro area in particular was subjected to a stern test concerning its identity, policy range and institutional character. To all intents and purposes, it was an unfinished, flawed creation in the form of a halfway house. It constituted a monetary union but fell far short of a fiscal union and had the greatest difficulty in constructing a fully-fledged banking union. The euro area crisis has also greatly increased support for traditionally anti-EU parties such as the Front National in France. It has spawned a large number of insurgent populist parties elsewhere in the EU which have proved increasingly critical of its management and of the EU idea at large.

The serious proportions of this crisis were all too evident by 2011/2012, by which time it was widely predicted that the euro area was heading for disintegration in the midst of chronic unemployment, little growth, a mass of public debt, rising budgetary deficits and soaring borrowing costs to member states like Greece, Italy, Portugal and Spain, prompting frequent references to a north–south division within the EU. In the period 2010–2013, only four of the 28 EU states throughout these years – Estonia, Finland, Luxembourg and Sweden – adhered to the Stability and Growth Pact requirement that their annual budget deficits should remain below 3 per cent of GDP (see Table 1.3). The unemployment figures presented a dire picture, rising for the twenty-fourth consecutive month to 12.2 per cent across the EU in April 2013 with a markedly higher rate among the under-25s of 24.4 per cent (Eurostat, April 2013). Government debt as a percentage of GDP also made grim reading; by 2012 the average for the EU as a whole amounted to 83.5 per cent. Some 19 of the 28 EU states effectively exceeded the 60 per cent permitted limit mentioned earlier; Greece (156.9 per cent), Portugal (124.8 per cent) and Italy (122.2 per cent) reported the highest while the British figure (2013) was 90.60 per cent.

Table 1.3 General government deficit/surplus (% of GDP) of the EU states, 2010–2013

	2010	*2011*	*2012*	*2013*
EU (28 states)	−6.4	−4.5	−4.2	−3.2
Belgium	−4.0	−3.9	−4.1	−2.9
Bulgaria	−3.2	−2.0	−0.5	−1.2
Czech Republic	−4.4	−2.9	−4.0	−1.3
Denmark	−2.7	−2.1	−3.9	−0.7
Germany	−3.0	−4.1	−0.9	−0.1
Estonia	0.2	1.0	−0.3	−0.5
Ireland	−32.4	−12.6	−8.0	−12.2
Greece	−11.1	−10.1	−8.6	−12.2
Spain	−9.4	−9.4	−10.3	−6.8
France	−6.8	−5.1	−4.9	−4.1
Croatia	−6.0	−7.7	−5.6	−5.2
Italy	−4.2	−3.5	−3.0	−2.8
Cyprus	−4.8	−5.8	−5.8	−4.9
Latvia	−8.2	−3.4	−0.8	−0.9
Lithuania	−6.9	−9.0	−3.2	−2.6
Luxembourg	0.6	0.3	0.1	0.6
Hungary	−4.5	−5.5	−2.3	−2.4
Malta	−3.3	−2.6	−3.7	−2.7
Netherlands	−5.0	−4.3	−4.0	−2.3
Austria	−4.5	−2.6	−2.3	−1.5
Poland	−7.6	−4.9	−3.7	−4.0
Portugal	−11.2	−7.4	−5.5	−4.9
Romania	−6.6	−5.5	−3.0	−2.2
Slovenia	−5.7	−6.2	−3.7	−14.6
Slovakia	−7.5	−4.1	−4.2	−2.6
Finland	−2.6	−1.0	−2.1	−2.4
Sweden	0.0	−0.1	−0.9	−1.3
United Kingdom	−9.6	−7.6	−8.3	−5.8

Source: Eurostat.

'Whatever it takes'

It was against this gloomy background and the increasing possibility of the collapse of the euro area that significant action was taken. Germany as a surplus country with a healthy external balance of trade and payments was under intense pressure to take positive measures. In a meeting (November 2011) with the US and French presidents, Obama and Sarkozy, Angela Merkel, the German chancellor, was subjected to such pressure that the normally imperturbable chancellor said angrily with tears welling in her eyes '*Das ist nicht fair*' (That is not fair); 'I cannot decide in lieu of the Bundesbank', she added, by which she meant that the Bundesbank, the German central bank, was so constituted in the 1950s as to be completely independent from politicians. In the event, she successfully resisted the main thrust of American and French arguments (Spiegel, 2014).

This episode was important in several respects. It was arguably the most critical juncture in the history of the euro area to date, prompting one member of the French delegation at the meeting to observe: 'It was the point where clearly the Eurozone as we know it could have exploded' (Spiegel, 2014). It was important, too, in giving momentum in the following month to a German-inspired proposal for a Fiscal Compact that took the form of the Treaty on Stability, Coordination and Governance which entered into force in January 2013. Significantly, the treaty had to be concluded as an intergovernmental rather than an EU measure (see Chapter 12). What the treaty underlined so far as Germany was concerned was the need to ensure stricter observance of the Stability and Growth rules and closer monitoring of any euro area state failing to observe the rules in the interests of greater fiscal discipline. The Bundesbank occupied a commanding position in determining the response to what were perceived as spendthrift euro area governments.

The treaty was the beginning of a concerted effort to save the euro area, culminating in the declaration (26 July 2012) by Mario Draghi, President of the European Central Bank, that the bank would do 'whatever it takes' to save the euro. Draghi himself belonged to the long line of EU technocrats stretching back to Jean Monnet and his associates in the 1950s. In the meantime and thereafter, improvised bailouts and muddling through (or 'kicking the can down the road' to use a common description) became the order of the day among the EU's political leaders whose lack of a proactive strategy and last-minute adjustments suggested an 'unbearable lightness of leaders' (*Financial Times*, 6 August 2011).

Bailouts took the form of either open support from the governments of euro area member states and the International Monetary Fund (IMF) or more tacit programmes of support from the European Central Bank. The latter eventually included the adoption of a quantitative easing (QE) programme commencing in March 2015 and involving the ECB in creating new money electronically by buying assets, typically government bonds, from banks and other financial institutions. The debt crisis was increasingly policed by the so-called Troika comprising the EU Commission, the IMF and the ECB with responsibility for laying down stringent austerity measures when bailouts or promises of bailouts were made to indebted euro area states. This arrangement with its German emphasis on a system for imposing discipline upon wayward countries was described as a 'discipline union', effectively meaning that member states 'are free to do precisely as they are told' (Wolf, 2014: 338).

Greece and the 'Grexit' threat

One state in particular put this austerity regime to the test – Greece. It has done so ever since the start of the crisis and predictably so in view of earlier evidence of Greek inability to adhere to the requirements of the original Stability and Growth Pact. The Greek case for joining the euro area was undoubtedly strengthened by the fact that there was systematic falsification of Greek public accounts throughout the period 1997–2003 which only came to light in 2004. In effect, Greece had misreported its financial data to the Eurostat (the EU's statistical office), producing figures that vastly overstated its fiscal health in the run-up to euro area membership when it had to meet the Stability and Growth Pact criteria. That revelation, together with widespread tax avoidance and evasion in the country, ensured that in the wake of the financial crisis of 2007–2008 its debt burden grew bigger and its economy became smaller. Greece was thus the most likely euro area state to exit from the euro area by choice or of necessity ('Grexit').

The key player in this drama throughout these years was Germany, so much so that by 2015 Greece was almost entirely dependent on Germany as the provider of the vast bulk of Greece's latest bailout programme of 240 billion euros. The possibility of 'Grexit' first came to the fore and most notably in German government circles in 2011/2012. Merkel's advisers divided into two camps. The 'domino camp' warned that Grexit would trigger panicked selling of all troubled euro area government bonds, potentially followed by large-scale bank runs in Italy, Portugal and Spain. The opposing view or 'infected leg' camp, expressed most forcefully by Germany's powerful finance minister, Wolfgang Schäuble, argued that cutting off Greece would allow the rest of Europe to return to health. That debate continued and the issue came into even sharper focus in February 2015 when the newly formed Greek government under the leadership of the left-wing Syriza party and with Alexis Tsipiras at its head secured a four-month extension to the bailout arranged in February 2012. Schäuble was even less impressed by the Greek case, and while Tsipiras came to power pledging to destroy 'Merkelism', the German chancellor herself described the new Greek leader as 'that unhelpful trouble maker' (*The Guardian*, 22 March 2015).

Meanwhile, in terms of furthering the process of integration, the period since the financial crisis of 2007/2008 has seen some, albeit minimal, progress. True, the euro area states eventually agreed to a banking union (March 2014) that pools sovereignty over banking supervision, and to a lesser extent provides for the closure or rescue of failed banks. However, they have shown little inclination to embark on a euro area fiscal union (i.e. common tax and spending policies) facilitating the transfer of resources to economies in need of assistance. Nor have measures to date done much to dent what is viewed as part of the root of the problem, this being the massive swing of Germany into a current account surplus over the past ten years that has been accompanied by a matching deficit extending to Greece, Ireland, Italy, Portugal and Spain (Wolf, 2014: 177, 179).

By early 2015 there were signs that the euro, now strengthened by the start of the ECB's programme of quantitative easing (March 2015), had survived the worst and that some degree of economic growth was underway across the EU. It remained the case, however, that the euro area still faced some fundamental predicaments. As several commentators have observed, the project is at risk since it seems impossible to go forward to a far stronger union or back to national monetary independence.

The migrant crisis

Greece also came to occupy centre stage in the unfolding of another major crisis that has shaken the very foundations of the EU at large in recent years: the influx of migrants from the Middle East and North Africa. In 2015 alone and according to the United Nations High Commission for Refugees, as of 19 November 2015 some 850,571 'refugees and migrants' had arrived by sea in Europe in this year, and just over 50 per cent of Mediterranean sea arrivals were fleeing from civil war in Syria, 20 per cent from Afghanistan (T. G. Ash, *The Guardian*, 30 November 2015). Other significant national groups fleeing from conflict and repression were Albanians, Eritreans and Iraqis. According to the International Organization for Migration, the latest figures for 2015 as of 21 December were 1,005,504 arrivals, the vast majority of whom – 816,752 – arrived by sea in Greece. A further 150,317 arrived by sea in Italy with much smaller figures for Cyprus, Malta and Spain, while 34,215 crossed by land routes, such as over the Turkish–Bulgarian border. The overall figure represented a fourfold increase on the figures for 2014.

The scale of this refugee crisis and the response of the EU and of individual member states are briefly noted here and discussed later. This population movement is clearly without parallel in post-1945 Europe, yet it has not yet matched the scale of migration from eastern to western Europe during and at the end of the Second World War – variously estimated at some 10–12 million people. The sheer volume of human traffic in recent years has nonetheless represented a serious challenge to the EU as an organization. It has raised question marks about the survival of the borderless Schengen area within the EU comprising 22 EU states and four non-EU states (see Chapter 4). It has tested the ability of the EU states to accommodate the migrants while dealing with the domestic consequences of this exercise against the background of a rising tide of populist nationalism across the EU with right-wing parties either in government or on the advance in Austria, Belgium, the Czech Republic, Denmark, the Netherlands and Poland. All in all, the refugee crisis offers something of a cameo sketch of the state of the EU by 2015 as governments struggled to square a workable immigration policy with popular support.

Deep divisions among the EU states over the handling of the immigration crisis became increasingly apparent during the course of 2015. Conflicting responses to this development became most marked as Chancellor Merkel of Germany relaxed the rules on Syrian refugees entering Germany, in addition to others seeking refuge from violence and warfare (September 2015). Germany thereby forfeited its right to return refugees to the EU state that they had first entered (known as the Dublin Regulation which makes the first EU country in which a refugee arrives responsible for any asylum claim). The result of Merkel's open door policy, which was quickly qualified by the reimposition of border controls in accordance with the Dublin Regulation, was that approximately 800,000 refugees made their way to Germany in 2015, a moving spectacle as 'The Statue of Liberty took up temporary residence in Berlin'. Meanwhile, the Dublin Regulation proved unworkable due to the sheer weight of numbers concentrated in just one or two countries: some 850,000 entered Greece in 2015 alone and 200,000 landed in Italy.

The German response formed a marked contrast to reactions elsewhere, especially in eastern Europe where Berlin was criticized for its unilateral, high-handed actions in pressing on with a scheme for distributing refugees by quota across the EU; Britain, Denmark and Ireland have special exemptions on justice and home affairs policies in the EU, including asylum matters, and do not need to take part. EU member states in eastern Europe – the so-called Visegrad 4 – the Czech Republic, Hungary, Poland and Slovakia – were set on stemming the migratory flow by reinforcing the EU's external border. Hungary took the lead in strengthening its border with Serbia by erecting a razor wire fence and proceeded to do likewise on its border with its fellow EU member state, Croatia.

Such attempts to seal borders to newcomers along the Balkan routes gave rise to a German-inspired plan to trade money, visa-free travel within the Schengen area and refugee quotas to Turkey in return for Turkey's efforts to minimize the number of refugees crossing the Aegean Sea to Greece. This plan was based on EU states volunteering to take in quotas of refugees directly from Turkey and to deport illegal migrants to Turkey. By early 2016, however, it was evident that support for the plan was fading even among Germany's allies on the issue – notably Austria, France and Sweden (*The Guardian*, 18 February 2016).

There are clearly parallels between the euro area and migration crises, most notably: the hybrid nature of European governance structures that are ill-prepared to face up to major external challenges; the preeminence of Germany as a key player and as Europe's political, economic and diplomatic centre; and the important role of a peripheral country – Greece – as a conduit for an external challenge that is becoming an internal crisis (Chryssogelos, 2015). Just as the euro area crisis was at its most intense in relation to handling Greece's problems, so the migrant crisis has pushed Greece to the forefront because, as noted earlier, many refugees and migrants have landed on Greek soil and have been allowed to pass into the rest of the EU under the Schengen regime.

The handling of these crises raises fundamental questions about the role, power and identity of the EU and its member states. In November 2015, Donald Tusk, president of the European Council, warned EU governments that they could not 'outsource' (i.e. to Turkey) the job of securing the external borders to the EU's Schengen area. His statement begged the question of who or what was to take responsibility for such matters. The crisis has laid bare the shortcomings of the EU, not least of these being the lack of a well-funded and well-resourced EU border and coastguard service, capable of managing the EU's external border. Similar questions arose about the limitations of the euro area, and more generally about the EU's existence in the international system at large. What is it? Economic giant and political dwarf? Feeble or powerful? A melting-pot or a bag of marbles in terms of state identity? Superstate in the making or largely a regulatory regime? Such questions were posed by a British scholar at the beginning of Britain's EC membership. They have been at the heart of debates about the EU and about Britain's involvement in the organization ever since (Shonfield, 1972: 9).

Conclusion

This chapter has drawn a distinction between Europe at large and the EU in particular in British minds. A wide variety of long-standing and disputed historical influences have figured as shaping British policy and attitudes towards the EU. A limited view of these influences suggests that the country has pursued a separate historical development from mainland Europe. Its global role, widespread interests and domestic practices and traditions have set it apart from any deep sense of continental European identity and history. An altogether different reading of the story, however, emphasizes a high degree of long-standing commonality between Britain and the continent extending from participation in medieval culture and power politics to involvement in the world wars of the twentieth century.

Whether Britain is a part of or apart from Europe has engaged the attention of historians in recent years in relation to the value and relevance of British involvement in the EU. We have noted that historians have divided opinions on the matter. Some emphasize Britain's exceptionalist identity and are usually inclined to support withdrawal from the EU. Others stress the country's European connections and typically support continuing membership of the EU.

The chapter has also featured the origins, evolution, key features and current problems of the EU. It has done so to provide an introductory frame of reference about the subject and to introduce some of the major landmarks in the history of the EU that figure elsewhere in the book.

2 Back to the future

> England is sticky with self-pity and is not prepared to accept peacefully and wisely the fact that her position and resources are not what they once were.
>
> (John Maynard Keynes, January 1946)

Introduction

This chapter focuses on the period 1945–1973 when British aloofness from the origins and early evolution of the EU in the 1950s was followed by a reappraisal of British policy resulting in three attempts to secure EU membership. It deals with some of the immediate and medium-term influences that shaped British policy and attitudes towards European integration after the end of the Second World War in 1945. We consider how far treatment of EU membership in this period was influenced by a historically minded, backward-looking perspective involving a network of long-standing ties rather than a forward-looking positive interest in a new project. The chapter examines the conditions and circumstances that first influenced the decision to stay out of the formative stages of the EU, and subsequently had an important bearing on the move towards membership.

Limited liability and continental commitment

In 1949 the Labour government under the leadership of Clement Attlee resolved that British policy should assist the recovery of Europe as far as possible but that 'the concept must be one of limited liability'. It was further agreed that the amount of assistance should not be so great as to leave Britain too weak to be a worthwhile ally of the United States. Nor should such assistance result in any form of co-operation with continental European states that surrendered British sovereignty and led the country down paths along which there was no return (Cairncross, 1982: 209).

This general conclusion was most immediately shaped by wartime experiences and early post-war conditions. It was also to govern British policy towards the beginnings of the EC in the 1950s, and it has remained in play down to the present day as symptomatic of the stresses and strains in seeking to strike a balance between limited liability and continental commitment.

The period 1945–1949 witnessed the resumption of a debate that in the 1930s had focused on British military strategy. In that period, limited liability meant providing only small land forces in a European war, while a continental commitment envisaged fighting a war with massive military support. Circumstances had greatly changed by the late 1940s. The strategic decisions, however, were not so very different. The reasons why the Attlee government opted to use limited liability as the benchmark of British policy towards the reconstruction of mainland Europe convey much about the parameters and setting of subsequent British policy towards the idea of European integration. If often used covertly, the language of limited liability has remained a useful tool of British political leaders ever since, even though – and sometimes because – the main thrust of their policy within the EC/EU has pointed in the direction of the continental commitment.

The impact of the Second World War

The Second World War had a profound and lasting impact on the post-war attitudes of British policymakers and public towards involvement in mainland Europe. Wartime experiences reinforced a deep-seated sense of insularity and detachment from the continent. Europe was regarded as a source of war, disorder and dictatorship, while widespread and lasting Germanophobia contributed to a pathological distrust of continental affairs.

Furthermore, Britain had escaped the mainland European wartime trauma of invasion, defeat and occupation. There was thus a far greater inclination in the country than on the continent to regard the wartime record, most especially the landmark events of 1940 like the Dunkirk evacuation and the Battle of Britain – 'their finest hour' as Churchill put it – as a matter of perpetual celebration and as part of a deeply ingrained folk memory. Such events were to be maintained by a memory bank of wartime exploits, myths and prejudices, so much so that in the course of time it seemed that Britain's future lay in its past. An endless stream of anniversaries continued to focus on British involvement in two world wars, particular events in the case of the Second World War being enthusiastically observed to a greater extent in Britain than elsewhere. Viewed in some quarters as an unhealthy obsession, such anniversary events served a number of functions whether as a reminder of Britain's past standing as a world power or as a means of seeking to uphold a common British identity, history and unity.

At the very least, the events of 1940 have formed an integral part of the creation myth of modern Britain, while the Second World War at large was in very different ways a foundation stone of later Eurosceptic and Europhile opinion. John Redwood, the well-known Conservative parliamentarian and opponent of EU membership, wrote of the contrast: 'Britain is at peace with its past in a way that many continental countries could never be … We do not have to live down the shame that many French people feel regarding the events of 1940–44. We do not have to live … with the collective guilt that Germany feels about the Holocaust' (Redwood, 2005: 12). Likewise, Liam Fox, the former Cabinet minister, declared that Britain was 'one of the few countries in the European Union that does not need to bury its 20th century history' (*The Guardian*, 4 March 2016), seemingly overlooking some of the unsavoury and hidden aspects of imperial rule.

Certainly, Britain shared none of the enthusiastic commitment to the idea of European integration as a form of liberation from a troubled past. West Germany was the most obvious example in this respect (see below). In later years, other European states also aimed to confirm and reinforce their European and democratic credentials as in the case of Greece, Portugal and Spain that emerged from military dictatorship in the 1980s and later the former communist states of eastern and central Europe. Prior to his country's accession to the EU in July 2013 as the latest new member state, Branko

Baricevic, the Croatian ambassador in Brussels, declared that 'the EU for us is not a question of choice. It is our destiny' (cited in Wellings and Baxendale, 2014). He thus expressed a prevailing view in the other eastern and southern European states in seeking EU membership, all of which was in marked contrast to the British view of EU membership as a matter of choice and of a hotly contested choice at that.

The wartime record was viewed as affirming rather than calling into question the strength and continuity of British culture, institutions and sovereignty. This condition was altogether different from that of defeated and occupied Germany. There, the immediate aftermath of war was known, if quite misleadingly, as zero hour (*Stunde Null*) and there were the beginnings of the extended process of coming to terms with the past (expressed in the appropriately lengthy German word *Vergangenheitsbewältigung*) and with the horrors of the infamous Hitler regime. There was no such radical break or discontinuity with the past in the case of Britain, no starting from scratch, and no need to establish new political systems or a modernized economic infrastructure as in Germany and throughout much of western Europe. Nor did post-war Britain require some zero hour myth of wiping the historical slate clean and starting afresh as was so evident in Germany at this time. In 1975 one British ambassador to West Germany commented that it required 'great, not to say gymnastic efforts to try to bridge the gulf between the British people's lively remembrance of the past and the Germans' oblivion about it' (quoted in Parris and Bryson, 2010: 35).

Britain and post-war Germany

Ironically, as one of the four military occupying powers in Germany, the Attlee government played an instrumental role in giving West Germany a federal political system that was long to remain anathema to British politicians both domestically and in terms of the organization of Europe. In addition, the British government also among other things helped to create a streamlined West German trade union movement that proved to be a model bargaining system and contrasted with the fragmented character of British trade union organization. It was perhaps also ironic that this was achieved under the foreign secretaryship of Ernest ('Ernie') Bevin, regarded by some as the outstanding British foreign secretary of modern times and a pugnacious defender of British interests with a bulldog patriotism in the Churchillian mould. Bevin was reluctant to visit Germany or to meet German politicians; 'I tries 'ard but I 'ates them' he confided in the British military governor in Germany (Bullock, 1983: 90) (he also had difficulty with his aitches).

Bevin's response was therefore unsurprising when one of his junior ministers, Frank Pakenham, who had special responsibility for post-war Germany in the Foreign Office, was anxious to show the Germans that the British felt no hatred for them. He was so determined to extend the hand of friendship that on his first trip to Germany he stepped out of the aircraft with outstretched arms looking to embrace the nearest German. Unfortunately, he did so before the mechanics had pushed forward the steps. He promptly did himself an injury; 'Serves 'im right' muttered Bevin whose view more fairly reflected that of the public at large, this accounting for the common saying that Europeans would not want to be led by Germans anywhere – even towards paradise.

German achievements since 1945, whether in the factory or on the football field, long remained unimpressive to some sections of British public opinion; 'Isn't it terrible about losing to the Germans at our national sport, Prime Minister?' commented Ken Clarke, the long-standing Conservative Cabinet minister, when England lost to Germany in the semi-finals of the 1990 World Cup, to which Margaret Thatcher retorted 'I shouldn't worry too much – we've beaten them twice this century at theirs'.

Britain's status as one of the three major victorious allies alongside the United States and the USSR seemed, outwardly at least, to confirm the country's position as a global power. The country was represented at the wartime and post-war conferences of the 'Big Three', and at war's end British armed forces comprised some five million personnel stationed across Europe, the Middle East, Africa and the Far East. Appearances, however, were deceptive and obscured the extent to which in its broadest, strategic outlines the Second World War consisted of four major combatants and two theatres of war: Germany and the Soviet Union in Europe, Japan and the United States in the Far East. This situation accounted for the comment attributed to Stalin, the Soviet leader, that 'England provided the time, America provided the money, and Russia provided the blood'. In any event, global power resources and status clearly marked Britain off from the other European states with their wartime experience of occupation, division and defeat. Oliver Franks, a leading British official throughout this period, succinctly summarized the deeply ingrained view of the British political establishment: 'Britain is going to continue to be what she has been, a Great Power' (*The Times*, 8 November 1954).

From Empire to Commonwealth

Besides the country's global power status, a further defining and recurring factor in the making of British policy towards Europe was the prevailing view in Whitehall that Europe could not be separated from the global dimensions of British foreign policy. Furthermore, it was a widespread view in government quarters that the European continent did not represent the major, exclusive area of British strategic interest. There was a marked difference in resources between Britain and much of mainland Europe in the early post-war years that considerably influenced British policy towards post-war European organizations. There was also a large reservoir of goodwill towards the British Commonwealth and Empire in view of its contribution to the war effort. The Britain 'standing alone' imagery often obscured the importance of manpower, resources and money from this source. Until the summer of 1944 there were more Commonwealth troops in the fighting line than Americans, comprising in total some 2.5 million from the Dominions, 2 million Indians, some 700,000 from African colonies, and 16,000 from the Caribbean (Colley, 2014: 125).

Britain's post-war recovery was assisted by assets denied to or only partially available to most European states: the markets and colonial resources of the British Empire and Commonwealth (or the Commonwealth as it was formally designated in 1949 to keep a republican India within the fold). Developments in this field were remarkably rapid as the process of decolonization took scarcely much more than a generation. At the turn of the century, when the British Empire comprised some 294 million people, imperial decay seemed unimaginable; Curzon, Viceroy of India in the period 1899–1905, would not allow the hymn 'The day Thou gavest Lord is ended' to be sung in the Raj on the grounds that it contained the words 'earth's proud empires pass away'. In 1942 Churchill declared that 'he had not been made His Majesty's First Minister to preside over the liquidation of the British Empire'. Five years later, however, India, the 'jewel in the crown' of the British Empire, achieved independence together with Pakistan, followed by Burma and Ceylon in 1948. Decolonization thereafter happened at breakneck speed elsewhere. Some 40 countries achieved independence from British rule over the next 30 years, markedly so in Africa during the period 1957–1963.

If the emergence of the Commonwealth came to mask Britain's declining power in the world, during the early post-war years at least British governments regarded the Commonwealth as a fundamental asset both in terms of strategic value and prestige and also as an economic, commercial and financial entity of the first order. It covered a quarter of the world's land mass, provided access to scarce raw materials and, as the world's largest free trading bloc via the operation of the imperial preference system, it offered an assured market for British goods and accounted for approximately 50 per cent of British trade. The Empire and Commonwealth constituted a major, defining framework for shaping British policy towards post-war schemes for European unity and co-operation. This multifaceted enterprise, with its mixture of tradition, sentiment and interest, was regarded as the indispensable arm of British power and independence in the world. It was a major component in the British people's sense of identity and integration at home and abroad. It has rightly been called a global mosaic of almost ungraspable complexity, comprising as it did self-governing Dominions, internally autonomous protectorates, dependent territories linked by treaty, and directly adminis-tered Crown colonies (Tombs, 2014: 778).

Certainly, Empire meant many things. To British schoolchildren before and during the 1950s it was an integral part of British history and a way of learning about the geography of the world, not always successfully; an opinion poll in 1947 found that 50 per cent of the respondents could not name a single colony, and one respondent named Lincolnshire as a possible colony (Sandbrook, 2005: 252). For the British consumer, the Empire meant lamb and butter from New Zealand, tea from India, chocolate from Nigeria, coffee from Kenya, apples, peaches and pears from South Africa, and tin and rubber from Malaya. It meant Imperial Leather soap with its trademark illustration of African servants carrying huge bars of soap aloft or Robertsons jam with its 'gol-lywogs'. Empire meant too the ability to travel round the world via ports that flew only the Union Jack, and to celebrate what was represented as a characteristically 'British' family of nations. Attlee later contrasted the principal features of this family of nations with the alternative of 'Continentalism' with its lack of a shared history or common way of life (*Sunday Express*, 4 February 1963) (see Chapter 11 for further discussion of the Commonwealth and Europe).

Besides the Empire and Commonwealth, there were other indicators of Britain's global reach and resources. There was most notably the sterling area that was largely though not wholly coterminous with the Empire and Commonwealth (apart from Canada and Hong Kong). It was the largest monetary area in the world and was headed by Britain as the central banker with all currencies in the sterling area tied to the pound. By this means London played a prominent role in the world's financial system at a time when sterling was used in some 50 per cent of the world's trade and international payments. Sterling thus had global status as a reserve currency alongside the dollar. Supporting the value of sterling in the fixed exchange rate system of the post-war world (until the early 1970s) was a key feature of government policy, especially as the value of foreign holdings of sterling assets exceeded the value of the country's foreign reserves. Recurring current account deficits and sterling crises in the early post-war decades were often treated more seriously than the country's industrial failings because of the impli-cations for government expenditure at home and abroad and in view of financial inter-ests. The maintenance of sterling as a reserve currency was long viewed in government circles as essential for the City's protection as a financial centre. Throughout this period and beyond, the comment of Winston Churchill as Chancellor of the Exchequer in 1925 continued to resonate: 'I would rather see finance less proud and industry more content'. It remained the case, in fact, that the interests of Britain's financial establishment – the Treasury, the Bank of England and the City – took precedence.

This key feature of the country's economy distinguished Britain from the continental states and has done so ever since as exemplified by the leading role of the City of London in the EU's financial services sector (see Chapter 10). That said, however, in the early post-war years at least, Britain had substantial manufacturing capacity and assets as compared with its continental neighbours. In 1951, it still accounted for one-third of the total industrial production of non-communist Europe (roughly equivalent to the combined industrial production of France and Germany) and enjoyed a pronounced lead over other European manufacturers in sectors like merchant shipbuilding, cars and aircraft. These advantages together with the largest military power of any west European state indicated that Britain's standing as a world power had substance and also meant that Europe was not a crucial or necessary element in Britain's post-war economic recovery.

A 'financial Dunkirk'

At the time, however, there was limited appreciation of the extent to which Britain had entered a phase displaying the characteristics of a second-class power on the global stage: military dependence on a powerful ally in the form of the United States, persistent economic vulnerability, crippling overseas debts, imperial overstretch and a narrowing range of options in international affairs. It seemed that the country had figured on the winning side in the war but was not a winner, a condition not unfairly described as that of 'a worn-out people with worn-out machinery'. During a wartime visit to the White House, Churchill startled Roosevelt when he emerged from the bath and declared that 'The Prime Minister of Great Britain has nothing to conceal from the President of the United States' (Reynolds, 1986). That was true literally and metaphorically, for the Roosevelt administration was familiar with the ways in which Britain had to repay US military support and supplies by running down its gold reserves, by selling off overseas assets, and by trading use or ownership of some of its overseas bases. During the war, Roosevelt himself had given Churchill fair warning that he had no intention of helping the British 'hang on to the archaic, medieval Empire ideas', and furthermore he was not averse to the idea of cutting out Churchill from his own dealings with Stalin.

Few were more alert to the perilous state of the British economy and public finances than the celebrated economist John Maynard Keynes. He was in no doubt that the country's massive external debts and losses meant that it faced 'a financial Dunkirk' and virtual bankruptcy; in short, the world's biggest creditor in 1914 had become the world's largest debtor. Keynes played a leading role in negotiating the first British post-war loan from the United States. In January 1946 and immediately after that punishing experience, he commented 'England is sticky with self-pity and is not prepared to accept peacefully and wisely the fact that her position and resources are not what they once were' (Kynaston, 2011: 423). Precisely the same condition was noted by Edward Stettinius, the US Secretary of State in the closing stages of the Second World War. Stettinius advised President Roosevelt never to underestimate the difficulty an Englishman faces in adjusting to a secondary role after so long seeing leadership as a national right. Stettinius here expressed one of the later, if often unstated, strands in the argument for exiting from the EU on the grounds that Britain did not found and does not lead the enterprise.

The formation of the Atlantic Alliance

The dominant historical narrative guiding British policymakers in their treatment of Europe in these early post-war years and beyond consisted of at least three major strands. First, the pre-war policy of appeasement had to be avoided at all costs. This requirement was particularly the case in seeking to contain what was perceived as the foremost geopolitical reality in Europe: the menacing Soviet presence and sphere of influence in eastern Europe. Second, there was a strong predisposition against irreversible European entanglements and open-ended commitments to continental security. 'We do not want any more Dunkirks', declared Ernest Bevin, the British foreign secretary and key member of the Attlee government, who was mindful of the fact that the main pillars of British defence policy at this time – the British mainland, control of the lines of sea communication especially via the Suez Canal (the 'Empire's jugular') and defence commitments in the Middle East – took priority over any possible peacetime undertaking to the defence of mainland Europe. How to square these two circles – containing vastly superior Soviet power in Europe while limiting the nature and extent of any commitment to Europe – found expression in the third strand, this being British involvement in developing early post-war European organizations.

Historians have offered different assessments of the underlying motivations of British policy towards Europe in this period. Some studies suggest that Bevin was principally concerned to restore Britain's credentials as a world power by organizing 'the middle of the planet' – including the west European states – in a power bloc comparable to the United States and the USSR. A more plausible explanation, however, focuses on the origins and impact of the enveloping Cold War. It stresses Bevin's role in shaping a western bloc based on the restoration of the close wartime relationship between Britain and the United States. This emphasis on the 'Atlanticist' strain in British policy is summed up in the view that the North Atlantic Treaty of 1949, with its military apparatus in the form of the North Atlantic Treaty Organization (NATO) a year later, was Bevin's crowning achievement.

The formative stages in the creation of this Atlantic Alliance indicated both British concern to develop a close relationship with the United States and London's reservations about overclose relations with France in the sphere of military strategy. Among other things, it was feared that substantive co-operation with France was bound to reveal British and US plans to evacuate their occupation forces from Germany in the event of a Soviet invasion. The British Chiefs of Staff especially did not wish to arouse French suspicions that 'we intend to desert them in the event of Russian aggression' (Cornish, 1995: 139).

There was a far greater willingness in London to participate in highly secret talks with the United States than with France. The dialogue between London and Washington was most evident in exchanges before and after the beginning of formal discussions resulting in the North Atlantic Treaty of 1949: the exploratory Pentagon talks of 22 March – 1 April 1948 were restricted to American, British and Canadian delegates. The French were excluded on security grounds – ironically so in view of the fact that one of the British delegates, Donald Maclean, was later to be exposed as a Soviet spy. He remained undetected for much the same reason as his fellow spy Guy Burgess who failed to land a job at Eton because the school had a more stringent vetting process than the British secret service.

The reconstruction of western Europe and the British model of European unity

Britain played a prominent role in the origins of the first generation of post-war European organizations. These bodies reflected a British understanding of European unity that emphasized intergovernmental co-operation and a pragmatic approach.

This strategy was designed to demonstrate to the Americans Britain's European leadership credentials. It also aimed to encourage US financial and military support for western Europe and for Britain in particular. Britain thus took the lead in responding to the offer of US aid by Secretary of State Marshall in June 1947, and in time was first in the queue for aid and received more than any other single country. The Attlee Labour government was also the prime mover in determining the character and aims of the organization – Organization for European Economic Cooperation (OEEC) – that was responsible for the distribution of aid and for undertaking the beginnings of trade liberalization following the protectionist regime of the inter-war and wartime period.

In March 1948, immediately after his Western Union speech two months earlier calling for some form of union in western Europe including Britain, Bevin was to the fore in forming a mutual security pact – the Brussels Treaty Organization (BTO) – that comprised Belgium, Britain, France, Luxembourg and the Netherlands. This initiative in turn shortly laid the basis for the North Atlantic Treaty of 1949.

More reluctantly but nonetheless influentially, Britain played a prominent role in ushering into being the Council of Europe in 1949 with its centrepiece of a consultative European Assembly. Bevin all the while emphasized the importance of a gradual, pragmatic, step-by-step approach based on intergovernmental co-operation. He thus expressed a lasting and deep-seated British suspicion of and opposition to what were viewed as utopian constitution-making, obsessive institution-building and impractical or abstract theory on the continent. He acquiesced in the formation of the Council of Europe but warned: 'If you open that Pandora's box, you never know what Trojan 'orses will jump out'. His worst fears about the Council of Europe and federalist opinion, however, were seemingly confirmed when the head of the British delegation reported on the federalists as 'conclaves of chatterboxes' and also observed that the French delegation consisted of a team of historical monuments incapable of any further action after the effort of the inaugural speeches (NA., FO 371/73099). Meanwhile, Oliver Harvey, British ambassador to France, cited the formation of the Council of Europe as an example of how the French maintained that 'the creation of European machinery would stimulate the growth of European consciousness, whereas the British held that until that consciousness had developed the machinery would be useless and probably dangerous' (NA., FO 371/89189, 2 March 1950).

Here then were the foundations of a British-led western Europe with a proprietorial attitude in Whitehall towards the functioning of such organizations. A varied mixture of arrogance, condescension and complacency often shot through the attitudes of London policymakers towards the mainland European states at the time. Edmund Hall-Patch, head of the British delegation to the OEEC and the personification of the patrician Whitehall mandarin, reported to ministers in July 1952 'The Europeans look to us for leadership; they are delighted when we are able to give it;

they respond to it in a remarkable manner' (NA., FO 371/77999). This view, however, was always combined with what was regarded as a hard-headed appreciation of the liabilities rather than the assets represented by these states. Three years earlier, the headmasterly Hall-Patch had warned ministers 'Do not put all your eggs in the European basket. It is a pretty shoddy contraption and there are no signs yet that the essential repairs are going to be made' (*Documents on British Policy Overseas* [hereafter *DBPO*], series II, vol. I, no. 466).

Opposition to the idea of a European customs union

The Treasury was particularly to the fore in resisting participation in any form of European economic integration that contemplated a customs union in the first instance and more radical schemes thereafter. The idea of a west European customs union did receive serious attention in the Foreign Office in 1947–1948. A paper on the subject justified its support for such a venture on the grounds that 'For better or for worse, our fate is in large part bound up with that of Western Europe' (NA., FO 371/71766, 27 February 1948). This paper represented a detailed, updated version of the strategy of continental commitment as against the concept of limited liability. The Foreign Office was here veering towards the former.

Had this view prevailed, the Attlee government would have figured at the forefront of precisely the project that the six founder member states of the EEC were to pioneer ten years later – a customs union comprising a tariff-free trading block and a common external tariff. The fact that Britain did not do so was due to weighty objections from the Treasury and the Board of Trade combined with strong reservations from the military about making any commitment to the European continent without a matching American commitment. As one senior British diplomat expressed the matter at the time: 'the mere words "customs union" produce a shudder in the Treasury and nausea in the Board of Trade' (NA., FO 371/67674, 16 October 1947).

There were several strands to this opposition, most notably that it would put at risk the country's far more important trading and financial interests beyond Europe. In particular, the country's ballooning trade and payments deficit with the dollar area meant that priority had to be given to increasing dollar-earning exports and reducing dollar-costing imports. Such a programme could not be advanced by a west European customs union, for as one Whitehall official commented 'we could not look on France as an overriding priority like Argentina'; the latter had dollars to pay for British goods and could provide necessary foodstuffs, while France lacked dollars to pay for imports and could not provide basic foodstuffs that could have reduced Britain's dollar payments (NA., FO 371/67673, 8 October 1947). A customs union, so it was repeatedly claimed, would also have an adverse impact on national economic management.

The clinching argument against a customs union was that it would eventually either dissolve or proceed towards economic union and political federation. There could be no 'halfway house' argued Treasury officials, rehearsing many of the later criticisms of the euro area: a monetary union but without arrangements for a fiscal and political union. Neither economic union nor political federation could be seriously entertained by the Attlee government. Furthermore, unlike their French counterparts, British policymakers had little or no interest in the idea of a customs union as part of a wider process of national economic planning and modernization.

The concept of European unity did elicit support in British circles most notably in the case of Bevin, at least until US financial and military aid was assured. Such support, however, had little in common with either the heady, plentiful federalist rhetoric on the continent at this time epitomized by the unofficial Congress of Europe at The Hague (May 1948) or with the type of European integration associated with the beginnings of the EC in the 1950s; 'The mystique of federalism has led too many astray' lamented one Foreign Office official (NA., FO 371/73099, 9 November 1948).

The idea of European unity by peaceful as opposed to the coercive means employed by a Napoleon or a Hitler was hardly novel. Much support for European unity during and immediately after the Second World War was founded on the belief that a new European community would permanently contain the dangerous force of nationalism, would accommodate defeated states that might otherwise succumb to a persistent sense of aggrieved isolation, and would make further war in Europe unthinkable. Many of the factors that made European integration an attractive proposition on the continent, however, simply did not appeal to a British audience. In Whitehall as among the public at large, it was the Atlantic Alliance and not a European union that offered the best mechanism for preserving peace and security in Europe and also for containing and controlling post-war Germany. The idea of European integration as advocated at the Congress of Europe and elsewhere was quite simply a solution to a problem that did not confront British politicians and public.

In all important respects, Britain was a status quo rather than a revisionist power in western Europe by this time. Policymakers endorsed change only in so far as west European organizations were subordinated to and meshed with the Atlantic defence and security framework buttressed by US military and financial aid. More precisely from a British perspective, the merits of intergovernmental co-operation, the weaknesses of what were perceived as unrealistic schemes for European federation, the desirable balance between European and extra-European interests, and the restricted interest in Western Europe, all demonstrated the meaning of the concept of limited liability.

Unsurprisingly, the British audience addressed by Albert Camus, the French novelist, in 1951 did not imagine its relationship with continental Europe in quite the same intimate terms: 'for better or worse', declared Camus, 'Britain and Europe are bound up together. It may seem an unfortunate marriage ... marriage may sometimes be good but never delightful. As our marriage is not a delightful one, let us try at least to make it a good one, since divorce is out of the question' (*The Listener*, 22 November 1951). Perhaps a Eurosceptical note is in order. Camus himself was twice married, had a string of affairs, and was on record as arguing passionately against marriage on the grounds that it was an unnatural state. In any event, the marital discord metaphor on Britain and Europe fell into disuse, only to be revived much later at the time of the post-2010 moves towards a referendum on EU membership and the debate about whether or not to maintain a 'loveless marriage'.

The parting of the ways

In 1950 there emerged an altogether different vision of the future of Europe: French-led rather than British-organized, European-focused rather than global, integrated and supranational rather than loosely structured and intergovernmental, farsighted rather than strictly limited in scope. The new approach to European unity first found expression in the proposal of Robert Schuman, the French foreign minister (9 May 1950), to place French and West German coal and steel production under a supranational High Authority open to the participation of other countries. Some of the distinctive features of this plan, as outlined by Jean Monnet (head of France's Modernization and Re-equipment Plan and high priest of post-war France's technocrats), were the emphasis on establishing a new basis for Franco-German relations and insistence on commitment to the supranational principle prior to detailed negotiations between interested states.

It was in this context that there emerged the idea that was to be a key factor in the subsequent process of European integration, namely that absorbing Germany into a new united Europe could serve to allay the economic and security fears of Germany's neighbours. At the same time Germany was here offered the opportunity to work its passage back to international respectability towards a 'Europeanized Germany' rather than a 'Germanized Europe'. From the outset, European integration was regarded less as an aspect of foreign affairs than as a continuation of domestic policy by other means. This idea of 'Europe' as a solution was later to be applied to other EU states, including Britain in the 1960s.

The negotiations between the six states (comprising Belgium, France, Italy, Luxembourg, the Netherlands and West Germany – commonly referred to as the Six in the literature) that accepted this invitation resulted in the Treaty of Paris (April 1951) and the formation of the European Coal and Steel Community (ECSC). Several years later, and after an abortive attempt by the Six in the meantime to create a European Defence Community (EDC), the foreign ministers of the Six met in Messina (June 1955) and set in train negotiations that finally resulted in the Treaties of Rome (March 1957) that established the European Economic Community (EEC) and the European Atomic Energy Community (EAEC). The ECSC, EEC and EAEC are hereafter referred to as the EC (European Communities).

For perfectly understandable if contested reasons, the British Labour government of 1950 and the Eden Conservative government of 1955 turned down the invitation to participate in both ventures. In parenthesis, it is worth noting that one Conservative politician, Harold Macmillan, who was soon to figure in the first abortive British attempt to join the EC, suggested that the Attlee government should accept the principle of the Schuman proposal and then enter into detailed negotiations. He advanced this argument by asserting 'Of course the Scottish people, who are the intellectuals of Britain, know there is nothing to be frightened of: one should accept everything *en principe* get round the table and start the talks', a view that was put to the test in September 2014 in the referendum vote on the principle of an independent Scotland.

There were certainly different interpretations of the words 'en principe' as between the British and the Six. For the Six, the expression clearly meant that they agreed in principle with the objective of the discussions, but if these should prove to be unacceptable when put into practical terms they would not be bound by them. The Dutch, in particular, held this view. They were most suspicious of the supranational idea, and they pressed for a representative assembly that was not part of Monnet's original technocratic model and that subsequently emerged as the forerunner of the European Parliament. The Dutch were also anxious to secure British involvement. Max Kohnstamm, a Dutch diplomat at the time, believed a British presence was needed as an alternative to 'Teutonic coherence and Gallic uniformity'. The British interpretation of 'en principe', however, was that if any state accepted the principle then that state was bound by the outcome, whatever the consequences (Heath, 1998: 148).

There was much that offended the Labour government and party about the Schuman Plan, as it seemed to undermine what passed for national planning under the Labour government and the principle of nationalization (though in fact the issue of ownership did not actually enter into the matter). No other pair of industries as a basis for European economic integration was more likely to arouse Labour Party passions than coal and steel, as both industries had been singled out as playing an integral role in the party's nationalization programme of 1945; coal was nationalized in 1946 and steel in 1949. There was thus unquestioning support for the view that Labour had not assaulted 'the commanding heights of the economy' in order to hand over control of the British coal and steel industries to a supranational European body. Herbert Morrison, the chief architect of the nationalization programme, pithily expressed the party consensus on the plan: 'It's no good, we cannot do it, the Durham miners won't wear it' (Donoghue and Jones, 1973: 481).

The substantive explanation at the time for the government decisions of 1950 and 1955 to stay out of the Schuman Plan and post-Messina negotiations changed little in this period. Loss of national sovereignty loomed large in both cases, though more so in the response to the Schuman Plan that explicitly referred to the principle of supranationality. The bulk of British trade lay with the Commonwealth (see Table 2.1). There were certainly signs of a change in trading policy when the Conservatives returned to power in 1951 and supported multilateral free trade; in protest Beaverbrook, the press baron and a keen advocate of Commonwealth trade, put chains on the crusader in his *Daily Express* masthead.

British interest in a global, multilateral trading system (as represented by the 1947 General Agreement on Trade and Tariffs) rather than in exclusively European trading arrangements formed a marked contrast to the European-focused customs union about to be hatched by the six EC states. Besides which, it was still the case that only 13 per cent of total British exports went to the states that later constituted the EC while 47 per cent went to the Commonwealth (1952) (NA., T 234/195). Furthermore, the imperial preference system, albeit on the wane, was judged to be incompatible with membership of a European customs union.

Other equally if not more important considerations also entered into the British response to the origins of the EC in the 1950s. In 1950 as in 1990 on the unification of

Table 2.1 Relative values of British trade with the Commonwealth, the sterling area and western Europe, 1952–1954 (annual average expressed as a percentage)

Area	Total external trade	Imports	Exports
Commonwealth			
Sterling	41	39	42
Non-sterling	7	9	5
Sterling			
Commonwealth	41	39	42
Non-Commonwealth	5	4	5
Non-sterling			
Commonwealth	7	9	5
ECSC countries	12	12	13
Scandinavia	8	8	9
Rest of non-sterling area	27	28	26

Source: NA., T 234/195.

Table 2.2 Coal and steel production 1938 and 1949 (millions of metric tons)

	Coal production		Steel production	
	1938	*1949*	*1938*	*1949*
UK	231.8	218.6	10.6	15.8
West Germany	153.8	120.9	17.9	9.2
France & Saar	61.2	66.0	8.8	11.0
Belgium and Luxembourg	29.6	27.9	3.7	6.1
Netherlands	13.6	11.8	0.1	0.3
Italy	1.9	1.5	2.3	2.1
Total	491.9	446.7	43.4	44.5

Source: NA., CAB 134/293.

Germany, the country did not share the same compelling reasons as France for partially losing national sovereignty and promoting an integrated Europe in order to accommodate and contain a recovering Germany. In 1950, France was particularly alarmed about the impact of the revival of Germany's heavy industrial arsenal in the Ruhr. It feared that this process threatened much-needed French access to German coal and also posed a challenge to France's heavy post-war investment in the steel industry. No such considerations amounted to overriding priorities in the case of Britain which enjoyed a dominant position in coal and steel production as compared with the Schuman Plan states (see Table 2.2). The British were primarily intent on ensuring the maintenance of national controls over the distribution of British coal, particularly in the face of American pressure to export more British coal to assist the European recovery. In these early post-war years of shortages, coal was an important instrument of foreign policy, as Bevin observed: 'If I had three million tons of coal which I could export ... I could have a foreign policy' (cited in Blackwell, 1993: 91). Then, too, in the Bevinite phrase of the day that was to be repeated time and again by British politicians over the years, Britain was not 'just another European country'. It was a power with global interests and status including nuclear weapons (after 1952) and a 'special relationship' with the United States that could not be compromised or weakened by overclose European ties.

Underlying such considerations, there was a set of attitudes deeply rooted in what British policymakers viewed as the 'lessons of history' that were drawn from the inter-war period and from wartime experience. One Whitehall mandarin remarked to Monnet shortly after the Schuman announcement: 'We are not ready and you will not succeed' (Charlton, 1983: 122); Monnet himself later pondered the question as to why Britain did not figure as a founder member of the EC. He concluded that 'it must have been because it was the price of victory – the illusion that you could maintain what you had without change'. In short, the course and outcome of the Second World War in Britain's case reinforced some traditional foreign policy attitudes rather than encouraging new departures.

Messina – 'a devilishly awkward place to get to'

Five years later, the British ambassador to France, in one of the less prescient dispatches sent by a British diplomat, advised that no very spectacular developments were to be expected as a result of the Messina conference of the Six in June 1955. Meanwhile, one of his Foreign Office colleagues observed that Messina was 'a devilishly awkward place to get to'. This view of mainland European travel was widely shared in the country at large. Indeed, the English football governing authorities at this time barred English clubs from the newly-created (April 1955) European Cup competition on the grounds that they would not arrive back from the continent in time to play Saturday matches. Matt Busby, the Scottish manager of Manchester United who believed Europe was the future, defied the ban. The club entered the competition in two consecutive seasons but lost many of its finest players in the Munich air crash (February 1958), an event which to some people demonstrated that foreign competition was not worth it (Weight, 2002: 263).

The fact that there was no British representation at Messina, however, was not due to geography but to history. In 1950 and again in their response to the Messina confer- ence, British policymakers looked to the past as a guide to the future. In view of three wars between France and Germany in 1870, 1914 and 1939, they could not imagine a Franco-German rapprochement and even less a marked improvement in bilateral relations between Paris and Bonn without British involvement and mediation. In his characteristically terse manner Attlee observed of the six EC founding member states, 'Know them very well. Very recently this country spent a great deal of blood and treas- ure rescuing four of them from attacks by the other two' (Hennessy, 2001: 173).

Strong doubts about the seriousness of French intentions were grounded in mem- ories of pre-war French 'Europeanism'; the Briand memorandum of 1929 on a fed- eral Europe was rightly viewed by the Foreign Office as unlikely to come to anything. More recent experience suggested that the Schuman Plan would suffer the same fate; it was regarded in London as simply the latest in a series of post-war ambitious French schemes for European unity that was symptomatic of France's major problems at home and abroad. Disbelief about French intentions was reinforced by hitherto stubborn French resistance to the recovery of post-war Germany and was also informed by the deep-seated ambivalent attitudes of British policymakers towards France.

Similar attitudes among British policymakers were evident at the time of the Messina initiative, all the more so in view of the recent failure of the Six to create a suprana- tional European Defence Community (EDC – originally known as the European Army) in August 1954. Churchill as prime minister had a pronounced antipathy towards the EDC project. He privately dismissed it as 'a sludgy amalgam' and 'a bucket of wood pulp' that conjured up visions of a motley, confused collection of Italian, Dutch and German privates being drilled by a French sergeant (Stirk and Willis, 1991: 95). He per- mitted no more than a form of British association with, rather than membership of, the scheme: 'Very pleasant, indeed, to be the guest of honour at the banquet of a society to which you pay no dues', was the caustic comment of the French wartime leader Charles de Gaulle on this arrangement (Werth, 1965: 227), here touching on some of the later characteristic features of British policy within the EC/EU (see Chapter 4).

The collapse of the EDC project gave the British government and especially Foreign Secretary Anthony Eden an opportunity to devise an alternative plan that allowed for a rearmed and fully sovereign West Germany. What emerged was a predictable British for- mula for intergovernmental European co-operation in the form of an enlarged Brussels Treaty Organisation to include Italy and West Germany and to be called Western European Union (WEU). The British undertaking to maintain a peacetime military presence on the continent did mark a shift from the traditional and primarily maritime character of British defence strategy in peacetime towards a more land-based continental presence. Furthermore, this commitment was sufficient to allay French fears about German rearmament and about the loss of national sovereignty, the key, controversial issues throughout the tumultuous EDC debate in France. However, this commitment was surrounded by escape clauses that allowed for the removal of British forces assigned to WEU. These clauses were soon to be activated (1957) when British defence strategy placed greater reliance on nuclear weapons than on conventional forces, thereby reasserting the country's role and capability as a global rather than a European power.

Eden's account of how this scheme originated was that it came to him suddenly while he was having his Sunday morning bath. This version of events, however, has long since been disposed of as misleading. Nevertheless, federalist opinion on the continent often viewed it as a strikingly authentic expression of Eden's casual regard for and limited interest in European unity. WEU was long to remain Britain's last major diplomatic success in western Europe. It was not viewed by Eden at least as an instrument for furthering European unity, but rather as a means for solving the specific problem of incorporating a rearmed West Germany into the western alliance. That much became apparent as WEU languished in later years. It maintained a shadowy existence until all of its functions were effectively incorporated into the EU and it closed down in June 2011.

'It will never happen'

The failure of the EDC project and the success of the British-inspired WEU scheme convinced London that the Six were unlikely to embark upon or to succeed in more adventurous schemes for integration. Again, long-standing memories of French weakness were to the fore. According to Whitehall assessments, France was in no fit state politically or economically to consider membership of a common market. In French government circles, there were widespread fears about Germany and reservations about exposing the highly protectionist French economy to the fast-growing West German economy. There were also rising political tensions in France that shortly resulted in the collapse of the Fourth Republic.

There were some fatal flaws in these British views of the Six's and particularly France's unpreparedness for further integration. Certainly the landscape of European integration at this time changed faster than the assessments of British policymakers and in ways that confounded their expectations. Some of the initial impressions of policymakers were based on a tendency to perceive what they wanted or expected to perceive. This approach was reinforced by political and social attitudes that often reflected a high degree of consensus and satisfaction with the status quo together with influential forms of insular and organizational groupthink. Furthermore, British membership of a European federation was, as Eden himself put it, 'something that we know in our bones we cannot do'. This comment drew a withering response from Paul-Henri Spaak, one of the EC's founding fathers and a constant thorn in the flesh of British ministers, 'That's a funny place to have thinking' (Charlton, 1983: 159, 182).

Throughout the 1950s British governments pursued a policy of association with the Six, reflecting a largely disengaged and sceptical attitude towards the collective efforts of the Six. This policy amounted to very little except most significantly continuing exclusion from the Six's planning and efforts. In that respect, the policy of association had some important side effects. Most immediately it relieved the government of having to take a major decision. A strong inclination to avoid taking such an irreversible decision was to be a recurring feature of British policy towards the EC/EU. So, too, was the complacent attitude in British quarters that the EC was most unlikely to materialize. The 'it will never happen' attitude was to be a recurring feature of British assessments of the EC/EU project.

In the period July–November 1955, immediately after the Messina initiative, Russell Bretherton, a Board of Trade official, attended meetings of the Spaak committee set up to explore plans for a possible common market of the Six. Bretherton performed the difficult role of participant without commitment. To some members of the committee he projected patronizing indifference and seemed to personify official British attitudes at large. Spaak noted his 'discreet scepticism' while Spaak's principal assistant, Robert Rothschild, commented that 'Bretherton usually had a rather cynical and amused smile on his face, and he looked at us like naughty children, not really mischievous, but enjoying themselves by playing a game which had no relevance and no future ... And then one day, he disappeared and never came again'. It is pure legend but nonetheless indicative of British attitudes that Bretherton left his final meeting with a flourish; 'Gentlemen, you are trying to negotiate something you will never be able to negotiate. But if negotiated, it will not be ratified. And if ratified, it will not work' (Spaak, 1971: 232; Charlton, 1983: 180).

Mainland European politicians and especially the so-called godfathers of the EC recognized this British outlook. One of their number commented when describing the attitudes of the British government towards the Messina initiative: 'their profound wish was that nothing should happen' (Marjolin, 1989: 282). More importantly, this episode illustrated what was to become a recurring effect of British policy towards the EC/EU, namely that Britain's absence from the negotiating table assisted the collective efforts of the Six and later of the enlarged EU in successfully pursuing further integration. The policy of association was eventually abandoned as the EC came into being and appeared to be a permanent fixture and a threat to British interests in western Europe.

Suez and the beginnings of an agonizing reappraisal

The period 1955–61 arguably marked the most extraordinary reversal in British policy towards Europe since the Second World War. In 1955 the Eden Conservative government had come down against Britain joining the Six in founding the EC. In November 1956, when Chancellor of the Exchequer, Macmillan had flatly ruled out any possibility that Britain might at some stage enter the common market that was then being discussed by the Six (*H.C. Deb.*, vol. 561, cols. 37–8). In 1961, however, the Conservative government under Macmillan's premiership decided to seek terms of entry to the EC – and this after the Conservatives had made no reference to such a possibility in the manifesto on which they fought and won the 1959 general election. How to explain this change over a relatively short period of time has attracted many answers, all of which start in some way or other with the Suez crisis of November 1956.

Eden succeeded Churchill as prime minister in April 1955. A year later, the Eden government was plunged into the most serious crisis confronting a post-war British government, first when President Nasser of Egypt nationalized the Suez Canal (July 1956), hitherto funded by the British- and French-dominated Suez Canal Company, and then by the outcome of British, French and Israeli military action against Egypt (31 October – 6 November 1956). This action was opposed by the United States, whose pressure was instrumental in achieving a ceasefire and a withdrawal of British and French forces from Egypt.

Suez as military failure and political disaster was a humiliating outcome of the first order. The most immediate political casualty of this episode was Eden himself who resigned in January 1957 amidst suggestions that he had been a 'rogue' prime minister or at least someone who had gone off his head (Shuckburgh, 1986: 362–3). The principal beneficiary was his successor Macmillan who had been among the first to urge military action against Nasser and the first to call time on any further military action as Chancellor of the Exchequer.

In a wider context, there is some substance to the view that Eden was the last British prime minister, as *The Times* commented at the time, to believe Britain was a great power, and the first to confront a crisis which proved that she was not. Suez (or 'Suezide') thereafter became a byword for British weakness. The episode finally exposed the country's decline in the international system that was masked by the victory of 1945, and thus ended the twilight zone of great power status. Oliver Franks, one of the key senior British officials of this period, described Suez as 'a flash of lightning on a dark night' that illuminated a political, diplomatic and military landscape that had long been changing (Hennessy, 1990: 97–8).

Suez also highlighted Britain's inability thereafter to attempt any global military action without first securing US acquiescence. That very dependence on the United States, however, was well understood in Whitehall before Suez as were many other developments like the retreat from empire (Peden, 2012). The fact that Macmillan quickly improved relations with the Americans was indicative of the extent to which Suez was, as Chris Bartlett puts it, 'essentially a passing thunderstorm in Anglo-American relations' (Bartlett, 1992: 77). In that respect a distinction can be made between the psychological impact of Suez in terms of the public perception of declining national self-esteem and international prestige and the limited impact of the Suez experience on Whitehall policymakers and policy. There was one important, relevant exception; Suez encouraged a turn from the Commonwealth towards Europe in the form of a proposal for a European free trade area (see below).

It was while on the defensive in the face of the developing EC that the Macmillan government undertook a review of European policy in the period 1959–1961. This review was to cover much ground, though historical assessments differ over the major factors at work. There is little disputing several aspects of this exercise, some of which had an enduring influence after Britain joined the EC. The application did not arise out of a single imperative or driving force. On the contrary, it demonstrated the interaction of often unquantifiable influences whether at the individual or collective level.

'The sick man of Europe'

'Why are we falling behind?' was very much the question of the hour in the press and in the broadcast media at this time. There was a gathering sense of gloom that, not much more than ten years after victory in the Second World War, Britain was not only in decline but was seen as being so by the rest of the world. The country was routinely labelled 'the sick man of Europe' over the next two decades (see Table 2.3). In economic terms, the particular cause for concern was not the country's annual average growth

Table 2.3 Britain: 'The sick man of Europe'
GDP growth rates of the EC states expressed as an annual percentage change

	1965–1970	*1973–1974*	*1978–1979*
Belgium	4.8	4.3	2.4
Denmark	4.4	4.3	3.5
France	5.8	3.9	3.2
West Germany	4.7	0.6	4.6
Ireland	4.5	1.0	1.9
Italy	5.9	3.4	5.0
Luxembourg	3.6	4.4	2.7
Netherlands	5.6	2.0	2.2
UK	2.2	0.3	0.9

Source: OECD (1970–80) *Main Economic Indicators*, OECD Publications, Paris.

rate as such – at 2.9 per cent (1950–1973) this was better than anything achieved in the previous 100 years and, for that matter, over the next 40 years down to the present day. What attracted increasing attention was rather the much better comparable figures for the major economies in the Six over this same period – West Germany 6 per cent, France 5.1 per cent, Italy 4.5 per cent. It was also the case that declinism and the accompanying idea of modernization were used to political effect by the Labour Party in criticizing 'the thirteen wasted years' of Conservative government (1951–1964).

The relative decline in Britain's manufacturing and exporting record was most marked in comparisons with West Germany and all the more so since only ten years earlier (1945–1949) Germany had been under military occupation while British manufacturing accounted for 38 per cent of the British economy (1948). In 1950 Britain produced more manufactured exports than France, Germany and Italy put together. In the period 1950–1960, Britain's share of world manufactured exports declined from 22 per cent to 16 per cent while West Germany's share increased from 7 to 19 per cent, finally overtaking Britain in 1958. There were other indices of laggardly growth as over the next ten years real earnings in Britain rose by 38 per cent but by 75 per cent in the EC.

There were many factors responsible for this relative economic decline that had little or nothing to do with the country's exclusion from the EC, some of which were of long-term standing: under-investment, low productivity, shortage of skilled workers, labour relations, complacent management, and lack of planned targets. A common critique of the British economy in the *Financial Times* of July 1961 concluded that for a whole variety of reasons – 'institutional, social, political and economic – a psychological climate has been created in this country which is a powerful obstacle to change'. Alongside such commentaries, there was an almost unquestioning view that the size of the market greatly determined the rate of economic growth and the scope for economies of scale. As in the early post-war years, the United States was cited as the desirable economic model, in this case demonstrating the advantages of a large market.

Against this background, it was hoped that by some automatic or osmotic process EC membership would stimulate economic growth, attract external and especially American investment, and promote economies of scale in a large market. Such hopes were not accompanied by any systematic, developed, long-term plan to link EC membership with economic reconstruction and industrial revival. In short, there was no British counterpart to Jean Monnet for whom the idea of European integration had developed out of his headship of France's post-war Modernization and Re-equipment Plan. Nor did many in the British political world at the time or later envisage precise forms of British involvement in a distinctive European industrial strategy. Michael Heseltine, later deputy leader of the Conservative Party, was one of the few to do so, especially during the Westland affair of 1986 when he strongly and unsuccessfully opposed the American bid for the British helicopter firm over a European consortium.

In British circles and particularly among supporters of EC membership, the case for membership was often advanced on the grounds that it would offer one of the few ways that government in a largely non-interventionist economic culture could bring pressure to bear on industry to make it more competitive. This argument seemed all the more persuasive in view of what were perceived as the limitations and failings of government attempts to rejuvenate industry and improve productivity by a mixture of exhortation, patriotic appeals to the Dunkirk spirit and wartime solidarity, cajolement and incentives. Failing all this in terms of creating a more competitive economy, as one free-market columnist put it, 'Only the judgement and the cathartic properties of a market of 260 million remain' (Kynaston, 2014: 318). Besides the case for exposing the domestic economy to external disciplines, the changing pattern of trade away from the Commonwealth to western Europe and the fearful prospect of exclusion from the EC's customs union increasingly pressed the possibility of membership to the fore.

There was another unpromising feature of exclusion from the EC (or Common Market as it was called in Britain at the time and into the 1970s, giving rise to the expressions pro-marketeers and anti-marketeers that will be used in this chapter). This was the fear of a French-led EC overshadowing Britain's post-war standing as the leading power in western Europe. Besides which, there was considerable US pressure on Britain to join the EC at a particularly awkward time, as Macmillan sought US assistance in updating the delivery system for Britain's nuclear weapons. Following Macmillan's visit to meet the newly elected President Kennedy in April 1961 the communist *Daily Worker* ran the headline 'Mac given his orders'. Certainly, it was the case that in so far as a single individual was responsible for mounting this first application it was Macmillan whose serpentine mind and manoeuvres were evident throughout this episode and whose agonizing over the issue was apparent at every stage.

Europe at sixes and sevens

The decision in 1961 to seek terms of entry for EC membership followed a period when Macmillan's government fruitlessly explored every avenue short of EC membership, including ill-directed, cackhanded attempts to sabotage the nascent EC that left lingering suspicions of British policy and diplomacy among the Six. The immediate British response to Messina was to propose the formation of a Free Trade Area (November 1956) that was to include the Six and any other western European states wishing to join. Macmillan, as Chancellor of the Exchequer, launched this proposal and pursued the matter as prime minister until it was was eventually rejected by France (November 1958). Paris seized the opportunity to portray the proposal as a suspicious British package and a typical expression of 'perfidious Albion' designed to sow divisions within the EC.

Britain and six other states (Austria, Denmark, Norway, Portugal, Sweden and Switzerland) subsequently formed the European Free Trade Association (EFTA) in

July 1959, known as the 'Outer Seven' as distinct from the 'Inner Six' (the Inner and Outer descriptions were revived on the later emergence of the euro area). Western Europe was thus divided into two trade blocs, a Europe at sixes and sevens in the newspaper headlines of the day. From the outset, the British were lukewarm about this new organization. EFTA was strictly limited to creating a free market in industrial goods by 1970 without imposing any common external tariff as in the case of the EC. It was regarded as an interim, second-best solution; David Eccles, President of the Board of Trade, spoke disparagingly of 'a climbdown – the engineer's daughter when the general manager's had said no'. Frank Lee, the most senior Treasury official, was equally unflattering in his description of EFTA as a heterogeneous and scattered grouping brought together by 'ties of common funk' (NA., PREM 11/2531, 11/3133).

The Macmillan government promptly embarked on an unsuccessful bridge-building exercise between the EFTA and the EC with a wide range of possible relationships from association to near-identification. The government had consistently overestimated the strength of its bargaining position during the Free Trade Area negotiations of 1957–1958. It did so again now and largely because of two underlying assumptions, these being that the embryonic EC would probably fail because of basic internal divisions and that, even if it did succeed, it would still be possible to work out some sort of arrangement with the EC short of full membership. By early 1960 both these assumptions proved false. Far from failing, the EC formally came into being in January 1958 and was forging ahead at an impressive rate: tariff reductions were taking place ahead of schedule; it was thriving economically; and it was displaying a much greater degree of political cohesion than most observers had expected. Moreover, the EC states showed no interest in establishing some form of associate relationship with Britain and the rest of EFTA.

Some of the British proposals at this stage reflected the utter confusion, panic, loss of confidence and indecision at the heart of government. They also foreshadowed later British attempts to escape full participation in certain EC/EU measures. Authoritative observers of the British system of government have noted that the idea that British governments have a special gift for decisiveness and for taking tough decisions is largely a myth (King and Crewe, 2013: 393).

There is certainly plenty of evidence in government files of the period to support the view that over the question of British membership of the EC Macmillan and his government prevaricated, procrastinated and deferred as often as they decided. In particular, Macmillan harboured doubts about whether to apply, how to apply, when to apply, on what terms to apply and with whom to apply, all of which seemed to confirm that on Europe, as one observer commented, Macmillan was 'Forever amber'. In other quarters he was repeatedly criticized for dithering (Evans, 1981), and also for displaying some of the traits that were pounced on by a young generation of satirists lampooning the Establishment. Meanwhile, Selwyn Lloyd, Foreign Secretary (1955–1960), was no driving force and was at best ambivalent towards the possibility of EC membership. On his first appointment as a junior minister in the Foreign Office in 1951, he had admitted to Churchill that he knew nothing of foreign affairs, spoke no foreign languages, had never been abroad except in wartime, and did not like foreigners (Bennett, 2013: 46).

There was too perhaps the lingering hope in London that the EC would eventually disintegrate or, as Macmillan confided to his diary as late as December 1958: 'It will be the EDC story all over again', yet another instance of a disbelieving mentality on the British side in the face of European schemes. Peter Thorneycroft, one of Macmillan's

Cabinet ministers, suggested that 'if we want the Common Market to fail, we need only let it alone' (NA., FO 371/122034). Yet this not uncommon delusion in Whitehall quarters overlooked the dangers of standing on the sidelines both at this time and later. It was already becoming evident that such a British position was often a pre-condition for the further development of the Six's plans. It helped to unify the Six and it removed Britain as a possible obstacle to progress. Furthermore, as Macmillan observed, standing on the sidelines immediately left France in a dominant position in western Europe. More importantly in the longer term it held out the prospect of a united Europe dominated by Germany; 'it is really giving them [Germany] on a plate what we fought two world wars to prevent', Macmillan had earlier minuted to a Treasury official (NA., T 234/100).

Backing into Europe

The eventual decision to apply for EC membership was taken not in a fit of euro-enthusiasm, but out of a reluctant, if not desperate, recognition that it represented a disagreeable necessity. The Macmillan government and subsequent governments took up the possibility of EC membership as a last resort, seeking to turn the tide of relative political and economic decline, and in the process lending some substance to the view that they thought the solution to the country's problems was to join a club (Bootle, 2014: 23).

In contemplating EC membership, the government sought to save as much as possible of past connections, all of which left the impression of trying to back into Europe as a conservative, tactical move rather than demonstrating an eager willingness to think in radically new terms.

There were several obstacles to putting a positive shine on the decision. One of the unspoken difficulties was how to explain the Conservative government's complete reversal of attitude on the question of EC membership after years of opposition to such a prospect. In July 1960, Gore Booth, head of the Foreign Office's Economic Relations Department and later Permanent Under Secretary, claimed it was unlikely that anyone in the political establishment would acknowledge the mistake of failing to join the EC at the outset and say 'OK we're wrong and will do it your way' (NA., FO 371/150363). To emphasize the 'never apologize, never explain' mantra of his peers he broke into German '*Das gibts nicht*' ('It's impossible'), a characteristically melodramatic touch from someone who, as president of the Sherlock Holmes Society, enjoyed dressing up as Moriarty in his spare time.

In the event, Macmillan, who had demonstrated his skills as actor manager at the time of Suez and who had emerged as the principal beneficiary of Eden's resignation after Suez, ensured that a humiliating U-turn was smoothed over without sounding too desperate in public, in much the same way as he used his theatrical skills to preserve the illusion of British greatness. On 31 July 1961, he made a low-key and lacklustre announcement of the decision to seek terms of entry to the EC, so much so according to one commentator that he 'sounded and looked to many of us like a company chairman badly in need of a holiday who was putting over with infinite caution the idea of a merger which might or might not come off' – an altogether strange presentation for what this same observer described as 'the most supremely important announcement delivered to Parliament and the country since the outbreak of the Second World War' (quoted in Kynaston, 2014: 317–18). For his own part, Macmillan a month earlier collapsed with exhaustion and complained in his diary that he had 'no more *élan vital*' and at the age of 67 was 'beginning (at last) to feel old and depressed' (quoted in Bennett, 2013: 72).

Macmillan's subdued announcement, however, was in marked contrast to his behaviour immediately afterwards and indicated that he was indeed about to go on holiday. According to his press secretary, while addressing lobby correspondents, he swung the chairman's gavel perilously backwards and forwards, talked about the First World War trenches and how they enabled him to stay calm, said he could still do the 18th hole at St Andrews in four strokes, and that he was now going to let off 300 or 400 cartridges – on which cue he suddenly got up and left (Evans, 1981: 156). Dealing with the EC/EU has had the strangest effects on most British prime ministers. In this case it seemingly confirmed the view of Harold Wilson, the future Labour Party leader and prime minister, that Macmillan's role as a *poseur* was always a pose.

It was equally difficult for Macmillan and government ministers to deploy positive arguments favouring EC membership that did not smack of more or less graceful national decline. At a Cabinet committee attended by Macmillan in May 1961, it was agreed that perhaps the strongest argument for joining the EC was based on the potential dangers of staying outside, but that this was 'a difficult argument to present publicly' (NA., CAB 134/1821). Some of the more positive arguments for membership focused on Britain's leadership aspirations, it being assumed, as Macmillan put it, that Britain could lead better from within the EC than outside. Here in the making was a toxic mixture of a deep sense of declining status, inflated leadership ambitions and a masked reversal of policy. This condition typified in many respects the beginnings of an enduring unwillingness or inability by the political class to educate the public about EC membership.

Not the least of the missing elements in this last respect was the potentially explosive issue of sovereignty that government sought to obscure or minimize as much as possible, as did later governments. Macmillan in particular was concerned to calm public fears about the loss of sovereignty. In November 1960, Edward Heath, the Foreign Office minister with special responsibility for European affairs and head of the British team in the 1961–1963 negotiations on the EC membership bid, sought the opinion of the Lord Chancellor, Lord Kilmuir, on the extent to which signature of the EEC Treaty of Rome might mean a loss of sovereignty. Kilmuir's view was that there would be a substantial surrender of sovereignty in at least three respects: Parliament would be required to surrender some of its functions to the organs of the EC, the Crown would be called on to transfer part of its treaty-making powers to those organs, and the courts of law would sacrifice some degree of independence by becoming subordinate in certain respects to the European Court of Justice (NA., FO 371/150369).

Kilmuir strongly advised against any attempt to gloss over the facts. Yet that was precisely what Macmillan did in the parliamentary debate following his 31 July announcement when he clearly aimed to allay fears of a loss of sovereignty (*H.C. Deb.*, vol. 644, 1–2 August 1961). It is fair to say that Macmillan was rarely impressed by Kilmuir's judgment on most matters: 'He was always beta minus ... the stupidest Lord Chancellor ever ... hopeless in Cabinet' (Sandbrook, 2005: 352). Predictably, Kilmuir figured as one of the seven ministers dismissed by Macmillan in the so-called 'Night of the Long Knives' (13 July 1962).

There were considerable fears about public attitudes towards the idea of EC membership underlying this handling of the issue of sovereignty. In July 1960 officials warned ministers that if the government changed its policy towards the EC it would have to contend with the ordinary Englishman's almost 'innate dislike and suspicion of "Europeans"' and that would require careful handling and intensive re-education (NA., CAB 134/1853). In September 1962 the results of the government's own findings, based on national opinion polls and soundings taken by Conservative Party agents, revealed that only 40 per cent favoured EC membership. The same soundings reported increasing distrust of foreign political connections and especially of being forced 'to surrender our independence to "Frogs" and "Wogs"' (NA., PREM 11/4415, 18 September 1962). While EC membership offered the possibility of projecting the Conservative Party as a rejuvenated, progressive, modernizing force after ten years in power by 1961, there was little evidence here to suggest that the party was likely to reap electoral dividends in making the issue a central feature of its forward thinking.

At the official level the combination of grandiose claims and the growing perception of Britain's relative decline in the international system affected all and sundry, even those who might have been expected to take a more clear-eyed view of matters. For instance, in the preliminary draft of a substantial and influential report commissioned by Macmillan and drawn up by Frank Lee, the most senior official at the Treasury, it was argued that EC membership was the most advantageous solution. Lee took the view that for far too long British industry had been feather-bedded by excessive reliance on Commonwealth trade and the sterling area. He also further stressed that there was no evidence that British leadership was desperately needed, eagerly awaited or required by the Six. He nevertheless concluded this draft with a flourish in the words of William Pitt: 'We will save England by our exertions and Europe by our example' (NA., PREM 11/3133). This conclusion was scarcely consistent with the burden of Lee's message. It was, nevertheless, indicative of the doublethink characteristics of British politicians and officials born when British imperial supremacy was at its zenith or on the turn. It seemed that only an element of self-delusion staved off any public expression of real or perceived decline (see Chapter 11 for further discussion of the Commonwealth and Europe).

Herbert Andrew, a senior Board of Trade official, drew an altogether different conclusion from Lee's paper. He claimed that 'Europe will change us, not we them', and he added for good measure that EC membership would have profound effects: 'It is as if another planet were crashing into us. The kingdom and the power and the glory will pass from us and leave us naked, face to face with our real selves at last' – unusually apocalyptic language for a Board of Trade official (NA., BT 11/5563, 9 May 1960). The marked disconnection between the intellectual and the emotional appreciation of Britain's changing position in the world was perhaps best expressed by Hoyer-Millar, the most senior official at the Foreign Office. He supported EC membership, thinking that it was the correct policy, but feeling otherwise. Against the background of such ambivalence, the construction of a coherent and convincing case for EC membership remained problematical.

Apart from generalized expressions about leadership aspirations, there was some crystal ball gazing in Whitehall: one Foreign Office paper suggested that the pound sterling might become the EC's common currency in the longer term. The attention of ministers and civil servants, however, was primarily focused on the legacy of Commonwealth connections and trade and, in particular, how to protect these interests in the course of negotiations with the Six. Besides the large network of family and friends especially in the white Dominions, in the popular mind the Commonwealth was primarily associated with food such as New Zealand lamb and butter, Indian tea and Kenyan coffee. Consequently, the negotiations that opened with the Six in October 1961 and lasted until the French veto in January 1963 were largely taken up with all manner of transitional arrangements for Commonwealth imports into the enlarged EC. Such imports ranged from the major problematical issue of Temperate Zone foodstuffs to the treatment of relatively minor items such as kangaroo meat and cricket balls.

International status under threat

Accompanying Britain's leadership aspirations in the EC there was a profound if often unacknowledged recognition of the country's decline in the post-Suez world, later fully acknowledged in the cottage industry of 'declinist' literature among historians and others. At the time, few books made a greater impact in dissecting what was perceived as the country's growing political, social and economic malaise than *The Stagnant Society* (1961) by Michael Shanks. There was much material to justify his view that the great psychological danger facing the British people was 'that we may bury ourselves under the rose-petals of a vast collective nostalgia, lost in a sweet sad love-affair with our own past' (Shanks, 1961: 28–9).

Political factors tipped the scales in favour of an application by 1961. In particular, matters of status and prestige weighed heavily on policymakers like Macmillan, sometimes referred to as the top table syndrome or mentality in international relations. This feature was particularly the case in view of the diminishing number of symbols of Britain's 'greatness' or world power rank and also in the light of the complex problems involved in the management of relative decline (or as a long-standing popular saying put it 'in the Britain of the 1950s we managed decline, in the 1960s we mismanaged decline, and in the 1970s we declined to manage'). At a time of changing power relations in the international system, as in Europe with the emergence of the Six, British policymakers were all the more sensitive about status in the international system and about the need to ensure that their allies 'understand and appreciate us and that our claim to rank as leader does not lapse by default' (NA., PREM 11/152119). They were also concerned about exclusion from a sizable new entity on their doorstep, or what one commentator has described as the delusions of sizism and proximity fetishism (Bootle, 2014: 316).

It was in these circumstances that one senior Foreign Office official argued that while Britain's relative power in the world declined, its non-material goods of good sense, first-class brains and ideas could more than compensate for the lack of real power in the world (NA., FO 371/143705). This conceit was to be repeated time and again in later years, as in the saying 'punching above one's weight'. There were, however, other officials in the Foreign Office and beyond who had the sense and brains to recognize that to rely on non-material goods for trading in international relations was not the most robust basis on which to conduct foreign policy.

Britain's status symbols and prestige in the international system appeared most at risk during the first six months of 1960, a critical period in terms of strengthening the case for an EC membership application. Arguably no other six-month period in the country's history since 1945 witnessed so many status symbols under threat or disappearing at an alarming rate. The abortive Four-Power summit of May 1960, occasioned by the shooting down of a US spy plane by the Soviet Union, was a public relations disaster for Macmillan who was far more committed to a positive outcome than any of the other participants. It was as a result of this experience, according to one of his closest advisers, that Macmillan realized Britain counted for nothing in terms of great power status (Charlton, 1983: 237); certainly the Four-Power (Britain, France, United States and USSR) gatherings of the post-war world ended at this point as the two superpowers subsequently engaged in their exclusive relationship.

During this same period, other long-standing symbols of Britain's international standing were under threat. At the time of the summit meeting, the issue of apartheid in South Africa threatened to tear the Commonwealth apart during a Commonwealth prime ministers' conference; Macmillan wrote in his diary (7 May 1960) 'Quite a pleasant Sunday – the Commonwealth in pieces and the Summit doomed!' (Horne, 1989: 226). It was scarcely surprising that Macmillan increasingly viewed diplomatic management of the Commonwealth as the latest version of the white man's burden; 'the new Commonwealth has nothing like the appeal for us that the old one had' Macmillan confided in Robert Menzies, the Australian prime minister, adding that 'I now shrink from any Commonwealth meeting because I know how troublesome it will be' (NA., PREM 11/3644). In short, there was little evidence here of post-imperial nostalgia. The accompanying, if subliminally-held rather than openly expressed, view that EC leadership offered a substitute for Empire, had its attractions in persuading some sections of Conservative Party opinion to back the case for entry. Meanwhile, the process of decolonization continued apace, symbolized by Macmillan's 'wind of change' speech in February 1960, by which time gale force winds best described the process.

Other developments conveyed a similar meaning in terms of the haemorrhaging of status symbols. Moreover, the sheer rapidity of change in a relatively short period of time magnified the perception of national decline. British leadership of the OEEC ended at this time as this body was turned into the Organization for Economic Cooperation and Development (OECD) under US leadership. In this same period (February 1960 but announced in April), the Cabinet cancelled Britain's Blue Streak missile project, and consequently an updated delivery system for Britain's nuclear weapons could be obtained only from the United States. Finally, in June 1960 President de Gaulle of France launched a plan for political union of the Six. This scheme eventually ended in failure (the Fouchet negotiations of 1960–1962) but immediately further emphasized the heightened prestige of France in western Europe and the diminished standing of Britain.

The veto and ancient rivalries

The far more devastating blow for Macmillan and his government was delivered by de Gaulle on 14 January 1963 when he vetoed the British application for EC membership. De Gaulle annoyingly (at least in British government circles) recycled arguments that London had previously used to justify Britain's exclusion from the origins of the EC. No doubt part of his veto speech raised questions that hung in the air over the next 50 years: 'England in effect is insular' declared de Gaulle, 'she is maritime, she is linked through her exchanges, her markets, her supply lines to the most diverse and often the most distant countries … She has in all her doings very marked and very original habits and traditions. In short, the nature, the structure, the very situation (conjuncture) that are England's differ profoundly from those of the continentals' (Western European Assembly 1963, 1964: 20–2). Few British politicians have matched this lucid exposition of the exceptionalist tradition in British foreign policy (see Chapter 11). Some have come close to doing so, not least one of the early anti-marketeers and Conservative MP, Derek Walker-Smith, who noted the distinctiveness of Britain compared to Europe and commented 'their evolution has been continental and collective, ours has been insular and imperial' (Young, 1998: 155).

The motives underlying de Gaulle's veto admit of different explanations ranging from the longer-term sense of dissatisfaction with his treatment at the hands of the British and the Americans during the Second World War to the immediate impact of the Nassau agreement (December 1962) between Britain and the United States concerning Polaris (see Chapter 11). Macmillan was certain that 'If Hitler had danced in London, we'd have had no trouble with de Gaulle'. Furthermore, it was Macmillan's view that de Gaulle wanted to be the leader of Europe and to be 'the cock on a small dunghill instead of having two cocks on a larger one' (Macmillan, 1973: 365).

De Gaulle did not doubt that if Britain had to make a choice between Europe and the United States it would always choose the latter as a partner; Churchill himself had said as much to de Gaulle during the Second World War: 'Every time I have to decide between you and Roosevelt [US President] I shall always choose Roosevelt'. From de Gaulle's perspective, Macmillan had followed exactly the same course in his relations with Kennedy, as exemplified by the Nassau agreement of December 1962 and the provision of US-built Polaris missiles. He had in effect chosen the limited liability strategy over and above one of continental commitment.

There was little appreciation in some British circles of the French view that no conceivable French national interest could be served at this stage by supporting Britain's EC membership application. France had yet to ensure that the EC was fashioned in accordance with French interests. Possibly some of de Gaulle's major antipathies and concerns in exercising the veto were unintentionally and succinctly expressed by Philip de Zulueta, Macmillan's influential Foreign Office Private Secretary, immediately after the veto. In a paper to Macmillan, de Zulueta advised that Britain's negative purpose must be to prevent the consolidation, still more the extension, of de Gaulle's Europe. Furthermore, the positive aim should continue to be to unite a wider Europe and to make her into a powerful and equal partner with the United States in the Atlantic Alliance (quoted in Wall, 2013: 42). Early French fears about Britain as the agent of the EC's disintegration were here seemingly more than justified.

Personal relations between Macmillan and de Gaulle throughout the negotiations between October 1961 and January 1963 were at best prickly. Occasionally in their several meetings during this period, de Gaulle's patronizing tone and Macmillan's allusive style made for a dialogue of the deaf. Before the veto, Macmillan had felt so slighted by de Gaulle that according to the Cabinet minutes of November 1962, when agreeing to sign a draft treaty with France to develop the Concorde supersonic airliner, he demanded that the 'e' in Concorde should be dropped on the British side. The 'e' was later restored by Tony Benn who, as Minister of Technology (1966–1970) in this pro-EC phase of his political life, insisted that the 'e' stood for excellence, England and Europe. He later added that the 'e' also stood for *Écosse* [the French word for Scotland] when a Scottish correspondent pointed out that the plane's nose cone was made in Scotland. As if adept in later years at repudiating much of his political life in the 1960s, Benn's comment much later that the 'e' might also have stood for 'extravagance' and 'escalation' amounted to a rewriting of history in view of his strong, influential support for the project in the 1960s.

De Gaulle's veto poleaxed Macmillan, who 'could not remember going through a worse time since Suez'. A deep sense of disappointment and anger affected at least the ministers and senior officials involved in the negotiations. Among the public at large, however, this feeling was less evident. A popular British retort at the time suggested an outwardly insouciant attitude: 'Take your dreams of independent power, and stick them up your Eiffel Tower' (Horne, 1989: 449; Wall, 2008: 1). The veto also shattered what had increasingly become the centerpiece of the Conservatives' modernization programme. It also demolished Macmillan's 'Supermac' image and made him the first of a long line of British leaders seriously damaged by the politics of European integration.

And yet at the very time when the country was seemingly unable to match the economic growth rates and manufacturing achievements of its near neighbours, it demonstrated what de Gaulle had referred to in his veto speech as its 'very original habits'. Two days before that speech, a pop group from Liverpool, the Beatles, released what was to be their first major hit – 'Please, Please Me' – and thereafter spearheaded British dominance in popular music. That, in turn, helped to lay the foundations of a widespread popular culture in the world, as Britain morphed from 'Workshop of the World to Cultural Superpower' (Sandbrook, 2015: xi). Among many other things this development meant that the French language, so dominant in EC proceedings during de Gaulle's time, was increasingly replaced by English. Indeed, one of de Gaulle's presidential successors, Jacques Chirac, stormed out of an EU summit in March 2006 when a French business leader chose to speak in English on the grounds that English was Europe's accepted business language.

Any expression of deep concern about the veto in Paris was squashed by de Gaulle himself. Paul Reynaud, a former French prime minister, immediately wrote to de Gaulle registering great regret at the veto. By return of post he received an empty envelope addressed to M. Reynaud and on which de Gaulle had simply written: 'If away, forward to Waterloo, Belgium'. In that regard, de Gaulle was not alone in demonstrating the whimsicality and long memory of an elderly alpha male political leader. According to several unsubstantiated reports, Churchill insisted that at his own funeral and on its way to its resting place his body should be brought through Waterloo railway station where it would have to be met by all special guests, including de Gaulle.

Labour's retreat into Europe and another veto

De Gaulle's veto was to be repeated four years later when the Labour government under Harold Wilson made the second attempt to join the EC. The Wilson government came to power (October 1964) determined to regenerate Commonwealth trading links and to modernize the British economy. It turned its back on Europe at the same time and sought to revive Commonwealth ties. Wilson himself boasted that he had 44 relatives in New Zealand alone. Neither the EC nor the EFTA figured on his agenda, and the 15 per cent surcharge that the incoming Labour government immediately imposed on all Britain's imports applied as much to Britain's EFTA partners as to the rest of the world.

Only two years later in November 1966, however, and after his return to power following the general election of March 1966, Wilson announced that the government intended to seek EC membership, the beginning of Labour's retreat into Europe. Many of the considerations that had persuaded Macmillan to pursue this course of action were also at work in Wilson's case, if anything to an even greater degree: the declining importance of Commonwealth trade (falling from some 44 per cent of total British trade in 1951 to 30 per cent in 1964), the disastrous failure of the government's National Plan (announced in September 1965), and the still laggardly performance of the economy as compared with the EC states (see Table 2.3).

There was, too, a clinging to great power status and to the idea of a global strategy at a time when there was a further reduction in Britain's global presence and commitments ('east of Suez'). Wilson himself declared that Britain was seeking to join the EC not for the economic benefits but to preserve its position as an important international power and to remain 'in the inner circle of diplomatic and strategic affairs' (Ponting, 1989: 205). There was at this time a worsening of the post-imperial crisis as developments intensified the need for alternative international arenas within which Britain could continue to be a significant global power (Gifford, 2014: 57). The decision to withdraw all British military forces from east of Suez in 1971 had dismayed the Americans; the reaction of Secretary of State Dean Rusk was 'For God's sake act like Britain', and he added for good measure on Britain's global retreat 'You're not going to be in the Far East. You're not going to be in the Middle East. You're not even going to be in Europe in strength. Where are you going to be?' (quoted in Bennett, 2013: 95, 117).

On the domestic front, the National Plan set an ambitious economic growth target averaging almost 4 per cent per annum over the next five years, as against the trend growth rate of the British economy of 2.5 per cent over the period 1950–2010. A severe deflationary package (July 1966) following a heavy run on sterling sounded the death knell of the Plan. The Plan as the centrepiece of the government's economic policy lay in ruins. In the ensuing vacuum, EC membership appeared as an alternative route to economic salvation, providing a strategic goal and potentially a sense of crusading mission offered by the Plan. It was thus an initially dominant regard for Britain's past trading connections together with the ruination of homegrown plans for economic growth that steered the Labour government towards the EC option.

On this occasion, however, the veto was exercised before the opening of negotiations. The bid was accompanied by the now familiar expression of European leadership aspirations. According to this view, Britain would be giving the Six the benefit of its long experience as a parliamentary democracy with 'the mother of parliaments'. It would also be providing the type of leadership eagerly awaited by the Six. George Brown, the foreign secretary and a keen supporter of EC membership, was so supremely confident in this respect that he informed Willy Brandt, the West German foreign minister: 'Willy, you must get us in [the EC] so we can take the lead' (Brandt, 1978: 161). This often unacknowledged reason for joining the EC was expressed by Margaret Thatcher at this time: 'I don't like the idea of a Europe without us there, directing and guiding its powers' (Moore, 2014: 186).

Arguably Brown's wholehearted commitment to EC membership, together with the support of Michael Stewart, his predecessor as foreign secretary, was a telling consideration in making the application. Certainly, he exercised considerable influence over government policy. He was not without serious character weaknesses – including a volatile temperament, an extraordinary capacity for rudeness and an excessive fondness for women and alcohol; his drinking habits caused Wilson to comment that Brown was 'a brilliant foreign secretary until four o'clock in the afternoon'. A *Private Eye* front cover of the time (February 1967) carried a photograph of Wilson, de Gaulle and Brown with balloon comments by each – Wilson to de Gaulle 'George is a little tired, Your Majesty' [*sic*], de Gaulle 'Non', and Brown 'You do the Hokey Cokey and you shake it all about' (the last being a not entirely gross parody of certain passages in the history of Britain's relationship with the EC/EU). Despite Brown's flaws and reputation for being 'tired and emotional', however, he had a strong following within the Labour movement. This support was reflected in a popular saying of the time: 'Better George drunk than Harold sober' (Pimlott, 1992: 329–31). The fact that de Gaulle took to Brown more than to Wilson made no difference to the outcome of the application. De Gaulle still exercised the 'velvet veto'.

Wilson exhibited many of his Walter Mitty characteristics throughout the episode, whether in extravagant claims about his abilities as a top-flight diplomat or in assessments suggesting that he had charmed de Gaulle. He misjudged de Gaulle, evidently believing that while the French president was opposed to British membership of the EC he might lack the strength to exercise a veto if the British government continued to beat at the door and did not falter in its purpose. Such an approach seemed unlikely to succeed, not least because a year earlier (March 1966) de Gaulle had not hesitated to upset an altogether bigger figure in the international system, the United States, when he announced France's withdrawal from military participation in NATO. He also insisted that all foreign, including American, military forces had to leave France. This last demand caused one American diplomat, mindful of the American war dead in two world wars, to enquire 'does that include the ones under the ground?' (Schoenbaum, 1988: 421).

'There is no alternative' and the defeatist thesis

Following de Gaulle's second veto, there was by now a widespread consensus in government circles that there was no viable alternative to EC membership, least of all apparently for a country experiencing economic crisis with the devaluation of sterling (November 1967) and its aftermath. At this time an 'I'm backing Britain' campaign (complete with theme tune recorded by Bruce Forsyth) encouraged the working population to work extra time without pay to boost productivity. The campaign fizzled out soon after it became known that the T-shirts bearing the slogan 'I'm backing Britain' had been made in Portugal (Sandbrook, 2006: 608).

Immediately after de Gaulle's first veto, Macmillan wrote in his diary 'The great question remains "What is the alternative to the European Community?" If we are honest, we must say that there is none'. This mindset became deeply entrenched in Whitehall during the rest of the 1960s. In the 1980s the acronym Tina (There is no alternative) was commonly used as a dogmatic assertion or an article of faith by the Thatcher governments that there was no alternative to free market capitalism. To a large extent, similar status was given to the importance of EC membership by the political establishment of the 1960s and early 1970s.

A classic exposition of this view found expression in a Foreign and Commonwealth Office (FCO) study of the options for British external policy if the third application for membership ended in failure (NA., PREM 15/369). Alec Douglas-Home, Foreign Secretary, and Geoffrey Rippon, Chancellor of the Duchy of Lancaster, broadly agreed with the conclusions of this paper, and they were part of the incoming Heath government of 1970 that opened negotiations on the third application for EC membership. The paper maintained that the arguments for EC membership were 'overwhelming'. It recognized, however, that the prospect of membership and potentially of a unified

Europe did not enjoy substantial support among the British public. There were four alternatives to EC membership:

* 'Go-it-Alone' policies;
* co-operation with European countries outside the EC;
* new forms of association with non-European countries;
* policies involving co-operation with the EC states.

As compared with EC membership, even the best of these options was judged to be not 'merely second but fourth or fifth best'. In effect, this view reflected the realization that they were not viable alternatives at all.

To some commentators at the time and since, this sort of analysis smacked of weakness and defeatism. It was in this vein that Margaret Thatcher held that the Suez debacle of 1956 marked the moment when 'the British political class ... went from believing that Britain could do anything to an almost neurotic belief that Britain could do nothing'. Pro-marketeers were routinely criticized for losing faith in Britain's ability to solve its problems outside the EC and for making extravagant claims about the assumed economic stimulus that EC membership would bring.

In October 1970, *The Spectator*, the leading pro-Conservative weekly, claimed that the British public was being taken into the EC under false pretenses. It was being misled by a formidable establishment masterminded by a group of British politicians and intellectuals unable to think of any acceptable diversion with which to conceal the country's political and economic weakness. At the same time, George Gale, its editor, declared that the magazine stood fast on the principle of national identity in opposing membership, insisting that to join the EC would be an unnatural and unhistorical and therefore ignorant folly. This view was indicative of the extent to which Heath did not endear himself to sections of the Conservative Party by being enthusiastically pro-EC. For his own part, Heath himself was not exactly enthusiastic about the party, describing it on one occasion as consisting of 'shits, bloody shits and fucking shits' (Moore, 2014: 131, 287).

Some historians later expanded on criticism of the decision to join the EC. The Heath government was accused of acting as an abusive parent towards the Commonwealth. It was further held that Britain had joined the EC under the moral cowardice of Heath in the dour, drab defeatist 1970s. The course and outcome of the third set of negotiations for EC membership bore out some of the charges leveled against the Heath government by such opponents of EC membership (*The Spectator*, 10 October 1970; Roberts, 2006).

Mission accomplished, 1970–1972

The coming to power of Edward Heath at the head of a Conservative government as a result of the general election of June 1970 resulted in the third and successful bid for EC membership. Heath took office with a determined commitment to seek EC membership. He possessed the temperament, experience and mindset to achieve his principal objective. He pursued this goal in such a single-minded, uncompromising manner that Thatcher and himself were arguably the only two post-1945 British prime ministers to have personally and fundamentally changed the course of British history by sheer persistence, force of character and conviction. Furthermore, Heath was undoubtedly one of the most European-centred of any British prime minister since 1945 with Tony Blair as a close contender in rhetoric if not deeds (see Chapters 3 and 10).

Unlike his contemporaries and the public at large, Heath believed that the EC was a dynamic and unfinished creation that might in the course of time evolve into a European federation. He believed, too, and to a greater degree than either Macmillan or Wilson, that EC membership was an important means of getting Britain to live with the modern world and most especially of advancing the process of economic modernization. The aim was to shake the country out of its malaise and set it on a more competitive course through greater investment and lower inflation. However, his efforts as a managerial modernizer were no more successful in that regard than those of his predecessors. It was nonetheless the case that in their judgment on the rationale for EC membership Macmillan, Wilson and Heath shared much in common. In the final analysis, they believed, to a greater or lesser extent, that the economic arguments for and against EC membership were not only finely balanced but secondary to the political argument; only by EC membership could Britain continue to exercise power and influence in a world now clearly dominated by others, most notably by the two superpowers.

'A medium power of the first rank'

In several important respects, however, Heath broke with the consensus view of Britain's role and presence in the wider world, while his backward glance at 'the lessons of history' focused only on the mistakes of the previous ten years of Britain's relations with the EC. A key feature of Heath's view of the world was his description of Britain's position in the international system: 'A medium power of the first rank', a view shared by Alec Douglas-Home, the former prime minister (1963–1964) who served as Heath's foreign secretary (1970–1974).

Unlike his predecessors and successors, Heath had no interest in the maintenance of a 'special relationship' with the United States, and always doubted whether Britain received anything in return from Washington for British support. He recognized, however, that shedding the special relationship for a natural relationship, as he put it, would be more difficult psychologically than the withdrawal from Empire. He steadfastly resisted attempts by the Nixon administration in Washington to establish more cordial relations. He was particularly critical of the Washington administration's handling of international trade and monetary policy, most especially the collapse of the dollar-based Bretton Woods fixed exchange rate system following the abandonment of the dollar's convertibility into gold (August 1971).

Nor did Heath feel any sentimental attachment to the Commonwealth, and was largely if not wholly unaffected by any sense of post-imperial nostalgia. He was invariably unimpressed by rhetoric about the future role and value of the Commonwealth. At a particularly fractious Commonwealth prime ministers' conference in Singapore (January 1971), he expressed such irritation with some of the other Commonwealth representatives for their criticism of certain aspects of British policy that one commentator concluded that the imperial menopause was over. By this time, the process of decolonization was at an end. Thereafter a long decline in popular and academic interest in the Empire and Commonwealth seemed to belittle its legacy. One of the last British governors of Aden claimed that when the empire finally collapsed it would leave behind it only two monuments: the game of Association Football and the expression 'Fuck off' (Weight, 2002). In fact, it left behind a deposit of post-imperial nostalgia, more evident among some of the country's political leaders than among sections of the population at large that were indifferent to the loss of Empire (see Chapter 11).

A more important aspect of Heath's European policy was his reading of the recent past in making a successful bid for EC membership. He was arguably in a better position than any other British politician to capitalize on his knowledge and experience as the chief negotiator in the Macmillan government's application for EC membership. He was thus well acquainted with the workings of the EC that are often overlooked, ignored or underestimated by other British politicians. He distinguished himself from the Macmillan and Wilson membership bids in two important respects.

'Swallow the lot, and swallow it now'

First, Heath's basic approach to the 1970–1972 negotiations was to concentrate on securing EC membership and to defer any attempt to modify EC institutions and practices until after the achievement of that goal. Jean Monnet had offered that advice to the Macmillan government in 1961. Heath's firsthand experience of leading the British team in the 1961–1963 negotiations had convinced him that there was no point in trying to obtain fundamental changes to existing EC treaties, arrangements and policies; 'Swallow the lot, and swallow it now' advised Con O'Neill, Britain's most senior official in the course of the negotiations, when emphasizing the importance of accepting all of the EC's existing legislative texts (*acquis communautaire*).

The successful negotiation of EC membership, however, was not without drawbacks, since it meant a reluctant acceptance by the British of terms about which they had serious reservations (see Chapter 3). The Heath government was left with little room for manoeuvre and no real alternative but to accept what was on offer, subject to some fairly minor concessions in certain areas such as imports of New Zealand meat and dairy products and of Caribbean sugar. Meanwhile, pro-marketeer opinion often explained negotiating strategy and tactics in terms of belated entry to the EC and the need to ensure a successful outcome. Lord Crowther, a leading advocate of EC membership in the House of Lords, stressed one of the important reasons for pursuing this approach: 'You do not haggle over the subscription when you are invited to climb aboard a lifeboat' (Young, 1998: 239). This view of EC membership as offering salvation for the country's political and economic ills seemed to confirm the speculation of Treasury officials in 1956. At that time, when the Six were founding the EC, such officials had expressed the view that in the longer term the question might become not whether Britain should go into Europe to save Europe as in wartime but whether Britain might have to move closer to Europe in order to save itself (NA., T 236/6018).

The second important aspect of the Heath negotiations for EC membership lay in the diplomatic field. Heath was determined to avoid any attempt to mobilize the so-called 'friendly Five' EC states against France on Britain's behalf. Both Macmillan and Wilson had unsuccessfully tried to do precisely that. Heath was in no doubt that British membership of the EC would only become possible when the French government was prepared to sanction it. The decisive breakthrough in that respect, that was assisted by de Gaulle's departure from office two years earlier, occurred as a result of a meeting between Heath and Georges Pompidou, the President of France (May 1971). The combination of personal chemistry between the two leaders and successful diplomacy proved irresistible. Thereafter, Britain signed the Treaty of Accession (22 January 1972) and became a full member of the EC (1 January 1973).

The domestic debate

The debate about Britain and the EC was immediately fuelled by opposition to Heath's handling of the issue. His passionate commitment to membership, while smoothing the path to entry in relations with the Six, left him open to the accusation that he was willing to pay any price or to sign a blank cheque to fulfil a cherished political ambition. It also exposed him to the charge that his European convictions were, like his interest in classical music, far removed from the common culture of most Britons and indicative of the High-Brow/Low-Brow gulf between the pro- and anti-marketeers that W. H. Auden, the poet, had detected at the time of the first application (*Encounter*, 1963). It was widely believed that Heath failed to honour his much-quoted undertaking that entry would only take place with the full-hearted consent of parliament and the people. Heath later conceded that he could have been more precise in his language when he talked of 'full-hearted consent', but maintained that his expression was unfairly exploited (Heath, 1998: 363).

It was also argued that Heath had belittled the loss of national sovereignty involved in EC membership. Certainly, the expression Common Market suggested little more than a trade deal in the public mind. It obscured any political and constitutional implications, and was far removed from the idea of a popular 'imagined community'. Furthermore, the EEC Rome Treaty's commitment to 'ever closer union' scarcely registered with the public. A detailed study of the parliamentary debate on the subject concludes that the fundamental rights and wrongs of EC membership were often semi-hidden behind an argument about the precise safeguards agreed with the Six for a number of interest groups likely to be hurt by EC policies.

Nevertheless, there is little foundation to the charge that the electorate was misled or that the political dimensions and effects of EC membership were insufficiently covered either by the pro-marketeers or the anti-marketeers (Ludlow, 2015). If the Heath government did not shy away from the sovereignty and primacy of EC law issues, it was nonetheless loath to dwell on the precise implications if only for fear of strengthening the anti-marketeer case. Certainly, the government made little or no effort to present membership as a fundamental change, nor did it stray far from the idea that this move represented continuity through change. In the circumstances, there is substance to the view of Richard Wilson, a former Cabinet secretary, that British entry into the EC was indicative of the British habit of undergoing big changes 'under anaesthetic' (Trewin, 2008: 670).

The issue did not figure greatly among the public at large. Leading anti-marketeers in parliament such as Enoch Powell, Peter Shore and Derek Walker-Smith were often portrayed as debating arcane points of order about sovereignty and national independence. One Cabinet minister at the time, Margaret Thatcher, was silent throughout a Cabinet meeting on sovereignty, claiming with regret in later years that she had regarded the arguments that Powell and others put forward about sovereignty at the time as 'rhetorical devices' (Moore, 2014: 237–8).

Such subjects rarely occupied the attention of a public increasingly habituated to regard EC membership as a bread-and-butter issue. For his own part, Heath defended his position by drawing a distinction between 'pooling' and 'surrendering' national sovereignty. His critics, however, frequently complained that he was guilty at best of being economical with the truth, at worst of deception (Castle, 1993: 444). The judgment that 'Ministers did not lie, but they avoided telling the truth' (Young, 1990: 247) was not the strongest basis for encouraging interest and trust in a new project.

Conclusion

British policy and attitudes towards the process of European integration in the period 1945–1972 so often served as a commentary on the country's past. The sheer weight of historical bonds, memories, traditions and interests shaped responses to the rapidly changing political landscape in western Europe. In particular, the weakening of longstanding ties together with the loss of global power and reach informed and influenced the debate about Europe.

What materialized after the emergence of the EC in the mid-1950s was strikingly different from the architecture of European and international relations that Britain had played a leading role in creating during the first decade after the Second World War. This phase in Britain's European policymaking was accompanied by:

- an emphasis on an Atlantic rather than a European community;
- a strong preference for intergovernmental co-operation rather than any supranational construction;
- a determination to strike a desirable balance between European and extra-European interests, prioritizing the idea of a global, multilateral free trading system over any exclusively regional European arrangement.

As we shall see in later chapters, these were to be enduring themes in British strategy and tactics towards the evolution of the EC/EU.

After 1955 British governments were on the defensive in western Europe. Initially they explored possibilities but increasingly recognized the diminishing appeal of alternatives to EC membership, and eventually applied for membership. Three common expressions may be said to capture the change of mood among most political leaders of both major political parties who came to espouse the idea of EC membership during the period 1956–1972. These were, in order of timing: the panic-ridden 'We've been caught out', the galvanizing 'We must do something', the fatalist 'There is no alternative'.

In the circumstances, relatively limited attention was given to what the country could or should bring to or obtain from EC membership. The membership option ultimately owed much to the belief that the EC could not be allowed to survive and thrive without the inclusion of Britain, and furthermore that membership could help to shore up the country's declining power and status in the international system.

Historical influences and conditions did not lose their potency or appeal following accession to the EC in January 1973. On the contrary, it was entirely in keeping with a continuing regard for past events that a particular political mood took hold of politicians and public alike during the first ten years or so of EC membership. They were far less focused on shaping a future in the EC than on looking back to and pursuing an almost continuous process of renegotiation to revise or modify the original terms of membership.

3   Belonging without believing

Our God,
We are now in the Common Market.
Some of us feel that this has been a mistake.
Some of us believe that this will bring opportunities for good.
Most of us just don't know.

(Special Church of Scotland prayer marking Britain's entry into the
European Community in 1973)

Introduction

This chapter considers British membership of the EC/EU in the period 1973–2010 (see
Chapter 12 for the period since 2010). It does so with a view to examining the distancing
between the original motives and inspiration underlying the emergence of the EC, as
discussed in the previous chapter, and British interests and perspectives. It deals with
the immediate reception given to membership by the political parties and public.

The chapter also examines the particular factors and circumstances that not only
affected the difficult transition to membership but also influenced the character of
Britain's membership thereafter. The circumstances surrounding the early period
of adaptation to membership helped to shape subsequent perspectives, policies and
attitudes. In that respect a central theme of the chapter concerns the extent to which
British politicians and public alike exhibited a sense of belonging to without believing
in the EU.

European dreams and visions

In the late 1940s a US congressman addressed a British political gathering at which
he was asked for his views about the British attitude towards the subject of European
unity. He promptly surprised his audience by likening the matter to a simple fairy story.
In short, a fairy princess dreamt that she was imprisoned in a tower when a handsome
prince suddenly appeared at her bedside. The princess exclaimed 'What are you going
to do now?' At which point the prince replied: 'Don't ask me. It's your dream' (*Foreign
Relations of the United States* [hereafter *FRUS*] 1947, vol. III).

Shortly after this event, a senior Whitehall official made the same point more pro-
saically when he likened British policy and attitudes towards European unity to some

lines in John Henry Newman's hymn 'Lead kindly light, amid the encircling gloom', the relevant lines being 'I do not ask to see/The distant scene: one step enough for me' (NA., FO 371/73099). There was perhaps a striking analogy between the circumstances that prompted Newman to write the hymn – as he was travelling on the continent seeking guidance in the midst of a deep personal spiritual crisis – and Britain's agonizing and highly problematical European Odyssey since 1945.

Some years later British political leaders appeared both unreceptive to the European 'dream' and reluctant visionaries. Matters of identity or destiny were seemingly not going to enter into or cloud the judgment of Whitehall policymakers. In 1956 Paul Henri-Spaak, the Belgian foreign minister, whose intergovernmental committee appointed by the Messina conference of 1955 was busy laying the foundations of the EC, visited London. His main aim was to inspire Conservative government ministers about European unity. In a meeting with R. A. Butler ('Rab'), the Chancellor of the Exchequer, however, his attempts to advance the cause of European unity evidently made little headway: 'I don't think I could have shocked him more when I tried to appeal to his imagination than if I had taken off my trousers', the Belgian observed after one particularly difficult meeting with Butler. For his own part Butler dismissed the Messina initiative as archaeological excavations designed to resurrect the dead body of European federalism. He later explained that the British decision to withdraw its observer from the post-Messina talks was taken through boredom (Charlton, 1983: 182, 194).

In hindsight, there can be few more eloquent testimonies than this to what is often perceived as some of the enduring characteristic features of British public attitudes down to the present day: the palpable lack of ideological and emotional commitment to the cause of European integration, the framing of EU membership largely in terms of an economic calculus, the emphasis on pragmatism and a suspicion of idealism, and a high degree of tedium about the subject among the public at large.

Such preferences formed a stark contrast to the attitudes of the founding fathers of the EC whether political leaders like Adenauer (West Germany), de Gasperi (Italy), Schuman (France) and Spaak (Belgium), or imaginative technocrats like Jean Monnet, Robert Marjolin, Étienne Hirsch and Pierre Uri. To be sure, an heroic mythology has gathered around their activities. They were clearly not immune to realpolitik and to jockeying for material or national advantage in their dealings. Moroever, and contrary to some British impressions at the time, they were far less inclined to sink their countries in tightly organized European structures than to use such structures to effect the recovery of their states from the disastrous experience of war (Milward, 1992). Nevertheless, they shared a burning sense of purpose, daring, vision and enthusiasm for the Community idea and for the goal of 'ever closer union'. They felt 'the future in their bones', or as the more ardent supporters of a federal Europe in the early post-war years advocated, 'a headlong flight into an unknown future, in order to escape from a fearful present' (Shonfield, 1972: 18).

Inauspicious beginnings

The process of British adjustment to EC membership in the decade after entry was long and troublesome. In other member states, whether fairly or not, Britain quickly acquired a reputation for being awkward and uncooperative. It was seemingly one of the least committed member states with a semi-detached status and a set of policies that consistently sought to minimize both the EC's development and its impact on Britain.

Meanwhile, substantial sections of opinion in the country remained either opposed to membership or at best doubtful as to whether the benefits outweighed the costs. Furthermore, public opinion was often confused about the objectives and desirability of EC membership. The polemical warfare of pro- and anti-marketeers generated much heat but little light on the subject. It was in these conditions that a political mood took hold that was less focused on future planning than on looking back to the original terms of membership and on pursuing an almost continuous process of renegotiation to revise or modify the terms.

The formal and informal process of renegotiation spanned the two Wilson Labour governments of 1974–1976, the Callaghan Labour government of 1976–1979 and the Thatcher Conservative government until 1984. The particular features of this process and the accompanying, often bruising, diplomatic activity will be dealt with in later chapters (especially Chapters 4 and 8). Suffice it to say, it was the final settlement of the vexed question of Britain's contribution to the EC budget – the Fontainebleau agreement (June 1984) – that brought to an end this first, highly contentious period in Britain's EC membership.

Several factors complicated and prolonged this problematical process of adjustment. First, Britain's relatively late and long-postponed entry into the EC put it at a decided disadvantage. It was joining an organization whose member states were already accustomed to a high degree of economic integration that had greatly assisted sustained economic growth. The EC's institutions and policies understandably reflected the interests of the Six and took no account of British concerns (see Chapter 8). A further and related difficulty was that Britain entered the EC with an array of extra-European trading and financial interests that fitted uneasily into the EC framework. What further compounded Britain's difficulties was that as a new member state it was joining a dynamic organization with a new sense of movement and purpose. At their meeting at The Hague in December 1969, the EC leaders agreed to the principle of EC enlargement and also to the creation of an economic and monetary union (EMU).

A further, major obstacle to a trouble-free transition to EC membership involved the worsening economic conditions of the time. British entry into the EC occurred when the virtually uninterrupted growth in the western international economy since the early post-war years was beginning to experience a check. The collapse of the Bretton Woods fixed exchange rate system in 1971, together with the quadrupling in the price of oil during 1973–1974, meant that British membership of the EC started against a gloomy background far removed from the buoyant economic conditions that had fostered the earlier development of the EC. In the period 1965–1978 the annual average growth rates of gross domestic product (GDP) for the EC states were far higher than that of Britain, while Britain's growth rate in the 1970s slumped to a greater extent than most of the other EC states (see Table 2.3 in Chapter 2). Meanwhile, there was a marked increase in the rate of inflation: from an annual average of 6.1 per cent for the EC and 7 per cent for Britain in the period 1968–1973 to 11.3 per cent and 15.7 per cent respectively in the period 1974–1979.

The change in British economic conditions was particularly dramatic in the period before, during and immediately after entry to the EC. In 1970 rates of inflation and unemployment were still in relatively low single figures, while there was a healthy balance of payments surplus. By 1975, however, the economy was in the throes of 'stagflation', with inflation running at over 25 per cent, a huge balance of payments deficit, falling production and investment, and rising unemployment. In the midst of deepening economic gloom, Jim Callaghan, Foreign Secretary, reportedly mused aloud at one Cabinet meeting in November 1974: 'When I am shaving in the morning I say to myself that if I were a young man I would emigrate. By the time I am sitting down to breakfast I ask myself, "Where would I go?"' (Morgan, 1992: 471). A few months later at the time of the 1975 budget, another Cabinet minister, Tony Crosland, crisply announced the end of an era: 'The party's over'. A few years later in 1979, the British ambassador to France observed: 'You have only to move about Western Europe nowadays to realize how poor and unproud the British have become in relation to their neighbours' (Parris and Bryson, 2010: 206).

It was eventually an historically high Public Sector Borrowing Requirement (PSBR) amounting to 9.6 per cent of GDP that finally sent sterling into a free fall on the international money market. In the period March–September 1976, massive sales of sterling reduced its value by 26 per cent. By September, the government's unsuccessful efforts to stop sterling's slide were dramatically exposed as Denis Healey, Chancellor of the Exchequer, was forced to make a hurried change in travel plans at Heathrow Airport in order to return to the Treasury as sterling continued to plummet on the foreign exchanges. 'Goodbye, Great Britain' a *Wall Street Journal* editorial concluded at the time, 'It was nice knowing you' (*Wall Street Journal*, 29 April 1975). In the circumstances, only an International Monetary Fund (IMF) loan of £3.5 billion was sufficient to shore up the pound. The British government agreed to reduce its planned public spending by £2.5 billion over the next two financial years. It also arranged to sell off £500 million of the government shares in British Petroleum (BP), the first major package of a longer term sale of state assets to the private sector. In the event, only half of the stand-by credits were drawn on by the government. Freedom from IMF controls – 'Sod off Day' as Healey put it in his characteristically blunt manner – occurred earlier than scheduled.

A further factor that complicated Britain's early years of EC membership was the domestic political situation during the period 1974–1979. There was a major constraint on the way the government dealt with EC business in that a deeply divided Labour Party held office without a strong parliamentary majority. Following the defeat of the Heath government in the general election of February 1974, Wilson returned to power at the head of a minority Labour government. As a result of a further election in October 1974, Labour was returned to office, but with an overall parliamentary majority of only three seats. This majority eventually melted away in 1977 when the Callaghan government negotiated a pact with the Liberals ('Lib-Lab pact'), by which it retained power until 1979. The absence of a strong majority government – an unusual condition in post-1945 politics, except in the periods 1950–1951, 1964–1966, 1995–1996 and since 2015 – greatly influenced the government's aims and objectives in the EC sphere. It also meant that the handling of EC issues was largely determined by the balance of forces within the governing party.

No fanfare for Europe

It is certainly true to say that a large body of parliamentary and press opinion favoured EC membership. In some cases, however, as among the public at large, there was limited interest in what seemed like an elitist rather than populist venture. At the time of the Wilson bid for EC membership in 1967, one of the front covers of the satirical magazine,

Private Eye, showed several elderly people, one with a handkerchief on his head, asleep in deckchairs, with the caption: 'The great debate begins'.

Little had changed several years later. The fanfare for Europe to mark entry into the EC completely failed to capture the public imagination; three out of four Britons opposed the venture. Immediately after the House of Commons vote in favour of the principle of EC membership (28 October 1971), Heath celebrated his 'greatest success as Prime Minister' on his return to Downing Street by playing the First Prelude from Book I of Bach's 'Well-Tempered Clavier' on his clavichord (Heath, 1998: 381). Few of the British public felt similarly inclined. Indeed, it seemed that most people accepted EC membership with resignation, if not indifference. *The Times* (2 January 1973) claimed that the issues were too complicated for mass enthusiasm. It might also have added that large sections of the public were content to remain half-hearted and ignorant. A woman in Liverpool was representative of this last category when asked by a Conservative Party official about her views on the Common Market, she replied 'Where are they building it, luv?' (Weight, 2002: 485, 497).

One of the most significant and enduring aspects of the Heath government's negotiation of EC membership lay in the internal convulsions and divisions within and between the political parties. These were first paraded when the House of Commons voted in favour of the principle of EC membership, and they have rarely disappeared from view ever since. Labour Party unity was the major casualty in the first instance. Sixty-nine Labour MPs, led by Roy Jenkins, deputy leader of the party, defied a three-line whip and voted with the government on 28 October while a further 20 Labour MPs abstained, thus helping to ensure a government majority of 112.

Immediately after its electoral defeat in June 1970, Labour Party opinion, greatly influenced by the growing strength of the Left, turned against EC membership. Wilson faced major problems in holding together a party bitterly divided over the issue and, less importantly, in seeking to act consistently with his own bid for EC membership in 1967. These conditions tested to the full his skills as a party manager; likening the Labour Party to a stage coach, he had once commented 'If you rattle along at great speed everybody is too exhilarated or too seasick to cause any trouble. But if you stop everybody gets out and argues about where to go next' (Smith, 1964). That was precisely what happened to the Labour Party when it went into opposition after defeat in the general election of 1970. Any attempt to avoid debate and division on the EC issue in these circumstances was far less easy than it had been in government in 1967. At that time, many in Wilson's Cabinet and in the party at large believed that the EC membership bid would be vetoed by de Gaulle and that it was therefore scarcely necessary to debate the matter. Wilson eventually agreed that on Labour's return to power the government would renegotiate the terms of entry and hold a referendum on the renegotiated terms (see below).

Signs of divisions within the Conservative Party at this stage were far more limited than in the Labour ranks. Nevertheless, as early as March 1970, John Biffen, a Conservative government minister in the 1980s, presciently warned that a struggle was just beginning for the soul of the party that would be focused on EC membership and would continue for years after entry. Indeed, the fact that 39 Conservative MPs voted against EC membership in principle was indicative of a strand of opinion within the party that in different circumstances was to command greater support. Some 40 years later, and in an uncannily similar fashion to Harold Wilson, David Cameron was to tread exactly the same path as Wilson by utilizing the renegotiation and referendum device to contain deep divisions over EU membership in the Conservative Party (see Chapter 12).

Renegotiating 'Tory terms'

The Labour Party's increasingly bitter divisions over the EC after 1970 placed Wilson in an acute dilemma. What he wanted to avoid at all costs was an irreparable split between the pro- and anti-marketeer factions. His chosen tactic for achieving this was to concentrate on the terms of entry. Wilson took the line that he was not opposed to entry in principle. However, he made the unlikely claim that he would not have accepted the 'Tory terms' negotiated by the Heath government, an inglorious if politically convenient compromise that left him open to the charge of inconsistency; Robert Carr, a Conservative Cabinet minister at the time, mocked the Labour Party for its U-turn and for having thus taken a package tour to Damascus (*Hansard*, 25 October 1971, col. 1362).

Other leading lights in the Labour Party at this time indicated all too clearly that EC membership was not a major point of ideology or theology (to use a favourite Wilsonian expression). Some changed their minds several times; Denis Healey did so three times in a matter of weeks. Others like Tony Crosland, who had earlier expressed pro-European opinions, failed to support the principle of EC membership in the decisive Commons vote in October 1971; he claimed that Europe did not rank among the issues that he really cared about (Radice, 1992: 194). In its manifestos for the general elections of February and October 1974, the Labour Party committed itself to a 'fundamental' renegotiation of the terms of entry before putting the issue of whether Britain should remain in the EC to the electorate.

The commitment to a 'fundamental' renegotiation was capable of different constructions in practice, ranging from a largely spurious face-saving effort on the one hand to radical changes in the original terms of entry on the other. Wilson himself had long since learnt the usefulness of employing the slippery concept of renegotiation in order to promise different outcomes to opposing factions in the party. Prior to the 1964 election, he had effectively limited the electorally damaging consequences of Labour's divisions over British possession of nuclear weapons by committing a Labour government to renegotiate the Nassau Agreement of December 1962 by which Britain obtained the US-built Polaris missiles. Following the election, however, the idea of renegotiation faded away and the agreement was maintained. In neither of the 1974 manifestos was it made clear whether voters would be consulted through a general election or referendum; it was not until 23 January 1975 that it was announced in the Commons that there would be a consultative referendum by June of that year at the latest cast in the form of a question – 'Do you think the United Kingdom should stay in the European Community (the Common Market)?' – an interesting and significant contrast to the question on the Cameron government's referendum paper for June 2016: 'Should the United Kingdom remain a member of the European Union or leave the European Union?'

Some of the original items on Labour's renegotiation agenda were soon revealed to be either irrelevant or relatively unimportant. It emerged, for example, that there was nothing to prevent Britain from retaining a zero Value Added Tax (VAT) rate on basic necessities. Furthermore, the perceived dangers from the EC leaders' commitment at their Hague summit of December 1969 to an economic and monetary union receded rapidly into the distance as turmoil on the international money markets ruled out the 1980 target date. Among the remaining items on the agenda, the most significant were reform of the CAP, a new deal on Britain's budgetary contribution to the EC (see Chapter 8), and improved arrangements for imports of Caribbean sugar and New Zealand meat and dairy produce.

Limited concessions were obtained in all these areas with assistance especially from Helmut Schmidt, the West German chancellor, and also from Giscard d'Estaing, the French president whose backing was gained by British agreement to a French proposal for direct elections to the European Parliament. Schmidt was particularly influential in supporting the British case on the EC budget, though later described the renegotiation as a face-saving cosmetic operation (Young, 1998: 283). Possibly, however, the massed ranks of anti-marketeers at the Labour Party conference addressed by him in November 1974 contributed to his later view that perhaps de Gaulle had been right after all in vetoing British membership of the EC. In any event, Schmidt's involvement in this episode was to establish something of a trend whereby German chancellors were prepared to assist British prime ministers experiencing difficulties with their own party over the issue of EU membership.

The renegotiation exercise was completed at the Dublin European Council of March 1975. The protracted wranglings over the issue served the purpose of projecting the image of Wilson as a tough campaigner. He played the populist nationalist card as the stout defender of British interests. He publicly dismissed the EC as a 'shambles' and ridiculed the EC Commission's plans for the harmonization of regulations, as horror stories of 'Euro beer', 'Euro bread' and so on filled the pages of the British tabloid press. All in all, he generally pioneered a form of highly ritualized Brussels-bashing that was to become the stock-in-trade of later British leaders. Wilson was equally determined to project the image of a strong negotiator, especially during the Dublin European Council where he appeared to dominate proceedings and insisted on finalizing the package of renegotiated terms of entry. It was widely assumed beforehand that the terms already agreed were satisfactory and that Wilson and the majority of his Cabinet would recommend acceptance. In fact, Wilson announced a football result at the start of his post-Council news conference, as if to confirm that the nailbiting atmosphere before the Council meeting was a charade and that he had always expected to reach an acceptable settlement.

Wilson conceded that he had failed to bring about major changes in certain respects, notably to the CAP. Nevertheless, he claimed that the new terms were substantially better than the original ones and justified a government recommendation that Britain should remain in the EC. However, it was relatively easy to portray the package of renegotiated terms as falling far short of a substantial advance on the original terms of entry.

Anti-marketeers argued that the changes were marginal and amounted to little more than a face-saving device, a view shared by large sections of the Labour Party. The Cabinet voted 16 to 7 in support of these terms, the minority view being expressed by the left-wing contingent in the Cabinet, notably Barbara Castle, Tony Benn, who was by now a particular source of irritation to Wilson – 'he immatures with age' – and Michael Foot. In view of these divisions, it was agreed that for the duration of the forthcoming referendum campaign ministers on both sides of the argument should be free to air their views. What could not be obscured was that Labour Party opinion as a whole was strongly against the government's renegotiated terms. In the critical Commons vote of 12 April 1975, the package failed to command support within the Parliamentary Labour Party (PLP): 137 voted for, 145 against. A fortnight later, a special Labour Party conference rejected the terms by 3.724 million votes to 1.986 million votes, roughly the same two to one margin as that by which the electorate was to support the renegotiated terms in the referendum of June 1975.

The referendum of 1975

After the Dublin European Council the date of the referendum was fixed for 5 June 1975. The decision to hold a referendum met with a mixed response. Some regarded it as a welcome extension of the British people's democratic rights; in other quarters, however, it was portrayed as a dangerous constitutional innovation that posed a threat to parliamentary sovereignty. The conventional wisdom, backed up by opinion polls, was that a majority of the public was opposed to EC membership and would reject it if given the chance. Unsurprisingly, therefore, the idea of holding a referendum was overwhelmingly popular with anti-marketeers, while it met with initial hostility from pro-marketeers at least until opinion polls in late 1974 indicated that the public mood was becoming more pro-membership. For its own part, the government justified the use of a referendum on the grounds that Heath had taken Britain into the EC without a mandate and that the issue at stake was one of unique constitutional importance. These arguments were rejected by the Conservatives and by most Labour pro-marketeers who claimed that the only reason a referendum was being held was to paper over Labour Party disunity.

An unequal contest: pro-marketeers versus anti-marketeers

The referendum campaign began in earnest in May 1975. It was an unequal contest. The pro-marketeers had access to far greater financial resources than their opponents. In addition, the umbrella organization that coordinated their actitivities, Britain in Europe, was considerably more efficient than its tiny, cash-strapped and somewhat ramshackle opposite number, the National Referendum Campaign. The pro-marketeers enjoyed the backing of practically the whole of the press with some ill-assorted exceptions: the communist *Morning Star*, the *Scottish Daily News* (a recently created co-operative), the *Dundee Courier and Advertiser* and *The Spectator*. Business sentiment was also overwhelmingly favourable to Britain staying in the EC, as was revealed in a survey published by the *The Times* on 9 April 1975.

All of the three main party leaders, Harold Wilson, Margaret Thatcher, who had replaced Heath as Conservative Party leader in February 1975, and Jeremy Thorpe, the Liberal Party leader, threw their weight – albeit with varying degrees of commitment – behind the 'yes' campaign. So too did the Liberal Party, the overwhelming majority of the Conservative Party and centre-right members of the Labour Party. In effect, the pro-marketeer camp commanded the support of the political mainstream. As against that, the opposing side consisted of a coalition of widely diverging political interests, riven by internal feuds and damaged by association with various extremist groups. Its principal spokesmen, Benn, Michael Foot and Enoch Powell, were certainly high-profile personalities, but they were also mavericks who aroused strong negative as well as positive feelings among the public.

Two issues dominated the referendum debate: a possible loss of sovereignty and the economic advantages and disadvantages of EC membership. The 'no' campaigners alleged that the inevitable result of EC membership would be a loss of political independence and absorption into a federal European superstate with the consequential narrowing rather than broadening of Britain's international horizons. The retort from the other side was that there was not the slightest possibility of rule by Brussels bureaucrats. Besides, what counted was how best to protect British interests, and in an increasingly interdependent world some pooling of sovereignty was not only unavoidable but positively beneficial.

Some of the leading anti-marketeers, notably Powell, Benn and Foot, sought to highlight the sovereignty issue. Opinion polls, however, indicated that voters were chiefly interested in the effect of EC membership on their living standards. The economic debate, however, was complicated and made more so by the difficulty of disentangling the various factors responsible for the undoubted deterioration in the British economy since 1972, as well as by varying and enduring 'guesstimates' about the likely impact of EC membership especially in connection with food prices and Britain's contribution to the EC budget (see Chapter 8).

The anti-marketeers sought to blame Britain's current economic difficulties wholly on entry to the EC, pointing to a disproportionately large balance of trade deficit with the original Six and a massive increase in unemployment as a direct consequence (see Table 3.1). The counter-argument was that the international crisis and deep-seated structural problems in the domestic economy were much more important as contributory factors. A report from the Confederation of British Industries (CBI), that gave powerful backing to the 'yes' campaign, reached the bleak conclusion that withdrawal from the EC would be disastrous for British industry.

In general terms, the 'yes' campaign sought to portray a grim future for Britain if it left the EC. Christopher Soames, one of the two Britons on the EC's Commission, declared: 'Frankly, it's damn cold outside', and he also quipped that at this moment in the nation's history 'you'd think twice about withdrawing from a Christmas Club, never mind the Common Market'. A similar message was conveyed by Roy Jenkins, who spoke of Britain being led into 'an old people's home for faded nations', as well as by the official 'yes' leaflet, with its talk of being 'alone in a harsh, cold world' (Butler and Kitzinger, 1976: 183). Framing the argument in this way was far more persuasive than the anti-marketeers' focus on abstruse points about sovereignty.

Table 3.1 UK balance of trade with the EC, 1970–1977 (£m)

1970	+39
1971	−191
1972	−591
1973	−1,191
1974	−2,027
1975	−2,412
1976	−2,127
1977	−1,733

Source: *Trade and Industry: News from the Departments of Industry, Trade, Prices and Consumer Protection*, 24 November 1978, London, HMSO.

One of the most sensitive aspects of the economic debate was the question of food prices and what the anti-marketeers viewed as a major threat to the long-standing British tradition of buying food cheaply on the world market. Because of an enormous increase in world prices over the previous two years, the general level of food prices within the EC in 1975 was no higher than outside. According to pro-marketeers, this was part of a long-term trend resulting from growth in demand and offered a timely warning that the days of cheap food were over. This interpretation was challenged by the anti-marketeers who maintained that artificially high food prices were an inbuilt feature of the CAP. Cabinet minister Barbara Castle became involved in one of the more lighthearted episodes in the campaign, the 'Battle of the Shopping Baskets'. As a publicity stunt she purchased a basket of food in London costing just over £4 and then went on a trip to Brussels to buy identical items at a cost of nearly £7. The point of this exercise was to provide a practical demonstration of what lay in store as British prices were brought up to EC levels. Her plan backfired, however, when Britain in Europe got wind of it, sent a woman to Oslo to do some shopping of her own and proved conclusively that the price of food was even higher in Norway, whose people had voted to reject membership of the EC in an earlier referendum.

As these and other arguments were traded during the referendum campaign, public opinion began to move strongly towards a 'yes' vote. By 5 June it was clear that the result would be a decisive endorsement of the government's recommendation. On a turnout of nearly 65 per cent of the electorate, 67.2 per cent voted for Britain to remain in the EC and 32.8 per cent voted against. There were some regional variations in the overall national pattern. The highest 'Yes' vote was in England (68.7 per cent), followed by Wales (64.8 per cent), Scotland (58.4 per cent) and Northern Ireland (52.1 per cent). Support for staying in tended to be strongest in the south-east of England, weaker in the north and weaker still in Scotland: only in Shetland and the Western Isles were there majorities against. To some extent, these local differences reflected the regional strengths and weaknesses of the two main political parties. The 'yes' vote was higher among Conservative electors than among their Labour counterparts, though even in the case of the latter the 'antis' were in a minority – something usually explained by rank-and-file loyalty to Wilson.

On the surface, Wilson had achieved his twin objectives of ensuring British membership of the EC while holding the Labour Party together. In the longer term, however, the consequences of the referendum were to prove disastrous for Labour Party unity. A particularly damaging feature of the referendum campaign for Labour was a tendency on the part of leading Labour pro-marketeers to discover in the course of cross-party campaigning that they had more in common with sections of the Conservative and Liberal parties than with the Labour Left. This loosening of the bonds of party unity played a major part in the formation of the breakaway Social Democratic Party (SDP) in 1981 (Jenkins, 1992: 424).

The impact of the referendum

The renegotiation exercise, culminating in the 1975 referendum, was a major triumph for Wilson. Even his detractors regarded it as such. He had achieved his objectives of keeping his party in power and in one piece – at least for the time being – and Britain in Europe (Pimlott, 1992: 659). He had kept the Labour Party together, despite the absence of majority support for the renegotiated terms at all levels of the Labour movement outside the Cabinet. That in itself was no mean achievement in view of the biting invective that his conduct attracted from the pro-marketeer Labour right and the anti-marketeer left-wing who variously regarded him as an unprincipled opportunist and a traitor. He had also obtained a result via the referendum that gave popular legitimacy to British membership of the EC. The referendum result lent some substance to the view that Heath had taken the British Establishment into Europe while Wilson took in the British people (Brivati and Jones, 1993: 205).

What failed to emerge through this episode was any positive view of how Britain intended to shape the EC's future or much evidence of depth of popular support for the project. Whether the size of the majority in the referendum for remaining in the EC was indicative of any great enthusiasm for British membership of the EC is open to serious doubt. At the time, the electorate's verdict was described as 'Full-hearted, whole-hearted and cheerful hearted' (*The Guardian*, 7 June 1975). Most historians, however, have concluded that the outcome owed more to caution, conservatism and acquiescence than to enthusiasm and positive feelings towards the EC. An authoritative study of the referendum concluded that 'the verdict … was unequivocal but it was also unenthusiastic. Support for membership was wide but it did not run deep' (Butler and Kitzinger, 1976: 280).

On the defensive: the Callaghan government and Europe, 1976–1979

In March 1976 Wilson unexpectedly and voluntarily announced his retirement from office. He was succeeded by Callaghan, an older man whose wide ministerial experience as Chancellor of the Exchequer, Home Secretary and Foreign Secretary, together with his skills as party manager, made him the obvious successor. The impact of EC membership on British politics and especially on Callaghan's Labour government of 1976–1979 did little to enhance public support for the project or to reconcile the Labour Party to membership.

Like Wilson, Callaghan pursued a defensive, semi-detached relationship with the EC. As foreign secretary during the renegotiation of the terms of entry episode, he had become convinced of the value of EC membership as a dull necessity rather than a matter of principle or as some form of idealistic ballast. In 1971, when President Pompidou of France remarked that French would remain the official language of the EC despite British membership, Callaghan had not hesitated to indulge in bruising, populist language; if sacrificing Britain's identity was what Common Market membership meant, then, as he put it, 'the President can have his answer – in French – *non merci beaucoup*' (Bell, 2004: 77). Callaghan as prime minister did not regard the EC as the principal or exclusive instrument for addressing the problems of continuing economic recession at the international level. His emphasis was on Atlantic co-operation, based on the premise that Europe and the United States had to work in tandem to pull the western economies out of recession.

Throughout its period of office, the politics of recession dominated the Callaghan government. The government was so subjected to domestic political constraints that it had limited room for manoeuvre in the conduct of its EC policy. The public expenditure cuts resulted in deep divisions within the Labour Party. The gulf between the government and party was most evident in a key institution like the National Executive Committee (NEC), where Callaghan – later describing some members of this body as viewing themselves as an 'alternative Government' – generally failed to command a majority for government policies. Anti-EC opinion was in the ascendancy, with a majority against membership on the NEC and with a party conference vote of two to one against the introduction of direct elections to the European Parliament (EP). Such conditions left an increasingly beleaguered government open to pressure to adopt a minimalist approach to the EC in order to assuage at least some of the party's opposition to the government's economic policy.

The problem of party management was made even more acute by the loss of a parliamentary majority and the emergence of the Lib-Lab pact in 1977, by which the strongly pro-EC Liberals extracted a government commitment to introduce legislation providing for direct elections to the EP. Callaghan also agreed to take full account of the Liberal Party's support for a system of proportional representation. There was no EC requirement for this last feature, and Callaghan himself was a confirmed opponent of such a measure. Proportional representation, however, was a vital necessity for the Liberals, who were likely to win few if any of the 78 British seats in the EP on the Westminster system of single-member constituencies and the first-past-the-post principle. In June 1977 the government introduced a bill implementing direct elections, with provision for proportional representation. In December 1977, however, the Commons rejected proportional representation. A majority of Conservative and Labour MPs voted against, Labour's divisions accounting for the fact that the government had allowed a free vote.

In view of this outcome and the need for further time to allow a boundary commission to draw up constituencies to operate on the British electoral system, Callaghan was obliged to inform the other EC governments that Britain – alone in this respect – was not in a position to hold the first direct elections as scheduled. Consequently, the first direct elections had to be put back until 1979. This episode further strengthened the image of Britain as a recalcitrant member state. The government was not prepared to risk its survival by more vigorous advocacy and prosecution of the case for direct elections, with or without proportional representation. In taking up that position, it was evidently not out of tune with the instincts of the British electorate, the large majority of whom did not vote in the first direct elections to the EP. The British turnout for the 1979 election was 32.6 per cent, compared with turnouts of over 60 per cent in the other EC states (with the exception of Denmark where the figure was 47 per cent).

Public perceptions of the advantages of EC membership underwent dramatic changes in the later 1970s. The EC's regular Eurobarometer polls of British opinion over the period 1975–1981 registered a fall in support for the view that EC membership was a 'good thing' from 47 per cent to 24 per cent, and an increase in support of the view that it was a 'bad thing' from 21 per cent to 48 per cent. The laggardly growth rate of the British economy during the period 1973–1979 – averaging 0.5 per cent per annum (excluding North Sea oil production) according to Treasury figures – made a mockery of earlier pro-marketeer claims that membership of a large buoyant market would galvanise the economy and serve to arrest its long-term relative decline.

There was, of course, much room for speculation that continued to fuel the debate about the economic pros and cons of membership. Debate was flooded with counterfactuals on all sides. Pro-marketeers insisted that Britain's economic performance would have been worse still but for EC membership. According to their analysis, to attribute the post-1973 economic malaise to the impact of EC membership was to mistake the symptom for the fundamental cause. The fundamental cause usually consisted of a lengthy list including the long-standing lack of competitiveness, poor quality and service, and the low productivity and investment record of British industry. The problems

Table 3.2 Eurobarometer opinion poll
(Spring 1983)
Feeling that one's country has benefited
from EC membership – national
results (%)

Belgium	90.7
Denmark	62.2
Germany	76.5
Greece	63.7
France	72.0
Ireland	66.7
Italy	83.0
Luxembourg	86.0
The Netherlands	87.6
United Kingdom	36.0

of British Leyland, the large car manufacture at the time, typified some of these features, not least when Prime Minister Callaghan took possession of one of their cars as the new official car and the window fell on his lap.

The anti-marketeers, however, concentrated their fire on the extent to which the EC accounted for an increasing proportion of total British trade – 43.8 per cent in 1980 compared with 30.9 per cent in 1972 – in ways that benefited the rest of the EC rather than Britain. In short, British manufacturers were failing to penetrate the rest of the EC market as effectively as the manufacturers of other EC states were invading the British market, thereby leaving a hollowed-out, deindustrialized economy. This view underlay the 'alternative economic strategy' of the left-wing in the Labour Party with its prescription of import and exchange controls in order to protect British industry. It aimed to obviate the need for austerity measures and inevitably entailed withdrawing from the EC. Denis Healey, Chancellor of the Exchequer, just fell about laughing when one left-wing Labour MP, who fancied himself as an economic expert, explained this programme to him.

It was scarcely surprising that on the tenth anniversary of British entry into the EC, *The Economist* (25 December 1982 – 7 January 1983), a long-standing supporter of EC membership, fairly reflected the passage from the heady optimism and extravagant promises of the pro-marketeers in the early 1970s to the more subdued assessments ten years later. In a substantial review, it was hard-pressed to cite many benefits derived from EC membership. In fact, it conceded that Wilson, who was roundly criticized by *The Economist* and most of the press in the first half of the 1970s for his pocket calculator or tradesman's approach to the issue, had after all correctly emphasized the importance of the terms of membership. Moreover, it was all too evident by now that some of the claims made by the anti-marketeers at the beginning of the 1970s rang true, especially concerning the budgetary costs of EC membership.

It was also on the tenth anniversary of Britain's accession to the EU that Roy Jenkins characterized Britain's relationship with the EC as 'semi-detached', fairly summarizing the limited commitment to the venture at this relatively early stage. By this time, public satisfaction with the EC and the British turnout for the elections of the first directly elected European Parliament were markedly different from opinion and trends in the other EC states (see Tables 3.2 and 3.3).

By the end of Callaghan's period of office, the problematical process of adjustment to EC membership was still in evidence. There were major constraints on the government's

Table 3.3 The turnout for the first directly elected
European Parliament in 1979

Belgium*	91.4
Germany	65.9
Denmark	47.0
France	61.3
Ireland	63.6
Italy	85.5
Luxembourg*	85.0
The Netherlands	57.8
United Kingdom	32.6

* Compulsory voting.

Sources: Office for Official Publications of the
European Communities, *Steps to European Unity*,
Luxembourg, 1987; Office for Official Publications
of the European Communities, *Europe as Seen by
Europeans: European Polling 1973–86*, Luxembourg,
1986.

room for manoeuvre, especially its minority status, its preoccupation with economic
difficulties and its inability to convey to much of its own party and the public at large
the benefits of EC membership. In these circumstances, it was not possible to advance
beyond a generally defensive and highly qualified approach to EC affairs.

'Megaphone diplomacy': Thatcher and renegotiation, 1979–1984

Between 1979 and 1990 there were three Conservative administrations headed by
Margaret Thatcher: the first from May 1979 to June 1983, the second from June 1983 to
June 1987 and the third from June 1987 until her fall from power in November 1990. This
section covers the period 1979–1984 that witnessed the second stage of renegotiation
and involved an intense, protracted struggle over what was widely described at the time
as the British Budgetary Question (BBQ).

The problem of Britain's contribution to the EC budget was one that Thatcher had
inherited and that Callaghan would also have needed to address if he had won the
1979 general election. The fact of the matter was that the financial arrangements that
Heath had agreed to in the early 1970s were disadvantageous to British interests (see
Chapter 8). In the course of the renegotiations of 1975, Wilson had tried to improve
matters by negotiating a rebate formula. This arrangement, however, was extremely
complicated, and had proved to be of little practical value. It was therefore left to
Thatcher to secure a better deal.

A deal was considered all the more necessary by 1979 as Britain was one of only two
net contributors to the EC budget – the other being West Germany. Its net payment
for that year amounted to approximately £900 million and the figure was scheduled to
go even higher in 1980 when the protection provided during the five-year transitional
period came to an end. By then Britain would be making an even bigger net contribution than West Germany, despite the fact that its GDP was much smaller. Thatcher
regarded this as an intolerable state of affairs and in characteristic fashion set out to
remedy it without delay.

One of Thatcher's great strengths, as well as one of her weaknesses, was a total inability to see the other side's point of view. Few things were more telling in this regard

than her problematical relationship with the Foreign Office at the beginning and at the end of her premiership. In the early 1980s Peter Carrington, Foreign Secretary, and his deputy, Ian Gilmour, were driven to despair by Thatcher's intransigent stand over Britain's contribution to the EC budget. By the late 1980s there was growing tension between Thatcher and Geoffrey Howe, Foreign Secretary. It culminated in Howe's removal from the Foreign Office, followed by his resignation from the government in November 1990 precipitating Thatcher's downfall in the same month. It is scarcely surprising that on one dark evening in the intervening period Thatcher stood at the door of No. 10, stared up at the bulk of the Foreign Office opposite, and said to an official 'Look at that, the place that keeps the light out of Downing Street' (Moore, 2014: 567).

The Foreign Office approach to business was to proceed by patient diplomacy and accommodation. It was based on the recognition that successful negotiations depended upon give and take and a willingness to compromise and to make reasonable concessions. Such a method was completely alien to Thatcher. It smacked of weakness and a lack of resolve in defending British interests. Her insistence that the word 'compromise' should never appear in any briefing paper meant that the Foreign Office had to find ways of couching their strategic suggestions round the unfailing notion of battle and victory (Trewin, 2008: 547). She was equally ill at ease with the word 'consensus', or as she put it in one speech: 'The Old Testament prophets didn't go out into the highways saying, "Brothers, I want consensus". They said, "This is my faith and my vision!"' (Moore, 2014: 408).

What possibly irked Foreign Office officials as much if not more than Thatcher's obstinacy was her use of populist phrases about getting Britain's money back. Harping on about getting Britain's money back made it more difficult to achieve objectives. It enabled other member states to camouflage their reluctance to take on a heavier budgetary burden themselves 'behind a smokescreen of sanctimonious rhetoric about our not understanding the nature of the Community's "own resources"…thus enabling them to avoid engagement on the specifics of a systemic remedy' (Hannay, 2013: 105).

Thatcher simply set out her demands and then refused to budge, whatever the pressure and however isolated she became. Her preferred method – variously described as megaphone or handbag diplomacy – appalled and disturbed the Foreign Office, which was accustomed to a smoother and more civil performance by British leaders. Indeed, the Foreign Office was usually left to repair the damage after Thatcher's set-piece battles with EC colleagues, so much so that the West German chancellor, Helmut Schmidt, and the French president, Giscard d'Estaing, at this time referred to Thatcher as a rhino and to Carrington as her zookeeper.

The Strasbourg and Dublin European Councils: setting the tone

That portrayal no doubt owed much to Thatcher's performance at her first European Council meeting in Strasbourg in June 1979. According to a later account by Roy Jenkins, president of the EC's Commission at the time, Thatcher spoke too shrilly and frequently and was soon involved in disagreeable exchanges with the French president, the West German chancellor and the premiers of Denmark, Ireland and the Netherlands. She thus performed the considerable feat of unnecessarily irritating two big countries, three small ones and the Commission within her opening hour of performance at a European Council (Jenkins, 1992: 495). Worse was to come at the Dublin European Council in November 1979. Schmidt informed Jenkins beforehand that he was prepared to be helpful in negotiating a settlement, provided Thatcher adopted a less hectoring approach. However, there was little prospect of that. She remained the person with whom, as the US President George Bush (Senior) put it, a conversation was 'a one-way street'.

From the outset of the Dublin meeting Thatcher insisted that she would accept nothing less than the return of 'our money', peremptorily rejecting the offer of an annual rebate of some £350 million that she later described as being only 'one third of a loaf'. The other leaders were infuriated by the challenge. Thatcher's reference to British money was viewed as a frontal assault on the concept of the EC's 'own resources'. They were also indignant at being subjected to a lengthy, harassing monologue in the course of which Schmidt famously fell asleep. His successor as West German chancellor, Helmut Kohl, was equally unimpressed by one of Thatcher's rants so much so that he excused himself by saying that he had to return to his office, only to be spotted by Thatcher shortly afterwards in a café tucking into cream cakes (*The Sunday Times*, 12 October 2014).

The Strasbourg and Dublin European Councils clearly demonstrated that the prospects of settling the budget question were adversely affected by a serious personality clash between Thatcher and a substantial majority of her EC counterparts. Relations between Thatcher and Giscard were particularly strained. She regarded the French president as cold, aloof and arrogant, while for his part he made little effort to hide his contempt for her. The acrimonious and fruitless discussions in Dublin were the prelude to almost five years of highly publicized haggling over Britain's budget contribution. Although it proved possible to put in place a series of short-term arrangements for the early 1980s, it was not until the summer of 1984 that an agreement was finally reached on a permanent rebate formula.

The first such short-term deal was negotiated by Carrington and Gilmour in May 1980. Thatcher was not easily persuaded. When Carrington and Gilmour took the terms of the projected deal to Chequers, they were coldly received. The fact that Thatcher eventually accepted this deal was indicative of the extent to which she was a pragmatic politician who, contrary to an aggressive public image, was willing to compromise, albeit in as covert a way as possible, whether in this particular case or later when signing the Single European Act and later still when agreeing to put sterling in the Exchange Rate Mechanism (see below).

Then and thereafter, the stiffest resistance to British demands came from the French under the leadership of François Mitterand who succeeded Giscard as president in May 1981. They were by no means alone in their reluctance to make concessions, however, since any reduction in Britain's net payments would inevitably entail financial sacrifices for others and for the Germans in particular (Wall, 2008: 6, 9, 25). On the opposite side of the negotiating table, Thatcher was obduracy personified, for a long time insisting on terms that stood no chance of acceptance. At the end of one EC summit press conference in March 1982, she declared: 'I am stubborn and I intend to go on being stubborn. I have much to be stubborn about' (Wall, 2008: 10).

Agreement at last: the Fontainebleau European Council of 1984

By 1984, however, there was a greater degree of willingness on both sides to reach a long-term settlement. A combination of circumstances provided Thatcher with the opportunity to obtain the permanent agreement that she was now seeking with a greater sense of urgency on terms that she judged to be acceptable. A victorious conclusion to the Falklands War in June 1982, followed by a Conservative landslide in the general election of May 1983 and some early signs of economic recovery, had all served to strengthen her domestic political position by the beginning of 1984.

At the same time changes of French and West German political leadership also worked in her favour. In 1979 Thatcher was the newcomer to EC politics, while Giscard and Schmidt were the experienced practitioners enjoying a long-standing political relationship. Now the roles were reversed and it was the new leaders of France and West Germany, Mitterand and Kohl respectively, who were the apprentices and whose collaboration, at this stage at least, was neither as close nor as effective as that of Giscard and Schmidt.

On the French side by early 1984, Mitterand was intent on disposing of the British budget issue during France's six-month presidency of the EC commencing in January 1984. He could scarcely help but improve on Giscard's relations with Thatcher, though how far, if at all, personal chemistry assisted the final agreement remains unknown. In any event, an agreement was finalized at the Fontainebleau European Council meeting in June 1984 (see Chapter 8). A less publicized aspect of this agreement but nonetheless indicative of the cautious, pragmatic side of Thatcher's politics, far from the unyielding, uncompromising public figure, was the accompanying agreement to increase the Value Added Tax (VAT) revenues flowing into the EC's coffers. This measure was scarcely consistent with Thatcher's efforts to impose tight limits on EC expenditure.

The Fontainebleau European Council of June 1984 also saw the distribution of a document by the Thatcher government entitled *Europe – The Future*. At the time moves were afoot in the EC to proceed to a European Union, most evident in the work of Altiero Spinelli, the Italian politician and European federalist, and subsequently in the Dooge Committee. *Europe – The Future* advocated the abolition of impediments to trade within the EC, emphasized the importance of retaining the national veto in EC affairs, and was virtually silent on questions of EC constitutional change. The British government liked to portray this particular contribution to the wider debate about the EC's future as a positive one. It claimed to offer progress on the basis of sensible and practicable reform, as opposed to the more fanciful ideas emanating from the Commission and other quarters.

It is possible, however, to view the British paper in a somewhat different light. In short, it can be seen as an essentially defensive tactic – an attempt to avoid complete isolation in EC circles and to divert the general enthusiasm for political integration and institutional reform into channels that were more congenial to Britain. Here, in many respects, was a classic British response at a time when the EC seemed about to make a major leap forward both in terms of a single market and also in the area of institutional change. The Thatcher government wanted to effect economic change within the EC but without increasing the powers of the EC. It thus played a double role in urging the EC onwards towards some reforms while working hard to prevent others. The aim of the exercise, as Thatcher's foreign policy adviser, Charles Powell put it, was to convince the 'Euro-enthusiasts' that Britain was prepared to move ahead while not succumbing to 'the drivel about European union' (Moore, 2015: 395, 397).

Europe – The Future did not amount to Thatcher's well-worked or systematic consideration of the future of the EC. That came later. There is in fact much substance to the view that in principle during the period 1979–1986 at least she adhered to the inherited pro-European doctrines which the Conservatives had made their own under Heath and which had helped them against a Labour Party divided on the issue (Moore, 2015: 408).

The Conservative government 1985–1997: advance and retreat

In the period 1985–2010 British membership of the EU involved both an advance and a retreat, sometimes simultaneously on different fronts in the domestic setting and in the EU at large. Advance and retreat in this context refer to the extent to which British governments and political parties supported or resisted major developments in the evolution of the EU during this period.

Certainly, there was a marked change in the attitudes of British political leaders at the beginning of this period and towards the end. For much of this period British prime ministers – Thatcher, Major and Blair – routinely expressed their desire to put Britain at the heart or at the centre of the EU. In the mid-1980s Thatcher insisted that Britain was 'ahead of the pack' in the EC in its support for the Single Market project. Her successor, Major, came to power in 1990 with the intention of putting Britain 'at the very heart of Europe'. The incoming Blair Labour government in 1997 indicated that it intended to play a central role in the direction of EU affairs instead of sulking on the sidelines.

In each case, such claims or boasts were eventually overtaken by disillusionment about the EU and about the tedious, interminable negotiations in this forum. Their prime ministerial successors, however, made no such promising early statements in what were altogether dissimilar conditions. Gordon Brown as prime minister in the period 2007–2010 was a reluctant visitor to EU gatherings, even to join his fellow EU leaders to sign a treaty. He had no interest in or feel for the European social democratic tradition and instead drew heavily on British and North American schools of political and economic thought. David Cameron as prime minister in the period 2010–2015 often cut an isolated figure on the sidelines in EU circles, partly at least to appease critics of Britain's EU membership in the Conservative Party; taking Britain out of the EU rather than taking the lead in the EU was much more in tune with the rising tide of Eurosceptic opinion in the party (see Chapter 12).

At no time was the process of advance and retreat in rapid succession so evident as during the Thatcher governments of 1985–1990. More precisely, Thatcher's leadership reflected some of the perils and pitfalls of belonging without believing in the EC project. In this period, as in the 1950s, the landscape of European integration often changed faster than the perceptions of British policymakers and in ways that confounded their expectations. Significantly, the word 'ambush' was used on several occasions by Thatcher in this period. She also used it later to describe her experience of dealing with an unexpected turn of events in the management of EC affairs in both the domestic politics of the Conservative Party and in the wider EC context.

One 'ambush' occurred at the very beginning of this phase in the EC's history that was to witness a decisive shift towards a degree of dynamism and integration comparable in scale and intensity to the formative years of the EC in the 1950s. By the mid-1980s there had emerged among a majority of EC member states widespread support for a greater degree of political and economic integration, partly arising out of the belief that the EC was becoming increasingly uncompetitive compared to Japan and the United States. This condition was commonly referred to in the press as 'eurosclerosis' and marked the earliest indications that the EC economic growth rates of the 1945–1975 period were not to be matched over the next 40 years.

The impetus to change and reform was associated with certain key individuals, notably Mitterand and Jacques Delors, formerly a French socialist minister and now president of the European Commission (1985–1992). The first breakthrough occurred at the Milan European Council of June 1985 where it was agreed in principle to establish a fully integrated single market by 1992. It was also decided to convene an intergovernmental conference (IGC) to consider a wide range of institutional reforms and a possible revision of the Treaty of Rome in order to carry them through.

Thatcher opposed the idea of an IGC and in doing so reflected a deep-seated British or at least Conservative distaste for European institution-building. She insisted, as she later put it in her famous Bruges speech (see below), that Europeans should not be drawn into arcane institutional debates or be distracted by utopian goals (Fontana and Parsons, 2014). In this particular instance, she was under the impression that an IGC could only be convened on the basis of the unanimous support of the EC's political leaders. In the event, however, Bettino Craxi, the Italian prime minister, who was chairing the session, called a vote – the first time ever in a European Council meeting – and the majority approved the IGC with only Britain, Denmark and Greece voting against. This was the first of several miscalculations by the British prime minister which she regarded as the Milan ambush, causing her to complain about the worst chaired international meeting she had ever attended and claiming that the French and the Germans had exhibited the sort of behaviour that 'would get you thrown out of any London club'. Yet there was no fundamental change of British policy, and the widespread view in Whitehall was the fear of isolation and of being 'left behind' (Wall, 2008: 63; Moore, 2015: 401–2).

Fatal attraction: Thatcher and the Single European Act

The proposals of the IGC formed the basis of the Single European Act (SEA) which was agreed in December 1985. The SEA's central objective was to reach a single internal market by the end of 1992 through the eradication of all impediments to the free movement of persons, capital and goods. What accompanied this commitment was equally important, especially in British circles. The SEA entailed a substantial extension of qualified majority voting (QMV) in the Council of Ministers, by which member states lost their opportunity to veto EU decisions. QMV allowed for flexibility in negotiations where the previous unanimity requirement had so often resulted in decision-making by lowest common denominator or stasis. Regardless of the merits of the new system, however, 'surrendering Britain's veto' is invariably how QMV is represented in the public domain.

The precise operation of the QMV system has changed over time, and is now based more on population than on the system of voting points negotiated with each EU enlargement. About 80 per cent of all EU legislation is adopted via QMV and thus severely restricts the opportunity of EU states to veto EU decisions. Since November 2014 a new procedure for QMV applies in the Council of Ministers; a qualified majority is reached if the following conditions are met:

- 55 per cent of member states vote in favour – in practice this means 16 of the 28 member states;

- the proposal is supported by member states representing at least 65 per cent of the total EU population. This means roughly 329 million out of the population of some 506 million;
- to block a decision from being taken there must be at least four member states voting against, representing more than 35 per cent of the population.

(European Commission (2014) 'The European Union Explained:
How the EU Works', Luxembourg)

The SEA also included the pledge to look at 'further concrete steps towards progressive realization of Economic and Monetary Union'. It also referred to the goal of improving living and working conditions. All these elements contained the potential for massive strides towards political and economic integration. Furthermore, the creation of a genuine single market, as soon became clear, would in itself have all sorts of implications for national policy in many areas relating to commercial activities, notably taxation, employment law, welfare provisions and border controls.

Thatcher strongly supported the Single Market project in so far as it meant the removal of all hindrances to the free movement of goods, capital and labour; the elimination of commercial restrictions was fully in accord with the government's staunch adherence to free market economics. She also ultimately acknowledged that the achievement of the Single Market meant abandoning the veto in the Council of Ministers in certain areas, to this day the most significant erosion of national sovereignty by any British government since 1973. Nevertheless, the SEA was accepted by the British government and it was also approved by the House of Commons with a minimum of opposition. Among those who voted for its acceptance were Conservative backbenchers like Bill Cash and Peter Tapsell, who were later to be among its bitterest critics on the grounds that it represented an intolerable erosion of national sovereignty. More puzzling is the attitude of Thatcher herself and why she signed up to an agreement that in time proved to be a fatal attraction.

Several explanations are on offer. In her own memoirs, she expressed the view that she felt unable to offer further resistance to the growing momentum for political integration, besides which she was misled and betrayed by duplicitous EC partners (Thatcher, 1993: 547–48, 555–6). Some of her closest confidants at the time, including Charles Powell, her foreign policy adviser, have echoed this charge. They have also alleged that Thatcher was badly misinformed by Foreign Office advisers about what precisely was involved in the SEA. However, this allegation was dismissed by one of the officials concerned, Michael Butler, according to whom Thatcher insisted on having every line of the act explained to her. On this episode, Butler himself, like most Whitehall officials, spoke with satisfaction of the process by which Thatcher's 'reason overcame her prejudices'. Another official, David Williamson, said that she boasted of having read it in minute detail. Certainly it seems implausible that a politician who was famed for mastery of a brief was unaware of what she was signing up to.

Arguably a more plausible explanation touches on some of the features of the belonging without believing mentality in the form of variously ignoring, misjudging or belittling the motives and plans of others, and all the while steadfastly refusing to subscribe to the dogma and pieties of the 'religion' of Europeanism. Thatcher wholly underestimated the seriousness of intent behind what appeared to be another in a long line of vague, ambitious commitments to the goal of European unity. That would certainly be consonant with her tendency to dismiss enthusiasm for political integration as 'airy fairy nonsense' based on 'cloudy and unrealistic aspirations'; on such matters she was, as one leading Conservative described her, 'an agnostic who continues to go to church' (Young, 1990: 184–5). She also subscribed to that long strand of thinking in some Conservative quarters of emphasizing pragmatism and realism while being deeply suspicious of idealistic schemes and utopianism; 'Utopia never comes, because we know we should not like it if it did' she declared in her Bruges speech (see below).

As the new Conservative leader at the time of the 1975 referendum, Thatcher had shown no great excitement in the arguments. She had such limited experience of foreign affairs that Harold Wilson called her 'the reluctant debutante' while Peter Carrington remarked that 'She hardly knew where Calais was'. Yet even at this early stage it was evident that 'she never bought the more visionary version of Europeanism'. She rejected any notion of a federal Europe and favoured only closer co-operation in the EC and not political union, claiming that she did not know the meaning of the latter. At the time of the Stuttgart EC Council (June 1983), when EC leaders signed the Solemn Declaration on European Union, she had reluctantly acquiesced on the grounds that the document had no legal force, and, as she was advised, to refuse to sign would run the risk of attaching more credibility to the document than it either warranted or deserved – a signature effectively nullifying the importance of the document (Moore, 2014: 306, 365; 2015: 389–90).

Given her desire to achieve a single market, subscribing to what she regarded as meaningless declarations no doubt seemed a small price to pay. It was all of a piece with this mentality that she later contemptuously declared that she did not expect to see a European central bank in her lifetime 'nor, if I'm twanging a harp, for quite a long time afterwards' (*The Independent*, 22 October 1988); in the event the European Central Bank was founded 15 years before she died. This particular version of the complacent 'it will never happen' mentality in British circles was soon to be joined by another example when her successor, John Major, described the plans for the euro as having 'all the quaintness of a rain dance and about the same potency' (*The Economist*, 23 September 2004).

This outlook also influenced Thatcher's initial failure to perceive the full implications of the SEA in the form of detailed plans for economic and monetary union (EMU). At their meeting in Hanover (June 1988) the EC heads of government, including Thatcher, supported a study of EMU by a committee chaired by Delors and comprising the central bankers of the EC states. The report of this committee favoured a three-stage approach to EMU, beginning with all the member states joining the Exchange Rate Mechanism (ERM) in the first stage, a transitional stage two and a stage three in which exchange rates would be fixed and the European Central Bank would be established (see Chapter 9). This report was submitted to the Madrid European Council (June 1989) and eventually formed the basis of the conclusions of the later IGC on EMU. Thatcher did not take the threat seriously enough, despite warnings from the Chancellor of the Exchequer Nigel Lawson about the dangers of EMU and about the fact that it would be an integral part of the EC system unlike the intergovernmental European Monetary System and its ERM framework.

There is little reason to doubt the conclusion of one authoritative study covering this episode that Thatcher misread the seriousness of intent of most of the other EC states over EMU and their determination to turn what she saw as vapid declarations into hard policy (Wall, 2008: 85). If, as this same study maintains, Thatcher woke up late to the impending reality of EMU, she was inclined to see it as a more cataclysmic event than some of her advisers and ministers. So much became apparent in her mounting suspicion of and hostility to Delors, whose presidency of the EC Commission was renewed in 1988.

The Delors and Thatcher feud

There developed between Delors and Thatcher something approaching personal hostility. Delors seemed to bring out the instinctive Euroscepticism and English nationalism in Thatcher. He had his own version of what the SEA entailed and it could not be further removed from her views. Delors insisted that it was not simply a question of sweeping away obstacles to a free internal market. The creation of a single market had to be accompanied by the following:

• full economic and monetary union;
• a greater role for the Commission and the European Parliament;
• the provision of comprehensive welfare measures throughout the EC as reflected in the Social Charter (May 1989).

In hindsight this episode arguably marked the high water mark of 'social market' ideas in EC corridors.

The emergence of this strain of thought in the EC illustrated yet again the advance and retreat syndrome in British attitudes towards EC affairs, and more particularly the different responses of the major political parties. At the beginning of the 1980s the Labour Party had committed itself to the withdrawal of Britain from the EC, a policy endorsed at the Labour Party conference of 1981 and part of its 1983 general election manifesto. However, this manifesto was famously described by Gerald Kaufman as 'the longest suicide note in history' for its left-wing prescriptions that were decisively rejected by the electorate as the party crashed to its worst defeat for 50 years. Following this election and under the new leadership of Neil Kinnock and Roy Hattersley, there was a reversal of policy that represented an advance towards embracing British membership of the EC in the course of time. Kinnock's 'conversion' to the cause of Europe was symptomatic of a general trend within the Labour movement as a whole during the second half of the 1980s. In 1988 the decision to withdraw from the EC was finally abandoned, and in the European Parliament elections in 1989 Labour fought on the basis of a solid commitment to closer co-operation with Britain's EC partners.

Among the factors responsible for this major development, EC developments undoubtedly assisted the change. The 'social market' philosophy embraced by the European Commission under Delors and a majority of the EC governments was most appealing to the Labour movement. This emphasis formed a marked contrast to the free market policies of the Thatcher government. By the later 1980s, moreover, little was to be heard in British Labour circles of the former staple complaint that the EC was a 'capitalist club'. On the contrary, the legal protection, working conditions and welfare provisions enjoyed by workers in other EC states were now an object of envy, especially as far as the trade unions were concerned. They looked to the Social Charter of May 1989, with its programme of minimum rights for workers and citizens, as a shield against the harshness of market forces. Trade union leaders were so attracted by Delors's speech at the TUC conference in September 1988 that one of their number, Ron Todd, general secretary of the Transport and General Workers' Union (TGWU), dramatically abandoned three decades of hostility to the EC: 'in the short term we have not a cat in hell's chance in Westminster. The only card game in town at the moment is in a town called Brussels' (Liddle, 2014: 37). Delors was serenaded by the conference as '*Frère Jacques*' – 'the only French song most of them knew', commented one observer rather snobbishly.

Thatcher's Bruges speech

The main thrust of Delors's speech was anathema to Thatcher, and she attacked the rather modest character of the Social Charter as 'Marxist'. Her strong retort came in the form of an address at the College of Europe in Bruges in the same month. She denounced the idea of a 'European superstate' and poured scorn on many of the policies advocated not only by Delors but also by most EC governments. She condemned Delors' projects, notably the Social Charter, as 'creeping back-door Socialism', she spoke out against centralized direction of the economy, and complained bitterly about the proposed new social dimension that would make the European economy less flexible and less competitive and impose a cost handicap on European industry.

The centrepiece of the speech, however, was its strident assertion of the crucial importance of the individual nations and complete distaste for anything that smacked of a supranational Europe: 'We have not successfully rolled back the frontiers of the state in Britain, only to see them reimposed at a European level, with a European super-state exercising a new dominance from Brussels'. Two years later, the front page of *The Sun* delivered the same message more loudly and pithily with a two-fingered gesture accompanied by the headline 'Up Yours Delors', together with the suggestion that at 12 noon on the following day its readers should face France shouting the headline's sentiment across the Channel (*The Sun*, 1 November 1990). There is no record as to whether any reader did so, but in any event this was a defining front page that set a benchmark for all subsequent tabloid broadsides against the EU.

The expression of Thatcher's views caused strained relations with other EC states. Arguably, however, this was due as much to the presentation as to the substance of the speech. At Bruges, she was on the powerful, hot gospelling, evangelistic form that she had no doubt first developed in her Methodist preaching activities as a young woman, a feature noted by one president of the Methodist Conference during a personal meeting with Thatcher in Downing Street, and an influence rightly acknowledged by her authorized biographer, Charles Moore, while overlooked or underrated in other studies (Gowland and Roebuck, 1990: 198–200; Moore, 2014: 6–8).

To a large extent, the content of the Bruges speech was a classic exposition of British views. It was also arguably indicative of the way in which Thatcher's hitherto schizophrenic attitude to the EC was increasingly overtaken by a more Eurosceptic stance. In the aftermath of her third general election victory (June 1987) it was no longer imperative to qualify public expressions of her views about the EU and she not only felt freer to voice criticism of the EU but consulted fewer and fewer people about the matter (BDOHP, 1 October 1997). Nevertheless, her first guiding principle as set out in the speech – 'willing and active cooperation between sovereign independent states is the best way to build a successful European Community' – sat uneasily alongside the fact that she had earlier signed the most integrationist of European treaties – the Single European Act (1986). How far others signed up to her first guiding principle became apparent when Blair took it almost word for word as his defining vision of the EU in a speech he made in February 2006 (Wall, 2008: 79). The similarity may be taken further to suggest that a study of the language of Thatcher and Blair when in power reveals them to have been much closer together on the issue than is sometimes suggested by conventional wisdom (Daddow, 2013: 216; see also below and Chapter 5).

The Bruges speech came to be seen as both seminal and terminal in Thatcher's leadership and in the European politics of the Conservative government and party. It was seminal in the sense that it was viewed as 'holy writ' by a generation or more of Eurosceptic Conservatives that was attracted by the nationalist and populist anti-institutional focus of opposition to the EC (Fontana and Parsons, 2014). Growing disenchantment with the EC immediately found expression in the formation of the Bruges Group (February 1989), the first of a number of Eurosceptic Conservative pressure groups that pursued what it took to be Thatcher's legacy of 'less' rather than 'more' European integration. In that respect, Thatcher personally set Britain on a far more anti-EU path than it was otherwise likely to take (Schnapper, 2014)

Other developments undoubtedly contributed to dissatisfaction with Britain's EC membership, most notably the pound's exit from the ERM in September 1992 (see below). If this trend was not quite the 'long withdrawing roar of the sea of faith', it certainly marked the beginning of a major transformation for a Conservative Party that for a generation or more had treated its pro-EC credentials, if diminishingly so, almost as an article of faith. The Bruges speech began the transition by which the Conservatives ceased to be 'the party of Europe' in British politics, and moved 'fitfully, by lurches, lunges and sidesteps, to a position now known as Euroscepticism' (www .margaretthatcher.org/archive/Bruges.asp).

While sedimentary layers of 'hard' and 'soft' Euroscepticism have built up in large sections of the Conservative Party, the Labour Party was also put on the defensive in its policy and attitude towards the EU (see Chapter 5). In that respect there is substance to the thesis that the five prime ministers from Thatcher to Cameron have intentionally or unwittingly nudged Britain closer to the EU exit door (Daddow, 2015). Their use of language about the EU has invariably emphasized Britain's exceptional status and global interests in a potent mixture of imperial nostalgia and the island story and the pursuit of a very distinctive EU policy record. Forty years of EU membership have thus scarcely shaken deep-seated beliefs about Britain's history and role and identity in the wider world (see Chapters 4 and 11). All such beliefs, moreover, whether in the form of the 'island story' or in some of the overstated trappings and posturings of 'great power' status, invariably overshadow, belittle and form a marked contrast to what is represented as a colourless, trading relationship within the EU.

This image was embedded in the minds of British politicians and public alike from the outset of EC membership. The emphasis on the common market as a bread-and-butter issue meant that there was often a correspondingly small reservoir of committed support for the values and purpose of the EU as a major political, social and cultural construct.

Europe and the 'palace coup' of 1990

The more immediate impact of the Bruges speech, however, concerned the extent to which it was also terminal. It set in train a course of developments that eventually led to Thatcher's downfall. To be sure, other factors contributed to this outcome, but there was no little significance in the fact that Geoffrey Howe, the foreign secretary at the time, was aghast when he first saw the amended version of a Foreign Office draft of the Bruges speech that represented Thatcher's authentic feelings. Howe, of course, was to be an influential figure in the proceedings that eventually led to Thatcher's departure from office two years later. There were here important traces of differences between Thatcher and Howe over the need for European institutions to oversee liberal, free market policies. Thatcher felt that free trade implied a lack of EC institutional authority and she equated the latter with utopian continental interventionism. In the circumstances, she increasingly felt British sovereignty had to be asserted against such EC institutions so that 'Ultimately her position became an unpragmatic and populist nationalism that trumped her neoliberalism' (Schnapper, 2014).

Thatcher's views at Bruges and elsewhere caused strained relations with the other member states. More importantly they brought mounting disquiet at home where there were signs that she was losing touch with the public mood and was increasingly perceived as a shrill, domineering ideologue. Her attitude towards the EC seemed to a growing number of critics to be narrow, blinkered, outdated and contrary to Britain's long-term interests. It was in such circumstances that the insecure, anxious side of Thatcher's character came to the fore.

Dissatisfaction with Thatcher's European policies – not least among Cabinet colleagues – was to play a significant part in her fall from power in the 'palace coup' of November 1990. There were many other strands of discontent besides the EC issue at the time like the political nightmare of the poll tax, the dangers of an overheated economy, and growing criticism of her personal style that was widely perceived as autocratic and uncaring. What ultimately sealed her political fate was the sense that she had become an electoral liability rather than an asset. Her stance towards the EC was nevertheless a major reason for her loss of support within the Conservative Party and more generally. Moreover, it was an EC issue – British membership of the ERM – that was the immediate cause of her terminal difficulties. Her final year in office proved to be a rapid switchback ride involving a marked advance and a determined retreat in EC matters.

The advance came in the form of the decision (June 1990) that Britain should join the ERM. Thatcher had opposed such a measure since coming to power in 1979. However, she had softened her opposition in June 1989 following 'a nasty little meeting' – another 'ambush' as she later called it – with Howe, Foreign Secretary, and Nigel Lawson, Chancellor of the Exchequer (Thatcher, 1993: 710–13; Howe, 1994: 576–84; Lawson, 1992: 928–34).

The retreat, such as it was, came four months later in October 1990 when Thatcher made it clear that entry to the ERM did not imply support for EC monetary union; 'No, no, no', she exclaimed in the course of parliamentary exchanges in which she defiantly rejected Delors' plans for monetary union. These remarks prompted the resignation of the long-suffering Howe from his position of deputy prime minister. A fortnight later, Thatcher herself made her resignation speech in the House of Commons (see Chapter 9).

Staying in but opting out, 1992–1997

The advance and retreat theme on the EC/EU was equally evident during the Conservative governments of John Major, Thatcher's successor, in the period

1990–1997. The advance came in the form of a treaty, the Treaty on European Union (TEU) signed at Maastricht (and thus commonly called the Maastricht Treaty) by Major and the other EU leaders in February 1992. This treaty turned the EC into the European Union (EU). Major, it seemed, was on his way to achieving his self-declared aim of putting Britain 'at the very heart of Europe'.

Later that year in September, however, disaster struck when the Major government had to beat a hasty and humiliating retreat as sterling exited from the ERM in the face of overwhelming pressure from currency speculators in the financial markets. This event undermined Major's economic policy, while his policy on the EU never recovered its sense of direction, and he himself described the event as a 'political disaster'. At the same time, however, there was in British government circles a suggestion that the EU was 'moving our way' as Foreign Secretary Douglas Hurd put it, as there were difficulties elsewhere in the EU about ratifying the Maastricht Treaty and about the survival of the ERM (Young, 1998: 450). This latest episode of British wishful thinking about the EU was overtaken by the subsequent survival of the EMU project and was in any case overshadowed by deepening divisions about the EU in the Conservative Party.

In the longer term, the traumatic experience of the pound's exit from the ERM told against the case for joining a monetary union. This episode together with the acute, accompanying problems of securing parliamentary ratification of the TEU also further exposed divisions on Europe within the Conservative Party. Sections of the party were in headlong retreat from the idea of British membership of the EU, while the TEU was ratified (August 1993) only after Major won a vote of confidence. There was no longer any inclination in sections of the Conservative Party of dismissing the EU as simply 'a common external tariff, the CAP, and internal tariff reductions – EFTA with knobs on' (quoted in Gifford, 2014: 105). To create some semblance of government and party unity, Major had perforce to placate this Eurosceptic opinion by adopting an increasingly obstructive policy in the EU, a course of action followed by the next Conservative prime minister, David Cameron.

By this time, Michael Palliser, British ambassador to the EC in the period 1973–1975 and later head of the Diplomatic Service, had cause to comment on the lack of trust in and negativity of the British stance in the EU. In his view, this condition was rooted in a 'congenital lack of enthusiasm' (Trewin, 2008: 397). By 1996 a majority of the Cabinet were Eurosceptics, and that strand of opinion became all the greater as the Conservatives went into opposition after their defeat in the general election of May 1997. In the circumstances, it is scarcely surprising that Major, who had no strong, long-standing personal commitment to the EU, described himself as 'a pragmatist, not an idealist, and a cautious pragmatist too', and he chose to characterize his reactive approach to EC/EU matters as 'procrastination on principle' (Major, 1999: 273, 581). What had emerged in the meantime within a large body of Eurosceptic opinion in the Conservative Party was the substance of a programme that with a few exceptions remained intact down to the present day:

- halt the drive towards a European superstate;
- repatriate the legal and political powers that had been ceded to the EU;
- uphold Britain's opt-out from the Social Chapter;
- defend the national veto in the EU;
- prevent any extension of majority voting in the EU;

- resist attempts to give bigger roles to the European Commission and the European Parliament;
- curb the jurisdiction of the European Court of Justice;
- never take part in EMU.

The experience of the Major governments of 1990–97 in tackling EU matters indicated that Thatcher's departure made her ideas more powerful than her rivals could have imagined, as her legacy steered the Conservatives to populist nationalism and anti-EU positions after 1990 (Schnapper, 2014).

The Labour government 1997–2010: advance and retreat

The Labour governments of 1997–2010 followed a similar pattern of advance and retreat but with an additional twist. The advance was much-trumpeted at an early stage in the first Blair government. It involved the ending of Britain's opt-out from the Social Chapter (announced May 1997) that Major had secured in the course of the negotiations resulting in the TEU. There was too an important move (October 1998) favouring the creation of a European defence identity. The Blair government was thus the first British government to end the country's longstanding objections to the EU taking on a military role resulting in possible competition with NATO. The St Malo Declaration (1999) paved the way for a form of European defence and for much closer co-operation on security issues between Britain and France. Another aspect of the EU's development strongly supported by the Blair governments, as was the case with earlier British governments only now on a much larger scale, was the enlargement of the EU to include many of the former communist states of eastern Europe (see Chapter 4).

Blair's attitude towards EU affairs and the British position in the EU marked a major change in tone and attitude from that of his predecessors, with the possible and doubt-ful exception of Heath whose views on the EU's future and institutional reform were far less pronounced than Blair's. Blair had no history as a committed supporter of the EU and had first stood as a parliamentary candidate in the election of 1983 supporting a manifesto committed to withdrawal from the EC. It is, nevertheless, difficult to deny that he believed in the project and that he did so for political reasons, viewing a pro-European position as an integral part of modernized social democratic politics under the label of New Labour. He instinctively grasped that the EU was fundamentally a political project. He dissociated himself from the 'declinist' arguments that had often shot through pro-European arguments in the past, and was equally unwilling to prior-itize the economic factors that accompanied the case. He genuinely wished to 'normal-ize' Britain's relationship with the EU, by which he meant that he wanted to resolve once and for all British ambivalence towards Europe and to end the uncertainty, the lack of confidence and the Europhobia (Liddle, 2014: 86).

Blair had a more positive, developed and imaginative view of the EU's future than any prime minister since 1973. He was, in short, a believer, but one whose major speeches on the subject, such as in Aachen in 1999 and in Warsaw in 2001, were sometimes derided as pious professions and empty rhetoric. His critics claimed that so often he failed to match words with action or to undertake a sustained follow-up; 'it was always a case of tomorrow' as one political commentator put it (Riddell, 2005: 151). There were, too, some intimations of regarding the EU as less than a top priority. At the beginning of his first administration in 1997, Blair appointed Doug Henderson as Minister for Europe because he had 'no strong views' on the subject. In addition, it can be argued that the fact that Blair changed his Europe ministers almost annually – there being three in 1999 alone – suggests that he was not entirely serious in his commitment to the EU (Smith, 2005: 708).

That said, however, on coming to power in 1997, the Blair government appeared favourable in principle to the idea of British membership of the euro area that was launched in January 1999 (see Chapter 10). Under the Maastricht Treaty, any country wishing to be in the euro area from the beginning was required to give notice of its intentions before the end of 1997. This stipulation left very little time for the incoming Labour government to make all the necessary practical and legislative preparations, especially since the government was committed by its election manifesto to hold a referendum on the matter and, more importantly, because Labour came to power 'with no worked-out European strategy or single currency timeline' (Liddle, 2014: 56).

Extraordinary though it may seem, Blair seems to have believed that he could persuade the prospective euro area states to allow some additional time for reaching a decision. At a meeting of advisers and senior officials, he allegedly indicated that he might telephone his friend, Helmut Kohl the German chancellor, to ask him if the project could be delayed until Britain was ready to take part. Needless to say, there was never the remotest chance of such a postponement at the British leader's behest. This was particularly the case in view of the preceding 50-year history of tardy responses by British governments to new EC developments and the many examples of British governments still debating the matter in hand while the other EU states had long since moved to the stage of implementing plans. True, there were occasional signs that the euro area plan might be delayed or abandoned. For the most part, however, here was but another example of British policymakers overlooking the pace of developments in the EU, and in particular underestimating the determined Franco-German impetus behind the monetary union plan.

Blair's attitude towards the euro was inextricably linked with his ambition to make Britain a leading player in the EU. He could not see how Britain could be Europe's leader if it did not belong to the euro area (Seldon *et al.*, 2005: 317, 2008: 205). At an early stage in his premiership he became frustrated at his inability to exert the influence he wished for in the EU. Nor was he in any doubt that one of the principal reasons for this failure was the fact that Britain remained outside the euro area; in December 1999 he gave vent to his impatience at the limitations imposed on his effectiveness by Britain's non-membership of the euro area. One of Blair's media advisers commented 'TB [Tony Blair] says that Britain's problem outside the single currency is that "It's trying to tell a club you're not happy with the way they're doing things without being willing to pay the membership price"' (Price, 2006: 177). This observation had substance as a feature of British government attitudes thereafter (see Chapter 12).

Although keenly aware of the political handicap of being outside the euro, Blair was unable to speed up progress towards a referendum on euro area membership. Arguably the only possibility of taking Britain into the euro area was in Blair's first administration and then as early as possible, capitalizing on Labour's huge parliamentary majority (179) as a result of the 1997 general election and overriding any objections on a wave of popularity. A referendum could only be held, however, after the Treasury had delivered a positive verdict on the five tests that had to be met before it could recommend euro area membership. In the event the whiphand was left with Gordon Brown, Chancellor of the Exchequer, and the Treasury.

As chancellor, Brown became more and more convinced that taking Britain into the euro would be an unjustified gamble. A key factor in sowing these doubts was Britain's enforced departure from the ERM in 1992 (see Chapter 9). That experience was probably the most important moment in Brown's European education and forever shaped his views about the difficulties of joining the euro area (Peston, 2005: 182, 186). His doubts were reinforced by those of senior Treasury officials and above all by the advice that he received from Ed Balls, his economic adviser and close confidant since 1994 who, as an economist by profession and a former journalist with the *Financial Times*, was a long-standing critic of EMU. In these circumstances and against such headwinds, there was a diminishing prospect of a successful attempt to join the euro area. In some respects for Blair the idea of British membership of the euro area was a case of believing without belonging, and ultimately represented a retreat from some early promise.

Labour's handling of the euro area issue was influenced by public opinion that registered growing hostility towards the EU during this period and a further retreat from the EU project by the public at large. During the premiership of Blair and Brown, British suspicion of or opposition to the EU, as reflected in press and parliamentary comment, became more pronounced (see Chapter 7). Paradoxically during this same period the EU was evolving in ways more in accord with British interests. The Maastricht Treaty was seen in retrospect as signifying the high water mark of federalist aspirations in the EU.

The EU's evolution largely in accordance with British interests was most apparent during the course of negotiations surrounding attempts to devise an EU constitutional treaty through the mechanism of the European Convention in the period 2001–2003 (see Chapter 4). The Blair government entered these negotiations with a pro-active, imaginative and positive attitude during the first phase of the Convention but later adopted an altogether more lukewarm, reactive attitude, frequently expressed with Eurosceptic overtones. Consequently, as Jacques Delors observed, Britain secured a draft constitutional treaty that met virtually all of its demands yet continued to fight the text nonetheless, thereby neither benefiting from its negotiation successes nor playing a key role in the EU (Menon, 2004a).

The case for the EU increasingly went by default during the second half of Blair's premiership when Blair virtually gave up trying to win British hearts and minds to the pro-EU cause. There is moreover substance to the view that Blair reworked rather than undermined core themes within the Eurosceptic tradition, at best normalizing relations with the rest of the EU at governmental level but ultimately falling short of the pledge made on the steps of Downing Street after the landslide election of 1997 to 'give the country strength and confidence in leadership both at home and abroad, particularly in respect of Europe' (Daddow, 2012). Certainly, Blair used up so much political capital on other foreign policy matters, notably the invasion of Iraq (March–May 2003), that he was unwilling or unable to challenge mounting criticism about the EU from the British media and public opinion (see Chapter 7). Significantly, he did not rate his European legacy very highly. EU matters as a whole during his premiership covered only a dozen pages in his 700-page memoir *A Journey*, possibly lending some substance to the view that he was an enigma or in Victor Hugo's phrase 'a sphinx without a riddle' (Tombs, 2014: 831). The verdict of Richard Wilson (Cabinet Secretary 1998–2002) on Blair's leadership perhaps applied most of all to his EU policy: 'He promised so much, but in the end so little was achieved' (*The Times*, 12 March 2016). The certitude and self-righteousness, often said to characterize his performance on the international stage, eventually seemed to desert him in the EU arena.

Table 3.4 Knowledge of European Union institutions in Britain compared with the EU average (%)

Institution	UK	EU average
European Central Bank	63	80
European Commission	70	80
Council of Ministers	44	66
European Parliament	83	90

Source: *Eurobarometer Standard Report No. 75* (Spring 2011): 40–5.

Table 3.5 Trust in European Union institutions compared with EU average (%)

	Tend to trust		Tend not to trust	
	UK	EU	UK	EU
European Central Bank	22	40	46	38
European Commission	20	40	51	37
Council of Ministers	17	36	45	35
European Parliament	23	45	57	38

Source: *Eurobarometer Standard Report No. 75* (Spring 2011): 40–5.

Few observers doubted that during this period Euroscepticism supplanted Europhile opinion as the dominant force in the British debate about Europe. In 2008, an EU-wide survey about attitudes towards the European Parliament found that the British were not only the most sceptical on many EU issues but also the most ignorant. The population of no other member state knew less and trusted less about the EU than the British, scepticism and ignorance seemingly appearing as two sides of the same coin (http://ec.europa.eu/unitedkingdom/) (see Tables 3.4 and 3.5).

The Brown premiership

During the Brown premiership (2007–2010), any pro-EU rhetoric in government circles drained away. In a speech in 2005, Brown had described himself as a 'pro-European realist', but it was unclear what exactly he meant by this label. Certainly, he had become much more seized of the idea that the pound had to steer clear of any absorption into the euro area, and in time he was to be seen very much as the saviour of the pound (see Chapter 10). Beyond that, however, there is little reason to dispute the conclusion of his biographers that he never had an overriding vision or strategy for the EU, that as chancellor he came to share the Treasury's traditional scepticism about the EU, and that he had a patchy understanding of the workings of EU institutions (Seldon and Lodge, 2010: 66). Furthermore, he had acquired a notorious reputation as chancellor for attending meetings of his fellow EU finance ministers (ECOFIN) to lecture on how they should be following his economic policies, while usually arriving late, delivering his piece and leaving early. Like Blair he saw himself as a modernizing European recognizing the value of the EU as a vehicle but with limits to his European Unionism.

Brown had perforce to tidy up his presentation in EU circles as prime minister and made a conscious effort to do so. The public impression left on key occasions, however, suggested that EU affairs figured low in the list of priorities and that EU membership really was a case of belonging without believing. In fact, his first major outing to a European Council meeting in Lisbon (December 2007) as prime minister to sign the Lisbon treaty turned out to be an unmitigated disaster. Against the background noise of a largely hostile, Eurosceptic British press, he signed the treaty away from the public gaze, on his own, and too embarrassed to look up into the cameras. This private sitting occurred after the other EU leaders had collectively signed the treaty, dined together and left for the airport – passing Brown's car as he arrived. There was a genuine explanation for this situation – a diary clash – but such behaviour simply drew attention to an incident that one official described as 'an absolute joke' and that was ridiculed by Britain's EU supporters and critics alike. Even *The Guardian*, one of the more supportive newspapers during Brown's premiership, was fiercely critical of his Lisbon performance: 'an insult to our European partners, and a national embarrassment to Britain' (*The Guardian*, 13 December 2007).

Some of the minor aspects of life in the EU remained the same at the end of Labour's period in power between 1997 and 2010. They were indicative of the still marked differences between Britain and the other EU member states. A small but noticeable contrast is evident on highways in the EU. Vehicles in EU states on the continent (with the exception of Finland) carry registration plates displaying the EU flag as a matter of course. The registration plates of road vehicles in Britain are rarely so decorated.

Conclusion

From the outset of British membership of the EU, this body was regarded as neither a fundamental project nor an integral part of national life. Rather it was treated as an awkwardly fitted, bolted-on extra. In that respect, the exclusively continental parentage of the project was but one factor that told against unqualified acceptance and made at best for grudging, half-hearted acquiescence. The problems of adjustment to EC membership were all the greater because British policymakers had to dispense with what they regarded (and still regard) as the superior merits of their own model of European co-operation. Adjustment was also difficult because membership meant engaging with 'foreign' notions of the divisibility of sovereignty and of multilayered political authority. Uninspiring common sense and a pragmatic approach have featured among the hallmarks of the British experience of EU membership. This background has greatly influenced the making and execution of British policy in the EU, the subject of the next chapter.

4   Leading from behind

Opt-outs, opt-ins and red lines

You're either at the table or you're on the menu.
(Washington political saying of unknown origin)

Introduction

This chapter focuses on the strategy and tactics of successive British governments in the EU policymaking arena, mainly in the period 1973–2010 (see Chapter 12 for further coverage of the period since 2010). It considers how far government has reflected different types of responses to the evolution of the EU. In particular, it discusses the extent to which government has figured as either a reactive or proactive force in its management of EU affairs and in its approach to initiating or resisting change in the organization. The chapter also examines the different types of responses to EU developments. It does so especially with a view to determining the nature and extent of government awareness of the implications of EU dynamism and the continuous process of Europeanization.

The chapter also deals with the impact of British policy on the making of EU policy at large. For this purpose, it highlights what are commonly regarded as some of the strategic preferences of successive British governments such as the enlargement of the EU, intergovernmental co-operation and 'negative integration'. By way of contrast, the chapter also traces the nature and extent of entrenched opposition to such matters as federalism and 'positive integration'.

Hardy perennials of British policy

There are certain structural features of Britain's relationship with the process of European integration that have endured over time and that, to a greater or lesser extent, are as evident now as 60 years ago. At the same time the influence of agency – whether in the form of a particular government, political party or individual political leader – has affected the nature and impact of structural factors and conditions. That said, few commentators dispute the view that Britain has rarely occupied the driving seat in the process of European integration. A fairly constant feature of British policy has involved a more or less covert attempt to reduce the pace of integration whether by prioritizing the enlargement of the EC/EU or by shaping outcomes with limited, if any, commitment to participation in any resulting project.

To a greater or lesser extent since the Schuman Plan of 1950 (see Introduction), British governments have approached the process of European integration with a view to maximizing their influence in any negotiations while minimizing their commitment to the outcome. Throughout they have demonstrated a dislike for irreversible commitments, most especially in recent years the 'ever closer union' motto on the EC/EU masthead. Indeed, this commitment was explicitly opposed by Cameron in May 2014 and cited as the 'most important' reform in any renegotiation of the terms of membership – the first British prime minister to declare such an aim (see Chapter 12). Ironically the Major Conservative government at the time of the negotiation of the Maastricht Treaty had fought hard to ensure the retention of the 'ever closer union' phrase in the face of strong support for a more federal-sounding commitment.

In some respects, therefore, government has reflected a pick-and-choose approach to EU business bordering on an almost freerider mentality, seeking to obtain the benefits of integration without contributing to the cost or at the very least insisting on opt-outs. A similar frame of mind is also to be found among Eurosceptic strains of thought that advocate withdrawal from the EU in favour of arm's-length freerider access to the EU comparable to that enjoyed by Norway or, less so, Switzerland (see Table C.2 in the Conclusion).

Successive British governments have therefore ideally preferred to remain in the slow lane to integration while attempting to direct traffic in the fast lane. This difference is often summed up in the distinction between 'maximalist' and 'minimalist' EU states in relation to the nature and extent of European integration. Thus, for example, following a disastrous performance for the Conservatives in the EP elections of May 2014 Cameron emphasized an ideally minimalist view of the EU, declaring that Brussels has 'got too big, too bossy, too interfering' and that it should be a case of 'nation states wherever possible, and Europe only where necessary' (*The Guardian*, 28 May 2014).

At the same time British governments have recognized that efforts to obstruct plans for further integration or to reduce the possibility of a multi-speed Europe were best mounted from within rather than outside the councils of the EC/EU. The French saying is particularly apt in the circumstances – 'They are wrong to be absent and, in their absence, the absentees are easily wronged by those who are present'. It was the fear that Thatcher was disregarding the practice of full, pragmatic engagement in EU deliberations in her final days as premier and was uniting the rest of the EU against Britain that most alarmed her pro-EC Cabinet colleagues and eventually contributed to her downfall. John Major, Thatcher's successor, was shocked to discover at his early meetings of the European Council that most of the other leaders of the EU states not only utterly disagreed with her but remarked that 'She is a unifying force … She unites all of us against her' (Major, 1999: 265).

This position, however, has long given rise to problems on all sides. It is clearly difficult to exercise any leadership from the rear of the column or when forever qualifying and retreating from certain aspects of EU membership. In fact, a recurring feature and important factor in the evolution of the EC/EU itself concerns Britain's absence from the early workings of major schemes such as the Schuman Plan, the Rome Treaties and the euro area. The 'golden age' of economic growth, trade expansion and institution-building of the Six, 1950–1973, coincided with the period of Britain's non-membership.

This absence has helped to ensure, if unintentionally on the British side, the successful launching of these initiatives. Furthermore, it has had the effect of walling off British governments from the strong sense of collective experience and identity generated through the formation and development of such projects. In each case, as we noted in Chapter 2, the initial British reaction to any initiative invariably consisted of a mixture of incredulity, disbelief and disdain for what was often regarded as euro-rhetoric and window dressing. British governments in the 1950s were deeply sceptical of the common market plans of the Six. Their successors in recent years have proved equally doubtful about the prospects of a lasting euro area.

Problems of coping with a multi-speed Europe

In addressing the problems of coping with the changing nature of the EU, British governments have often faced a particularly difficult challenge, requiring them to perform a complex balancing act in the face of conflicting domestic and international pressures. While attempting to block or at least delay unwelcome changes, they have simultaneously sought to avoid being left behind or becoming completely isolated. At the same time, they have needed to formulate a policy in response to proposed changes which was acceptable to both pro- and anti-EC/EU opinion in Britain. This was the formidable task that confronted Heath, Wilson, Callaghan, Thatcher and their successors.

Occasionally, government has sought refuge in espousing the cause of a 'two-speed' EU while seeking opt-outs from certain treaty provisions. The idea of a two-speed or multi-speed Europe first emerged in the 1980s. It meant that some of the EC states, that were able and willing to integrate in a particular way, should be free to do so in the expectation that the other member states would follow them in due course. What this involved in practice became evident in the Maastricht Treaty negotiations when the Major government secured two opt-outs, one of which allowed Britain to defer a decision on participation in the third and final stage of EMU while the other concerned the Social Chapter of the Maastricht Treaty. The first of these two opt-outs meant that Britain was not obliged or committed to adopt the euro without a separate decision to do so by its government and parliament.

Variable-geometry Europe was another concept that increasingly crept into EC parlance at this time. This expression was used to describe an EC within which a group of member states was able and willing to integrate in a particular way but was fully aware that other member states had no intention of following them, thereby making for a permanent difference in the degree of integration. This concept had a particular appeal to the British government in that it relieved the government of the necessity of participating in an EC/EU wide uniform approach to integrative projects (Wall, 2008: 64). At the same time, however, such an arrangement held out the unwanted prospect of a two-tier EC/EU with Britain in the second division. The more recent and relatively untested process of 'enhanced co-operation' allows a vanguard of countries to press ahead with reforms when full EU agreement is impossible. It is the workings of this process, especially in regard to the commitment of ten euro area states to a financial transaction tax (the so-called 'Robin Hood' tax) that has met with British opposition (see Chapter 10).

In many respects, British governments over the past 25 years have wrestled with the implications of these developments, most notably as their preoccupations have not been shared by other member states on the road to a greater degree of integration. This condition was evident in 1989–1990 when the Thatcher government deliberated about joining the ERM. Significantly, the other EC states had by this stage operated the ERM for almost ten years and were thinking beyond ERM to the creation of EMU. Similarly, in the period since 2010 increasing Conservative support for a renegotiation of the terms of membership was far removed from the main focus of attention of the euro area member states. The latter were principally concerned to cope with the effects of the financial crash of 2007–2008 on the euro area and latterly the influx of refugees. In that respect their collective concerns and efforts were concentrated on such problematical matters as plans for a euro area banking union. Insofar as Britain figured on this agenda it did so largely as an irritant through early skirmishes on the 'frontier' between the euro area and the non-euro area members of the EU. Britain was to the fore in this struggle in seeking to shield the City of London from the unwanted effects of new EU rules and especially from euro area-based initiatives (see Chapter 10).

Besides such differences, the opt-out from the final stages of EMU highlighted the extent to which Britain became marginalized on this key issue. This much was evident before the euro area formally came into being. In November 1997 it was proposed to give extensive powers to a council that came to be known as Euro-11. This body comprised the 11 original member states of the euro area, and it seemingly usurped the role of the EU's Council of Economic and Finance Ministers (ECOFIN).

This episode pointed the way to a longer term problem concerning the relationship between the euro area and the EU states like Britain (and Denmark, Greece and Sweden at this time) outside the euro area. There was an immediate, some might say, characteristic British reaction to this proposal. It took the form of a confused strategy that sought at one and the same time to smother the council at birth, restrict its functions as narrowly as possible and obtain a place on it for Britain. This latter demand drew the dismissive comment from the French prime minister, Lionel Jospin, that 'the UK which invented clubs, should not say it is unfair to be excluded' (*Financial Times*, 9 December 1997). British humiliation was completed at the inaugural meeting of Euro-11 in June 1998 during the course of Britain's presidency of the EU. Gordon Brown, Chancellor of the Exchequer, insisted on his right to chair the opening proceedings, but was then obliged to stand down in favour of the finance minister of Austria, the next country to take over the presidency. His conduct provoked an outraged reaction from other finance ministers, and the whole incident provided a telling illustration of the extent to which Britain had become sidelined on the issue of EMU.

How then is the British track record of opt-outs and exemptions in the EC/EU to be understood whether in relation to the euro area or in other policy areas such as the Schengen open borders arrangement and more recently still on the issue of co-operation on matters of crime and justice. How are the often ambivalent attitudes of policymakers to be explained – wishing to exert influence within the EU while also wanting to keep some distance from the project?

Tony Blair probably gave more thought than most British political leaders to the problems, contradictions, dilemmas and conflicting pressures facing any British policymaker in the EU context. In doing so, however, he reflected the mixed record of his premiership concerning EU affairs. In November 2001, he observed that 'We will not have influence if we only ever see Europe as in opposition to Britain and become backmarkers for further co-operation, always arguing thus far but no further'. Two years later, however, in June 2003 and against the background noise of a British press hostile to the EU, he returned to a familiar message 'it is important to recognize that we have our red lines and we are maintaining them'. The 'red lines' were around policy areas that included taxation, criminal justice, foreign policy, social security and defence, these being areas in which Britain was unwilling to lose its national veto.

The very public emphasis on 'red lines' and on non-negotiable or negative policy objectives by British governments has frequently figured as they have entered major EC/EU negotiations. In the case of the negotiation of the Lisbon Treaty of 2007, Blair at the very end of his premiership in June 2007 stressed the importance of four red lines, while the incoming Brown government a month later set out its four red lines. In that respect while there were differences in emphasis between Blair and Brown, both adopted an established governing position that for all its 'awkwardness' meant that Britain could lead and shape the direction of integration from inside (Gifford, 2014: 140).

The latecomer

One of the persistent features of British policymaking in the EC/EU context, most markedly so in the early period of membership, was the continuation of pre-entry habits of thought within the British political elite. According to one inside observer, who was a member of the team that negotiated British entry into the EC, some of the early strains that arose between Britain and the other EC states were caused to some extent at least by a tendency on the part of British policymakers to adopt an aloof and superior attitude. This feature was allegedly accompanied by a failure to adapt to the country's new role within the EC. In short, successive political leaders were locked in a mindset that accorded priority to links with the United States and the Commonwealth rather than with Europe. Furthermore, what they lacked was a real understanding of the drive to unity engendered on the continent by the experience of defeat and occupation during the Second World War (Denman, 1996).

There is considerable substance to such an interpretation, even if it underestimates the extent to which British leaders during this early period were trammeled in their conduct of EC policy by serious internal and external constraints that were largely beyond their control. There were very real material difficulties in adapting to EC policies as a latecomer. Several of the EC's policies were especially burdensome for Britain. In particular, new arrangements for financing the EC, agreed by the Six in December 1969, together with the principal item of expenditure on the EC budget, the CAP, left Britain at a double disadvantage.

In the first place, the EC's financing arrangements meant that in future its 'own resources' were to come from levies and tariffs on all external imports, plus up to 1 per cent of receipts from Value Added Tax (VAT). As Britain imported more from outside the EC than any of its prospective partners, it followed that its contribution to the EC budget would be disproportionately large. Second, the bulk of the money raised for use by the EC was devoted to the CAP. Britain's agricultural base was relatively small. It therefore stood to gain less than the other EC states from its financial resources. It was for this reason that the issue proved so contentious for many years after accession to the EC (see Chapter 8).

Such disadvantages amounted to the price that had to be paid for Britain's tardiness in seeking and securing EC membership. By the time the Heath government managed to obtain entry to the 'club', the original members had understandably drawn up rules and policies that suited their own interests. France, in particular, had always demonstrated a keen determination to settle key issues before British entry. In 1961, de Gaulle had insisted on reaching the first set of agreements on the CAP before the first British application for EC membership was given serious consideration. Similarly, his successor, Pompidou, was equally intent on achieving new arrangements for the financing of the EC before attending to the third British application; he calculated that British participation in producing a finance mechanism would in all probability have an outcome that was less favourable to France. Then, too, Britain had to accept a new policy in the form of the Common Fisheries Policy (CFP) that was first agreed in 1970 without any consultation even though the country had a greater interest in this sector than most of the other EC states. In fact, Britain together with the other applicant countries (Denmark, Ireland and Norway) had fishing industries three times the size of that of the Six. Understandably, critics of EC membership like Enoch Powell complained that the fate of Britain's fishing industry would be in the hands of 'the landlubbers of Brussels' (Enoch Powell, extract from a speech at Ardglass, Co. Down, 31 July 1976). There was therefore a good deal of substance to the view, as expressed by one leading British diplomat, that when Britain finally took up its seat at the EU table in 1973 'the hand it was dealt came from a stacked deck' (Cooper, 2012: 6).

Besides the difficulty of adapting to policies ill-suited to British interests or of seeking to mitigate the impact of such policies, however, there was a deeper problem of cultural and psychological adjustment at the root of the protracted struggle to come to terms with life in the EC. The fact of the matter was that Britain was joining an organization that was not of its making and was doing so after a period – 1945–1955 – in which it had played the dominant role in the creation of early post-war European organizations. Arguably this period was the most constructive phase in British foreign policy and diplomacy in the European arena since 1945. In many respects the British authorship of the plan to resolve the problem of German rearmament by ushering into being an enlarged Brussels Treaty Organization in the form of the Western European Union in 1955 remains to this day Britain's last major diplomatic success in western Europe. Thereafter, the country was on the defensive in the face of the origins and evolution of the EC/EU, when it became less a case of acting than of being acted upon in the European arena.

Reacting to events

A preference for a reactive rather than proactive stance is often cited as one of the hallmarks of British government policy towards the EC/EU together with strategic indecision and a lack of vision. Some of these features were and are the inevitable consequence of having to respond to external events, in this case the dynamics of European integration. Others are in accord with those definitions of British foreign policy associated with Salisbury, prime minister and foreign secretary for much of the later nineteenth century. Salisbury's preference in foreign affairs was 'to float lazily downstream occasionally putting out a diplomatic boat-hook to avoid collisions' while at the same time recognizing that 'Whatever happens will be for the worse, and therefore it is in our interest that as little should happen as possible' (Cecil, 1921: 130; Roberts, 1999: 84). Most prime ministers in the past 50 years have rarely experienced the simple manoeuvres of the former and have often vainly hoped for the latter in their handling of EC/EU business.

Government conduct of EC/EU matters has often reflected a pragmatic approach, an imperturbable diplomatic style, and the piecemeal treatment of issues as they arise and on their merits. Such methods tend to emphasize, as one classic study of British foreign policy notes, the external event rather than the goal or purpose that the British government wishes to pursue. This mode of operation and conduct is easily construed as an example of ad hoc indirection or a policy of drift often presented as masterly inaction (Vital, 1968: 99, 110; Trewin, 2008: 358). Furthermore, it frequently appears that British governments marginalize themselves in EC/EU policy areas when they prove more effective in blocking ideas emanating from other member states than in putting forward their own ideas (Wall, 2008: 77). British governments like the governments of other member states have of course pursued their national self-interest in EU circles. Unlike some other member states, however, they have proved less adept at cloaking national interest in pro-European language.

In February 2006, the year before he stepped down as prime minister, Blair reflected on the British role in the EU: 'There was always a feeling that at best the British role was to be the pebble in the shoe; the thing that made others stop and think; but not the one that did the walking' (Blair, Oxford speech, 2 February 2006). The official British tone in EU affairs has frequently been viewed as carping and dismissive rather than one of constructive criticism. Yet British governments have nonetheless played a positive role in the institutional and administrative development of the EU. They have done so by drawing attention to gross failings in the so-called inter-institutional balance between the EU's main institutions (turf wars) or highlighting cases where the Commission in particular has exceeded its remit. More generally, the British role and influence in EC/EU affairs has been most evident in the evolution of the Single Market, the Lisbon agenda, European defence co-operation, and on such matters as the development of consumer protections and energy regulations.

The making and implementation of British government policy towards the EC/EU cannot be divorced from the general character and substance of the foreign policy-making process. In an assessment of the underlying flaws of British foreign policy-making in recent decades, one authoritative, insider's account identified the following:

- an overweening trust in pragmatism and reaction to events as they occur,
- an inability to plan ahead and set clear objectives,
- a disinclination to define publicly an international role for Britain and persuade public opinion of its merits.

(Coles, 2000: 33)

Each of these features appears time and again in British policy towards the EC/EU. Whitehall's response to some of the major developments in the history of the EC/EU, especially its underestimation of the drive towards European integration, often demonstrated a failure to adjust to reality and an unwillingness to learn from the past or at least to probe unexamined assumptions. These features have been combined with an inflated sense of Britain's capacity and influence as the leading player in Europe that is often cited as the main objective. A strong element of panic set in when the EC/EU developed at a pace beyond British expectations, as when Macmillan in 1960 unsuccessfully pressed the Six to delay the acceleration of their tariff-cutting programme or when Blair in 1997 toyed with the idea of a quick phone call to Chancellor Kohl of Germany to see if he would be agreeable to postponing the launch of the euro (Peston, 2005: 200).

Dealing with the neighbours

The limited government effort to communicate the dynamics of EU activity to the public at large is often mixed with a failure on the part of government to comprehend EU developments as seen from the vantage points of other member states. Again, this is an entrenched characteristic evident from the early pre-EC membership days. In the late 1940s Jean Monnet, architect of the Schuman Plan, visited London for discussions with government officials. He found that they had little understanding of, and even less interest in, his commitment to a single European economy. Monnet's experience of this encounter proved particularly eventful in 1950 when he and other French policymakers had no intention of waiting on Britain for a positive response to the Schuman Plan.

Throughout the 1950s British governments made little effort to appreciate the driving forces behind the origins of the EC, most evidently so in the ill-fated, British-inspired Free Trade Area scheme of 1956–1958. This plan was concocted without regard to the interests of other possible member states. It was noted in a review of this episode that the introverted nature of the Whitehall policymaking exercise meant that much time and energy went into the management of interdepartmental and departmental differences and 'the effort and achievement of having formulated a plan breeds some arrogance and lack of willingness to understand the Europeans' ideas' (NA., FO 371/150154).

Arguably not much has changed over the years. It is a matter of common observation that the British government machinery in the EC/EU context is particularly effective in developing a well-coordinated interdepartmental approach with government negotiators in Brussels acting in unison. At the same time, however, this same machinery has tended to conform to the Whitehall culture and norms of policymaking. This practice has been at the cost of flexible and effective bargaining in the altogether different policymaking environment of the EU and has invariably betrayed weaknesses with reference to long-term strategic planning of EU policy (Miller, 'How the UK Government Deals with EU Business', House of Commons Library, 2012).

In the 1960s, both Macmillan and Wilson placed much emphasis on using the diplomatic leverage of the so-called 'friendly Five' in seeking to win French support for British membership of the EC. Neither of these prime ministers, however, did much to cultivate close ties. Moreover, in terms of understanding French views neither man made sufficient use of the best tools the Foreign Office offered them, including the British embassy in Paris only a few hundred metres from the French presidential palace (Boehme, 2004). Indeed, in the case of the Wilson administration, George Brown, foreign secretary and a keen supporter of British membership of the EC, was so dismissive of reports from the British ambassador (Patrick Reilly) in Paris warning of de Gaulle's scepticism about the possibility of British membership of the EC that there was a complete breakdown of trust between Brown and Reilly. Brown prematurely relieved Reilly of his ambassadorship in 1968 and forced him to take early retirement.

In the forty years of British membership of the EC/EU since 1973 governments of whatever political hue have proved unable to develop a consistent, coherent overarching set of alliances with other EC/EU governments. In particular, a comparable development to the Franco-German relationship that has for so long determined the nature and pace of European integration has eluded British governments. This pattern was as evident under the Labour governments of the 1970s as under the Labour governments of 1997–2010, and as evident too under the Thatcher Conservative governments of the 1980s as under the Coalition government of 2010–2015. Thatcher, Brown and

Cameron, in particular, have proved particularly averse to the idea of alliance-building and compromise in the EU, except in the latter case when preparing the ground for the renegotiation exercise of 2015–2016.

In the period before joining the EC, it was widely regarded as axiomatic in British governing circles that the country would enjoy a status equal to that of France and West Germany in EC circles. Strategic management of the EC, it was held, would be based on an informal triumvirate or *directoire* comprising these three states. In the event, this was far from being the case. By the early 1970s, close collaboration between France and West Germany was underpinned by the extensive network of institutional links that had developed between Paris and Bonn since the conclusion of the Franco-German Treaty of Friendship and Cooperation in 1963. This treaty symbolized the post-war *rapprochement* in Franco-German relations. More substantively, it made provision for meetings at regular intervals between the heads of state and government and ministers of foreign affairs of both states. It also established a special commission, comprising government ministers from both states, charged with coordinating Franco-German co-operation.

No such apparatus or routinized form of co-operation has emerged between London and either Paris or Berlin. For much of the first decade of British membership of the EC there was a particularly close working relationship between Helmut Schmidt, the chancellor of West Germany, and Giscard d'Estaing, the president of France. This formidable partnership effectively relegated Britain to an unduly low status under the Callaghan administration of 1976–1979 and the first Thatcher administration of 1979–1983. In neither case and for largely domestic political reasons was there much interest in pursuing close ties with either Paris or Bonn. The close Franco-German relationship remained in being for the very simple reason, as Schmidt put it, that 'we are so frightened of ourselves that we hang onto France; the French are so frightened of us that they hang onto us' (BDOHP, 3 July 1996).

Twenty years later, however, there was a concerted effort under Blair's premiership to secure a place at the EU's top table with France and Germany. However, Blair's attempts at trilateralism eventually ran into the sand. Various elements accounted for this failure including a souring of relations as a result of the Iraq war. Most notably, there was a clash of personalities between Blair and Jacques Chirac, the president of France, including one of a number of spectacularly angry scenes when Chirac presented Blair with a *fait accompli* in the shape of a package of proposals on agricultural reform that he had agreed beforehand with Gerhard Schröder, the chancellor of Germany. Besides this latest episode in the long-running Franco-British *mésentente*, however, the most important obstacle by far to Blair's plans to establish an informal triple partnership was the special relationship between France and Germany that had now endured for more than 40 years. It was built on a community of interests that no transient ideological or personality differences could undermine. It was also backed up by a dense bilateral network of institutional co-operation. Chirac eventually put an end to Blair's trilateralist aspirations in February 2004 when he rejected the idea that the Franco-German relationship should be opened up to Britain.

A long-standing sense of a community of interests in bilateral or multilateral terms has often seemed singularly lacking in the British handling of EU negotiations. The approach to EC/EU negotiations and especially the pragmatic examination of issues on a case-by-case basis has told against the making of the sort of strategic alliances that cut across multiple issue areas as in the case of the Franco-German core alliance or the Benelux bloc. Under the Blair premiership, for example, the government practised what was called 'promiscuous bilateralism', meaning working with whichever EU state or states had interests that coincided with Britain's on a particular issue (Smith, 2005: 709).

The experience of membership on these terms, and especially the inclination to view the rest of the EU through a largely British prism, has often revealed both a desperate scrambling around to seek allies to resist domestic pressures and also an ignorance of what is and is not possible in the EU forum. A recurring feature of the former condition is evident in the way in which British political leaders have especially sought German support in order to face down domestic critics of their EC/EU policies, while at the same time demonstrating limited backing for or interest in some of the strategic objectives of German governments.

This pattern was first evident in relations between Wilson and Helmut Schmidt at the time of the renegotiation of the terms of entry culminating in the referendum of 1975. Schmidt was particularly influential in pressing the British case on the EC budget and in brokering talks between Wilson and Giscard d'Estaing. Furthermore, he made a telling contribution by addressing the massed ranks of anti-marketeers at the Labour Party conference in November 1974. He spoke in flawless English and made one of the most effective conference speeches that Denis Healey, Chancellor of the Exchequer at the time, had ever heard, later adding that 'However much we distrust Europe, we still like Europeans – when they speak our language!' (Healey, 1990: 454). There is little or no evidence to suggest that Schmidt obtained anything in return for his labours.

There was a similar though on this occasion unsuccessful attempt by a British government to secure German assistance at a time of a national emergency. In 1992 and immediately prior to the exit of the pound sterling from the Exchange Rate Mechanism (ERM), the Major government and in particular Norman Lamont, the Chancellor of the Exchequer, sought to keep the pound in the ERM by trying to persuade the German government to cut their interest rates or, at the very least, to stop raising them (see Chapter 10).

It seemed improbable that the German government would subordinate its national priorities to those of Britain, any more than London would do so in similar circumstances. This possibility appeared even less likely since only two years earlier the process of German unification had met with very lukewarm British support. Thatcher had reluctantly and at a late stage accepted the necessity for German unification in 1990. She had long recognized that the Berlin Wall was an abhorrent symbol of Soviet oppression. She was, however, intensely suspicious of the motives underlying long-standing West German support for European integration with France in tandem, and that in turn fuelled her Euroscepticism. She had agreed very readily with Charles Powell, her key foreign policy adviser, that 'German reunification is an area where we have to say one thing and think another' (Moore, 2015: 396). There was, too, the famously frosty relationship between Thatcher and Chancellor Kohl that caused the latter to refer to her as 'that woman'. Kohl commented in his memoirs (2005) that Thatcher 'always gave me headaches' and that she played 'an unfriendly, dangerous role during the process of German unification'. The feeling was mutual, as Kohl occupied a lowly position in Thatcher's list of favourite foreign leaders, so much so that she described him as 'the German equivalent of Ted Heath' (Moore, 2014: 312).

In the aftermath of 'Black Wednesday' – the day on which the pound fell out of the ERM – several commentators and some participants in these events commented on the apparent inability of British ministers and officials to grasp either how governments on the continent actually worked or how the world as seen from Paris or Berlin might possibly differ from the world as viewed from Whitehall and Westminster (King and Crewe, 2013). The fact that Britain had no share in the post-war Franco-German rapprochement at the heart of the EC was all too evident in Thatcher's reaction to one of the abiding images of Franco-German reconciliation: the French President Mitterand and the West German Chancellor Kohl holding hands on the horrific First World War battlefield of Verdun (September 1984). Asked if she found the scene moving, Thatcher replied: 'No, I did not. Two grown men holding hands!' (Moore, 2015: 389).

The reactions of British policymakers to the events leading up to Black Wednesday were all of a piece with their limited understanding of what the ERM represented in the minds of policymakers elsewhere in the EU. This was evident at the time of Britain's entry into the ERM in 1990 (see Chapter 9). There was at this stage in British government circles little appreciation of the extent to which France and Germany were now committed to full economic and monetary union within the EU. Mitterand and Kohl, the prime movers of the scheme, no longer viewed the ERM as a flexible apparatus but as a project hard-wired to result in a single currency area.

The same limited understanding of what was afoot among the prospective members of the euro area was also in evidence when Blair at the head of the incoming Labour government in 1997 thought that at this late hour he might enlist Kohl's support in delaying the emergence of the euro area. There was no likelihood of securing such a concession. Years later in the aftermath of the US/British invasion of Iraq, relations between London and Berlin were distinctly cool. Blair's European speeches impressed some mainland European audiences. Others, however, noted that he had a weakness for words and rhetoric; German sources close to Chancellor Merkel claimed that Blair 'never stuck his neck out for Europe' and that 'all the political risks he took were towards Washington and never Europe' (*The Guardian*, 20 February 2008), a judgment not easily overturned.

Attempts to curry favour with Germany in order to assist the partisan purposes of the Conservative element in the British Coalition government were again evident in 2013–2015 when Cameron sought the support of Angela Merkel, the German chancellor, in his bid to renegotiate the British terms of EU membership. Prior to promising a referendum before the end of 2017 on British membership of the EU, Cameron had demonstrated little interest in mounting a concerted attempt to develop a co-operative relationship with Germany. The commitment to hold a referendum on renegotiated terms of entry nevertheless meant that he continued to make a concerted effort to secure German support for the British case, most obviously so in February 2014 when Merkel visited London and gave qualified support to Cameron's renegotiation stance on the EU (Seldon and Snowdon, 2015: 429). Significantly, however, the German government was particularly unhelpful in its refusal to participate in the British Balance of Competences Review announced in July 2012 (see Chapter 12 for the origins and purpose of this review).

Long-standing policy interests

There is a deep-seated aversion in British governing circles to visionary thinking about the EC/EU. This feature has reinforced the mainland European parentage of the organization. It has also reflected an essentially pragmatic approach to the subject. 'If you have visions, you should go see a doctor' advised Helmut Schmidt, one of the chancellors of Germany since 1945 least inclined to practice conviction politics. Such advice would meet with approval in British policymaking circles when contemplating basic or existential questions about the future of the EU. In many respects the British response to such circumstances has focused less on plotting a course for the future and more on protecting British interests by means of 'red lines' and possible opt-outs in the face of a dynamic EU.

Over the years, however, British governments have followed a broadly consistent line in terms of their preferences. Indeed, there are certain long-standing aspects of the British engagement with the EC/EU that can be traced back to the very beginnings of the post-war debate about European integration in the late 1940s:

*   the emphasis on minimal goals;
*   strong support for intergovernmental co-operation and a pronounced antipathy towards the idea of a federal Europe;
*   the quest for unconditional and ideally free rider access to the economic benefits of EC/EU membership;
*   the preoccupation with reconciling Britain's European and extra-European interests and commitments while seeking to make a positive contribution to the development of the EU's Common Foreign and Security Policy (see Chapter 11);
*   the prioritizing of enlargement over further integration;
*   the projection of European integration as primarily an economic rather than a political phenomenon;
*   considerable distaste for an open-ended commitment to the goal of 'ever closer union';
*   deep suspicion of any European rhetoric that suggests an irreversible journey to an unknown destination;
*   an aversion to a tight, little inward-looking Europe;
*   a strong preference for viewing EU membership as a fall back or minimal, defensive position rather than as a base camp for an advance towards further integration.

Some of these features are interconnnected and several are dealt with elsewhere in this book. Here we consider several that have stood the test of time: opposition to a federal Europe, support for enlargement of the EU, a strong preference for 'negative' rather than 'positive' integration, and an intermittent commitment to modernization in the EU context. Each illustrates both the reactive and proactive features of British policymaking. Each also figures in major phases of British policymaking towards the EU over the past 25 years in the course of major sets of treaty negotiations.

The much used and abused F word

Few words in the British dictionary of European integration have caused such strong aversion and misunderstanding as the word federal and the idea of a federal Europe. Much misuse, distortion and misinterpretation attend these words in British political discourse about European integration. A federal Europe invariably invokes the image of a monstrous behemoth of an omnipotent, highly centralized European superstate that robs the individual states of all power and sovereignty.

At every juncture in the evolution of the EC/EU, Britain has figured prominently as an opponent of what politicians and public have variously construed as a federal Europe. They have stood on the principle that the British system of government founded on parliamentary sovereignty rejected federal or shared power. In the making of the Maastricht Treaty of 1992 it was the Major government that, contrary to the views of the other EU governments, insisted that the final treaty should not contain any reference to a federal destiny or vocation as the end goal of the EU.

There are, to be sure, elements in the EU's structure of governance that can be defined as federalist in character, notably QMV, the supremacy of EU law over national law, the decisive role of the European Court of Justice, the independence of the European Commission and the existence of the EP. Federalism in Britain's debate about the EU, however, is invariably taken to mean the exact opposite of how it is understood elsewhere in the EU or in other parts of the world such as the United States with its federal system of government.

This condition gives rise to a meaningless discourse based on diametrically opposing definitions of terms. Certainly, there are different definitions of federalism, but however defined none corresponds to what is routinely described as federalism in the British debate, and none mistakes centralization for federalism. John Killick, a senior British diplomat whose career began in Germany helping to devise the West German constitution or Basic Law, has observed that the word 'federal' or 'federation' means something absolutely different in Germany from British understandings of the subject, and that the West German constitution was so devised 'precisely because we didn't want too much power at the centre' (BDOHP, 14 February 2002). In short, while federalism in Germany means decentralization and the avoidance of a unitary state, it means almost the opposite in British political discourse.

Over and against their understanding of and distaste for a federal Europe, British policymakers have consistently upheld the idea of intergovernmental co-operation. This method of operation involves a traditional form of co-operation between states in which participating states do not confer powers upon supranational institutions and embark on joint action only as and when each state sees fit. In many respects the OEEC under British leadership in the years immediately after the Second World War remains to this day for British political leaders the ideal model of exclusively European co-operation with no higher authority imposing policies upon the member states.

The larger the better?

Another major, enduring feature of British policy towards the EU has involved strong support for the enlargement of the organization. The Thatcher government in the 1980s threw its weight behind the accession of Greece (1981), Portugal and Spain (1986) with a view to reinforcing the transition of these former military dictatorships to a democratic system of government. This development was further helped by long-standing ties between Britain and Portugal, most recently in the EFTA.

The Major government of the 1990s in its turn was eager to support the case for EU expansion. It did so first by advocating the inclusion of Austria, Finland and Sweden in 1995 (the latter two having been Britain's trading partners in the EFTA). Furthermore, it supported in principle the extension of EU membership to the former ex-communist states of eastern Europe recently freed from Soviet control, with a view to strengthening their democratic institutions.

This last development came to fruition under the equally committed Blair government in securing the accession to EU membership of the Czech Republic, Estonia,

Hungary, Latvia, Lithuania, Poland, Slovakia and Slovenia in 2004 (known collectively as A8) together with Cyprus and Malta with their strong historical ties with Britain, and the accession of Bulgaria and Romania in 2007 (known collectively as A2). The accession of Croatia in 2013 was approved by the Cameron government, though on this occasion controversy over 'benefits tourism' emanating from central and eastern Europe was taking centre stage in British politics (see below). Finally, in this respect British governments have figured as prominent advocates of Turkey's application for EU membership, a vexed, long-running saga dating back to Turkey's first application for EU membership in 1987. The Coalition government of 2010–2015 also advocated the future accession of all the western Balkan countries, not least as a means of bringing long-term peace and stability to the area and of resolving the enmities that drew British military forces into conflict there in the 1990s. At every stage in the expansion of the EC/EU, British governments have also attached great weight to the economic advantages of trading in a much larger internal market.

EU enlargement, therefore, has figured as one policy area in which Britain was most proactive and was perhaps the most committed, influential supporter in driving the process. Certainly, there was general agreement on the principle of enlargement among other EU governments, but some of them tended to be less enthusiastic than Britain.

France was rarely more than lukewarm about the prospect of EU expansion and not just in the 1960s when it twice blocked Britain's EC applications. French governments feared that enlargement would result in institutional paralysis and also lead to a diminution of their own influence within the EU as the EU's centre of gravity shifted eastwards. The instinctive preference in Paris was to concentrate instead on deeper integration. At the time of the EU extension into central and eastern Europe, the reservations felt by the German government centred on the financial implications of enlargement, as the Berlin government was simultaneously paying a hefty price to absorb the former East German state into a unified Germany. The costs of admitting central and eastern European states into the EU would undoubtedly be huge and if past experience was any guide Germany was almost certain to pay a disproportionately large share of the bill. Elsewhere, some of the smaller EU member states were worried about a possible reduction in their voting power in the Council of Ministers as a result of enlargement. Furthermore, member states like Greece, Ireland, Italy and Spain, that had hitherto received generous EU subsidies, were reluctant to see these diverted to economically backward newcomers in central and eastern Europe.

Besides declared reasons for backing EU enlargement, there were in British government circles several implicit or coded reasons for supporting this process. Chief among these and accounting for the British preference for 'widening' (i.e. increasing EU membership) rather than 'deepening' (i.e. enhancing the depth of integration) the EU was the belief that a larger EU would dilute the tendency to centralize power in Brussels.

As noted in the Introduction, the precise relationship between widening and deepening in the EU has varied in character over time. Clearly, the idea of a wider, looser and flexible EU has long been a declared aim of British governments, though the idea of a covert operation to this effect should not be overstated, least of all in view of the fact that opt-outs have partly insulated Britain from the deepening process (HM Government, 'Review of the Balance of Competences between the United Kingdom and the European Union EU Enlargement', December 2014: 58). In some cases, notably under Blair's premiership, enlargement was viewed as beneficial in itself to the accession states.

There were also other perceived advantages to be derived from pressing 'widening' as the priority, not least of these being a possible weakening of the potency of the Franco-German axis. There was, too, the opportunity of seeking out useful potential allies among the new EU member states of central and eastern Europe, most of which not only shared the Blair government's Atlanticist outlook and commitment to free market economics, but were also disinclined to support the idea of speedy supranational integration. On the euro area front, moreover, the enlargement of the EU served to increase the number of EU states outside the euro area, thereby reducing the risk of British isolation. Furthermore, many contributors to the Cameron Coalition government's Balance of Competences exercise maintained that Britain had benefitted from a larger EU that was more able to negotiate on equal terms with the likes of China, India and the United States. In short, a larger EU, so it was argued, 'has acted as an influence-multiplier for UK foreign policy priorities in many areas' (HM Government, 'Review of the Balance of Competences between the United Kingdom and the European Union EU Enlargement', December 2014: 7).

It was in keeping with the long-standing emphasis on EU expansion that a large part of Thatcher's Bruges speech in September 1988, often cited simply as an influential landmark in the evolution of Euroscepticism in the Conservative Party, was actually devoted to making the case for an enlarged EC to include the countries of eastern and central Europe. Then, too, John Major, her successor as prime minister, made a speech at Leiden University in September 1994 in which he maintained that widening the EU came before 'deepening' it.

Such British advocacy of enlargement was reciprocated by the support of some of the new member states for key aspects of British foreign policy. In the course of events leading up to the Iraq war of 2003, three of the then prospective EU member states – the Czech Republic, Hungary and Poland – supported the US–British interpretation of United Nations Organization (UNO) resolution 1441, as opposed to that of the French and Russians which stressed the need for a further vote to provide a legitimate basis for war. President Chirac of France was furious, especially since the US defense secretary, Donald Rumsfeld, had spoken disparagingly a few days before of France and Germany belonging to what he termed 'old Europe' (Riddell, 2005: 141–2).

Chirac's angry response to the central and eastern European states that backed the United States was to tell them that they were not yet full EU members and that it behoved them to adopt a low profile. The effect of his rebuke was the opposite of what he intended. It caused the Poles and the rest to draw closer to the British and the Americans. In these circumstances there appeared to be a possibility of Britain heading a group of EU states acting as a counterbalance to the Franco-German partnership and sharing Britain's outward-looking, free-market and pro-Atlanticist/NATO outlook, with English increasingly serving as the *lingua franca*.

Most immediately, however, such a grouping was unsustainable and fell apart in 2005 amidst bitter wrangling between the British, the Poles and other new member states. The particulars of this episode are dealt with in Chapter 11, suffice it to note here that British support for the EU's enlargement into central and eastern Europe proved a mixed blessing in that it was eventually accompanied by some unintended and unwanted consequences, notably relating to Britain's EU budget rebate and to the issue of immigration into Britain from the new EU member states of central and eastern Europe.

EU expansion and the immigration issue

While EU expansion in the first decade of the twenty-first century had an immediate impact on Britain's budget rebate (see Chapter 8), it was more of a long-burning fuse in relation to the free movement of EU citizens into Britain from central and eastern Europe. Eventually, however, this issue was to dominate Britain's EU politics through to the renegotiation of the terms of membership and the referendum in June 2016. In the relatively benign economic conditions of the pre-2007–2008 financial crash and without drawing much attention to the matter, the Blair government had permitted unrestricted access to Britain by nationals of the new member states of 2004 (the A8 countries). It waved aside the imposition of transitional controls. Meanwhile, apart from Ireland and Sweden, all of the other EU states had to a greater or lesser extent restricted the right of entry (for a maximum of seven years) on nationals from the eight new member states. What materialized was the biggest influx of people in such a short period of time in the country's history (see Table 4.1).

EU membership for Bulgaria and Romania (known as A2 countries) in 2007 was accompanied by across the board, transitional controls on the free movement of citizens from this source. It was a measure of how far immigration from elsewhere in the EU to Britain had moved from a marginal to a central issue in British politics, however, that when these controls were finally lifted in January 2014 it was widely expected especially in the anti-EU press that large numbers of Bulgarians and Romanians would enter the country; disappointingly for the waiting press from this source, however, the first flight from Bucharest to Britain on 1 January 2014 contained only two Romanians, both of whom had firm job offers. True, this did not reflect the large number of migrants from this source thereafter, but the fact that both had job offers was indicative of the general character of migrants from elsewhere in the EU. By 2015, some 1.9 million people born elsewhere in the EU were employed in Britain (The Migration Observatory, University of Oxford, 5 October 2015).

During the period 2010–2015, immigration from elsewhere in the EU became a centrepiece of the United Kingdom Independent Party's (UKIP) platform in the European

Table 4.1 Estimate of the resident population of the UK (by non-British nationality) 2004–2012 (figures in thousands)

Year	EU14	EU8	EU2	Non-EU
2004	951	125	20	1,852
2005	945	233	27	2,000
2006	981	404	28	2,191
2007	971	567	33	2,354
2008	975	677	64	2,433
2009	1,006	745	87	2,486
2010	1,038	829	118	2,457
2011	1,091	1,038	135	2,489
2012	1,092	1,074	155	2,509

EU14 – pre-2004 EU member states.

EU8 – states that joined the EU in 2004.

EU2 – Bulgaria and Romania that joined the EU in 2007.

Source: Office of National Statistics, *Annual Population Survey* (2004–2012).

Parliament. The party's popular appeal was registered in the EP elections of May 2014 when it emerged with the largest number of seats of any British political party (see Chapter 5). It was in these circumstances of a twin threat from UKIP and from their own Eurosceptic backbenchers that throughout the remainder of the 2010–2015 parliament Cameron and Conservative ministers sought to reduce welfare benefits to migrant labour from the rest of the EU. They also called into question the free movement of EU citizens within the EU – a fundamental principle of the EU – most notably by threatening to bar the entry of new states to the EU unless accompanied by restrictions on the free movement of citizens from such sources. They also considered an emergency brake on citizens from less well-off EU states.

This position scarcely impressed some of the governments in central and eastern Europe. In some cases there was considerable disagreement between Britain and governments in the area over Conservative proposals to change EU migrants' access to benefits in the UK. According to one secretly taped expletive-laden conversation involving the Polish foreign minister, Radoslaw Sikorski, in the spring of 2014, Sikorski reportedly said that Cameron had 'fucked up' his handling of the EU by resorting to 'stupid propaganda' to appease Eurosceptics. It was unclear from the transcript as to whether Sikorski was referring to Britain's proposed revision of the principle of free movement within the EU or more specifically plans to curb EU migrants' access to benefits (*Wprost news magazine*, 23 June 2014). Polish concerns were indicative of the large influx of Poles following the country's accession to the EU. Polish nationals made up the biggest single group of foreign nationals in Britain, amounting to some 14 per cent of the total number of non-British nationals resident in Britain (HM Government, 'Review of the Balance of Competences between the United Kingdom and the European Union Single Market: Free Movement of Persons', Summer 2014: 27).

Negative and positive integration

Another enduring characteristic of British policy towards the EC/EU has involved a marked preference for 'negative' as opposed to 'positive' integration. Negative integration essentially entails the removal of existing restrictions on economic, commercial and financial transactions between states. In the early post-Second World War years, the OEEC led by Britain embarked on the first steps in this direction by starting to dismantle the infrastructure of trade restrictions and monetary controls derived from the interwar and wartime period in Europe, starting in particular with the reduction or abolition of trade quotas. Few, if any, commentators doubt that Britain has historically been one of the strongest advocates of a liberal approach to trade and investment in the EU and in the global economy. With the support of like-minded states such as Germany and Sweden, it has influenced EU trade and investment policy as much as any other EU state and more than most (HM Government, 'Review of the Balance of Competences between the United Kingdom and the European Union Single Market: Free Movement of Persons', Summer 2014: 61).

By contrast, positive integration involves the introduction of new common policies between states whether, as in the case of the EC/EU, in the form of the CAP or the creation of the Single Market. Positive integration in the EC/EU context has met with a mixed response on the British side with a bias towards a shallower version of political and economic integration than is evident in other EU states and also a determination to avoid competence creep of additional powers for the EU, including extended jurisprudence for the Court of Justice (Wallace, 2012: 543). As noted earlier the Thatcher government figured prominently in supporting the making of the Single European Act of 1986 and the still incomplete development of the Single Market. That proactive stance, however, has been accompanied by a reactive and often critical voice in some British circles, suggesting at least misunderstanding, if not ignorance, of some of the implications of a commitment to a single market.

A common British criticism of the EU is that it involves an overwhelming amount of red tape, bureaucracy and regulations that limit, if not cancel out, any benefits from EU membership. Cameron typified this strand of opinion when he criticized the EU in January 2014 for 'burdensome, unjustified and premature regulatory burdens'. There are certainly unnecessary restrictions and burdens imposed on business by the EU administration, in much the same way as they are imposed by national bureaucracies. There is also little regard for the cost of enforcing regulations. Furthermore, the EU does itself no favours in the public eye when, for example, it attempts to ban the use of unmarked olive oil jugs on restaurant tables or limit the power settings of vacuum cleaners.

Two pieces of employment legislation resulting from the EU are often raised as the most controversial in this respect: the Working Time and Temporary Agency Workers Directives. The former deals with such matters as restrictions on night work, rest breaks, paid annual leave, and the requirement for a maximum working week of 48 hours (with provision for the individual to opt out of this element). The latter involves the equal treatment entitlements of agency workers after 12 weeks with the same hirer in the same role. According to one estimate based on British government figures, over two-thirds of the annual cost to business from EU regulation arose from these directives (HM Government, 'Review of the Balance of Competences between the United Kingdom and the European Union Social and Employment Policy', Summer 2014: 60–1).

There is, however, a good deal of substantial evidence that challenges the view of the EU as a source of burdensome 'red tape'. Ken Clarke, as a government minister and a veteran pro-EU supporter, attacked the myth that 'heroic British ministers' were restraining a flow of EU regulations that tied up businesses in red tape. He challenged the critics to name a regulation forced on the British government by the EU, dismissing their reference to the Working Time Directive with its opt out element (*The Guardian*, 27 January 2014). One of the Balance of Competences exercises reviewed the operations of the Single Market. It concluded that the advantages of EU action – such as a level playing field for British businesses and a single transparent set of rules with scope for legal redress – outweighed the costs arising from administrative burdens, regulatory costs or policy trade-offs (HM Government, 'Review of the Balance of Competences between the United Kingdom and the European Union Single Market: Free Movement of Goods', February 2014).

Another review in this same series reported more mixed opinion. It noted that in a Confederation of British Industry (CBI) poll 52 per cent of businesses said that they benefited from the introduction of common EU standards, while exactly the same percentage of businesses believed that if Britain were to leave the EU, the overall burden of regulation on their businesses would decrease (HM Government, 'Review of the Balance of Competences between the United Kingdom and the European Union Social and Employment Policy', Summer 2014: 43). A different and earlier source reported that the benefit–cost ratio of EU regulations in Britain was 1.02, meaning that for every £1 of costs that EU regulations imposed, they delivered £1.02 of benefits (House of

Lords Select Committee on the European Union (Sub-committee B), *Inquiry into Relaunching the Single Market*, 7 October 2010). In this field, as in so much else involving the precise impact of the EU, it is difficult to disaggregate the costs arising from EU action from what costs may have existed anyway as a result of domestic legislation.

It is also the case that Britain together with some other EU states (notably Ireland, the Netherlands and some of the central and eastern European states) favour a light touch, comparatively economically liberal approach that is at variance with the EU's regulatory process. According to an OECD 2014 report, product and labour market regulations in Britain are already among the least restrictive in the developed world. The OECD ranked Britain as having the fourth lightest employment law regime in the developed world. Besides, 'red tape' in many cases consists of safeguards defending both people and places from predatory corporations (*Financial Times*, 12 June 2014; *The Guardian*, 19 November 2014).

That said, the EU has good reason to concern itself with regulation if only to make the Single Market work on a level playing field across all member states. A common set of rules is said to be cheaper to administer than having to demonstrate compliance with multiple regulatory frameworks (i.e. 28 national regimes on the basis of the current EU membership), and it offers the following benefits:

- Reduces the compliance costs for their members, when compared with the costs of having to deal with a number of different national regimes.
- Removes many of the non-tariff barriers to trade, enabling exporters to reap economies of scale.
- Enables exporters to benefit from reduced costs, shorter delivery times, and less risk of interruption to goods movements at the border.

> (HM Government, 'Review of the Balance of Competences
> between the United Kingdom and the European Union
> EU Foreign Policy', July 2013)

In the absence of common minimum standards and rules that are necessary for mutual recognition and are set by the EU, the Single Market would collapse under the weight of conflicting national regulations and 'free ride' abuses. Arguably this basic premise is largely absent from the British debate about the EU, especially when the Single Market is either routinely mistaken for a free trade area in public discourse or attracts other fundamental misunderstandings. For all her support for the venture, Thatcher herself did not understand that creating a single market necessarily involved not just deregulation, but the harmonization of regulations across the EC which impinged on matters hitherto the prerogative of national governments (Campbell, 2003: 309). In effect, a truly single market with a genuinely level playing field requires a single legal framework, identical industry, labour and environmental standards, and courts that will enforce them throughout the single jurisdiction.

It is also fair to say that the popular appeal of any campaign to cut EU red tape can have unintended consequences. One recommendation of the Cameron Coalition government's 'Business Taskforce on EU Red Tape', which was asked to find regulations to scrap, was to push for full implementation of the EU's Services Directive (Centre for European Reform, 2014: 41). In fact, however, a deepening of the still incomplete EU market for services would be impossible without more regulation, all the more so as the market for services is of necessity more highly regulated than the market in goods.

Britain has considerable interest in completing the Single Market in services that has made much more laggardly progress than the free movement of persons and visible goods. Only about 20 per cent of EU services are allowed to be traded across European borders in the Single Market (2015), and this at a time when some 70 per cent of EU GDP is made up of services. The poor implementation of the EU's legislation (Services Directive) is often cited as a key reason for laggardly progress with national restrictions remaining as barriers, besides which services are generally less easy to trade than goods. Over 40 per cent of intra-EU trade in services is taken up by travel and transport services which are by definition cross-border in their nature.

The European defence industry, with a turnover of 96 billion euros and organized largely on national lines, is often cited as a striking example of the advantages that could be reaped from a fully developed EU-organized defence services sector, especially at a time of spiralling high costs, duplication and declining military budgets. Some research has suggested that a truly Single Market in defence would reduce EU defence procurement costs by 10–20 per cent, while other studies conclude that Europe might be paying 30–40 per cent more than it should for its military equipment. With the largest defence industry in Europe, Britain would be well-placed to capitalize on the removal of national restrictions and obstacles in this sector (HM Government, 'Review of the Balance of Competences between the United Kingdom and the European Union The Single Market: Free Movement of Services', Summer 2014: 50).

During the past 20 years or so the gap between the British preference for negative integration and distaste for positive integration has become increasingly acute. In many respects it has proved possible to bridge this gap only by an ever-lengthening list of opt-outs ranging from non-participation in the euro area and the Schengen agreement to the issue of opt-out of the EU's justice and home affairs and a non-signatory of the Fundamental Charter of Human Rights, with the accompanying possibility of opt-ins in all cases. Among other things, this lengthening list of opt-outs limits the possibility of substantive as opposed to cosmetic concessions resulting from the renegotiation of the terms of EU membership exercise undertaken by the Conservative government (see Chapter 12).

Britain has the highest number of opt-outs and special clauses of any EU member state, indicative of the extent to which the country has become most detached from the core of European integration. There comes a point when the number of possible opt-outs is exhausted, after which challenging the fundamental principles of the EU increasingly appears as the sole option. Arguably this loosening of integrative ties with the rest of the EU can no longer be obscured by effective diplomacy or clever drafting, and recent years have marked a definite caesura (Federal Trust Report, 2013: 58). In the event, there were some further gains and concessions, symbolic or otherwise, that could be squeezed out of the other EU states, as demonstrated by the February 2016 agreement following the renegotiation of the terms of Britain's relationship with the EU (see Chapter 12).

Modernization and EU membership

Modernization has figured as a second order aspect of British policy towards the EU, most particularly in terms of the idea of reinvigorating a laggardly British economy through osmotic contact with more dynamic continental economies. The EU and modernization theme, however, has featured intermittently, strongly so when associated with a keen emphasis on EU membership and less so when EU membership has fallen from favour. It was more evident in the 1960s and 1970s and later under the Blair governments of 1997–2007 than in the 1980s and in the period since the financial crash of 2007–2008. Under the Thatcher governments of the 1980s domestic panaceas for what were perceived as Britain's economic ills dominated the scene, while following the financial crash of 2007–2008 and the onset of economic recession the EU, especially in its euro area travails and weaknesses, was widely viewed in British political circles as a model to be avoided at all costs.

The first attempt to achieve EC membership was conducted at a time when domestic efforts to rejuvenate industry and improve productivity through a mixture of exhortation, patriotic appeals to the 'Dunkirk spirit', cajolement and incentives had palpably failed. In the early 1960s and increasingly so thereafter the modernization theme and declinist accounts of Britain were very much to the fore, as part of the wider social rush to modernity in this period.

There was growing criticism of the slowness to change of an arrogant, class-ridden and complacent managerial elite. Michael Shanks, a leading contemporary exponent of the modernization message, observed that Britain was in danger of becoming 'a lotus island ... shielded from discontent by a threadbare welfare state and acceptance of genteel poverty' (Shanks, 1961). In these circumstances, it was commonly assumed that EC membership would make British industry more competitive by exposing it to greater foreign competition inside the EC. For Macmillan himself EC membership provided the prospect of a 'necessary cold shower' or a course of creative destruction for British industry, as it was viewed in some quarters. After more than a decade in power, moreover, modernization offered the Conservative Party the opportunity to advance its cause as the party of the future and to portray the Labour Party as old-fashioned.

Wilson and to an even greater extent Heath were seized of the importance of EC membership in pursuing the process of modernization. In the case of Wilson, however, the attempt to secure EC membership was as much a consequence of failed domestic plans for modernization as an initial, integral part of a modernizing tendency. Heath, however, came to power in 1970 with a strong commitment to modernize and regenerate the British economy. A radical reform of industrial relations and exposure of domestic industry to fierce competition within the EC were key elements in his modernization programme. EC membership in this frame was viewed as modernizing and liberalizing the British economy by stealth. By the early 1970s, moreover, the far higher standard of living of the Six was fast becoming a matter of common knowledge. EC membership was increasingly viewed as a principal means of emulating the successful economic advances of the Six.

The link between the EU and modernization theme was resurrected under the Blair governments of 1997–2007. Whatever their differences over EU policy, Blair and Brown shared the belief that Britain needed to modernize through closer engagement with the EU. In Blair's case this was part of the centerpiece of his representation of what New Labour and the Third Way were about. Much debate has surrounded the idea of the Third Way, described by some critics as voguish and insubstantial and by others more cuttingly; Joe Klein, the American commentator, portrayed New Labour as 'little more than a humane rhetorical image that technocrats like Tony Blair created to prove to themselves that they haven't become middle-aged conservatives' (Seldon, 2007: ix; *The*

New Yorker, 28 April 1997). In other circles, New Labour was described less cuttingly as the SDP for slow learners.

For his own part, Blair's preoccupation with the Third Way epitomized his determination to shake up existing political and economic structures both in Britain and in the EU as a whole. Domestically, it involved moves towards multi-level governance most especially through the process of devolution (see Chapter 6), the adoption of proportional representation in regional and EP elections, and the introduction of a directly elected London mayor.

Pro-Europeanism was a crucial part of Labour's modernization and of its return to electability after the near-death experience of the early 1980s, and in that respect it was essentially a project rooted in domestic politics (Liddle, 2014: xxiii). That said, however, Blair's overriding objective for the EU was to equip it to meet the new challenges presented by globalization. He thus advocated the abandonment of shibboleths that had long held sway among most of the EU member states. This attitude was shaped less by a resolve to prevent another major European war (a key feature of the rhetoric supporting the original EC) than by a mission to modernize and promote greater efficiency. His ambition was to provide the framework for a thriving enterprise culture, through deregulation, the elimination of remaining obstacles to a single market, especially in energy, telecommunications and financial services, and the promotion of more flexible market conditions, this being viewed in some quarters as a Thatcherite Mark 2 programme.

This Blairite emphasis was to provide the basis for a rare, pro-active burst of British interest in creating a new framework for EU developments. Blair was not alone among EU leaders in seeking such reforms, but he played a prominent role in the initiative. His main allies in the early years of his premiership included the centre-right Spanish and Italian prime ministers Jose Maria Aznar and Silvio Berlusconi. They were particularly influential in helping to secure at the Lisbon European Council of March 2000 the adoption of the proposals intended to make the EU 'the most competitive and dynamic knowledge-based economy in the world' within ten years and with a view to increasing the EU's GDP growth rate by 3 per cent per annum.

This Lisbon Agenda stood as a powerful symbol of the direction in which the Blair government wanted the EU to move, focusing as it did on increased investment in education, training and research. In the event and even before the global financial crash of 2007–2008 derailed things completely, a mid-term review in 2004 indicated that the EU's record had fallen far short of the Lisbon goals; 'Lisbon is a big failure' commented Romano Prodi, the president of the European Commission in October 2004. Meanwhile, the EU and modernization theme of New Labour featured far less so after the end of Blair's premiership, except among sections of the electorate that viewed modernization as a proxy for globalization and the accompanying loss of domestic employment.

Opt-outs and red lines, 1990–2010

The precise nature and significance of Britain's EU policy in the period 1990–2010 and the resort to opt-outs and red lines can be illustrated with reference to the making of the Treaty on European Union (TEU – hereafter Maastricht Treaty) 1990–1992 and the emergence of the Lisbon Treaty in the period 2001–2007.

The Maastricht Treaty, the Major government and the first parting of the ways

The making of the Maastricht Treaty marked an important tipping point in the approach of a Conservative government to the conduct of EU business. Major succeeded Thatcher as prime minister in 1990, expressing the hope that Britain would be 'at the very heart of Europe' (*The Times*, 12 March 1991). On the conclusion of the treaty negotiations, he viewed the outcome as an unqualified triumph for his diplomacy, a case of 'game, set and match' according to one of his spokespersons. In the intervening period, however, the course of the negotiations revealed the first important parting of the ways since 1973 between Britain and most of the other member states.

The Maastricht Treaty was another milestone on the road to a potential European federation. No subsequent EU treaty was to move as far in this direction as this treaty which also coined a new name for the EC – the more federal sounding 'European Union'. The centrepiece of the treaty, however, was the commitment to forge an economic and monetary union (EMU) by means of three stages with the final stage to be completed by 1999 at the latest. The treaty also made provision for a Social Chapter (see below) covering such matters as improvements in living and working conditions, fair remuneration, social protection and worker participation. In addition, the treaty included a commitment to a Common Foreign and Security Policy (CFSP) that envisaged a more influential role for the EU in the international system (see Chapter 11).

There were also significant changes to the EU's institutional architecture. Some of the EU's institutions acquired new powers and a further range of policies fell within the EU's ambit. There was one other new area of co-operation besides CFSP, this being Cooperation in Justice and Home Affairs (JHA). The structure of the newly entitled EU was also transformed according to three pillars. The EC formed the first pillar, where there was a relatively high level of integration encompassing the Single Market, Community Policies and eventually EMU. The second pillar consisted of the provisions for CFSP. The third pillar comprised the provisions for JHA. The term 'European Union' was an umbrella term that referred to joint activities in all three pillars.

The Major government signed the Maastricht Treaty, but could only do so by insisting that the principle of differentiated integration or variable geometry should apply in the case of specific British concerns. One such concern was the Social Chapter that had its origins in the Social Charter that Thatcher had rejected in 1989.

The Social Chapter gave greater powers to the EU to legislate on such matters as improvements in living and working conditions, fair renumeration and social protection. It also envisaged a greater role for employer and employee representatives to be consulted on social policy legislation. Major ensured that the Social Chapter was relegated to a protocol in the TEU, thereby excluding Britain from its provisions. He did so partly on the grounds that competitive labour costs gave Britain the leading edge in the EU marketplace, a view contested by John Smith, the leader of the Labour Party, who argued that the British people could not understand why they should be denied the social rights, opportunities and advantages enjoyed by other EU citizens. This division of opinion reflected a fundamental debate about whether the EU was an economic union or had a legitimate set of social goals at its core, and in particular about whether or not social policy was an intrinsic element of the Single Market.

Britain together with Denmark also secured the right to opt out of the third stage of EMU. This stage involved the irrevocable fixing of the conversion rates of the currencies of the prospective member states of EMU, culminating in the introduction of the euro as the single currency. Major approached the Maastricht Treaty negotiations on the issue of EMU with a similar view to that of past and present British leaders in the face of a fundamental EU change not to their liking; 'to delay the single currency if we could, and to insert safeguards if we could not' and all the while 'procrastinating on principle' (Major, 1999: 272–3).

In view of these opt-outs and also the accompanying objections to anything that smacked of federalism and political union, it was scarcely surprising that on most issues Britain was isolated, playing the role, as Major put it, of 'the abominable no-men in the negotiations' with its reputation as 'the in-house awkward squad' (Major, 1999: 266, 273).

Shortly after the signing of the Maastricht Treaty, Britain also steered clear of the substance of a measure that further undergirded the collective unity of most of the EU states: the Schengen Agreement (so named after the town in Luxembourg where the agreement was signed). This agreement was drawn up in 1985, took effect in 1995, and was integrated into the EU framework by the Amsterdam Treaty (1997). This treaty also established a protocol allowing Britain to decide whether to opt into certain legislation adopted in the area of freedom, security and justice.

The Schengen Agreement abolished checks at the internal borders of the signatory states, thereby creating a passport-free travel area and a single external border. Here in reality was what one British foreign secretary, Ernie Bevin, had once declared was the main aim of his foreign policy 'to go down to Victoria Station here, take a ticket and go where the hell I like without anybody pulling me up with a passport' (Bullock, 1983: 198), the restoration of a pre-1914 world in which people could move easily between different European states and before travel restrictions became common after the First World War. Bevin's aim, however, remains as unfulfilled today as it did in his day, for Britain is missing from the list of 'Schengen' states except for certain specific purposes such as the Schengen Information System (SIS) that allows the police across Europe to share data on law enforcement. The Council of the European Union agreed in 2000 that Britain could participate in the majority of the police and judicial co-operation elements of the Schengen Agreement, but this did not affect Britain's retention of border controls (HM Government, 'Review of the Balance of Competences between the United Kingdom and the European Union Police and Criminal Justice', December 2014).

Full membership of the Schengen system currently comprises 22 EU states and four non-EU states (Iceland, Norway, Liechtenstein and Switzerland). Six EU states are not part of the passport-free travel area (Bulgaria, Croatia, Cyprus, Ireland, Romania and the UK). In recent years the Schengen Agreement has been sorely tested by the mass influx of refugees from the Middle East into Europe and also by the impact of terrorist outrages in France in January and November 2015 (see Conclusion).

The key rules adopted within the Schengen Agreement included:

- a removal of checks on persons at the internal borders;
- a common set of rules applying to people crossing the external borders of the EU member states;
- harmonization of the conditions of entry and of the rule on visas for short stays;
- enhanced police co-operation (including rights of cross-border surveillance and hot pursuit);
- stronger judicial co-operation through a faster extradition system and transfer of enforcement of criminal judgements;
- establishment and development of the Schengen Information System.

All in all, Major secured considerable concessions in the making of the Maastricht Treaty. In that respect, the later criticisms of Maastricht by Eurosceptic Conservatives and UKIP are far removed from what was actually achieved by Major. Indeed, to represent the Maastricht Treaty as another Munich, as has been the case in such quarters, represents a glaring example of myth making and a gross distortion of events. It is also indicative of the extent to which the public debate in Britain about the EU is sometimes regarded as 10 to 15 years behind the times.

The making of the Lisbon Treaty and red lines

The Lisbon Treaty of 2007 emerged from the wreckage of a failed attempt to forge a European constitutional treaty in the period 2001–2004. This process had its origins in the European Council's decision (December 2001) to establish a European Convention under the chairmanship of the former French President Valéry Giscard d'Estaing. The Convention's most important achievement was the negotiation of a 'Draft Treaty Establishing a Constitution for Europe'. This item was submitted to the European Council (July 2003) and, after some negotiation, was finally endorsed by the governments of the member states (June 2004). Ratification of the treaty, however, required the unanimous consent of the member states, and in the event the treaty fell at this hurdle; it was decisively rejected in France (May 2005) and in the Netherlands (June 2005). According to one of the participants in the Convention, the Labour MP Gisela Stuart, not once in 16 months did representatives question 'whether deeper integration is what the people of Europe want' (Sampson, 2004: 362). In the aftermath of this rejection, a new scaled down treaty – the Treaty of Lisbon – was agreed (June 2007), signed by all EU states (December 2007) and entered into force in December 2009.

The Treaty of Lisbon dispensed with all the 'hate' words – 'constitution', 'flag', 'anthem' and 'laws' – that had aroused public opinion against the idea of a European constitutional treaty. While the new treaty was not called a constitution, it nevertheless inherited many features from the failed constitutional treaty. There was to be a strengthened role for the EP, a president of the European Council appointed for two-and-a-half years, a High Representative for the Union in Foreign Affairs and Security Policy, and the extension of QMV in the Council.

It fell to Blair's Labour government to plot a course through these proceedings between 2001 and 2007. In doing so, the government underwent a marked change of substance and tone in its handling of this venture. In the early stages of the Convention's deliberations, the British input was upbeat about the EU and reflected a positive, proactive attitude with clear priorities that met with success and were designed to make the EU more effective. This approach chimed in with Blair's pro-EU rhetoric at the time and also with his decision on coming to power in 1997 to reverse the Major government's opt-out from the Social Chapter, though even at this early stage Blair was reluctant to pursue an unambiguously pro-EU line (Smith, 2005: 703–21). Particular British proposals in the Convention included the creation of a permanent chair for the European Council. They also made provision for national parliaments to play a role in the oversight of subsidiarity (this concept had featured in the Maastricht Treaty and concerned the level of governance – EU, national, regional or local – at which action should be taken). The British proposals also provided for the strengthening of the European Commission (Menon, 2004a: 1).

By early 2003, this constructive phase in British policy was replaced by a more nega-tive stance. It seemed that policymakers were reverting to a default position so char-acteristic of British policy towards the EU, increasingly renowned for what they were against rather than for what they were for in EU matters. British negotiators now dem-onstrated a preference for blocking initiatives they opposed rather than for putting for-ward a proactive agenda of their own. By May 2003, Blair himself threatened to use his veto at the IGC on the proposed constitutional treaty if certain elements of the consti-tution were not dropped or amended, insisting in particular that if the word 'federal' and references to QMV on tax fraud and social security rights were not removed then he would wield the veto.

The expression of non-negotiable objectives or 'red lines' now became increasingly common. References to the need to strengthen the Commission vanished to be replaced by blanket criticisms of supranational institutions and fears about the development of a European superstate. In fact and paradoxically, the final draft of the constitutional treaty largely coincided with the preferences and priorities of the British representa-tives (Menon, 2004a: 1). True, the extensions of QMV could be construed as a move in the federalist direction, but the fact of the matter was in the most sensitive areas of QMV – justice and home affairs and social security – Britain obtained the right either not to participate or to insist on unanimity. Besides which, a number of other QMV measures relating to the euro area did not apply to Britain. This outcome, however, counted for little compared with the rising tide of domestic political opposition to the constitutional treaty that ultimately shaped government policy (see Chapter 7). The Blair government was fearful of further inflaming Eurosceptic opinion in the country and of antagonizing the Eurosceptic media.

At the European Council meeting (June 2007) to thrash out the details of the Treaty of Lisbon, Blair stressed the four red lines that would underpin the British approach to the negotiations. Britain would not accept a treaty that allowed the Charter of Fundamental Rights to change British law in any way, would not agree to something that displaced the role of British foreign policy and foreign secretary, would not agree to give up the British ability to control its common law and judicial and police system, and finally would not agree to any moves towards QMV in respect of tax and benefit mat-ters. For the most part these were comparable to the red lines set out in a White Paper by the Brown government in 2007, differing only in specifying one such red line as being protection of Britain's existing social and labour legislation. Such episodes seemed to illustrate the observation of Shirley Williams, co-founder of the Social Democratic Party, that 'Perhaps Whitehall keeps tests and conditions on its mantelpiece, as cooks keep jelly moulds, there to be used for any purpose' (Williams, 2003: xi).

In the event, British concerns about such matters were dealt with satisfactorily, espe-cially with regard to dropping symbols of EU statehood such as the anthem and the flag. The Lisbon Treaty did make the Charter of Fundamental Rights legally binding on the EU and came into force at the same time as the treaty (December 2009). The Charter brought together in a single document the fundamental rights protected in the EU under six titles.

This action, however, was accompanied by some considerable and lengthy confu-sion in British circles about whether or not the Charter came with an opt-out clause or Protocol (30). According to one official report, contradictory statements by the Brown government were followed by the Coalition government's failure to explain the effect of the Charter. Eventually, however, some clarification came from the latter with the indication that there was no opt-out Protocol (House of Commons European Scrutiny Committee, Session 2013–14). The matter, however, remained a bone of contention. A promise to reform the Charter appeared in the Conservative Party election manifesto of 2015, and subsequently featured in Cameron's renegotiation of the terms of EU membership brief with its commitment to enshrine in domestic law that the EU Charter of Fundamental Rights did not create any new rights.

In many respects, the Blair government ended up with the worst of both worlds. It not only played down its own achievement in negotiating a text which suited it relatively well but also helped to reinforce the negative stereotypes about the EU that had been its stated intention to challenge (Menon, 2004a: 49). The Treaty of Lisbon significantly rowed back from the federalist impulses underlying the Maastricht Treaty and reflected a more intergovernmental emphasis. It simply did not correspond to the federalist phobias that were being successfully fanned by the Eurosceptic British press and the Conservative opposition.

This domestic audience, however, increasingly determined how any EU measure by government was to be received. According to some reports, it was very much in keeping with trying to distance himself from a treaty that largely accorded with the original British negotiating objectives that Gordon Brown as prime minister tried to sign the Treaty of Lisbon (December 2007) without drawing attention to the event.

Whitehall perspectives and procedures

The often tortuous course of British policy and diplomacy in the EU arena is typified and partly explained by the way in which most governments since 1973, especially on coming to power, have offered strong professions of support for the EC/EU and for a major British role in the organization. There were certain exceptions in this respect, most notably the Brown government of 2007–2010 and the Coalition government of 2010–2015, the latter comprising two parties so much at odds over the subject that government policy towards the EU approached a condition of stasis at times. However, the resolve of those governments employing an initially positive declaratory stance subsequently weakened and they beat a retreat to a more sceptical view of the matter by the end of their period in office.

In the case of the Blair governments of 1997–2007, the Eurosceptic *Daily Telegraph* commented 'It happens, sooner or later, to all British prime ministers. They begin with hopeful talk about putting Britain at the heart of Europe. They end up isolated' (*The Daily Telegraph*, 19 June 2005). Other far less Eurosceptic sources were equally convinced that this was the case in Blair's EU journey and indeed at an earlier stage. According to Chris Patten, the Conservative politician and former member of the EU Commission, it appeared that as early as 1999 Blair was going through the stage common to all British prime ministers, starting with every intention of making progress on Europe but 'then getting turned off … and thoroughly pissed off' (Trewin, 2008: 602). In that respect, Blair mirrored Thatcher's own journey from initial, limited enthusiasm in her case to cynical disillusionment about 'the drudging routine of EU summits and interminable negotiations for seemingly nothing in the way of EU reform that could be sold to a skeptical British audience' (Daddow, 2013: 223).

Part of the reason for the persistent tendency of governments to retreat from their initial resolve lies in the often finely balanced calculations surrounding the cost of exclusion from and the price of inclusion in the EC/EU. As often as not, the national

debate over EC/EU membership has focused on a preoccupation with the largely measurable price of membership rather than with the more speculative political cost of
staying out of the EC before 1973 or out of particular EU projects such as the euro
area. This much is evident in the long-standing, marked differences between Whitehall
departments about the nature and extent of involvement in the process of European
integration.

The contrast between the Foreign Office (FCO – Foreign and Commonwealth
Office since 1968) and the Treasury, for long the two key departments in the making of
European policy, is a case in point. Both departments were broadly in agreement about
European policy until the first application for EC membership. They disagreed only
over tactical responses to the emergence of the EC. Since 1960, however, the FCO posi-
tion has undergone a greater degree of change than that of the Treasury.

During the 1960s the FCO convinced itself that there was no alternative to EC
membership. It has subsequently highlighted the political advantages of involvement
in the formation, if not full membership, of any new EC/EU project. David Owen,
Foreign Secretary (1977–1979), later claimed that the Foreign Office was dominated
by Europeanists who considered Britain's EC relationship as their first priority (Owen,
1991: 245). Certainly, the emphases of individual foreign secretaries, among other
things, have influenced the extent to which EC/EU membership has received a high
profile, more obviously so during the foreign secretaryship of George Brown, Geoffrey
Howe, Douglas Hurd and Robin Cook than in the case of Selwyn Lloyd, David Owen,
Jack Straw and Philip Hammond. During the period 2010–2014 under the foreign secretaryship of William Hague, who proved less Eurosceptic in office than in opposition,
the FCO enhanced its position on the Whitehall EU stage. Following the decision of
the Cameron government in July 2012 to undertake a two-year review of the Balance
of Competences between Britain and the EU, as noted above, the Foreign Office was
assigned the task of supervising the review and thus of influencing the outcome (see
Chapter 12).

By way of contrast, the Treasury has consistently adopted a cautious, sceptical stance
ever since the first attempt to secure EC membership. On occasions, in fact, it has proved
particularly unhelpful to chancellors wishing to contribute to the debate about British
membership of the EC. When Roy Jenkins, Chancellor of the Exchequer (1967–1970)
wanted to deliver a speech about the benefits of EC membership, he was informed that
the Treasury did not have a single civil servant capable of drafting a text; at the time, it
was still a matter of common observation that there were more classical scholars in the
Treasury than economists. Then, too, as one Treasury official commented in 1992 on
the eve of the pound's exit from the ERM and when the Treasury needed foreign, and
especially German, assistance: 'We were never much good with foreigners' (Stephens,
1996: 233).

Arguably the Treasury has figured as one of the most Eurosceptic departments in
Whitehall from an early stage. In the late 1940s it intransigently opposed the idea of
participating in a west European customs union and thus overruled some Foreign Office
opinion in favour of British involvement. In the early 1970s at the time of the Heath
application for EC membership, it warned that EC plans for an economic and monetary union could lead to a European federal state and that Britain could be left with
less control over its own affairs than the individual states in the United States. Prior to
becoming prime minister, Harold Wilson once said that 'Whichever party's in office, the
Treasury's in power'.

Unsurprisingly, therefore, the Treasury played an influential role in determining the decision in 1978 to keep the pound out of the Exchange Rate Mechanism (ERM) of the European Monetary System – EMS (see Chapter 9). The Treasury official, Kenneth Couzens, appointed to the small EC committee to consider the plan for an EMS was sceptical from the outset; his first evaluation for Prime Minister Callaghan contained eight 'cons' and two 'pros' (Franklin, 2013: 761). More importantly, the heavyweight chancellor of the time, Denis Healey, opposed the idea of entering the ERM.

Several considerations have influenced this Treasury position, besides its short-termist perspective and ready use of any economic arguments to oppose further involvement in the process of European integration. Concern about the impact of EC/EU membership on Britain's interests beyond Europe has loomed large. The cost of membership has also figured as a key consideration whether in relation to the country's general economic performance or with reference to particular difficulties such as the British contribution to the EC/EU budget. The Treasury emphasized the heavy costs rather than the potential benefits of joining the EC at the time of the Heath application. It argued against acceptance of the Fontainebleau budget rebate deal in 1984, wishing to hold out for a better offer.

The tumultuous events of 'Black Wednesday' in September 1992 had a devastating effect on Treasury morale and the pound's exit from the ERM greatly reinforced the Treasury's underlying scepticism and hardened its opinion against any similar experiment in future. True, the ERM was largely viewed as an anti-inflationary device and not as a staging post towards plunging the pound into full economic and monetary union. Exiting from the ERM was perceived at the time as a complete and unmitigated disaster; departmental papers released in February 2005 under the Freedom of Information Act clearly indicate that Treasury officials were appalled at the extent to which the decision to enter the ERM in 1990 had been affected by political factors, especially by tensions between Thatcher and Lawson. The Treasury's scepticism was reinforced under the Labour governments of 1997–2010, while the euro area's woes since 2007 have ruled out indefinitely any suggestion of joining the euro area. In fact, the Treasury's ultra-cautious approach to joining the euro during Gordon Brown's period of office as Chancellor of the Exchequer (1997–2007) played an influential role in maintaining Britain's exclusion from the euro area, especially in designing the five tests that had to be satisfied before entry to the euro area (see Chapter 10).

Such divisions as these at the heart of government have often underlined the lack of agreed strategy or vision about the longer-term direction and management of change within the EC/EU context. This feature has sometimes hobbled ministers from making the case for a particular policy such as entering the euro area. It has also lent weight to the view that the absence of a single overarching concept, design or 'Idea of Britain' to inform more detailed objectives and diplomatic activity has prevented clear and credible policies on Britain's role in Europe and has also avoided the need for hard choices (Coles, 2000: 43–7).

The appearance of division and confusion in policymaking is related to another persistent and striking feature of British involvement in the EC/EU: the perception of European integration as a two-edged sword holding out both a threat and an opportunity. At a very general level, the anti-marketeers of yesteryear and their Eurosceptic successors have focused on the threat posed to national sovereignty and independence. Meanwhile, pro-marketeer or Europhile opinion has viewed membership as an opportunity to undertake a much-needed process of modernization. For much of the period since 1997 and especially since the financial crisis of 2007–2008 and the onset of economic recession, however, the sense of threat has increasingly overshadowed the idea of opportunity. Thus, as one well-informed commentator has put it, even in Whitehall it is quite hard to find any real sense that Europe is an opportunity rather than a threat (Stephens, 2005). Furthermore, according to one insider's account, there is also an instinctive dislike of EU legislation across Whitehall departments, where the common response to a proposed piece of EU legislation is 'No unless' as compared with the 'yes if' response of most of the other EU states (Wall, 2008: 200). British negotiators in Brussels, according to one senior civil servant, are rarely required to make a positive case, and their single most frequent question passed to their colleagues in London is 'can we live with this?' not 'do we like it?' or 'is it any good?' (Charter, 2012: 12).

British officialdom in Brussels

Some of the problems in representing Britain in the EC/EU policymaking milieu are evident in the testimony of senior officials permanently stationed in Brussels. There is a marked contrast between the routine conduct of business in Brussels by British officials and the deeply adversarial nature of the British political system. In particular, there is a difference of perspective between senior British officials, who are permanently or regularly involved in EC/EU matters via the UK Permanent Representation to the EU (UKRep), and government ministers who are on day trips to Brussels and who are concerned with the management of the media as well as the substance of official proceedings.

The UKRep negotiates and lobbies in the EU on behalf of the British government while government departments consult UKRep on the conduct of EU business and EU developments. In short, the UKRep is the crucial link between the British government and the EU institutions, acting as the eyes, ears and communicator of the government. It advances national aims and interests in EU negotiations in the Council, and also seeks to exert influence in the Commission and the EP.

Evidence from this source and also from the wider contribution of British civil service culture at large throws light on several aspects of the British handling of EU policymaking. A study of some eight senior officials that have headed UKRep since 1973 concluded that the signals given by London in its EU policies have ranged from the confused to the downright hostile. Furthermore, successive British governments faced such venomous criticism at home in their dealings with EU matters that this increasingly tended to leave the country looking at worst isolated and out of step with other EU states (Menon, 2004b: 45). In such circumstances, governments have pursued a different political agenda from other member states, resulting in minimal influence except negatively through securing opt-outs or advocating à la carte integration. These conditions have also meant that the government was reluctant to take pride in Britain's contribution to the EU, causing José Manuel Barroso, President of the European Commission (2010–2014) to comment: 'You will never persuade people to support an organization which you pretend does not exist' (http://europa.eu/rapid/pressReleasesAction).

The handling of EU business as between Whitehall and Westminster and as between the executive and the legislature presents a number of contrasting conditions and elements of continuity. At the highest political level several long-standing distinctive features in the field of handling EU business stand out, most notably the absence of a highly centralized approach, a high degree of coordination between departments capable of effectively processing day-to-day EU business, and the increasing importance of the Prime Minister's Office since the establishment of the European Council in 1975.

Meanwhile, some of the well-chronicled weaknesses of the British approach to handling EU business include a tendency to conform to the Whitehall norms of policymaking at the cost of flexible and effective bargaining in the different policymaking environment of the EU itself. In addition, there are recognized weaknesses in terms of the long-term strategic planning and issues of European policy and the predominance of 'Whitehall logic' (Miller, 'How the UK Government deals with EU Business', House of Commons Library, May 2012). Furthermore, it was not until Blair announced a 'step change' in Britain's relations with the EU that it became a requirement that ministers, MPs and civil servants should step up bilateral contacts with their opposite numbers in other EU states. This move recognized that one of the weaknesses of the British political system was the difficulty of persuading British politicians to network across the EU (Liddle, 2014: 99).

Significantly, it remains the case that there is no Cabinet minister responsible for EU affairs. There is a minister of state for Europe within the Foreign Office whose brief includes the EU and much else besides in the European arena. The current holder of this office (at the time of writing), David Lidington, has held this post since 2010, an unusually lengthy period of time as compared with some nine holders of this appointment in the period of the Blair governments of 1997–2007. In some respects, this rapid turnover is indicative of the extent to which the EU and Brussels are viewed less and less as useful staging posts or preferments for high flying politicians and officials. David Hannay, a former British ambassador to the EC, maintains that the British political class are not well-suited by professional experience for senior appointment in the EU, often lacking serious knowledge of a language other than their own, possessing limited inclination to acquire the necessary international skills, and fearful that a Brussels appointment means no way back into British politics (Hannay, 2013: 142).

There is a marked contrast between earlier British appointments to the EU of known, top level political figures such as Roy Jenkins (President of the European Commission 1977–1981) and Chris Patten (one of the British appointments to the Commission 1999–2004) and more recent, largely anonymous personnel such as Catherine Ashton and Jonathan Hill. Ashton's appointment to the grandiosely entitled post of High Representative of the Union for Foreign Affairs and Security occurred under the Brown government when the front runners, Peter Mandelson and Geoff Hoon (Defence Secretary) – who were put up to the EU by Brown for this appointment – were ruled out; Brown later quipped: 'There was no real support for Geoff because no one knew him; there was even less support for Peter, and they all knew him' (Seldon and Lodge, 2010: 349). Jonathan Hill, the Cameron government's candidate for the Commission in 2014, was so unknown that the President of the Commission, Jean-Claude Juncker, reportedly had to Google his name to find out who he was (*The Guardian*, 11 September 2014).

British personnel and EU institutions

It is also the case that relatively few Britons are to be found in the ranks of the EU bureaucracy. In relation to its 12.5 per cent share of the EU's population, Britain remains significantly under-represented among the staff of the major EU institutions (Foreign Affairs Commons Select Committee, 1 July 2013, www.parliament.uk/business/committee).

In 2013, Britain accounted for just 4.6 per cent of the 24,000 permanent officials of the European Commission as compared with France (9.7 per cent), Germany (8.4 per cent) and Poland (4.9 per cent) which did not join the EU until 2004. In fact, the number of British nationals on the staff of the European Commission has fallen by 24 per cent in seven years. Much the same trend is evident in the other major EU institutions. Since 2010, the British share of policy staff has fallen from 4.8 per cent to 4.3 per cent in the bureaucracy of the Council of the EU, and from 6.2 per cent to 5.8 per cent in the European Parliament.

According to a statement in October 2014 by Barroso, the outgoing president of the European Commission, the number of British officials in EU institutions was less than half of what it should be and falling quickly (www.euractiv.com/content/barroso-speech-chatham-house).

Unsurprisingly, there is a marked decline in British influence as a generation of officials that went to Brussels after Britain joined the EC in 1973 retire and are not replaced; British EU mandarins, once hailed as the 'Rolls-Royces' of European officialdom, are now becoming extinct. The numbers of British nationals moving up in the EU institutions remain too small to compensate, so much so that Foreign Secretary Hague identified what he called a 'generation gap' in the British presence, especially in the European Commission. Cameron as prime minister reportedly demonstrated an apparent failure to attach much importance to filling influential administrative positions in the EU machine with individuals sympathetic to his agenda, focusing instead on headline-grabbing political posts (Ashcroft and Oakeshott, 2015: 503). Some EU states like France and Germany insist that the Commission should annually send them a detailed breakdown of staff to monitor their nationals' progress. Britain does not do so.

It is also a measure of the EU's expansion that Britain's formal representation in the EU's institutions has substantially decreased over the years. According to evidence presented to a government review, since joining the EC in 1973 Britain's voting power in the Council of Ministers has decreased from 17 per cent to 8 per cent, in the European Parliament it has decreased from 20 per cent to 9.5 per cent [of seats], and in the European Commission it has decreased from 15 per cent to 4 per cent (see Chapter 5 for the role and influence of British political parties in the European Parliament). Such changes are not of course confined to Britain, but they do mean that 'Britain's ability to block bad European laws has diminished' as more countries have joined the EU. During the past 15 years, moreover, the number of contested votes in the Council of Ministers involving Britain has increased, and Britain has figured as the member state that overall has voted against the majority most often (HM Government, 'Review of the Balance of Competences between the European Union and the European Union EU Enlargement', December 2014: 64).

At the lowest end of the supply chain of British personnel to the EU bureaucracy, it is evident that British graduates for any number of reasons – poor language skills, the toughness of the competition, the unpopularity of the EU project at home, and uncertainty about Britain's EU membership – do not view EU-related employment as an attractive career. Significantly, the entry points for EU posts are not thickly peopled by British graduates. In 2011, the College of Europe – arguably the best preparatory institution for EU-related careers – had only 13 UK-based students out of a total of 438, far outnumbered by other EU states such as Italy (57), France (49), Poland (33), and even by Ukraine (14) that is not a member of the EU.

Furthermore, Britons have proved fewer in number and less able than the nationals of other EU states in tackling the Concours, the notoriously difficult entrance tests to work in all EU institutions. The examination is taken in an applicant's second language. This requirement has proved such an obstacle that the British government requested that the examination could be taken in English. However, this was one opt-out that Britain failed to win on the grounds that such a measure would be illegal. In 2012, 1,066 Britons took the Concours and only five passed, as compared with 24 passes out of 2,891 German candidates and 17 passes out of 2,866 French candidates. Given these conditions and the poor image of the EU, therefore, few Britons are actually confronted by the situation as described by one former British senior EU official: 'It might be comfortable to have an EU job in Brussels, but it can be distinctly uncomfortable to say what you do in, say, a Doncaster pub on Friday evening' (*The Times*, 24 November 2013).

Conclusion

This chapter has considered the evolution of British government policy towards the EU. It has reviewed some of the long-standing priorities, strategic preferences and tactics of government engagement with EU politics, including: strong support for co-operation, a pronounced antipathy towards the idea of a federal Europe, the prioritizing of EU enlargement over further integration, the deep suspicion of any European rhetoric suggesting an irreversible journey to an unknown destination or towards 'ever closer union', and the protection of British interests by opt-out arrangements.

We have noted some of the particular determinants of policy, ranging from longer-term differences of perspective in Whitehall departments to the more recent moves towards holding a referendum on EU membership. We have also considered both the reactive and proactive features of British policymaking, and identified a variety of episodes illustrative of the substance and style of government handling of EU matters from the 'high' politics of treaty making to more mundane business. All in all, the balance sheet suggests a mixed record of encouraging advances in some fields while stoutly resisting integration measures in other areas.

The various twists and turns in government policy, however, can only be fully appreciated and understood in the context of the country's political culture and history. The next chapter therefore deals with the EU issue as a persistent source of conflict in the field of inter- and intra-party divisions and as an integral part of the personal, party, ideological and other aspects of British politics.

5 Party games and politics

In politics you must always keep running with the pack. The moment that you falter and they sense that you are injured, the rest will be on you like wolves.

(Rab Butler, Conservative Cabinet minister, 1941–1945 and 1951–1964)

Introduction

At the start of the successful set of negotiations to secure British membership of the EC, Geoffrey Rippon, the Conservative government minister at the head of the British delegation in Brussels, was presented with a *fait accompli* by the EC states in the form of a Common Fisheries Policy (CFP). This unexpected presentation came as a complete shock to the British delegation. Rippon, however, did not immediately ask the EC states for further details, nor did he consult Heath or the Foreign Office about how best to respond. Instead, he promptly consulted a large map of Britain and traced its coastline from one Conservative parliamentary seat to another. His principal concern was to work out how many Conservative MPs might be at risk if Britain adopted such a policy.

This minor episode is illustrative of the main theme of this chapter which focuses on EU membership in the context of British political culture and domestic politics. Chapters 2 and 3 examined some of the changing attitudes of the major political parties towards the EC/EU that occurred as a result of either developments within the EC/EU or shifting perceptions of the EU. This chapter deals with European integration as a persistent source of conflict in the field of intra- and inter-party divisions and competition, and also in terms of personal, party, ideological and other aspects of British politics. The treatment of the subject is necessarily highly selective in its identification of particular aspects and its use of examples to illustrate what can be viewed as characteristic features under this heading.

The analysis especially singles out features that cannot be overlooked in any survey of the meanings and understandings of the EU in British domestic politics. This section also considers some of the latent functions served by EU membership in the subterranean currents and trends of British political life. These have had little or nothing to do with the particular issue and more to do with a wide variety of strategic and tactical considerations on the part of parties and individuals. In the process the EU has been portrayed in a wide variety of contradictory images serving diverse, ulterior purposes.

Leaders and rivals

We start at the top of the political tree. Personal rivalry and conflict in the upper echelons of government have figured as endemic, if immeasurable, features of the country's relationship with the process of European integration. It is fair to say that in their handling of the question of EC/EU membership, British prime ministers have constantly aimed to ensure that the issue has not undermined either their own authority or their ability to overcome deep party divisions. In particular, they have sought to counter or neutralize any move by senior ministerial colleagues to advance their leadership ambitions by exploiting opposing views on the issue.

This pattern of behaviour was evident from the 1950s onwards. In the first instance, relations between Macmillan and Butler always remained strained following the outcome of their contest for the premiership in 1957. They were further worsened by differences of opinion over European issues and especially over how to react to the emergence of the EC. Macmillan's first response in the form of the Free Trade Area proposal (see Chapter 2) met with some scepticism on Butler's part who sardonically enquired as to whether the EC states would be 'all eager to receive us on our terms' (NA., FO 371/ 122033).

Butler's backing for Macmillan's EC application was uncertain throughout the early part of the negotiations concerning the first application for EC membership. He was the most senior minister sceptical about membership and all the more so as he belonged to the strongly imperial and protectionist wing of the Conservative Party. He also feared possible damage to his own position in an agricultural constituency: 'My seat is fundamentally at stake' (Howard, 1987: 295–6). Until Butler at last fully committed himself to the EC application as late as August 1962, Macmillan was left uneasy by reports in the Beaverbrook press that he was poised to lead a revolt against him in defence of British agriculture and the Commonwealth. Throughout this period, Macmillan was much preoccupied with the danger of splitting his party over agriculture. The disturbing historical precedent he had in mind was that of 1846 when Robert Peel's repeal of the Corn Laws had caused a deep schism in the Conservative Party.

Harold Wilson as Labour Party leader, particularly during the period 1970–1974 in Opposition, was equally concerned to ensure that none of his leadership rivals used the EC issue to advance their claims. He was obsessed by this danger and was renowned for his anxiety about plots and conspiracies against his leadership. He viewed Jim Callaghan and Roy Jenkins as the two ministers from whom he had most to fear. Callaghan was rightly regarded as the more serious potential threat because of the wide support that he enjoyed throughout the Labour movement; he lurked like a pike in the shadows in the words of Jenkins who effectively scuppered his own ambitions to lead the party by resigning from the deputy leadership of the party (April 1972) following the Shadow Cabinet's decision to support the idea of a referendum on EC membership. Jenkins was highly critical of Wilson's handling of the issue, though shortly before his death in 2003 he wrote a positive reassessment of Wilson, praising the wily tactician's success in 'keeping the train on the track through rough terrain' (*The Guardian*, 4 January 2013). At this later vantage point there was no doubt a greater degree of sympathy for Wilson's complaint at the time that he had been 'wading in shit for three months to allow others to indulge their conscience' on the question of EC membership (Healey, 1990: 360).

More importantly, Wilson countered the Callaghan threat in several ways. Most notably, he employed his own brand of anti-EC rhetoric in grandstanding fashion. He also 'shadowed' his main rival's tortuous policy shifts over the EC. He thereby denied Callaghan any tactical advantage in his handling of EC membership and in his penchant for expressing truculent insularity.

On returning to power in 1974, moreover, Wilson was in a stronger position than he had been in managing the issue while out of office. He made Callaghan foreign secretary and put him in charge of the EC renegotiations prior to the referendum of 1975 in what Roy Jenkins grandly termed 'the European education of Mr Callaghan'. Wilson thus tied his foreign secretary to the course and outcome of the renegotiating exercise.

The major threats with a European dimension to Thatcher's premiership witnessed a rather different form of animosity. It was Geoffrey Howe's resignation speech, particularly focusing on the failings of Thatcher's attitude towards the EC, that precipitated a set of events eventually leading to her resignation. One of Thatcher's closest associates, Charles Powell, her private secretary, claimed that Thatcher was suspicious of Howe's ambitions and saw him trying to build up a rival power base (BDOHP, 18 July 2000). Nevertheless, it was the pro-EC Michael Heseltine, who had challenged Thatcher during the Westland affair (1986) when she could have been forced out of office, who emerged as a leading contender to succeed her in 1990. The fact that he and other Cabinet ministers were critical of her isolationist position towards the EC, gave rise to the view in some Conservative circles that she had been betrayed by a pro-EU cabal of ministers including, besides Heseltine, such Cabinet figures as Ken Clarke, Geoffrey Howe, Douglas Hurd and John Major. The episode had far reaching consequences for Conservative Party divisions over the EU. Most immediately, it meant that the EU policy of the Major governments (1990–1997), especially over the Maastricht Treaty, was all the more savagely attacked on this account (see below).

Another example of how EU matters entered into rivalry between political leaders occurred in the period 1997–2007. In short, British policy towards the EC/EU was one aspect of the highly personal conflict between Tony Blair and Gordon Brown. Blair feared that Brown could be in a strong position if he split from himself over Europe and in particular over the question of British entry into the euro area (see especially Chapter 10). There were no major, ideological differences between the pair; their disagreements over the EU largely obscured the extent to which their rivalry was about personal power and advantage.

A far less antagonistic relationship was obtained between Cameron and Chancellor of the Exchequer Osborne. Nevertheless and significantly, Cameron ensured that Osborne was tied to a 'successful' renegotiation by making him formally responsible for the outcome along with himself. This arrangement also had the advantage of ensuring that supporters of Osborne, who saw him as the heir apparent to Cameron and who had no fixed views about EU membership or at least fell short of being confirmed opponents of EU membership, would support the government position during the referendum campaign.

A further common aspect of premierships over the past 60 years has concerned the extent to which political leaders have experienced the unanticipated turn of events presented by EU developments. Neither Macmillan nor Wilson expected to be filing applications for EC membership within less than three years of their electoral victories in 1959 and 1964 respectively, nor did their party manifestos even hint at such a possibility.

Edward Heath was subjected to a minor, unexpected incident that delayed by an hour the signing of Britain's treaty of accession to the EC on 22 January 1972 in Brussels. A young German woman hurled a bottle of ink at his head and shoulders. She was not protesting about Britain joining the EC but about the redevelopment of Covent Garden. This unfortunate start to the country's EC membership was scarcely improved by much of the British press a day later when it gave more coverage to the ink throwing than to the signing.

More significantly, Thatcher supported the Single European Act (SEA) of 1986, but soon recoiled in horror at the economic and monetary implications of the Act. Her successor, John Major, shepherded sterling into the Exchange Rate Mechanism (ERM) in 1990, only to be faced by its unceremonious exit from the ERM two years later. A similar, unanticipated turn of events in the Blair premiership occurred when Blair decided to hold a referendum on the proposed EU Constitutional Treaty, having strenuously argued against such a proposal and only a few months earlier boasted that he had no reverse gear. Shortly before the general election of May 2010, David Cameron declared that 'I don't want Europe to define my premiership' (Seldon and Snowdon, 2015: 165). He came to power with no strong vision for or of the EU. There was no hint of renegotiating Britain's terms of EU membership and of holding a referendum on the outcome: the landmark, strategic events of his premiership.

The issue of EU membership has also surprised or ambushed political leaders who have had no formal powers in the matter. Alex Salmond, Scotland's First Minister (2007–2014), caused a public row (or stooshie to use the local expression) when he made the contested claim in October 2012 that he had sought legal advice on the position of an independent Scotland in the EU. This incident was one of the opening shots in the lengthy campaign preceding the referendum on an independent Scotland (September 2014).

There is another curiously common aspect to most premierships which is to say that prime ministers have invariably made key speeches on EU membership to foreign rather than British audiences. In doing so, they have sometimes left the impression of viewing EU membership as a matter of judgement for the political elite and of involving the management of public ignorance and expectations. Macmillan set the trend in addressing a foreign audience as one of his more expansive speeches on EC membership was at the Massachusetts Institute of Technology (April 1961), the venue of a similar speech some 50 years later by Gordon Brown. In the intervening period, Heath's Godkin lectures delivered at Harvard (March 1968) represented his most extensive study of foreign affairs including Europe. The College of Europe in Bruges was the scene of Thatcher's well-known speech on Britain and Europe. Blair used several foreign platforms like the French National Assembly (February 1998), Ghent (February 2000) and the Polish Stock Exchange (October 2000) to expound his views on the subject. Cameron broke with this 'tradition' by giving his two major speeches in London: Bloomberg (January 2013) and Chatham House (November 2015)

Don't mention Europe

It is also fair to say that for a variety of reasons the mainstream political parties have sought to avoid public debates about EU membership. Only rarely has this proved otherwise. The general election campaign of 2001 was an exception when William Hague, Conservative Party leader, ran a campaign against entry to the euro area and to save the pound, but failed to mobilize voters in doing so. This emphasis was in marked contrast to the Conservative election manifesto of 1970 in which Heath made very little of what was to prove his most important single achievement of securing British membership of the EC.

Otherwise, there has been an unmistakable conspiracy of silence on EU matters on the part of the major parties. They appear to perceive EU membership as a 'shield' rather than a 'sword' issue: 'one on which they might have to defend their position, but not one on which they would rationally opt to take a lead' (Smith, 2012: 1286). Even the Liberal Democrats, long regarded as dogged supporters of EU membership, have in recent years become more divided in their views and more reticent to take the lead by speaking out about the subject. On several occasions, opponents of EC/EU membership have complained about the tactics of successive governments in this regard. They have particularly singled out the ways in which governments have manufactured and deployed a predictable cycle of complaints, criticisms and ultimatums. Governments have also done so with synthetic, stage-managed, nailbiting rows to spin the appearance that they were fighting for something substantial, the renegotiations of 1975 and 2015/2016 being two cases in point according to this school of criticism.

Few prime ministers have taken on and followed through a large-scale and systematic attempt to win the argument on Europe. Heath and Wilson did so for specific purposes, the former to secure EC membership and the latter to maintain membership but doing so with a low-key role that reflected, among other things, his difficulties over divisions in the Labour Party. It has often remained the case that the delivery of a speech strongly defending EU membership was a task best left to a junior minister 'on the occasional wet night in Dudley' (Stephens, 2005). Few political leaders have had the confidence, boldness and power to challenge assumptions and myths about the EU.

The question of British membership of the EC/EU has been most keenly, constantly and divisively debated within individual political parties as much as if not more than in electoral competition between the parties. It is therefore useful to consider this dimension in the first instance.

Intra-party conflicts

A principal preoccupation of political leaders in this field has concerned the management of internal party splits. Treatment of the EC/EU as a temporary no-go area in British politics has often reflected the importance of concealing party divisions for electoral considerations. In some respects, the effort conjures up the picture of spending a vast amount of time trying to keep people in the boat and never actually rowing it anywhere. The complex management of intra-party conflicts over EC/ EU membership is evident in the ways in which both major political parties – Labour under Wilson in the period 1970–1975 and the Conservatives under Cameron in the period 2010–2015 – decided to determine the future of Britain's membership of the EC/EU by resorting to a referendum on the subject.

The origins, course and outcome of the referendum of 1975 on British membership of the EC reflected deep-seated divisions within the Labour Party between pro- and anti-marketeers. The idea of a referendum had slowly emerged as a mechanism for overcoming such divisions. When Tony Benn first raised the suggestion in late 1970, it aroused little interest among his colleagues. He had done so at the time as a pro-marketeer, but shortly afterwards he emerged as an anti-marketeer, making the transition from the thrusting young technocrat of Wilson's Cabinet in the 1960s to a socialist firebrand in the 1970s.

Wilson, for his part, was lukewarm towards the idea of a referendum. It was only gradually, as Labour's internecine quarrels over EC membership intensified, that he began to appreciate its potential usefulness as a device for preventing the party, including the Cabinet, from tearing itself asunder. The referendum would be a 'life raft', as Jim Callaghan put it, aboard which the warring factions could clamber. By this means, Wilson not only held together the pro- and anti-marketeer factions in the party but also strengthened his own leadership that was indissolubly linked to his handling of the question. With the benefit of hindsight, however, it can be seen that Wilson's success was only partial and short-term. The referendum put an end neither to discord between Labour's pro- and anti-marketeers nor to the corrosive national debate over EC membership.

Cameron and the Conservative Party pursued a similar tortuous course to Wilson's Labour Party in alighting upon the idea of renegotiating the terms of British membership of the EU and holding a referendum on the outcome. Cameron did so for much the same reasons as Wilson, most notably with a view to fending off threats to his leadership and to pursuing a course of action that temporarily at least held the Conservative Party together, and avoided the worst effects of division and fragmentation.

Neither renegotiation nor referendum had figured in the Conservative election manifesto of 2010. Cameron initially opposed the idea of a referendum, mindful of the fact that, as his critics often pointed out, he had made a 'cast iron' pledge while in opposition to hold a referendum on the EU Lisbon Treaty of 2007. He had failed to fulfil this pledge on coming to power in 2010. He continued to resist the idea at the head of the Coalition government in 2010. However, his position radically changed in the face of the rising tide of Eurosceptic opinion in the Conservative parliamentary party and what was perceived as the growing threat of UKIP (see below). One of the signal events in this respect occurred in October 2011 when 81 Conservative backbenchers defied party orders on a three-line whip and supported the idea of a referendum on EU membership. This was the biggest post-war rebellion on Europe and larger even than the 41 Conservative MPs who had defied Major over the Maastricht Treaty in 1993.

The beginnings of a prolonged period of appeasing this body of opinion in the parliamentary party was registered in Cameron's Bloomberg speech (January 2013) with the pledge to hold a referendum on EU membership by the end of 2017 following a renegotiation of the country's relationship with the EU (see Chapter 12). That move was followed up by various efforts to paper over deep divisions within the party including an unsuccessful attempt (July 2013) supported by Cameron to bind the next parliament to hold a referendum on EU membership, regardless of the long-standing requirement that no parliament can bind its successor.

Following the general election of May 2015 and the return to power of a Conservative government, there were further concessions as Cameron followed in Wilson's footsteps, notably declaring (January 2016) that members of his government, including Cabinet ministers, would be allowed to speak out against the official line during the referendum campaign. The referendum pledge during the Cameron Coalition government was dictated entirely by the politics of the Conservative Party and was opposed by the other political parties, except UKIP. Nevertheless, every effort was made to accuse the opposition of denying the electorate its democratic rights, this being but one case of how the referendum could be used as a tactical device by government (see below).

Inter-party competition

The absence of any long-term national consensus concerning the value and purposes of European integration has figured as a more or less permanent feature of the British political landscape for 50 years. Competition between the major parties and the changing balance of forces within these parties have invariably put at risk any axiomatic assumptions about the issue.

Party opinion about the EC/EU has rarely, if at all, conformed to the larger Left/Right division in British politics. As often as not the left wing of the Labour Party has shared similar positions to the right wing of the Conservative Party on EC/EU membership, though for markedly different ideological and other reasons. Thus, a young Jeremy Corbyn in the referendum of 1975 voted like Enoch Powell to withdraw from the EC, the one perceiving the EC as a capitalist organization with scant regard for workers and welfare systems and the other emphasizing that the EC was a major threat to national sovereignty. In a later existence as leader of the Labour Party, the former muted his hostility to EU membership for fear of the threat of open civil war in his party to his detriment. The latter left a lasting legacy as a prophet for a later generation of Eurosceptic Conservatives.

A broad consensus between the Conservative and Labour parties existed only in the period 1945–1960 when British aloofness from the origins of the EC commanded widespread support. Since then, however, EC/EU membership has proved a major political battleground between the parties, except for occasional periods of ceasefire when the leadership of both parties has preferred not to talk about the subject. Broadly speaking, as noted in earlier chapters, whereas in the 1960s and 1970s the Conservatives were regarded as the 'pro-European' party, the bulk of the Labour Party treated EC membership as anathema and eventually supported withdrawal from the EC in the early 1980s. By the 1990s these roles had reversed, after each party had moved in opposite directions in the intervening period for a variety of reasons, some of which had little or nothing to do with EC/EU affairs.

Inter-party competition has often seemed most intense when the actual differences between party leaderships were in reality wafer-thin. This was evident at an early stage in the 1960s when mutual antipathy between Wilson and Heath spilled over onto the question of EC membership. A second order explanation for Wilson's decision to apply for EC membership in 1967 is that as the master tactician and political manipulator he was motivated to some extent by calculations of party advantage. He knew that Heath strongly supported EC membership and would want to make it a major issue at the next general election. He therefore took action to deprive the Conservative Party of electoral ammunition. Rarely unable to resist a sideswipe at Heath, Wilson accused him of subservience to the French: 'One encouraging gesture from the French Government', he said, 'and the Conservative leader rolls on his back like a spaniel' (*The Guardian*, 19 March 1966). Wilson hastened to explain that some of his best friends were spaniels, while Heath stormed 'Lies … revolting, poisonous lies' (Ziegler, 2010: 191). Such canine imagery became part of the vocabulary of inter-party discourse on Europe; 30 years later in the 1997 general election it was the Conservative Party that claimed that Labour would act like a spaniel on EU membership (Heath, 1998: 356).

Wilson was also adept at using language about the EC to put the Conservatives on the defensive and to fend off criticism of his own handling of the matter. His frequent, pejorative references to the 'Tory terms', when describing the Heath government's negotiation of EC membership, had the effect of painting the Conservatives in the worst possible light. It also obscured the extent to which a Labour government, had it won the general election of 1970, would have settled for broadly similar terms of entry. Indeed, George Thomson, the Labour government minister who was chosen by Wilson to do the initial soundings on the 1967 application to join the EC, explained to a Labour Party special conference (July 1971) why the EC entry terms that Heath had negotiated were ones he would have recommended to a Labour government if it had won the 1970 general election (*The Guardian*, 6 October 2008).

Exchanges between Callaghan and Thatcher in 1979 over the Callaghan government's decision not to enter the Exchange Rate Mechanism (ERM) of the European Monetary System also exemplified the extent to which the major parties sought to gain the upper hand while actually agreeing with each other on the substance of the matter in hand (see Chapter 9). The Conservative Party was so divided over the issue as to be relieved at not having to take a decision. Nevertheless, it did not hesitate to capitalize on the position of Callaghan's Labour government. Thatcher portrayed the failure to join the ERM as a sign of Britain's economic weakness under Labour and 'a sad day for Europe' (*H.C. Deb.*, 6 December 1978). Only after 11 years in power and under duress did she herself agree to enter the ERM.

The policy of the Blair governments towards the EU in the period 1997–2007, stripped of Blair's pro-EU rhetoric, can also be viewed as serving a party political purpose governed by electoral considerations. In short and in addition to the analysis in Chapters 3 and 10, it is possible to maintain that New Labour was less interested in developing a distinctive policy of principled support for European integration than in stealing the electoral clothes of the Conservative and Liberal Democratic parties. We have noted elsewhere similarities between Blair and Thatcher with respect to their use of language about the EU. The point can be taken further, however, in questioning the extent to which Blair's attitude towards the EU actually represented a break with the past. On one interpretation, in fact, far from creating a break with past practices Blair instead prolonged a historic trend in British European policy since 1945 'by opportunistically using the issue of "Europe" as a tool to settle scores against opponents from within his party and against other parties' (Daddow, 2007a: 2). It puzzled Peter Mandelson, one of the architects of New Labour, that the Conservative Party made such a display of its preoccupation with the EU: 'Why do the Tories keep banging on about Europe? We're divided too, but we keep it under our hats' (quoted in Major, 1999: 590).

Inter-party competition could also become intensely personal at times. A notable example of such occurred in 2009 when the post of the first permanent president of the EU came to be filled. The response to the possibility of Blair occupying this post indicated all too clearly the partisan divisions and antipathies that informed British responses to this possibility. William Hague, the Conservative Shadow Foreign Secretary at the time, was adamant that Blair 'should be let nowhere near the job' (*The Guardian*, 15 July 2009). He subsequently emphasized his opposition to such an appointment at a meeting of 26 EU ambassadors in London when he commented that giving Blair the post would be a 'hostile act' and that Blair would be appointed 'over my dead body'. His audience was taken aback by his comments. They knew there were differences between the Labour and Conservative parties over the EU. However, they imagined – as other commentators did – that Blair's appointment would be of benefit for Britain exercising its influence within the EU through such a big European post. There was perhaps limited understanding of how no British-generated move, position or policy within the

EU could be divorced from British domestic party rivalries and competition. In this particular case, as one Conservative source put it, Hague had been 'badly hit by his loss to Blair in the 2001 general election' (*The Guardian*, 21 October 2009).

Finally, inter-party competition has proved particularly evident when the EU has been deliberately used to counter or nullify what one party – usually in opposition – has viewed as extremist elements in the other party. Brussels, in effect, has been regarded by both major parties at different times as offering protection from the domestic political programme of its major opponents. Thus, for example, Conservative support for the cause of remaining in the EC in the 1975 referendum was in part influenced by the view that EC membership could help to counter left-wing policies associated with Bennite opinion in the Labour government and party. A similar situation obtained in the late 1980s only on this occasion it was the Labour Party that viewed Brussels in the form of Jacques Delors, the socialist president of the European Commission, as offering welcome protection for the rights of British workers in the face of Thatcherite policies.

New political practices

EU membership has had an impact on British political culture and practices in several respects. One of the most striking innovations concerns the introduction and use of the referendum. Prior to 1975, the referendum represented a constitutional novelty. No such device had ever been used on the British mainland, and to date only the question of EU membership has attracted a UK-wide referendum.

The decision to hold the 1975 referendum met with a mixed response. In some quarters, it was regarded as a much-needed, welcome extension of the British people's democratic rights in a political system that included a hereditary head of state and an unelected second chamber (the second largest legislative body in the world after the National People's Congress of China). There was, besides, a House of Commons described at the time as 'an elective dictatorship' by a former Lord Chancellor Hailsham and mean-ing, among other things in this context, executive dominance over the legislature in all aspects of EU policymaking. None of these features, incidentally, has moderated the common criticism of the EU for its 'democratic deficit' in some British political circles. Arguably executive dominance has proved less pronounced in recent years, partly as a function of coalition government and more recently as a result of the government's small parliamentary majority and the enhanced influence of backbenchers, evident in pressing the case for a referendum on EU membership (see Chapter 12).

In other quarters, however, the use of a referendum was portrayed as a dangerous con-stitutional innovation that posed a threat to parliamentary sovereignty. It smacked of unwanted continental practices and suggested that the recourse to popular sovereignty through a referendum could just as easily undermine as save parliamentary sovereignty. While left-wing opinion in the Labour Party viewed the referendum as fully in keeping with the emphasis placed on participatory democracy at that time, other sections of the party led by Jenkins maintained that a referendum was setting a dangerous precedent and threatened the thesis advanced by Edmund Burke in the eighteenth century that MPs were representatives, not delegates, and had to be allowed to exercise their own judgement. This view was also the official line taken by the Conservative Opposition in the early 1970s, with Geoffrey Rippon denouncing referendums as 'wholly contrary to our constitutional practices'. When the matter was debated in the Commons (11 March 1975), the newly elected Conservative Party leader, Margaret Thatcher, pointed to the difficulties that could well arise if, for example, the vote went against the government's recommendation (*H.C. Deb.*, vol. 888, cols. 310–14).

Another constitutional innovation resulting from EU membership has involved adoption of a proportional representation voting system for the European Parliament (EP). This system has operated in Britain since 1999. In England, Scotland and Wales the voting system is the *d'Hondt* system of proportional representation involving the regional closed list whereby political parties put forward names of candidates in rank order, the number of candidates being no more than the number of seats allowed for each region. In Northern Ireland the system involves Single Transferable Vote (STV). In 2002, the EU agreed to uniform election procedures for elections to the European Parliament which, while broadly defined, determined that proportional representation would be the method for election to the EP, using either a list system or STV. Proportional representation has since become more common in some UK domestic elections and is now used in a variety of forms for the election of the Northern Ireland Assembly, the Scottish Parliament, the National Assembly for Wales, the London Assembly and the London mayor.

The first-past-the-post system for electing the Westminster Parliament, however, remains intact, as does the unelected House of Lords. Such traditional practices are viewed by some as indicative of a long-standing belief that there is no reason to manufacture a written constitution or to undertake major constitutional experiments, apart from the important exceptions of devolved powers especially in Scotland (see Chapter 6).

Away from the public gaze and often at a lower level of activity, EU membership or what is sometimes called 'the Europeanization of UK government' has had a widespread impact. The most notable areas encompass civil servants often working in a largely EU-determined environment, local authorities seeking EU funding or implementing EU-generated programmes, and universities heavily involved in EU-wide funding and research projects.

We have noted elsewhere the pronounced antipathy towards the mainland European tradition of written constitutions. British governments have brought this distinctive feature to their handling of the basic, underlying constitutional rules and procedures of the EU. The British preference for an uncodified or unwritten constitution with scope for evolutionary change looms large in this context. So, too, does the development of informal procedures and the penchant for piecemeal institutional changes, and for one definition of the British constitution as simply 'what happens' according to one legal theorist (*The Guardian*, 25 November 2005). A typical example of piecemeal change and a rare example of importing continental practices into Britain's EU membership occurred towards the end of the Cameron government's renegotiation of the terms of EU membership in February 2016. In order to win the support of Boris Johnson, the London mayor, for his renegotiated terms, Cameron was expected to declare that the UK supreme court or another official body should be vested with powers akin to the German Constitutional Court to assess whether legal acts by the EU's institutions remain within the scope of the powers of the EU.

That rare exception apart, however, there is still no inclination on the British side to imagine that anything useful can be learnt from the EU or from its member states in the field of political practices and constitutional procedures. The Blair governments' handling of domestic constitutional reform in the period 1997–2007 did not even make a gesture towards learning from mainland European experience. In addition, the Blair

governments also failed, like their predecessors, to understand that there was no prospect 'of reforming the institutions of the EU in the image of the British constitution'
(Johnson, 2004: 307). In a similar manner, the incoming Brown government published
a Green Paper, 'The Governance of Britain', that made no reference at all to the EU. It
thus failed to take account of the fact that Britain's governance was inextricably bound
up with the governance of the EU, an omission that 'almost baffles belief' according to
one authoritative assessment (Marquand, 2008).

EU membership and the emergence of new political parties: 'Gang of Four' and 'Sod the lot'

A further important impact of EU membership on the landscape of British politics
has concerned the emergence of new political parties, notably the Social Democratic
Party, (SDP), the United Kingdom Independence Party (UKIP) and the Referendum
Party. In the process, a multi-party system has come into being and the question of EU
membership has become an increasingly important element in competition between the
parties.

The SDP was born out of bitter internal quarrels in the Labour Party in the later
1970s as the Left gradually established a dominant position within the party and
drove it in an increasingly anti-marketeer direction. There was a marked refusal to
accept the verdict of the 1975 referendum and a determination to reverse Labour
support for EC membership. These efforts met with success when the 1981 Labour
Party conference passed a resolution calling for a negotiated British withdrawal from
the EC, a stance that was adopted as official Labour Party policy for the 1983 general
election.

Pro-marketeers in the Labour Party viewed these developments with a mixture of
alarm, distaste and despair. They felt increasingly alienated, especially after Michael
Foot, the veteran spokesman of the Labour left, succeeded Callaghan as party leader
in 1980. In the following year the so-called 'Gang of Four' – Roy Jenkins, David Owen,
Bill Rodgers and Shirley Williams – took the dramatic decision to leave the Labour
Party and form a new political movement, the Social Democratic Party. Dissatisfaction
with Labour's new stance on EC membership was by no means the only factor that precipitated their departure, and in many respects EC membership was proxy for a wider
unresolved struggle for the soul of the Labour Party (Liddle, 2014: 34). EC membership
was the decisive factor according to one of the principals (Owen, 1991: 66–7). In particular, the 'Gang of Four's' experience of cross-party co-operation in support of EC
membership during the 1975 referendum campaign played a significant part in loosening ties with their left-wing colleagues. It also paved the way for future collaboration
with the Liberals that eventually resulted in a merger with the Liberals (1988) to form
the Social and Liberal Democrats (SLD), and known as the Liberal Democrats since
1989 (Jenkins, 1992: 424).

The major, contentious debate over the Maastricht Treaty in the early 1990s gave
rise to two new parties at the opposite end of the spectrum of opinion to that of the
SDP. The smaller and more short-lived of these, the Referendum Party, was founded in
1994 by the billionaire James Goldsmith. This single-issue party resurrected the idea of
another referendum on British membership of the EU. It contested the general election
of 1997, finishing fourth with approximately 3 per cent of the vote but winning no seats.
The party ceased to exist shortly after Goldsmith's death (July 1997). Its successor, the

Referendum Movement, eventually merged with an anti-euro group funded by the millionaire Paul Sykes who subsequently bankrolled UKIP.

UKIP has proved to be a more lasting and substantial creation than the Referendum Party, both in terms of popular support and in influencing the handling of the issue of EU membership by the Conservatives in government since 2010. The party had its origins in the Anti-Federalist League founded by the historian Alan Sked as a single party that was renamed UKIP in 1993. Its subsequent growth owed much to broadening its appeal away from that of a single-issue party to supporting a set of right-wing populist policies including reducing immigration, supporting tax cuts, restoring grammar schools, and denying climate change. This development was accompanied by the emergence of Nigel Farage as leader in 2006. He remained so but for a brief spell in 2009–2010 (11 months) and an even briefer spell (three days) in 2014.

Farage and his party have rarely lacked publicity. Elected officials have variously called women sluts, have referred to foreign aid recipients as 'bongo bongo land', have been jailed for benefit fraud, and have blamed floods on gay marriage – a combustible mixture of racism, sexism and homophobia. Farage's wife reportedly described the party's headquarters as a 'freak show', understandably so as it was said to include such exotica as one aide sitting with an 'orgasmatron' wire massager on her head. Meanwhile, staff regularly took off their clothes and used a whiteboard on the office wall to name people that they wanted to have sex with, loyally including Farage's name (*Daily Mail*, 14 January 2016). Such reports and stories have done little or no harm to the party's popularity, and nor did Cameron's dismissal of the party as comprising 'fruitcakes, loonies and closet racists' (*The Guardian*, 4 April 2006).

According to one history of the party, its strongest appeal is among the 'Left Behind' voters (Ford and Goodwin, 2014), these being defined as mainly white, working-class, older men with few or no advanced academic qualifications and with a strong nationalist, Eurosceptic outlook. Such supporters are loosely described as white face, blue collar, grey hair. Contrary to some impressions, however, they are more likely to be former Labour voters than 'Tories in exile'. The results of the 2015 general election indicated a marked swing to UKIP in traditional Labour heartlands in England and Wales. This trend was arguably all the stronger because the Blair government chose not to impose transitional controls on immigration from the eight central and eastern European states that joined the EU in May 2004. Nevertheless, Farage has long regarded Thatcher as a major source of inspiration, while UKIP has strong similarities with the right wing of the Conservative Party, so much so that it was once described as a 'Dad's Army offshoot of the Tory party'.

A further feature of UKIP voters is that many hanker after a past 'golden age' with a particularly keen sense of nostalgia for Britain's imperial past. A *Private Eye* cover mocked up an exchange between the driver of a purple UKIP taxi and a passing punter: 'Where to, Guv?' the cabbie asks. His charge replies: '1957 – and step on it' (*Private Eye*, 26 November – 11 December 2014). In similar vein, at the party's conference in September 2015, Farage himself paraded on the platform with a sign saying 'We want our country back'.

The widening appeal of this right-wing populist party lay in its emphasis on opposition to the EU and concerns about immigration. Its standing as a populist force was reflected in its limited ideological framework and its constant emphasis on deep distrust of the established political parties and Whitehall's deeply engrained culture of secrecy. During the 2010 general election campaign a UKIP poster featuring Brown, Cameron and Clegg was captioned: 'Sod the lot'. The fusion of opposition to EU membership and fears about mass immigration has given rise to a particularly potent, insurgent force. Some observers maintain that Farage himself has changed from the jovial EU-baiter to an anti-immigration polemicist, citing his attempt to blame a motorway traffic jam on open-door migration and feeling 'awkward' about hearing foreign tongues on a commuter train; UKIP's opponents have called it the 'BNP [British National Party] in blazers' on that account.

The party first came to prominence in the European Parliament elections of 2004 when it secured third place and won 12 seats, while in the 2009 election it came second equal with Labour and won 13 seats. Thereafter it replaced the Liberal Democrats as a recipient of the protest vote. It enjoyed stunning success in the local elections of 2013 when it gained 25 per cent of the vote, by which time its threat to Conservative parliamentary seats forced Cameron to promise a referendum on EU membership. The party increasingly benefited from the fragmentation of British politics, the loosening hold of the established parties in some of their traditionally strong constituencies, and the emergence of a volatile electorate. It has also shaped a distinctive narrative by tapping into Eurosceptic, conservative and populist traditions with a populist form of Euroscepticism standing in contrast to the elite-based form of Euroscepticism of the Conservative Party (Tournier-Sol, 2015). They also lend substance to the view that people who self-identify as English are significantly more likely than those who live in England but self-identify as British to regard the EU as a bad thing and to favour restricting immigration.

UKIP's biggest breakthrough occurred in the European Parliament elections of 2014 when it received the greatest number of votes of any British party (27.49 per cent of the total votes cast) and the largest number of seats (24) of any British party in the European Parliament elections. In the general election of 2015, however, it returned only one MP, Douglas Carswell, who had earlier defected from the Conservatives and who was soon at loggerheads with Farage.

Zero sum and variable sum politics

Public and especially press presentations of British negotiating strategies and tactics within the EU are often at variance with the dynamics, method and character of the EU policymaking process. In short, coalition building and variable sum politics at the heart of the terms of trade in Brussels do not fit easily into the binary conception of politics dominant at Westminster. Among other things, the Westminster system ultimately rests on the view of politics as a zero sum game of winners and losers, the idea of a positive or variable sum set of outcomes often being viewed as an alien concept associated with continental coalition governments.

The winner-takes-all culture is as evident at the ballot box in elections for the British parliament as in the workings of parliamentary politics. Over the years, this condition has often resulted in popular images of British involvement in EC/EU business as aggressive, uncooperative, unconstructive, confrontational. Unsurprisingly, one British ambassador to West Germany reportedly pleaded for more thought to be given to the style of British policy in Europe, noting that the plain speaking [*sic*] of the House of Commons did not translate well into continental languages, especially in countries that lived by coalition and compromise (Wall, 2008: 76). The experience of coalition government at Westminster in the period 2010–2015 did little to change this image.

From Harold Wilson's premiership through to that of David Cameron's, the 'Battle of Britain' rhetoric of heroic stands, no surrender and glorious victories, has reflected the need of government to impress both the parliamentary opposition and discordant elements within the government party – ever eager to exploit any suggestion of government weakness in Brussels – and sections of the public either neutral or hostile to the EU. A victory or 'win-win' scenario for British negotiators is portrayed as a loss for the EU while the deepening of European integration is represented as a loss for British sovereignty. Roy Denman, a senior Board of Trade and subsequently EC Commission official, recalled a minor incident when, on returning from a meeting in Paris, his driver enquired 'Did we win, sir?', an enquiry that spoke volumes for the winning or losing mentality and suggested to Denham at least that 'something has been lacking in the education of British politicians' (BDOHP, 4 May 1999). Other senior Whitehall officials have made similar comments. Michael Palliser, Permanent Under-Secretary and Head of the Diplomatic Service (1975–1982), once observed that British government ministers 'feel perhaps more than ministers from other countries, to be in the business of winning victories, which is pretty good nonsense really' (BDOHP, 28 April 1999). In the process, politicians project onto the EU the very faults and weaknesses of the British system of government.

The application of the concept of zero sum politics in this context fundamentally misrepresents the conduct of EU business. The winner-takes-all mentality invariably requires that government represents EU politics in the simplistic form of set piece battles as opposed to a continuous process of negotiation which is the reality of how the EU conducts its business. Any compromise has to be fudged or hidden from view. Furthermore, while every major change or treaty is presented as a final destination rather than a stepping stone, so a wary public becomes all the more suspicious when this proves otherwise.

The problems of allaying fears and managing expectations have proved particularly evident when the EU states have engaged in an evolving Intergovernmental Conference (IGC) over a protracted period of time, as in the case of the Single European Act, the Maastricht Treaty on European Union, the failed Constitutional Treaty, and the Lisbon Treaty. These episodes often leave the impression that any transaction in Brussels can be reduced to a simple binary choice with no middle way between the idea of co-operation between sovereign states and a federal Europe. Such a representation of British involvement in EU politics reinforces presentations of the issue in terms of false choices that distract attention from underlying issues. It also deepens distrust of the government and adds to misunderstandings about the nature of European integration among the electorate (Oliver, 2015: 91).

A further common feature that reinforces these conditions is the persistent tendency of political leaders to be hidden from the public when it comes to disseminating information. The British involvement in the making of the Treaty of Lisbon is a case in point, and all the more important in view of the continuing controversy over the treaty within the Conservative Party. Government handling of the matter arguably conformed to other such occasions involving the lack of transparency of the negotiation process at the domestic level, the emphasis on 'red lines' and little else, and the squandering of yet another chance to have a full and informed discussion about the country's relationship with the EU (Blair, 2010: 6, 25; see also Chapter 4).

Scepticism about Euroscepticism

There are grounds for some scepticism about the usefulness of the concept of Euroscepticism as narrowly applied to the policies and attitudes of British political parties towards the EU. It may be an overstatement to suggest that 'We are all Eurosceptics now', but it is not an exaggeration to maintain that at the very least there are several Euroscepticisms (Usherwood, 2014). The expression itself was first used to describe the reservations of some Conservative backbenchers in the late 1980s about the Single European Act and its aftermath. It gained traction as a result of Thatcher's Bruges speech (see Chapter 3) and subsequently attracted widespread use during and after the debate over the Maastricht Treaty.

The expression Euroscepticism has since become an elastic, ill-defined, catch-all label that obscures as much as it reveals about the precise motivations and stance of individuals, groups and political parties towards the EU. Confusion is all the worse in that the expression can be made to serve both descriptive and pejorative functions. In the Conservative Party of 2016, every conceivable shade of Euroscepticism was on display ranging from the doubters about EU membership who wished to remain or leave and the doubters about EU membership who wished to remain or leave depending on the outcome of the process of renegotiation.

At one end of a spectrum of opinion, it is relatively easy to identify individuals and agencies opposed in principle to EU membership under any circumstances, albeit for a wide variety of political, ideological, cultural and other reasons. The latter usually relate to a defence of parliamentary sovereignty, opposition to European federalist aspirations, a visceral hostility to France or Germany especially when both states are perceived as operating in tandem, and a view of Europe as a source of instability and disorder. Such principled opponents of the EU have been variously labelled as irreconcilables, fundamentalists or 'Eurorejects'. They are sometimes regarded by their critics as swivel-eyed zealots or as an awkward squad looking as if nursing a well-informed grievance.

Parliamentary figures such as Tony Benn and Peter Shore represented this strand of opinion in an earlier generation. Bill Cash and Bernard Jenkin are typical of more recent exponents. They subscribe to the viewpoint of 'hard' Euroscepticism and would probably maintain opposition to EU membership even after losing a referendum on the issue, as Benn and Shore did after the 1975 referendum. According to this viewpoint, EU membership and the underlying principles of integration associated with the EU amount to a fundamental cause of problems and are not simply indicative of some other more important problem.

That said, however, in some cases 'hard' Euroscepticism may be a vehicle for a large number of other equally, if not more, important causes of complaint and protest. UKIP as a coalition of the disaffected may be a case in point in that while its original purpose was 'hard', unreserved opposition to EU membership that may no longer be so. In short, Euroscepticism in this case may be symptomatic of deeper, more fundamental causes whether relating to economic change, loss of identity, globalization or the impact of immigration. As the party of discontent and protest claiming to speak for voiceless people with deep-seated problems, UKIP would not necessarily disappear if Britain left the EU but would rather focus on some other supposed source of social or economic grievance.

Two sets of polling figures point up the often secondary rather than primary importance of Euroscepticism in this respect. They also incidentally serve as a warning from the psephologists against assuming that public opinion on any issue can be ascertained from the performance and popularity of the political parties. First, according to the Ipsos MORI Political Monitor, with its long-standing reputation for tracking British attitudes towards the EU, the percentage of the people polled between November 2012 and October 2014 who voted to stay in the EU increased from 48 per cent to 56 per cent. Another major polling organization, YouGov, reported similar trends with support for EU membership increasing from 28 per cent in May 2012 to 45 per cent in February 2015. As noted above, however, this period coincided with fast-growing support for UKIP. This indirect evidence of the limited impact of EU membership in spite of the surge in UKIP support was further reinforced by the 2014 Ipsos MORI poll showing that 11 per cent of UKIP voters actually supported EU membership, while another 10 per cent were 'not sure' about the matter. In effect, this evidence suggests that EU membership as such is not much more than a symbol of underlying issues mentioned above (Ford and Goodwin, 2014) and that UKIP is no longer a single-issue party.

One, by no means uncontested, division under the Eurosceptic label is the distinction between 'hard' and 'soft' Euroscepticism, the former as noted above referring to the unqualified, principled opponents of EU membership and the latter describing the supporters of a more or less reformed EU with no principled objection to the EU. It is problematical, however, to pin down the precise attitudes of those who may be said to come under the umbrella of 'soft' Euroscepticism. There may be only a finely nuanced difference between a Eurosceptic 'headbanger' and a Eurosceptic 'non-headbanger', to use the language of Zac Goldsmith, the Conservative MP and candidate for London mayor (*The Guardian*, 25 January 2016). 'Euroscepticism' in this respect is a 'broad church' with a wide variety of campaigning views and interests. These range from business-based organizations like Business for Britain and OpenEurope to more political and largely Conservative-manned groups such as the Bruges Group, 'Better off Out' and the Fresh Start Project. It is not always clear to the general public that seemingly independent, research-based agencies have a partisan character (see Chapter 7).

There is much middle ground between the polar opposites of 'hard' Eurosceptics and Europhiles, the latter having become either almost an endangered species in British politics or so given to silence as to let their side of the argument fall by default. For the large majority in the middle, the 'in-betweeners' so to speak, whether in parliament or among the public at large, it is often the case that they have no fixed views and uphold no 'eternal truths' about European integration. They occupy a sceptical but pragmatic position and are likely to veer towards the retention of the status quo, if most polls in recent years are to be believed (see below).

Some MPs can be influenced in one direction or another by any number of factors that have little or nothing to do with EU membership. A combination of some of the hidden wiring and persuaders of the British political system can decisively affect personal attitudes towards the particular question of EU membership, especially when calculations of advancement, opportunism and ambition enter into account. In January 2016, it was reported that some two-thirds of Conservative MPs supported withdrawal from the EU as matters stood at the time. The response of one senior Conservative Party figure to this news, however, was that if 'things are very tight some will be bought off by offers of patronage and will be reluctant to take a different line to the prime minister'. Furthermore, many MPs would not want their careers blighted by being on the wrong side of such an important debate (*The Guardian*, 9 January 2016). More than one-third of Conservative MPs are on the government payroll, and that in itself is a powerful tool for ensuring support for the Downing Street view. In some cases, moreover, a factor as important, if not more so, than detailed arguments about

EU membership concerns Cameron's successor and, for the major contenders, calculations about how best to place themselves to establish or burnish their credentials.

It is also the case that, for reasons of personal hatred, disappointment at lack of ministerial promotion or sacking from ministerial jobs, some Conservative parliamentarians might use the EU issue to demonstrate their hostility towards the party leadership in what has long resembled a Conservative Party blood feud. In some cases, politicians without interest in, or hope of, ministerial preferment have proved impervious to the usual blandishments and strong-arm tactics of the Whips' Office. Such considerations indicate that the question of EU membership may be said to have reflected a number of latent functions.

Some latent functions

The EC/EU membership has served several latent functions in the context of political conflicts within and between political parties. In short, the substance of the issue has proved secondary to its significance in assisting a number of ulterior strategic, tactical and electoral purposes in a variety of guises and forms. Expressed in an extreme form, it is possible to argue that much criticism of the EU is not necessarily or particularly about the EU and all its works. In the rhetoric of national governments and political parties, the EU is one of the easiest of targets to blame for a host of problems, regardless of whether or not these are directly or even indirectly due to the existence of the EU. In the process, the organization has taken on a complex and contradictory identity ranging from that of a weakling in the international system to that of a superstate in the making.

The debate about EU membership in political circles has often figured less as a matter of assessing the intrinsic merits, advantages and disadvantages of membership than of serving a host of extraneous aims. In effect, the EU has been utilized as a manifestation of some other unrelated or disparate issue. Sometimes, the problems of determining the underlying meaning of particular expressions and positions on the question are so full of hidden messages that they call to mind the comment of Metternich, the leading diplomat of nineteenth-century Austria, who on hearing about the death of his French rival and counterpart Talleyrand observed 'What did he mean by that?'

Examples abound of the ways in which the EC/EU has been used as a safety valve or lightning rod for deflecting attention away from party weaknesses and for minimizing the degree of dissent within a party on other matters. Management of EC/EU membership has also proved useful as a means of destabilizing, discrediting or weakening an opposing political party. Governments and parties under pressure on other fronts have also mercilessly used the EC/EU as a bogeyman, as if it was an entirely separate entity. Whitehall officials have been similarly inclined to blame Brussels bureaucrats for interventions which used to be blamed on themselves. At times, the EU has been unfairly blamed for economic failures that are national in origin. At other times, politicians have emphasized the economic dimensions and benefits of EU membership in order to divert attention away from other more problematical aspects such as the sovereignty question.

The use of the EC/EU as a distracting or diverting device in the context of domestic politics has proved particularly attractive to governments and parties under intense pressure. In this case, distraction and diversion involve rather more than the use of routine tactics such as 'dead cat' rhetoric or the practice of releasing unwelcome government announcements on a 'bad news day'. In the case of the EU there has been a more strategic and sustained use of the EU in this regard. Two episodes from the 1960s set a long-term pattern in this respect.

First, at the time of the Macmillan application for EC membership in 1961, Gaitskell, the Labour Party leader, stipulated that five 'essential conditions' had to be met to secure the party's support for EC membership: binding safeguards for trade and established relations with the Commonwealth; freedom from constraint on the issue of foreign policy; accommodation of the EFTA states, especially the neutrals; freedom to plan the economy; and safeguards for British agriculture (incidentally, five conditions or 'tests' became the Labour Party's favourite number when determining the viability of EC/EU affairs; it applied that number of tests on the question of entering the euro area under the first Blair Labour government of 1997–2001).

It is fair to say that Gaitskell's conditions had little to do with a genuine concern for or interest in EC membership in particular or European integration in general. It was rather the case that the conditions were used as 'weapons in the game of political opportunism and skulduggery' (Broad and Daddow, 2010: 13). In particular, they aimed to wrong-foot the Conservative government and also to address the deep divisions in the Labour Party. Through publicizing the conditions, Labour was able to present itself as the British party that rejected the idea of EC membership 'at any cost', mocking the Conservative administration for 'negotiating on its knees' with the EC states.

By avoiding a firm decision for and against EC membership, Gaitskell was also able to buy time, diverting attention from his own party's position and divisions. The last thing that he wanted was another bout of vicious infighting between Left and Right that had followed Labour's devastating and unexpected defeat in the 1959 general election. He had set out to make the party more electable by jettisoning its commitments to nationalization and unilateral nuclear disarmament, resulting in bitter rows at the annual party conferences in 1959 and 1960. In theory, his five conditions did not preclude EC membership, but his audience at the 1962 party conference rightly believed that for all practical purposes Gaitskell was declaring against EC membership. He thus pleased the anti-marketeers in the party, who viewed the EC as a 'capitalist club'. They were predominantly though not exclusively left wing in outlook, and they had just lost the debate over nationalization and unilateral disarmament. The pro-marketeers, Gaitskell's closest allies, were mortified; the conference scene at the end of Gaitskell's speech caused his wife to exclaim 'Charlie [Charles Pannell], all the wrong people are cheering' (Jenkins, 1992: 146; Brivati, 1996: 413–16).

Second, the EC as a distracting device was to a certain extent evident when the Wilson Labour government in 1966–1967 alighted on the idea of applying for EC membership. As noted in Chapter 2, several factors account for this move, including the failure of the government's much-vaunted National Plan aiming at an economic growth rate of almost 4 per cent per annum over a five-year period. The Plan collapsed under the weight of severe deflationary measures (July 1966) following a heavy run on sterling. This outcome so stripped the government of the central plank of its economic policy that the entire affair was immediately dubbed Labour's 'Suez'.

In these circumstances and in psychological terms, the idea of EC membership provided a strategic goal, a new modernization strategy and potentially a sense of crusading mission to make up for the failure of the Plan. For the Wilson government as for Macmillan's, EC membership represented an escape from decline. It helped to fill the vacuum at the centre of the government's economic strategy. In short, an application for EC membership could at the very least serve as a diversion from the catastrophic failure of the government's domestic policy. It also offered an alternative route to economic salvation for what one government minister, Benn, described as a 'defeated cabinet' that was persuaded to see EC membership as an external solution to Britain's economic problem (Benn, 1988: 490). Richard Crossman, also a Cabinet minister, maintained that the application was being pursued as a way out of crisis by deflecting from underlying problems as well as helping to outflank the Left of the party (Crossman, 1976: 349). Ben Pimlott, Wilson's biographer, makes the same point, maintaining that among other things the application was a 'gigantic attempt' to distract attention from domestic and foreign policy problems (Pimlott, 1992: 435). In making the application, Wilson stuck to Gaitskell's conditions, but by this time they were used 'for any purpose', according to Shirley Williams, a junior minister in Wilson's government at the time (quoted in Broad and Daddow, 2010: 14).

EC membership as a useful running sore or favourite whipping boy was most evident in Thatcher's handling of the EC budget question during her first government (see Chapter 8). The fact that the budget rebate issue spanned the entire period of Thatcher's first administration (1979–1983) was arguably not entirely due to the nature of the problem. There was also an element of political calculation behind her aggressive, unyielding dealings with the rest of the EC at this stage. According to Ian Gilmour, who was directly involved in negotiations concerning the budget rebate as Lord Privy Seal (1979–1981), Thatcher deliberately prolonged the crisis over Britain's budgetary contribution. She thereby hoped to use it to boost her flagging political standing in the midst of what at the time was the worst economic recession since 1945. By 1981 she was the most unpopular prime minister on record, and was still on probation within the Conservative Party, some of whose leading figures had not properly accepted her (Moore, 2014: 676). Economic recession in the period 1979–1981 resulted in the loss of approximately 20 per cent of the country's manufacturing capacity and some two million manufacturing jobs. In addition, there were large government expenditure cuts and tax increases, most notably in the budget of March 1981.

Gilmour was in no doubt about the reasons for Thatcher's reluctance to endorse an agreement that he and Foreign Secretary Peter Carrington reached in Brussels concerning the rebate (May 1980). He claimed that so far as Thatcher was concerned: 'a running row with our European partners was the next best thing to a war; it would divert public attention from the disasters at home' (Gilmour, 1992: 240). In short, a continuing EU budget grievance was far more valuable than its removal at a time of mounting hostility to her monetarist policies and as rioting swept through British cities and her popularity slumped.

To be sure, Gilmour was not the most impartial of witnesses. As a leading 'wet' in the first Thatcher government, he was basically out of sympathy with most aspects of its programme and was soon dismissed from his post (September 1981). Nevertheless, others have also commented on Thatcher's use of the EC issue as a way of diverting attention from domestic difficulties and drumming up popular support at home. Hugo Young in his biography of Thatcher argued that at a time of enormous problems for the government in the early 1980s, when its popularity had sunk to a desperately low point, it served Thatcher's interests well to be seen putting up an heroic defence of national interests against the other EC states (Young, 1990: 189–90). Some historians of the subject have concurred with this judgement, one of whom maintains that the harsh line employed by Thatcher was largely determined by domestic political considerations (George, 1990: 162–3).

There was a comparable example of this towards the end of Thatcher's premiership according to some sources. Worsening economic conditions by 1989 and the growing unpopularity of the government and of Thatcher in particular meant that there was every reason to distract attention from economic problems (see Chapter 9). In the European Parliament election of that year, the Conservative campaign was characterized by an attack on the EC summed up in one of the party's posters: 'Do you want to live on a diet of Brussels?' Nigel Lawson later described the campaign as a form of crude and embarrassing anti-Europeanism and recalled, 'with a shiver of apprehension', that Thatcher saw the EP election campaign as a trial run for the next general election campaign and that with the short-term economic outlook looking unpromising 'she saw a crude populist anti-Europeanism as her winning strategy' (quoted in Gifford, 2014: 97).

This use of a substantive EU issue to serve ulterior purposes is evident in other ways. For example, during the protracted economic recession following the major crisis of 2007–2008, British government ministers during the Cameron Coalition government often highlighted the weaknesses of the EU market when accounting for the country's laggardly economic recovery. There was some substance to this view given the importance of the EU market to Britain. Nevertheless, the persistent references by Chancellor of the Exchequer Osborne and the Treasury to the struggling EU as 'the greatest threat to Britain's economic recovery' (*The Times*, 4 October 2014) served to obscure domestic factors responsible for this plight. Such references also had the effect of laying the blame for the failure of the government's export-led recovery programme entirely at the feet of the EU, and as noted below distracted attention from the impact of the government's austerity programme.

The uses of referendums

The question of EC/EU membership has also figured as a weapon in major internal party struggles. This feature was evident at an early stage in the history of British membership of the EC. At the time of the 1975 referendum, Harold Wilson effectively used this device in dealing with left-wing, anti-marketeer opinion in the Labour Party. At least part of his strategy and tactics in handling the renegotiations and referendum campaign were designed to counter and, if possible, inflict a defeat on the left wing.

The Labour Party's swing to the Left following the general election of 1970 was partly a result of disillusionment with the Wilson governments of 1964–1970. It was also the product of the industrial strife generated by the Heath government's 1971 Industrial Relations Act. The 1970s saw a pronounced growth in the influence of the Left at the constituency level, on the party's National Executive Committee (NEC) and in the trade union movement.

The course and outcome of the referendum campaign assisted Wilson in several important respects, most notably in dealing with the rising tide of left-wing opinion in party circles led by Tony Benn, the government's industry minister. This strand of opinion was associated with an interventionist economic strategy in accordance with 'Labour's Programme 1973' including proposals for nationalization, a National Enterprise Board and planning agreements. Some of these proposals, especially nationalization, scarcely appealed to Wilson. Furthermore, the protectionist and isolationist character of the programme reflected a strong anti-marketeer flavor, so much so that Jenkins publicly denounced Benn, saying that he found it impossible to take him seriously as an economics minister. (One of the ironic outcomes of the referendum campaign was that Benn, who as noted above originated the proposal for a referendum, saw his anti-marketeer views rejected by this mechanism, while Jenkins who had opposed a referendum had his pro-marketeer cause endorsed by this means.) For his own part, Wilson vetoed the idea of a controlling state interest in 25 of the country's largest manufacturers, caustically commenting to Benn at this time: 'Who's going to tell me that we should nationalize Marks and Spencer in the hope that it will be as efficient as the Co-op?' Moreover, Wilson reportedly became so exasperated with Benn's anti-marketeer campaign that he was driven to the verge of resignation (Ziegler, 1993: 394, 431).

In these circumstances, the referendum campaign itself absorbed time and energy that might otherwise have been devoted to pressing for an even more left-wing domestic economic policy. Bernard Donoghue, one of Wilson's personal assistants at this time, commented on the spectacle to the effect that Benn's army of the left was diverted from the dangerous fields of British industry onto the deceptively inviting marshes of the EC. Once committed and trapped there, Benn was blown up by a referendum of the British people.

This outcome afforded Wilson the opportunity to make Cabinet changes including the transfer of Benn from industry to energy; he reportedly claimed that he was going 'to use Tony Benn to display my sense of humour' (Ziegler, 1995: 440). This move gave Wilson some degree of satisfaction following his irritation with Benn's conduct during the referendum campaign. Benn himself remained irrepressible in his new post, revelling in the opportunity to pursue an obstructive attitude towards the EC. He proudly claimed that an EC Council of Energy Ministers was delayed while he attended a local Labour Party meeting. Meanwhile, one diplomat was assigned the task of stopping Benn 'from breaking up too much china in Brussels' (Hannay, 2013: 93).

This episode in Labour Party history is illustrative of the ways in which referendums, whatever their value in enhancing the democratic process and public involvement in decision-making, can be made to serve multifarious purposes. In short, they can be used as a tactical device by governing parties and leaders. As such, referendums at large and in particular EU referendums are open to several criticisms, not least of these being that:

- political elites and well-funded interest groups are better placed to exploit them, and that in turn perpetuates the problem of elitism;
- minority groups can be isolated;
- debates can lead to the oversimplification of complex issues with simple slogans and binary choices based upon playing to the fears and biases of uninformed voters;
- the answer given can be about something other than the question asked – 'if you ask a specific question in a referendum' declared the former French President Mitterand 'you will always get an answer to a completely different question'; voters cast their vote because of feelings about other issues such as the incumbent government;
- voters can easily allow themselves to be swayed by the media, interest groups, parties and political leaders, not least in the absence of sufficiently developed opinions about the EU.

(McCormick, 2014: 217)

One study of the 28 referendums that have been promised or held over the course of the history of the EC/EU (a large majority since the Maastricht Treaty) concludes that most were driven by the strategic political considerations of governments that used referendum pledges for domestic, defensive reasons (Oliver, 2015: 80–1).

The EC/EU has also long served as a cover or mask for hydra-headed protest politics and for representing opposition to party leadership. John Major as prime minister found some of his Conservative parliamentary Eurosceptics a heavy cross to bear. Within the Cabinet itself there were several ministers who made no secret of their Eurosceptic sympathies, conducting a form of guerrilla warfare against the official line through a combination of coded messages and open dissent. The ministers most prominently associated with such activities were Michael Howard, Peter Lilley, Michael Portillo and John Redwood – the 'bastards' as Major called them in one of his periodic fits of exasperation, not realizing that he was speaking into a live microphone at the time. Besides their views on the EU, they were attempting to strengthen their challenge for the Conservative Party leadership in the event that electoral defeat precipitated Major's downfall.

Similar forces and tendencies were at work during the Cameron Coalition government of 2010–2015. There can be little doubt that at the root of Cameron's problems with some of his backbenchers was their lack of trust in him, not least because of his early record as party leader (see Chapters 3 and 12). More importantly, his commitment to a referendum was primarily caused by mounting concern among Conservative backbenchers alarmed at the growing threat from UKIP. There were also frustrations at being in government with the more pro-EU Liberal Democrats, and some Conservative backbenchers barely concealed their contempt for these coalition partners. The promise of a referendum was an attempt to defuse what William Hague (Foreign Secretary 2010–2014) described as a 'ticking time bomb' in the party, while for the purpose of public consumption it was presented as a national imperative demanded by the people at large. The public at large, however, was no more obsessed by the EU in the second decade of the twenty-first century than it had been years earlier (see below). John Major's earlier judgement on the subject had some lasting validity: 'The notion that Britain in 1997 was racked by anxiety over Europe is pure nonsense. Conservative politicians were. The electorate was not' (Major, 1999: 697).

In many respects, Cameron's decision to hold a referendum was comparable to previous commitments by British leaders to hold a referendum on EU matters: John Major on membership of the euro in 1992, Tony Blair on the euro in 1999, Blair on the proposed EU constitutional treaty in 2005, and the Cameron Coalition government's European Act (2011). While none of these referendums have come to pass – referendums being more talked about than utilized in British politics – each grew out of deep-seated, internal tensions within the parties in government and served as a form of government and party management.

A further example of the latent functions served by the EU specifically relates to the period of the Cameron Coalition government. It is linked to an explanation concerning the use made of a populist anti-EU stance. The Conservative leadership in this government, notably Cameron and Osborne, on coming to power quickly revived a neo-liberal view of the state and the economy and adopted a series of austere budgets in the teeth of the deepest recession in recent British history. Given these conditions, Cameron sought to use a populist anti-EU stance with full-scale demonizing of the EU in 'an effort to mask and compensate politically for the unpopularity of his economic policies' (Schnapper, 2014). In effect, the EU provided a convenient scapegoat by distracting attention away from deflationary domestic policies by means of symbolic gestures in defence of Britain's national sovereignty against the EU. This stance also allowed Cameron to put clear distance between the Conservatives and the Labour Party that, as noted above, refused to support the Conservative-inspired idea of a referendum on Britain's EU membership. One consequence of symbolic gestures in this case, however, was that it built up expectations of major concessions and gains in any renegotiation of the terms of membership, a point to which we will return in a later chapter.

Euroscepticism and English nationalism

A final much debated example of a latent function concerns the links between Euroscepticism and English nationalism. The substance of this view is that opposition to European integration provides the best organized outlet for nationalism in present-day England and that contemporary English nationalism is characterized by a defence of British sovereignty (Wellings, 2011: 1). In contrast to a wide variety of views about English nationalism in recent years – that it is 'absent', 'dare not speak its name', or is 'politically weak' – it can be argued that Euroscepticism has been deployed as a proxy for English nationalism and that the key to understanding English nationalism is to focus on sovereignty in explaining the emergence of British Euroscepticism.

The Conservative Party, while disinclined to encourage English nationalism for political gain, has been quite willing to use Euroscepticism for such a purpose. Internal debates and divisions in the Conservative Party about the role and limits of the state or about national identity would not dissolve away or disappear in the absence of divisions over EU membership. In effect, Euroscepticism has been deployed as a surrogate for English nationalism. The defence of British institutions, identity and sovereignty has been a key feature of the Conservative view with European integration serving as a useful counterpoint. The conflation of England and Britain through the defence of parliamentary sovereignty has proved all the more important and difficult from this standpoint with the withdrawal of the Conservative Party into its English heartlands. This trend has continued to the point where the party has become almost an England-only party. As a result of the 2015 general election, the party has no MPs in Northern Ireland, one MP in Scotland and 11 MPs in Wales. Furthermore, an accompanying feature of devolution is that England has attained a special place in Europe as a nation without state, the largest nation without its own political institutions and 'nonchalant' about nationhood (Tombs, 2014: 877, 883).

In mainstream politics, few were more alert to what he viewed as the dangers of Englishness and English nationalism than Gordon Brown. During his premiership especially, he regarded Britain's problem with the EU as essentially about how the British saw their identity. His attempt to define a modern, confident sense of British identity was greatly motivated by the case for strong British engagement with the EU and by the need to defeat Scottish nationalism. Most importantly in this context, he feared that 'Englishness' encouraged the political forces that wanted to 'pull up the drawbridge' with the rest of Europe (Liddle, 2014: 92).

The political parties and the European Parliament

British representation in the European Parliament (EP) has often reflected a very distinctive character and also mirrored divisions and attitudes in domestic politics. There are currently 766 Members of the European Parliament (MEPs), 73 of whom represent British EP constituencies (see the Introduction and Appendix for the precise role and powers of the Parliament in the EU system). The Parliament is divided into EU-wide groups, as noted below; the groups appear in order of the number of seats won at the European parliamentary election of May 2014:

European People's Party (Christian Democrats) (221)
Progressive Alliance of Socialists and Democrats in the European Parliament (191)
European Conservatives and Reformists (70)
Alliance of Liberals and Democrats for Europe (67)
European United Left/Nordic Green Left (52)
Non-attached members – members not belonging to any political group (52)
The Greens/European Free Alliance (50)
Europe of Freedom and Direct Democracy Group (48).

The relationship between these groups and British political parties reveals some of the enduring features of the British contribution to parliamentary life. With the sole exception of the pro-European Liberals/Liberal Democrats, the British parties in the Parliament have often encountered difficulties in adjusting to the character and emphases of the major political groups.

At times the British political parties have seemed out of kilter with their ideological counterparts elsewhere in the EU and particularly in the case of the representatives of the other EU states with a large number of seats, notably France (72), Italy (72) and Germany (99). Prior to 1973, Parliament largely consisted of members who were supportive of the idea of European integration and prepared to organize themselves into trans-national groups based on ideological faultlines. By way of contrast, party fragmentation and internal divisions characterized the impact of British EC membership on the party groups in the Parliament (Smith, 2012: 1291). The discordant notes of the domestic debate about EC/EU membership were hereby exported to the EP forum, occasionally loudly in the histrionic outbursts of the DUP leader Ian Paisley heckling during a parliamentary speech by Pope John Paul II (12 October 1988) or a Nigel Farage launching into a face-to-face tirade against the EU president, Herman van Rompuy (24 February 2010). Meanwhile, it remains the case that British MEPs still have the right to vote in a number of policy areas such as the euro area and immigration where Britain has obtained opt-outs.

From the very early days of Britain's EC membership, the EP acquired a new dimension through the British representatives, evident in the initial reactions of the Conservative and Labour parties. In the first instance, the Labour Party refused to send representatives to the EP until after the renegotiation and referendum of 1975. Thereafter and for the next ten years or so it supported candidates who were opposed to Britain's EC membership, the most notable of whom was Barbara Castle, the former Cabinet minister, who stood as one of the Labour candidates in the first direct elections to the EP in 1979. There were also difficulties in the early years in developing Labour's links with the European Socialist Party (PES) which is currently known as the Progressive Alliance of Socialists and Democrats (PASD).

Meanwhile, through this early period of membership the Conservatives rejected affiliation with what was known at the time as the Christian Democratic Group (currently the European People's Party – EPP), a centre-right formation with whom the Conservatives might have been expected to ally themselves. They did not do so in the first instance partly because of the strong support for a federal Europe in the Group and partly because of the Roman Catholic connections of the Christian Democrats in West Germany and Italy. Instead, the Conservatives formed their own grouping along with two Danish MEPs known as the European Democratic Group.

One study of the British political parties in the European Parliament suggests that they can be labelled or characterized as follows: Reliable (Liberals), Ambiguous (Labour), Reluctant (Conservative) and Dismissive (UKIP) (Thillaye, 2014).

The Liberals/Liberal Democrats have had a relatively short-lived presence in the EP with fluctuating fortunes. They had no representatives in the EP until 1994 when they won two seats. In the election of 1999, however, they won ten seats, greatly assisted by the introduction of a list form of proportional representation in that year, as was the Green Party that secured representation for the first time. The Liberal Democrats' representation increased to 16 in 2004 but then fell to 11 in 2009 and disastrously collapsed to one MEP as a result of the 2014 election. In the period 1999–2014, when they enjoyed their largest representation, the Liberal Democrats generally adopted a pro-EU attitude, played a constructive role in the parliamentary grouping known as the Alliance of Liberals and Democrats for Europe (ALDE), and adopted a pragmatic approach to British interests while seeking to reconcile these with the EU's at large and in particular with the euro area.

Unlike the other British political parties, the Labour Party is a member of the main centre-left bloc, the PASD, one of the two major groupings in the EP, the other being the EPP. It is thus in a better position than the other British parties to bring influence to bear in the legislative process. During the period 1989–1999, when Labour representation in the EP heavily outnumbered Conservative representation, it played a particularly influential role in the PASD. That was far less the case as its seats in the EP declined from 29 (1999) to 13 (2014). Moreover, Labour's representation in the PASD has long been overshadowed by the numerical weight and preferences of the German and Italian socialists.

Under Blair's premiership especially, there was a limited interest on Blair's part to cultivate close links with continental socialists. Indeed, he often much preferred the company of such non-socialist leaders as the centre-right/right-wing Spanish and Italian prime ministers Jose Maria Aznar and Silvio Berlusconi. There were particular disagreements between Labour and the French socialists in the PASD, as the latter fundamentally disagreed with what they viewed as the broad thrust of the market-oriented features of Blair's Labour government. There were also tensions between Labour and the rest of the PASD group over British-only issues such as the British rebate, the CAP and social regulation, and also over the candidature of Martin Schulz of the German Social Democratic Party for the presidency of the European Commission in November 2013.

Under the Labour Party leadership of Ed Miliband, however, there was a greater degree of interest in cultivating closer links within the PASD. It was also the case that Miliband opposed the Conservatives' commitment to a referendum on EU membership, while at the same time allowing for some strong criticism of the EU for fear of being outflanked by other parties. In sum, the Labour record was a mixed story of 'attraction-repulsion', not unlike the way in which it abandoned its opposition to a referendum immediately after defeat in the general election of May 2015.

The Conservatives have experienced the most difficulty over the years in forming a lasting partnership in a political group. As noted above, they remained aloof from the EPP until 1992 when, under the Major premiership, it was arranged that Conservative

MEPs would sit with the EPP Group as 'allied members'. The arrangement fell apart when, at the time of his bid for the Conservative Party leadership, Cameron pledged to withdraw Conservative MEPs from the EPP. This decision took effect in 2009, ironically at a time when the federalist emphases of the EPP, that had so alarmed the Conservatives, were far less in evidence. The Conservatives hereby abandoned the largest group in the EP.

The Conservatives subsequently formed their own group, the centre-right ECR, in which they constituted the largest element, at least until the EP election of 2014. Withdrawal from the EPP had important political consequences, not the least of these being absence from the leaders' meetings of the highly influential EPP. The decision had particularly important implications in terms of fostering close relations with the German Chancellor Merkel whose party, the Christian Democratic Union, played a leading role in a Group that was highly regarded by Merkel herself (see Chapter 12). Cameron hereby placed himself in an isolated position outside this circle, a move criticized as 'autistic' by the then French Europe Minister Pierre Lellouche (Smith, 2012: 1294).

The performance and attitudes of UKIP in the 2009–2014 EP largely indicated a strong preference for isolation, a weak attendance record and a limited interest in co-operating with any other like-minded representatives. The party's absence and non-voting rates were particularly striking. According to one study it had a non-voting rate in the EP of 55 per cent and an average participation rate in debates of 68 per cent. It was consistent with this record that the UKIP leader, Nigel Farage, was not present when the EP voted on such important matters as the EU's Multiannual Financial Framework (MFF), the CAP reform, the European External Action Service and the banking union. He also had one of the lowest scores in the parliament for participating in roll-call votes (Thillaye, 2014).

In the 2009–2014 parliament, moreover, UKIP's detached attitude was combined with limited interest in and loyalty to the Europe of Freedom and Democracy (EFD) group (subsequently known from June 2014 as the Europe of Freedom and Direct Democracy – EFDD). The party respected the EDF's voting guidelines in only 52 per cent of cases in this parliament. To be sure, there was little common ground between UKIP and the two other main delegations in this group – the Solidarna Polska and the Lega Nord – and the group's lack of cohesion, far more evident than in any other group, was due in no small measure to UKIP's aversion to building coalitions or engaging in compromise deals. The party largely regarded the EP as a source of funding and high visibility in pursuit of its opposition to the EU and with zero influence on the decision-making process.

The impact of the EP election results of May 2014

The marked change in the composition of British representation in the Parliament following the election of May 2014 is indicated in Table 5.1.

The arrival of UKIP in force, the reduction in the number of members from the two major parties, and the diminished influence of British representation as a whole has to date presented an altogether different and weakened British presence from that in the 2009–2014 parliament. In the latter body, British parties were the single driving force behind two EP groups, the ECR (Conservatives) and EFD (UKIP), and were leading elements of two further groups: the PASD (Labour) and ALDE (Liberal Democrats) (Salamone, 2014).

Table 5.1 European Parliament election results May 2014: British representation

Party	MEPs	
	2009–2014	*2014–2019*
Conservatives	25	19
Labour	13	20
Liberal Democrats	11	1
UKIP	13	24
Greens	2	3
SNP	2	2
BNP	2	1
Plaid Cymru	1	1
Sinn Féin	1	1
DUP	1	1
UUP	1	1

Source: www.europarl.europa.eu/elections.

This picture has dramatically changed since the 2014 election. The reduction in the number of Conservative seats means that Conservative influence in the ECR is no longer so commanding, especially since its representation is now the same as the other major party in the group – the Polish Law and Justice Party – while the addition of a number of new parties to the group has further undermined the Conservative position.

UKIP belongs to and heads the right-wing group, the EFDD. As a result of the 2014 election, the party emerged as the largest British party in the EP with some 24 seats. Astonishingly in the view of some observers, it secured one seat in Scotland where it was widely regarded as an English nationalist party and where Farage on a visit to Edinburgh in May 2013 was hounded out of a pub by a barracking crowd. He was rejected by one taxi driver, turfed out of another, had to seek refuge in the pub with its sign above the door reading 'Enjoy your visit', and was eventually whisked away in a police riot van (*The Guardian*, 16 May 2013).

UKIP's outright rejection of the purposes and policies of the EU continues to leave it in an isolated position within the EP chamber, large in number but virtually impotent in terms of influence. Thus, following the election of 2014, though UKIP was entitled to chair one of the parliamentary committee leadership positions, this move was blocked by other parties, thereby underlining the extent to which Britain's largest EP party was also the least influential. Since the 2014 election, the EFDD has so far proved to be a fragmented body as some of its members in the previous parliament either defected or failed to be elected with cases of financial fraud involving at least two of the UKIP MEPs. At one stage, the EFDD only had MEPs from six EU states, just below the number needed to qualify for official group status and for UKIP to qualify for £1 million a year in taxpayers' funding. To obtain the required number, it recruited a Polish MEP from the Congress of the New Right whose leader, Korwin-Mikke, attracted notoriety for his views about the Holocaust and denying the vote to women (*The Guardian*, 20 October 2014).

Labour Party gains in the 2014 election suggest that of all the British parties it is best placed to influence legislation as part of the PASD grouping. However, as the major opposition party in domestic politics it did not do as well as might have been expected on the basis of the past record.

EP elections and activities have served a number of purposes in British political life that have had little or nothing to do with the EP or the handling of issues by the EU. First, voters have demonstrated limited interest in the EP as reflected in the low turn-out for elections (see below), notwithstanding the common complaint of a 'democratic deficit' in EU affairs and the fact that since the Lisbon Treaty the EP has more power than ever to shape the organization as co-legislator. EP elections are often perceived by voters as a second-order type of election, scarcely engaging with EU policies and more often than not simply presenting a mid-term opportunity to express an opinion on national politics and most particularly to capitalize on the protest vote against the performance of the party in power.

The major party in opposition in domestic politics has invariably regarded an EP election as an opportunity to attack the national government and to build a platform for winning national elections. During the period 1979–2014 and in the competition for seats between the Conservative and Labour parties (with the single exception of the EP election of 1984), the major party in opposition has always won the largest number of seats, Labour did so when in opposition at the time of the 1989 and 1994 elections and the Conservatives did so when they were in opposition in the period 1999–2009. This pattern was less evident in the 2014 election when Labour in opposition might have been expected to pick up far more seats than the Conservatives, while UKIP overtook both major parties.

Public opinion and EU membership

There are particular complications in determining and representing public opinion, or to reverse a common saying – people may be like politicians because what they say, and what they do, and what they think are three different things. It is the case that there is no single convincing time-series of public opinion soundings or polls involving an identical question on the EU throughout the period since 1973. The EU's comprehensive Eurobarometer, launched in 1973, comes closest to providing such a measure, though the wording of some questions has changed over time.

Public opinion polls about the general question of British membership of the EU and particular views about the acceptable evolution of the EU often obscure a gallimaufry of motives, some of which have little or nothing to do with the activities of the EU. Then, too, a shift in public opinion can be determined to a great extent by a change in the way the issue is framed, thereby eliciting a wide variety of responses. That said, as compared with the major political parties that have undergone internal convulsions and dramatic changes in their attitudes towards the EC/EU over the past 50 years, public opinion has, if anything, proved steadier and more constant. True, that position might be based on the public's 'total ignorance' of the EU, as one senior Foreign Office mandarin put it, adding that 'the country as a whole has much more common sense to it than parliament' and that the prevailing public mood (in 1999) was that 'we are not sure if we like this [EU membership] very much but it clearly doesn't make sense to leave it' (BDOHP, 28 April 1999). In short, there is an important distinction to be made between party- or parliamentary-based Euroscepticism and public Euroscepticism. A more informed public does not necessarily change opinion; a Standard Eurobarometer survey (July 2015) concluded that learning more about the EU may be just as likely to lead people to have a negative view of the EU as a positive one.

To a large extent the outcome of the referendum of 1975 set the pattern for the next forty years. The referendum result did not signal unreserved acceptance of EC membership. The substantial 'yes' majority reflected a preference for the status quo rather than enthusiastic approval (Butler and Kitzinger, 1976: 280). Nor had the opportunity given to the electorate to express its opinion on the subject completely dispelled a widespread feeling that the decision to join the EC lacked popular legitimacy. In this connection, great play continued to be made with Heath's much-quoted undertaking that he would only take Britain into the EC 'with the full-hearted consent of Parliament and the British people'.

There were some regional variations in the overall pattern of voting in the referendum of 1975. To some extent such differences reflected the regional strengths and weaknesses of the Conservative and Labour parties. Support for staying in the EC tended to be strongest in the south-east of England, weaker in the north and weaker still in Northern Ireland and Scotland where Shetland and the Western Isles were the only areas to record majorities against membership. Continued membership of the EC received 67.2 per cent of the vote in Britain as a whole: 68.7 of the vote in England and 66.5 per cent of the vote in Wales. The comparable figures for Scotland and Northern Ireland were 58.4 per cent and 52.1 per cent respectively (see Chapter 6 for public opinion in Northern Ireland, Scotland and Wales since 1975).

After the referendum, the attitude of the British public towards EC membership remained less than enthusiastic. This was the unequivocal message that emerged from numerous opinion polls, as well as from the first direct elections to the EP (1979), in which the British turnout of 32.35 per cent was far lower than that of any other member state. Such a mood hardly encouraged the adoption of bold, positive policies by whatever government was in power. In any case much of the caution and scepticism to be found among the public was mirrored in governing circles.

Popular interest in the European Parliament elections continued to remain low. The turnout was always below 40 per cent in the period 1979–2014, falling to as low as 24 per cent in 1999. The British turnout was always the lowest turnout of any EU state, at least until the enlargement of the EU into eastern Europe where turnouts in some cases like the Czech Republic, Poland, Slovenia and Slovakia consistently fell below 30 per cent. The relatively low British turnout has proved less marked in recent years as the average EU turnout has declined from 61.99 per cent (1979) to 42.61 per cent (2014) (see Table 5.2).

Growing disenchantment with the EU on the continent largely accounts for this trend, while evidence from other sources suggests that British public attitudes towards the EU are not far out of line with opinion elsewhere in the EU. A four-country study by YouGov, a leading polling organization, in March 2014 reported that while only 5 per cent of British voters favoured a more integrated EU with more decisions being taken by the EU, they were far from alone in holding this view, the comparable figures for France, Germany and Sweden being 15 per cent, 12 per cent and 5 per cent respectively. Furthermore, France (26 per cent) and not Britain (24 per cent) scored highest in terms of the percentage of voters wishing to leave the EU altogether (*The Times*, 22 March 2014).

Besides such data, other polls indicate a low level of knowledge ('knowledge deficit') in Britain about how the EU works, more than half the population admitting to not understanding the EU. That, in turn, had a direct impact on the precise wording of the referendum question on Britain's EU membership. In October 2013 the Electoral

Table 5.2 European Parliament election turnout percentage for the United Kingdom and the average EU turnout 1979–2014

	1979	*1984*	*1989*	*1994*	*1999*	*2004*	*2009*	*2014*
UK	32.35%	32.57%	36.37%	36.43%	24%	38.52%	34.7%	35.60%
Average EU turnout	61.99%	58.98%	58.41%	56.67%	49.51%	45.47%	42.97%	42.61%

Source: www.europarl.europa.eu.

Commission reported on its own studies of the proposed referendum question at that time ('Do you think the UK should be a member of the European Union?'). Their studies revealed that enough Britons did not know that Britain was *already* an EU member as to create confusion and a flawed result. The referendum question eventually settled and agreed was: 'Should the United Kingdom remain a member of the European Union or leave the European Union?' (McCormick, 2014: 218). How this re-wording eventually helped ill-informed voters and benefited one side more than another in the referendum campaign are no doubt matters to be addressed by research in years to come.

In the 1990s and especially after the pound's exit from the ERM in 1992, public opinion was increasingly opposed to EMU and to any suggestion of a federal Europe. Blair's idea of harnessing modernization to a positive appreciation of the EU faced difficult circumstances from the outset and ultimately proved so unsuccessful that he abandoned the effort. In the run-up to the 1997 general election, a MORI poll reported that respondents were evenly split between staying in and withdrawing from the EU – 40 per cent in each case (*The Times*, 17 April 1997). In the face of this and other evidence suggesting a growth of Eurosceptic sentiment among voters, Blair responded by writing articles in *The Sun* in which he proclaimed amongst other things his 'love for the pound' and his determination to slay the 'dragon' of a European superstate (see Chapter 10).

There is much evidence to indicate that unqualified opposition to EU membership has proved strongest in that section of the electorate that has been responsible for the rise of UKIP and far less evident among voters in higher-income managerial and professional occupations. Supporters of continued EU membership tend to be younger, more educated and more likely to work in relatively financially secure occupations. They are noticeably more likely than other groups to work in higher or lower managerial and professional occupations, and less likely to work in lower-income semi-skilled and routine jobs. They are also nearly twice as likely to have stayed in the education system beyond secondary school or their eighteenth birthday (see Table 5.3). While a strong sense of the loss of national identity forms the bedrock of UKIP opposition to the EU, the instrumental benefits of EU membership loom large among non-UKIP voters (Curtice and Evans, 2015: 6).

Ipsos MORI polls on public attitudes towards the EC/EU since 1973 highlight some of the fairly constant trends in public opinion. According to these polls, during the period 1977–2014 a majority of respondents supported British membership of the EU except in the years 1978–1983 and again in 2011–2012. The possible economic benefits of the EC/EU have loomed large in favouring membership, while at the same time there has been little inclination to become even more integrated with the organization. Other polls and surveys have identified the mid-1990s as marking the beginnings of a more Eurosceptic attitude among the public.

Table 5.3 Social background of 'inners', 'outers' and 'undecided' voters

Traits	Inners	Outers	Undecided	Full sample
Social class				
Higher managerial/professional	21	14	14	17
Lower managerial/professional	35	28	29	31
Intermediate occupations	20	23	26	22
Small employers/self-employed	6	7	6	6
Lower supervisory/technical	6	9	6	7
Semi-routine	8	12	12	10
Routine	4	8	7	6
Education (age left school)				
16 or younger	24	48	36	35
17–18	22	24	28	22
19 or older	54	29	37	44
Gender				
Male	53	50	34	49
Female	47	50	66	51
Age				
18–34	35	18	31	29
35–54	31	34	37	33
55+	33	48	31	38
N (Unweighted)	14,490	10,272	4,212	30,027

Note: Numbers in each column represent the weighted percentage of the 'inners' (who want to remain in the EU), 'outers' (who want to leave the EU) and 'undecided' individuals who belong to a given group.

Source: 2014–2017 British Election Study (Waves 4 and 6) – cited by Goodwin and Milazzo (2015).

One authoritative study discerns a changed climate of opinion in this direction in 1996 with a greater degree of Euroscepticism (the term being defined in this context as support for either leaving the EU or reducing its powers). This movement of opinion occurred at the time of the EU's decision to ban the export of British beef after British ministers admitted that there was a link between eating meat from cows suffering from Bovine Spongiform Encephalopathy (BSE or 'mad cow disease') and the incidence of a new variant of Creutzfeldt-Jakob disease in humans. This episode 'triggered a dramatic and what proved to be a long-term change in attitudes towards the EU' (Curtice and Evans, 2015). In many respects, while the Maastricht Treaty debate saw the emergence of more critical opinion about the EU among the political class, it was the beef ban that had a comparable effect on public opinion.

Some poll results for the period 1996–2014 demonstrate an enduring set of preferences about Britain's future role in the EU in the form of responses to four options. Support for Option 1 – 'Britain and other EU states moving towards closer political and economic integration' – fell from 24 per cent of respondents in April 1996 to 14 per cent in October 2014. Support for Option 2 – 'Britain's relationship with Europe remaining broadly the same as at present' – increased from 24 per cent of respondents in April 1996 to 29 per cent in October 2014. There was also an increase in support for Option 3 – 'Britain returning to being part of an economic community without political links' – from 28 per cent to 34 per cent. Finally, Option 4 – 'Britain leaving the EU altogether' – was supported by 19 per cent of respondents in April 1996 registering a slight fall to 17 per cent in October 2014 (www.ipsos-mori.com/researchpublications).

Table 5.4 Attitudes towards Britain's continuing membership of the EU, 1983–2014

	1983	1984	1985	1986	1987	1989	1990	1992	1997	2014
	%	%	%	%	%	%	%	%	%	%
Continue	53	48	56	61	63	68	76	72	54	57
Withdraw	42	45	38	33	32	26	19	17	28	35
Unweighted base	1,761	1,675	1,804	3,100	2,847	3,029	2,797	2,855	1,355	971

Source: Curtice and Evans (2015).

An extensive YouGov poll in October/November 2015 on voting intentions in a referendum on EU membership reported no gap between those wishing to remain in the EU and those wishing to leave. The poll was conducted at a time when the process of renegotiation was incomplete and when the overall figures – 41 per cent to remain and 41 per cent to leave – changed considerably depending on the outcome of the renegotiation. Such figures need to be treated with considerable caution. What is undeniable is the increasing degree of disenchantment with the EU in the past 20 years. However, this is scarcely without parallel over a longer time period, and even allowing a generous margin for error this evidence at least indicates a likely result of a referendum on Britain's membership of the EU (see Table 5.4).

Some of the YouGov survey results concerned assessments of the most important areas for reform, expectations about the likely outcome of renegotiation, and attitudes towards the EU. The two most important areas for reform were greater control of borders and immigration (52 per cent) and limits on benefits EU migrants are eligible for (46 per cent). Expectations of Cameron's renegotiation exercise were modest, most respondents (74 per cent) thought he was likely to achieve only minor reforms or none at all. There were considerable differences between 'best' and 'worst' case scenarios – the achievement of major reforms would result in 50 per cent supporting EU membership and 23 per cent leaving, while no reforms would result in 32 per cent remaining versus 46 per cent leaving. Of course, whether 'reforms' are perceived as small or major is as much a matter of presentation as of substance.

A separate YouGov survey at this time involving six EU states including Britain, explored attitudes towards the EU. The three most common adjectives to describe the EU among British respondents were 'wasteful', 'arrogant' and 'remote', while the least used adjectives were 'accountable', 'efficient' and 'honest'. The results were similar to the other states and not too dissimilar for respondent attitudes towards their own national governments. However, these are polls that at best reflect tendencies.

Conclusion

In a highly selective fashion, this chapter has picked out some of the salient features of the handling of EU membership in the context of domestic British politics. We have noted how and why attitudes have changed over time in a Eurosceptic direction, however that expression is defined. The chapter has considered some of the ways in which the character of domestic politics has often involved an awkward fit with some of the key features of the EC/EU and of mainstream continental politics. The management of the question of EU membership has proved increasingly problematical to the point where the country is revisiting the question of future membership of the EU.

The crowded events and developments of recent years have if anything contributed to a swelling Eurosceptic tide, some of the reasons for which we will return to later, notably the build-up of Eurosceptic opinion in the Conservative Party, the growth of UKIP, the silence of the pro-Europeans who have let their side of the argument fall by default, and the impact of the euro area crisis that has tarnished the EU brand.

In the next chapter, however, we visit those parts of Britain where public opinion about the EU has undergone changes in the past 40 years, suggesting that if England can be described as a 'Eurosceptic Isle', the rest of the British Isles may not be so.

6   Devolution and European Union membership

Scots'll make great Europeans. When we hear the English say, We don't want to be ruled from a distant capital where they speak differently from us and impose an alien currency on us, we think: hold on, we've had that for three centuries … London, Brussels, what's to choose? Better to be wee and ignored in a potential superpower than wee and ignored in a post-imperial backwater.

(Ken Nott in *Dead Air* by Iain Banks)

Introduction

This chapter is given over to a discussion of the European politics and interests of Northern Ireland, Scotland and Wales (hereafter referred to collectively as the devolved nations). They represent three of the four territorial components that make up the multinational state of the United Kingdom, described in some quarters as 'a centralized and pluri-national state' and 'a state of unions'.

Several reasons account for this coverage. First, separate treatment of the devolved nations offers a corrective to the largely English or nominally British analysis of the subject in some texts. The subject invariably figures as a postscript in general studies, reflecting the deeply ingrained English habit of using 'England' as a synonym for the entire British Isles. This practice is very much in the manner of the nineteenth-century Cambridge historian, J. R. Seeley, whose celebrated book on modern British history was entitled *The Expansion of England*. Such an approach is all the more questionable at a time when the relationship between 'Englishness' and 'Britishness' is problematical to say the least.

Second, the subject has forced its way to the forefront of British politics by virtue of the devolution of powers to the devolved nations that was agreed in 1998 and took effect a year later. More recently, the EU membership issue loomed large during the campaign preceding the Scotland referendum on independence (September 2014). More recently still, it has also emerged as a controversial matter in the context of the UK-wide referendum to be held in June 2016. Both the future of the constitutional arrangements of the devolved nations as well as the possibility of markedly different voting patterns across the UK in the EU referendum have given rise to warnings and predictions about the future survival of the UK.

Third, there is arguably a marked contrast between an Irish, Scottish and Welsh experience of 'Europe' and what might broadly be considered an English perspective. It is commonly maintained that in the past 20 or so years, the former have distinguished themselves from the latter by their support for the EU. We consider some of the reasons why that might be so. A more important difference, however, is that, unlike the English, the Irish, Scots and Welsh have long been accustomed to multiple identities – their own and a wider British one (or Irish one). In this realm of identity politics, the Scots and Welsh at least 'are unfazed by the discovery of a third European identity', while the English 'can't get used to the notion of multiple identities' (David Marquand in *The Guardian*, 18 December 2011). Charles Kennedy, former leader of the Liberal Democrats, was at ease with such a condition: 'I find no contradiction between being a Highlander, a Scot, a citizen of the U.K. and a citizen of the European Union at one and the same time'.

We first consider the institutional character and range of EC/EU policies concerning regions and stateless nations (the latter being historical unions of previously independent and self-governing parts). This section includes an assessment of the importance of the Treaty on European Union in cultivating the idea of a 'Europe of the regions' and the subsequent evolution of this idea. The chapter considers the devolution settlement of 1998 and the precise role and limitations of the devolved administrations in EU affairs. The policies and attitudes of the political parties confined to the devolved nations receive attention, particularly detailing Scottish developments, together with reference to public opinion. Finally, the chapter considers all of these elements in relation to the UK referendum on EU membership.

'Europe of the regions'

In its origins and during the first three decades of its existence, the EC made virtually no provision for regional or sub-state administrations. Such entities were overshadowed by the intergovernmental and supranational politics of the highly centralized EC. Representation at the supranational level was denied them. Meanwhile, national governments treated EC business as falling within the field of foreign policy and consequently within their exclusive competence. The regions were thus increasingly far removed from the EC decision-making system.

Some degree of change in this situation was effected as and when national governments proposed to transfer powers to the EC in areas where they themselves shared competence with regional administrations or where the latter had exclusive competence. In these circumstances, first evident in the aftermath of the Single European Act and even more so by the time of the (Maastricht) Treaty on European Union, such administrations could bring pressure to bear on government. This trend was particularly evident in a federal system as in the case of the powerful German Länder and the Belgian Sub-national Entities, both of which achieved influence over the conduct of European affairs in their respective countries. It has also featured in respect of the Autonomous Communities in Spain.

The opportunity to advance this case emerged in the 1980s but found strong expression during negotiations resulting in the signing of the Treaty on European Union. By this time, the German Länder in particular had secured several mechanisms within the German federal system, and they enjoyed collectively considerable influence over EU matters which fell within their competence. Moreover, they had a potential veto over further transfers of competence to the EU. This process of the 'Europeanization' of domestic policy was indicative of the eroding away of the dividing line between domestic and European policy matters. National governments could no longer monopolize European policy on the grounds that it belonged to the realm of foreign policy and was thus their exclusive preserve.

Several key aspects of the Treaty on European Union gave substance to the idea of a 'Europe of the regions'. The Treaty basically acknowledged that its territories or regions had a role to play in EU policymaking where the treaties so allowed. Furthermore, the principle of subsidiarity laid down that where possible decisions in the EU should be taken at the lowest level where appropriate and that powers should be exercised as close to the citizen as possible. The Treaty also made provision for a Committee of the Regions (CoR). This body had no decision-making status within the EU apparatus. However, it did involve some recognition that the EU's regions and stateless nations should have a formal role in the policy process where appropriate. The regions and territories were, so to speak, the building blocks of the EU.

There appeared to be considerable momentum behind the regionalization of Europe by this stage, especially among minority nationalist parties that seized the opportunity to press for greater recognition of their demands for independence. This was so much the case that theorists of European integration seeking to understand and to explain the workings of the EU as a political system developed a theory of multi-level governance. According to this theory, EU policymaking basically involved the regions or sub-state actors playing an important role alongside states and supranational institutions. Thus, devolved governments pressed for greater decentralization within the EU at the time of the abortive EU Constitutional Treaty and the subsequent making of the Lisbon Treaty.

Some of the early promise, however, was not fulfilled in later years. Indeed, the notion of a 'Europe of the regions' arguably began to fall out of favour for a variety of different reasons. There was limited evidence of the widespread mobilization of regions to bring influence to bear successfully at the EU level. Furthermore, it became increasingly clear that EU politics was still dominated by the central governments of the member states. In effect, national governments ensured that they themselves acted as 'gatekeepers' in limiting the input of sub-state actors. Governments were equally determined to restrict the application of the principle of subsidiarity to the relationship between the member states and the EU institutions rather than applying the principle as a mechanism for empowering the sub-state level (Elias, 2008).

Meanwhile, the Committee of the Regions did not quite live up to early promise. From the outset its assorted membership of stateless nations, federal regions and municipalities often had little in common to generate much momentum and notice in EU circles. It tended to produce complex resolutions rather than detailed treatment of key policy issues with a view to feeding the results into the policy process at the right time (Keating, 2014). There was a widely held view that the status of regions remained too subordinate within the EU. If there were diminishing prospects for a 'Europe of the regions', the process of the decentralization of power in many EU states nonetheless emerged as a major feature of European politics, as in the case in Britain.

Devolution

Prior to the devolution settlement of 1998, Britain was a multinational, unitary state within which the devolved nations each had their own territorial branches of government with different degrees of autonomy. Following the establishment of the

Scottish Office (1885), Scotland had a form of administrative devolution that provided for a degree of autonomy concerning the implementation of domestic policies that were purely Scottish. Northern Ireland secured a type of executive devolution under the Government of Ireland Act (1920) that endured until the imposition of direct rule (1972) by Westminster as a result of 'the Troubles'. Wales did not secure its own territorial branch of government until 1965. Initially at least, the Welsh Office had a much smaller remit than its counterpart in Scotland, though in 1975 it secured significant economic powers. Scotland and Wales each had its own Secretary of State who was a member of the Cabinet.

Britain's accession to the EC in 1973 had an immediate impact on the political life of Scotland and Wales, though this was far less the case in Northern Ireland. The latter possessed little, if any, substantive autonomy following 'direct rule'. There was a recognition in Scotland and Wales that both stood to lose autonomy as decision-making looked set to become physically and politically even more remote. While previously enjoying direct access to decision-makers in London most especially in Cabinet through their Secretary of State, it was now the case that their access to decision-making would be indirect, in those areas of policy which fell within the EC ambit. At an early stage, nevertheless, it was recognized that while EC membership represented a threat it also presented the opportunity of engaging in a new political arena whether for lobbying or later for more active participation.

Britain's entry into the EC coincided with growing demands for constitutional change. The struggle for change was most pronounced in Northern Ireland where one side in a prolonged armed conflict aimed to achieve the reunification of Ireland. In Scotland and Wales there was mounting pressure for greater autonomy with a rising tide of nationalist opinion in both countries. The first response was a Royal Commission on the Constitution (1969) that was eventually followed by a government White Paper under the Wilson Labour government that proposed legislative devolution for Scotland and Wales. This proposal came to grief in 1979 when it failed to secure the required majorities in referendums held in Scotland and Wales. The issue of EC membership surfaced in both of these cases, first in the production of the 1969 White Paper when two dissenters from the report maintained that devolution would be a recipe for confusion with ambiguity over the divisions of competence, and second over the issues of how the proposed devolved administrations could best be represented in Brussels. At an even earlier stage than that, a close link was forged between European integration and nationalist demands – at least in Scotland. In 1961, at the time of the first British application for EC membership, the Scottish National Party (SNP) leadership wrote to Prime Minister Macmillan demanding the 're-convention' of the English and Scottish parliaments. It did so on the grounds that under the terms of the Act of Union of 1707 Westminster lacked the authority to cede sovereignty to the EC.

The current process of devolution started under the Blair Labour government in September 1997 when, as a result of referendums in Scotland and Wales, a majority of voters chose to establish a Scottish Parliament and a National Assembly for Wales. In Northern Ireland, devolution was a key part of the Belfast (Good Friday) Agreement supported by voters in a referendum in May 1998. Parliament subsequently passed three devolution acts: the Scotland Act 1998, the Northern Ireland Act 1998, and the Government of Wales Act 1998 (effectively superseded by the Government of Wales Act 2006). These acts established the three devolved legislatures.

Reserved powers

There were some significant variations between the powers accorded to these legislatures. The relevant point in this context, however, is that in all cases international relations and EU affairs remained the responsibility of Westminster, commonly referred to as 'reserved powers'. The British government retained its responsibility for managing both international relations and relations with the rest of the EU including leading on all policy and legislative negotiations. A Memorandum of Understanding affirmed that the relationship between the UK government and each of the territorial administrations would be one of collaboration. Joint Ministerial Committees were expected to provide a formal setting for consultation between the central government and the devolved administrations, meeting four or five times annually. A set of Concordats between central government and the devolved administrations recognized the interests of the latter in several aspects of international and EU relations, providing in particular for the coordination of EU policy issues and the mechanisms for dealing with EU business between central government and the devolved administrations. The Memorandum of Understanding and Concordats were superseded but not substantially altered by the 'Memorandum of Understanding and Supplementary Agreements' (October 2013) which, like the original, did not amount to a binding agreement with legal obligations.

Members of the devolved legislatures nominate ministers among themselves to comprise an executive, known as the devolved administrations and headed by a First Minister (www.gov.uk/guidance/devolution-of-powers-to-scotland-wales-an-northern-Ireland). Currently (October 2015), the Scottish government is a working majority government comprising the SNP. The Welsh government is a minority government formed by the Labour Party. The Northern Ireland Executive is a five-party power-sharing executive comprising the largest parties in the Assembly: the Alliance Party of Northern Ireland, the Democratic Unionist Party (DUP), Sinn Féin, the Social Democratic Labour Party (SDLP) and the Ulster Unionist Party (UUP). What, then, are the roles, functions and emphases of the devolved administrations in EU affairs?

Broadly speaking, the formal constitutional relationship with the EU is similar across the three countries. The devolved administrations are responsible for implementing EU obligations where they relate to devolved matters. This requirement effectively means that the devolved legislatures are responsible for transposing and implementing a wide spectrum of EU legislation including areas such as agriculture, fisheries and the environment. Thus, for example, while the UK government represents the UK in EU negotiations, fisheries management itself is a devolved matter. Each devolved administration has control over the management of their own commercial fishing fleets, within a UK-wide system. Furthermore, the EU in 2007 agreed to devolve some conservation measures to the Scottish administration.

The devolved administrations are also responsible for administering the spending of EU funds such as Structural Funds (principally designed to reduce disparities between regions in the EU) and the Common Agricultural Policy. In areas where the British government has competence, such as Single Market legislation, the devolved administrations have an interest in monitoring how EU laws will impact on their countries. Finally, in this respect, the devolved legislatures have to ensure that all of their legislation is compatible with EU law (House of Commons Library, June 2015). This requirement is embedded in the Acts of 1998 and may prove problematical in the event of a British vote to leave the EU (see below).

The value of EU membership in the devolved nations

Northern Ireland

The perceived benefits of EU membership to Northern Ireland have ranged from its political value in addressing the problems of a divided society to the impact of economic factors and financial assistance.

EC/EU membership has directly and indirectly changed the context within which to address the problems of the region. It has most notably facilitated several developments in seeking to resolve longstanding conflicts, particularly in terms of relations between the London and Dublin governments and also relations between Northern Ireland and Dublin. Prior to EC membership, there was often a tense relationship between Britain and Ireland centring on Northern Ireland. The EC membership of both states contributed to a greater degree of co-operation between both governments. The Anglo-Irish Agreement (1985) signified the degree of change in relations. More particularly, it drew on EC-inspired notions of transnational governance in giving the Irish government a role in the public affairs of Northern Ireland. The eventual outcome of this process and the creation of transnational institutional structures found expression in the 1998 Good Friday Agreement with its provisions for a territorial Northern Ireland Executive and Assembly, a transnational North/South Ministerial Council, and a transnational British-Irish Council and British-Irish Intergovernmental Conference (Phinnemore *et al.*, 2012).

The EU was not directly involved in negotiations resulting in the Good Friday Agreement. It was nonetheless influential in that many key actors in the peace process acknowledged that the agreement was derived from many European sources, including EU principles and treaties. More particularly, the European Commission has provided vital support for the process at the local community level through its Peace and Reconciliation programmes covering Northern Ireland and the Border Region of Ireland. Peace I (1995–1999), Peace II (2000–2006) and Peace III (2007–2013) suggest 'a sophisticated and sustained example of a "peace-building from below" strategy', engaging public, private and third sector organizations on both sides of the Irish border and forming many cross-border partnerships for conflict transformation (Phinnemore *et al.*, 2012). The content of the current Peace IV (2014–2020) programme, agreed by the Northern Ireland Executive and the Irish government, places a strong emphasis on promoting cross-community relations and understanding in order to create a more cohesive society. It is financed by some 229 million euros from the European Regional Development Fund (ERDF).

Following the agreement to re-establish power-sharing arrangements in Northern Ireland (May 2007), Barroso, the president of the European Commission, was the first senior international political figure to visit Belfast where he agreed to set up a unique Task Force for Northern Ireland within the Commission services to maximize the opportunities on offer from the EU. The territory has long received considerable financial assistance from the EU through its status as an Objective 1 peripheral region – this being defined as a region whose development is lagging behind and attracts maximum EU support. Northern Ireland has long had the highest unemployment of any UK region (except incidentally at one point in 'the Troubles' when a large military presence was mistakenly counted in as part of the local gainfully employed labour force). Objective 1 status in the period 1989–1999 resulted in £1.7 billion of EU funding for Northern Ireland, with agriculture, fisheries and rural development particularly featuring as beneficiaries.

Scotland

As in the case of Northern Ireland, EC/EU membership has offered a framework within which to consider new understandings of British politics and of Scotland's place in the Union and in the wider world, a theme to which we will return below. In terms of the precise value of EU membership to Scotland, the Scottish government's own assessment of the economic, social and cultural benefits appeared in a paper published in March 2015, 'The Benefits of Scotland's EU Membership' (www.gov.scot/Resource/00473833.pdf).

Access to the Single Market featured as a major advantage, particularly since the EU was the main destination for 46 per cent of Scotland's international exports with an estimated value of £12.9 billion (2013). A 2013 survey also indicated that eight of Scotland's top ten international export destinations were EU member states (Belgium, Denmark, France, Germany, Ireland, Italy, Spain and the Netherlands), the value of exports to these countries being worth just over £10.7 billion (Scottish Global Connections Survey 2013). Some 336,000 jobs in Scotland were estimated to be directly associated with exports to the EU in 2011.

According to the Scottish government, EU membership has also played an important role in increasing the amount of Foreign Direct Investment (FDI) in Scotland. In 2013 there were over 2,100 foreign-owned companies in Scotland, employing approximately 302,000 people with a combined turnover of £1,201 billion. Some 40 per cent of these companies were ultimately owned by firms based in the EU.

The other important economic and financial aspect of EU membership has involved EU funding through European Structural Funds, the Common Agricultural Policy (CAP) direct payments, and through winning competitive funding. During the funding round between 2007 and 2013, Scotland received £1.3 billion of structural funds. The current funding package for Scotland for the period 2014–2020 is made up of European Regional and Social Funding (985 million euros), the EU contribution to the Rural Development Programme (844 million euros), and CAP direct payments to farmers totalling 3.5 billion euros and funded through the European Agricultural Guarantee Fund (EAGF). The total amount of competitive funding won by Scottish universities (2007–2014) was 572 million euros, almost 1.3 per cent of the research funding programme for the whole of the EU.

The Scottish government has also claimed a leading role in climate diplomacy by setting high ambitions and marshalling support from elsewhere in the EU. Again, according to Scottish government figures, electricity delivered from renewable sources accounts for a greater proportion of gross electricity consumption in Scotland (42 per cent) than across the EU overall (23.5 per cent). Similarly in the sphere of greenhouse gas emissions during the period 1990–2012 these fell faster in Scotland (–29.9 per cent) than in the UK (–23.3 per cent) or across the EU (–18.5 per cent).

Wales

Many of the benefits of EU membership cited by political leaders in Northern Ireland and Scotland have found expression among Welsh politicians. In May 2015 Carwyn Jones, leader of the Labour Party in Wales and First Minister of Wales since 2009, was far more effusive in his support for EU membership than the Labour Party leadership elsewhere in Britain. In a rare British acknowledgement of Europe Day (9 May), he declared that

EU membership was 'vital for our economic success'. He further noted that the EU was Wales's largest trading partner, with more than 500 firms in Wales depending on that trade. In addition, more than 450 firms from other EU states were located in Wales and employed over 50,000 people (quoted in House of Commons Library, June 2015).

Like Northern Ireland and Scotland, Wales also draws considerable benefits from EU funding. Indeed, by any measure the three countries currently and collectively receive a proportionately larger share of funding than England, amounting to 3.397 billion euros as compared with a figure of 6.174 billion euros for England. Wales receives a larger amount of funding than either Northern Ireland or Scotland, totalling some 2.145 billion euros.

Some of this funding is of particularly crucial importance to certain sectors of the Welsh economy. The effects of EU membership first became apparent in rural Wales through the workings of the Common Agricultural Policy. It is estimated that the CAP provides around 80–90 per cent of the basic farm income in Wales. More generally, it was the decline of heavy industry in the 1980s that highlighted the potential significance of EC membership. The 1988 reform of the EC's European Regional Development Fund (with its focus on the poorest and most backward regions) and the doubling of regional aid to Wales eventually had 'a hugely significant effect in Wales'. The West Wales and Valleys region has received considerable Objective 1 funding since 2000 on the grounds that it has failed to cross the threshold of 75 per cent of average EU GDP (Jones and Rumbul, 2012). The issue of EU funding has not been without controversy in Welsh politics, particularly when disagreements with the Blair government on the question of EU funding mechanisms eventually led to the removal of Alun Michael from the post of First Secretary for Wales (1999–2000).

According to a Welsh government source in 2013, EU structural funds had helped over 47,000 people in Wales into work, had assisted nearly 128,000 to gain qualifications, and had facilitated the formation of over 5,000 new enterprises and 18,000 jobs (House of Commons Library, June 2015). Evidently, the omission of Wales from the map of one EU yearbook in 2004 did not adversely affect the country's access to EU funding (Jones and Rumbul, 2012).

Nationalism and European Union membership

Each of the governments of the devolved nations have contained or currently include elements that are committed to exiting from the United Kingdom and creating their own nation-state. The Northern Ireland Executive has Sinn Féin representatives, whose aim is the unity and independence of Ireland as a sovereign state. It also includes the Social Democratic and Labour Party, a nationalist party committed to political and non-violent means of uniting Northern Ireland with the Republic of Ireland. The Scottish government is a working majority government comprising the SNP with an independent Scotland as its principal goal. The Welsh nationalist party – Plaid Cymru – shared power in coalition with the Labour Party in 2007–2009. It has since figured as an opposition party winning only 15 of the 60 seats in the Welsh National Assembly elections of 2007 and 2011 and reflecting the very limited support for independence in Wales. Unlike Scotland, Wales has not made the transition from cultural nationalism to political nationalism that was dramatically registered in the SNP's victory in the Holyrood election of 2011 and its landslide victory in the UK parliamentary election of May 2015 when it won 56 of the 59 seats in Scotland.

Divisions of opinion in Northern Ireland over the EU have reflected the polarized character of politics and society in the province. During much of the period of direct rule, British ministers were understandably more concerned about resolving the conflict than defending the province's EC/EU interests. As compared with Scotland and Wales, the degree of Europeanization in Northern Ireland was relatively limited and, due to the absence of political leadership, it was the civil service that was often to the fore in addressing EC/EU affairs.

For a considerable period of time (1979–1999), two of the province's three Members of the European Parliament (MEPs), John Hume of the SDLP and Ian Paisley of the DUP, represented contrasting perspectives on the EC/EU. Hume, leader of the SDLP (1979–2001) and a convinced Europhile, expressed a widespread view among progressive nationalists that European integration would facilitate the reunification of Ireland. It would do so by diminishing the importance of borders, by transferring political sovereignty, and by reconciling previously warring populations (Phinnemore *et al.*, 2012).

Paisley, leader of the DUP (1971–2008) and First Minister of Northern Ireland (2007–2008), was an intransigent opponent of European integration. He believed that the EC/EU like Irish nationalism was a major threat to British sovereignty over Northern Ireland. He also engaged in some notorious rants against the Pope and Roman Catholicism. On one occasion in the European Parliament he interrupted a speech by Pope John Paul II to denounce him as the Antichrist, though Seat Number 666 in the Chamber that Paisley claimed was reserved for the Antichrist was unoccupied at the time. He was forcibly removed from the proceedings for his interjection.

The bitter divisions between such unionist and nationalist leaders did not hinder some degree of co-operation. Paisley was willing to join in Hume's lobbying efforts in relation to the crucial issue of economic assistance for the province's conflict-damaged economy. During the 1980s, they presented a united front in order to maximize financial assistance from Brussels, continuing to do so in the 1990s until the establishment of the Peace I programme in 1995. Following Hume's retirement (2004), the SDLP lost its European Parliament seat to Sinn Féin, and thereafter the region's MEPs reflected various shades of Eurosceptic thinking (Phinnemore *et al.*, 2012).

There is evidence to suggest that in the past decade or so opposition to EU membership has weakened within the traditionally Eurosceptic Sinn Féin, the largest nationalist party. Similarly, Peter Robinson, the First Minister of Northern Ireland and leader of the DUP (2008–2016) acknowledged that, while he was personally in the 'eurosceptic classification', Northern Ireland 'has done well out of EU peace funding' and that leaving the EU would potentially damage the local economy. Indeed, several months after Cameron announced support for a referendum on EU membership (January 2013), Northern Ireland's political leaders warned that Britain leaving the EU would be a 'huge mistake' that could deter foreign investors, disrupt bilateral trade with the Republic of Ireland amounting to some £1.6 billion, and damage the region's fragile economy (*Financial Times*, 7 July 2013). Furthermore, it is possible that a British withdrawal from the EU would be a source of enormous instability and turbulence for Ireland and that the political arrangements established by the Good Friday Agreement would not be entirely protected from this instability (Institute of International and European Affairs, August 2012).

Such concerns were also evident in the reactions of the Dublin government to the possibility of Britain leaving the EU. Enda Kenny, the Irish prime minister, expressed deep unease at the prospect of a British exit, suggesting that it would be a 'serious difficulty' for Northern Ireland and that the success of the Northern Ireland peace process was in part linked to the UK and Irish Republic's joint membership of the EU. Similarly, a report in 2015 by the Irish Parliament's joint committee on EU affairs warned that in the event of Britain's exit from the EU some of the cross-border bodies established under the Good Friday Agreement to build confidence among nationalists could become redundant (*The Guardian*, 25 January 2016).

Scotland and Wales have more in common with each other than with Northern Ireland in their approach to and handling of EU affairs since the devolution settlement of 1998. While this arrangement reserved European matters and international affairs to Westminster, it was nonetheless acknowledged that the administrations in Scotland and Wales had a role to play, as did the Scottish Parliament and the National Assembly for Wales. Both Scottish and Welsh ministers have invariably taken a close interest in European issues because of their impact on devolved matters. Furthermore, each administration formulated its own distinctive foreign affairs agenda and also established bureaux in Brussels – Scotland Europa and the Wales European Centre – that pre-dated devolution and that were heavily involved in lobbying on behalf of their respective territories (Wright, 2005). All three territories also joined RegLeg which emerged in 2001. This Conference of Regions with Legislative Power comprises representatives of regional governments, but is not a formal EU institution.

The early years of SNP policy towards the EU

In 2004, the Scottish Executive defined the aims of its European Strategy as:

*   To position Scotland as one of the leading legislative regions in the European Union, with a thriving and dynamic economy.
*   To bring effective influence to bear on the UK Government, EU Member States, regions and institutions on EU policy issues affecting Scotland.

(Scottish Executive External Relations Division, January 2004)

At the same time the Scottish Executive issued a publication – *International Outlook: Educating Young Scots about the World* (2001) – that emphasized the importance of the European dimension in the school curriculum, asserting that 'we are already European citizens, with rights and responsibilities' (quoted in Brocklehurst, 2015).

At this time a Labour–Liberal Democrat coalition formed the Scottish Executive. Ten years later, however, a majority SNP government was in power, advocating altogether more ambitious, if controversial, plans for Scotland's relationship with the EU. Of the three devolved nations, Scotland has proved to be the most advanced in pressing the UK government to take account of its interests. The country also experienced a prolonged debate over EU membership before and during the referendum campaign on an independent Scotland and subsequently in the context of the Smith Commission that was established by Cameron immediately after the September 2014 referendum.

SNP policy and attitudes towards EC membership since 1973 have undergone considerable change. In recent years, moreover, the question of Scotland's relationship with the EU in the event of independence has raised unresolved problems. Meanwhile the outcome of the UK-wide referendum on EU membership has prompted much speculation.

The SNP has long represented itself and Scotland as a keen supporter of EU membership. Such support, however, was not always the case and has often rested on untested professions in the absence of an independent Scotland. The SNP has always viewed the issue of EU membership in the context of the SNP's cardinal principles: 'the obtaining of self-government within the UN and Commonwealth by democratic means and the furtherance of Scottish interests' (Wilson, 2009: 44). Furthermore, the handling of the precise issue has often been determined by the party's fluctuating fortunes, by its attention-seeking strategy and tactics, by domestic political opportunities and, almost to a lesser extent, by changes in the evolution of the EC/EU.

Both academic and personal accounts of distinct phases in the party's policy and attitudes towards the EC/EU over the past 60 years are more or less at one in identifying four phases: 1950s; 1960s–1970s; 1980s–1990s; post-2000 (Wilson, 2009, 2014; Tarditi, 2010). In the 1950s and through to the first British application to join the EC, the party supported the idea of European integration. It did so often for the same reasons that it returned to this position in later years. For much of this period, European integration had its attractions as appearing less threatening and less invasive for Scottish identity than the UK Union. It also demonstrated a contrast between a supposedly internationalist party and an isolationist UK government (Tarditi, 2010: 10–11).

Following the failure of the first British application for EC membership and through the rest of the 1960s into the 1970s, there was a major change in the party's position. Shortly before the unsuccessful Wilson application for EC membership in 1966, the SNP conference insisted that all negotiations should recognize Scotland as an independent country (Mitchell, 2014: 119). By the time of the Heath negotiations for EC membership, there was a hardening of SNP attitudes against the EC with the insistence that an independent Scotland would not be bound by any signature of the British government to the Treaty of Rome. The campaigning slogan at the time – 'No Voice. No Entry' – was accompanied by hostility to perceived European centralization, bureaucracy and elitism. The latter challenged the party's decentralist traditions and was anathema to SNP members 'who had been fighting London control and saw little benefit in exchanging that jack boot for a European model' (Wilson, 2009: 46, 56, 101). The achievement of Scotland's independence and membership of a supranational EC were here viewed as two wholly irreconcilable processes, a view that has lingered in some sections of the party ever since.

The SNP campaigned for a No vote in the referendum on continued membership of the EC in 1975. Equally, if not more importantly, it regarded the referendum campaign as a means to prove the illegitimacy of the UK government and its policies in Scotland. It was hoped that a clear majority of the Scottish people would think the same. They didn't, and that eventually prompted a review of the party's policy.

Independence in Europe

At the 1983 SNP conference Gordon Wilson (SNP leader 1979–1990), chiding the party over its isolationist approach, argued that the EC offered 'a first class way of pushing the advantages of political independence without any threat of economic dislocation' (Wilson, 2009: 225–6). An explicitly pro-EC policy was one of three areas where Wilson sought changes, the others being the abandonment of the party's opposition to NATO and its hardline opposition to devolution (Mitchell, 2014: 231). Several years earlier in 1979, the election of the first SNP MEP, Winnie Ewing, increasingly highlighted the advantages of association with the broad protective umbrella of European integration. Ewing remained an MEP until 1999, initially highly critical of the EC but later becoming one of the party's strongest supporters of membership.

What further encouraged a more pro-EC policy in the 1980s was a growing recognition in several quarters of the value of the EC. Scottish local authorities found that Brussels was more amenable to their requests for support than the Thatcher government in London. Similarly, trade unionists found the EC institutions more sympathetic to their interests than London. EC regional funds came with the condition that EC support was recognized and EC symbols became a familiar part of the Scottish landscape.

Prior to the European Parliament elections of 1989, the SNP campaigned for the first time on the slogan 'Independence in Europe' that was coined by Jim Sillars, the architect of the new approach, who was an SNP MP (1988–1992) and deputy leader of the SNP (1991–1992). This mantra, all the more potent for the vague, ill-defined meaning of the catch-all expression 'Europe', served two main purposes. It projected a positive international rather than isolationist outlook, seemingly escaping from the unwanted connotations of 'separation', 'secession' and 'division' on the quest for independence. 'Independence in Europe' also countered the view that an independent Scotland would lose influence and security. EC/EU membership would effectively bring Scotland all the underpinning it might need as a relatively small state in the international arena.

'Independence in Europe' was also indicative of a calculation as to how best to position the party on the EC/EU as a secondary issue in order to advance the primary goal of independence. Commentators have variously described the change to a pro-EC stance in terms of the EC playing the role of an 'external support system' and as a route to independence that was not dependent on Westminster. In short, 'England could be bypassed' (Tarditi, 2010: 18). The EC also offered an alternative point of reference in which UK policy developments could be challenged or mediated (Brocklehurst, 2015).

The slogan also took the place in the public's mind of the 1970s catchphrase 'It's Scotland's oil'. That expression, as Wilson later commented, was coined against the background of 'silly' UK government-inspired arguments about oil that had to be countered 'given the essential gullibility of the Scottish people' (Wilson, 2009: 86) – an unusual public statement by a political leader.

It was no coincidence that the 'Independence in Europe' slogan emerged at a time when Prime Minister Thatcher was painting the EC in increasingly unattractive colours and, more importantly, when the introduction of the Community Charge ('poll tax') in Scotland in 1989 and in England and Wales in the following year was resulting in mass protests. The poll tax episode was but one stage in the secular decline of the Conservative Party in Scotland. The party had held 66 out of 71 parliamentary seats in Scotland in the general election of 1955. In all general elections since 2001, however, it has held only one seat, increasingly making the Conservatives close to an England-only party.

By the late 1980s the EC became all the more attractive to some sections of Scottish public opinion as a welcome refuge from Thatcherite views on the poll tax, the EU, devolution and privatization. Thatcherism was becoming 'Scotland's Other' (Mitchell, 2014: 234). Against the background of mounting Conservative Euroscepticism, there emerged a degree of contrariness ('if the Tories are worried about Europe, we are not going to be'). This feature, together with folk memories and tales about the 'auld alliance' with France and links with Nordic culture, has marked one section of Scottish opinion ever since, though the reason why many Scots have car registration plates with the name of their country in French (*Écosse*) is debatable, if not mystifying.

Both at the time and later – following the Conservatives' return to power in 2010 as part of a coalition government – the SNP's desire to distance itself from the UK government's position on the EU was very similar to its strategy on multiculturalism, immigration and welfare reform. It sought to present Scotland as a much more open, progressive, outward-looking and tolerant nation than Britain/England (Hepburn, 2014). This contention was as untestable or untested as some of the party's pro-EU expressions. At the very least, however, it was questionable in view of the ethnic make-up of the two capital cities – Edinburgh and London – 8 per cent of Edinburgh's population being non-white (a figure twice the average of Scotland as a whole) compared with over 50 per cent of London's residents describing themselves as non-white and representing some 300 languages in a quintessentially cosmopolitan city, 41 per cent of whose residents were not born in the UK (*The Guardian*, 17 September 2014).

Levels of EU migration (from other EU states outside the UK) to Scotland are lower than in the rest of the UK, and immigration has a much less significant effect on employment in Scotland than in the rest of the UK. Data from the 2015 Labour Force Survey indicate that among those employed in Scotland, 92 per cent have been born in the UK. In the UK as a whole, however, around 16 per cent of employees have been born outside the UK (Bell, 2015). Consequently, issues relating to EU immigration such as migrant benefits are unlikely to have the same salience with the Scottish electorate and may arguably boost support for EU membership.

The convenience of identifying with the EU has also presented the SNP with an opportunity to appear as a credible European mainstream party at a time when other parties, notably the Labour Party, were undergoing a similar change (see Chapter 3). Furthermore, by the late 1980s European integration became all the more attractive because of the reform of structural funding in the EC. At the same time, there was also the compelling vision of a 'social Europe' associated with Jacques Delors, president of the European Commission (see Chapter 3). Nevertheless, the SNP regarded some EC institutions with suspicion, not least the Committee of the Regions, which it viewed as assigning Scotland a sub-state position keeping the country subordinated within the UK.

How far the adoption of the 'Independence in Europe' slogan represented effective, glossy marketing rather than a detailed, deep-seated interest in the EU became evident some years later. In 2000 Wilson observed that while major developments had taken place in the EU since 1990 (notably the Maastricht Treaty, the enlargement of the EU and the formation of the euro area) the SNP's European policy was in 'a stage of intellectual neglect' and had 'lain fallow' (Wilson, 2014: 73). Besides the lack of political and intellectual leadership, there was little regard for addressing key questions such as how exactly an independent Scotland would exert more influence within the EU than the much larger UK. That position, however, was consistent with the view that the SNP's variable position on the EU has been determined more by 'the domestic structures of political opportunities than by those at the European level' (Tarditi, 2010).

Since 2000, the SNP's position on the EU has become, if anything, more cautious and eventually more critical of EU policy. The party has given less prominence to EU membership for fear of exposing divisions of opinion within the party over the issue. The party conducted a U-turn in its support for the euro, criticized the lack of democratic accountability, opposed the abortive EU Constitution of 2005, and registered scathing criticism of the Common Fisheries Policy (Hepburn, 2014). In some respects, the party differed little, if at all, from the views of pro-EU elements in the mainstream British parties, while it included a sizable minority opposed to EU membership (Wilson, 2014: 179). Furthermore, the SNP government was no more inclined than the British government to abandon the budget rebate or any of the British opt-outs from the EU whether in relation to the euro area or the Schengen Agreement.

According to Wilson's account, the issue of EU membership dropped from public view until the post-2008 euro crisis and the controversy attending the independence referendum of 2014, and even then polling showed that the Scottish public had little interest in Europe (Wilson, 2014: 73, 215). Later evidence from an authoritative Nat Cen Social Research study also noted that there was little difference between Scotland and the rest of the UK in terms of public attitudes towards the idea of an unreformed EU. John Curtice, co-author of the study, concluded that '60 per cent of people in Scotland can also be classified as Eurosceptic, just five points below the figure for Britain as a whole' (quoted in *The Guardian*, 24 February 2016).

It was perhaps indicative of the limited interest in the EU issue in the party and among the public at large that Alex Salmond, the SNP First Minister (2007–2014), was criticized for giving a 'muddled and incomplete' answer about his government's legal advice on an independent Scotland's future membership of the EU (*The Guardian*, 10 January 2013). During the lengthy independence referendum campaign, in fact, the SNP was at its least coherent and convincing when addressing EU matters, especially on the euro and the currency of an independent Scotland. This was so much the case that Tom Devine, the Scottish historian, who voted 'Yes' for independence in the referendum and who is regarded in some circles as the SNP's court historian, subsequently disclosed that he would not do so again because 'There has not been any systematic tackling of the intellectual and economic weaknesses of the Yes campaign' (*The Times*, 27 February 2016).

A key change in SNP handling of EU matters since 2000 has involved the way in which devolution has opened up a new political space hitherto occupied in part by the EU. In short, once the Scottish Parliament came into being 'EU policy gradually lost relevance in the party agenda' (Tarditi, 2010: 35). That trend became even more pronounced as and when the SNP came to power, first as a minority administration after the Scottish parliamentary election of 2007 (when the party rebranded the Scottish Executive as the Scottish Government) and subsequently as a majority administration following the election of 2011. The party has meanwhile transformed its Westminster representation from ten seats in the general election of 2005 to 56 seats in the 2015 general election, a political dominance all the greater as the number of Westminster parliamentary seats in Scotland was reduced from 72 to 59 in 2005. Given these conditions, there is still substance to a conclusion arrived at in 2010. This is to the effect that, once having obtained a more visible and relevant role in the Scottish context, the SNP rapidly marginalized the European issue, becoming often indifferent to the specific policies and activities at the EU level, and more critical towards some aspects of European integration (Tarditi, 2010: 39).

In the run-up to the independence referendum, the SNP government published two documents that varied in their coverage of EU membership. A 649-page blockbuster entitled *Scotland's Future: Your Guide to an Independent Scotland* was launched in a blaze of publicity in November 2013 at a press conference where the London media were cheekily given international accreditation. Only eight pages in this publication were devoted to 'Scotland in the European Union'. Part of this section addressed the question of possible procedures under which an independent Scotland could become a signatory to the EU treaties, none of which could be said to have captured the imagination of the Scottish public.

At the same time, another Scottish government paper – *Scotland in the European Union* – offered more substantial coverage. In the circumstances, however, some of its content was necessarily speculative and occasionally platitudinous. It emphasized the better and fairer treatment, so it was claimed, that sectors of the Scottish economy would enjoy with an independent Scottish government in control. These points were made with reference to the EU's CAP and Common Fisheries Policy (CFP). Such were the failings of successive British governments in CAP negotiations that, according to this paper, Scotland had the lowest per hectare rate of support for rural development in the EU and was third lowest in the EU for direct payments to farmers.

On the CFP, it was argued that the EU's land-locked states such as Austria, Luxembourg and Slovakia had more formal influence over that policy than Scotland with the longest coastline in the EU and home to one of the EU's most important fishing industries and communities. Scotland accounted for some 61 per cent of the total landings value of fish in the UK (2012) and 90 per cent of the UK's aquaculture (*Scotland in the European Union*, 2013: 15, 44; HM Government, 'Review of the Balance of Competences between the United Kingdom and the European Union Fisheries Report', Summer 2014: 23–4; Scottish Government, 'Scotland's Priorities for EU Reform', February 2014: 10–11). Unsurprisingly, the SNP has long called for the repatriation of the CFP with a view to assigning it to the Scottish Parliament and not Westminster.

The issue of EU membership, however, largely entered the independence debate in terms of whether, when and how an independent Scotland could retain/renew/apply for EU membership. The matter attracted conflicting assessments. Nobody in government either in London or elsewhere in the EU (and least of all in countries with independence movements, notably Spain, Cyprus and some of the east European states) publicly shared the SNP view that Article 48 of the Treaty on European Union offered a suitable legal route to facilitate the transition to EU membership for an independent Scotland. Article 48 of the Lisbon Treaty allows for the EU rulebook to be amended by existing EU states, while the pro-Unionist case cited Article 49 to indicate that an independent Scotland would be required to apply for EU membership as a new applicant state. Needless to say, there was no need for a definitive answer to what would have been an unusual situation in EU history and for which no specific treaty provisions were in place – the secession of a country from an EU member state or, in SNP parlance, the dissolving of the 1707 Union partnership.

For the time being at least, the matter remains unresolved in view of the majority vote (55.30 per cent) against independence in the referendum. Yet the issues and the questions continue to hang in the air, as do the linkages between a referendum on Scotland's independence and a referendum on British membership of the EU, especially a referendum result taking Britain out of the EU. Meanwhile, the Scotland referendum experience persuaded at least one senior SNP figure, Jim Sillars – the architect of 'Independence in Scotland' – to support a vote to leave the EU in the referendum of June 2016. Sillars insisted that the only way to secure Scottish sovereignty was to vote against continued EU membership, since Brussels would otherwise remain an obstacle to independence (*The Guardian*, 3 March 2016).

One strand in the case for Scotland staying as part of the UK, as deployed by the 'No' campaigners in the September 2014 referendum, was much the same as that used by supporters of British membership of the EU. Globalization had eroded the capacity of nations to exercise sovereignty, and sharing sovereignty was a way to reclaim power and to impose order on an increasingly unregulated international political economy. Yet part of the 'Yes' case in the Scotland independence referendum campaign was based on a very different response to globalization. It reflected a desire to express a more distinctive and reassuring local identity. In some cases, moreover, the 'Yes' vote represented hostility to the prospect of becoming an independent state only to have to lose or pool sovereignty by joining the EU. By way of contrast, as one Member of the Scottish Parliament (MSP) put it, 'there is no point arguing about losing sovereignty to Europe, because we don't have any sovereignty' (Tarditi, 2010).

On the issue of EU membership within a continuing UK, the SNP listed its proposals in a submission to the Smith Commission. The Commission was set up immediately after the referendum in September 2014 and published its report detailing Heads of Agreement on further devolution of powers to the Scottish Parliament (27 November 2014). The SNP government proposed that:

- Scotland should have guaranteed rights to engage directly with the EU institutions in areas of devolved competence;
- a statutory mechanism should be put in place to enable Scotland to jointly develop, influence and represent UK policy positions on broader EU matters such as treaty change;
- the Scottish government and parliament should be given the ability to influence the policy priorities and contribute to the business planning of the departments, agencies, embassies, consulates and offices overseas that promote the UK's commercial and cultural interests;
- Scotland should have competence to negotiate, sign and ratify international agreements that relate to devolved matters;
- Scotland should have a formal role in determining the UK's priorities and policies on international agreements relating to reserved matters that affect Scottish interests;
- the Concordats on Coordination of European Union Policy Issues and on International Relations between the UK Government and the Devolved Administrations should be put on a statutory footing.

> (SPICe The Information Centre, 'Proposals to the
> Smith Commission on Further Powers in the EU and
> International Affairs', 30 October 2014, www.scottish.parliament.uk)

This list of ambitious proposals drew heavily on practices in some of the other EU member states, notably Belgium, Germany and Spain. It highlighted several of the pitfalls and problems involved in working with a devolved system of government in the context of the European Union. It can be argued that, unless the arrangements for bringing Scottish influence to bear in determining the UK line in the EU operate effectively, the basis of the devolution settlement within the UK could be undermined. Furthermore, since Scottish government ministers bear no political accountability for the UK line in devolved areas, the Scottish Parliament may be unable to exercise effective scrutiny over EU legislation that impacts on the exercise of its own competence.

For the most part, the Smith Report reiterated that EU and foreign affairs still came under reserved powers and that the devolved administrations already had a formal role (outlined in the current Concordats) in contributing to and agreeing the final UK negotiating position. The report did contain two notable proposals. First, a devolved administration minister should lead the UK delegation in EU negotiations in the absence of the lead UK minister. Such a practice was already allowable under the original Memorandum of Understanding but it was here embedded as a presumption. As in the past, it would remain the case that the UK government had the final word and that Scottish ministers could not publicly dissent from the official line. Second, it was proposed that in meetings involving a UK minister and devolved administration ministers, another UK government minister should represent the position of England (or England and Wales in certain policy areas). Such measures, however, fell far short of the proposals of the SNP government. Meanwhile, the SNP continued to enjoy the best of all possible worlds, burnishing its untested pro-EU credentials, deploying some critical views of the EU when useful, and all the while holding the UK government to account for failing to offer an adequate defence of Scottish interest in the EU forum.

Public opinion and EU membership

As was noted in Chapter 3, the results of the 1975 referendum on British membership of the EC indicated that the strongest support for continued membership was in England (68.7 per cent of the vote) and especially south-east England, while there was weaker support in the devolved nations: Northern Ireland 52.1 per cent, Scotland 58.4 per cent and Wales 64.8 per cent. If polling figures in recent years are to be believed, almost the opposite is the case with London as a major exception in strongly supporting continued EU membership. According to an Ipsos MORI poll published in February 2013, 53 per cent of the Scottish respondents voted to stay in the EU while 34 per cent voted to leave. A Chatham House YouGov survey (January 2015) found that Scottish respondents were more pro-European than English ones. Furthermore, a majority of respondents in London and Scotland voted to stay in the EU, while a majority of respondents in the south, Midlands/Wales and northern England voted to leave.

More recent and more detailed surveys and polls have painted a similar picture. A survey undertaken by the University of Edinburgh Academy of Government and published in March 2015 contained the following results about views on Britain's long term EU strategy by country (per cent) (see Table 6.1).

The commentary on this exercise noted that there was no majority for an exit from the EU in any part of the UK but a strong majority throughout for a reduction of the powers of the EU. It concluded that the differences between the four countries were rather nuanced and not as large as sometimes made out, suggesting like some other sources that the Scottish public was marginally rather than substantially more supportive of EU membership than Britain as a whole. True, Nicola Sturgeon, who succeeded Salmond as First Minister and SNP leader in November 2014, declared in June 2015 that polls in Scotland consistently showed strong support for EU membership.

Some commentators, however, have expressed a few qualifications to such a view, noting that since 2000, data has registered a hardening of views on the EU in Scotland with more people saying that Britain should leave and more people saying that the powers of the EU should be reduced (House of Commons Library Research Briefings, 9 June 2015). Another survey concluded that while a majority of Scots favoured EU membership, the

Table 6.1 Views on Britain's long term EU strategy by country (%)

	England	Scotland	Northern Ireland	Wales
Leave the EU	31	22	26	28
Stay in the EU and try to reduce the EU's powers	43	46	45	41
Leave things as they are	16	20	17	19
Stay in the EU and try to increase the EU's powers	7	8	8	7
Work for the formation of a single European government	2	3	5	4
Total (100%)	3,646	1,457	549	1,082

Note: Don't know responses were excluded from this analysis; percentages are weighted, sample size is unweighted.
Source: Eichhorn *et al.* (2015).

idea of Scots taking a more positive and enthusiastic interest in the EU as compared with the English was a far from accurate picture (Eichhorn and Kenealy, 2015).

Another poll and survey on the subject under the auspices of the NatCen Social Research unit (October 2015) and supervised by a leading psephologist, John Curtice, however, reported some different returns based on interviewing 30,000 people. This exercise found that in England 45 per cent of respondents said that they wanted to stay in the EU and 35 per cent to leave (the respective figures for London being 48 per cent and 32 per cent). In Wales support for staying in the EU was somewhat higher – 50 per cent wanted to stay and 33 per cent to leave – while in Scotland 58 per cent backed staying and only 28 per cent wanted to leave. Besides this YouGov poll, a Survation poll pointed in the same direction when its respondents were asked the exact question to appear on the referendum ballot paper – 'Do you think that the United Kingdom should remain a member of the European Union or leave the European Union?' (Curtice, 2015).

In Wales and Northern Ireland, the changes in attitudes towards EU membership over the past 25 years have proved less dramatic than in Scotland. In the case of Wales, the differences may be marginal. According to a YouGov poll for Cardiff University (January 2015), 44 per cent supported EU membership while 36 per cent voted to leave, suggesting that 'Wales sits uneasily in the middle on the EU, between an England tending towards scepticism and a Scotland that polls normally show is rather more positive about Europe'. Evidently, years of substantial EU funding, mentioned earlier, have not made much of an impression on many Welsh people. An earlier poll in 2013, conducted for WalesOnline, reported that in the region known as West Wales and the Valleys, in receipt of some £3 billion in aid from the EU since 2000, there was an almost two-to-one majority (43 per cent to 23 per cent) in favour of leaving the EU. In an all-Wales poll, only 17 per cent of respondents thought that Wales benefitted more than the rest of the UK from EU membership, while 30 per cent thought that Wales benefitted less from EU membership than the rest of Britain (Scully, 2015a).

Polling data suggest a more positive perception of and greater engagement with the EU in Northern Ireland than in Wales. An academic survey in 2002 found that Northern Ireland voters displayed more positive views on participation in the EU than the rest of the UK. In the European Parliament election of 2004, a higher proportion of the electorate voted (48 per cent) than in any other region in the UK. A Flash Eurobarometer survey (2008) also presented Northern Ireland as the region of the UK most positive about the EU (Phinnemore *et al.*, 2012). It should be noted that the distinctiveness of the party system in Northern Ireland has long meant that the country does not figure in many UK-wide opinion polls.

Nevertheless, Table 6.1 suggests that little has changed in the period since 2008, and nor has one of the fundamentals in that the impact on Northern Ireland of British withdrawal from the EU would be different from that of the rest of Britain. Northern Ireland is the only region of Britain to share a land border with another EU member state. Consequently, withdrawal would mean that an external border of the EU would run through the island of Ireland. This situation might have implications in several areas including co-operation between the London and Dublin governments in dealing with cross-border crime and terrorist activity. Significantly, in June 2015 the Irish Parliament's committee on EU affairs was so alarmed at the possibility of withdrawal and the impact on cross-border institutions introduced under the Good Friday Agreement that it called for Ireland to be given a formal role in any negotiations (*The Guardian*, 25 June 2015).

Referendum politics

The prospect of a referendum on British membership of the EU in June 2016 has given rise to much speculation about the likely consequences if the majority vote in England differs from the majority vote in the devolved nations. At a relatively early stage, the SNP and Plaid Cymru, the latter under the leadership of Leanne Wood, jointly pledged to insist that Britain's withdrawal from the EU should follow only if a referendum showed majorities for exit in all four countries of the UK – known as a 'double majority' rule (*The Guardian*, 29 October 2014).

The rationale for this demand, as expounded by Sturgeon, involved linking the referendum on an independent Scotland with the referendum on British membership of the EU. During the two-year campaign regarding the former, Sturgeon declared that Scotland was told time and again that it was a valued and equal member of the UK multinational state. It followed therefore that 'none of the nations that make up the UK should be at risk of being forced out of the EU against their will' (House of Commons Library Research Briefings, 9 June 2015). She also made the more questionable claim that the issue of EU membership was central to the referendum campaign on an independent Scotland in that the 'No' campaign had claimed that the only way to protect Scotland's EU membership was to vote 'No' to independence.

By such means, the issue was linked to the possibility of holding a second referendum on an independent Scotland, withdrawal from the EU being viewed as 'democratically indefensible' and as a justifiable reason or 'trigger' for another referendum. The possibility of a second referendum on an independent Scotland has given rise to the widespread use of the word 'neverendum', a word coined by French-speaking nationalists in Quebec to continue having referendums on sovereignty until voters finally produce their desired outcome.

The 'double majority' view has not so far secured majority support in opinion polls. A detailed opinion poll, published in March 2015, reported that the majority of people in all four constitutive parts of the UK viewed a UK exit from the EU as a decision that should be taken by the population as a whole and not by separate parts. According to this poll, the view that an overall majority of the UK vote should decide the matter attracted 68 per cent of respondents in England, 60 per cent in Northern Ireland, 55 per cent in Scotland and 64 per cent in Wales (Eichhorn *et al.*, 2015). Hence, while there was significant support for the Sturgeon proposition that a majority in each of the four countries would be required for the UK to decide to leave the EU following a referendum, it was a minority position even in Scotland.

The Conservative government strongly opposed the idea on the grounds, as Cameron put it (29 October 2014), that there is one UK and one in/out referendum that would be decided on a majority of those who vote. At the same time, a leading Scottish Conservative dismissed the Sturgeon proposal as fanciful and self-serving, and as evidence that she had been taking lessons from her predecessor Salmond on 'the art of gripe and grievance politics' (EurActiv Newsletters, 30 October 2014). The House of Lords European Union Committee in July 2015 strongly advised the UK government to engage fully with the devolved institutions so that they were closely involved in the process of renegotiating Britain's EU membership and were not presented with a *fait accompli* (House of Lords, European Union Committee, 3rd Report of Session, 2015–16)

A British decision to withdraw from the EU primarily on the back of an English vote to leave the EU could be highly problematical in terms of relations between the UK government and the devolved nations, causing a constitutional crisis and leading to the break-up of the UK. To date, this is one of the least discussed aspects of a British withdrawal from the EU, especially among organizations supporting withdrawal. At the SNP conference in October 2015, Sturgeon claimed that the demand for a second Scottish independence referendum would be 'probably unstoppable' if the UK voted to leave the EU without the majority of voters in Scotland also voting to leave (*The Guardian*, 16 October 2015). It is of course possible that some SNP voters might vote to leave the EU in the hope of hastening the possibility of a second independence referendum.

It was perhaps indicative of some panic in the hierarchy of the Conservative Party that in December 2015 William Hague, the Conservative former foreign secretary, a long-standing critic of the EU, was nonetheless minded to vote for Britain to remain in the EU for fear that a referendum vote to leave could lead to the break-up of the UK: 'To end up destroying the United Kingdom and gravely weakening the European Union would not be a very clever day's work' (*The Guardian*, 23 December 2015).

It has been suggested that although the Westminster Parliament may repeal the European Communities Act of 1972 in the event of a referendum vote to leave the EU, this action would not bring an end to the domestic incorporation of EU law in the devolved nations. It would still be necessary to amend the relevant parts of devolution legislation. Although the UK parliament may amend the devolution acts – as power but not sovereignty passed to the devolved nations in 1998 – the British government stated from the outset of devolution that it would not normally legislate on a devolved matter or on any change to the powers of the devolved nations without the consent of the devolved legislatures. This arrangement was known as the Sewel Convention, as enunciated by the now disgraced John Sewel, the Labour government Scottish Office minister who promoted the Scotland Act in the House of Lords in 1998. The Smith Commission proposed that this Convention, never endorsed by the UK parliament, should be put on a statutory footing.

In these circumstances, the devolved legislatures might be reluctant to grant assent to a British withdrawal from the EU, in which case the need to amend devolution legislation 'renders a UK EU exit constitutionally highly problematic' (House of Commons Library Research Briefings, 9 June 2015). Moreover, the prevailing doctrine of popular rather than parliamentary sovereignty in Scotland (see Introduction) might form the basis of Scotland's own right to determine whether or not it exits the EU. There is, therefore, some substance to the view that a British exit from the EU risks shattering the fragile balance and stability of the UK by threatening the peace settlement in Northern Ireland and by raising the possibility of a second independence referendum in Scotland (Douglas-Scott, 2014).

There is one other possible scenario worth noting. A Scottish 'yes' to EU membership could turn an English 'no' into a UK 'yes'. Such an outcome seems less likely and more far-fetched than an English 'no' vote carrying the devolved nations out of the EU. However, some calculations have been made using a July 2015 poll that had 51 per cent of English respondents voting to leave the EU and 66 per cent of Scottish respondents voting to remain. On this basis it is estimated that when translated into actual voting numbers the Scotland result could tip the UK as a whole into a 'yes' to the EU against the wishes of the majority 'no' in England. Furthermore, if Wales and Northern Ireland came out at least moderately pro-EU, then an English 'no' cannot win the day unless it achieves at least 53 per cent of the total vote (Hughes, 2015). A Wales-based survey and poll concluded that if the referendum turnout was to differ across England, Scotland and Wales in roughly the same way as it did in the general election of 2015 then the 'yes' side would be very marginally ahead 'But it would be achingly close' (Scully, 2015b).

A 'yes' result would of course inflame English opponents of EU membership. At the same time, however, it would be a mixed blessing for the SNP. It would endorse their pro-EU professions, but it would count against the higher claims of their national independence crusade, removing one means of triggering a second referendum on an independent Scotland. Such a result would be a highly satisfying and hugely ironic twist to this tale, at least for any pro-EU Scot who also believed that English-born resident voters in Scotland (approximately 300,000) had tipped the balance against the 'yes' vote in the independent Scotland referendum (some 72.1 per cent of English-born voters voted 'no' while only 47.3 per cent of Scottish born voters voted 'no'. The final referendum result was 2,001,926 'no' votes and 1,616,989 'yes' votes).

Conclusion

In this chapter, we have discussed the ways in which EU membership has directly and indirectly changed the context within which to address the problems of the devolved nations – Northern Ireland, Scotland and Wales. It remains the case that EU matters and foreign affairs in general are classified as 'reserved powers' under Westminster's direct control. Nevertheless, as we have noted, this system has not prevented devolved bodies from expressing concerns, from lobbying for their particular interests and from actively monitoring the points at which an EU dimension and law impact on a range of domestic matters that fall within their remit.

EC membership was often perceived as a threat in its early stages. It appeared that decision-making power was further removed politically and physically from the devolved nations. Each had to rely on government departments in London to represent their interests in Brussels. The limited degree of support for remaining in the EU in the referendum of 1975 reflected dissatisfaction with this arrangement.

In the past 20 years, however, European integration has offered the devolved nations the prospect of a new political arena with which they could engage. In often different ways for each territory, the EU has provided a platform for tackling key questions about the European identity and interests of each territory, and about the relationship between nationalism and EU membership. EU funding has directly assisted this purpose and has been perceived as beneficial to a greater extent than elsewhere in the UK. That in turn has contributed to a more favourable image of the EU in these territories than in England where the press – the subject of the next chapter – has played a formative role in shaping public opinion.

7 The press and the European Union

There is certainly clear evidence of misreporting on European issues.
(Lord Justice Leveson, Report of the Leveson Inquiry,
November 2012, Volume 2: 687)

Introduction

This chapter explores the treatment of Britain's membership of the EU by the press. It considers how and why large sections of the British press in recent decades have come to regard the EU as an alien, external force that finds expression in an 'us and them' discourse. Some of the aspects covered include the nature and extent of widespread ignorance about the dynamics of European integration, the emergence of Euroscepticism as the dominant narrative, and the limited effects of the pro-EU case. The chapter considers the construction and impact of negative stereotypes. It also touches on how the often complex features of EU affairs are sliced up, framed and dumbed down into sensationalized soundbites or lurid headlines that are recycled to reinforce particular views about the EU and about Britain's role in the organization. Finally, the chapter examines relations between successive prime ministers and the press over the question of EU membership and also between the public and the press.

Some problems

This subject bristles with problems. Most obviously, there are difficulties in measuring the precise impact of the press on public opinion, on government and on political parties alike, and on the often feverish political atmosphere surrounding the issue of EU membership. There is also a host of problematical features regarding discourse analysis. This field of study encompasses such matters as the meaning and use of language, the unspoken or unacknowledged assumptions underlying language and behaviour (what is not said is often as important as what is – the hidden wiring, so to speak, behind the message), and the careful crafting of the message or 'message discipline'. In addition, the subject of Britain and the European Union belongs to that class of controversy in which the framing of events constantly changes as conflicting narratives have waxed and waned and as particular words, phrases and concepts have struggled for dominance or have been deliberately avoided for fear of hostile reactions (see Daddow, 2012 for an authoritative discussion of this subject).

There is not the space here to cover all aspects of a debate that ranges from the agenda-setting functions of the press and its role as a shaper, mirror or magnifier of public opinion to such matters as whether politicians, rightly or wrongly, believe that newspapers influence public opinion. In terms of the media, this chapter focuses exclusively on the press. It does so partly on the grounds that studies of the effects of broadcast journalism in this field are very limited and in any case this source gives less coverage to EU affairs, though an impressionistic two-minute report by a TV reporter in Brussels may have more impact than the word pictures of an anonymous, London-based tabloid reporter. More importantly, the focus on the press is based on the well-founded, widespread view that newspapers rather than broadcasters have occupied the dominant agenda-setting role in this field. In short, broadcasters have followed the lead of newspapers in establishing the daily agenda, especially in following up negative headlines generated by the press in the first instance. Robert Peston, the BBC's former economics editor, claimed that BBC news 'is completely obsessed by the agenda set by newspapers' (*The Guardian*, 7 June 2014). Meanwhile, the infant upstart of the communications industry – the social media – still falls far short of the collective influence of the press.

Scepticism and ignorance

There are at least two interrelated and largely incontestable general statements that can be made about this subject at the outset and that are discussed below. First, scepticism and ignorance are often two sides of the same coin so far as British attitudes towards the EU are concerned. Second, large sections of the British press, far from enlightening the public about the subject, have authored and perpetuated many myths about the EU from an insular-minded standpoint, often drawing on a large stock of stereotypes about other member states.

In some quarters, therefore, journalism as the first draft of history can be decidedly misleading and distorted. Tabloid portrayals of the EU seem credible because the level of public knowledge of EU processes is so low. In these circumstances, public debate easily slides into a miasma of fear, fantasy and prejudice. At best the EU is regarded as remote, complex, interfering or boring in so far as it attracts any attention among the public at large. In March 2008, an EU-wide survey about attitudes towards the European Parliament found that the British were not only the most sceptical on many EU issues but also the most ignorant. The population of no other member state knew less and trusted less about the EU than the British (Eurobarometer, March 2008). A later survey in March 2011 concluded that 18 per cent of British respondents felt informed about the EU, while 82 per cent said they knew little or nothing (Eurobarometer, March 2011). There is no evidence to suggest any significant change in recent years.

Seemingly massive exposure to arguments about the EC/EU have done little to dispel a high degree of unfamiliarity with the purposes and workings of the EU. During the 1975 referendum campaign, Roy Hattersley, who was then a junior minister at the FCO, expressed doubt as to whether 'ten per cent [of the public] voted on the merits of the issue or even according to their reaction to the question on the ballot paper. They put a cross against their prejudices' (Hattersley, 1995: 158). Thirty years later, little appeared to have changed as another junior FCO minister claimed that the poor level of policy discussion and debate in political parties was most evident on Europe (MacShane, 2005: 13–14).

Unsurprisingly, interest in the EU occupies a low position on most polls as a decidedly second-order issue. Particular subjects like immigration attract much attention, but for the most part public attitudes suggest a strikingly marked contrast to the frenzied obsession about the EU in some political circles. In 2008, an Ipsos MORI survey, charting the most important issues facing Britain, reported that only between 2 per cent and 7 per cent of voters cited Europe among their concerns, far behind their main concerns about crime, immigration, health, defence and the economy. A similar Ipsos MORI poll in September 2013 found that only 1 per cent of respondents viewed EU membership as the most important subject facing Britain. Furthermore, only 22 per cent of UKIP voters considered EU membership the number one issue (*The Guardian*, 13 February 2015). Indeed, most such surveys indicate the low salience of the issue among the public at large not only in Britain but also elsewhere in the EU where domestic matters figure more prominently than international affairs.

Perception and reality

Several misconceptions result from this ignorance and lack of interest. Popular impressions of the cost of EU membership to Britain often reveal a large gap between myth and reality, fuelling the common complaint associating the EU with a 'waste of money'. A survey carried out in 2011 invited people to estimate the size of Britain's annual net contribution to the EU budget. Most of the general public considerably overestimated the UK's net contribution. The median response was £27 billion, more than three times the actual figure of £8.1 billion. The mean response of £74 billion represented an average estimate more than nine times the actual size of Britain's net contribution (Chatham House, 2012). Such misconceptions, in turn, have a significant impact as politicians focus on voter perceptions rather than on the actual data.

The wide gap between what appears to be the case and what in fact is the case is evident in other quarters. Reports of fraudulent spending of EU funds are regularly splashed across the headlines of the Eurosceptical press with the accompanying insistence that a grossly incompetent, if not corrupt, European Commission is responsible for such an outrage. In fact, however, national governments have exclusive responsibility for ensuring the proper use of EU funds; the Commission is denied legal powers to interfere in such an area of 'national sovereignty' (Palmer, 2013). There are also considerable differences between the real and imagined size of the EU budget. A Eurobarometer poll (March 2011) reported that 75 per cent of British respondents believed that the EU budget was larger than the British national budget. In fact, the British budget at this time was almost six times larger than the EU budget.

A further example of the difference between appearance and reality lies in the contrast between widespread impressions and detailed evidence. For example, in October 2014, UKIP was riding high in the polls and Conservative critics of EU membership were very much in the ascendancy. Yet Ipsos MORI, the polling organization that has a long-standing reputation for tracking British attitudes towards the EU, reported in October 2014 that 56 per cent of the people polled voted to stay in the EU, the highest support for EU membership since December 1991 (Ipsos MORI Political Monitor, October 2014). A similar poll in November 2012 reported that only 48 per cent of respondents supported EU membership, while UKIP's share of the vote in the intervening period had increased from 3 to 16 per cent. Another major polling organization, YouGov, reported similar trends with support for British membership of the EU at an all-time high of 45 per cent in February 2015, an increase from a low of 28 per cent in May 2012. In effect, support for staying in the EU had grown over the period when support for the anti-EU UKIP strengthened in the polls.

In a similar vein, there is a marked contrast between the voluminous criticism of the EU in large sections of the British press (see below) and the limited calls to exit the organization. In fact, only one newspaper to date (October 2015), the *Daily Express*, has formally come out in favour of withdrawal with its 'Get Britain out of Europe' campaign that commenced in November 2010, though others like the Telegraph group are often cited as pursuing the same objective more covertly.

The message and the messengers

The Europhile case

The dominant narrative in the press and in public life at large about British membership of the EU has undergone a pronounced change over the past 50 years. In short, Eurosceptic opinion, whether defined as ostensibly supporting a 'reformed' EU including Britain or favouring complete withdrawal from the EU, has made major advances in the past 25 years. Such opinion is very much in the ascendant while the once major pro-marketeer force, that swept all before it in the 1960s and 1970s, has become a weak Europhile rump.

The pro-marketeer language of the 1960s and early 1970s that became embedded in the press not only seemed to convey empty promises in the light of experience but ultimately failed to capture public imagination. Pro-marketeer language was designed to blunt the edge of any suggestion that EC membership represented a radical break and to communicate the idea of continuity through change – hence the widespread use of the expression European 'common market' rather than 'European Community', the pledge of accession on the basis of the 'full-hearted consent of the British people', the 'pooling' rather than the 'loss' of national sovereignty. Such handling of the matter was accompanied by the language of fear: the fear of being left behind, the bleak prospect of standing alone, and the EC as a 'lifeboat' for the British economy.

Some of the weaknesses of this approach soon became apparent. As was noted in Chapter 3, the economic recession that accompanied the early years of Britain's EC membership in the 1970s made a mockery of the original promise of rising prosperity as a result of membership. Any positive effect of membership was barely discernible. More importantly, the pro-marketeers and their latter-day descendants the Europhiles failed to build a lasting mass base of support for EC/EU membership. Nor did they offer a popular alternative narrative to that of the Eurosceptics. Rightly or wrongly, their public image as an elitist group has rarely struck a popular note, and opponents of EU membership have easily foisted on them unappealing labels, branding them as metropolitan, liberal and intellectual in recent years.

The seeming absence of a populist stance has also registered in the way that pro-EU opinion has objected to government by referendum on European issues, opposing the idea of a referendum in 1975, again at the time of the Maastricht Treaty and also on the abortive Constitutional Treaty. A Chatham House/YouGov Survey (January 2015) noted a significant difference of opinion between what might be defined as elitist opinion (i.e. opinion-formers) and the public on the issue of a referendum on British membership of the EU. Opinion-formers narrowly opposed a referendum (50 per cent against and 46 per cent in favour). The public strongly supported a referendum (60 per cent in favour with 24 per cent opposed). This division of opinion is also reflected in the amount of support for remaining in the EU: 72 per cent in the case of opinion-formers and 40 per cent in the case of the public ('Internationalism or Isolationism?' The Chatham House/YouGov Survey, January 2015).

Jacques Delors, a former president of the EC Commission and one of the pioneers of the Single Market and the euro, once famously warned: 'You can't fall in love with a Single Market!' Raymond Aron, a fellow Frenchman and political philosopher, earlier (1954) claimed that the European idea lacked the characteristics of messianic ideologies and concrete patriotism. In short, the idea was the creation of intellectuals, this accounting for 'its genuine appeal to the mind and its feeble echo in the heart' (Haas, 1958: 29). So much has proved to be the case in Britain where the campaign of the pro-marketeers and Europhiles has elicited no strong emotional commitment to their cause and has lacked the cutting edge of Eurosceptic presentations. Their message has failed to offer a feel-good dimension about Britain and the EC/EU. Indeed, it has often relied on public opinion which, whatever its suspicions of or opposition to the EU, has at least until recent years tended to believe that further involvement in the EU was inevitable. While opinion polls during the early years of the first Blair government showed majorities against joining the euro, these same polls nonetheless revealed majorities expecting Britain to join the euro.

The Europhile case has frequently come under attack for deploying unappealing arguments about the EC/EU membership as the main or sole solution to Britain's economic problems. Speculating about how best to 'get inside the British head and make it more excited' about EU membership, Robin Cook, the former foreign secretary, was in no doubt what was unlikely to inspire the public; 'You must be joking' was his considered response to the view that the public would be captivated by any announcement that the Blair government's five tests for entry to the euro area (see Chapter 10) had been satisfactorily met (Trewin, 2008: 738).

Some years later in March 2015 Gordon Brown made the same point in conceding that laudable factsheets about trade or well-meaning manifestos on the minutiae of EU reform were no match for the gut emotional appeal of Eurosceptic claims that Europe was making Britain a foreign country:

> 'Sadly we pro-Europeans', observed Brown, 'are in danger of fighting with the wrong weapons: a worthy, London-establishment-led corporate-finance fact-based campaign of "the great and the good" … whose prominence will be used by anti-Europeans to justify the allegation that Europe is for an elite who don't understand the real Britain'.
>
> (*The Guardian*, 9 March 2015)

Pro-EC/EU opinion has also attracted criticism for failing to instill into the population at large any sense of a common European culture. The essentially negative, if valid, case presented by government and Europhiles alike, that Britain would be worse off outside the EC/EU, has rarely aroused popular support (Wall, 2008: 210). Pro-EU opinion has long relied on the absence of any well-worked alternative to EU membership. In the debate on the Maastricht Treaty in 1992, Tristran Garel-Jones, the Conservative Minister for Europe, posed the question that always caused some awkward silences among Eurosceptics: 'Can the anti-federalists, the Euro-sceptics and little Englanders offer a positive alternative?' (Schnapper, 2014).

Besides the argument based on the absence of any alternatives to EC/EU membership, the pro-marketeers and Europhiles have also attracted criticism for a persistent unwillingness to explain the precise impact of membership on such matters as national sovereignty. More broadly still, there is strong evidence to suggest that the pro-marketeers failed to educate the public about the EC and instead mounted a propaganda campaign to manufacture consent for EC membership (Mullen and Burkitt, 2005). None of this is to underestimate the difficulties of the pro-EU case, both in countering what are perceived as simplistic Eurosceptic slogans and solutions or in seeking to expose the use of the EU as a whipping boy for a range of problems that have little or nothing to do with the organization (see Chapter 5).

The Eurosceptic case

Unlike their opponents, the anti-marketeers and Eurosceptics have exploited a rich seam of opinion and language invariably inclined to view Britain's EU ties in terms of injured national sovereignty, lost independence and outraged national identity. In the process, the often prejudiced language against the EU has also found its way into the expressions of pro-EU arguments, thereby seemingly validating the views and attitudes of opponents on the issue.

The Eurosceptic press, most notably *The Daily Telegraph*, the *Daily Mail* and *The Sun*, has unhesitatingly projected the EU as the hostile 'other' or 'as somewhere else' across the English Channel. It has drawn heavily on military metaphors of surrender and defeat in defence of British sovereignty and independence. In doing so, it has often depicted the EC/EU as an imposition from above masterminded by wily foreigners in league with defeatist politicians at home. However differently framed, whether as a hostile, bureaucratic and undemocratic superstate posing an existential threat to national sovereignty or as a bargaining forum within which Britain has limited influence, the Eurosceptic discourse about the EU is designed to alert and alarm the public. It aims to generate a deep-seated sense of separation and subjugation in support of the case for withdrawal from the EU.

Such a portrayal is indicative of a striking change in British press attitudes towards the EC/EU over the past 30 years. At the time of the referendum of 1975, the press overwhelmingly supported EC membership with a fairly simple, compelling narrative as noted above. The *Financial Times* and *The Guardian* had long favoured membership, while *The Times* and *The Daily Telegraph* threw their weight behind the cause. Meanwhile, the popular daily newspapers especially, *The Sun* and the *Daily Mirror*, were hotly in favour of membership, the latter helpfully including for its readers a 'Guide to the Euro-Dollies', a series of 'Euro-Dolly' pin-up photographs together with advice on how they kiss and how Englishmen rate with them (Kitzinger, 1976: 345–6). This press consensus included even the *Daily Express* and the *Sunday Express* which, in the early 1960s under the influence of their proprietor Beaverbrook, had taken a staunchly anti-EC line and continued to do so until the Commons vote in favour of the principle of membership in October 1971. Only an ill-assorted and highly marginalized group, comprising the communist *Morning Star*, *The Tribune*, the *Scottish Daily News* (a short-lived workers' cooperative newspaper in 1975), *The Spectator* and the *Dundee Courier and Advertiser*, opposed EC membership at this stage.

In recent years, however, the reverse is very much the case. With very few exceptions, notably the *Financial Times*, *The Guardian* and *The Independent*, the press has become more solidly Eurosceptic than at any time over the past 50 years, strongly so in the case of the foreign-owned press of the Murdoch empire (*The Times*, *The Sunday Times*, *The Sun* and *The Sun on Sunday*), the Telegraph Group (*The Daily Telegraph* and *The Sunday Telegraph*), the Harmsworth Group (*Daily Mail*, *The Mail on Sunday* and the *London Evening Standard*), and the *Daily Express* and the *Sunday Express*. These out-lets make few, if any, concessions to the pro-EU case, while any debate in print is largely confined to papers like the *Financial Times*, *The Guardian*, *The Independent* and the weekly *Economist*.

The character of much British press coverage of EU matters has attracted a good deal of critical comment concerning its malign influence and its treatment of the subject as unburdened by factual accuracy and untroubled by popular ignorance. One of the most detailed studies of the subject concludes that 'the majority of the reading public is indeed insulted by the quality of the press performance with regard to European issues'. According to this study, tabloid discourse especially is assertive, engages in crude stereo-typing and xenophobic outbursts, distorts issues, omits information, and is heavy with ideological force (Anderson and Weymouth, 1999: 185).

It is certainly the case that the increasing dominance of Eurosceptic discourse has dic-tated the terrain on which wider debates about the EU are conducted. How the issue is framed very much influences public opinion, especially if viewed through the lens of the nation-state and casting the relationship between Britain and the EU in terms of separa-tion and threat. There is convincing evidence that framing the EU in terms of oppor-tunity and of potential benefits is correlated with higher levels of support for the EU. By way of contrast, presenting the EU in terms of a zero-sum conflict between states, a risky undertaking and a utopian ideal of the political elite which fails to take account of political reality or popular wishes, is associated with greater cynicism and opposition to the organization.

The influence of the Eurosceptic narrative is all the greater as the EU is portrayed through a variety of unattractive descriptions: undemocratic, artificial construct, European dreamers and idealists, Brussels steamroller, euro-fundamentalists, and a particular favourite in recent years of economic recession the idea of Britain 'shack-led to the corpse of Europe'. There is also evidence to suggest that opponents of EU membership seem to have stronger views than supporters (Kellner, 2012). Significantly, Eurosceptic positions escape the very terminology that such positions use towards Europhile expressions – rarely if ever, for example, are those who oppose the expansion of the EU's powers described as idealistically nationalistic (Hawkins, 2012).

Europhobia and mythology

A large section of the press has so persistently conveyed the view that all manner of ills, villainy and killer headlines can be placed at the door of the EU that Europhobic is often a more accurate label for this mentality than Eurosceptic. The monstering of EU figures like past and present presidents of the European Commission such as Delors and Juncker is also a common feature of such coverage with a shoal of stereotypical images. At the time of the Convention on the Future of Europe that was headed by the former French President Giscard d'Estaing, *The Sun* described Giscard as an 'arrogant condescending French snob' who 'was planning to end Britain's freedom'. The fact that Giscard's views on such matters as a federal Europe were virtually the same as those of the British government seemed to escape this sweeping judgement. Similar treatment was meted out to any British politician who offended *The Sun*'s Europhobic sensibilities; on the day after a government White Paper on the IGC following the release of the Convention's report, *The Sun* (10 September 2003) printed a photo of Blair in an undertaker's hat on the front page under the headline 'Last Rites: Blundertaker Blair is set to Bury our Nation'.

Besides exuding an arrogant, bombastic insularity, the examples of factual errors, distortion, misrepresentation, fiction and a generally infantilized approach to EU matters in such press coverage are legion and legendary. In evidence to the Leveson Inquiry, Alastair Campbell, Blair's former press secretary and director of communications and strategy, effectively summed up the inventions of a number of national dailies concerning the EU. According to his own self-assessment, Campbell was 'something of a Eurosceptic by Blairite standards'. Furthermore, he not only knew more about the common practices of the press than most of his contemporaries but he was also described as the architect-in-chief of New Labour's rapprochement with the Murdoch press (Liddle, 2014: 59). Citing in particular *The Sun*, the *Daily* and *Sunday Express*, the *Daily Star*, the *Daily Mail* and *The Daily Telegraph* as 'broadly anti-European', Campbell continued:

> At various times, readers of these and other newspapers may have read that 'Europe' or 'Brussels' or 'the EU superstate' has banned, or is intending to ban kilts, curries, mushy peas, paper rounds, Caerphilly cheese, charity shops, bulldogs, bent sausages and cucumbers, the British army, lollipop ladies, British loaves, British made lavatories, the passport crest, lorry drivers who wear glasses, and many more. In addition, if the Eurosceptic press is to believed, Britain is going to be forced to unite as a single country with France, Church schools are being forced to hire atheist teachers, Scotch whisky is being classified as an inflammable liquid, British soldiers must take orders in French, the price of chips is being raised by Brussels, Europe is insisting on one size fits all condoms, new laws are being proposed on how to climb a ladder, it will be a criminal offence to criticize Europe ...
>
> (www.bnegroup.org/blog/archives/945)

Lost in translation

As Campbell conceded, some of these examples may appear trivial and comic. However, they all point to a more serious charge, this being newspapers' scant regard for fact as they relentlessly and remorselessly hammer a particular message into their readers. What is lost in translation in stories said to have emanated from Brussels and written up by reporters, subsequently rewritten by sub-editors, and then edited by editors is a very limited degree of veracity, knowledge, understanding and perspective.

At best there is a grain of truth in some of the stories and an ethos that more closely resembles the entertainment industry than professional journalism. At worst, the press routinely presents 'news' in which insinuation and vilification substitute for accurate reporting, all the while fostering a wildly inaccurate Europhobic mythology as the prism through which the EU is commonly observed in Britain. A case in point concerns the London mayor, Boris Johnson, who was the Brussels correspondent of *The*

Daily Telegraph in the 1990s. One European newspaper correspondent in Brussels in the mid-1990s recalled that many of the Euro-myths and half-truths at this time – smaller condoms, square strawberries and fishermen forced to wear hairnets – were invariably Johnson creations (*The Guardian*, 26 February 2016). According to Charles Moore, the highly Eurosceptic deputy editor of the newspaper at the time, Johnson 'was always a bit vulnerable because his stories weren't always wholly accurate' (*The Guardian*, 16 February 2015) – evidently an early foray into the business of light entertainment.

In case it is supposed that Campbell 'may have exaggerated for effect', as Leveson observed, there is abundant evidence from other sources about how the Eurosceptic British press processes and presents EU-related tales in the form of popular mythology comprising scare stories, rumours and half-truths – usually reflecting the view that facts are much less potent than perceptions or fantasy. The Euromyths website section of the London office of the EU Commission includes the following examples of tabloid-fuelled hysteria and unfounded reports: that the EU was changing the definition of an island; that 21-gun salutes had to be muffled; that warning signs would soon be required for mountains telling climbers that they were high up; that women had to hand in their used sex toys; and finally, as if to give a new dimension to the cleavage between Britain and 'Brussels', that the EU had declared 'a crackpot war on busty barmaids by trying to ban them from wearing low-cut tops'; this last item, like so many others, was given a spurious degree of accuracy by reference to an EU Optical Radiation Directive.

A further feature of much press coverage of Britain and the EU is the parochial character of the treatment. A preoccupation with the domestic angle on any EU story has often meant that the press has relegated a major item to the sidelines. Campbell reportedly noted that following one informal meeting of EU leaders, when the key piece of news by all accounts concerned a Franco-German disagreement, the British press was running around like headless chickens asking where was the story: 'i.e. where was the Britain-versus-the-rest story'; according to Campbell, it seemed to be the case that everything had to be fed through an anti-Europe frame of mind (Young, 2008: 594).

In Campbell's view, this episode was but one example of how the domestic press provided inferior coverage and analysis of Britain's EU policy as compared with the mainland European press with its journalists much more at ease discussing political ideas and philosophy, not just 'stories' (Campbell, 2011: 535; Trewin, 2008: 594). Forty years ago even British tabloid newspapers had a network of correspondents across Europe including those covering the EC. Currently, however, there is a striking paucity of British media representation on the ground in Brussels and in other European capitals. The tabloid British press has virtually no representation in most European capitals and especially in Brussels, meaning that it is more often than not simply 'flying blind' as it writes and interprets stories in London about events in the EU (*The Guardian*, 11 April 2013).

A corollary of this very limited direct representation is that the press is fed stories by seemingly independent think tanks that may in fact be geared to serve a partisan cause or political campaigning. Open Europe, one such think tank, is a ready source of EU stories and reports for the press. It describes itself as a non-partisan and independent policy think tank, committed to crafting and putting into action solutions to the European Union's most pressing challenges. Some observers, however, have suggested otherwise, claiming it is committed to a limited vision of the EU, a distaste for ever closer union, support for a new model of European co-operation and a penchant for showing the EU in the worst possible light. According to one source, well over half the stories about the EU in the British daily press are directly inspired by Open Europe press releases and tip-offs (www.economist.com/blogs/charlemagne/ 2010/03). Other stories originate from a similar anti-EU organization, Business for Britain. The comparable organizations on the pro-EU side, British Influence and the Centre for European Reform, occupy a much lower profile like pro-EU opinion at large in recent years, thereby leaving the ground open to predominantly anti-EU opinion.

It is also the case that the press and publicity facilities of the European Commission Representation in Britain with four press officers (2013) do not begin to match the resources of the Eurosceptic press. Nor are there any European-wide newspapers or publications to serve as a counterbalance to national press channels, though there are publications like the EU's *Press Watch* and websites like Fullfact.org that seek to expose myths and scrutinize official claims and statistics. For the most part, however, the Eurosceptic tabloid press has been able to pursue its agenda with at best a minimal and uncoordinated riposte either from EU-friendly politicians or from other media. Meanwhile, with few exceptions, politicians across the spectrum have been complicit in denigrating the EU for party gain.

More seriously, the EU as an organization has attracted criticism for its failings in terms of communication and publicity. A leading think tank, Demos, described the EU as 'the ultimate public relations disaster' (Leonard, 1998). The reasons for this 'communication deficit' and failure to project a message with clarity and simplicity were principally threefold.

First, a high level of public ignorance about the EU was partly a result of the fact that most EU policies and assistance are not perceived to stem from the EU but are associated with local and national government – the latter often shamelessly taking credit for such policies. It has been suggested that the governments of the member states should assume responsibility for promoting the EU, though in the case of British government antipathy to EU matters that might be 'comparable to leaving Herod in charge of the orphanage' (Anderson and Weymouth, 1999: 155).

Second, the report considered that the EU was spectacularly bad at claiming the credit due to it for its successes affecting the daily lives of the public such as the European Working Time Directive and the distribution of European Structural Funds. Opinion polls reveal that billboards advertising EU-funded projects have proved influential over the years, while the claimed, generalized benefits of the EU – peace, prosperity, security, trade and investment – have less impact on the public. Some very significant developments receive little or no attention such as, for example, EU Commission proposals in February 2015 to establish a single European market in energy supplies. These proposals aim to loosen Russia's stranglehold on Europe's gas supplies and its use of energy supplies as a political weapon and for blackmail purposes.

Finally and most importantly, the EU has often invested in the wrong projects. It has failed to recognize that such policies as the CAP attract far less interest and attention from the population at large than such matters as tackling international crime and terrorism and protection of the environment. Then, too, there are the persistent failings of the EU institutions to engage public interest. The European Parliament, for instance, is supposed to give the public a direct voice in the EU, but it is rather the case that the public learns very little about how the European Parliament might be of use and relevance to it (Anderson and Weymouth, 1999: 157).

Mobilizing 'history'

The strength and character of Eurosceptic/Europhobic criticism of the EU and of Britain's EU policies, however, do not wholly rely on myths, falsehoods and public vilification. Such attacks invariably launch into the subject by setting a particular issue or government measure in the context of a 'patriotic' version of Britain's history and greatness. This approach aims to resonate with the reader and is able to command all the best tunes and lines. Every effort at all levels is made to portray the 'island story' told by H. E. Marshall in *Our Island Story* (1905) in an updated form – 'the great, world-beating story of the UK' as David Cameron put it commenting on this as his favourite childhood book (*The Guardian*, 7 February 2014)

The telling of the patriotic story is often carried out with a passion, intuition and an ability to touch on 'the taste buds' of politics rarely evoked by the well-reasoned arguments of the pro-EU case. As one study of the subject observes, the historical stories used by such press sources are more familiar to the British public and more persuasive as a result (Daddow, 2007b).

Only rarely has the pro-EU case found expression in the sharp, colourful invective often employed by Eurosceptic opinion in the press. One such case, significantly from a foreign source, appeared in the *New York Times* where Richard Cohen described Eurosceptics as 'the pin-striped effluence of an ex-imperial nation banging on about finest hours and the Luftwaffe, politically inept – less the fighting spirit of the Normandy hedgerows than the self-regarding hypocrisy of the giant offshore hedge fund that Britain often resembles' (*New York Times*, 11 December 2011). (The reference here to 'hedge fund' was particularly apposite in view of the extent to which the Conservative Party and UKIP were reportedly bankrolled by City of London donors and in particular by hedge fund firms and their owners (*The Guardian*, 2 January 2015).)

A typical example of the Eurosceptic genre was the approach of *The Sun* to the idea of British membership of the euro area in 1998 and to the signing of the Treaty of Lisbon by Brown in 2007. *The Sun* reached for one of the most iconic figures of twentieth-century British public life and some of the most memorable political oratory of the century when it expressed unflinching opposition to the euro and promised '*We will fight, fight, fight.* And even if we lose, we hope people will use the words of one of our greatest statesmen, Winston Churchill, and say ... *This was their finest hour*' (*The Sun*, 24 June 1998). (Some of Churchill's other sayings are cited less often in the Eurosceptical press, such as his hopes for 'a Europe where men and women of every country will think as much of being Europeans as of belonging to their native land and wherever they go in this wide domain will feel truly "Here I am at home"' (quoted in Sampson, 1968: 4).) On the day Brown signed the Lisbon Treaty, moreover, *The Sun* reproduced his signature with the simple caption 'Surrender signature', evoking memories of appeasement and the Munich agreement of 1938. It headlined the government's refusal to hold a referendum on the subject by deliberately misquoting Churchill, 'never have so few decided so much for so many' (*The Sun*, 13 December 2007). These and other examples are indicative of how opposing EU policies by using the 'straight-talking' language of the 'common man' has become the characteristic position of the Murdoch press down to the present day (Daddow, 2012).

The Europhile case in the press and elsewhere has clearly lacked this kind of 'history' on its side and has singularly failed to combine a 'patriotic' appeal with a European dimension. It has invariably proved unable to utilize such potent images, events and memories in order to penetrate the clutter of the modern media with a set of powerful symbolic messages. The press has whipped up popular qualms about EU membership, but it is scarcely wholly responsible for the often aphasic grasp of the key features of European integration, nor for the absence of a sense of shared history between Britain and the other major EU states. Mainstream British political culture at large, and not just the press, has encountered difficulties in coming to terms with the historical foundations, language and rhythm of European integration.

In the press and elsewhere in British public life, the image of Britain as the reluctant European and 'outsider' has not only survived 40 years of EU membership but has gone largely unchallenged. No British leader since 1973 has ever proposed that Britain should leave the EU, but it is equally the case that no such leader has seen fit to challenge 'the strong notion of outsiderliness underpinning Britain's status as a reluctant partner in the organization' (Daddow, 2015). Eurosceptic opinion has increasingly filled the space left by the absence of a robust, imaginative pro-EU case.

If there is little doubt that in the past 20 years or more the press has become much more vituperative in its coverage of EU activities, is it therefore more influential? Some evidence would suggest so to a certain extent, at least in relations between British prime ministers and the press on questions of Britain's EU membership.

Prime ministers, the press and the EU

It is a truism that prime ministers can't live with the media, but they can't live without them either. There is, to be sure, an unseen, seedy side to this relationship, obscured from the public's gaze as deals are struck between the two parties, often on one side at least in accordance with the advice of the former prime minister Lloyd George on how to handle the press: 'What you can't square, you squash; what you can't squash, you square'. Methods for managing the press, however, have varied greatly and with differing degrees of success over the period since 1961 when the Macmillan government first considered EC membership. The anti-marketeer Beaverbrook in the 1960s never exercised the influence over Macmillan as Murdoch is alleged to have brought to bear over the Labour governments of 1997–2010 and the Conservative-dominated Coalition government of 2010–2015. Certainly, it is difficult to imagine Macmillan flying anywhere to see Beaverbrook in the way that both Blair and Cameron flew round the world to pay court to Murdoch on a number of occasions, this being indicative of the extent to which large sections of the British press with their patriotic outpourings are actually owned by a handful of foreign or foreign-based personnel.

Friction between prime ministers and the press over policy towards the EU has proved particularly marked since the Major governments of 1990–1997 and first conspicuously so at the time of the making and ratification of the Maastricht Treaty in the period 1990–1993. In earlier years Heath had benefited from the press consensus favouring EC membership. However, Heath was not unlike the Labour Party leader Clem Attlee, who never bothered to read the newspapers; he preferred to remain aloof from a press that he regarded as frivolous. Indeed, how little Heath thought and cared about the press was most evident when, as he later recalled, at the end of his discussions with President Pompidou of France that effectively sealed the British bid for EC membership 'The President and I looked across at each other with delight, for we had secured success and also triumphed over the media' (Heath, 1998: 372).

Throughout Thatcher's premiership in the 1980s, EU policy matters including the signing of the Single European Act did not attract press opposition, and in particular the cheerleading of the Murdoch press helped to sustain Thatcher's hold on power. Interestingly enough there is not a single reference to Murdoch in the index of Thatcher's two-volume memoirs. Moreover, her biographer makes only one significant reference to Murdoch, this being in connection with his bid for control of *The Times* and *The Sunday Times* in 1981 that required her government's approval. It is fair to assume that at the very least she informally supported the bid (Moore, 2014: 549). Thereafter she was supported by his newspapers almost to the end of her premiership, as was the case with Rothermere's Associated Newspapers, the Telegraph group and Express Newspapers.

It is scarcely surprising, therefore, that David Hannay, British ambassador and permanent representative to the European Communities in the period 1985–1990, was able to comment on this spell of office that: 'We did not then have that solid block of the Black, Murdoch and Rothermere presses going full steam all the time, with which many of my successors had to contend' (Menon, 2004b: 21). Nevertheless, the 1980s saw the beginnings of a qualitatively different tone in tabloid treatment of European affairs and markedly so in the Murdoch press, tipping the balance from a legitimate 'proud sense of insularity' symbolized by Thatcherite discourse on British nationhood into rank stereotyping and strident jingoism (Daddow, 2012: 1232).

The Major experience of the press

Relations between Major and the press and especially the Murdoch titles over policy towards the EU were far more antagonistic in the period of Major's premiership between 1990 and 1997 than had been the case in the 1980s. The parliamentary passage of the European Communities (Amendment) Bill in connection with the ratification of the Maastricht Treaty on European Union was accompanied by a right-wing press increasingly opposed to the Treaty. It was also supportive of opponents of the Bill in the Conservative parliamentary party as the party began a bitterly divisive contest over Europe during the next 20 or so years. According to Major, almost all the Conservative press at this time and all the more so after 'Black Wednesday' and sterling's exit from the ERM in 1992 was 'captured by the anti-European cause' and 'enmeshed itself closely with the more active elements of the Euro-sceptic cause' (Major, 1999: 358–9).

By the end of Major's premiership the tabloid press especially was into a triumph and disaster mode of reporting Britain's EU membership. This condition was most evident after the EU announced (March 1996) a worldwide ban on all exports of British beef and derivatives, following the government's admission that there might be a connection between Bovine Spongiform Encephalopathy (BSE) in cattle and Creutzfeldt-Jakob disease (CJD) in humans. Initial attempts to secure the lifting of the ban led to an explosion of xenophobic and anti-EU feeling in the press. The acronym BSE was represented as standing for 'Britain Screwed by Europe', while one newspaper, the *Daily Express*, started a 'Stop the Euro-Rot' campaign.

In May 1996 the government embarked on a campaign of blocking EU business until agreement was reached – the so-called policy of non-cooperation in Europe (with the unfortunate acronym PONCE). This policy was described by British officials as 'cumulative irritation rather than general buggeration' (*The Independent on Sunday*, 26 May 1996). The tabloid press immediately moved from the disaster to the belligerent headline. In the *Daily Mail* the 'Humiliation of Britain' headline was followed a day later by the 'Major Goes to War at Last' on the announcement of the policy of non-cooperation, or as *The Sun* put it in its inimitable style 'Major Shows Bulls at Last' (*The Sun*, 22 May 1996). The tabloid orgy of xenophobic hysteria was particularly directed at Germany as a leading opponent of lifting the beef export ban. Crude gibes about Chancellor Kohl's girth mingled with references to the Second World War and the emergence of a 'Fourth Reich'. Unsurprisingly, the press was delighted to report that British beef was on the menu for the official banquet on Kohl's visit to London.

Blair and the Murdoch press

How far the issue of EU membership in itself was responsible for this development is debatable. Suffice it to say, at the beginning of the general election campaign in 1997 the most symbolic loss of support for Major was the decision of *The Sun* to switch its support to Blair and the Labour Party. Understandably, 'the sheer irrationality of this decision' surprised Major, because a Labour government was far more likely to take the pound into the forthcoming euro area than the Conservatives and thereby upset *The Sun*'s prejudices against such a move. In his later evidence to the Leveson Inquiry, however, Major flatly contradicted the views of others (see below) on the relationship between the government and the Murdoch press when he declared: 'he [Mr. Murdoch, chairman of News Corp] made it clear that he disliked my European policies which he wished to change. If not, his papers could not and would not support the Conservative government' (evidence of former Prime Minister John Major to the Leveson Inquiry, 14 May 2012).

In the period immediately preceding the general election of 1997, it became apparent how far Blair was prepared to pander to *The Sun* when he was inclined to employ Eurosceptic language concerning the EU. Shortly after *The Sun* came out for Labour in the election campaign, Blair's article on 'Why I love the pound' was later judged by Roger Liddle, Blair's special adviser on European policy (1997–2004), to be 'The most egregious example of Blair's appeasement of Murdoch' (Liddle, 2014: 47–8). In his illuminating study of the making of Eurosceptic Britain, Chris Gifford maintains that a Eurosceptic nationalism was integral to New Labour's European strategy. It became essential for neutralizing the press and maintaining the support of the Murdoch empire (Gifford, 2014: 146).

Liddle, like Blair himself, insisted that Murdoch had no sway over government policy. He nonetheless maintained that there were more subtle and deeply significant influences including the internal struggle for power between Blair and Brown which gave the Murdoch press huge leverage to exert pressure (Liddle, 2014: 48). Blair was by no means alone in using Eurosceptic language to advance his own ends. In the contest for the Conservative Party leadership in 2001, which he lost, Ken Clarke, the standard bearer of the pro-EU cause in the Conservative Party, claimed his EU views were irrelevant and promised to oppose the Nice Treaty, for which declarations he won the backing of the Eurosceptic *Daily Mail*.

Lance Price, Blair's former spin doctor, recalls that when he worked at Downing Street Murdoch was 'like the 24th member of the Cabinet. His voice was rarely heard [the same could have been said of many of the other 23] but his presence was always felt' (Price, 2006: xii). In similar vein, Price maintained that Murdoch might not even have had to lean on Blair to ensure that no British government minister said anything positive about the EU. According to this source, anticipatory compliance was Murdoch's most powerful weapon, allowing Murdoch himself to claim at the Leveson Inquiry that 'I have never asked a prime minister for anything' (*The Guardian*, 1 July 2006; Cook, 2003: 170). At the same inquiry, Blair insisted that he had made no deals with the Murdoch press, a view disputed at the time by Price himself who quotes the reassuring advice of Paul Keating, the former Australian prime minister, to Blair: 'You can do deals with [Murdoch] without ever saying a deal had been done'.

No less debatable are the roots of Murdoch's bitter, long-standing opposition to the EU and the euro. Economic and commercial considerations rather than a sensitive concern for British sovereignty are rumoured to account for this position, most notably the failure to establish a Europe-wide satellite channel in the 1980s together with the potential of the EU regulatory authorities to hamper the growth of the Murdoch media empire and to act as a bulwark against the emphasis of the Murdoch press on unregulated markets and unfettered free enterprise (Price, 2006: 323).

At an early stage in his premiership in June 1998, Blair was given a warning of what to expect when some favourable comments which he made about the euro at the Cardiff European Council prompted a series of vitriolic articles in *The Sun*. In typically knock-about fashion, one of these posed the question whether the prime minister was 'the most dangerous man in Britain' (*The Sun*, 24 June 1998). Blair's attempts to coax Murdoch into a less anti-European position proved fruitless, while his general concern about treatment at the hands of the press caused Mandelson to quip that 'what Tony means by strategy is what's in the weekend papers' (Liddle, 2014: 58). Mandelson, however, later commented that 'There are now newspapers that are just propaganda rags, there is no balance, no even-handedness. It is just straight forward Europhobia' (BBC, 25 February 2013).

Campbell constantly warned Blair that the press had to be treated as players in and not spectators of EU affairs, and Campbell himself was under no illusions about 'the poisonous media culture' that was 'a screaming pain in the backside' (Campbell, 2012: 155, 159). That meant, among other things, that government was acutely sensitive to treatment of European stories by the press. One Blair Cabinet meeting on the EU, according to Campbell, involved tactical as much as strategic discussion as the whole time the Cabinet had to work 'round an impossible media that would not allow an honest debate' (Campbell, 2011: 589–90). Unsurprisingly, Jonathan Powell, Blair's Chief of Staff in the period 1997–2007, later conceded that the Blair government had worried too much about media moguls, particularly over Europe (*The Guardian*, 19 July 2011). Possibly that judgment underestimated the impact of the dark arts of under the radar intimidation chronicled by other sources (Channel 4 – How Murdoch ran Britain: Dispatches, 25 July 2011).

Shortly before he left office, when his aides thought he had been 'liberated' from the media at last (Price, 2006: 380), Blair likened the British media to a feral beast. In doing so, it seems unlikely that he overlooked the way in which the predominantly Eurosceptic media, and especially the agenda-setting capabilities of a dominant right-wing press, had greatly constrained his attempts to normalize Britain's EU membership. At his final EU Council press conference as prime minister, he was invited to address the criticism that he had never managed to win the argument for Europe with British voters. On discovering that the hostile questioner was from the Europhobic *Daily Telegraph*, Blair ruefully commented 'Well thank you for your help in winning this argument over the years!' (www.number10.gov.uk/Page12094). Furthermore, at the Leveson Inquiry Blair acknowledged that the misinformation published about Europe by some sections of the press made it difficult for him 'to adopt particular policies or achieve certain political ends in Europe that he might otherwise have done' (www.bnegroup.org/blog/archives/945).

Against all that, however, Blair was not prepared, as one of his former advisers on European policy put it, to let loose an effective and well-financed pro-European campaign for which he could have undoubtedly raised the money. Nor did his government systematically attempt to counter misinformation with hard facts, for which he could have mobilized the civil service machine (Liddle, 2014: 102).

Throughout the period of Labour government between 1997 and 2010, neither Blair nor Brown was willing to confront or contest Eurosceptic opinion-forming circles in the press. Neither man was inclined to turn on the press proprietors as Stanley Baldwin had done in 1930 when he criticized them for exercising 'power without responsibility: the privilege of the harlot throughout the ages'. Indeed, they were quite prepared to fall back on the 'standing up to Europe' language (or muscles in Brussels to use a later catchphrase). In doing so, they reflected the predominance of the Eurosceptic discourse in the press and of how they had to operate within a discursive environment that was 'infected' by Thatcher's European views (Blair, 2010: 533). Blair and Brown were also given to blaming the press for their muted stance on the issue of British membership of the EU, as when Blair commented in 2001 that he didn't have a problem on EMU but that he had a media problem (Campbell, 2011: 270–1).

It is debatable as to why the character and achievements of the EU policy of the Blair governments in the period 1997–2007 failed to effect a marked change in British public opinion towards a more favourable view of the EU. Jonathan Powell, Blair's highly influential chief of staff, summed up a widespread view in Labour government circles that 'What we managed to do was shift Britain's position in Europe. What we failed to do was change British public opinion about it'. There was thus no bridging of the gap between policy and public opinion and between 'establishment Europeanism and public scepticism' (Daddow, 2011: 21). It is difficult to dispute the view of another 'insider' that Blair failed to pursue some of his most ambitious dreams in part, at least, because he thought the attempt would cost him too much support in the media (Price, 2010: 15). As early as 1999, according to another account, Blair realized that he could only advance his European plans by confronting Murdoch. His overriding priority, however, was to win a second full term and he therefore compromised by keeping Europe and the euro on the boil, but not allowing the brew to boil over (Liddle, 2014: 94).

Conflicting views about British membership of the EU have regularly found their way into the press not only in article form but also in a series of leaks often reflecting opposing views in government. For nearly a month in the early period of the first Blair government, for example, sensational reports appeared in a number of newspapers, including the *Daily Mail*, *The Independent* and *The Times*, most of them inspired by leaks and briefings from members of the warring Blair and Brown factions. It was rumoured that Brown was trying to bounce Blair into an early decision in favour of joining the euro currency. An altogether different suggestion had them working together to 'talk up' the likelihood of British membership of the euro area. Confusion reigned on this as on other occasions as the Blair government was frequently accused of failing to present a coherent policy on the euro.

A more serious example of this practice occurred in November 2005 when, according to one account, Brown was suspected of leaking details of Britain's negotiating strategy over the EU's budget. The details included a willingness to make a concession on the rebate while Blair was negotiating with other EU leaders about the matter. Officials in Number 10 regarded this move as a betrayal and held Brown personally responsible, believing that he wanted to undermine Blair for conceding too much and that he aimed to impress the Eurosceptic press, notably the *Daily Mail* and the Murdoch press, with his Eurosceptic credentials (Price, 2010: 383). It was a measure of the gulf between Blair and Brown that Blair reportedly complained that Brown discussed the euro more openly with Murdoch than with himself, again with a view to burnishing his Eurosceptical credentials (Campbell, 2012: 254).

The influence of press opinion during the years of the Blair administrations was most apparent on the question of the abortive EU constitutional treaty and the issue of the euro. Blair initially insisted that the treaty would not be a matter for a referendum. In April 2004, however, he discovered the reverse gear he had previously said he did not have, telling the Commons that the electorate 'will be asked for their opinion' on the matter. Although he took care not to mention the word 'referendum', everybody understood that was what he meant. Blair's explanation for this change of mind was that Michael Howard, the Conservative leader, had earlier (24 March) given a pledge to renegotiate the treaty unless it was approved by a referendum and that, added Blair, would weaken Britain's position in the EU (*The Guardian*, 21 April 2004). A suitable response to this explanation came from the *Financial Times*, which described it as 'tripe' (*Financial Times*, 20 April 2004).

The Sun, predictably, ascribed the enforced U-turn largely to pressure from its ten million readers. If *The Sun* was 'the tabloid that wields the most clout at No. 10' (Peston, 2005: 197), one of its readers, Rupert Murdoch the proprietor, was more influential than the rest put together, as he acknowledged at the Leveson Inquiry: 'If politicians want my views they should read *Sun* editorials'. It was reported that when, in 2004, Blair decided not to hold a referendum on the proposed EU Constitutional Treaty Murdoch personally ensured that the word 'traitor' appeared in the reporting of the issue in the *News of the World*. At the same time Murdoch told Blair that he would switch his support to the Conservatives at the next election unless he agreed to a referendum. He did, and within a matter of days *The Sun* secured the scoop. Press rumours had abounded that the American economist Irwin Stelzer, Murdoch's trusted emissary often referred to as his 'representative on earth', had been involved, and these were given some credibility by a confirmation from Downing Street that a senior figure from Murdoch's News International Group had held a meeting with Blair in March 2004 (*The Guardian*, 19–20 April 2004; *Financial Times*, 20 April 2004). On this as on other issues, however, *The Sun* was reflecting as much as shaping public opinion. The day before Blair's announcement of his U-turn a *Sun*/YouGov poll reported that only 16 per cent of respondents said they would vote 'yes' in a referendum. At a House of Commons Media Select Committee in 2012, Murdoch himself admitted that 'Europe' was the only issue that had caused heated discussions between himself and Blair during Blair's premiership.

Europe and, in particular, the issue of a referendum on the Lisbon Treaty came to the fore in the early days of Brown's premiership at the time (October 2007) of arguably the key decision of the Brown premiership not to hold a general election in the autumn of 2007. Immediately before this decision was taken, Brown was left in no doubt by Murdoch himself and also by Stelzer that the Lisbon Treaty – due to be signed in a few months time – should be put to a referendum and that Brown's attitude to the referendum issue would be a decisive factor in deciding who both *The Sun* and the *News of the World* would support at the next general election. In the event, Brown resisted this pressure and refused to agree to a referendum, the possibility of a defeat in any such referendum weighing more heavily in his mind than any desire to spike the guns of News International (Price, 2006: 405–6). Nevertheless, his low profile signing of the Lisbon Treaty at a time when the Eurosceptic press was wholly opposed to the treaty proved to be a public relations disaster. His failure to be photographed signing the treaty along with all the other EU heads of government drew wounding comment from the press. The episode was also indicative of the extent to which the Murdoch press and the Eurosceptic press at large had moulded a cultural and moral climate that necessitated such behaviour by politicians.

Cameron and the press

At an early stage in Cameron's leadership of the Conservative Party in opposition, the importance of seeking the support of News International was evident in the laborious negotiations that eventually led the Murdoch press to switch its allegiance from Brown's Labour government to the Conservatives and to change its initial view of Cameron as a 'lightweight toff'. This move was facilitated by an unambiguous pledge made by Cameron to the readers of *The Sun* in September 2007 that he would hold a referendum on the Lisbon Treaty. The timing of this move was of critical importance as the Cameron leadership appeared to face its greatest crisis as the Conservatives trailed by 20 points in the public opinion polls and Brown seemed poised to call and win a general election. For his own part, Cameron later claimed at the Leveson Inquiry that he had never traded a policy in return for support from a media outlet and, in particular, that he won the leadership of the Conservative Party without the backing of the newspapers.

In power during the period 2010–2015, Cameron did not attract the same volume of critical comment from the tabloid newspapers as experienced by Major and Blair. He had close relations with senior personnel in Murdoch's News International, most notably Rebekah Brooks, the former editor of the *News of the World* and *The Sun* and later chief executive officer of News International (2009–2011) who texted Cameron on the eve of his October 2009 party conference speech 'professionally we're definitely in this together' and 'Yes we Cam!' In addition and from the same stable, there was Andy Coulson, former editor of the *News of the World* and Cameron's disgraced communications director.

Evidently, Cameron was not beyond criticism when his views about the EU were perceived as insufficiently Eurosceptic. The editor of one newspaper reportedly serialized a biography of Cameron with sensational but unsubstantiated rumours about his student life, because he believed that Cameron had gone too soft on Europe and immigration (*The Guardian*, 22 September 2015). This was a minor irritant, however, compared with the torrent of press criticism that accompanied the publication of the Tusk-Cameron document (2 February 2016) on the state of progress in the renegotiation of Britain's EU membership (Tusk being the president of the European Council). Cameron's expression of support for remaining in the EU on the basis of these still incomplete terms drew withering, if ill-considered, criticism that the document was of marginal importance if not meaningless (see Chapter 12). The tabloids competed for the most melodramatic headline; the *Daily Mail* used a 1940 quote – 'Who will speak for England?', *The Sun* chose to go with the Dad's Army theme – 'Who do you think you are kidding Mr Cameron?' – while the *Daily Express* headline was 'Cameron's EU deal is a joke'.

Cameron conceded at the Leveson Inquiry that politicians and the press had grown too close in the past two decades. His policy and attitude towards the EU generally went with the grain of Eurosceptic opinion in the press at least until the process of renegotiation, though the press was less influential than opinion within the Conservative parliamentary party in accounting for the various twists and turns in Cameron's EU policy. Furthermore and significantly, a few days after the Eastleigh byelection (February 2013) at which UKIP won second place, there was a meeting between Murdoch and Farage following which Murdoch evidently believed that Farage reflected his own opinion on Europe. Meanwhile *The Sun*'s associate editor, Trevor Kavanagh, compared UKIP favourably as against the Coalition leadership in a piece headlined 'UKIP are Not as Odd as the Odd Couple' (*The Guardian*, 22 March 2013).

It is also the case that public opinion has rarely demonstrated the same degree of support for or hostility to the EU as the press. This difference is indicative perhaps of the limits of the influence of the press and especially the tabloid press in shaping opinion. At its most influential, the press may 'successfully accelerate but never reverse the popular attitude', as Hugh Cudlipp, a leading figure in twentieth-century British journalism put it, or more minimally it may simply reflect rather than create popular attitudes through a distorting and superficial prism. Besides, two-thirds of adults do not read the tabloid press, and the circulation figures of all newspapers have plummeted over the past 40 years (see Table 7.1).

In the wake of the Leveson Inquiry, it was scarcely unexpected that according to one poll only 9 per cent of respondents trusted *The Sun* and 17 per cent the *Daily Mail* (Federal Trust Report, 2013: 21–2). A Eurobarometer poll (March 2011) found that some 48 per cent of respondents indicated that reports about the EU in the press tended to be unnecessarily negative, a view for which there was a majority opinion even among respondents who expressed consistently unfavourable opinions about the EU. This same poll also reported that nearly half of the respondents expected their government to inform them about the EU, placing the government in a far higher position

Table 7.1 Circulation figures of a selection of British newspapers: 1987, 2000, 2014

	2014	*2000*	*1987*
The Sun	2,213,659	3,557,336	3,993,000
Daily Mail	1,780,565	2,353,915	1,759,000
Daily Mirror	992,256	2,270,543	3,123,000
The Daily Telegraph	544,546	1,039,749	1,147,000
Daily Express	500,473	1,050,846	1,697,000
Daily Star	489,067	502,647	1,289,000
The Times	384,304	726,349	442,000
Financial Times	234,193	435,478	280,000
Daily Record	227,639	626,646	N/A
The Guardian	207,958	401,560	494,000
The Independent	66,576	222,106	293,000

Note: Figures shown are average circulations for January of each year.
Source: Audit Bureau of Circulations.

than any other information provider. Evidently, most newspaper readers do not labour under the misapprehension that they are reading the unmediated absolute truth, nor mistake propaganda for journalism. Perhaps only the politicians have exaggerated the power of the press and paid a heavy price for it (Price, 2010: 16).

Conclusion

In the period since Britain joined the EC in 1973, the terms of the debate in the press about the subject have demonstrably changed, as one authoritative assessment of the matter has put it, from 'permissive consensus to destructive dissent' (Daddow, 2012). Most especially the Murdoch press and the *Daily Mail* – the latter often viewed as the 'benchmark audience' in government circles during the Blair premiership (Trewin, 2008: 734) – have dramatically affected coverage of EU membership and in ways that have made politicians fearful of taking up an explicitly pro-EU posture.

Nevertheless, there are limits to the influence of the press in shaping public opinion and in determining public perceptions. Unlike the press, the public has rarely judged Britain's membership of the EU as a highly salient issue, and again unlike the press the public is divided over the issue of EU membership in ways that are scarcely reflected by the press or by the opinions of a few newspaper proprietors (see Chapter 5). The subject of the next chapter has yielded much critical newspaper coverage over the years, and has also intermittently, sometimes dramatically, attracted public attention.

8 The 'Bloody British Question'

We are simply asking to have our own money back.
(Margaret Thatcher, November 1979)

Introduction

The British contribution to the EU budget has long figured as a running sore in Britain's relations with the other EU states. At a particularly contentious time in this saga between 1979 and 1984, the British Budget Question (BBQ) was sometimes referred to by Roy Jenkins, president of the EC Commission 1977–1981, as the 'Bloody British Question' (Jenkins, 1992: 491). This period culminated in the negotiation of a budget rebate ('abatement') by the Thatcher government in 1984, described as 'the most long drawn out and bitter battle yet fought in the EU' (Wall, 2008: 8), though possibly overtaken in that regard by deep-seated crises in the euro area since 2008–2009. In any event, the negotiation of EU budgets and the question of the rebate ever since have proved to be highly controversial matters.

Among European diplomats the answer to the question why the EU currently sets its budget (see below) only every seven years is simple – because the process is so painful that they could not dare to do it more often. The subject has presented a major test for British prime ministers, especially as it involves negotiations about the most quantifiable aspect of the EU's activities – the size and disbursements of the budget and the survival of the British rebate. In his description of the 2005 EU budget negotiations in which he was directly involved, Tony Blair commented that even talking about the rebate was tantamount to political blasphemy, that to question it was to betray the nation and to challenge it was like introducing Darwin to an ardent creationist. Few, if any, of Blair's predecessors and successors as prime minister would dispute the view that the EU budget issue has attracted flag-waving confrontations and involved 'a nightmare of detail, political cross-currents, national pride and prime ministerial egos, all played out in vivid public technicolour' (Blair, 2010: 535, 541).

This chapter comprises a case study of this still topical matter. It first considers the nature and extent of Britain's original problem with the financing of the EC. It then examines the partial solutions to the problem and the origins of a lasting settlement in the form of a budget rebate known as the Fontainebleau agreement of 1984. The chapter covers subsequent British government efforts to defend the rebate. It discusses the extent to which the rebate issue entered into and influenced Britain's relations with other EU states and also reflected a set of 'book-keeping' British attitudes towards the EU budget at large with cuts in the budget being pursued for their own sake.

The EU budget

The evolution, composition and size of the EU budget require brief consideration in order to give some context to the particulars of British policy and attitudes in this field. In the early years of its history, the EC was directly funded from the national exchequers of the Six. In December 1969, however, the Six agreed that the EC should have its own budget or 'own resources'. The revenue was to come from customs duties and agricultural levies on all imported products from outside the EC, plus up to 1 per cent of receipts from Value Added Tax (VAT). At this time (1970) EC expenditure was equivalent to 2 per cent of member states' public expenditure, and 0.7 per cent of member states' GDP.

Since 1970 and especially since 1988, the EU's revenue and expenditure system has consisted of two main elements. The most important and the one attracting periodic controversy at the highest political level (involving as it does unanimous adoption by the European Council), is the now septennial Multiannual Financial Framework (MFF). This mechanism provides the basis for financial programming and budgetary discipline by ensuring that EU spending is predictable and stays within the agreed limits.

The current MFF for the period 2014–2020 (agreed by the European Council in February 2013) set a maximum amount of EUR (euros) 960 billion for commitment appropriations (sometimes referred to as the credit card limit or the maximum amount that can be pledged for projects) and EUR 908 billion for payment appropriations (the funds that are forecast to be paid out in a given year). The other element is the EU's annual budget that is governed by several principles, including the requirements that all revenue and expenditure is brought together in a single document, that budget operations relate to a given budget year, and that expenditure must not exceed revenue.

In percentage terms, the expenditure part of the budget has changed more substantially than the revenue side over the past 40 years. In 1970, agriculture accounted for 86.9 per cent of the EC's budget, but that share had fallen to just over 40 per cent by 2012. There has been no change in the sources of revenue since 1988 when, following an agreement in 1984 to increase the receipts from VAT to 1.4 per cent, it was also decided that there should be a national contribution based on the gross national income of each member state.

The MFF agreement for the period 2014–2020 specified that the maximum annual amounts of own resources that the EU may raise during a year was to be 1.23 per cent of the EU gross national income (GNI). This figure together with the fact that the national budgets of the member states account for 44 per cent of GDP on average lends some necessary perspective to any claim that the EU is a federal power in the making. The budgets of federal states are very much larger proportionately than the EU budget. In federal states like Germany and the United States, federal public expenditure is around 20 to 25 per cent of GNP (HM Government, 'Review of the Balance of Competences between the United Kingdom and the European Union EU Budget', Summer 2014: 36).

Furthermore, the governments of the EU member states still have exclusive fiscal control over the personnel and infrastructure costs for social security, pensions, health, justice, education and defence that constitute a large proportion of national budgets (Spence, 2012: 1250, 1254). Thus, British public spending on pensions and health care alone is much more than the whole of the EU budget. It is estimated that the EU budget amounts to about 53 pence per person per day on average for the 500 million people of the EU – less than the price of a cup of tea.

The problem

The successful negotiation of terms of EC membership by the Heath government left a legacy of problems and conflict, one of which centred on the British contribution to the EC budget. Almost inevitably, the question of the British contribution to the EC budget became the focal point of a more or less continuous process of renegotiation long after Britain joined the EC. The 'own resources' arrangement was disadvantageous to Britain in several respects:

- it imported more from outside the EC than any of the EC states, and consequently its contribution to the EC's revenue stream would be greater than that of the other EC states;
- it would be further penalized by the fact that the large bulk of EC funding was devoted to the CAP;
- its agricultural base was relatively small, and thus it stood to gain less than the other member states from the CAP.

In short, Britain would be making a contribution to EC expenditure that was wholly disproportionate to the benefits it received and also to the size of its GDP as a share of the EC's total GDP. True, in the early stages of EC membership, calculations concerning the full British contribution to the budget belonged to the realm of guesstimates in view of the five-year (or possible seven-year) phasing-in period. As one British diplomat involved in the negotiations put it, Britain and the EC were arguing about 'the impact of a budget of unknown and unknowable size an unknown number of years ahead' (Hannay, 2013: 50).

Yet there was no denying that the nub of the problem by the end of the transitional period would be the large size of the net budget contribution facing the British government, this being the difference between what Britain paid into the EC's coffers and what it received back. Britain has figured as a net contributor to the EU budget in every year since it joined except in 1975 (see Table 8.1). By 1978, in fact, and before the end of the transitional period, the British net contribution (some £822 million) was the second largest to that of West Germany.

This financial penalty was the price that had to be paid for failing to secure EC membership at an earlier stage and the inability to influence the 'own resources' decision. The Heath government sought to cushion the shock of adjustment to the EC budgetary regime by negotiating a five-year transitional period. It also managed to extract what proved to be a largely worthless assurance during the initial negotiations (November 1970) that the EC would be impelled to find equitable solutions in the event of an unacceptably high British contribution to the EC budget. However, there was no accompanying, unambiguous definition of terms like 'equitable' and 'unacceptably high'. Nor did the Heath government have much success in reducing its net contribution by other means. It was hoped to claw back some of the money paid by Britain to the EC through the EC's newly formed European Regional Development Fund (ERDF). In the event, the introduction of this policy was delayed until 1975, by which time the prospect of

Table 8.1 Britain's EU contributions, rebates and receipts (£million)

Year	Gross total	Rebate	Gross contribution	Public sector receipts	Net contributions
1973	181	n/a	181	79	102
1974	181	n/a	181	150	31
1975	342	n/a	342	398	−56
1976	463	n/a	463	296	167
1977	737	n/a	737	368	369
1978	1,348	n/a	1,348	526	822
1979	1,606	n/a	1,606	659	947
1980	1,767	98	1,669	963	706
1981	2,174	693	1,481	1,084	397
1982	2,863	1,019	1,844	1,238	606
1983	2,976	807	2,169	1,522	647
1984	3,204	528	2,676	2,020	656
1985	3,940	227	3,713	1,905	1,808
1986	4,493	1,701	2,792	2,220	572
1987	5,202	1,153	4,049	2,328	1,721
1988	5,138	1,594	3,544	2,182	1,362
1989	5,585	1,154	4,431	2,116	2,315
1990	6,355	1,697	4,658	2,183	2,475
1991	5,807	2,497	3,309	2,765	544
1992	6,738	1,881	4,857	2,827	2,030
1993	7,985	2,539	5,446	3,291	2,155
1994	7,189	1,726	5,463	3,253	2,211
1995	8,889	1,207	7,682	3,665	4,017
1996	9,133	2,412	6,721	4,373	2,348
1997	7,991	1,733	6,258	4,661	1,597
1998	10,090	1,378	8,712	4,115	4,597
1999	10,287	3,171	7,117	3,479	3,638
2000	10,517	2,085	8,433	4,241	4,192
2001	9,379	4,560	4,819	3,430	1,389
2002	9,439	3,099	6,340	3,201	3,139
2003	10,966	3,559	7,407	3,728	3,679
2004	10,895	3,593	7,302	4,294	3,008
2005	12,567	3,656	8,911	5,329	3,581
2006	12,426	3,569	8,857	4,948	3,909
2007	12,456	3,523	8,933	4,332	4,601
2008	12,653	4,862	7,791	4,497	3,294
2009	14,129	5,392	8,737	4,401	4,336
2010	15,197	3,047	12,150	4,775	7,375
2011	15,357	3,143	12,214	4,112	8,102
2012	15,021	3,172	11,849	4,954	6,895
Total	283,667	76,474	207,193	110,909	96,284

Note: 2012 figures are estimated.

Sources: 'The EU Budget', House of Commons Library Standard Note; HM Treasury *European Union Finances*, July 2012, Cm 8405.

large-scale receipts was receding rapidly, partly because of the continuing growth of expenditure on the agricultural sector, partly because of the impact of the world economic crisis, but also because of West Germany's unwillingness to provide the necessary level of funding – this being one of the earliest intimations of West Germany's long-standing role as the EC's principal paymaster.

France, Britain and the EC budget

The question of the British contribution to the EC budget gave rise to a long-standing conflict between Britain and France. Early intimations of entrenched positions on both sides were evident in dealings between de Gaulle and Macmillan at the time of the first British application for EC membership in the early 1960s. For his part, de Gaulle emphasized the importance of agriculture for France – 'an essential element in the whole of our national activity' – as he put it when formally announcing his rejection of the first British application for EC membership (*The Times*, 15 January 1963). It was the Six's acceptance of the inclusion of a CAP in the common market that finally persuaded France to sign the EEC Rome treaty. France has always figured as the biggest agricultural producer in the EC/EU accounting for some 18 per cent of its total farm output which in turn has made it the principal beneficiary of the CAP with about 17 per cent of total CAP payments (2013). By way of contrast, as de Gaulle tediously reminded Macmillan, Britain's food chain lay outside Europe in the form of the Commonwealth preference system. The fact that the CAP came into operation in 1962 was at least in part due to French determination to push through the principle of the CAP before considering Britain's application for EC membership.

The CAP regime was deeply unpopular in Britain even before the country joined the EC. It was widely regarded as an expensive and wasteful system that produced artificially high food prices. In addition, it was commonly portrayed from the outset, especially by the tabloid press, as a racket for subsidizing inefficient French farmers and other continental farmers at the expense of the British taxpayer and consumer. This burden was considered all the greater as for more than a century the British consumer had enjoyed relatively cheap food imports from the Empire/Commonwealth. There has, in fact, been a long-standing disagreement about whether EU membership has increased or decreased costs to the consumer. Arguments have centred on at least three concerns: British tariffs if outside the EU, the effect of CAP payments and subsidies for producers on prices paid by consumers, and the effect of regulations on producer costs (HM Government, 'Review of the Balance of Competences between the United Kingdom and the European Union Agriculture', Summer 2014: 35).

The origins of the EC's 'own resources' budget and the question of Britain's contribution to the budget during the early years of membership also threw into sharp relief major differences between London and Paris. On the 'own resources' decision of 1969/1970 France was determined to ensure that arrangements for the EC's financing of the CAP and the financial mechanism for providing the EC with its own resources were firmly in place before the beginning of negotiations on the Heath government's application for EC membership. London would not therefore be in a position to influence the outcome.

France was also to the fore, though less successfully so, in determining the level of Britain's contribution to the EC budget during the early years of membership. Britain's opening proposal was for an initial payment of 3 per cent of total contributions, rising to a maximum of 15 per cent over five years and with provision for reviews if the burden became too great. President Pompidou of France dismissed this proposal as a good example of the British sense of humour. The French countered with a figure of 21 per cent and no relief in the early years. It was eventually agreed that there should be a five-year phasing in period (with provision for a possible two-year extension), by the end of which Britain would be contributing around 19 per cent of all payments towards the budget (Heath, 1998: 372–3; Campbell, 1993: 355, 357).

Partial solutions

The first attempt to address the net budget deficit occurred as part of the renegotiation of the terms of entry exercise undertaken by the Wilson Labour government in 1974–1975. Wilson sought to tackle the question by means of a general system of rebates. It was not a success, either in offering a simple formula for determining any rebate or in yielding any tangible results. Nevertheless, it had the advantage of appearing to address the problem, and that was enough for Wilson in terms of the referendum. Basically, the Commission was authorized by a summit of EC leaders (December 1974) to propose a general corrective mechanism. This mechanism was designed to trigger a rebate for net contributors whose per capita GNP was less than 85 per cent of the EC average, whose rate of growth of per capita GNP was less than 120 per cent of the EC average, and whose transfers to the EC budget exceeded by more than 10 per cent its share of EC GNP. This complicated financial mechanism never actually came into play, mainly because of changing economic conditions with North Sea oil coming on stream from 1975 and also because Britain's share of the EC's GNP never exceeded 10 per cent. To all intents and purposes, it was a cosmetic formula governed by referendum politics.

Meanwhile, as the seven-year transition phase drew to a close there was the immediate prospect of a steep rise in British contributions. In 1973 Britain's net payment to the EC was £102 million. By 1979 that figure had risen to £947 million, a sum that was exceeded only by the other net contributor, West Germany, and this at a time when Britain's per capita GDP ranked seventh in the nine-member EC.

It was this situation that confronted Thatcher's Conservative government on coming to power in 1979. Thatcher was determined to secure a lasting settlement. The principal weapon in her armoury was dogged persistence; 'What she liked best was being defiant' recalled John Gummer, one of her speech writers at the time (Moore, 2014: 338), and the budget question offered her plenty of scope to demonstrate this trait. The issue was perfectly straightforward as far as she was concerned; the current situation was demonstrably unjust and politically indefensible. It followed that if the British case was put with sufficient conviction and resolve, it must eventually win general acceptance. She quickly demonstrated that she was fully prepared to reiterate the same arguments *ad nauseam*, even at the risk of alienating all the other EC leaders and becoming completely isolated. As her self-assurance grew, her negotiating style increasingly came to resemble a form of brinkmanship carried to extreme lengths. As one British diplomat observed, she would 'take the wheel of the European car and drive it at full speed to the cliff's edge, confident that the others would lose their nerve before she did' (Wall, 2008: 177).

At the first European Council meeting attended by Thatcher (Strasbourg, June 1979), there were ominous signs that agreement on the British rebate might prove problematical. At this meeting chaired by Giscard, Thatcher was outraged that the French president understandably ranked energy policy, world economic problems and the EMS higher on the agenda than the British budget question. This spat then turned into a series of fractious exchanges not only with Giscard but also with several other leaders, including Schmidt. Her squabble with Schmidt was especially unfortunate, as West German co-operation, then as now, was indispensable to any budget settlement. Thatcher immediately and thereafter disliked the process and style by which the EC did its business, and in Giscard's view 'She was hostile to the European Community from the beginning' (Moore, 2014: 446).

The Strasbourg meeting, however, signified only the opening shots in the battle over the budget. More substantial differences became apparent at the next European Council meeting (Dublin, November 1979). In a speech prior to this Council meeting (October 1979) and in an unlikely image of herself, Thatcher declared that she could not 'play Sister Bountiful to the Community while my own electorate are being asked to forego improvements in fields of health, education, welfare and the rest' (Thatcher, 1995: 79). From the outset at Dublin, she insisted that she would accept nothing less than the return of 'our money', peremptorily rejecting the offer of an annual rebate of some £350 million, which she later described as being only 'one third of a loaf'. The other EC leaders were indignant at being subjected to a lengthy and hectoring monologue, in the course of which Schmidt famously feigned sleep.

More importantly, EC leaders were infuriated by the challenge that Thatcher's reference appeared to mount to the concept of the EC's 'own resources'. Helmut Schmidt, the West German chancellor, challenged the Thatcher view claiming that to act on it would mean the end of the EC in a matter of weeks. He later suggested that there were greater issues at stake than the British contribution to the EC budget – such as world recession. He and other continental critics accused her of demanding the so-called *juste retour* – the recovery of exactly the amount that Britain paid out to the EC budget. No doubt, this view of Thatcher as the bookkeeper or exponent of housekeeping economics lay behind the sneering comment of Giscard d'Estaing, the notoriously snobbish and haughty French president, who dismissed her contemptuously as the 'grocer's daughter'.

Given Thatcher's rhetoric, such a view was understandable but not entirely fair or accurate. In fact she was always prepared to accept a position where Britain was a net contributor. Her principal objective was to achieve on a permanent basis a broad balance between British outgoings and receipts. This outcome was to be effected within the framework of a fundamental restructuring of the EC budget aimed at controlling total expenditure and reducing the proportion of it devoted to agriculture – two of the main threads in British policy towards the EU budget down to the present day. The French retort to all this was that Britain had already renegotiated its financial contribution in 1974–1975, and if it wanted to pay less into the EC it had only to concentrate its trade in the EC and thereby reduce its payments under the 'own resources' formula.

Thatcher's abrasive negotiating style was, in part, simply a reflection of her personality; as she announced it herself she was 'not puttable offable'. A forceful and combative individual, she positively relished disputes with her EC counterparts, as Giscard acknowledged on her death in April 2013 when he referred to her unshakeable will and untameable character. Her 'them and us' mentality was as evident in her contempt for some of her contemporary EC leaders in the early days of her first administration as it was soon to be in her description of some of her fellow citizens as 'the enemy within'; about the former she scathingly commented that with the exception of Schmidt: 'They are a rotten lot' (Jenkins, 1992: 495).

It is fair to say, however, that her notorious prickliness was to some extent a response to the way in which she was initially treated on coming to power by Helmut Schmidt, the West German chancellor, and Giscard d'Estaing, the French president. They were well-established, senior figures within the EC, as they had been in power since 1974. Furthermore, they had resurrected the strong Franco-German axis of the early 1960s and had become accustomed to acting in tandem on EC affairs. They tended to deal with the recently elected British prime minister as though she was an interloper, and the fact that she was a woman probably did not help matters (Tugendhat, 1986: 122). There were some first-hand British observers, including Peter Carrington, the foreign secretary (1979–1982), Christopher Tugendhat, a European commissioner (1977–1981), and Roy Jenkins (president of the Commission), who laid at least some of the blame for the acrimonious tone of Thatcher's early discussions on the budget on the alleged failure of Giscard and Schmidt to adopt a more welcoming attitude towards her. Tugendhat claimed that the French and German leaders showed a complete lack of statesmanship during the early days of the Thatcher government in failing to mount a serious effort to find a prompt solution to the British problem. By making a 'derisory' offer at the Dublin European Council, they effectively drove Thatcher into a corner and provoked her into taking up a more unyielding stance than she might otherwise have done.

The rancorous and fruitless discussions in Dublin were the prelude to almost five years of what has been termed megaphone diplomacy over Britain's budget contribution. At the Luxembourg European Council (April 1980), there appeared to be a real possibility of an agreement. It was proposed by Schmidt that Britain's net contribution for 1980 should not be allowed to exceed the average for 1978 and 1979. It was further proposed by Giscard that the net amount to be paid out by Britain in 1981 should be the same as in 1980. In short, Britain would be receiving an annual rebate of some £760 million for the two years 1980–1981. This offer represented a significant advance on that made in Dublin, so much so that Carrington recommended acceptance, as did Thatcher's two senior advisers, Robert Armstrong, the Cabinet secretary, and Michael Palliser, the permanent under-secretary at the Foreign Office. To the surprise of most observers, however, Thatcher rejected it (Jenkins, 1989: 592–3; Gilmour, 1992: 236). It was during the making of this decision that Carrington attended a Cabinet meeting. He needed to leave early, got up still arguing, walked to the door without looking and promptly bumped into one of the Doric pillars: 'My God', he exclaimed, 'I've hit another immoveable obstacle' (Moore, 2014: 493).

Substantial progress was made at the Brussels Council of Ministers (May 1980) when Karl von Dohnanyi, the West German Minister for European Affairs, devised an ingenious variant on the Luxembourg formula. This proposal reduced the British contribution to two-thirds for two years with an option for a third year if structural change in the CAP had not been achieved. Carrington was favourably impressed and, after an all-night negotiating session, an agreement was finally reached at 6 a.m. Returning elated to London, Carrington and Gilmour, Lord Privy Seal attached to the Foreign Office, were immediately summoned to Chequers. They were received coldly; according to Gilmour they could not have met with a more hostile reception if they had been the bailiffs – or even Heath making a social call accompanied by Delors (Thatcher's bogeymen). After a blazing two-hour assault, Thatcher grudgingly acquiesced.

There are conflicting explanations as to why she did so. According to Thatcher's later account, she herself concluded that the package offered the 'great advantage' of providing a three-year solution, while its other elements, including a 5 per cent increase in farm prices, were 'more or less acceptable'; 'the deal marked a refund of two thirds of our net contribution and … huge progress from the position the Government had inherited' (Thatcher, 1995: 86). A somewhat different version of events is offered by Gilmour who depicted Thatcher as having her hand forced by strong pressure from within the Cabinet, a resignation threat from Carrington and a skillfully judged press leak by Gilmour himself suggesting that she had won a resounding diplomatic triumph (Gilmour, 1992: 237–41).

An arrangement on Britain's budgetary contribution was thus in place for the next two years. Thatcher's campaign did not cease even at an EC heads of government meeting (March 1982) to celebrate the twenty-fifth anniversary of the signing of the Treaty of Rome she was there to press the case. In no mood for celebration, she arrived 'all in deepest black' and 'would not have looked out of place at a state funeral' according to *The Times* (Wall, 2008: 9). In June 1982 another temporary deal – this time for one year – was negotiated by Francis Pym, who had just become foreign secretary following Carrington's resignation over his handling of the Falklands crisis.

Meanwhile, the Treasury under Howe developed a proposal aimed at fixing an upper limit, set in relation to GDP, on the budgetary burden of each member state. While it was intended to be of general application, in practice it was so self-serving that Britain would be the principal beneficiary standing to recover some 70 per cent of its current net contribution. Unsurprisingly, therefore, the scheme was given a frosty reception by the other EC states. What made it even more unpalatable to them was the fact that it was so complicated as to be virtually unintelligible to most people (Wall, 2008: 19). Eventually, domestic circumstances after the successful Falklands war of 1982 and the return to office of the second Thatcher government following the general election of 1983 facilitated a resolution of the budget problem.

Agreement at last – the Fontainebleau agreement of 1984

By 1983 it had become increasingly clear that a permanent solution to the British budget problem was needed. The matter was continuing to sour relations between Britain and the rest of the EC, was taking up an inordinate amount of time, and was diverting attention from other important issues. In the longer term the advent to power of new leaders in France and West Germany – François Mitterand took over from Giscard in May 1981 and Helmut Kohl replaced Schmidt in October 1982 – was to assist the process of reaching an accommodation on the issue. During 1982 and 1983, however, there were no signs of a breakthrough. On the contrary, attitudes seemed to be hardening on both sides. In May 1982 Peter Walker, the minister of agriculture in Thatcher's first administration, attempted to veto the annual increase in EC farm prices, but ministers from the other member states overrode his efforts to exercise the right of national veto embodied in the Luxembourg Compromise of 1966 (Thatcher, 1995: 85; Wall, 2008: 10–17).

In June 1983 Thatcher told the European Council in Stuttgart that she would not agree to a resolution of other issues before achieving a permanent settlement of the budgetary dispute. That settlement had to consist of two essential elements: a mechanism for ensuring that the contribution of each member state was related to its ability to pay, and a reduction in the share of EC spending allocated to the CAP. In response, Mitterand took an equally tough stance at the Athens European Council (December 1983), insisting that the aim of the meeting should be to agree on another temporary arrangement rather than a permanent formula (Thatcher, 1993: 337–8). Thatcher's suggestion that Britain's net contribution should be broadly similar to that of France did nothing to improve the atmosphere. A headline in *Le Monde* aptly captured the intransigence displayed by both leaders when it characterized their confrontation as 'Iron Lady versus Man of Marble'. Mitterand famously described Thatcher as having 'the eyes of Caligula and the mouth of Marilyn Monroe'. For her own part Thatcher greatly appreciated Mitterand's 'very staunch' support for the British cause during the Falklands War of 1982.

It was precisely at this point, however, in early 1984 that Mitterand adopted a more flexible approach. He was intent on disposing of what he had come to see as an intolerable distraction from the current drive for deeper integration of the EC that was to culminate in the Single European Act of 1986. After France assumed the presidency of the EC in January 1984, he made a determined effort in that direction. He immediately announced his intention to ensure that all aspects of the budgetary problem were settled by the time of the March European Council and then set off on a round of visits to other heads of government.

Mitterand's stated deadline was not met, but the Brussels European Council (March 1984) saw a considerable narrowing of the gap between Britain's position and that of the rest, particularly the French. It was agreed that there should be an increase in the proportion of VAT revenues allocated to the EC. In addition, Thatcher made a major concession on the contentious issue of how to calculate any rebate that Britain might obtain. The British government had hitherto maintained that the tariffs and agricultural import levies that it paid over to the EC should be counted as part of Britain's gross contribution to the budget. The other EC governments, however, never accepted this argument, insisting that tariffs and levies were not national contributions, but were simply being collected on the EC's behalf. The French now sought to reconcile these conflicting positions by means of a formula on VAT contributions that was to apply only to member states that in the previous year had paid more in VAT contributions than they had received from the budget by an agreed amount – that amount to be determined later. Thatcher accepted this formula as a basis for negotiation (Howe, 1994: 400–1; Thatcher, 1993: 538–9).

By the time of the Fontainebleau European Council (June 1984), there were few outstanding points of substance to be resolved, and the settlement that was reached there closely followed the lines laid down in Brussels three months earlier. Agreement was achieved without too much difficulty on a rebate of one billion ecus (European Currency Unit – the European unit of account) – a massive advance on the £350 million offered in 1979. Making arrangements for subsequent years proved rather more troublesome. Kohl and Mitterand initially had in mind an annual rebate equivalent to 60 per cent of the difference between Britain's VAT contributions and its receipts for 1985 and each year thereafter. Thatcher wanted 70 per cent and sought to play France and Germany off against each other. Her efforts to arrange a private meeting with Kohl, however, were rebuffed; it is unclear whether this was because, as Kohl later commented in his memoirs, Thatcher 'always gave me headaches' (*The Sunday Times*, 12 October 2014). In any event, a meeting between Thatcher and Mitterand brought an increased offer first of 65 per cent and then of 66 per cent – in cash terms slightly more than one billion ecus.

A further element in the overall package was a definite increase in VAT revenues from 1 per cent to 1.4 per cent of the national total, with the possibility of a further increase to 1.6 per cent in 1986. This decision was scarcely consistent with Thatcher's efforts to impose tight limits on EC expenditure, but was arguably characteristic of the cautious, pragmatic side to her politics. Throughout, she was well aware of strong Eurosceptic opinion at home among Conservative and Labour MPs who noted the increase in VAT revenues and the absence of any reform of the CAP. In any event, the increase to 1.6 per cent was crowded out by what was represented as the achievement of the budget rebate agreement.

Assessments of the Fontainebleau agreement

Assessments of the course and outcome of this long-running saga have varied considerably. As regards the tactics employed by Thatcher, opinions differ widely on the question of how effective they were. Her truculent, aggressive style of diplomacy owed little to subtlety. It consisted in essence of setting out the British position and then refusing to budge, no matter how intense the pressure that was exerted or how great the risk of total isolation. Critics of Thatcher's reliance on sheer bloodymindedness have argued that it was more often than not counter-productive; its main effect was to stiffen the attitude of other leaders and thus lessen the chances of coming to a sensible agreement. Others have reached precisely the opposite conclusion. Robin Renwick, a senior official in a Foreign Office whose upper echelons often winced at the idiosyncratic methods Thatcher employed for conducting foreign relations, was closely involved in the final stages of the negotiations leading up to the Fontainebleau agreement; in his opinion a successful outcome there was only possible because of Thatcher's stubbornness and extraordinary tenacity (Wall, 2008: 39).

Thatcher, of course, was not alone in taking up an intransigent position and in demonstrating an unwillingness to compromise. The French, in particular, were equally capable of digging in their heels when important national interests were felt to be at stake. The blanket refusal of both Giscard and Mitterand to contemplate a reduction in the share of the EC budget spent on agriculture was a major obstacle to an agreement on the British rebate. Nevertheless, Mitterand's efforts in seeking a solution to the problem departed from the normal conduct of relations between London and Paris over the EC/EU budget (see below).

There is little disputing Thatcher's success in securing a fair deal over Britain's contribution to the EC budget. From a narrowly financial point of view, she clearly achieved her goal. Michael Butler, who was directly and closely involved in proceedings as the British ambassador and permanent representative to the EC in the period 1979–1985, concluded that the Fontainebleau agreement was a 'major victory for the UK' (Wall, 2008: 37). Hugo Young commented: 'The Thatcher technique was brilliantly successful in a certain task. It got the money back' (Young, 1998: 325), while Tony Blair later described the deal as part of hallowed mythology.

On the debit side of the balance sheet, however, the financial gains were secured at a very heavy political cost. Relations between Britain and the EC were badly strained and the experience of five years of acrimonious disputes left a legacy of deep bitterness and mistrust on both sides. At the personal level, Thatcher emerged from the episode with an even lower opinion of her EC colleagues than before, more firmly convinced than ever that they were almost without exception unprincipled, hypocritical and untrustworthy. Furthermore, the budget row reinforced her distaste for the way the EC worked, and as her biographer notes it was one of a number instances in which she confronted the problem of all negotiation in the EC: how much should a matter of principle, such as national independence, be sacrificed for a specific, material advantage or for the Foreign Office concept of 'influence'? (Moore, 2014: 495). She, for her part, had forfeited whatever goodwill that had existed towards her when she first came to power.

Attacking the budget, defending the rebate

While the Fontainebleau agreement satisfactorily addressed the British case for a rebate, it did not deal with the remorseless growth of the EC budget that Thatcher also had in her sights. Indeed, on several occasions in the 1980s the EC was brought to the verge of insolvency. The fundamental problem was the CAP; it was extremely expensive and absorbed a large proportion of the total EC budget (65 per cent in 1986). The British strategy for ensuring tight controls over the budget was to set strict limits on the growth of spending and to press for a radical control of the CAP. However, the large farming constituency within the Conservative Party ('The National Farmers Union was the Conservative Party at prayer' in the words of Geoffrey Howe) meant that even Thatcher was not prepared to be as tough on CAP reform as she sometimes appeared to be (Wall, 2008: 81–2). British agriculture benefited from the CAP, even returning to its 1870s acreage while rising cereal prices meant East Anglian farmers joked about a new crop rotation 'barley, barley, world cruise, barley' (Tombs, 2014: 803).

In yet another crisis over the EC budget in 1987, the Thatcher government agreed to an increase in overall resources only on condition that it would be accompanied by binding agreements to restrict the production and price levels of surplus agricultural products such as milk, beef and cereals (Howe, 1994: 522–3; Thatcher, 1993: 728–37). British tactics throughout all the tortuous negotiations over the budget in the period 1984–1988 conformed to a common pattern. The government initially took the line that it could not possibly agree to any increase in spending. At length and after a great deal of argument, however, it finally acquiesced in return for tighter curbs on the amount devoted to agriculture. The procedure was 'messy and negative' (Riddell, 1991: 193), and it was furthermore a recipe for discord between Britain and the other EC states.

A major step towards the reform of the CAP advocated by Thatcher took place after she had left office. In May 1992 the European Council agreed to substantial reform of the CAP. This decision was taken largely as a result of pressure to curb surpluses (in the form of the so-called 'butter mountains' and 'wine lakes') and reduce subsidies in order to complete the Uruguay Round of trade negotiations under the auspices of the General Agreement on Tariffs and Trade (GATT). What was to become known as the MacSharry reform, after the commissioner for agriculture at the time, cut the link between guaranteed prices and overproduction and started the shift from product support (through prices) to producer support (through direct payments to farmers largely based on farm size). The reform aimed to improve the competitiveness of EU agriculture, to stabilize agricultural markets, to diversify production and to protect the environment.

New Labour and the EU budget

Reform of the CAP continued to figure as an objective in British circles in line with the strategic objectives of liberalizing the EU's policy both within the EU and in relation to international trade in agricultural products. CAP reform appeared in the Labour Party manifesto on which the party fought and won the general election of 1997 under Blair's leadership. Blair regarded the CAP as one of the most serious impediments to modernization within the EU. It still absorbed a massive share of EU expenditure on a downward trajectory but still some 50 per cent in 1997. Furthermore, the MacSharry reform of 1992 had failed to achieve the desired cutbacks. The EU Commission warned in one of its papers of July 1997 (*Agenda 2000: For a Stronger and Wider Union*) that further action was required to avert a crisis of overproduction. The Blairite view was that EU funding could be channelled more productively into education, research and technological innovation so as to equip the EU to meet the challenges posed by globalization. In the course of Blair's first administration and even more so during the second administration, British policymakers were increasingly faced with a two-pronged attack that focused on Britain's budget rebate and arose out of the enlargement of the EU into central and eastern Europe in 2004 and 2007.

It was the prospect of enlargement in the first instance that triggered a prolonged and bitter debate. This issue brought to the surface latent dissatisfaction among some member states, and Germany in particular, about their respective contributions to the EU budget. Germany was by far the largest net contributor, followed by Britain, the Netherlands and Sweden. All the other member states were net gainers. Berlin began a sustained campaign for reform that culminated in a demand at the Cardiff European Council (June 1998) for a cap on Germany's budget contributions and a rebate similar to that enjoyed by Britain since 1984. The Netherlands and Sweden also pressed for a better deal for themselves. Such changes, however, could only be effected by unanimous vote and depended on the willingness of others to make concessions. The uncompromising response from Blair was that whatever else might be changed the British rebate was not negotiable (*H.C. Deb.*, 18 June 1998).

It was far less easy to maintain such intransigence as the accession of Poland and the other central and eastern European states loomed large. Major reform of the CAP was imperative, not least because any attempt to extend the existing regime to regions in eastern and central Europe where at least a quarter of the population worked in agriculture would be financially ruinous. By 2004–2005 the interrelated questions of the EU budget, reform of the CAP and the British rebate were at the top of the EU Council's agenda. President Chirac of France had long wanted to get rid of the hated '*chèque brittanique*', regarding it as no longer justified because of the growth in Britain's relative prosperity since 1984. He was far from alone in this respect. The Germans and the Dutch were still calling for a rebate of their own if the British continued to receive theirs. Meanwhile, the other EU member states were wholly unsympathetic to Britain's case. Indeed, it became increasingly common in EU circles to highlight the contrasts between the prosperity levels of Britain and the 12 states that joined the EU in the period 2004–2007, all of which were expected to contribute to the British rebate. It was strongly argued that the new, poorer states should get relatively more from the budget in line with the EU 'solidarity' principle.

The issue first assumed a particularly high profile in the context of the Commission's proposal for a 35 per cent increase in the EU budget (MFF) for the period 2007–2013. The increase was designed to take account of the EU's enlargement. The British response was to reject categorically any idea of abolishing the rebate. Gordon Brown, Chancellor of the Exchequer, offered a robust defence of its retention at an ECOFIN meeting (November 2004). He pointed out that even with the benefit of the rebate Britain was the second largest net contributor to the EU budget since 1984, paying twice as much as France; in 2011–2012, when CAP still accounted for 43 per cent of EU expenditure, France received five billion euros more than Britain which was among the poorest net contributors with the lowest per capita receipts from the EU budget (HM Government, 'Review of the Balance of Competences between the United Kingdom and the European Union EU Budget', Summer 2014: 53). In line with long-standing British policy, Brown also attacked the proposed increase in the EU budget as unrealistic and unacceptable, all the more so since the Commission was currently criticizing member states for exceeding a 3 per cent deficit in their own budgets. In January 2005 Blair managed to persuade his EU colleagues to postpone further consideration of the issue until after the approaching British general election was out of the way, but the respite was brief.

Only a few weeks after winning a third term in office (5 May 2005), Blair attended the Brussels European Council. He went aiming to preserve the rebate, to reform the CAP and to trim and restructure the EU budget. The stage was set for a tough battle. The Treasury had spent a year preparing to defend the rebate and Brown was reported to have appointed some of the department's 'brightest stars' to negotiate the 2007–2013 MFF (*The Guardian*, 21 January 2005). All the indications were that the government was not in the mood to compromise; Jack Straw, Foreign Secretary, threatened to use the veto to protect the rebate shortly before the Brussels summit.

The Brussels European Council meeting ended in deadlock. Chirac reiterated a now familiar argument that the British rebate was outdated and had lost whatever justification it ever had. Currently worth £3.2 billion a year, the rebate was set to rise even higher in line with the growth in the EU budget. What made this especially indefensible to Chirac and others was that the twelve new, predominantly poor member states would be contributing to it. Blair continued to insist that the rebate was not negotiable and pointed out that over 23 per cent of agricultural subsidies under the CAP went to France compared with only 9 per cent to Britain. Chirac was unimpressed. Even at this stage, however, Blair was beginning to see that some sort of compromise might be necessary given that not a single one of the other 24 member states supported the British viewpoint.

This outcome was profoundly disappointing for Blair. He had hoped to use the British, six-month presidency of the EU commencing in July 2005 to promote a programme of far-reaching changes. Much of his time during the six-month long presidency, however, was taken up seeking to reach agreement on the various financial issues left unresolved by the Brussels European Council. The basic obstacle to a deal remained Chirac's refusal to accept a reduction in the scale of agricultural subsidies and Blair's insistence that this was an essential precondition of a British concession over its rebate. According to Blair, Gordon Brown, Chancellor of the Exchequer, demanded that France should accept the demise of the CAP, a publicized view that enraged the French; Brown's constant interventions on the subject so dismayed Blair that 'In the end I just stopped taking calls from him' (Blair, 2010: 542). Certainly, as chancellor, Brown had good reason to resist an extra budgetary burden, but his prime ministerial ambitions also suggest that he had political reasons to be seen to be 'standing up for British interests'. In any event, this episode was arguably the one time in his premiership when Blair 'courageously' stood up to Brown on Europe (Liddle, 2014: 178), while he did not do so on the altogether more important issue of the euro (see Chapter 10).

The protracted wrangle over finances was not in fact settled until 16 December, a fortnight before the end of the British presidency. Blair agreed to a reduction in the growth of the British rebate between 2007 and 2013 by the amount that the twelve new member states would have had to contribute. There was to be an increase in the EU budget, although not by as much as the Commission had wanted. In addition, as a sop to the British government, it was decided that there would be a mid-term review of the CAP in 2008. This last concession was of no practical importance, since the 2002 agricultural settlement already made provision for a review in 2008. For the Blair government what counted was being able to show that it had managed to wrest some French counter-concession over the CAP to justify the proposed cuts to the British rebate. Following this settlement, the rebate remained equal to 66 per cent of Britain's net contribution to the EU budget, subject to the following points:

- The rebate applies only in respect of spending within the EU. Expenditure outside the Union (mainly EU overseas aid), amounting to around 5 per cent of total budget expenditure in 2011, is excluded.
- From 2009 onwards non-agricultural expenditure in the member states that have acceded to the EU after April 2004 is excluded. This was phased in up to 2011, and the effect was limited up to a total of 10.5 billion euros (in 2004 prices) up to the end of 2013.
- The UK's contribution is calculated as if the budget were entirely financed by VAT.
- The rebate is deducted from the UK's VAT contribution a year in arrears.

The agreement was far from ideal from the British viewpoint and securing it had involved political as well as financial costs. British proposals to trim parts of the budget, particularly regional funding, attracted critical comment; José Manuel Barroso, president of the Commission, warned Blair against behaving like the sheriff of Nottingham by taking from the poor to give to the rich (*The Guardian*, 1 December 2005). Worse still, there was a marked deterioration in relations between Britain and the new member states. They had reacted with outrage to British proposals for a reduction in agricultural subsidies which they saw as detrimental to their interests. The Poles threatened a veto, and the Polish and French foreign ministers sent a joint letter to the *Financial Times* on 14 December saying that the British proposals were completely unacceptable. In time, Poland was in fact the largest net recipient of EU funds, amounting to 12 billion euros (2012).

It was generally agreed on the domestic front that Blair had needed the settlement in order to prevent the achievements of the British presidency from seeming meagre. However, that was precisely the reaction of most commentators; one critical journalist awarded the outcome a miserly '*nul points*' (*The Guardian*, 24 January 2006). Blair highlighted the fact that for the first time the British net contribution to the EU budget would in future be about the same as that of France. The Eurosceptic press, however, was unconvinced. It lambasted the settlement as an abject surrender, a betrayal and a blow to the British taxpayer. Blair later and justifiably commented that such a reaction would have been the same even if he had 'led Jacques Chirac in chains through the streets of London' (Blair, 2010: 542). The rebate remained a source of controversy. In September 2010, Janusz Lewandowski, the EU budget commissioner, declared that 'The British rebate has lost its original justification' on the grounds that farm subsidies – the main reason for the original rebate – now accounted for a substantially smaller proportion of the EU budget, while the per capita income of Britain had increased considerably since the 1980s (https://euobserver.com/economic/30735).

The tussles between Thatcher and Chirac and also between Blair and Chirac, as noted above, perpetuated the tensions arising out of the size and use of the EU budget. These differences were also evident in more recent years under the Cameron Coalition government of 2010–2015, most notably in the negotiation of the Multiannual Financial Framework (MFF) for the period 2014–2020. The precise outcome of these negotiations represented a landmark event. For the first time in its history the EU's long-term budget was to be cut in real terms, if only by 0.3 per cent of the EU-wide GNI (gross national income); the overall payments for commitments and payments were 3.5 per cent and 3.7 per cent respectively less than under the previous MFF for 2007–2013. In the course of the two-and-a-half years of negotiations preceding this decision, the

Cameron government was determined on two goals, namely to preserve the British rebate at the same level as had been agreed under the previous 2007–2013 MFF (some three billion pounds/3.6 billion euros) and to effect a cut in the funding under the MFF; 'at best a cut, at worst a freeze' was how Cameron approached the exercise.

A beleaguered Cameron could not have settled for less, and according to one report he lost his temper in a conversation with one Eurosceptic, Conservative MP on the subject (Ashcroft and Oakeshott, 2015: 495–6). The government was defeated in the House of Commons (31 October 2012) by a rebel amendment from the Eurosceptic Tory backbenches supported by Labour that called for a real terms cut in the EU budget; 53 Conservative MPs defied their party's whip. While this was a non-binding vote on the government, such opinion could not be lightly dismissed by this stage. Besides, the rebate was an integral part of the Thatcher legacy, and as Cameron remarked on Thatcher's death (April 2013) 'When you negotiate in Brussels, it is still her rebate you're defending'.

By 2015 the official Treasury figure of the saving as a result of the rebate was £78 billion, the most valuable financial agreement ever negotiated by the country according to one former diplomat (*The Daily Telegraph*, 8 April 2013; Moore, 2015: 380). According to one estimate, without the rebate Britain would have a net contribution to the EU budget twice that of France and half that of Germany, reinforcing the strongly-held view of successive British governments about the retention of the rebate to deal with a budgetary distortion. For the year 2015, Britain paid £17.8 billion into the EU budget, but received back from the EU £4.9 billion (rebate), £4.4 billion (regional and agricultural subsidies) and £1.4 billion (grants to private companies), resulting in an actual cost to the country of £7.1 billion (HM Treasury, *European Union Finances 2015*).

The headline figure served Cameron's purpose, and Britain's gross contribution to the EU budget is likely to fall (as a share of UK GNI). According to budgetary details, however, Britain's net contribution (i.e. what it pays into the EU after what it gets back and the rebate are taken into account) was still likely to increase, this being due to the fact that the share of the EU budget going to the new member states that had joined since 2004 would increase, and since Britain receives no rebate on this spending, its net contribution would increase (www.openeurope.org.uk/Article?id=9905).

In achieving its two main goals, the Cameron Coalition government was involved in preliminary skirmishes with France. France was intent on ensuring that the CAP was not adversely affected and was also less convinced than the Cameron government of the case for budget discipline and austerity. There emerged, however, something of a tacit compromise more or less to the effect that France would not call into question the British budget rebate if London did not press for radical reform of the CAP. In the event, direct payments under the CAP are to fall in real terms, but just under 40 per cent of the EU budget will still be spent on farm and rural subsidies. The EU decision-making system has over time both assisted and thwarted British purposes in this field. The unanimity voting principle in the Council of Ministers has served British interests in blocking increases in the EU budget but at the same time has allowed France to obstruct British-driven reforms to CAP spending (HM Government, 'Review of the Balance of Competences between the United Kingdom and the European Union EU Budget', Summer 2014).

More importantly, the course and outcome of this set of MFF negotiations highlighted two aspects of British policy towards the EU budget, one signifying an important change since the early days of EU membership and the other indicative of a persistent attitude towards the issue. In the first place, while so much of Britain's EC/EU budget issue since the early 1970s involved, as we have seen, an isolated Britain fighting its corner against the rest, the negotiations surrounding the 2014–2020 MFF witnessed a striking change. Britain formed an alliance with Denmark, Germany, Sweden and the Netherlands in favour of a budget cut and thereby overcame French and Italian calls for an increase. As in the past, Germany held the balance of power, and Chancellor Merkel, for whom the budget figures were something of a sideshow, acted as broker and in Bismarckian style played different alternatives against each other depending on the issue at hand. Alliance formation and striking out from a minority position, therefore, registered a marked difference on the British side in this sphere.

A further changing aspect of budget negotiations is the extent to which the British rebate has resonated with other EU states anxious to reduce their own net contributions to the EU budget. The MFF negotiations for the period 2014–2020 resulted in lump sum rebates for the Netherlands, Sweden and a new rebate demanded by Denmark. Germany, the Netherlands and Sweden are to benefit from caps to their VAT-based contributions, while Austria secured a cap on its share of the British rebate. Given this outcome, it is difficult to dispute the verdict that the majority of EU spending will continue to be in the form of growth-destroying farm subsidies and irrational recycling of regeneration cash between richer countries. Meanwhile, to meet these costs a Commission proposal to build cross-border infrastructure that had the potential to generate economic growth was, among other things, abandoned. In that respect, the decisions on the MFF for the period 2014–2020, far from equipping the EU for a globalized role, will weaken rather than strengthen the competitiveness of the European economy, according to one authoritative commentator, and will also fail to effect a radical change in priorities to focus on areas where the EU adds value (*Financial Times*, 17 February 2013).

A book-keeping exercise?

Arguably, this outcome suits British purposes, notwithstanding British rhetoric about the need for greater competitiveness and reform within the EU. British policymakers have hardly ever, if at all, regarded the EU budget as a principal engine of economic growth and modernization, though they have over the years highlighted research and innovation and international development as priority areas for budgetary allocations. Their major priority, however, has focused on reducing the headline figures for overall EU expenditure, restraining the size of the budget, and thereby limiting Britain's contribution to the EU. Among other things, the indirect benefits of EU membership tend to be overlooked in any assessment of the EU budget. It is estimated that over the period 1992–2006 EU membership in itself was responsible for an increase of approximately £25 billion in Britain's GDP (Spence, 2012).

Furthermore and especially in recent years, government has rarely publicized budgetary allocations that have benefited Britain to a disproportionate extent. It thus scarcely receives publicity that in the last seven-year (2007–2013) EU research and technological funding programme Britain won a bigger share of research funding than any other member state except Germany, contributing 11 per cent of the budget and securing 15.4 per cent of the sums awarded (HM Government, 'Review of the Balance of Competences between the United Kingdom and the European Union Research and Development', November 2013: 10). Meanwhile, in the most prestigious research funding of all – the EU's European Research Council (ERC) – Cambridge, Oxford, Imperial and University College London were among the ten most successful university recipients in the EU. It was on the basis of this record that leading academics and scientists warned that a British exit from the EU would be catastrophic (*The Guardian*, 12 November 2015).

Conclusion

An unchanging feature of the British approach to the EU budget has been the projection of what can only be described as a book-keeper rather than public investor view of the budget. The emphasis or mood music may have changed slightly over time, but the clarion calls for budgetary restraint, constraint and discipline have invariably focused on keeping the British rebate, cutting the cost of the CAP and limiting the size of EU budgets so as to reduce the British contribution.

Throughout the 2014–2020 MFF negotiations, Cameron focused exclusively on payments, arguing that the figure better reflected the amount of money leaving the Treasury. Concentrating on that figure also had the benefit of being lower than any other figure in the EU budgetary equation and was thus less objectionable to Eurosceptic opinion in Britain.

The value of Britain's budgetary strategy and tactics over the years is at the very least questionable. A detailed study of the subject concludes: 'Britain's rather single-minded concern for discipline and restraint has not allowed it to draw full political benefit from the EU budget, either on its targets or on its control' (Spence, 2012). Barroso, the outgoing president of the EU Commission, commented in October 2014: 'it's a shame that the political debate here [in Britain] focuses only on absolute figures when quality of spending is so much more important' (www.euractiv.com/content/barroso-speech-chatham-house). Barroso was here reflecting a view held elsewhere in the EU about the British preoccupation with the economic dimensions of the EU and how such conduct was regarded as very strange (Liddle, 2014: 8).

While the question of Britain's budget rebate is indicative of one of the distinctive features of Britain's standing in the EU, so too on a much larger and significant scale is the subject matter of the next chapter – the pound and the European monetary system.

9 Brief encounters and quick exits

The pound and Europe 1970–1992

> When the pound did not move, I knew the game was up. I felt like a TV surgeon in
> Casualty realizing his patient was dead. All we had to do was unplug the system.
>
> (Norman Lamont, Chancellor of the Exchequer,
> on the day the pound exited the Exchange
> Rate Mechanism – 16 September 1992)

Introduction

This and the next chapter deal with the process of monetary integration within the EU
since the 1970s as it has influenced and impacted on British policy and interests. The
treatment identifies and accounts for British responses to major developments in this
field. In particular, the coverage aims to explain the country's exclusion from the euro
area that currently comprises 19 of the 28 EU member states, with some two-thirds
or 337 million of the EU's population (Lithuania being the latest EU state to adopt
the euro in January 2015). In this chapter, we focus on the beginnings of European
monetary integration in the period 1970–1992 and especially Britain's membership of
and departure from the Exchange Rate Mechanism (ERM – see below), the staging
system for the formation of the euro area.

The origins of the European Monetary System

In 1972, the Heath government took the first faltering steps towards establishing a new
relationship between the pound sterling [hereafter pound] and the currencies of the other
EC states. The course and outcome of this short-lived episode curiously foreshadowed
the twists and turns of later developments in this field.

At the Hague summit of EC leaders in December 1969, where agreement was struck
to open negotiations with four applicant states including Britain, it was also decided
to proceed towards economic and monetary union (EMU) by 1980. This initiative was
partly driven by growing turbulence in the international money markets by this time
and also by the problems of managing a common price system in the CAP at a time of
wildly fluctuating exchange rates. The first practical step towards the goal of EMU, as
set out by the Werner Plan (so named after the Luxembourg prime minister who chaired
the committee set up to consider precise proposals) of October 1970, was the creation
of the 'snake in the tunnel'. This mechanism aimed to ensure that the exchange rates

of each of the national currencies of the EC member states were tied together within a narrow band of fluctuations.

Britain was not at the time a formal member of the EC. Heath nevertheless agreed that the pound should participate in the scheme. By the time the pound joined in May 1972, however, the whole system was already coming under severe strain as a result of a major turning point in the post-1945 history of the western monetary system: the collapse of the dollar-based Bretton Woods system of fixed exchange rates as the United States ended the convertibility of the dollar into gold (August 1971). At the same time, many fixed currencies such as sterling also became free-floating. As a result of intense speculative pressure on the pound on the international money markets, it was forced out of the 'snake in the tunnel' only months after joining (July 1972). The Treasury refused to re-enter without assurances that the West German central bank, the Bundesbank, would underwrite the pound's parity. The Germans were not prepared to contemplate such a move without a prior commitment to the coordination of economic policies. This disagreement produced a sharp deterioration in relations between Bonn and London. It also foreshadowed a similar difference of opinion between Britain and Germany that was to emerge at the time of the pound's exit from the ERM 20 years later (see below).

The exiting of the pound from the 'snake in the tunnel' scarcely attracted much attention, and nor did the mechanism itself which limped on as a mini-deutschmark area comprising only five of the nine EC states (the deutschmark being the currency of West Germany and later of a united Germany). The Werner Plan was abandoned altogether. A few years later, however, the next major monetary policy initiative was undertaken by the EC states in the form of the European Monetary System (EMS). This scheme was more modest than the idea of EMU by 1980; it made no provision for a European central bank and a single currency. It surfaced as a result of close Franco-German relations and was introduced in 1979.

The EMS aimed to create a zone of monetary stability in western Europe. It was designed to limit fluctuations between the currencies of the member states through the operation of the Exchange Rate Mechanism (ERM), the centrepiece of the EMS. The ERM was a device that linked the currencies of the member states and placed limits on the extent to which each currency was permitted to fluctuate against other currencies in the system. To assist this purpose, the European Currency Unit (ECU) was introduced, the value of which was determined by a basket of currencies of the EMS states and against which each currency was to have a central rate. These central rates, in turn, provided the basis for a parity grid comprising each pair of currencies in the system and permitting each pair of currencies to fluctuate within a margin of plus or minus 2.25 per cent. There was provision for automatic intervention by the central banks in order to ensure that a pair of currencies operated within this margin.

The problems of living with *Modell Deutschland*

The most significant feature of this scheme was its West German authorship under Chancellor Helmut Schmidt. By this time West Germany had not only emerged as Europe's economic superpower but also presented a model – *Modell Deutschland* – of sustained economic growth, price stability, low unemployment and balance of payments surpluses. Schmidt's leadership in the EMS project was primarily driven by an interest in promoting a more stable monetary environment for West Germany's large stake in intra-EC trade. In addition, and further afield, there was a growing concern in Bonn (capital of West Germany) about the plummeting value of the dollar against the deutschmark that was impacting adversely on West German prices at home and abroad. Schmidt was a strong critic of the Carter administration in Washington. He took a particularly dim view of the American failure to maintain the value of the dollar since the collapse of the Bretton Woods fixed exchange rate system, regarding American management in this respect as 'absolutely intolerable' (Jenkins, 1989: 247). Schmidt was thus increasingly inclined to develop an EC scheme for promoting monetary stability.

The ERM like the earlier 'snake in the tunnel' was designed to re-establish exchange rate stability that had come to grief on the collapse of the Bretton Woods system. It was designed to establish a system of fixed, but adjustable, parities. The particular advantage for West Germany, so it was hoped, was that the ERM would increase the attractiveness of other EC currencies and thus take some of the pressure off the deutschmark, a consideration that was also evident in the later German decision to adopt the euro.

For the other EC states, however, the central question posed by the EMS, as in the earlier operations of the 'snake', was whether or not they could afford to enter a system in which the deutschmark was the benchmark currency in all but name, thereby tying themselves to the low inflation and highly competitive disciplines of the West German economy. More precisely, there surfaced the question of which country – a strong currency country like West Germany or a weak currency country like Britain (the pound as recently as 1976 had lost 25 per cent of its value in a six-month period) – was to take corrective action in the event of major exchange rate fluctuations. Was the Bundesbank, the emblem of West German economic success since 1945, to give unlimited support to any ERM currency that found itself in trouble, or was the onus to be on the weak currency country to take the appropriate deflationary action? Alternatively, were there to be symmetrical obligations, with parallel reflationary and deflationary measures being undertaken by strong and weak currencies respectively?

These were not simply questions of the period. Rather they pointed to fundamental problems that, albeit in different circumstances and forms, were to feature in the trials and tribulations of the euro area down to the present day, not least in terms of the disputed responsibility of surplus countries like Germany to reduce imbalances within the euro area.

The EMS and ERM machinery were exceptional in the history of the EU in at least two respects. First, the system was not based on the EC treaties and did not emerge as a Commission-inspired proposal. Rather it was the outcome of traditional inter-state relations, more precisely close relations between Schmidt and Giscard d'Estaing, the French president; the latter was determined to preserve the Franco-German relationship as the EC's pacemaker and also viewed the maintenance of a strong franc (*franc fort*) via the ERM as a useful external discipline for the French economy. Second, no EC state was obliged or required to join the system, as was amply demonstrated by the British decision (December 1979) to withhold the pound from the ERM. The Callaghan government (1976–1979) did agree to participate in the other aspects of the EMS such as arrangements for the partial pooling of member states' gold and foreign currency reserves to create the ECU.

The disastrous experience of the pound's short-lived involvement in the 'snake' undoubtedly influenced the response of the Callaghan government to the EMS project. This entire episode was the first major example of British exceptionalism since becoming an EC member state. It also reflected, however, several elements of continuity in British handling of the particular issue of monetary co-operation and EC/EU initiatives at large.

Participation without commitment

The initial British response to the EMS proposal was supportive of the idea of monetary stability. From the outset, however, Callaghan was mainly intent on postponing a decision. He feared that staying out of the ERM might cause a run on the pound. This understandable concern drew heavily on recent memories of the pound's collapsing value in 1976 and also reflected his traumatic experience as Chancellor of the Exchequer at the time of the 1967 devaluation of the pound. Early discussions of Schmidt's plan in Labour government circles and beyond demonstrated a characteristically British willingness to participate in top-level deliberations but without any commitment to the exercise. One of Callaghan's advisers on European policy at this time also later noted that the British discussion about the EMS scheme demonstrated a common failure in British dealings with the EU: continuing to address the intrinsic merits of a policy even after it had been decided (Franklin, 2013: 764).

At the Copenhagen European Council meeting (April 1978), Callaghan agreed with Giscard and Schmidt that detailed proposals should be considered by a small working group comprising a nominated adviser from each of the three states: Clappier (France), Couzens (Britain) and Schulmann (West Germany). In fact, it was a Clappier-Schulmann paper that was forwarded to the next meeting of the European Council. Couzens had strict instructions not to agree to anything, and he largely occupied the role of a sceptical bystander. He lacked any political backing from London, and thus cut a similar figure to Bretherton at the time of the post-Messina negotiations in 1955.

Several telling considerations weighed heavily against full British membership of the EMS. First, the Schmidt plan coincided with the unveiling of Callaghan's scheme for a joint European–US effort to rejuvenate the languishing western economies. Callaghan's major contribution in this respect – a paper entitled 'International Initiative on Growth and Currency Stability' (March 1978) – was based on the premise that Europe and the United States had to work in tandem to pull the western economies out of recession. This initiative also expressed the long-standing British preference for dealing with the strategic issues of international economic co-operation in such a way as to ensure US involvement and to emphasize the importance of western international economic institutions like the IMF and the OECD.

The prospect of a tightly organized European monetary bloc did not commend itself to Callaghan if it was likely to jeopardize the chance of co-operation with the Americans and threaten the possibility of 'a revived Anglo-American project of economic globalization' (Gifford, 2014: 11). With his strong Atlanticist rather than European predisposition, Callaghan needed no reminding from one senior Treasury official who, in Sir Humphrey Appleby mode, reportedly commented on the possibility of putting the pound in the ERM: 'But it is very bold, Prime Minister. It leaves the dollar on one side. I do not know what the Americans will say about it' (Radice, 1992: 105).

It was a matter of conventional wisdom that Britain moved in what economists called the 'Anglo-Saxon' (i.e. United States and Britain) economic or business cycle as opposed to the European or 'German' one. For much of the period since 1945, the United States has been the main destination (by country) for British exports, totalling some $109 billion in goods and services in 2013. Besides which, Britain has long figured as the largest source of foreign direct investment (FDI) in the United States, accounting for nearly 18 per cent of all FDI there in 2012 (www.cbi.org.uk). Furthermore, and especially under the fixed exchange rate system of the early decades after the Second World War, the United States underpinned sterling to maintain its value as a reserve currency, most notably as the system became unstable in the 1960s and as sterling was viewed by the Americans as the first line of defence for the dollar in the international monetary markets. In short, Callaghan's response to the EMS initiative and to the wider economic crisis of the times reaffirmed the strong preference of British governments since 1945 to deal with global economic affairs under American economic and financial leadership rather than through a regional European approach.

Second, British involvement in the wider international economy suggested that there was no compelling reason to sink the pound in an exclusively European construction. The long-standing global dimension (or globalization to use a later expression) in British policy gave a special or exceptionalist note to the government's handling of the particular issue at stake. Unlike the other EC states, Britain had extra-European financial and commercial interests that were still more heavily concentrated in North America and the Commonwealth than in Europe. At the same time, the country was attracting foreign investment and multinationals from the United States and Japan. Such considerations together with the pound's role as an international currency meant that the attention of City opinion was focused on the wider world economy and especially on the pound–dollar exchange rate. In this quarter, there was little interest in, or support for, the inclusion of the pound in an exclusively European framework.

Nor was there strong demand from British industry. Its earlier support for EC membership was now less evident, partly due to growing disenchantment with EC bureaucracy and harmonization plans and partly because the EC market was not of overriding importance for British exports. A smaller proportion of Britain's total manufacturing exports (38.8 per cent) went to the rest of the EC than was the case with all of the other EC states except Denmark: the comparable figures for France, Italy and West Germany (in 1986) were 47.5 per cent, 51.4 per cent and 47.5 per cent respectively. The value of Britain's intra-EC trade in 1980 was lower than that of any other EC state (see Table 9.1). This condition remained the case throughout the 1980s. In 1987, intra-EC trade accounted for as much as 49.1 per cent of British trade, but this was well below the EC average of 58.6 per cent and ranked second lowest, next to Denmark. The same pattern was evident in later years; in 2003 intra-EU trade accounted for 56.9 per cent of total British trade, but this was still well below the EU average of 66.5 per cent and ranked second lowest, next to Greece (Office for Official Publications of the European Communities, *Annual Abstract of Statistics*; Eurostat, 2004). For the value of British trade within the EU and with non-EU countries see Table 9.2.

Third, there was a decidedly negative response in government quarters as the full implications of the Schmidt plan became apparent. True, the Foreign Office supported EMS membership on strategic and economic grounds. According to Denis Healey, who was Chancellor of the Exchequer at the time, this response was scarcely surprising as the Foreign Office supported anything that included the word 'European', which effectively meant that wider political considerations in favour of becoming a full member of the EMS went by default (Healey, 1990: 439; Franklin, 2013: 761).

Elsewhere in Whitehall and especially in the Treasury, however, a far more influential body of opinion concentrated on the probable deflationary consequences of tying

Table 9.1 The value of the intra-European Community trade
of each EC member state expressed as a percentage of each
state's total exports in 1958 and 1980

	1958	*1980*
Belgium/Luxembourg	35	71
Denmark	58	50
Germany	35	48
France	28	51
Ireland	83	74
Italy	32	48
The Netherlands	57	73
United Kingdom	20	42

Source: European Communities 1982.

Table 9.2 The UK's annual import and export trade statistics (2012)

	£billion
Goods exported from the UK to other EU states	149.8
Goods imported into the UK from other EU states	207.0
Difference	−57.2
Goods exported from the UK to non-EU countries	146.7
Goods imported into the UK from non-EU countries	199.3
Difference	−52.6

Source: www.hmrc.gov.uk/statistics/trade-statistics.htm.

the value of the pound to the deutschmark in the ERM. Healey like Callaghan took
the view that the proposed scheme was little more than a reincarnation of the 'snake',
with a 'European' element that was largely a matter of political window dressing. In
effect, the Germans were trying to persuade the other weaker EC currency countries
to serve as a lead balloon on the rising value of the deutschmark that threatened West
Germany's buoyant export trade.

The Treasury view was greatly affected by the relatively poor performance of the
British economy as compared with the major economies of the other EC states. During
the period 1974–1978, Britain's annual output grew by only 0.25 per cent, compared
with 1.5 per cent in Germany and Italy and 2.5 per cent in France. During this same
period the British rate of inflation averaged over 18 per cent as compared with 10 per
cent in most other EC economies and 5.5 per cent in Germany. This economic record,
and especially the accompanying slide in the value of the pound against the deutschmark, did not augur well for the pound in the ERM. The fact of the matter was that the
government would be required to take deflationary measures to keep the pound in the
ERM, thereby adversely affecting growth and employment.

According to Treasury estimates, the inclusion of the pound in the ERM would mean
a progressive increase in its value of 6 per cent by the end of 1979 to 20 per cent by the
end of 1981, with an accompanying reduction in GDP of 1 per cent in 1980 and as
much as 5 per cent in 1981 (in fact and unforeseeably in 1978, the pound's value on the

money markets rose sharply in the period 1979–1981 as a result of its petrocurrency status and the doubling in the price of oil in 1979/1980 in the wake of the revolution in Iran in January 1980). In the circumstances of 1978, however, full British membership of the ERM was perceived as abandoning the one instrument that British governments had long used to adjust British prices in the international economy – devaluation.

The EMS and party politics

The prospect of full membership of the EMS lacked substantial support in Callaghan's Cabinet and in the Labour Party at large. Furthermore, with a general election in the offing, Callaghan was disinclined to allow yet another European issue to expose government and party divisions. In that respect, Schmidt's plan was an unwanted complication at an inopportune moment. In the Cabinet, Tony Benn, the Secretary of State for Energy, was one of the most vociferous opponents, arguing that full EMS membership would lead to the further deindustrialization of Britain. He also expressed the view that Britain could stop the venture in its tracks by exercising a veto – an idea which one of his ministerial colleagues later described as 'for the birds' (Dell, 1995).

The bulk of Cabinet opinion, however, including pro-Europeans like Edmund Dell, the Secretary of State for Trade, was less partisan and took the view that, on balance, there was little to be gained and much to lose from placing the pound in the ERM. Dell himself later commented that the most striking contrast during the EMS negotiations was between the continental conviction that politics should have priority over economics while in London there was scepticism as to whether this was really possible. This observation was no less applicable to some aspects of Britain–EC differences long before and after this episode, most notably in British-based observations on the political origins and stability of the euro area flying in the face of economic and monetary realities.

Labour Party considerations ultimately prevailed against joining the ERM. Callaghan himself knew that he 'could not travel fast' in EC affairs due to opposition in the party (Callaghan, 1987: 493; Morgan, 1997: 614–16). There was considerable hostility to EMS at the 1978 Labour Party conference. Any remaining doubts in Callaghan's mind about the inadvisability of full membership of the EMS were here swept away. Shortly afterwards, following Cabinet discussions in November–December 1978, it was formally decided to withhold the pound from the ERM, while being a member of the EMS – an outcome that to some resembled a 'half way house' preserving a fig leaf of influence.

In relaying this decision to the other EC leaders, Callaghan sought to minimize the significance of the decision and to avoid the impression that this was a question of being for or against the EC. As on previous and also later occasions – the Major government's opt-out from the single currency being a case in point – it seemed that the British government was intent on maximizing the advantages of association with an EC initiative while avoiding full commitment. It was entirely in keeping with this mentality that the Callaghan government agreed that, if the EMS was to be set up as an EC scheme, it had to be devised in a way that met several British requirements. The first of these was that the door must be left open to Britain to join the ERM at any time it wished, and that there must be scope to amend the scheme to make it more acceptable. In short, however late the British arrived at the EC party, provision had to be made to change the rules of the game and also the games themselves to accommodate the late arrival.

Meanwhile, the Conservative opposition under the leadership of Margaret Thatcher since 1975 was so divided over the issue as to be relieved at not having to take a decision.

At the same time the Conservatives capitalized on Labour's position; Thatcher was able to comment that the failure to join the ERM was a sign of Britain's economic weakness under Labour and 'a sad day for Europe' (*H. C. Deb.*, 6 December 1978). As her official biographer notes in his coverage of this episode, however, the documents and letters of the time perfectly foreshadow – in tone, in content, in personalities, even in the choice of words – the matter that was to cause such extreme bitterness and division in her own Cabinet by the late 1980s (Moore, 2014: 381).

Some members of the Conservative Shadow Cabinet like John Knott, who as a treasury minister in the Heath government had vivid memories of the ill-fated attempt to put the pound in the 'snake', had no wish to repeat the experience. Others like Geoffrey Howe were unequivocal supporters of the idea. Still others like Nigel Lawson, who was later a convert to the idea of putting the pound in the ERM as Chancellor of the Exchequer, adopted a classic British line when confronting a new EC proposal. He hoped for a quick collapse of the scheme, so that 'we could propose some alternative and more sensible framework for European economic convergence'. He added for good measure that if the government did not enter the ERM the Conservatives could always attack Callaghan 'for being afraid of the big bad Benn' (Moore, 2014: 380); at this time as earlier Benn was routinely demonized in the Conservative-supporting newspaper titles.

It was scarcely surprising that on coming to power after the general election of 1979 the Thatcher government withheld the pound from the ERM for the next 11 years. While Thatcher had campaigned for a 'yes' vote during the 1975 referendum, it was a matter of common observation that she had done so with only a fraction of the commitment and vigour displayed by Heath. Indeed, her approach to the EC was much closer to Callaghan's. Like him she was unimpressed by extravagant rhetoric about European unity and instinctively suspicious of ambitious projects for the future development of the EC. More precisely, she was against placing the pound in the ERM, not least because such a move clashed with her free market principles and she strongly disliked the idea of trapping the pound in such a system. She favoured floating exchange rates, believing that fixed rates (however adjustable) were inherently unworkable, or as she put it in one of her famous sayings: 'There is no way in which one can buck the market' (Thatcher, 1993: 703). Given these circumstances, then, why did Thatcher eventually agree to place the pound in the ERM?

Opting in and opting out 1990–1992

Few short periods in the history of the pound brought such a rapid occurrence of events as the years 1990–1992. The Thatcher government opted to place the pound in the ERM in October 1990. Less than two years later in September 1992 the pound unceremoniously fell out of the ERM. In the intervening period the Major government signed the Maastricht Treaty on European Union (February 1992); it thereby secured an opt-out for the pound from the final stage of a three-stage process to forge an economic and monetary union by 1999 complete with a single currency.

A combination of factors and circumstances account for these changes, most notably the evolution of the EC in the late 1980s, Conservative Party politics especially within the Cabinet that eventually and fatally weakened Thatcher's leadership, and economic problems that had not been solved or eliminated by 11 years of Conservative government and seemingly required a European solution studiously avoided throughout most of Thatcher's premiership.

In the aftermath of the Single European Act of 1986, there emerged a fierce debate in EC circles that left its mark on the organization in the 1990s. Some states, most notably the core or founding member states, saw the Act as a means of promoting further political, economic and monetary integration. This view was strongly championed by Jacques Delors, the former French economics and finance minister whose presidency of the Commission (1985–1994) restored its role as a dynamic force in promoting new schemes, most famously in a three-stage plan for full economic and monetary union – EMU (April 1988) – and also a social charter of workers' and citizens' rights (May 1989). In the meantime, Delors further angered his critics when he told the European Parliament (July 1988) that in ten years' time 80 per cent of economic, financial and social legislation affecting members of the EC would emanate from Brussels.

There is evidence to suggest that in the later 1980s Thatcher misread the seriousness of intent of most of the other EC states over EMU and their determination to turn what she saw as airy declarations into hard policy (Wall, 2008: 85). If, arguably, she woke up late to the impending reality of EMU, she was inclined to see it as a more cataclysmic event than some of her advisers and ministers. So much became apparent in her mounting suspicion of and hostility to Delors. In fact, there developed between Delors and Thatcher something approaching a personal feud. The relationship perhaps reflected on Thatcher's side her view of European Commissioners – 'tiresomely foreign' – of French negotiators – 'preternaturally cunning … cleverer than us … They will run rings round us' (Moore, 2014: 488) – and of Brussels negotiations that were likened to a game of snakes and ladders by one diplomat 'Oh no … In Brussels they are all snakes!' she exclaimed (Hannay, 2013: 124). In any event, the pair exchanged mutually hostile 'addresses', Delors's at the annual conference of the Trades Union Congress in Brighton (8 September 1988) and Thatcher's at the College of Europe in Bruges on 20 September 1988 (see Chapter 3).

By the late 1980s Thatcher occupied a minority and often discounted position in EC councils. That in itself was less of a major political problem than the fact that by this stage there were significant differences of opinion between herself and Cabinet colleagues about the ERM and EC monetary union. It is difficult to separate out these issues from the many other strands of discontent at this time. The poll tax was proving to be a nightmare, while the economy was becoming dangerously overheated. Above all, there was growing criticism of Thatcher's personal style which was widely regarded as autocratic and uncaring. Her handling of the EC budget issue had clearly struck a chord with domestic opinion in the early 1980s. By the late 1980s, however, her attitude towards the EC seemed to a growing number of critics to be narrow, blinkered, outdated and contrary to long-term national interests. What ultimately sealed her fate was the sense that she had become an electoral liability rather than an asset. Certainly, her stance towards the EC and particularly ERM membership was an immediate cause of her terminal difficulties and was of longer term standing than the poll tax in terms of Cabinet divisions.

The case for joining the ERM

From the mid-1980s onwards, several of Thatcher's Cabinet colleagues increasingly believed that entry to the ERM would enhance economic stability and provide a more effective weapon against inflation than control of the money supply (monetarism). Despite strong, accompanying differences of opinion about how best to measure and control the money supply, this factor was viewed as the key solution to some of the systemic problems of the country's public finances and high inflation record, not least by Nigel Lawson, Chancellor of the Exchequer (1983–1989). The extent to which control of the money supply was increasingly viewed as an inadequate policy instrument, however, became evident in a meeting held in November 1985 when a majority of senior government ministers supported ERM entry.

Accounts differ as to what exactly was said at this meeting, but there is little doubt about the fundamental disagreements on display. Willie Whitelaw, then Lord President of the Council and Thatcher's fixer and enforcer – 'every Prime minister needs a Willie' she famously remarked with unwitting humour – is said to have summed up the sense of the meeting by concluding that the chancellor, the foreign secretary and the governor of the Bank of England all supported ERM entry and that was good enough for him. Thatcher retorted that it was not good enough for her and that if the government decided to go in, it would have to do so without her. Lawson regarded this episode as the saddest event of his time as chancellor. Howe, foreign secretary at the time, later concluded that if Thatcher had supported ERM membership at this time rather than succumbing to the idea later (see below) the pound would not have been so vulnerable in the early 1990s (Howe, 1994: 449–50; Lawson, 1992: 497–500; Stephens, 1996: 48–51; Moore, 2015: 420).

This episode marked the beginning of a protracted bout of ministerial wrangling, with Thatcher effectively exercising a veto until 1990. In this period she often felt 'ganged up against' as reports were presented to her advocating ERM entry and expressing regrets about absence from the ERM 'which is said to cloud our European credentials' (Moore, 2015: 682). While unable to take the pound into the ERM, Lawson did the next best thing by pursuing a policy of 'shadowing the deutschmark', i.e. acting as though the pound was actually inside the ERM by keeping it at a fixed rate against the deutschmark. By the spring of 1988, Thatcher openly criticized this policy, and thereafter differences between Thatcher and Lawson became increasingly public. The quarrel was inflamed by the embarrassing intervention of Alan Walters, Thatcher's personal economic adviser, who was described by one anonymous mandarin as the man who provided her 'with the algebraic equations for her flat-earth economics' (Stephens, 1996: 129). Unsurprisingly, Lawson found the situation intolerable and resigned (26 October 1989).

Shortly before Lawson's resignation he and Geoffrey Howe, Foreign Secretary, had obliged Thatcher to soften her opposition to ERM membership at the Madrid European Council (June 1989). They had threatened to resign unless she agreed to change her current stance. The loss of two such senior figures would have been politically disastrous and Thatcher therefore reluctantly capitulated. Since 1979 she had fallen back on the vague and well-worn formula that the pound would enter the ERM 'when the time was right' (or 'ripe'). At Madrid, however, more precise conditions were laid down and it was now a question of when, rather than whether, the pound's entry to the ERM would take place.

Entry to the ERM

Despite this move, Thatcher remained unhappy about the prospect of ERM membership. She rightly saw it as a preliminary step towards full EMU, complete with a single currency and a European central bank, with the consequential loss of sovereignty. In October 1990, however, she was persuaded of the need to go in by the joint efforts of

John Major, who had replaced Lawson as chancellor, and Douglas Hurd, who had become foreign secretary (October 1989). Major and Hurd held a strong hand. They were both on better terms with Thatcher than Howe and Lawson. Their leverage was increased by the fact that she could not afford to risk any further resignations after the musical chairs of 1989. Besides, the economic and financial situation seemed to demand a change of policy. By the spring of 1990, the government's anti-inflation policy was in shreds, destroyed by the boom of the late 1980s following Lawson's 1988 tax-cutting budget. Interest rates were at a higher level than at any time since 1981 and the pound was dangerously vulnerable to speculative pressure. The situation was exacerbated further by Britain's economic decline; while GDP had fallen in France, Germany and Italy in the period 1989–1991, Britain was the only member state that recorded negative growth during this period (Blair, 2002: 165).

By this time, too, Thatcher's opposition was weakening. She was almost totally isolated on the question. The resignation of Nicholas Ridley (July 1990), Secretary for Trade and Industry, removed an important anti-ERM voice from the Cabinet. Ridley was accustomed to speaking his mind. It was for his forthright views on the French, Germans and monetary union that he was forced to resign; he referred to monetary union as 'a German racket designed to take over the whole of Europe', to the French as 'poodles' of the Germans and to the EC commissioners as 'unelected, reject politicians' (*The Spectator*, 12 July 1990). In fact, most accounts would place more weight on French initiative in persuading a reluctant Germany to embark on monetary union. More importantly in this context, however, Ridley was widely – and probably correctly – assumed to be uttering Thatcher's own thoughts that were in turn symptomatic of the depth of unease that had grown up about her attitude towards Europe. Thatcher later wrote that by this time Ridley was 'almost my only ally in the Cabinet' (Thatcher, 1993: 722).

Thatcher finally gave her consent to ERM entry at a meeting (4 October) with Major and officials from the Bank of England and the Treasury. At least one report of this meeting suggests that she appeared to be principally concerned with how the news should be released to the press – thus giving substance to Gilmour's jibe that she was the 'mistress of irrelevant detail', or as her biographer more forgivingly put it – when under stress she 'soon hurried off down the byways of minutiae' (Moore, 2014: 665). She also insisted that the right to determine interest rates had to remain with the British government, not seeming to realize that this would not be possible (Stephens, 1996: 171–3). Nobody saw fit to disabuse her.

This decision and its timing were dictated almost entirely by domestic political considerations. It was not a well-planned, wholehearted endorsement of the principle, but rather an example of being bundled willy-nilly into a working system without any of the sort of concessions that, as noted earlier, Callaghan had insisted on in 1979. The whole episode was very much a case of a British government turning to the EU *in extremis*. What the government was intent on securing was a cut in interest rates – and mortgage rates in particular – before the Conservative Party annual conference that was held only a few days after the decision to enter the ERM. It was felt that this could only be done without endangering the value of the pound if it was in the ERM and backed by the resources of the Bundesbank. Significantly, the announcement of ERM entry was accompanied by a cut in bank rate from 15 per cent to 14 per cent.

Even after ERM entry, Thatcher remained deeply sceptical, and that was fatally conveyed in her highly critical comments about monetary union during and after the Rome

European Council of October 1990. She defiantly rejected Delors's plans to bring it about – 'No, no, no', she exclaimed in the course of parliamentary exchanges on the Rome meeting. Those remarks, in turn, prompted the resignation of the long-suffering Howe from his position of deputy prime minister at the beginning of November. His resignation speech (13 November) was a devastating critique of Thatcher's whole attitude to Europe, and this from a politician not noted for biting invective; on an earlier occasion his critical comments were cruelly likened by Denis Healey to 'being savaged by a dead sheep' while this speech was colourfully described by one writer as 'the anger of the Sex Pistols conveyed in the voice of Eeyore' (O'Farrell, 1998). Howe's speech played a major part in precipitating a challenge to Thatcher's leadership of the Conservative Party and her subsequent resignation from the premiership (22 November 1990). At the end of her premiership as at the beginning, there were proportionally far more rebels against her leadership in the Cabinet than on the parliamentary backbenches. In that respect she was the victim of a 'palace coup'.

'Black' or 'white' Wednesday

The circumstances in which the pound entered the ERM ultimately contributed to its eventual exit, and in both cases there was an element of groupthink mentality at work with ministers and officials carried along by what seemed to them to be the logic of events. One Whitehall official commented in the period immediately before the entry of the pound into the ERM: 'Everyone agrees. So we must be wrong' (King and Crewe, 2013: 259).

As Major noted in his memoirs, the occasion of the pound's exit from the ERM saw many of the original supporters of the policy claiming to have warned of the inevitability of disaster from the outset – a case of the 'golden age of hindsight' in his view (Major, 1999: 162). It was nevertheless clear to some observers at the time and increasingly so thereafter that the pound entered the ERM at too high a rate against the deutschmark – DM2.95 – and at a time when inflation was well above the ERM average. By any objective criteria, October 1990 was arguably one of the least propitious times in the entire Thatcher premiership to undertake such a move. All in all, as several observers put it, it was a case of joining the ERM at the wrong time, at the wrong rate and for the wrong reasons.

It was in the light of this experience that the Treasury in the period of Blair's Labour government was so determined to establish precisely what criteria had to be met for the pound to re-enter the ERM and join the euro area. For her own part, when out of office, Thatcher appeared to disown the ERM entry decision and spoke of it as if it had not been made by her government, a technique she often deployed of permitting a decision but distancing herself from it and later describing the decision as a very costly 'folly' (Moore, 2014: 463; Thatcher, 1993: 726).

How far entry to the ERM did not presuppose British acceptance of moving towards involvement in a full monetary union became apparent in the course of negotiations surrounding the making of the Maastricht Treaty on European Union signed in February 1992. For the first time the Maastricht Treaty set out not only the objective of EMU, but also the timetable and means by which it was to be achieved. Major was simply not prepared to accept this measure. He revived an idea that he had first put to Thatcher when he was Chancellor of the Exchequer in April 1990. He negotiated a special opt-out arrangement whereby Britain would be allowed to defer a commitment to participate in the third and final stage of EMU until the government and parliament had made 'a separate decision to do so'. Only Denmark of the other EU states obtained a similar opt-out.

Entry to the ERM was a central element of Major's strategy towards Europe when he succeeded Thatcher. It underpinned his government's macro-economic policy. A major problem was that the pound entered the ERM just as this mechanism was becoming less stable. As a result of the unification of the two Germanies (1990), there was greater inflationary pressure on the German economy. The Bundesbank was determined to retain a high interest rate in order to reduce this threat. This policy had the effect of lowering the value of currencies of the other member states with the result that they were driven ever closer to the lower limit of the ERM band.

A possible solution to this problem was a devaluation of the other ERM currencies against the deutschmark. France flatly opposed such a measure. Another solution was for Germany to cut its interest rate. Appeals by Major and Lamont to Germany to do so, however, fell on stony ground. The stage was thus set for the drama of 16 September 1992 when the Major government quit the ERM after the pound came under overwhelming pressure from currency speculators and fell beneath its ERM 'floor' of DM2.778.

At 7.30 p.m. on Wednesday 16 September 1992, Norman Lamont, Chancellor of the Exchequer in Major's Conservative government, announced the suspension of sterling from membership of the Exchange Rate Mechanism. On an appropriately gloomy evening outside the Treasury, he reported to the waiting press that it had been 'a difficult and turbulent day at the office'. His announcement was to rank alongside other major landmarks in the twentieth-century history of the pound, notably the pound coming off the Gold Standard in 1931 and the first post-1945 devaluation of the pound in 1949.

Wednesday 16 September began with the Bank of England interest rate at 10 per cent. By 10 a.m. and in the face of a tidal wave of selling the pound on the foreign exchanges, that figure had risen to 12 per cent and rose again hours later to 15 per cent in a vain attempt to prop up the value of the pound. According to Treasury papers released in 2005, some £3.3 billion of the country's reserves drained away in a matter of hours. Lamont later recalled the precise moment when international currency speculators defeated the efforts of the Conservative government to stem the tide: after interest rates had been raised to 12 per cent he watched the Reuters screen for the market's reaction: 'When the pound did not move, I knew the game was up. I felt like a TV surgeon in Casualty realizing his patient was dead. All we had to do was unplug the system' (*The Daily Telegraph*, 16 September 2012).

This massive, humiliating and politically damaging defeat for the Major government and the accompanying devaluation of the pound accounts for the description of the day as 'Black Wednesday'. Only a few months earlier, Major had declared that the pound would become one of the world's strongest currencies, a claim that John Smith, the Labour Party leader, described as a certain detachment from reality of which Walter Mitty would be proud. In the event, the sense of disbelieving impotence scarred a generation of politicians and sent out a strong warning to the next generation of political leaders, Conservative and Labour. As one observer put it, the markets had taken on a central bank and actually won, while another vividly described how the government's 'Black Wednesday' was 'Delirium Day' in the City – the balance of power had shifted irrevocably towards the markets (Kynaston, 2011: 588).

Some sections of Eurosceptic opinion also came to a similar conclusion and saw at the very least a silver lining in this seemingly unmitigated disaster. Lamont himself, who like Major had staked enormous credibility on being able to keep sterling in the ERM, was nonetheless reportedly heard singing in the bath at the outcome. 'White Wednesday' was a more appropriate shorthand to this strand of opinion, for in an unplanned, forced and serendipitous way sterling's exit from the ERM, combined with the counter-inflationary value of the two-year ERM membership since October 1990, could be held to have assisted the country's recovery from recession. Certainly it freed the pound from the ERM straitjacket and seemed to justify criticism of the entire Maastricht Treaty infrastructure and the goal of economic and monetary union. The hurried decision to suspend ERM membership was one of several options considered during the course of the day, except that is a further increase in interest rates. After quitting the ERM the pound was allowed to 'float' on the markets with the result that devaluation followed.

Conclusion

Over the period 1970–1992, British policy and attitudes towards the idea of EU monetary integration involved long periods of a distant or arm's-length relationship punctuated by brief and ultimately unsuccessful attempts at a relatively close relationship – a case of brief encounters and quick exits. The explanations, as we have seen, range from systemic obstacles to bad timing. Divisions within government and between political parties militated against any national consensus on the issue. The lack of strong, sustainable pressure in the business and financial world favouring a major change also contributed to this condition. Unlike the other EU states, that were primarily European-oriented in their approach to monetary matters, Britain's extra-European financial and commercial interests told against overclose EU relations in this field.

10 The pound, the euro and the City

The problem is not the euro ... the British are obsessed with the damn euro.
(Kenneth Clarke, Chancellor of the Exchequer,
1993–1997, November 2014)

Introduction

This chapter examines why British governments since the pound's exit from the ERM have kept out of the euro area. It deals with some of the arguments surrounding the question of euro area membership. It does so against the background of an explosive mixture of events: the major financial crisis of 2007–2008, the near collapse of the banking system, the accumulation of mountainous sovereign and private debt, and the onset of the worst economic recession since the 1930s.

The chapter considers the particular problems arising from these conditions, especially the difficulties of functioning as an EU member state outwith the euro area. It also covers in this connection the nature and significance of the City of London as a global financial capital with European interests but operating outside the euro area. The City here is used as shorthand expression for British-based financial services that are not confined to London. In fact, two-thirds of financial services jobs were reportedly outside London in 2013, and the financial services sector figured particularly prominently in Scotland with a share higher than the equivalent figure for any region outside London and the south-east (HM Government, 'Review of the Balance of Competences between the United Kingdom and the European Union The Single Market: Financial Services and the Free Movement of Capital', Summer 2014: 36).

So near and yet so far: the Labour government and the euro 1997–2001

The policy and attitudes of the Labour governments under Blair's premiership (1997–2007) to the question of euro area membership encompassed a wide range of possibilities. At one end of a spectrum of opinion there were several seemingly promising intimations about joining the euro but at the other and ultimately decisive end there was a decidedly negative response.

In the run-up to the 1997 general election, Labour displayed a united front on the EU. It was anxious to enhance its pro-Europe credentials and to contrast this position with the bitter feuding over Europe in the Conservative ranks. At the same time, however, the party took a cautious line for fear of attracting criticism from the Eurosceptic press. The party's election manifesto contained little on the subject of Britain's relations with the EU to distinguish it from the Conservatives, and it conformed to a long-standing practice of the major parties over the past 60 years in giving minimal attention to the subject in their election manifestos. The only real difference of substance in the run-up to the 1997 general election was on the issue of the Social Chapter. Labour pledged to end the opt-out negotiated at Maastricht while the Conservatives were committed to maintaining it. There was here all the makings of what has been described as a European 'policy vacuum' on the part of the incoming Blair government (Peston, 2005: 201).

On coming to power in 1997, the Blair government appeared to be in earnest about adopting a more co-operative approach to its EU partners than had been the case in the later stages of the Major government. The appointment to a key post in the Department of Trade and Industry of the prominent industrialist David Simon, who was known to be an enthusiastic supporter of the single currency, was generally interpreted as a sign that the government favoured British participation (Seldon *et al.*, 2005: 317). This impression was powerfully reinforced when Gordon Brown, Chancellor of the Exchequer, disclosed his intention to hand over control of interest rate policy to the Bank of England. True, Brown insisted that the decision had nothing to do with preparations for the euro. Most expert observers, however, viewed the move as an important preliminary step towards meeting the Maastricht convergence criteria (i.e. the tests for euro membership – exchange rate stability, low inflation, low interest rates and sound public finances). It appears that this was the prevalent assumption even at the Bank of England and the Treasury (Peston, 2005: 130).

It is often argued that the early part of the first Blair government was probably the best time to sign up for the euro and thus to join the first wave of euro area member states in 1999, especially in view of the fact that the government had the largest parliamentary majority (179) of any British government since 1945. It is also claimed, however, that there was never any real possibility of that happening. According to Terence Burns, then Permanent Secretary at the Treasury, there was 'not a cat in hell's chance of joining in the first wave' (Seldon *et al.*, 2005: 318). This view did not reflect any difficulty in meeting the Maastricht criteria. Ironically and unlike many of the other EU states, including France and Germany, Britain was at this time easily able to meet these criteria. Brown indicated as much in his first budget (2 July 1997), thereby provoking groundless Eurosceptic fears that the government was making preparations for entry on the launch date of the euro.

Several factors account for the hesitation, reluctance and, some might say, timidity of Blair and his colleagues in handling the issue of the euro. Much expert opinion at the time strongly suggested that entry to the euro in January 1999 would be risky and might well have a damaging impact on the economy. The Treasury, in particular, had serious misgivings about a fundamental lack of convergence between the British and other EU business cycles (just as a basic lack of economic convergence between its members was to show up some of the shortcomings of the euro area in the post-2007 crisis).

The Treasury's negative view was in keeping with its generally consistent record of scepticism towards the EC/EU in general (see Chapter 4) and the EMU in particular. The experience of 'Black Wednesday' and the events leading up to it had a devastating effect on Treasury morale, and an exhaustive internal enquiry was immediately begun into what went wrong. Treasury papers released in February 2005 suggest that officials were appalled at the extent to which political factors and a superficial political

Table 10.1 MORI public opinion polls November 1997–July 1998
Do you agree that Britain should be part of a single European currency?

	Agree	*Disagree*	*Don't know*
November 1997	30%	52%	18%
January 1998	32%	52%	16%
March 1998	30%	54%	15%
May 1998	31%	54%	15%
July 1998	33%	50%	17%

consensus in favour of ERM entry had influenced the decision to enter the ERM in 1990 (www.hm-treasury.gov.uk). (Only the eventual opening of all the files for this period may demonstrate whether or not such observations were designed to dissociate the Treasury from the original decision to put the pound in the ERM.)

In any event, one of the main lessons that the Treasury drew from this episode was that any future attempt to participate in EMU must be dealt with on a purely financial and economic basis. Another was that it should only proceed if and when genuinely sustainable convergence had been established between all economies concerned (*Financial Times*, 10 February 2005). This amounted to a flexible escape card that now reflected a deep-seated aversion to locking the pound into any irrevocable mechanism. Such considerations loomed large in Treasury thinking from the mid-1990s and account for the department's ultra cautious approach to the idea of joining the euro.

The mixed message from industry and commerce about the euro was a further factor contributing to government indecision. There was general support for joining the euro at some point – a 'contingent yes' was the verdict of a CBI poll in July 1997 (*The Independent*, 27 July 1997). The business community was nevertheless dubious about doing so in January 1999. Besides the lack of preparation, the main reservations concerned the immediate impact that such a move would have on domestic interest rates and the international value of sterling.

A further factor telling against adoption of the euro at this early stage concerned government sensitivity to public opinion and press attitudes. Numerous opinion polls revealed strong public opposition (see Table 10.1). As noted in Chapter 7, the majority of newspapers – especially the organs of the Black and Murdoch empires – were all fiercely opposed to signing up for the euro. Blair's preoccupation with the damage that could be inflicted by *The Sun*, in particular, was to be a permanent feature of his premiership. A significant move in this respect was his decision prior to the 1997 general election to offer a referendum on the euro. He hoped to neutralize Europe as an election issue and make it more likely that the Murdoch press would endorse Labour. In the process, however, as Roger Liddle, formerly Blair's special adviser on European policy, observes 'the referendum pledge was a major victory for Euroscepticism' in that there could never be a certainty, however favourable the circumstances, that such a referendum would be won (Liddle, 2014: 46–7).

Another obstacle to early entry to the euro was the disagreement in the upper echelons of the Blair government. The principal figures in the government – Blair, Brown and Robin Cook (Foreign Secretary) – were not of one mind about the issue and worked against the adoption of a clear and coherent policy; Blair's special adviser on Europe observed that this was 'a recipe for totally dysfunctional decision-making'

(Liddle, 2014: 76). Blair appreciated the potential benefits of membership of the single currency to the government and to his own leadership aspirations in the EU. He was, however, anxious about the economic and political risks of such a move. Brown was favourably inclined to joining the single currency, and strongly opposed Blair's decision to hold a referendum on the issue. That said, he was not as keenly in favour to the extent that he was thought to be and was already beginning to change his mind. At this stage, Cook was the most sceptical of the three, and in a speech prior to the general election he had ruled out entry to the euro for the duration of Labour's first term (Peston, 2005: 195).

To a greater or lesser extent, this constellation of factors remained in being throughout the first Blair government and beyond. In 1997, however, positive messages about joining the euro became the norm. True, Blair and Brown quickly realized that taking part in the first wave was not a feasible option, though neither was prepared to say so publicly (Scott, 2004: 213). Blair wished to preserve as important a role as possible in the critical negotiations preceding the launch of the euro. Already at this stage, however, he employed the well-used tactic of other British prime ministers of sending mixed and contradictory messages to different audiences. He emphasized 'formidable obstacles' to euro entry to appease the Eurosceptic press and opinion. Meanwhile he reassured Jacques Santer, president of the EU Commission, that though Britain was unable to join the euro in 1999 he hoped that 'any delay would be short', all of which suggested to one of his biographers that 'the euro saw Blair at his most enigmatic' (Scott, 2004: 213; Seldon *et al.*, 2008: 294).

In a major speech on the single currency 17 July 1997, Brown declared that the government was 'throwing open the EMU debate' and he also announced the appointment of a group of business leaders to advise on practical preparations for adoption of the euro. He reiterated the official Labour line that a decision on entry to the euro would be taken on the basis of a 'hard-headed assessment' of whether it was in the national interest. In principle, the government favoured entry and saw potential benefits in the elimination of exchange rate risks, lower international transaction costs, a long-term reduction in interest rates and a greater degree of financial stability. Three months later in a parliamentary speech (27 October 1997), Brown left no doubt about the government's basically favourable attitude when he said 'We are the first British government to declare for the principle of monetary union'. At the same time, he set out five key economic tests by which the government would judge whether it was in the national interest to adopt the euro (see below).

Brown's announcement contained some promising affirmations about entry to the euro. It also suggested, however, several indications of future developments that punctured any muscular pro-euro rhetoric. It was accompanied by a Treasury document with a technical assessment of how far the British economy met these tests; its conclusions were strongly negative. Brown's statement also ruled out the possibility of entry to the euro in the current parliament. More importantly, the fact that it was Brown rather than Blair who made the announcement was an early pointer to who would play the dominant role in determining policy on the euro. There was never any doubt after this announcement that it was Brown and his Treasury team rather than Blair and the No. 10 Policy Unit who had the ultimate say; to all intents and purposes Blair had given Brown 'a permanent veto over British policy on the euro' (Riddell, 2005: 135). Brown's stranglehold over euro policy was most evident in his insistence that joining the euro had to be decided solely on the basis of the rigorous economic criteria set out in the five tests, thereby brushing aside any attempt by Blair and others to weaken or qualify this approach.

Positive efforts to keep the idea of euro entry high on the agenda consisted of encouraging campaigning initiatives and a gradualist strategy seeking support for the EU in general. In November 1997 Brown's message to the CBI was: 'Let's get down together to the serious business of preparation' (*The Independent*, 11 November 1997). In February 1999, Blair announced a National Changeover Plan that provoked fury from the Conservatives and the Eurosceptic press that accused him of trying to bounce the country into the single currency. In view of such opposition and limited public support for the euro, later that year Blair and Brown were joined on an all-party Britain in Europe platform by the pro-European Conservatives Ken Clarke and Michael Heseltine together with Charles Kennedy, leader of the Liberal Democrats. Blair reasoned that the debate about euro entry could only be won by winning the wider debate about Europe. Not everyone agreed. Charlie Falconer, a Cabinet minister, thought that it would be absurd for Blair to go on a Britain in Europe platform and refuse to speak about the euro: 'That would be like going to an anti-abortion meeting and saying "I'm not prepared to talk about abortion, just about childbirth in general"' (Price, 2006: 123, 152).

Sustained support for euro entry, however, was greatly stymied by serious differences of opinion both between senior ministers and between their assorted aides that were not conducive to presenting a coherent policy on the euro. At the ministerial level, Brown was often involved in clashes over the euro with two of its staunchest supporters, Cook who had rapidly changed his mind about the euro after becoming foreign secretary, and Peter Mandelson, the holder of three ministerial posts in the first Blair government. Personal animosities and grudges probably counted at least as much as differences over policy between Brown and his two colleagues. Brown had not forgiven Mandelson for switching his support to Blair during the 1994 Labour Party leadership contest. Meanwhile it was a matter of common observation that Brown and Cook always took pleasure in being on opposing sides in any argument (Bower, 2007: 247).

Brown was regularly reported as being grumpy, furious or livid at the activities of both of his colleagues. As Mandelson complained, he had quickly developed a 'territorial fetish' over the government's policy on the euro (Bower, 2007: 317). Even Blair was excluded from the decision-making. On being refused a draft statement of the EMU assessment, he said of his chancellor that 'it's like dealing with a child' (Campbell, 2012: 566), while he reportedly sounded like a child when he commented to Clare Short, one of his ministers: 'I really wish Gordon would let me join the euro' (Short, 2004: 124).

Brown certainly enjoyed an extraordinary degree of independence in the conduct of all aspects of economic and social policy, including that on the euro. This position was partly due to the notorious deal reached in 1994 at the Granita restaurant in Islington, by which Brown agreed not to stand in Labour's leadership contest in return for being given both a free hand in those policy areas and (according to Brown) an assurance that Blair would make way for him in the not too distant future. The situation also reflected the fact that Blair had little knowledge of or interest in economic policy and was content to leave it to his chancellor, especially since the economy appeared to be thriving under his stewardship.

In the run-up to the 2001 general election, Blair sought to clarify the government's plans to take Britain into the euro. The government's official position in the meantime, 'prepare and decide', seemed little different from the 'wait and see' policy of the Major government which Blair had derided when in opposition. In February 2001,

Blair promised that a re-elected Labour government would decide within two years whether to hold a referendum. He also promised that the Treasury's assessment of the five economic tests for entry would be held within two years, about which and much to his annoyance Brown had not been consulted. It was a series of events during the course of Blair's second government (2001–2005) that put paid to any prospect of joining the euro. On the euro as on other aspects of government policy, Blair and Brown increasingly found themselves travelling in opposite directions.

Blair's attitude towards the euro changed from initial caution to enthusiastic support. His motives were overwhelmingly political, both in supporting the principle of euro entry and in drawing back from pressing the matter to the exclusion of other considerations; adopting the euro was 'simply not politically sellable' and 'the economic case was at best ambiguous' was his judgement in the briefest of references to the subject in his book (Blair, 2010: 537). There is thus some substance to the view contained in the memoirs of John Prescott, Blair's deputy prime minister, that it was a case merely of Brown being 'more sceptical' than Blair on the euro (Prescott, 2008: 303).

The Treasury's five tests

What effectively ended the debate about entry to the euro for the foreseeable future, however, was not Blair's view but Brown's assessment and the weight of Treasury opinion. On becoming chancellor, Brown was generally thought to be one of the most Europhile members of the government and strongly in favour of entry to the euro. In Opposition before 1997, he had given wholehearted backing to ERM membership and often spoke in favour, at least in principle, of joining the euro. Once in office, however, he effected a surreptitious retreat from his earlier support for euro membership.

A key factor in sowing doubts in his mind was Britain's enforced departure from the ERM in 1992. It was a 'searing experience' for Brown in that not only had Labour hitched its wagon to the failing policy of ERM entry but Brown's personal credibility was on the line as well (Liddle, 2014: 40). The experience was probably 'the most important moment in his … European education', while the fear of joining the euro at the wrong rate and the wrong time 'overwhelmed his innate pro-Europeanism' (Peston, 2005: 182, 186). Brown's doubts were reinforced by those of senior Treasury officials and above all by the advice that he received from Ed Balls, his economic adviser, close confidant since 1994, and long-standing critic of EMU with weighty papers to his name on the subject. An economist by profession and a former journalist with the *Financial Times*, Balls was so influential that Michael Heseltine, deputy Prime minister in the Major government, jokingly commented on a complex Gordon Brown speech that 'It wasn't Brown's, it was Balls' (Conservative Party conference, 1994).

Besides particular doubts about the inherently deflationary tendencies of the EU's Stability and Growth Pact and of the role allotted to the European Central Bank (ECB), Brown and his aides had little incentive to join the euro. The British economy was performing well and did not appear to be suffering unduly from being outside the euro area. In short, Britain was no longer the 'sick man of Europe'. Between 1958, when the EC was set up, and Britain's entry in 1973, GDP per head rose 95 per cent in France, Italy and West Germany compared with only 50 per cent in Britain. After becoming an EC member, however, Britain slowly began to catch up so that in the period 1973–2013 Britain became more prosperous than the average of the three other large European economies for the first time since 1965. According to Nick Crafts, one of the country's leading economic historians, Britain's really big problem in the 1960s was very weak competition; 'Trade liberalization was a major factor in improving competition … It removed weak firms, made management better and improved industrial relations – more than Thatcher'. While Crafts conceded that no one can know exactly how much the EU directly benefited Britain, a 10 per cent rise in prosperity was a reasonable estimate (*Financial Times*, 24 February 2016).

Equally importantly, especially in the light of the ERM debacle of 1992, there was the strongly held view that a state with its own currency always had options, including the option to create its own money. In the aftermath of the financial crisis of 2007–2008, that degree of freedom was to be most visibly demonstrated by the programme of Quantitative Easing (QE) introduced in 2009 and supervised by the Bank of England. QE involved the Bank in creating new money electronically by buying assets, typically government bonds, from banks and other financial institutions like pension funds. Such action could not have been undertaken unilaterally if Britain had been in the euro area. It is equally the case that as a euro area member Britain would have breached the Stability and Growth requirements concerning the maximum budget deficit as a percentage of GDP (3 per cent), the British figure being as high as 11.4 per cent in 2010 reducing to 5.8 per cent in 2014.

The endgame for any possibility of euro membership under this Labour leadership was played out in June 2003 when Brown made his statement (9 June 2003) on the five tests by which the government would judge whether it was in the national interest to adopt the euro. Five seems to be a favoured number in Labour circles when setting tests for the EC/EU. It was the same number of unfulfilled and arguably unfulfillable conditions that the Labour Party insisted had to be met at the time of the first British application for EC membership in 1961–1963; in both cases they covered up indecision on a central issue as one Labour insider put it (Liddle, 2014: 20).

The tests set out by Brown were:

- Are business cycles and economic structures compatible so that the UK and other euro area members could live comfortably with euro interest rates on a permanent basis?
- If problems emerge, is there sufficient flexibility to deal with them?
- Would joining EMU create better conditions for firms making long-term decisions to invest in the UK?
- What impact would entry into EMU have on the competitive position of the UK's financial services industry, particularly the City of London's wholesale financial markets?
- In summary, would joining EMU promote higher growth, stability and a lasting increase in employment in the UK?

(www.hm-treasury.gov.uk)

The central conclusion of the statement and of the accompanying Treasury assessment was clear enough; only one of the five tests – that relating to the effect on the financial services industry – had been fully met. This statement was packaged in such a way as to offer something to both supporters and opponents of entry to the euro area within the Labour Party while also convincing the other EU states that Blair was serious about joining. It was a typical case of the government facing both ways at the same time, a posture that inevitably invited Conservative scorn: 'This isn't prepare and decide. It isn't even wait and see. It's hope and pray', declared Michael Howard, the Shadow Chancellor (*The Times*, 10 June 2003).

Appearances were deceptive in the wake of Brown's statement. Outwardly, there seemed to be little or no change in the government message on the euro. Blair announced that there was to be a 'road show' designed to highlight the benefits of the euro. Characteristically, he also went out of his way to reassure EU colleagues that Brown's statement should be seen as a positive sign and that Britain was actually taking a big step towards joining the euro (*Financial Times*, 9 June 2003). All this, however, was little more than window-dressing, all the more so as economic growth and stability under Brown's management weakened the case for euro area membership. Meanwhile London's primary role as a global finance centre was not threatened by the emergence of the euro (see below).

Abandoning the euro option and 'saving the world'

The reality was that Brown's statement effectively ended the prospects of entry to the euro area for the foreseeable future. David Blunkett, the Home Secretary, noted at the time: 'I think the issue is dead for some years to come' (Blunkett, 2006: 511). *The Economist* headline was to the point: 'Five tests and a funeral' (*The Economist*, 1 May 2003). The promised road show never materialized and the ministerial committee that Brown had established to monitor progress towards convergence between Britain and the euro area proved to be 'more virtual than real' (Wall, 2008: 171). Blair and Brown continued to engage in pro-euro rhetoric. A reduction in the size of the Treasury assessment team from 100 to ten officials, however, in the months after Brown's statement provided a more accurate gauge of government intentions and of Brown's dogged refusal to surrender to Blair's enthusiasm for the euro.

From 2003 onwards events and circumstances combined to make the prospect of euro entry increasingly remote. By the time Brown succeeded Blair as prime minister in June 2007, even the pro-euro rhetoric had vanished from sight. In a meeting with euro area leaders in Paris on 12 October 2008, to which he was specially invited by President Sarkozy to give an address, Brown was taken aback when Sarkozy cheekily suggested that if he wished Britain to join the euro his peers would be delighted for him to stay for the rest of the meeting. According to one biography, there was much laughter from Brown's fellow leaders but not from Brown who looked disconcerted and unsure how to take such a flippant remark (Seldon and Lodge, 2010: 176).

By this time, the world had changed dramatically with the financial bloodbath and credit crunch precipitated by events in New York, especially the US government bailing out of mortgage financiers Fannie Mae and Freddie Mac and the bankruptcy of the Lehman Brothers bank in September 2008. Similar conditions quickly spread to London and the euro area where the seizing up of credit flows and the dire straits of most banks highlighted the need for government intervention to save financial capitalism from itself, and in time created an existential challenge for the euro area.

Only a few weeks earlier, Brown had addressed the euro area leaders in Paris when some in his audience including Sarkozy had shown little understanding of the gravity of the situation and even less urgency in mounting a collective response. In an earlier phone call to Sarkozy, Brown through an interpreter had boomed down the line 'We need to look at naked short-selling'. The expression was new to the interpreter who interpreted it literally, causing one Cabinet official who was listening in to speculate about the sex-attuned Sarkozy trying to understand it and thinking 'those crazy British speculators, selling bonds with no clothes' (Seldon and Lodge, 2010: 164). Sarkozy's English was so limited that he ended phone conversations with Brown by saying, 'I kiss you, Gordon!' (Ashcroft and Oakeshott, 2015: 504).

Joining the euro could not have been further from Brown's mind at the Paris meeting as he experienced one of the high points of his premiership in the EU forum and as he turned in an instant 'from a Prime Minister under siege to one on a mission' (Seldon and Lodge, 2010: 139). On this occasion, in contrast to his often deeply unpopular and uncongenial behaviour as Chancellor of the Exchequer at EU gatherings and at the signing of the Lisbon Treaty only ten months earlier, he was lecturing to a very attentive and grateful EU audience on how to respond to the calamitous financial circumstances of the time. He won their minds, if not their hearts, to the case for immediate concerted action.

In a speech as Chancellor of the Exchequer (27 September 1999), Gordon Brown claimed that there would be no return to 'Tory boom and bust economics' under the economic management of Blair's Labour government. The expression has passed into some books without the 'Tory' prefix. No matter, it was still a boast that seemed to defy the history of the nature and dynamics of capitalism or at least of lightly regulated, if not, unrestrained 'casino' capitalism. The City became known as the 'Wild West' of global finance following the deregulating and modernizing process initiated by the so-called 'Big Bang' (27 October 1986). The latter freed up finance by removing traditional restrictive practices and enabled London to regain its position as the world's pre-eminent financial centre. Certainly, the words 'boom and bust' came back to haunt Brown as prime minister when the boom ended in bust in 2008 and the ensuing slump proved to be the deepest and longest to affect Britain and the rest of the EU since at least the 1930s and exposed the glaring weaknesses and flaws of City culture.

The seriousness of the situation was evident in Brown's parliamentary speech of 10 December 2008 in which he announced that with the co-operation of other countries the world's banking system had been saved and not one depositor had lost any money in Britain. It was in the course of this speech with a slip of the tongue and to the merciless amusement of the Conservative Opposition, that Brown initially said that 'we not only saved the world ...' He conveniently overlooked the extent to which Blair and himself had favoured light regulation of the banking sector, had held up bankers as exemplars of all that was best about Britain and had showered them with honours. They had also given bankers a say in government policy as in the case of Fred Goodwin, the disgraced Chief Executive of the Royal Bank of Scotland (RBS), who regularly visited Westminster to ensure that any adverse legislation or regulation 'would be watered down or seen off' (*The Guardian*, 13 October 2008; Fraser, 2014: 178, 182, 425–6).

The key developments on the British side in the making of this speech had occurred at the time of the Paris meeting. True, the earliest intimation of a major problem in Britain was in September 2007 when Northern Rock experienced the biggest run on a British bank for more than a century; £1 billion was withdrawn by depositors in a day. Only emergency financial support from the Bank of England together with government steps to guarantee people's savings ended the queues outside Northern Rock branches. In October 2008, however, the crisis assumed much larger proportions. On the day of the Paris meeting of EU leaders, the government announced plans to pump £37 billion of taxpayers' money into three British banks: RBS (that was within hours of total collapse), Lloyds TSB and HBOS. Nationalization, a taboo word for more than a generation, came back into circulation. Two weeks later (24 October 2008) there emerged the earliest indication that the country was on the brink of a recession; for the first time in 16 years the economy shrank by 0.5 per cent between July and September 2008.

Recapitalization of the banks and concerted action as prescribed by Brown at the Paris meeting were immediately taken up by the other EU states. Some states like France acted with greater alacrity than others like Germany where Chancellor Merkel was initially cautious of concerted action – 'It's up to each country to clean up its own shit' (Seldon and Lodge, 2010: 176), reflecting the long-standing German commitment to fiscal discipline. That attitude was rarely far below the surface over the next few years as German policymakers wrestled to limit any euro area-wide commitment that would involve Germany as being primarily responsible for shouldering the sovereign and private debts of other member states. In all cases Brown persuaded the euro area states to take concerted action. None had experienced quite the same banking carnage as in Britain, bank losses there being equivalent to 20.9 per cent of GDP – more than three times the US figure and nearly ten times the EU average. The most dramatic evidence in this respect was the collapse of the Royal Bank of Scotland's (RBS) share price in the Autumn of 2008 when dealings in its shares were suspended. Alistair Darling, Chancellor of the Exchequer, later recalled that this was a pivotal moment: 'The game was up. If the markets could give up on RBS, one of the world's largest banks, all bets on Britain's and the world's financial system were off' (quoted in Gifford, 2014: 149).

Furthermore, no other EU state experienced the same degree of systemic corruption and misdoings that were to come to light about the City's activities in the period down to 2015 (see below). The worst of the euro area crisis (to date) lay ahead in 2011–2012 and centred on sovereign debt. Nevertheless, all EU states had an interest in concerted action as their banks were not insulated from developments elsewhere; much if not all of the global business of the domestic banks of the other EU states was done in the City of London (Levitt, 2012: 1265).

Coalition government, the euro area and economic recession

Any assessment of the nature and significance of developments since 2010 is both relatively easy and complicated. All EU member states are part of Economic and Monetary Union, which means that they coordinate their economic policies for the benefit of the EU as a whole. However, not all EU states are in the euro area, and at the time of writing the euro area comprises 19 of the 28 EU states, while all of the remainder (Bulgaria, Croatia, Czech Republic, Hungary, Poland, Romania and Sweden), apart from Britain and Denmark with their opt-outs, are obliged to adopt the euro as their sole currency once they meet certain criteria. The latter are known as 'convergence criteria' and are formally defined as a set of indicators that measure:

- Price stability (not more than 1.5 per cent above the rate of three best performing member states), to show inflation is controlled.
- Soundness and sustainability of public finances, through limits on government borrowing (government deficit as a percentage of GDP not more than 3 per cent) and national debt to avoid excessive deficit (government debt not more than 60 per cent as a percentage of GDP).

- Exchange-rate stability, through participation in the Exchange Rate Mechanism (ERM II*) for at least two years without strong deviations from the ERM II central rate.
- Long-term interest rates, to assess the durability of the convergence achieved by fulfilling the other criteria.

   (* ERM II was set up in January 1999 as a successor to the ERM to ensure that exchange rate fluctuations between the euro and other EU currencies do not disrupt economic stability within the Single Market.)

                                                                    (ec.europa.eu/economy)

The relatively easily understood aspect of this subject and period as it relates to Britain is that the country has remained outside the euro area with no indication of joining any time soon. In its declaration of May 2010 – *The Coalition: Our Programme for Government* – the Cameron Coalition government, comprising the Conservatives and the Liberal Democrats, stated its determination to ensure that 'Britain does not join or prepare to join the Euro in this Parliament' (www.gov.uk); thus, even the traditionally enthusiastic pro-EU Liberal Democrats stopped talking about the issue. Nor did such a possibility figure in Labour Party circles. The Labour leader Ed Miliband and the Shadow Chancellor Ed Balls reportedly claimed that joining the euro would not happen in their political lifetime (*The Guardian*, 24 February 2014), a sufficiently elastic promise or threat all too indicative of widespread opposition to such a possibility.

   The more complicated part of the subject centres on at least two major features, each of which has been magnified or compounded by the lengthy period of economic recession and mounting government budget deficits. First, there is the problem of managing the financial services dimension of the EU Single Market that involves all member states. Second, there are the attendant difficulties of handling relations between those EU states in the euro area (19) and those EU states (9) like Britain outside the euro area (sometimes referred to as the 'euro area-outs').

   The euro area crisis exposed some of the difficulties in reconciling the interests of the euro area and the EU. The 'euro area-outs', in particular, feared that the continued integration of the euro area would develop to the detriment of the EU's decision-making capacity, notably in the field of the Single Market financial services remit. The principal concerns and objectives of British policymakers in this field have focused on defending what they have viewed, rightly or wrongly, as the interests of the country's financial services as predominantly represented by the City of London [hereafter City]. In seeking to shield the City from any undesirable EU rules and practices and especially rules and practices originating in the euro area, British policymakers have patrolled, as it were, the 'frontier' between the euro area and the rest of the EU with a view to challenging any unwanted decisions, this resulting in a number of skirmishes and incidents.

Criticisms of the euro area project

British policy and attitudes towards the euro area since 2010, at least as represented by the Conservative element in the Coalition government and by the party at large, have varied in character. Eurosceptic opinion, especially that favouring an exit from the EU, has viewed the euro area as a fundamentally flawed system with a limited life. Other bodies of Eurosceptic opinion supporting continued membership of a 'reformed' EU have implored the euro area states to take often unspecified remedial action for fear of the calamitous effects of a collapsing euro area including the particularly adverse impact on British trade. The failings of the euro area have also provided an easy excuse for hard-pressed politicians seeking to escape any blame for shortcomings in domestic economic management (*Observer*, 29 April 2012).

Critics of the system have had plenty of ammunition to hand in focusing on the weaknesses of the euro area project and thereby justifying the pound's continuing exclusion from the area. On its formation in 1999, so it was argued, the euro area was not 'an optimal currency area', the criteria for which are normally similar business cycles, free movement of capital and labour across borders, wage flexibility, and automatic fiscal transfers to stabilize economies. The declared effects of a single monetary policy and therefore a single interest rate ('the one size fits all' monetary and exchange rate policy) on economies with disparate economic and financial features have loomed large in such circles, though the British single interest rate regime has rarely accommodated all sections of the British economy and society.

The criticism has proved even more potent as the euro area states have shown little inclination to embark on a euro area fiscal union (i.e. common tax and spending policies) facilitating the transfer of resources to economies in need of assistance. However, they have agreed to a banking union (March 2014) that pools sovereignty over banking supervision and, to a lesser extent, over the closure or rescue of failed banks. The idea of a banking union originated in the problems of the post-2008 euro area. It was based on the recognition that a monetary union required a banking union due to the intimate connection between currency stability and the stability of the banks within a currency union, and the particular need to sever the link between weak sovereigns (i.e. states) and weak banks.

The failings of the euro area in its origins and governance have also attracted attention. The questionable qualifications of some of the original members of the club were initially overlooked only to be glaringly revealed in the recent years of financial turmoil. Strict adherence to the rules would almost certainly have excluded several of the member states at the outset, namely Belgium, Greece, Italy and Portugal. Excluding two of the founder member states of the EC, however, was politically unthinkable. Ken Clarke, Chancellor of the Exchequer (1993–1997) in the Major government and one of the few Conservative figures still supporting British membership of the euro area, later recalled when he asked ' "Why the hell have you let the Italians in?" I got a whole lot of stuff about: "Oh, Imperial Rome, the birthplace of European civilisation"' (*The Guardian*, 21 November 2014). Much the same applied to Greece in view of its pride of place in European history. John Major recalled that during his premiership when the question came up as to whether Greece should be admitted to the euro area, the leaders of other member states insisted: 'you cannot say no to the country of Plato'.

The Greek case for early membership of the euro area was undoubtedly strengthened by the fact that there was systematic falsification of Greek public accounts throughout the period 1997–2003 which only came to light in 2004. In effect, Greece had misreported its financial data, producing figures that vastly overstated its fiscal health in the run-up to euro membership when it had to meet certain entry criteria. That revelation, together with widespread tax avoidance and evasion in the country, ensured that in the course of time after 2010 as its debt burden got bigger and its economy became smaller Greece was the most likely euro area state to exit from the euro area by choice or of necessity ('Grexit') as was noted in Chapter 1.

The City, the EU and the euro area

As mentioned in Chapter 4, the ostensible reason for Cameron vetoing the Fiscal Compact turned on his failure to secure agreement to a draft protocol setting out provisions said to be essential to protect the City in any new arrangements for financial regulation and supervision. However, there was no overwhelming body of City opinion in favour or against this move. City opinion about the impact of the euro area and about the issue of British membership has been divided (Levitt, 2012: 1262–3), not unexpectedly in view of the fact that the City is not a homogeneous or monolithic bloc. A government review of the sector noted that the Single Market provided benefits to Britain's financial services, but that these were not felt equally by all parts of the sector and that there were alternative views on the scope for Britain to operate outside the EU (HM Government, 'Review of the Balance of Competences between the United Kingdom and the European Union: The Single Market: Financial Services and the Free Movement of Capital', Summer 2014: 34). Besides, the City, not unlike football's English Premier League, is so penetrated by the diverse interests of non-British ownership, capital, and personnel that it is almost a case of simply conducting its operations on English turf.

A leading historian of the City has commented that in the late 1990s there developed no coherent, overall City view about what British policy should be towards the euro area (Kynaston, 2011: 602). Arguably little has changed in the last 15 years, and the balance of City opinion was perhaps fairly reflected in a major research study published by the Hongkong and Shanghai Banking Corporation (HSBC) in February 2015. It was, to say the least, even-handed in its conclusions. On the one hand, an EU single market in services and a capital markets union would play to British strengths, while leaving the EU would mean losing the chance to influence plans. On the other hand, in the event of Brexit the City could remain a global financial centre as most of its 'fundamental attractions' would not change (cityam.com, 25 February 2015). According to a survey of financial sector executives conducted by TheCityUK (2013), 37 per cent of respondents considered a (partial) relocation to the EU as likely if Britain left the EU, while 81 per cent of respondents regarded a Brexit as detrimental to Britain's competitiveness as a financial centre.

The City: the EU's financial capital

There is certainly much speculation about the way in which the regulation and supervision of financial services within the euro area in particular and in the EU at large may have an adverse impact of the City. Far less debatable is the City's dominant role in the field of EU and global financial services, a position that owes little to the evolution of the EU. In its relatively modest 1950s appearance and following the declining significance of the sterling area for international trade, the City was little more than an international clearing centre for sterling-based transactions. Several key developments sparked its revival, notably the emergence of the Eurodollar market in the 1960s, the end of exchange controls in 1979, the 'Big Bang' in 1986 and the unshackling of financial capitalism, and the subsequent emergence of integrated global trading banks.

The City is the EU's financial capital, far overshadowing possible rivals like Frankfurt and Paris. In 2013, the City handled two-thirds of EU financial services, and London was home to more listed international companies than any other stock market in the

Table 10.2 International market share by country (2013)

	UK	France	Germany
Cross-border bank lending	17%	9%	9%
Foreign Exchange turnover	41%	3%	2%
Exchange-trade derivatives	7%	–	8%
Interest rate OTC derivatives	49%	7%	4%
Hedge fund assets	18%	1%	–
PE investment value	10%	5%	2%
Fund management	8%	3%	2%
Marine insurance	22%	4%	5%

OTC – Over-The-Counter
PE – Price-Earnings
Source: The City/UK.

world (see Table 10.2). Furthermore, EU banks held £1.4 trillion of assets in London, about 17 per cent of the country's total bank assets, while some 40 per cent of the global total of euro-denominated foreign exchange trading took place in London (*Financial Times*, 1 April 2013). The City is also at the centre of what makes Britain the largest net exporter of financial services and insurance in the world with a trade surplus of $71 billion in 2013, more than double that of any other country (UNCTAD STAT data). Financial services comprised 26 per cent of British exports in 2011 (*Financial Times*, 20 February 2013). Some 44 per cent of British overseas assets were invested in the EU in 2014, and over one-third of Britain's trade surplus in financial services came from trade with other EU states in 2012 (HM Government, 'Review of the Balance of Competences between the United Kingdom and the European Union', Summer 2014: 39). Furthermore, the British insurance industry is the largest in Europe and third largest in the world, London is the second largest global centre for legal services, and the City is the fourth largest banking centre globally (TheCityUK.com, June 2014).

In terms of its contribution to the British economy, in 2013 the financial services sector accounted for 9.6 per cent of British output, 12 per cent of tax revenue, and 1.1 million jobs (*The Times*, 6 March 2013). Set against these familiar City claims of major contributions to the national economy, however, are the huge costs imposed by the financial crisis in the form of bailouts, the damage to the City's reputation as a result of massive malpractices, and the extent to which the interests of the British state and of the City are viewed less and less as synonymous. At its peak, total British government support for the banking sector, which included contingent guarantees, as well as cash outlay, exceeded £1tn (76 per cent of UK GDP) (HM Government, 'Review of the Balance of Competences between the United Kingdom and the European Union The Single Market: Financial Services and the Free Movement of Capital', Summer 2014: 37).

Given the City's dominant position in the markets, a not uncommon argument in support of Britain exiting (Brexit) from the EU is that the City would still possess formidable competitive advantages including: political stability, openness to foreign business and personnel, deep and liquid capital markets, widely understood language and legal systems, timezone hub between Asia, Europe and the United States, and historic trading ties (factors, incidentally, that were also turning the City into a global centre for laundering corrupt funds amounting to many hundreds of billions of pounds annually according to a 2015 government report, and accounting for the nickname Londongrad (*The Times*, 17 October 2015)).

According to one strand of the Brexit case, the City would simply become 'Hong Kong West' following Britain's exit from the EU. It is precisely at this point, however, that different views have emerged, most immediately about the EU's Single Market in the area of financial services and in the longer term about the impact of the possible future evolution of the euro area on the City's role and position.

During most of the early years of the euro area's history the City enjoyed beneficial standing. At the time of the launching of the euro, fears about life outside the euro area were rated as groundless by some influential figures; Eddy George, Governor of the Bank of England (1993–2003), was untroubled by such concerns, declaring that 'The euro is just a bigger Deutschmark – we have seemed to do perfectly satisfactorily handling the mark, just as we have the dollar and the yen'. The City played an influential role in ensuring a smooth changeover to the euro. More generally, there is evidence to suggest that the City's philosophy and interpretation of what a single market for financial services should look like 'largely held sway in the EU until the 2008 crisis' but that it does so no longer (Levitt, 2012: 1275). Before the banking crisis, the British government was rarely, if ever, outflanked in a vote on financial services regulation in the Council of Ministers (Liddle, 2014: 212). For much of this period, Britain was treated as a 'pre-in' – Brussels jargon for a state that will join the euro area at a later stage. There was moreover evidence to hand that the City was profiting from the existence of the euro; by April 2000 it was handling more international euro-denominated transactions than Paris and Frankfurt put together (Kynaston, 2011: 602).

Impact of the 2007–2008 crisis on the City

The crisis of 2007–2008, however, changed the European environment in which the City operated and put a different complexion on matters. The crisis had an immediate twofold effect. First, it exposed several economic and institutional weaknesses in the euro area principally focusing on a lack of central oversight and functions. In short, the euro area lacked the central crisis-fighting tools needed to prevent a meltdown. Most importantly, there was an absence of a lender of last resort to sovereign governments. Furthermore, while each euro area state had an independent fiscal policy it could not pursue its own monetary policy. Second, the crisis spurred the euro area states into devising means to stabilize the economy and to save the currency union, ushering into being new institutions including the creation of the European Stability Mechanism (ESM) and the European Financial Stability Facility (EFSF). Britain chose to stay out of both institutions, thereby reflecting an underlying desire to avoid as much as possible any pan-European supervision and to escape making any direct contribution to EU bank bailout funds. Standing on the sidelines in this respect together with the Cameron veto of the Fiscal Compact increasingly meant that any British desire to be an outsider on the inside was becoming ever harder to fulfill (*Financial Times*, 28 February 2013).

Substantial evidence to the Cameron Coalition government's 'Review of the Balance of Competences on Financial Services' suggested that Britain had a degree of influence on financial services measures in the EU. However, it was widely believed that Britain had a disproportionately low level of influence considering the national importance of the country's financial sector in terms of its size and contribution to the economy compared to other member states. One submission sought to prove the point by demonstrating that although Britain accounted for 36 per cent of the EU financial wholesale market and 61 per cent of the EU's net exports in financial services, it had far less formal influence in EU institutions with some 9.5 per cent of seats in the EP and just over 8 per cent of votes in the Council of Ministers (HM Government, 'Review of the Balance of Competences between the United Kingdom and the European Union', Summer 2014: 58). Other member states had greater protection on regulation of their strategically important industries compared to Britain on EU financial regulation – France and its agricultural sector being historically a case in point.

In continental circles with President Sarkozy of France to the fore, there was a widespread view that the financial crisis and credit crunch of 2007–2008 originated in the problems, excesses and weaknesses of 'Anglo-Saxon' capitalism (meaning the American and British form of deregulated financial markets). Criticism particularly highlighted the liberal or light touch regulatory framework and freewheeling culture within which the City operated as compared with the west European (or 'Rhineland capitalism' and the 'social market economy') model of capitalism in which a far greater regulation of market forces is accepted as necessary and appropriate (Hyman, 2008). Significantly in this respect and consistent with the long British tradition of open capital markets' policies, the Thatcher government removed all exchange controls in 1979, some 15 years before the Maastricht Treaty prohibited restrictions on the free movement of capital.

In recent years, growing suspicion of, if not hostility towards, Britain and the City has emerged in the treatment of several issues in the field of financial services. True, a more regulatory approach to some matters has emerged on the British side. The Vickers Independent Commission on Banking, whose proposals (2012) were accepted by the government, took a much tougher stance on bank recapitalization, issues of governance and the question of ring fencing retail and investment banking than many euro area states.

This assumes that the original Vickers proposals, to be fully implemented by 2019, are not weakened as a result of special pleading and lobbying by the banks in the meantime. To date, the Conservative government has proved sympathetic to the concerns of the bankers by scaling back the bank levy and by softening the ring fence rules; in November 2015 Sajid Javid, the Conservative government business secretary, declared an end to 'banker bashing'. Furthermore, the decision of the Financial Conduct Authority to drop a review of banking culture only months after its launch was widely criticized in view of the financial crisis and rate-rigging scandals (*Financial Times*, 4 January 2016). Meanwhile, opposition to ring fencing was publicly expressed by Howard Davis, the chairperson of the Royal Bank of Scotland (RBS), despite the fact that RBS had so spectacularly and ruinously failed in 2008, triggering the largest bank bailout in the world at great cost – £45 billion – to the taxpayer, and despite the fact that ring-fencing rules were designed to prevent it doing so again. Davis reportedly argued that the original ring-fencing decision was 'a political decision, for political reasons' (*The Sunday Times*, 1 November 2015), as if the original decision to save RBS from its folly had not been a 'political decision'.

There is some evidence to suggest that Britain and the euro area states do not have serious differences over prudential regulation (Springford, 2014). Indeed, since the 2007–2008 crisis there is further evidence to indicate that the supposed freedom of the British financial system and of the British government to make choices independent of the euro area has led to their making very similar choices to those prevalent in the euro area (Federal Trust Report, 2013: 35). In many respects, Britain faces what has been identified as the same trilemma in international financial economics as other countries – between financial stability, internationalized finance and national sovereignty; it is possible to have two of these options but not three (Springford and Whyte, 2014, www.cer.org.uk). In Britain's case, the trilemma is all the more acutely felt as one of the world's financial centres that is outside the euro area but in the EU.

On other issues, however, a marked contrast emerged between British preferences and evolving euro area interests. Bankers' bonuses and the proposal for a Financial Transactions Tax (FTT – commonly known as the 'Tobin tax' after the economist James Tobin who came up with the idea) have proved particularly contentious. The British government opposed the idea of capping bonuses at 100 per cent of salary, not least for fear of losing what it chose to describe as the best people in the industry. The cap on bonuses took effect in January 2014. In the event, banks and insurers found ways of sidestepping the cap, and the measure scarcely dented the £91 billion of bonuses paid out by the banks and insurers since October 2007 (*The Guardian*, 23 February 2015). There was, moreover, little evidence here of any substantive change in banking culture with its 'too big to fail or jail mentality', its practice of enjoying benefits while leaving the taxpayer to bear the losses, and its strong preference for investing in property, overseas speculation, tax avoidance and financial derivatives. In May 2014, Christine Lagarde, managing director of the IMF, maintained that the behaviour of the financial sector had not changed fundamentally in a number of dimensions since the 2007–2008 crisis (*The Guardian*, 27 May 2014).

The FTT aimed to create a common system of taxation for financial transactions across participating EU member states. It was taken forward by 11 member states under the enhanced co-operation procedure whereby nine or more member states can take forward a proposal where agreement cannot be reached among all member states. The British government's legal challenge to the FTT on trading in stocks, bonds and derivatives – 'a heat-seeking missile' aimed at the City as John Major colourfully put it – was thrown out by the European Court of Justice (April 2014). The FTT is seen as one method to raise revenue from an undertaxed financial sector, to make banks pay for causing the crisis in the first place, and to seek recompense for the billions in help that banks have received from governments and central banks. In fact and ironically, the proposed FTT is far lower (0.1 per cent) and less punitive than Britain's stamp duty rate on shares (0.5 per cent).

The course and outcome of the bonus and FTT proceedings highlighted the weakness of the government's position in defending the City. The cap on bonuses was the first occasion on which Britain was outvoted on a financial services reform in the EU. This episode also meant that some of Britain's former allies like Germany, that previously sided with Britain on financial services legislation to offset French demands for stricter controls, were now less likely to support British positions on matters relating to financial services. Suspicion of American and British forms of financial capitalism such as the little regulated sector like hedge funds, for whom the EU is anathema (Levitt, 2012: 1275), was now joined by irritation at how Britain hectored the euro area while declining to take part in what Germany saw as solutions to the crisis (*Financial Times*, 28 February 2013, 3 March 2013). The constant badgering about sound finance was all the more objectionable in view of Britain's huge indebtedness; in the period 2009–2013 (excluding 2011) the country figured amongst the top four of the 28 EU states with the highest government deficit as a percentage of GDP (Eurostat).

The banks and the euro area

Throughout much of the euro area after 2007–2008, there emerged a stronger inclination than in London to ensure that the banks were kept on a very short leash, that bonuses were capped, that the proposed FTT currently supported by 11 euro area states was adopted, and that any consequential loss of senior staff from the European banking industry was regarded not as a threat but a promise (*Financial Times*, 3 March 2013). By way of contrast, Martin Wolf, chief economics commentator of the *Financial Times*, welcomed banking reforms yet maintained that the banking industry is still taking 'the public for a ride' and that the argument the industry makes is that 'it is too important to reform. In fact, it is too important not to be reformed' (*Financial Times*, 19 June 2013). Meanwhile, the self-justifying appeal of the British banks at the time was that they were 'too big to fail'.

Some elements within the euro area have not hesitated to draw their own conclusions about the rash of scandals and criminal behaviour of banks and other City institutions in recent years. There is a lengthy charge sheet: rigging the Libor market, manipulating the Euribor (Euro Interbank Offered Rate), mis-selling mortgages and payment protection insurance policies, gold price manipulation, credit default swaps and money laundering; 'It's a terrible list' admitted Douglas Flint in an understated way, as chairman of HSBC that was one of the British-based banks involved in such activities (*The Guardian*, 26 February 2015). This was not so much a matter of earlier 'gentlemanly capitalism' with unspoken rules about what 'wasn't done' as a case of financial capitalism red in tooth and claw.

The historian of the RBS debacle offered a more expansive charge sheet than Flint of the 'vices' of this and other banks at the time: 'shabby, reckless, greedy, dysfunctional and corrupt' (Fraser, 2014: 404). Meanwhile, Keith Bristow, director general of the National Crime Agency, warned that illegal activities by banks risked undermining the 'reputation of the UK' and could trigger a sharp fall in tax revenue generated by the City (*London Evening Standard*, 26 February 2015). Mark Carney, governor of the Bank of England, held the same view, arguing that light-touch regulation had eroded fair capitalism while scandals had undermined trust in the financial system (*The Guardian*, 28 May 2014). Eighteen months later, there was still evidently more work to be done, though Carney claimed that 'the era of heads-I-win, tails-you-lose capitalism' was drawing to a close. At the same time Chancellor of the Exchequer Osborne promised the public that the scandal-battered financial sector was being cleansed of wrongdoing and that City fraudsters and bankers guilty of multimillion-pound rip-offs should be treated like other criminals if they broke the law (*The Guardian*, 12 November 2015).

Such pious concern, however, sits uneasily alongside the fact that no senior figure in the British financial establishment to date has been held criminally liable for any of the above practices. Furthermore, a report by the Financial Conduct Authority in July 2015 found that some banks and lenders had yet to take even basic steps towards ensuring that there could be no repeat of the Libor, foreign exchange and gold price manipulation scandals (*The Times*, 30 July 2015). This finding lent weight to the view that the big banks have surely drawn at least one lesson from the crash and its aftermath: 'that in the end there is very little they will not get away with' (*The Times*, 30 July 2015; *The Guardian*, 30 September 2015).

To some observers, it has increasingly seemed that the financial sector was not out of control but beyond control. According to this view, any form of EU regulation was therefore deemed far less of a threat to the City's standing than the ethical standards and practices of City institutions with senior staff routinely disclaiming responsibility, accountability or blame for any wrongdoing in a system that rewarded risk without a penalty for failure.

Coalition government and euro area reforms

Some of the EU measures adopted in the wake of the financial crisis of 2007–2008 have accorded with City interests or were successfully contested by the Coalition government. European Commission plans to put the London-based and scandal-mired Libor lending rate under the direct control of a European supervisor in Paris were beaten off in September 2013 (the London Interbank Offered Rate – Libor – is the benchmark governing the rates at which banks are prepared to lend to each other in the wholesale money markets).

The Coalition government also achieved a satisfactory governing system in the case of the European Banking Authority (EBA). This institution was set up in 2011 to maintain a level playing field for banking regulation and to conduct stress tests for banks. It sets the rules for the EU via a 'double majority' voting system so that any measure requires a majority of both euro area members and non-members. If more EU member states join the euro area (currently only Romania has a target date for doing so – January 2019), Britain could theoretically end up having a veto on all financial rules. The voting system in this body gives Britain and the other non-euro area members of the EU a blocking minority together. In sum, the EU states like Britain outside the euro area have secured a measure of protection against the risk that members of the banking union ignore the interests of the Single Market. These protections include:

- a prohibition on discrimination by the European Central Bank;
- a requirement by the ECB to enter into a memorandum of understanding with supervisory authorities of non-participating member states;
- voting safeguards in the EBA to address the risk that banking union members vote as a bloc;
- a requirement for EBA members to strive for consensus.

> (HM Government, 'Review of the Balance of Competences
> between the United Kingdom and the European Union
> Economic and Monetary Policy', December 2014: 47)

A more general and arguably greater threat to British financial services and City interests in the EU is that since November 2014 and in accordance with the provisions of the EU Lisbon Treaty the euro area has majority voting strength (QMV) in the EU Council of Ministers (see Chapter 3 for QMV details). Voting as a bloc, therefore, the euro area could outvote countries like Britain outside the euro area on all decisions made by QMV which in practice includes all financial services covered by the Single Market. In a worst case scenario, therefore, City interests could be put at risk by the emergence of a strong coalition of euro area states defining its own interests over and against City interests and caucusing to this effect. Such a euro area bloc could utilize the QMV practice either to mount successful opposition to British policy or to limit the further development of the still unfinished financial services sector under the Single Market, a long-standing British goal; examples of where there are still barriers in the internal market in financial services include insurance, EU securities law, and the ability of financial institutions to provide long-term finance (The CityUK.com, June 2014).

If these are longer term risks and concerns based on questionable assumptions such as a unified euro area bloc on any one issue, several developments to date have hinted at some of the dangers to City interests. As a sign of the times, Britain went to the

European Court of Justice to challenge the demand by the ECB that clearing houses that process financial transactions denominated in euros above a certain threshold have to be located within the euro area; the Court ruled against the ECB (March 2015) on the grounds that the ECB did not have the power to demand such a move.

Nevertheless, concern has been expressed in British banking circles that the euro area banking union presents an existential challenge to Britain with the potential for diminished opportunity in the EU rule making process and marginalization from the centre of influence. In short, there could be an unequal contest between 'euro ins' and 'euro outs' with the dominant views of the European Central Bank favouring the former (HM Government, 'Review of the Balance of Competences between the United Kingdom and the European Union The Single Market: Financial Services and the Free Movement of Capital', Summer 2014: 69). There are in fact at least two types of risks to non-euro member states of the EU like Britain. Besides the risk that the measures securing closer integration among the 'euro ins' fail to respect the rights and interests of the 'euro outs', there is the risk that 'euro ins' fail to achieve the fiscal, economic and financial integration needed to place the euro currency on a secure long-term basis resulting in adverse effects on the 'euro outs'. In the circumstances, the British government has sought to ensure that euro area related policy is compatible with the Single Market, is non-discriminatory, and respects the fundamental freedoms and principles that underpin the whole of the EU. Significantly, the relationship between 'euro ins' and 'euro outs' featured as one of the main items in the renegotiation of the terms of British membership of the EU (see Chapter 12).

France, in particular, has figured prominently in seeking to advance the idea of an integrated euro area excluding Britain and downgrading the City's role. In December 2012, Christian Noyer, Governor of the Bank of France, predicted that an increasing share of euro-denominated trades would be conducted in the euro area under the supervision of the ECB: 'We're not against some business being done in London but the bulk of the business should be under our control. That's the consequence of the choice by the UK to remain outside the euro area'. Gerhard Schröder, the former German Chancellor, shared the same view: 'It's tough but you cannot say: "I will not be there but I want a say"'. In such quarters, there seemed to be no rationale for allowing the euro area's financial hub to be 'offshore'. Such ambition was dismissed by Boris Johnson, Mayor of London, as 'a naked attempt to steal London's financial crown' (*Financial Times*, 3 December 2012).

The City as a global player

As a key player in the global financial world, City interests in and concerns about the euro area have reflected this larger context. We noted in Chapter 9 that the City response to the emergence of the EMS in the late 1970s was very much influenced by extra-European interests, and in particular by the dense network of transatlantic financial relations. This dimension forms another contrast between the City and the euro area in that the City belongs to a global market. It thus always assesses EU tax and regulatory proposals with that in mind in case they threaten its global competitiveness and drive business offshore (Levitt, 2012: 1267).

The current position and prospects of the City concerning the EU at large and the euro area in particular admit of very different accounts. At one end of a spectrum of opinion, there is the view that outside the euro area and even more so outside the EU the City would be severely and adversely affected; its euro listing and trading business will gradually switch to Frankfurt while its international and emerging markets operations will move to New York or Hong Kong. In particular, what is presented as the 'remorseless logic' of euro area integration would marginalize Britain to such an extent that it would be outvoted and outmanoeuvred by the euro area states and that it would be forced to leave the EU. In effect, the non-euro members of the EU could become second-class or at best 'country members' of the club.

At the other extreme, it is argued that on the basis of the record of the past 15 years the City's position and standing are unlikely to be greatly affected. It will remain as the financial capital of the EU while at the same time expanding its business outside Europe as it has done since the formation of the euro area, if slightly more problematically since the financial crisis of 2007–2008. In short, some of the fears expressed at the time of the formation of the euro area are unlikely to be realized. According to this view, euro area member states will not undertake any radical moves beyond what is necessary to stabilize the euro. Any fears that a euro area caucus will materialize and marginalize Britain, particularly on Single Market legislation, may therefore be overblown (Springford, 2014). Besides, as we have noted, Britain can successfully use the European Court of Justice to defend its Single Market rights and interests in the financial services sector. Significantly, however, the question of the relationship between the euro area states and the non-euro area EU states emerged as a key issue in the renegotiation of Britain's EU membership in 2015–2016 (see Chapter 12).

The possibility of Brexit would be a welcome prospect to some City interests such as hedge funds that are contributing to various Brexit campaigns and UKIP (*The Guardian*, 2 January 2015; *The Sunday Times*, 1 November 2015). It would, so it is claimed, offer freedom from EU regulations and 'red tape', thereby allowing the City to compete more successfully with other global financial centres. Brexit would also be in line with a salient feature of the City's history over the past 40 years: its escape from state control (Kynaston, 2011: 408). Yet it is also possible that the idea of a 'bonfire of red tape' may be as improbable in the financial services sector as in any other EU sector following Brexit.

In some respects, the City is the last symbol of Britain's global power and reach. Unlike the British state, the City has grown in global significance from a still predominantly international clearing centre for sterling-based transactions in the 1950s into a global financial centre. At the same time, it has managed to straddle the European Union and global stages with a fair degree of success. Whether the country's political leadership has also done so is the subject of the next chapter.

Conclusion

In this chapter we have traced the history of Britain's relationship with the euro area from the slim possibility of euro area membership in Blair's first government to ruling out euro membership indefinitely under the Cameron Conservative government. The rising tide of Eurosceptic opinion in the country, the perceived flaws in the euro project, the interests of Britain's financial industry and the problems of the Eurozone in the wake of the 2007–2008 financial crisis, have all kept euro area membership as at best a very distant possibility.

The absence of a groundswell of popular support for abandoning the pound has also played its part. A key economic argument against such a move has turned on the loss of any discretion to use monetary and exchange rate policy in ways tailored to suit national circumstances. An equally powerful political argument against joining the euro venture or even flirting with such an idea was the requirement to hold a referendum on the matter before entry. Asked why he would not hold such a referendum, Blair reportedly replied: 'I am not going down in fucking history as the prime minister who took Britain out of Europe' (*The Guardian*, 31 March 2015). The celebrated economist, John Maynard Keynes, expressed his view more elegantly: 'He who controls the currency controls the country'.

11 Britain, the European Union and the wider world

Great Britain has lost an empire and has not yet found a role.
(US Secretary of State, Dean
Acheson, 5 December 1962)

Introduction

This chapter focuses on the relationship between Britain's European and EU role and commitments and the country's identity, power and interests in the wider world. In particular, it considers the global perspectives that have informed and influenced policy and attitudes towards EU membership, and also the precise ways in which Europe and Britain's place in the world are tightly interconnected. The subject involves different conceptions, approaches and emphases. Both the making and the study of British foreign policy over the past 70 years have attracted a wide spectrum of opinion.

This section first explores several images of Britain's place in the world. These are rooted in or framed by narratives and understandings of the country's role and identity in the international system. One such long-standing, potent image projects the country as occupying an exceptionalist position in the international system. An altogether different emphasis, however, can be said to centre on the country's relative decline and loss of great-power status. In these and other cases, no assessment of British involvement in the EU is possible without recognizing the importance of extra-European ties and interests.

The chapter then pays particular attention to British involvement in the evolution of the EU's handling of foreign and security policy affairs. It covers the early period of such activity known as European Political Cooperation (EPC) and more importantly the subsequent emergence of the EU's Common Foreign and Security Policy (CFSP) together with its civilian-military operational arm known as European Security and Defence Policy (ESDP). It considers the extent to which British governments have viewed the EU's role in this field as a standalone, dominant entity or as a subsidiary element based primarily on intergovernmental co-operation, driven by traditional bilateral relations between member states, and wary of accepting the centrality of the EU in defining the country's role in the world.

This order of treatment – from the global to the European – in itself fairly demonstrates the priorities and outlook of the British foreign policymaking establishment. Attempts to model Britain's changing place in the world have involved a number of well-worn metaphors such as: 'special relationship', transatlantic 'bridge', 'punching above one's weight', 'pivotal power', 'global hub', 'thought leader', 'networked world' (Harvey, 2011). All such images have one thing in common, besides attempting to frame Britain's place in the world and thereby formulating a coherent foreign policy. They emphasize the global dimensions of British foreign policy as well as the idea that the country can pursue a foreign policy facing many directions simultaneously. Few such descriptions have had the lasting appeal and potency as that coined by Winston Churchill in 1948.

At the heart of three inter-linked circles

In October 1948 at a Conservative Party meeting in Llandudno, Churchill first gave expression to what was to become in time a classic exposition of the exceptionalist view of Britain's place in the world. This presentation advanced the idea of Britain as being at the intersection between three inter-linked circles (later rendered as three interlocking circles): the British Commonwealth and Empire, the English-speaking world including the British Dominions and the United States, and a United Europe that was significantly specified as the last circle. If the political scientist views such imagery as a neo-realist model of international relations, it certainly represents an idealized version of Britain's role in world affairs, whether in the form of the Commonwealth 'family of nations' or the 'special relationship' with the United States. The exceptionalist feature of this portrayal lay in the fact that Britain was 'the only country which has a great part in every one of them' (Churchill, 1950). According to this formulation, Britain occupied a unique position in the world with a wide range of strategic, political, economic and cultural assets and ties deriving from its imperial standing and great power status.

To a greater or lesser extent, such imagery has powerfully influenced definitions of Britain's role and position in the world. Its value to policymakers partly lay in its attractions in reinforcing a sense of continuity in the conduct of foreign policy. It was also useful in avoiding a strategic choice in favour of one circle at the expense of another. Furthermore, it upheld Britain's position on the world stage. Critics of this position have noted, however, that this was to set in aspic British foreign policy to the detriment of strategic reappraisal and adaptation to a post-imperial standing. In short, it offered a comforting and often unquestioned framework. Douglas Hurd, British foreign secretary in the period 1989–1995, later commented that part of the trouble with the enduring appeal of the three circles model was that it mistook a snapshot for a long-term analysis at a time when the three circles were changing shape and size quite rapidly (Hurd and Young, 2010: 346).

While Churchill was coining the three circles model, the Attlee Labour government of 1945–51 was establishing what it viewed as the ideal type of European co-operation set in the context of Britain's global interests and influence (see Chapter 2). By 1950, in fact, the key features of Britain's claim to great power status in the post-war world were either in place – the sterling area, the maintenance of sterling as a global currency, the Commonwealth trading system based on imperial preference, and leadership of west European organizations – or were shortly to materialize like the acquisition of the atomic bomb in 1952. The global perspective and great power rhetoric of post-war politicians were further enhanced by Britain's leading role in numerous international organizations such as its status as one of the five permanent members of the United Nations Security Council, the Commonwealth, the OEEC (later OECD – the

Organisation for Cooperation and Development), NATO, the International Monetary Fund (IMF) Executive Board, the Bank for International Settlements, and in later years the G7/8 and G20 groups of leading industrialized countries.

The Attlee government also believed that the western international system had developed along satisfactory lines by this time through the emergence of the Atlantic Alliance and the revival of close relations between Britain and the United States. There was little reason to expect or to encourage any new west European organization beyond the OEEC, the BTO and the Council of Europe. Indeed, Foreign Secretary Bevin in April 1950 declared that it was necessary 'to get away from talk about Europe', to recognize that Europe did not constitute a separate and self-contained unit, and to acknowledge the importance of the Atlantic Pact (*DBPO*, series II, vol. II, no. 52).

'Kith and kin': the Commonwealth and Europe

In Chapter 2, we noted the interrelationship between British policy towards Europe and Britain's Commonwealth links prior to EU membership. During much of the period 1945–1960, British governments portrayed Commonwealth commitments and interests as the major external barrier to closer British involvement in European integration. The Commonwealth was widely viewed by policymakers and public alike as the centrepiece of Britain's claim to great power status. At war's end and in the immediate post-war years, the Commonwealth was the world's largest trading bloc at a time when approximately 50 per cent of international trade and payments was transacted in sterling. London was the hub of a Commonwealth network of political, economic, commercial and financial ties that incorporated the white self-governing Dominions of Australia, Canada, New Zealand, South Africa and the Irish Free State (until 1948), the newly independent countries of India and Pakistan (1947) and Ceylon (1948), and a host of colonies in Africa, Asia, the Caribbean and the Mediterranean still under direct control, at least until the rapid process of decolonization after 1956.

There was a strong consensus of opinion in British politics about the value of the Commonwealth. A deep sense of pride was further heightened by the common wartime effort. Churchill's strongly held imperialist views were summed up in a memorandum of December 1944 to the Foreign Office: 'Pray remember my declaration against liquidating the British Empire ... "Hands off the British Empire" is our maxim' (NA., FO 371/50807). Anthony Eden, foreign secretary at the time, scarcely required such a reminder. He himself later described Commonwealth ties as 'sacred' and demonstrated where English loyalties and interests primarily lay in the wider world of the 1950s when he observed: 'What you've got to remember is that, if you looked at the postbag of any English village and examined the letters coming in from abroad to the whole population, ninety per cent of them would come way beyond Europe' (Charlton, 1983: 157).

Equally importantly, Labour Party leaders shared the same feelings. They were convinced that the Commonwealth – described by Attlee as 'one of the greatest political ventures of all time' – was the indispensable base of British strength and leadership in the world (Blackwell, 1993: 14). A Labour Party pamphlet (1950) on European unity accurately summarized a national consensus in its reference to the strong cultural bonds and emotional ties between Britain and the rest of the Commonwealth: 'In every respect except distance we in Britain are closer to our kinsmen in Australia and New Zealand on the far side of the world than we are to Europe. We are closer in language and in origins, in social habits and institutions, in political outlook and in economic interest' (*European Unity*, a statement published by the NEC of the British Labour Party, May 1950: 4). This profound sense of identification with 'kith and kin' in the white Dominions remained in being even as the strategic and economic value of the Commonwealth declined in importance. At the time of the Macmillan government's announcement in July 1961 of its intention to seek terms of entry to the EC, Harold Wilson, then Shadow Chancellor of the Exchequer, expressed a popular sentimental regard for Commonwealth ties when he declared: 'If there has to be a choice, we are not entitled to sell our friends and kinsmen down the river for a problematical and marginal advantage in selling washing machines in Dusseldorf' (*H.C. Deb.*, vol. 645, col. 1665).

The Commonwealth as emblematic of the country's world power status remained intact until at least the late 1950s. Thereafter, however, British policymakers' perceptions underwent marked changes. The degree of change was still often clouded by the popular appeal and mystique of the Commonwealth. Furthermore, policymakers frequently insisted that it was difficult to gauge the importance of Commonwealth ties as they were so imponderable and 'not a matter of a pure economic calculus' (*DBPO* (1986), series I, vol. III, no. 200–2). Nevertheless, by 1960 there was a growing body of opinion in Whitehall that increasingly viewed the imperial preference system as a wasting asset. Macmillan himself recognized some years earlier that the associated sterling area was becoming a deadweight. Reflecting on the dangers of Britain acting as banker to the sterling area at a time when sterling crises were an endemic feature of the British economy, he commented in December 1956: 'We have inherited an old family business which used to be very profitable and sound. The trouble is that the liabilities are four times the assets' (quoted in Kynaston, 2011: 438). In effect, Britain's gold and dollar reserves were too small in relation to its short-term liabilities or its overseas trade to withstand a run on sterling.

It was also increasingly the case that the opportunity for British leadership of the Commonwealth was rapidly diminishing to leave an organization that was regarded in some Whitehall circles, especially the Foreign Office, as politically sometimes 'more of an embarrassment than an asset' and that was fast losing the image of a white man's club under the impact of the second wave of decolonization (1957–1963). The expulsion of South Africa from the Commonwealth in 1961 on account of its apartheid system marked the emergence of a new constellation of forces. This episode clearly upset the long-standing dominance of Britain and of the white Dominions in the management of Commonwealth affairs.

Certainly, the Commonwealth was to demonstrate its survival capacity in a host of ritual, ceremonial, cultural and international aid functions. It currently comprises some 54 states and involves institutions and activities ranging from the Commonwealth Heads of Government Meeting (CHOGM – popularly characterized as a Cheap Holiday on Government Money) to the Commonwealth Games. The fiction that Commonwealth countries are not really foreign is maintained in the practice of calling embassies in those states 'high commissions' (Cooper, 2012: 6). More importantly in this context, the Commonwealth and the accompanying post-imperial complex have found expression in a number of ways, most of which have tended to reproduce claims of Britain's great power status while subordinating the place of Europe and of the EU in British hearts and minds. Meanwhile, however, the trading importance of the Commonwealth to Britain has considerably diminished. British exports to Empire countries comprised 49.9 per cent of total overseas trade in 1938. By 2008, however, British exports to the

Commonwealth countries were just 8.8 per cent of total exports. During the same period, the comparable figures for British imports from this source fell from 40.4 per cent to 8.6 per cent (Charter, 2012: 219).

A host of poignant memories and sentimental dreams of empire and of global leadership has gathered around and continued to colour expressions of Britain's role and identity in the wider world. Enoch Powell, the Conservative maverick figure of the 1960s and 1970s who made the transition from supporter of empire to 'Little Englander', dismissed the Commonwealth as 'a sticking plaster for the wound left by the amputation of empire' (*Oxford Dictionary of National Biography*). There nonetheless remained in being a deep-seated nostalgic view of empire and of global reach and leadership, eloquently expressed by Powell himself when describing his return to Britain to enlist in 1939 at the beginning of the Second World War:

> had I been asked 'What is the state whose uniform you wish to wear and in whose service you expect to perish?' I would have said the British Empire ... I also know that on my death bed, I shall still be believing with one part of my brain that somewhere on every ocean of the world there is a great grey ship with 3 funnels and 16 inch guns which can blow out of the water any other navy it is likely to face.
>
> (quoted in Muller, 2002: 106)

Imperial legacy

Memories of empire could not be easily dissolved away or forgotten. The country may 'have conquered half the world in a fit of absence of mind', as the late nineteenth-century Cambridge historian J. R. Seeley put it, but it did not demit imperial office in quite so mindless a way. In some cases memories of empire had immediate consequences in influencing foreign policy. The Suez crisis of 1956 was to a considerable extent an expression of post-imperial nostalgia, reflecting the formative foreign policy experience of Prime Minister Eden in the inter-war and wartime period when British political leaders acted and saw themselves as representative of a major global power (Hannay, 2013: 278). Thereafter, memories of empire and of former pre-eminence in world affairs retained potent appeals in the great power rhetoric of political discourse. Furthermore, the enduring legacy of empire lingered on in a multitude of ways, including the imperial pomposity of an anachronistic honours system, the Foreign and Commonwealth Office murals depicting the origin, expansion and triumph of the British Empire, and the diverse forms of popular culture in film, television and literature.

A preoccupation with asserting a global leadership role for Britain, initially based on empire and subsequently on post-imperial nostalgia, has figured as a key element in the making of British foreign policy. This emphasis, in turn, has had a lasting influence on British policy and attitudes towards the EC/EU, not least according to the view that a world outlook has led in practice to less concern or respect for Europe. The memory of empire fed into and underpinned the assertion of a leadership role in the world. Britain's claim to a special place and mission in the wider world was further reinforced by what was debatably represented as the smooth transition from Empire to Commonwealth. The quest for post-imperial European and global leadership remained in being even when there appeared to be an attempt to escape from Britain's imperial past. For instance, while treating empire as clearly belonging to a past era, Tony Blair nonetheless declared in language easily mistaken for imperial fantasy that: 'We are a leader of nations, or we are nothing' and that Britain's frontiers 'reach out to Indonesia' (Deighton, 2002: 109).

Such sentiments find expression in other Commonwealth circles and in often trivial ways. According to Ali Williams, the legendary All Black rugby player, the English 'always carry this consciousness of their grand past and would like to be reminded of their great empire', this accounting for why 'big rugby nations like Australia, New Zealand and South Africa are so determined to beat England' (*The Sunday Times*, 13 September 2015). A few weeks later, Australia duly inflicted a humiliating defeat on England in the 2015 Rugby World Cup, the first occasion on which the host nation has been bundled out of the competition in the opening stages, producing the cutting comment from *The Mail on Sunday* (4 October 2015) that 'only the worst hosts leave their own party this early'.

A mixture of motives and considerations accounted for such views at any particular time including concerns about national and personal prestige and purpose, and the influence of history, tradition and inertia. In addition, there was the enduring ambition to project Britain as the joint world policeman with the United States or at least as a house prefect of the international system (see below). Even when objective conditions clearly underlined Britain's relative decline in the international system, there remained a keen determination to lay claim to a global leadership role. Sometimes, it seemed as if bombastic assertions were designed to obscure from the public the scale of the retreat and to ease the transition from a global pre-eminent status to a more regional European standing. In itself, that transition 'caused problems to the national psyche' and arguably required 'an almost superhuman attitudinal adjustment' (Lord Neuberger, *The Daily Telegraph*, 14 February 2014).

Towards the end of the period 1947–1970 that witnessed the decline of the empire, Harold Wilson as prime minister still insisted that Britain's frontiers extended to the Himalayas and this at a time (1965) when the Commonwealth member states of India and Pakistan made use of Soviet rather than British mediation in their conflict over Kashmir. Meanwhile, leading Cabinet supporters of British membership of the EC like Brown (Foreign Secretary) and Stewart (Secretary of State for Economic Affairs) argued that EC membership was essential to keep up Britain's international status and place at the 'top table'.

It is at such points that exceptionalist and declinist standpoints on the character of British foreign policy part company. The former emphasizes the distinctive features of Britain's global standing including the country's place at the top table of world affairs and global organizations together with its possession of nuclear weapons and deployment of military forces in various policing and peace-keeping roles across the world. Douglas Hurd as foreign secretary in 1993 portrayed a proud, self-important Britain aiming at 'punching above its weight' on the international scene. At the same time, Garel-Jones, an FCO minister, was said to have argued against the case for adopting a totally EC-oriented role by asserting that 'History has dealt us a more important role' (Trewin, 2008: 367).

Critics of the exceptionalist narrative of British foreign policy since 1945, however, have focused on a declinist account of British foreign policy since 1945, most famously expressed in Dean Acheson's comment at the head of this chapter. They have emphasized the loss of great power status (see Chapter 2) and have done so in such a way that Thatcher referred to exponents of this view as 'an army of professional belittlers' (Harvey, 2011: 5).

A not uncommon feature of this perspective is that British political leaders have struggled to reconcile popular British perceptions of great power status with the country's reduced resources and standing in the world. Announcing the end of Britain's east of Suez role, a Defence White Paper (February 1966) highlighted the essence of Britain's dilemma when it declared that there was no point in being a world policeman if you didn't have the resources to fulfil such a role. For the most part, however, the country's political elite rarely attempted to educate the public about the full nature and extent of Britain's reduced power and status in the wider world. Far from facing up to the challenge of coping with the retreat from past glory and the language of empire, according to this view, politicians have steadfastly refused to adjust to reduced circumstances in their public pronouncements. Instead, they have preferred to seek refuge in some of the overstated trappings and posturings of 'great power' status. They have done so with the accompanying imperial conceit of having to show international leadership on any issue. The reluctance of British political leaders to accept a fundamental change in Britain's world role was once likened by Richard Crossman, a Labour government Cabinet minister in the 1960s, to a 'status barrier': like the sound barrier it 'splits your ears and it's terribly painful when it happens' (quoted in Bennett, 2013: 111).

Critics of such behaviour regard the idea of Britain 'punching above its weight' as 'a reckless thing to try to do', and they might also accuse Britain of 'thinking beyond its weight' in presuming that the world is waiting to hear the British view on international affairs (LSE IDEAS, November 2015). According to the historian Paul Kennedy, the divergence between Britain's shrunken economic state and its overextended strategical posture 'is probably more extensive than that affecting any of the larger powers, except Russia itself' (quoted in Sampson, 2004: 133). Alec Douglas-Home, Heath's foreign secretary (1970–1974), had few illusions in that respect. In his memoirs, he observed that Britain was 'a medium-sized power' and that there were two errors commonly made about British foreign policy: the failure to recognize that its role in the world had changed, and the assumption that because Britain's power had diminished it had no influence.

Since 1945, all British governments, with the possible exception of the Heath government of 1970–1974, have maintained that Europe could not be separated from the global dimensions of foreign policy. In the same vein, they have insisted that the European continent did not represent the major, exclusive area of British strategic interest. Any form of regional or European co-operation was at best a subordinate and diminutive piece in the global jigsaw and at worst an impediment to what British policymakers viewed as the higher priorities of global co-operation and interdependence or what might be described as post-imperial connectivity (Niblett, 2015: 7).

The 'one world approach' and globalization

The emphasis on global co-operation or interdependence in the early decades after the Second World War was often referred to as the 'one world (or collective) approach'. It found particular expression in pressing the case for the liberalization of international trade and payments and the lifting of restrictions on inconvertible currencies. This programme was designed to dismantle the barriers to international trade and payments erected during the inter-war period and the regime of wartime controls. These aims were combined with marked opposition to any exclusively European arrangement on such matters. As detailed in Chapter 2, this emphasis partly accounted for Britain's refusal to consider tariffs in a purely European setting during the 1950s, thereby excluding itself from the origins of the EC. During this period, the EC was often dubbed 'Little Europe' and, most notably among opponents of EC membership, this description was intended to convey the impression of the EC as a very restricted, regional entity.

In more recent decades many of the features of the 'one world approach' have found their way into the concept of globalization. However defined, globalization has often overshadowed European integration in some parts of British political discourse about the external environment, occasionally downplaying the relevance of the EU and reducing it to a redundant or anachronistic feature.

Set against this background, the EU has figured in British circles not as an end in itself but either as a means of achieving global goals according to supporters of EU membership or as an obstacle to securing Britain's global interests in the view of opponents of EU membership. The labelling may have changed but the global perspective has remained more or less intact over the years. It was the theme of a speech by Harold Macmillan on a visit to Boston in the United States in 1961 and also by Gordon Brown, albeit featuring different issues, on a visit to the same place in 2008. Significantly, the Brown government's initiative at this time was entitled Global Europe and was designed, in accordance with long-standing British preferences, to encourage the EU to spend less time on its structures, institutions and laws and more time on its global role, 'a globalized context which we are best placed to oversee/supervise' according to one report of Brown's views on the subject (Keesings Contemporary Archives, 1961: 18053–54; *The Guardian*, 19 April 2008; Trewin, 2008: 812).

The main thrust of this analysis as expressed by both Blair and Brown while in government over the period 1997–2010 was that Britain's exceptionalist position in the international system meant that it was equipped to benefit from the twin processes of globalization and interdependence, especially in view of its universal language, continuing exposure to the global economy and path-breaking role in pursuing neo-liberal economic policies and deregulation. The globalization of the economy, finance and information technology meant that national governments could not escape the reality of global interconnectedness. Globalization was to be embraced, not feared, as it provided new opportunities for growth (Schnapper, 2014).

Under the Cameron Coalition government of 2010–2015 the global theme was presented as Britain adapting to 'a networked world'. Rejecting the thesis of decline, Cameron at an early stage in his premiership reflected exceptionalist leanings by emphasizing Britain's distinctive combination of foreign policy assets. According to this view, the country was well-placed to pursue an active global role and was 'at the centre of all big discussions' (Harvey, 2011).

We will return later in this chapter to consider the particular impact of British interest in extra-European affairs on shaping policy and attitudes to the foreign and defence policy profile of the EC/EU. Suffice it to say here that a global perspective has prompted British political leaders since 1945 to insist that the country's principal overseas interests lay beyond Europe. This view has served to divert attention away from occupying a full role in the EC/EU. It has also perpetuated in the domestic context an inflated impression of Britain's standing on the international stage, especially in view of the country's limited military and economic strength. The resources and effort poured into upholding the image of Britain as a world power have arguably worked against the process of full adaptation to the EC/EU. As a result, it can be argued, Britain has often punched below its weight in the EU for lack of sustained political engagement (Deighton, 2002; Wallace, 2005).

The relationship between Britain's global position and policy towards the EC/EU has, of course, undergone a transformation, most notably in the form of EC/EU membership that ranks among the small number of fundamental changes executed by British governments since 1945. As we noted in Chapter 2, this development reflected among other things an acute sense of national decline. EC membership was viewed by its advocates as a means of buttressing the claim to global leadership, while in other quarters the possibility of British leadership of the EC was mocked as a substitute for empire on the basis of a delusion. At the same time, Britain's self-styled important role in world affairs placed it apart from and in front of other major European powers. In this respect EC membership was a case of change but within a deeply laid continuity, at one and the same time avoiding unqualified commitment to the process of European integration and maintaining the pretense that EC membership was vital but would change nothing. The view of Britain as apart from and superior to the continental European powers was increasingly regarded as a piece of fiction by these powers. Nevertheless, it served the purpose of conveying to a domestic audience a particular image of Britain as occupying a pivotal role in international affairs, whether in the form of the Churchillian 'three circles' or in later years by the claims of the Labour government in the period 1997–2010 that Britain was best placed to bring Europe and the United States together.

From Commonwealth to Anglosphere

Following Britain's entry to the EC in 1973, the Commonwealth element in British foreign policy, that had figured so prominently in negotiations surrounding attempts to join the EC in the 1960s and early 1970s (see Chapters 2 and 3) and had retained a nostalgic and political pull, fell away into the background. It was increasingly overshadowed by an EC-focused trading pattern and political forum. It seemed that at least part of one of Churchill's three inter-linked circles – 'the English-speaking world including the British Dominions and the USA' – had become increasingly outmoded in defining British strategy and interests in the wider world. In the later 1990s and increasingly thereafter, however, this particular circle attracted renewed interest in the form of what was to be known as the Anglosphere with its roots in the Commonwealth tradition but now developed in a global rather than an imperial context.

A key feature of the idea of an Anglosphere is that the English-speaking nations are distinguished by a set of institutions and characteristics that the other advanced nations of Europe and Asia lack, notably a common law tradition, respect for private property, continuous representative government, free trade and a culture that nurtures civil society and entrepreneurial enterprise (Bennett, 2004: 54). These values, so it is argued, are not shared 'by the corporatist, socialist, corrupt and even authoritarian political cultures prevalent on the European continent, and of which the EU is itself an expression' (Laughland, 2008). That being the case, an Anglosphere organization would be 'a monument to the British exceptionalism that anti-integrationists often cite as a reason for British withdrawal or disengagement from the EU' (Wellings and Baxendale, 2014). The English-speaking nations in this context are usually defined as including Australia, Canada, New Zealand, the United States and the UK. Some definitions range further afield to include English-speaking Caribbean islands as well as India and Singapore. According to some versions of this perspective, it seems that not for the first time in our story the country's future appeared to lie in its past and especially in a revival of ties with the white Dominions.

The concept of an Anglosphere has not to date entered the realms of international relations and politics in any institutional or organic form. Indeed, Robert Conquest, the historian who has written on the subject, has acknowledged that his proposed Anglosphere Alliance was 'a work of cultural and political science fiction' (quoted in Wellings and Baxendale, 2014). That possibility has not stopped supporters of such a venture from suggesting a variety of possible titles: 'English Speaking Union', the 'Anglosphere Association', the 'Anglosphere Network Conference' and the 'Anglosphere'. It has also been viewed in some quarters as providing the governing intellectual framework for the referendum campaign to quit the EU (*New Statesman*, 10 February 2015).

The emergence of this concept owed much to several considerations that weighed heavily with opponents of EU membership. It was especially associated with Eurosceptic opinion within the Conservative Party and with the view of combining nationalism and globalism. Such Conservative opinion was especially galvanized at the time of the Maastricht Treaty negotiations and subsequently expanded on the theme during the period of Conservative Opposition (1997–2010) and the Cameron governments after 2010. A key impulse underlying the idea of an Anglosphere has revolved around the need to respond to the question posed by supporters of the EU and famously so by Garel-Jones, the Conservative Minister for Europe in the Major government: 'Can the anti-federalists, the Euro-sceptics and little Englanders offer a positive alternative?' [i.e. to EU membership]. The Eurosceptic wing of the Conservative Party has adopted the Anglosphere as an alternative to European integration, reinforcing the centrality of British national narratives at the heart of an increasingly Eurosceptic Englishness and forging closer relationships with countries that have similar political structures, systems and values.

In the course of time, the idea has attracted varying degrees of support from some high-profile Conservative politicians including Margaret Thatcher, Norman Lamont, Liam Fox and others (Wellings and Baxendale, 2014). The idea also resonated with leading Conservative figures in the Cameron Coalition government. Cameron and Foreign Secretary Hague in particular favoured cultivating closer links with Commonwealth countries, reviving the image of Britain at the intersection of Churchill's inter-locking circles, but discarding much grandiose post-imperial rhetoric and focusing instead on the world of commercial diplomacy. They had reason to do so as they and their party increasingly disengaged from the EU and sought out allies that did not challenge a dominant British view of the past and traditional allies (Wellings and Baxendale, 2014).

The Anglosphere idea has also found support for mining and reflecting the Commonwealth appeal and Eurosceptic identification with Britain's maritime traditions rather than continental inclinations. It provides a platform from which to reject the declinist, defeatist view of Britain in favour of the country's exceptionalist standing in the wider world, less a case of a retreat to a fading past, albeit with echoes of a neo-Elizabethan age, and more a matter of pursuing the vision of an outward looking, seafaring country with a global perspective. The idea of *Britannia Unchained* was at the heart of Churchill's comment to the French leader, Charles de Gaulle, before the D-Day landings in 1944, 'If Britain must choose between Europe and the open sea, she must always choose the open sea!' Seventy years later this same view was expressed by Boris Johnson, the London mayor. He pressed the case for 'a wider destiny for our country' and described the earlier decision to join the EC as betraying other Commonwealth countries at a time when the British establishment was defeatist and obsessed with the idea of being excluded from the most powerful economic club in the world (*The Daily Telegraph*, 24 August 2013). According to this view, freed from the constraints of the EU, Britain would be able to revive its global mission by fully exploiting economic opportunities in the world at large (Gifford, 2014: 174).

A further case for embracing the Anglosphere idea focuses on the failings of the EU. Robert Conquest has argued that the political arrangements of the west including the EU were all increasingly deficient and needed to be replaced by a more fruitful unity between the Anglosphere nations. In addition, Conquest and others have highlighted fundamental changes in the world order that make an EU-focused strategy outmoded in the face of British commercial and financial interests beyond Europe. According to this account, an independent Britain released from EU ties and reinventing its open trading heritage could prosper in a global economy dominated by the rise of Asia. The Anglosphere idea has served to divert attention away from EU membership in much the same way as another major feature in British foreign policy: relations with the United States.

The 'special relationship'

A fundamental feature of the external environment for British policymakers since 1945 has involved the so-called 'special relationship' between Britain and the United States. This relationship has attracted markedly different judgements that are beyond the scope of this study, including the rejection from an American perspective of the idea of an exclusive relationship and some acknowledgement on the British side, beyond the routine rhetoric, that 'a' rather than 'the' special relationship is more appropriate (Hannay, 2013: 285). Here, the emphasis is on British perceptions and assessments of this relationship in the European context and most especially on some of the changing and enduring implications of this relationship for British policy towards the EC/EU.

Several aspects of British policy towards the United States have had a lasting bearing on policy and attitudes towards the EC/EU. First, British governments since 1945, with the exception of the Heath government of 1970–1974, have strongly upheld the view that Britain's main bilateral relationship in the world is with the United States. They have also acted on the understanding that there should be no repetition of the disastrous impact of the Suez crisis of 1956 on relations between London and Washington, and that this relationship should be maintained at whatever cost and in attractive imagery. Macmillan as Eden's successor after Suez moved quickly to repair relations and in typical Macmillan style envisaged Britain as playing the role of ancient Greece to Washington's ancient Rome. Macmillan and his successors always stressed the importance of the Atlantic Alliance as the principal forum for the conduct of relations between western states. Significant maritime experience and interests constitute an important if underrated factor distinguishing between Britain and the United States on the one hand and Europe as a whole (Cyr, 2012: 1317). This heavily 'Atlanticist' complexion of British foreign policy has involved a keen determination to safeguard the British position as the foremost ally and principal cheerleader of the United States in

Europe. It has entailed a systematic attempt to ensure that any EC/EU proposals in the defence and security field have not conflicted with or undermined NATO (see below).

No other NATO member state since 1950 has matched Britain's unwavering support for the organization. A prominent position within NATO as the most faithful US ally has served several functions other than the explicitly defence and security ones. Most notably, it has enabled the British government to maintain the idea of the 'special relationship', to keep up appearances on the world stage and the capacity 'to punch above its weight', and to project a triumphalist representation of British foreign policy. It was for this reason among others that the parliamentary vote (August 2013) against British military action in Syria was held to be significant. There was widespread criticism in the press of Cameron's lack of preparation and sense of tactical understanding (Seldon and Snowdon, 2015: 343). Furthermore, this parliamentary defeat undermined Cameron's standing in Washington and placed 'some strain on the Anglo-American relationship' according to Defence Secretary Hammond. It also seriously questioned the notion of occupying a pivotal role in the global order, indicating the extent to which Britain had moved 'from being on the team on the field to being on the reserve bench of international security' (Niblett, 2015: 3).

Britain's standing in NATO via the 'special relationship', it can be argued, has increased its sense of superiority over its mainland European allies and has prolonged British delusions of grandeur (Marsh and Baylis, 2006: 187). The country's credentials in this regard have rarely passed unnoticed or unquestioned on the continent, often complicating co-operation with other European countries. De Gaulle feared that Britain as an EC member state would act as an American Trojan horse. This view was endorsed much later by Gerhard Schröder, the former German chancellor. He maintained that Britain's 'special relationship' with the United States not only weighed on its European-focused future but meant that Britain more than any other European state was prepared to anticipate American wishes and turn them into European political issues.

In British government circles, the advantages of a close relationship with Washington in terms of financial, intelligence, military and defence support have invariably counted for more than any gains from the EC/EU relationship. Co-operation in the military and intelligence fields arguably gives some substance to the idea of a 'special relationship'. In the field of nuclear weapons, Britain has been entirely dependent on American nuclear weapons delivery systems from Polaris in the 1960s and 1970s to Trident since the 1980s. How far these systems are operationally independent is a matter of debate, though such dependence on US technology and maintenance suggests that they could not conceivably be used without US consent. In any case, it is the totemic significance of nuclear weapons in British politics that appears to matter above all else. One of the most potent expressions favouring British possession of nuclear weapons was long ago expressed by the Labour Party Shadow Foreign Secretary Aneurin ('Nye') Bevan. Hitherto a critic of nuclear weapons in a party invariably divided by the issue, Bevan famously opposed unilateral nuclear disarmament at the Labour Party conference of 1957 on the grounds that such a policy would 'send a British Foreign Secretary, whoever he may be, naked into the conference chamber'. At the time of the acquisition of Trident in 1980, on expensive terms that included the long familiar trade of allowing US military use of a British overseas base (Diego Garcia), Peter Carrington, the foreign secretary, cited another influential consideration regarding the possession of nuclear weapons, noting that failure to acquire Trident 'would have left the French as the only nuclear power in Europe. This would be intolerable' (Moore, 2014: 572–3).

In the grey area of intelligence and security activities, meanwhile, the close relationship between British and American intelligence agencies in the Second World War has continued ever since in the form of collaboration between the Government Communications Headquarters (GCHQ) on the British side and the US-based National Security Agency (NSA). It is a matter of dispute and of unconfirmed reports as to how far GCHQ receives funding from the US government and what the Americans expect in return for their investment. It is also a matter of speculation as to how far the US authorities use GCHQ as a cheap, permissive spying outpost with 'light oversight' compared to the regulation of the NSA by American political authorities (*The Guardian*, 1 August 2013, 9 May 2014). Unsurprisingly, one of the reported reasons for the delay in the publication of the long-awaited Chilcot inquiry into the 2003 invasion of Iraq has cited sensitivities between the British and US intelligence agencies.

The second aspect of London's relations with Washington concerns the extent to which all British governments since 1945, again with the exception of the Heath government, have set great store by what they have regarded as Britain's unique and invaluable role as a bridge or intermediary between Europe and the United States. True, the bridge idea had a wider application than in transatlantic relations, meaning Britain's diplomatic assets in finding common ground between other countries; James Callaghan as foreign minister (1974–1976) declared that the British were 'the bridge builders' in relation to improving what were then known as North–South relations. It was in the context of transatlantic relations, however, that this well-worn bridge metaphor had most resonance and served as a central frame of reference. Its post-1945 origins lay in Britain's leading role in enlisting US economic and security support in the late 1940s and especially in the formation of the OEEC and NATO (see Chapter 2). British prime ministers from Macmillan to Brown have regularly employed this imagery, with the occasional extra gloss as applied by Blair 'Call it a bridge, a two lane motorway, a pivot or call it a damn high wire' (Wallace, 2005).

The self-appointed function of the British government in such a position was, as Blair put it, to keep its sights firmly on both sides of the Atlantic. There were problems in doing so. One French diplomat unhelpfully pointed out that the problem with being a bridge is that you get walked over. In fact, the 'bridge' has generally carried only one-way traffic from Washington to Europe, while the idea that the British government might seek to take the lead in achieving a common EU view before communicating that view to Washington was never entertained under Blair's premiership (Wall, 2008: 215; Trewin, 2008: 555). In any case, the idea of acting as a bridge or as a transatlantic intermediary in the course of events leading up to the invasion of Iraq was out of the question. Blair's bridge simply collapsed in the midst of deep divisions within the EU over the Iraq war. Britain's global values and interests were here perceived as markedly different from what were viewed as European values and identity in other EU states, especially France and Germany.

Unsurprisingly, David Miliband, foreign secretary (2007–2010) in Brown's government, distanced himself from the image of Britain as a bridge on the grounds that it epitomized an ambivalent relationship with Europe 'suggesting Europe was a bilateral relationship rather than an institution of which we are a party' (Harvey, 2011: 8). Miliband hereby traded in the exceptionalist idea of Britain's bridge building role for the equally exceptionalist notion of the country's role in the world as a 'global hub'. Nevertheless, he acknowledged that the United States was Britain's 'single most important bilateral relationship. We are committed members of the EU' (July 2007). There was effectively nothing 'special' about Britain's EU membership, unless it lay in the area of the country's unresolved identity as a truly European nation. Time and again, the United States has always trumped the EU as a model for the expression of Britain's identity in the international arena (Daddow, 2013: 214).

The idea of acting as a bridge in transatlantic relations has proved even less likely under Cameron's premiership since 2010 as the government has partially disengaged from the EU to consider its position. Furthermore, it has in any case scarcely elevated relations with Washington to the 'mountain top' experience of the Thatcher and Blair years. Indeed, following its return to full NATO membership (2009), France increasingly nudged aside Britain to become the US military's key European power. This development was most evident in the alignment of its policy towards Iran's nuclear programme with Washington. France also stood alone with the United States in 2013 in support of possible military action against the Assad regime in Syria for its use of chemical weapons.

Meanwhile, the Cameron Coalition government may be said to have reasserted an exceptionalist outlook by emphasizing Britain's distinctive combination of foreign policy assets and its position, as Cameron put it, 'at the centre of all the big discussions' with an increasing recognition of the shift in global power from west to east (Harvey, 2011: 9). This emphasis suggested a revival of Britain at the intersection of Churchill's interlocking circles with a marked preference for shedding instinctive deference towards the United States and for moving on from the obsession about Europe (Niblett, 2015: 7). During the Cameron Coalition government, the so-called special relationship appeared to be fraying at the edges with later revelations from Obama about the failings of the British and the French in the aftermath of the invasion of Libya in 2011. Arguably more importantly, Obama disclosed that he had warned Cameron at this time that the 'special relationship' would be at risk if Britain did not commit to spending 2 per cent of its national income on defence in line with NATO targets (*The Guardian*, 11 March 2016) – a particularly wounding comment for a British political and military establishment that had long prided itself on acting as Washington's most faithful ally in Europe.

Under the Obama presidency since 2009, US foreign policy has also increasingly shifted from an Atlanticist to an Asiatic and Pacific set of priorities, reflecting the major changes in the balance of global power. Furthermore, at the personal level, the 'Anglo-Saxon' character of the 'special relationship' was far less evident from the outset of Obama's presidency than it had been under any other post-1945 US president. Significantly, a bronze bust of Churchill from the British government's art collection was loaned to President George W. Bush and enjoyed pride of place in the Oval Office during much of his presidency (2001–2009). On coming to office in 2009, however, Obama wasted little time in removing it from the Oval Office. It was after all during Churchill's second premiership (1951–1955) that Britain suppressed Kenya's Mau Mau rebellion, and among Kenyans allegedly tortured by the British colonial regime included one Hussein Onyango Obama, the president's grandfather.

The idea of acting as a bridge between the United States and Europe has also meant, among other things, that British governments came to know and care more about the workings of the US system of government than those of any mainland European country. Churchill's comment that 'No lover ever studied every whim of his mistress as I did those of President Roosevelt' had its parallel in the instruction issued to the new British ambassador to Washington on taking up his appointment in 1997 to 'get up the arse of the White House and stay there' (*The Independent on*

Sunday, 13 November 2005). In both cases, it occasionally seemed that some of the principals in London acted as if the United States could be regarded less as a foreign country and more as part of the 'Anglo-Saxon' world. Furthermore, it was often assumed that Washington would somehow on the basis of mutual understanding, goodwill and sentimentality about the 'special relationship' take British interests into account in its policies.

The binding ties of history, culture and language made for *a* special relationship, but the idea of *the* special relationship was a British and not an American conceit (except as a ritualistic expression on the visit of a British prime minister to Washington). Nevertheless, this relationship contributed far more to a sense of British identity than anything in continental European quarters. In sum, it had deep-seated roots in 'a military alliance, a model of capitalism, a form of government, a global ideology, and a popular culture' (Gamble, 2003: 86). Meanwhile, the preoccupation of the British media with US politics has offered a long-standing and striking contrast to its negligible interest in and coverage of the politics of other EU states (see Chapter 7).

A blend of robustness in defence of British and European interests combined with a willingness to pay attention to American concerns has often seemed to elude British foreign policy over the decades (Hannay, 2013: 70). Exceptions to the rule tend to stand out like Wilson's refusal to send British troops to support the Americans in Vietnam or Thatcher's handling of the Soviet–western Europe gas pipeline project, mentioned below, and her privately expressed opposition to the US invasion of Grenada, a member of the Commonwealth (October 1983).

Thatcher, in particular, placed considerable importance on relations with the United States. She gave immediate backing in 1979 to President Carter's strong stand against the Soviet invasion of Afghanistan. More importantly, she later went on to develop an extremely close rapport with Ronald Reagan throughout the period 1981–1989. It was grounded in personal friendship and shared political convictions: an unquestioning belief in free market economics and a profound aversion to the Soviet Union summed up for some in the spoof *Gone with the Wind* film poster featuring Reagan and Thatcher with the caption 'She promised to follow him to the end of the earth. He promised to organize it'. The relationship particularly proved its worth in the major crisis of Thatcher's period of office, the Falklands war of 1982, when the supply of US satellite information, intelligence and military hardware were of vital importance to the British effort: 'Give Maggie everything she needs to get on with it' was Reagan's clear command to the Pentagon after some hesitation in reaching that decision (Broussard, 2014).

Third, British governments, most markedly so in the case of the Macmillan, Callaghan and Blair administrations, steadfastly resisted the idea of being forced to choose between the United States and Europe. They always publicly regarded this as a false choice and invariably insisted that a special relationship with Washington could be combined with close relations with the EC/EU. Some of the problems of attempting or failing to do so, however, have to a greater or lesser extent featured ever since the 1940s. As one Foreign Office paper of 1958 observed, maintaining a special relationship with Washington could be at the expense of building close relations with European states, yet only through close relations with and a leadership role in Europe could Britain bring influence to bear in Washington (NA., FO 371/132330, 7 January 1958). More than 40 years later a similar point was made by a German foreign ministry spokesman when he argued that successive British governments had laid themselves open to a 'double self-mutilating whammy'. They had failed to recognize that a country that does not matter in Europe will never be taken seriously by Washington and they had actively invested in their special relationship with the United States a positive reason not to be involved in Europe (Trewin, 2008: 727). Furthermore, the closeness of relations with Washington ultimately rested on the leverage Britain exercised in Europe.

Successive British political leaders have given little credence to such views. They have often underestimated the extent to which their emphasis on the special relationship has weakened relations with major mainland European neighbours. They have also overestimated the amount of weight and influence that Britain on its own can bring to bear on Washington. The difficulties of maintaining a balance between the European and transatlantic dimensions of British policy have proved all the greater because of the British emphasis on the 'special relationship'.

Finally, the 'special relationship', as prioritized and treasured by British governments, has provided an opportunity to avoid full commitment to the EU, ironically so in view of long-standing American support for Britain's full integration into the EU. It has also deprived Britain of any European alternative to the role of America's adjutant, giving rise to the view that the 'special relationship', for much of the period since Churchill coined the expression and first cast it in cosy propaganda, has amounted to a 'misguided sentimental investment' that has paid few dividends for Britain (Charmley, 2004, 1995: 360–1). In addition, the 'special relationship' has also served to obscure the nature and extent of Britain's declining role in world affairs. Shadowing Washington, as one historian has commented, has allowed British policymakers who still hunger for the big international stage some continued admission, though now far removed from Attlee's aspirational comment on Britain and the United States as being 'equal in counsel if not in power' (NA., FO 800/517/US/50/57).

There is substance to the view that much emphasis on the adverse impact of EU membership on British national independence in British political circles has deliberately attempted to deflect attention away from the major, if largely unnoticed, challenges to British independence from US influence. Among other things, Washington has demanded less than the EC/EU in terms of the *overt* loss of formal national sovereignty and independence. One school of thought, however, has argued that on occasions such as the involvement of the Blair government in the US-led invasion of Iraq under the administration of George W. Bush, Britain ceased to be sovereign in the conduct of its relations with Washington and made the sort of sacrifice of national independence never required in the EU (*The Guardian*, 6 December 2008, review of *The Hugo Young Papers* by Chris Patten). Less debatable is the damage done to Blair's reputation as a result of this event; David Miliband, foreign secretary in the Brown government (2007–2010), later described Bush's election as US president as 'the worst thing ever to happen to Tony Blair' (*The Times*, 6 March 2013). In these and other circumstances, the 'special relationship' seemed to serve as a grandiose term for Britain's subordination to the United States with little or no payback from Washington.

Lecturing the Europeans

John Milton, the seventeenth-century poet and polemicist, once advised his fellow countrymen: 'Let England not forget her precedence of teaching nations how to live' (*The Doctrine and Discipline of Divorce*, 1644). The application of this mission statement by British political leaders in the course of time was to be easily mistaken by outsiders as a form of sanctimonious interventionism and moralizing delivered in a hectoring tone of voice. Arguably this was all the more so with battered moral authority after two long, painful and 'lost' wars in Afghanistan and Iraq. Steeped in the history of running and then shedding an empire, British governments have frequently viewed themselves as eminently well-qualified to offer advice to foreigners, no global issue being beyond their interest even if far beyond the reach of their power in a post-imperial age.

Over the past 70 years the subject of British sermonizing has ranged far and wide from the benefits of Atlantic co-operation to the moral value of the Commonwealth. However, it has particularly concentrated on Europe and European integration, lending weight to the view that throughout the period since 1945 British political leaders have travelled across the Atlantic to learn and across the English Channel to preach (Wallace, 2005).

Sermon texts used by British political leaders since 1945 have focused on the general theme that only Britain knows what is good for Europe. The subject matter has included such items as:

- the benefits of British schemes for European co-operation;
- the inadequacies of mainland European models of integration;
- the failings of any new EC/EU initiative;
- the weaknesses of the euro area and the necessary, seemingly unachievable, changes to facilitate British entry;
- the importance and uniqueness of Britain's self-styled role as either a transatlantic 'bridge' or a 'global hub'.

The preaching to European audiences has extended from the benefits of 'socialism in one country' in the late 1940s to the proclaimed strengthening of the democratic credentials of the EC through admitting Britain with its 'mother of parliaments' in the 1960s and 1970s. During the period of Thatcher governments in the 1980s mainland European audiences were treated to lectures on the dogma and superior merits of 'Anglo-Saxon' free market capitalism in the form of economic liberalization and deregulated markets. In addition, Thatcher was on hand to declare that, contrary to Dean Acheson's well-known comment that Britain had lost an empire and not yet found a role, Britain had now found a role 'in upholding international law and teaching the nations of the world how to live' (Moore, 2014: 710), to which Blair, as noted above, added the view that 'We are a leader of nations or nothing', thereby drawing on a long-standing Labour Party self-styled view of offering unique 'moral leadership' to the world.

As Chancellor of the Exchequer in the period 1997–2007, Brown pursued the same line. He reportedly attended EU finance ministers' meetings only when it suited him to do some 'Eurobashing' (Trewin, 2008: 722–3). He was particularly renowned for lecturing his fellow EU finance ministers on why they should follow his example of prudent management of public finances, making himself even more unpopular as he usually arrived late for meetings, delivered his piece, and left early. According to one source, his normal approach to EU meetings was 'Speaking rather than listening, and suspicion rather than friendship' (Seldon and Lodge, 2010: 66), and in lauding his own economic policies he was quite prepared to refer to what he perceived as the weaknesses of other EU states such as the alleged deficiencies of the German social market economic model. As noted in Chapter 3, Brown signed the Lisbon Treaty in 2007 but downplayed its significance and made no attempt to publicize it. His emphasis on the booming globalized financial sector (at least until the financial crash of 2007–2008) meant that he was far more US- than European-oriented in outlook. He rarely missed an opportunity to advise EU audiences that in the face of globalization Europe was 'too slow in adapting to change' (Brown, 2005: 8).

The resentment of other EU and especially euro area states at unwanted British criticism was if anything even more evident under the Cameron Coalition government of 2010–2015. This was particularly the case as Britain was mired in economic recession and as the euro area crisis worsened in 2011–2012. Cameron and George Osborne, Chancellor of the Exchequer, were very much to the fore in lecturing the euro area states on what they needed to do to put their house in order. Osborne like Brown before him rarely missed an opportunity to single out the weaknesses and inadequacies of the EU, notwithstanding Britain's low wage, low productivity, large trading deficit and highly indebted model of economic activity. Among other things, the persistent reference to the struggling EU as 'the greatest threat to Britain's economic recovery' (*The Times*, 4 October 2014) obscured domestic factors threatening economic recovery. It also had the effect of laying the blame for the failure of the government's export-led recovery programme entirely at the feet of the EU.

This customary practice continued under the Cameron Conservative government. In October 2015, Theresa May, Home Secretary, lectured the Europeans about putting their house in order over the treatment of migrants: 'On returns [of migrants to their country of origin] we need to see Europe upping its game, and we stand ready to support that' (*The Guardian*, 9 October 2015). What 'support' meant in this context was unclear, particularly since Britain took no part in common EU asylum policies, was the only EU state declining to contribute to the new quotas system sharing refugees, and promised to take 20,000 Syrian refugees by 2020 as compared with what was estimated to be Germany's intake of migrants of 800,000 in 2015 alone.

At best, euro area leaders often found such advice from the sidelines unhelpful, all the more so because of British unwillingness to contribute to any of the support mechanisms for the euro, apart from relatively modest and indirect International Monetary Fund (IMF) contributions. John Holmes, a former British ambassador to France, commented that EU leaders were 'unamused' by such interventions and 'found Cameron's lectures rather irritating' (*The Guardian*, 18 May 2012). President Sarkozy of France went even further and strongly rebuked Cameron at one European Council meeting: 'You missed a good opportunity to keep your mouth shut. We are sick of you criticizing us and telling us what to do. You say you hate the euro and now you want to interfere in our meetings' (*The Sunday Times*, 4 November 2012). This incident was a not untypical spat in chequered Franco-British relations especially as only a year earlier Cameron and Sarkozy had appeared together in Benghazi celebrating the role of British and French military force in unseating the Libyan leader Gadaffi.

The Merkel government in Berlin also took umbrage at the way in which Cameron insisted that the Coalition government was sticking with its austerity programme and that a government cannot borrow its way out of debt crisis. At the same time he insisted that the German government should relax its fiscal discipline and thereby get the euro area out of its debt crisis (*Observer*, 20 May 2012). This demand was particularly galling from a German point of view. Britain was not a member of the euro area, was about to abandon its original aim to clear the British budget deficit by 2015 and appeared to be acting in a hypocritical manner, seemingly giving substance to Churchill's well-known comment that Britain's usual export was hypocrisy.

An accompanying feature of this lecturing mode was an underlying assumption that however problematical Britain's future in the EU became the other member states would be extremely anxious to keep Britain in the club. This form of high level self-absorption found expression across the years. In the 1960s British advocates of EC membership took the view that the EC states desperately needed, required or eagerly awaited British leadership. They did so, however, without producing much proof to support such a contention.

A comparable conceit was evident in the parliament of 2010–2015. In the autumn of 2014, when a parliamentary bill was introduced for a referendum by 2017 following renegotiation of Britain's EU membership, Philip Hammond, the foreign secretary, was in no doubt that 'We are lighting a fire under the European Union by this piece of legislation' (*The Times*, 18 October 2014). He also declared that the other EU states would sit up and take notice of Britain's demands.

By this stage, however, the other states were almost inured to British opt-outs, pleas for concessions, red lines, threats and a veto. Some of the EU principals already made clear that they had their own red lines. Chancellor Merkel of Germany warned Cameron that he could not 'cherry pick' the parts of EU treaties that he liked, for therein lay the unravelling of the Single Market. President Hollande of France was equally emphatic that 'Europe à la carte' was not on the table. Besides, British grievances figured low on the EU agendas of the other member states, at a time when the major priorities were the problems of economic stagnation, the future of Greece in the euro area, the war in the Ukraine, the impact of Middle East conflicts on the streets of European capitals, and the massive influx of migrants from the Middle East. Barroso, the outgoing president of the Commission and the most anglophile occupant of the post for many years, had the temerity to suggest that Hammond's language was more appropriate for a defence secretary (Hammond's previous post) than a foreign secretary. He was immediately dismissed as an 'unelected bureaucrat' by Grant Shapps, who was at the time the unelected chairman of the Conservative Party and subsequently the disgraced Conservative government minister.

The European Union and 'high politics'

From European Political Co-operation to the Common Foreign and Security Policy

There is a familiar if debatable division between 'high politics' and 'low politics' in histories of the European Union. The former normally refers to foreign, security and defence policy, while the latter expression is an umbrella term for the economic and commercial activities of the EU. This section of the chapter discusses the evolution of the EU's institutions, role and activities in the sphere of foreign, security and defence policy. It does so principally with a view to analysing the nature and extent of British interest and influence in this EU forum.

The first tentative steps of the EC in the field of foreign policy occurred in the form of European Political Cooperation (EPC). This venture followed two earlier abortive attempts – the European Defence Community (with its accompanying European Political Community plan) and the Fouchet negotiations of 1960–1962 (see Chapter 2). The issues raised by these failed attempts and by EPC have had long-standing significance down to the present day, most notably touching on the EU's role as a foreign policy actor and its identity in the field of defence and security.

The EPC was launched informally in 1970 following the summit conference of EC leaders at The Hague (December 1969). It took effect in 1973 when EC foreign ministers drew up the Copenhagen Report. This report established the basic obligation of the member states to consult each other on all important foreign policy questions before adopting their own final positions. Some months later in December 1973, the EC foreign ministers published the Document on European Identity. It sought to define more closely the relations of the EC member states with other countries of the world as well as their responsibilities and position in world affairs. The main feature of EPC was consultation among the EC member states on foreign policy issues. For most of its history, EPC operated outside the formal EC framework and in accordance with the principle of intergovernmental co-operation. It came into being at a time when the EC was increasingly described as an economic giant but a political dwarf and when Henry Kissinger, the US Secretary of State, reportedly and famously enquired 'If I want to call Europe, who do I call?'

EPC had some influence in the field of so-called 'soft power' or non-military power. Most notably, it helped to ensure that the EC acted as a single entity in the 1970s at the time of the Conference on Security and Cooperation in Europe (CSCE) in the period 1973–1975. In fact, the EU was ahead of the United States in pressing for positive results, in much the same way as the EU's Venice Declaration of 1980 was in advance of Washington in referring for the first time to the right of self-determination for the Palestinian people. The CSCE forum resulted in the Helsinki Accords that registered mutual recognition by the Western Powers and the Soviet Union of the territorial and political status quo in Europe, and also gave rise to the Organisation for Security and Cooperation (OSCE).

The record of EPC in coordinating the foreign policies of the EC states, however, was mixed and invariably modest. There was far less evidence of coordination or solidarity in the face of the quadrupling of the price of oil by the Organization of the Petroleum Exporting Countries (OPEC) in 1973–1974. In fact, this episode pointed up deep divisions between the EC states. A number of states, with Britain in the lead, sought bilateral deals with oil producers to guarantee their future supplies, or as one oil company executive put it at the time 'Everyone got on their bikes, cycled to the Middle East, and made their own deals with the oil producers'.

In the 1980s there was some evidence of EC solidarity and of British leadership especially in the context of transatlantic relations. In at least two cases the effectiveness of the Thatcher government's views in negotiations with the Reagan administration was all the greater for expressing a widely shared consensus among EC states. In 1982 and with the backing of the EC states, Thatcher helped to reverse a US decision to impose sanctions on European companies (including the British company John Brown) involved in the project to build a gas pipeline between the Soviet Union and western Europe. A similar example occurred two years later when Thatcher, with the support of the EC states, persuaded Reagan to limit the Strategic Defence Initiative (SDI) (a programme for an anti-ballistic missile system also known as Star Wars) to the research stage and to leave deployment as a matter for later negotiations. This outcome demonstrated to one close observer of these events that British influence in Washington could be greatly augmented if it was part of a European mainstream view (Hannay, 2013: 119–20).

The Single European Act (1986) formally enshrined EPC as part of the EC institutional structures, effectively formalizing intergovernmental co-operation in foreign policy without changing its existing nature or methods of operation. A few years later, however, the Treaty on European Union (Maastricht Treaty) resulted in the creation of a new, more developed superstructure covering foreign, defence and security matters.

The Maastricht Treaty created the EU, which comprised three pillars: the European Communities comprising the three original Communities of the 1950s, the Common Foreign and Security Policy (CFSP), and Justice and Home Affairs (JHA). CFSP provided a basis for intergovernmental co-operation and common action among the EU states covering all areas of foreign policy (excluding trade and the environment) and all questions relating to the EU's security, including the progressive framing of a common defence policy that might lead to a common defence (Article 24 (1) Treaty on European Union). This last gave rise to the European Security and Defence Policy (ESDP) that came into being at the Helsinki European Council in 1999.

From the outset the ESDP figured as an integral part of CFSP as its civilian-military operational arm. At the same time, the EU leaders also called for the EU to be able to deploy a Rapid Reaction Force (RRF) of up to 60,000 combat troops at 60 days' notice for missions including crisis management, peacekeeping, and peace-making operations. Since 2002, the EU has conducted 30 civilian and military operations, ten of which were military operations including the naval mission to prevent piracy off the Somali Republic's coast and the police and justice mission in Kosovo. Importantly, the RRF is not a 'euro-army' and is not a standing force as it is drawn together on an ad hoc basis. In short, the EU unlike NATO is not an instrument for high intensity conflict situations. Its unique selling points in the field of international security are the diplomatic, civilian, military, developmental and financial tools that it can utilize in promoting international peace. It should be noted that six of the 28 EU member states do not belong to NATO: Austria, Cyprus, Finland, Ireland, Malta and Sweden.

The primary responsibility for setting the strategic direction and objectives of all aspects of EU foreign policy rests with the European Council (the heads of state or government of the member states) with the president of the European Council in the chair. The Treaty of Lisbon (2007) created the post of High Representative of the Union for Foreign Affairs and Security Policy, whose role is to conduct the foreign policy of the EU. This post, however, does not have the monopoly on the EU's external representation. The Lisbon Treaty also gives the president of the European Council responsibility for the external representation of the EU, at a separate level, without prejudice to the powers of the High Representative. The Lisbon text does not specify how the work is to be divided between the two, allowing practical experience to determine their respective roles. The Treaty of Lisbon also introduced a name change as the ESDP was replaced by the Common Security and Defence Policy (CSDP).

A further aspect of the Lisbon Treaty concerns the creation of the European External Action Service (EEAS). Its primary role is to assist the High Representative in the conduct of CFSP. One of its key functions is to staff and operate EU delegations in third countries and international organizations, replacing the former Commission and Council delegations abroad. A final feature of this institutional infrastructure should be noted, namely that under CFSP the European Parliament has no role in the adoption of decisions. Its function is limited to asking questions and making recommendations to the Council and the High Representative, and holding a debate on CFSP twice a year. A parliament that debates foreign and security policy only twice a year does not on the face of it suggest that this area of EU activity has proved hugely significant or subject to democratic control.

Arguments for and against the CFSP
For:

- All member states face the same security threats so they should work together to protect each other.
- The United States can no longer carry the majority of the burden of defence through NATO – the EU needs to pull its own weight.
- CSDP allows Europe to pursue its own defence agenda, rather than that laid down by the United States.

Against:

- Democratically elected representatives should make decisions about war and peace. CSDP is run by an unelected and therefore less accountable High Representative.
- CSDP diverts resources away from existing organizations such as NATO.
- Confusion and difficulties arise as EU defence somewhat duplicates both NATO's and individual member states' defence activities.

CFSP and CSDP do not mean that the EU develops a view on every foreign and security issue that is binding on all member states. It is rather the case that this institutional apparatus is utilized to produce a united stance on areas of concern to all or most member states. It is designed to ensure that the EU states have a joint view on what a common foreign and security policy means in practical terms. This aim has proved all the more important as internal movement within the EU and especially within the Schengen Area has become easier. Furthermore, this activity has grown in importance as the EU has become greatly concerned with potential security threats along its external borders and also increasingly preoccupied in recent years with the massive influx of migrants from North Africa and the Middle East.

Indeed, at an early stage in its evolution, the CFSP was sorely tested and found wanting during the conflicts accompanying the break-up of the decaying corpse of Yugoslavia in the 1990s. EU efforts to broker peace as Yugoslavia began to disintegrate were eventually defeated by the individual member states themselves when they separately recognized the new breakaway republics as sovereign states. Furthermore, the EU was sidelined in international efforts to end ethnic conflict in Bosnia-Herzegovina, as the United Nations, NATO and the United States in particular led international intervention. Similarly, international intervention in Kosovo in 1999 was largely a NATO affair. Such developments appeared to highlight the limits of the EU's common foreign and security policy, in the process attracting arguably some misplaced criticism about the precise role and powers of the CFSP. In any event, these events acted as a spur to changes that emerged as a result of the Franco-British St Malo summit meeting in December 1998 (see below) and following the above-mentioned Helsinki European Council in December 1999.

A former EU official of the EEAS has rightly cautioned that EU foreign and security policy has attracted more attention than it perhaps deserves. At times it seems that there are more people writing about the subject than there are making policy (Cooper, 2012: 1197). With that caveat in mind, this section highlights the impact of some of the key emphases and contributions associated with British involvement in this field. It also considers how this particular piece of the EU jigsaw has served British interests and how EU external action has helped or hampered the realization of British objectives. And finally, it covers what are perceived as the advantages and disadvantages of this sphere of activity in relation to the Review of the Balance of Competences between Britain and the EU undertaken by the Cameron Coalition government in 2012 in association with the government's commitment to hold a referendum on EU membership by the end of 2017.

The limits of intergovernmental co-operation

Significantly Britain was present at the creation of the EPC. The government was not confronted therefore with having to accept a set of institutions and troublesome policies such as the CAP and the EU budget that were made without a British input in the first instance. There is little doubt that the workings of the EU's foreign, defence and security policy procedures not only suit British requirements but conform to the classic British idea of European co-operation. The emphasis is on intergovernmental co-operation which means that the balance of competence lies squarely with the member states. In effect, all significant decisions in this area are made by unanimity. Each member state has a power of veto over such matters as the deployment of EU military operations and civilian missions. It is also the case that each member state retains full sovereign control of its military forces, civilian personnel and other security assets. No British personnel can be deployed in an EU mission unless the British government makes a deliberate decision to do so. Member states can also act unilaterally or via other international organizations like NATO when they see fit (HM Government, 'Review of the Balance of Competences between the United Kingdom and the European Union Foreign Policy', July 2013).

There is equally little doubt that Britain has brought to the making of the EU's foreign and defence policy considerable assets that have in turn allowed the country to play a prominent role in shaping the EU profile. Indeed, one authoritative account of this role has argued that in the EU's foreign affairs 'nothing is done against British interests, and little without British active participation'. The assets that Britain brings to the EU table include a high-quality, worldwide diplomatic network – according to some non-British observers the best in Europe – a web of relationships to match, and high grade military forces (Cooper, 2012: 1197, 1200).

The impact of British concerns and influence has proved particularly striking in the field of the common defence and security policy. Paradoxically, while the CSDP would arguably not have come into being without British and French leadership at the time of the St Malo summit of 1998, the policy would be much more effective without British reluctance to make use of it. A great deal of that influence derives from the British position as the leading European military power, accounting in 2010 (and before the expenditure reductions of the 2010 Defence Review) for some 22.4 per cent of defence expenditure in the EU and some 20.8 per cent of the average number of troops deployed (Biscop, 2012: 1297).

British influence in the making of policy in this sphere was evident from the outset. During the negotiation of the Treaty on European Union, Article 42 (7) of the treaty committed member states to come to the aid of any member under attack 'by all means in their power'. At British insistence, however, and to guard against this clause potentially undermining NATO's crucial collective defence role, the treaty text made clear that commitments and co-operation in this field had to be consistent with NATO commitments which for its member states remained the foundation of their collective defence.

Safeguarding the role and importance of NATO to Europe's defence acquired paramount importance in British handling of EU matters in this field. Prior to the advent of the CFSP, the Western European Union (WEU), the mid-1950s creation to usher a rearmed West Germany into NATO (see Chapter 2), attracted revived interest in the 1980s as an instrument for the EC's defence and security. It expanded from its original membership of seven states to include ten EC states with the membership of Greece, Portugal and Spain. The WEU was written into the Treaty on European Union as the default subcontractor for any military operations which the EU member states would want to undertake (Biscop, 2012: 1300).

There were, however, major strategic differences at the heart of this organization, usually involving Britain and France. The substance of the British view was that the WEU and the CSDP were clearly subordinate to NATO and valuable only insofar as they stimulated support for NATO and played a complementary role. Most importantly, British policymakers persistently rejected attempts to make the EU responsible for territorial defence in Europe. NATO had to remain the primary European and transatlantic defence organization, having guaranteed Europe's defence for more than 60 years. The EU should act militarily only where NATO cannot or chooses not to act, or where it can add particular value. The contrasting French view echoed the Gaullist emphases of the 1960s. It advocated a greater degree of strategic independence from the United States and a more defined European defence identity separate from NATO with the further development of the CSDP. This emphasis, however, as noted above, was increasingly qualified as France resumed full NATO membership (April 2009). Following the adoption of the Treaty of Lisbon, all the functions of the WEU were effectively incorporated into the EU and the WEU was closed down in 2011.

In the meantime, there was a keen British determination to ensure that the WEU was not used as an instrument to drive a wedge between the United States and its European allies. Time and again, the emphasis was on how NATO command and control could be used for European operations. The case for doing so was plainly stated by David Lidington, Minister of State for Europe in the Cameron Coalition government who remained in this post after the 2015 general election: 'First and foremost, NATO remains the bedrock of Britain's national security' (Lidington, 2012).

British resistance to any EU initiative that undermined or usurped the position of NATO has proved particularly evident in response to the proposal for a permanent standing operational headquarters for the EU. This idea first emerged at the time of the Iraq crisis in 2003 and was supported by Belgium, France, Germany and Luxembourg. It was strongly opposed by Britain and the United States on the grounds that it amounted to an unnecessary duplication of NATO. What materialized was an arrangement whereby the EU outsourced the conduct or command and control of military operations to NATO. Thus the alliance's Supreme Headquarters Allied Powers Europe (SHAPE) took on the functions of operational headquarters, arguably presenting an obstacle to EU planning especially in emergency, crisis situations (Biscop, 2012: 1304–5).

Some institutional developments in the European defence field have nonetheless found Britain taking the initiative especially in collaboration with France, the other major military power in the EU. A key factor in this move was what was perceived as the ineffectiveness of EU foreign, security and defence policy in Bosnia and in the later Kosovo conflict with dependence on US-led NATO military intervention. A possible additional consideration on the British side was the opportunity to project leadership in Europe. Blair was particularly obsessed by the fear that exclusion from the euro area would adversely affect British leadership in Europe and on the global stage. It was against this background that a St Malo meeting between Blair and President Chirac of France took place in December 1998 and resulted in the St Malo Declaration.

This Declaration affirmed that the EU must have the capacity for autonomous action backed up by credible military force and acting in conformity with NATO as the collective defence of its members. British governments had hitherto resisted the formation of a specifically EU military force. The Blair government, however, hereby supported the principle of an EU military force. Major qualifications, however, remained in being. Britain was to the fore in persuading the Washington administration that this move would not be detrimental to NATO. In the event, the St Malo Declaration opened the way for the eventual deployment of EU forces abroad in the form of the Rapid Reaction Force, mentioned above.

The subsequent response to major developments has been variable in character, sometimes giving substance to a common foreign and security policy, sometimes attracting misdirected criticism, and on other occasions highlighting fundamental strategic differences between the EU member states. Some aspects of British leadership and involvement in the EU's external affairs were underrated or unmentioned for reasons discussed in Chapters 4 and 5. As a Conservative government minister noted in 2012, it was during Britain's presidency of the European Council (July–December 2005) under the Blair government that more CSDP operations were launched than under any other presidency before or since, adding that Britain has led two of the EU's most influential military missions – in Bosnia-Herzegovina and off the Horn of Africa – and provided civilian and military personnel to many others. This same source concluded that 'It may not suit the stereotype, but the contribution that Britain and France have made to CSDP has been indispensable [*sic*]' (Lidington, 2012).

Case studies: Iraq, Libya, Iran and the United States

The US-led invasion of Iraq in March 2003 revealed deep divisions within the EU. Some EU states headed by Britain and including Denmark, Italy, Portugal, Spain, the Netherlands and the eight EU candidate states in central and eastern Europe supported this action, Britain and Poland participating militarily in the US-led 'coalition of the willing'. They justified their actions on the grounds that the Saddam Hussein regime in Iraq had 'weapons of mass destruction'. Other EU states, however, led by France and Germany and including Belgium, Greece, Luxembourg and neutral states such as the Republic of Ireland opposed the invasion and flatly rejected the claim that Iraq had weapons of mass destruction, a view that subsequently proved to be correct. The absence of a second UN resolution supporting military intervention amounted in their view to a flouting of international law.

Undiplomatic language on both sides further inflamed the situation. Donald Rumsfeld, US Secretary of State for Defence, dismissed France and Germany as 'old Europe'. French President Chirac advised the candidate EU states in central and eastern Europe that they were junior partners in the EU and should therefore remain quiet. Chirac also directed his fire at the Blair government so much so that co-operation on defence matters between the two countries and symbolized by the St Malo Declaration appeared under threat; Chirac is said to have ordered his staff not to assist British dip- lomats in the further development of the ESDP (Cini, 2007: 249).

The toppling of another dictator, however, General Gadaffi of Libya, did involve Britain and France acting in concert, including joint activity as the two permanent European members of the UN Security Council. A UN Security Council resolution in March 2011 authorized its member states to take all necessary measures to protect civil- ians and civilian populated areas under threat of attack in Libya. Britain and France took the lead in mounting an air operation to enforce a No Fly Zone. US military assistance was required and offered, and accepted, notably in relation to air-to-air refu- eling, targeting, and precision-guided munitions. Washington, however, did not wish to take the lead and had no intention of committing ground forces. In the circumstances it was finally agreed to absorb the air campaign into NATO with political control by an expanded NATO format including participating Arab countries (HM Government, 'Review of the Balance of Competences between the United Kingdom and the European Union Foreign Policy', July 2013: 34).

This outcome admits of different interpretations in terms of the role and signifi- cance of the EU. Most obviously it suggests a failing of EU security and defence policy. Britain and France acted in the Libyan operation on the basis of their NATO rather than EU status, while Germany refused to take part in any military operation in or over Libya. There was a palpable lack of any collective European view on the scope of Europe's responsibilities in the security field. Certainly, this episode broke new ground in that the Europeans initiated action on a crisis in their neighbourhood. However, the inability of the EU as such to provide any substantial military support was viewed by one group of Conservative parliamentarians as providing 'the final evidence of the irrelevance of the CSDP' (HM Government, 'Review of the Balance of Competences between the United Kingdom and the European Union Foreign Policy', July 2013: 35).

An altogether different view of the matter, however, emphasizes that the EU's com- mon foreign and security policy is not designed to deal with issues arising from sub- stantial US involvement, leadership and resources. The EU is therefore being criticized for failing to undertake a task for which it is not equipped. Its strengths lie not in 'hard security policy' but in addressing the aftermath of conflict in the form of humanitar- ian assistance and development aid. It may nonetheless be the case, as one study puts it, that Libya demonstrated that there is still not enough Europe in European security, either politically or militarily, and that in future there is likely to be less America in European security (Biscop, 2012: 1309).

In spite of its military assistance, the Libyan operation underlined US refusal on this occasion and later in Syria to commit ground forces. This position, all the stronger with the withdrawal of American forces from Iraq (2011) and from Afghanistan (by 2017), was accompanied by increasing US pressure on the EU states to make a greater contribution to Europe's defence and security. That in itself was scarcely new as the Americans had long sought to persuade European states to make a greater contribution to NATO. What was relatively new was the accompanying acceptance of a greater degree of European defence identity and, it has been argued, an attitude of benign neglect towards the defence of Europe (Biscop, 2012: 1312). There is in fact abundant evidence to suggest that the United States no longer regards CSDP as a duplication of or threat to NATO. It is rather the case that the shift in the US strategic focus of attention away from Europe towards Asia is increasingly accompanied by the view that the EU should use CSDP to take more responsibility in international security and defence especially in stabilizing its own neighbourhood. In this context, British attempts to block further European military co-operation now find less favour in Washington than in the early decades of NATO's history.

The role of the EU in relations with Iran is often cited as indicative of the EU's success in foreign policy and also as adding weight to particular British concerns in the area. Arguably, lessons were learnt from the EU's disarray over the invasion of Iraq that made for the EU's much better handling of Iran's nuclear programme (Cooper, 2012: 1199). Since 2004 the EU has played a prominent role first as a mediator between Iran and the international community and subsequently as an assertive actor capable of formulating its own policy. The substance of this policy was that military action against Iran's ambitions to develop a nuclear bomb was unacceptable and that the EU's position should be governed by the doctrine of effective multilateralism, meaning the EU's close involvement with other international institutions like the UN in the search for diplomatic engagement and a peaceful solution.

In 2006, the five permanent members of the UN Security Council (China, France, Russia, the United Kingdom and the United States) plus Germany began a diplomatic engagement with Iran to secure a peaceful, negotiated solution to the nuclear issue and the use of sanctions to persuade Iran to negotiate seriously. The High Representative of the European Union for Foreign Affairs and Security Policy was involved from the outset, this accounting for the shorthand representation E3/EU+3 meaning the three European states, the EU High Representative, and China, Russia and the United States. The role of the High Representative in convening the negotiations and in acting as an honest broker throughout the diplomatic proceedings was widely acknowledged in July 2015 when an agreement was reached whereby Iran was offered sanctions relief and an end to its international isolation in exchange for its pledge to stop its quest for a nuclear bomb. EU policy towards Iran throughout this period was driven by its need to access Iranian energy reserves, as the country reportedly possesses the biggest combined energy deposits in the world, with the fourth largest oil reserves and the second largest natural gas reserves.

During the lengthy negotiations with Iran, it can be argued that the EU acted as a multiplier for British influence on Iran. British interests in effect could be pursued through two channels – as an EU member and as a state represented in the negotiations. As the latter, acting on its own so to speak, it could not have brought to bear the same kind of pressure exerted by the EU, not least when in 2012 the EU imposed an oil embargo on Iran and thus demonstrated the ability to impose far more painful sanctions than Britain could do alone (HM Government, 'Review of the Balance of Competences between the United Kingdom and the European Union Foreign Policy', July 2013).

A similar consideration is evident in relations between the EU and United States, particularly where the EU has exclusive competence such as on trade. Current negotiations on a Transatlantic Trade and Investment Partnership (TTIP) are a case in point. While this proposal has attracted critics, a less contested feature of the scheme is the extent to which EU membership adds value and weight to British policy. EU–US trade represents the world's largest intercontinental commercial flow. In particular, the EU and the United States account for 47 per cent of the world's GDP and one-third of global trade flows. The daily bilateral trade in goods and services is worth almost two billion euros, while aggregate investment stocks are over two trillion euros (HM Government, 'Review of the Balance of Competences between the United Kingdom and the European Union Foreign Policy', July 2013: 52). Whether desirable or not, there is little disputing the view that Britain acting on its own as a negotiator is unlikely to command the influence derived from EU representation.

A common feature of these and other such case studies concerns the distinctive position of Britain in the international system. On any foreign policy issue Britain has access to a complex network of alliances and partnerships in the world at large. This position is almost unrivalled among European states with the possible exception of France. In that respect, other EU states have less diplomatic reach and fewer options beyond the EU. Germany as Europe's economic superpower for much of the past 70 years has preferred the role of a regional European power in the defence and security field, sometimes attracting criticism for being 'a bigger version of Switzerland'. Berlin has long demonstrated persistent ambivalence at the idea of employing German military force in a war situation, most notably refusing to do so during the Gulf war (1990–1991) and at the time of NATO military intervention in Libya (2011). The former episode was particularly viewed in right-wing Conservative circles as a welcome revitalization of the Anglo-Saxon partnership as compared with 'the flabbiness of a European Community dominated by a lobotomized German economic giant' (quoted in Gifford, 2014: 110).

It is a matter of common observation among British foreign policymakers and diplomats that a wide range of options in international affairs is an asset. Evidence submitted to the Review of the Balance of Competences (July 2013) indicated that 'The UK still finds herself in a position of privilege, with the options of acting in unilateral, limited multilateral or wider alliance modes' and that according to another witness 'In a complex world a choice of identities is a plus not a minus' (HM Government, 'Review of the Balance of Competences between the United Kingdom and the European Union Foreign Policy', July 2013: 34). Set against that background, the EU figures as one forum among many in which to pursue British interests, not of supreme or unique importance but nonetheless holding out a number of advantages to be weighed against what are perceived as disadvantages.

The advantages and disadvantages of working through the EU in foreign and defence policy

One representation of the advantages and disadvantages of working through the EU in foreign and defence policy is to be found in the extensive Review of the Balance of Competences between Britain and the EU with reference to foreign policy (July 2013). On the basis of evidence submitted from a wide variety of sources, this Review summarized its conclusions about the value added and comparative disadvantages for Britain of working through the EU in the foreign policy field. The following is an abbreviated version of these conclusions, some of which figure elsewhere in this book.

How the EU adds value:

- Strength in numbers.
- Britain's position in the EU gives it more influence internationally.
- Size/economic weight of the Single Market and commercial benefit.
- The reach and magnitude of EU financial instruments.

- Maximizing the use of British resources.
- The range and versatility of the EU's tools.
- The EU's perceived political neutrality.
- The EU is often effective where the member states, and in particular Britain, France and/or Germany, are fully aligned and driving policy.
- Coordination of assistance to an overwhelming crisis.

The disadvantages of working through the EU:

- Decision-making by unanimity or qualified majority voting can lead to 'lowest common denominator' results.
- The EU would benefit from clearer, stronger strategy.
- Uneven leadership.
- Institutional divisions can impede policy implementation.
- Slow decision-making.
- The complexity of funding instruments can impede policy implementation.
- Tensions between EU policy and the interests of member states.

In this 93-page review, three observations sum up the limited importance of this issue in the context of any renegotiation of Britain's terms of EU membership. First, it was noted that the EU was not seen as punching its weight on foreign policy, or as one commentator put it: 'The issue is not legal competence, but competence in general'. Second, the majority of the evidence presented in the Review maintained that it was generally strongly in Britain's interest to work through the EU in foreign policy and that on balance Britain 'gets more out than it puts in, although the achievements are often modest'. Third, as all significant decisions regarding European defence matters continue to rest with the member states, one contributor to the Review commented 'There is nothing to repatriate on the defence side' (HM Government, 'Review of the Balance of Competences between the United Kingdom and the European Union Foreign Policy', July 2013: 63, 76, 89). In combination, these views indicate very clearly why British involvement in the EU's common defence and security policy scarcely features as a subject in any renegotiation of the terms of British membership of the EU, or for that matter in many Eurosceptic lists of criticisms of British membership of the EU.

Conclusion

This chapter has reviewed the relationship between the global perspectives, dimensions and dynamics of Britain's foreign policy and the country's role and commitments in the field of the EU's external relations. We have discussed in particular the impact of Britain's extra-European interests and ties on the country's role in and contribution to the EU. In the former case, we have considered the influence of a 'great power' mentality, the nature and significance of the Commonwealth dimension and the imperial legacy, and the influence of the 'special relationship' with the United States. In the latter case, we have noted some of the distinctive features of Britain's contribution to the EU and also assessed evidence of what the country has gained from the relationship in external relations.

At the time of the first British application to join the EC in 1961, some critics of this policy dismissed the prospect of British membership of the EC as a substitute for

Empire. It is certainly possible to point out similarities or parallels between the Empire and the EU: the EU's Single Market as a deeper version of imperial preference, the EU's free movement of workers and the free access of Commonwealth immigrants to Britain before 1962, the right to vote of Commonwealth citizens in British elections and the right to vote of EU citizens in British elections for local and European Parliament elections.

None of which is to say that the EU has simply replaced the 'British Empire and Commonwealth circle' of the Churchillian model of Britain's world role. Nor can it be said that Britain has discovered a new role in world affairs in response to the comment of Dean Acheson, the US Secretary of State, December 1962, to the effect that Britain had lost an empire and not yet found a role. For some the loss and lack of definition are all too apparent: 'We don't know who we are as a nation, we don't know where we are in the world' according to an anonymous Conservative MP quoted by William Wallace in a House of Lords debate (November 2014).

For their own part, British policymakers have long insisted that the country has many roles in world affairs and that British foreign policy is necessarily multidimensional, omnidirectional and flexible. Where they part company from their peers in some other EU states is in a steadfast refusal to acknowledge the paramount importance of the EU circle to Britain's role in the world. It is sufficient that the evolution and emphases of the EU's common foreign and security policy have generally served British interests and reflected British influence.

12 Still leading from behind

The Conservatives and the European Union since 2010

Include me out.
        (Sam Goldwyn, American film producer)

Introduction

This chapter considers the question of Britain's EU membership during the Cameron Coalition government of 2010–2015. It also examines more briefly and tentatively the treatment of the EU issue following the general election of May 2015 and the return to power of the Cameron Conservative government. In particular, the chapter traces the emergence of the idea of a referendum on Britain's EU membership, the accompanying debate within the Conservative Party and among the public at large, and the handling of the process of renegotiation.

There were several defining moments in the evolution of British policy towards the EU under the Cameron Coalition government. To a greater or lesser extent, each signalled Conservative disengagement from the EU, and each revealed a by now familiar fixation or obsession with EU matters within the Conservative Party. During this period, the idea of Brexit (Britain's exit from the EU) increasingly became a badge of honour among some Conservative ministers and backbenchers. Meanwhile, Cameron's handling of the issue often resembled an increasingly forlorn attempt to deal with opposition to EU membership and to appease the unappeasable.

In coalition

A Coalition government came to power following the general election of May 2010. Under the leadership of David Cameron, it comprised Conservative and Liberal Democrat representation with the former in the dominant position. This new government with its 77 parliamentary seat majority presented to outside observers a wide variety of views and positions on the EU. The Conservatives eventually committed themselves to renegotiating Britain's terms of EU membership and to holding a referendum on the matter by the end of 2017, in the event of a Conservative victory in the 2015 general election. Meanwhile, a still pro-EU Liberal Democrat element refused to countenance this Conservative commitment.

Neither renegotiation nor referendum figured in either the Conservative election manifesto of 2010 or in the Coalition Agreement on Europe (May 2010). This Agreement declared that there was to be no further transfer of sovereignty or powers to the EU over the course of the 2010–2015 parliament. This declaration laid the basis for the European Union ('EU') Act of 2011 and for the so-called referendum lock. The main provisions of the Act were:

- Any future proposal to transfer power by Treaty change from the UK to the EU shall be approved by an Act of Parliament, and by a referendum.
- Acts of Parliament, and in some cases a referendum, are required to approve certain other decisions under the EU Treaties including the use of *passerelles* [a legislative tool which allows for changes in scope of EU action or changes to ways measures are agreed, without specific Treaty change].
- Directly applicable or directly effective EU law is only recognized and available in national law by virtue of the European Communities Act or another Act of Parliament.

> (HM Government 'Review of the Balance of
> Competences between the United Kingdom and the
> European Union Police and Criminal Justice', December 2014: 28)

'Banging on about Europe'

What was long forgotten as the EU became a fixation or obsession within the Conservative Party was Cameron's warning at the Conservative Party conference in October 2006 that the electorate cared far more about other matters than 'banging on about Europe'. Prior to entering parliament and according to one account, Cameron referred to the EU in disobliging terms and held that the EU was a stitch-up between the French and the Germans. There appears to be some confusion over his precise views at this stage. As a special adviser at the Treasury, he reportedly told Norman Lamont, the Chancellor of the Exchequer, that he was 'Eurosceptic, but not as Eurosceptic as you'. On later seeking a parliamentary seat, he insisted on classification as a 'Eurosceptic' but acknowledged that he did not favour withdrawal from the EU (Ashcroft and Oakeshott, 2015: 125–6, 490), seemingly appearing as a Eurosceptic but not stridently so.

Cameron's first encounter with 'Europe' as a matter of personal party management occurred at the time of his bid to become Conservative Party leader. During the election campaign for the leadership in 2005 he promised to withdraw the Conservative Members of the European Parliament (MEPs) from the European People's Party (EPP). The EPP was the largest political bloc in the Parliament and principally comprised centre-right, national Christian Democrat and conservative parties. To a large extent this pledge was part of the loose change that bought Cameron the support of the right wing in the Conservative Party that strongly opposed the EPP's support for a federal EU. In 2009, the Conservatives helped to form the European Conservatives and Reformists (ECR) group in the Parliament.

From the outset, several discernible features of Cameron's handling of the EU membership issue have attracted the attention of commentators. First, he had no pronounced convictions or beliefs about the EU: 'Let me get this straight. I am no Euro obsessive' he declared in May 2003. As leader of the Conservative Party in opposition, moreover, he took the view that on coming to power 'we cannot afford to waste time having a row with Europe' (quoted in Charter, 2012: 70). Certainly, he recognized the economic importance of membership, acknowledged the relationship between membership and toxic issues like immigration, and held a generalized view about EU membership and Britain's standing in the world. Beyond that, however, he was unencumbered by any strong ideological commitments or preferences about Europe, seemingly personifying ambivalence. He was unwilling to view Europe as a 'die-in-the ditch' issue, as one of his Cabinet colleagues put it, eschewing descriptions such as Europhile and Eurosceptic, and belonging to neither the Heathite nor Thatcherite schools of thought on European integration. In many respects he resembled Harold Wilson rather than Harold Macmillan (with whom he is sometimes likened) in his management of the European question, most obviously in the twists and turns accompanying the commitment to renegotiation and a referendum. One biography notes in its preface that long after he became prime minister, the impression persisted that Cameron 'was more interested in holding the office than in using its power to achieve anything in particular' (Ashcroft and Oakeshott, 2015). According to another source, Cameron was ideally equipped to be prime minister because 'he doesn't believe in anything very much' (*The Spectator*, 18 February 2016).

Cameron himself declared that he did not see EU membership as a resigning matter in the event of a referendum vote that went against his advice. He claimed that his authority rested on holding the vote and abiding by the result in accordance with his party's 2015 election manifesto (*The Guardian*, 10 January 2016). Some strands of Eurosceptic opinion, however, argued that his authority was undermined as he was ultimately forced to hold a referendum on membership.

Second, a further public impression of Cameron's persona suggests a laissez-faire approach to issues and what some of his critics viewed as a casual disregard for the possible implications and consequences of decision-making, often demonstrating a peculiar compound of a languid style and chutzpah in personal relations. The decision noted above about withdrawing from the EPP is a case in point. It meant most immediately that as leader of the opposition he distanced himself and his party from the EPP. The EPP included the German Christian Democrats, the party of German Chancellor Angela Merkel whose later support was, rightly or wrongly, regarded as crucial in assisting British policy in the EU before and during the process of renegotiating the terms of membership. Time and again, the Conservative Party found itself locked out from the deliberations of the influential EPP at crucial moments as in the case of the Juncker appointment (see below). Worse still from Merkel's point of view, following the EP elections of 2014 the Conservative MEPs formed a bloc with her bitter domestic political opponents, the anti-EU and anti-immigrant party Alternative für Deutschland (AfD). Meanwhile, Cameron sought to cultivate close personal relations with Merkel, believing that she was the key to a successful renegotiation of Britain's terms of EU membership.

Third, Cameron's management of the Conservative Party on the question of Britain's EU membership has long attracted critical comment as a protracted exercise in seeking to appease the unappeasable on the question of EU membership. This has involved less a case of leadership than of speaking as little as possible about the matter until forced to do so and of taking the line of least resistance or by means of temporary expedients seeking to fend off or neutralize opposition. Thus, Paddy Ashdown, the former Liberal

Democrat leader, observed that Cameron 'has highly developed skills in the art of following where he should be leading' (*The Guardian*, 7 September 2015).

The problems of detecting Cameron's precise views on the question of EU membership are all too evident in the marked contrast between two of his reported opinions. During a conversation with Chancellor Merkel in November 2012 about his negotiating position ahead of the referendum he declared: 'I need to make a pitch to the country. If there is no acceptable deal, it's not the end of the world. I'll walk away from the EU' (Seldon and Snowdon, 2015: 264). Privately, in January 2014, however, he assured the French President Hollande that he wanted Britain to stay in Europe (Ashcroft and Oakeshott, 2015: 506). Such reports, of course, involve different audiences at different times, but nonetheless raised questions about Cameron's position.

We will first examine these not uncommon impressions in terms of the performance of the Cameron Coalition government.

Veto

The first major event in the direction of 'walking away' and the politics of disengagement actually occurred at the European Council in December 2011 when Cameron vetoed the proposal for an EU treaty-based Fiscal Compact (see Chapter 10). The veto followed his failure to secure safeguards against the possibility of greater fiscal coordination within the euro area distorting the EU Single Market.

This veto, supported only by the Czech Republic, was a strange affair in that it was circumvented by the other 25 EU states and became known as 'the veto that never was'. Unable to introduce the Fiscal Compact as a full EU treaty, from which Britain would have been granted an opt-out, the 25 EU states simply introduced it on the basis of intergovernmental co-operation and accordingly signed (January 2012) what was to be known as the Treaty on Stability, Coordination and Governance (TSCG). The veto had little practical effect except in the context of domestic Conservative politics. Moreover, Cameron's initial, seemingly churlish insistence that the 25 EU states could not use EU premises for their monthly meetings was subsequently abandoned. Meanwhile, Britain was permitted to occupy a not unfamiliar role as an observer at such gatherings.

There were markedly different accounts of the nature and significance of this episode in terms of Cameron's behaviour. They ranged from the view that he had passed an important political virility test to criticism of his lack of preparation and cack-handed diplomacy. His particular attempt to secure safeguards for the British financial services sector [hereafter the City] pointed to a major dilemma that faced British policymakers. At one and the same time, they wanted to prevent the euro area from rigging rules to harm the City, while acknowledging that deeper euro area integration was a prerequisite for a stable and prosperous euro area in the interests of British trade (see Chapter 10).

The Eurosceptic press hailed the veto as a welcome, spectacular PR coup, suggesting that Cameron had at last won his spurs. A commentator in *The Times* was mock delirious: 'This was Cameron's Agincourt moment. This was his Spanish Armada. This was the moment when King Dave joined the pantheon of Great Britons who have heroically resisted continental Europe's recurrent quest for unity – and hegemony' (*The Times*, 10 December 2011). Days after the veto, Cameron was warmly received by the 1922 Committee (of all backbench Conservative MPs) with a full-on orgy of 'desk banging and hysteria'. Veteran opponents of British membership of the EU in the parliamentary

Conservative Party like Bill Cash and Bernard Jenkin detected a 'watershed' and the path to 'fundamental renegotiation' (Seldon and Snowdon, 2015: 177).

Other more critical comment viewed Cameron's conduct as an abject failure in that he had opposed the idea of a treaty that would not actually have applied to Britain. In addition, he had pressed a sectional interest, the City, at a time when the euro was argu-ably at the lowest point in its history and required substantial backing. Furthermore, walking away from the negotiating table for observer status was very much an action at variance with Britain's long-standing policy towards the EU and even attracted critical comment in the City (*Financial Times*, 26 June 2012). Constantly playing to the Eurosceptic gallery at home, moreover, scarcely cultivated allies elsewhere in the EU: '*Auf Wiedersehen, England*' was how the most influential German news magazine, *Der Spiegel*, reacted to this episode.

Still other critics viewed the veto as the action of a fathomless opportunist who would have been seriously surprised or disappointed by any other outcome. It was also noted that this defence of City interests was taking place when the City was providing half of all Conservative Party funding. Privately, Cameron himself reflected that the positive reaction showed an entrenched Euroscepticism among most British voters, giving rise to thoughts about whether any party could enter the 2015 general election campaign without some sort of referendum pledge (Ashcroft and Oakeshott, 2015: 495).

At the time, however, he was still battling against the idea of a referendum on EU membership. Only two months earlier (October 2011), 81 Conservative backbenchers had defied party orders on a three-line whip and had supported a referendum on British membership of the EU. This episode was the biggest post-1945 rebellion on Europe and larger even than the 41 Conservative MPs who had defied Major over the Maastricht Treaty in 1993.

Cameron's room for manoeuvre was also constrained by the existence of the European Union Act of July 2011. This parliamentary measure made any substantial transfers of power from Westminster to Brussels subject to a referendum, and thus placed major obstacles to further involvement in the process of integration. Regardless of content or application, an EU treaty signed by Cameron at this stage would have further inflamed Eurosceptic opinion within the Conservative Party. It was in any case out of line with Cameron's view favouring the repatriation of powers from Brussels. The latter had fig-ured as a Conservative Party commitment in its general election manifesto of 2010 together with ruling out euro membership indefinitely. These commitments indicated how far Eurosceptic opinion had advanced in the party and continued to do so with the 2010 intake of Conservative Party MPs.

The Cameron case for 'less' rather than 'more' Europe was diametrically opposed by Angela Merkel, the German chancellor. In a speech in the German Bundestag (September 2011), she left no doubt that 'If the euro falls, Europe fails'. She further maintained that the completion of economic and monetary union and the building of political union in Europe 'does not mean less Europe, it means more Europe' (*The Times*, 14 November 2011). Merkel's view was all the more important, because this treaty was largely a German-inspired creation at a time when the markets would not accept that sufficient action had been taken to prevent euro area states from defaulting on their debts. Cameron's concerns seemed all the more parochial against the immediate background of an acute euro area crisis. At the time, Greece was imploding politically, and Italy was on the brink of being cut off from global financial markets as its sovereign debt approached two trillion euros – the fourth largest debt pile in the world.

In the aftermath of the veto there commenced a debate that revolved around the country's possible loss of influence and greater isolation for failing to sign the treaty. For the government, David Lidington, the Minister of State for Europe in the Cameron Coalition government who remained so after the general election of May 2015, acknowledged a 'theoretical risk' of British isolation. He noted, however, that similar warnings accompanied the British decision not to adopt the euro and that such warnings had proved unjustified in the light of subsequent events.

A widely held criticism of the veto echoed the American political saying that 'You're either at the table or you're on the menu'. It was feared that the other EU states would 'gang up on the UK', and that Britain would be in solitary confinement in the EU 'barred from key meetings, rendering us voteless and voiceless' according to Emma Reynolds, the Labour Party's opposition Shadow Europe Minister (*H.C. Deb.*, 29 February 2012). A more authoritative expression of this view came from Dominic Grieve whose experience of EU business as Attorney General (2010–2014) in the Cameron Coalition government caused him to conclude that the case for EU reform 'cannot be achieved by critics being outside the conversation … we need a dialogue and not a British monologue' (Palliser Lecture, 2015).

The Juncker episode

Although not quite as dramatic as exercising a veto, the controversy over the successor to Barroso as president of the EU Commission in 2014 nonetheless encapsulated much about the approach of Cameron and the Conservative Party to EU matters. From the outset, Cameron was a determined opponent of the leading candidate for this post, Jean-Claude Juncker, on the grounds that he held EU federalist views. Juncker was the lead candidate (*Spitzenkandidaten*) in the European Parliament (EP) where he had the support of the EPP, the largest political bloc in the newly elected EP (May 2014), the bloc that the Conservatives had left in 2009. Juncker was also the favoured choice of Angela Merkel. Under the Lisbon Treaty of 2009, the president of the Commission is elected by the EP after a candidate is put forward by the European Council while taking into account the EP election results. Cameron argued with some justification that this took the decision out of the hands of the European Council and that the EP was seeking to enhance its power against the European Council. However, he lacked any political influence with respect to the EPP due to his earlier decision to take the Conservative Party out of this bloc.

Cameron issued dire warnings about the likely implications of Juncker's appointment for successfully renegotiating Britain's EU membership (see below). There was limited regard on the British side, however, for why Juncker's appointment would be bad for the EU at large, this being indicative in some quarters of an inability or unwillingness to represent what is judged to be a British national interest as a European necessity. Meanwhile, sections of the British press rallied to the cause and subjected Juncker to their tender mercies, smearing him for his alleged drinking habits and resorting to tasteless headlines: 'Junck the drunk'.

This whole affair was strangely reminiscent of a similar event 20 years earlier when John Major aimed to appease Eurosceptic opinion in the Conservative Party by vetoing the appointment of Jean-Luc Dehaene, the Belgian prime minister, to replace Delors as president of the European Commission. Major's Eurosceptic critics were temporarily appeased by his show of defiance. The fact that he was obliged to accept another candidate, Jacques Santer, the prime minister of Luxembourg, whose views were indistinguishable from those of the original candidate, was beside the point. In this instance, Major's determination to fight for British interests, as in Cameron's case, could be interpreted very differently, by supporters as demonstrating a bulldog spirit and by critics as evidence of a weak leader masquerading as a strong man in the face of criticism within his own party.

In June 2014, Cameron called for a vote in the European Council on the Juncker candidature, an unprecedented move on such occasions. The result of the vote – only Britain and Hungary opposed the candidature in a 26/2 split between the member states – was somehow represented by Cameron as 'a bad day for Europe' together with what was to become a familiar warning of its likely adverse impact on any British renegotiation of EU membership. The outcome was variously represented in the British press as a form of splendid isolation or a humiliating failure of judgement. The latter was expressed by Boris Johnson who dismissed the attempt to block the Juncker appointment as 'the quintessence of turd-polishing pointlessness' (*The Sunday Telegraph*, 8 June 2014).

It was in response to this affair that Michel Rocard, the former prime minister of France (1988–1991), declared that the British 'vetoes' of Dehaene and Juncker were all of a piece with long-standing British wrecking tactics in the EU, these being principally motivated by the view that 'You do not like Europe'. According to Rocard, British governments had long aimed to keep the EU a 'political dwarf'. They favoured paralysis and also stood in the way of the reform and democratization of the EU that they professed to support. Rocard's parting advice to the British government was starkly put: 'go before you wreck everything' (*Le Monde*, 6 June 2014). Nor was this a case of French sources predictably casting Britain in the worst possible light. This view was widely shared across the Rhine where a *Der Spiegel* editorial charged British governments with persistent blackmail tactics. It further claimed that Cameron was riding roughshod over the EP election results of May 2014 in opposing Juncker's candidature, and concluded that there was now a clear choice between a more democratic EU and Britain's continued EU membership (*Der Spiegel*, 3 June 2014).

The Bloomberg speech

Besides what his critics viewed as his maladroit handling of the Juncker candidature, Cameron was also taken to task for his timing of the pledge to hold a referendum on British membership of the EU by the end of 2017 and following a renegotiation of Britain's relationship with the EU. This commitment was made in his long-awaited speech at the Bloomberg offices in London (23 January 2013). He likened the making of the speech to the drawn-out joys of tantric sex. In any event, it was arguably the most significant foreign policy speech of his premiership. It was also a speech that he had not wanted to make but had to do so as pressure piled up on him from all sides to make some kind of defining statement of his thinking. Conservative Cabinet and parliamentary opinion in favour of a commitment to a referendum on Britain's EU membership had become virtually unstoppable by this stage (Seldon and Snowdon, 2015: 257–8).

In this speech, Cameron insisted that as an 'island nation' Britain had a distinctive view of Europe but was not 'un-European'. He identified five principles for his 'vision for a new European Union, fit for the twenty-first century':

• Competitiveness: 'creating a leaner, less bureaucratic Union, relentlessly focused on helping its member countries to compete'.

- Flexibility: 'We need a structure that can accommodate the diversity of its members – North, South, East, West, large, small, old and new. Some of whom are contemplating much closer economic and political integration. And many others, including Britain, who would never embrace that goal'.
- Power back to members: 'power must be able to flow back to the member States, not just away from them'.
- Democratic accountability: 'we need to have a bigger and more significant role for national parliaments. There is not, in my view, a single European demos. It is national parliaments, which are, and will remain, the true source of real democratic legitimacy and accountability in the EU'.
- Fairness: 'whatever new arrangements are enacted for the euro area, they must work fairly for those inside it and out'.

(House of Commons Library
Research Papers, 29 April 2014: 64–5)

This speech raised as many questions as answers. It remained unclear what exactly would be left of the EU if all of these criteria were met to the satisfaction of a future Conservative government – possibly a free trade area comparable to that unsuccessfully explored by the Macmillan government in the period 1956–1958. It was equally unclear to the other member states what precisely Cameron had in mind in terms of any renegotiation.

Furthermore, this renegotiation and referendum commitment was viewed in some quarters as demonstrating a profound ignorance of the way the EU works, at least if anything more than a cosmetic exercise was envisaged. In short, a timetable choreographed to suit the domestic politics of a British political party showed scant regard for the realities of EU politics and limited understanding of the likely obstacles to any settlement by that date. As one informed commentator put it, Cameron's timetable for achieving a renegotiation of the terms of membership and a referendum by the end of 2017 could only be conceived 'in cloud cuckoo land' and that the odds were overwhelmingly against achieving such an outcome on this timescale (Dick Tavern in *The Guardian*, 2 May 2014). Dominic Grieve, the former Attorney General in the Coalition government, later expressed similar criticisms, maintaining that there was a total lack of clarity as to how a government would proceed to unravel a relationship that had developed in complexity over more than 40 years and leaving a question hanging in the air: 'Which parts of the several thousand pieces of EU legislation that are currently incorporated into our statute law would be retained?' (Grieve, 2015). The body of EU legislation, i.e. the *'acquis communautaire'*, is, in fact, thought to comprise some 150,000 pages.

In some EU circles, there were considerable doubts about Cameron's strategy and tactics. Herman van Rompuy ruminated aloud about 'How do you convince a room full of people, when you keep your hand on the door handle?' More tellingly, Guido Westerwelle, the German foreign minister, made clear just how far from reality was Cameron's aspiration of a substantial renegotiation, commenting ' "You either do what I want or I'll leave" is not an attitude that works, either in personal relationships or in a community of nations' (*The Times*, 30 January 2013).

Prior to the EP elections of May 2014 and largely as a result of the rising tide of support for UKIP, Cameron gave a 'cast iron' guarantee of an in/out referendum by the end of 2017 under his premiership, regardless of whether or not he had managed to negotiate a package of reforms beforehand. 'Cast iron' was precisely the language that he had used when he offered the unfulfilled guarantee (September 2007) to hold a referendum on the Lisbon Treaty. That failure was long regarded by sections of Eurosceptic opinion in the Conservative Party as betrayal and caused a lack of trust in Cameron's leadership. In the event, the EP election results in May 2014 were disastrous for the Conservatives. UKIP emerged with the largest number of seats (24), while Labour was in second position (20) and the Conservatives trailed in third position (19); the first occasion for more than a century that neither the Labour nor Conservative parties had won a national election. In conversation with President Hollande of France at this time, Cameron explained that the referendum was 'the price we have to pay to contain the rise of Europhobia in England', to which the bemused Hollande replied 'But the opposite just happened', referring to UKIP's gains (Ashcroft and Oakeshott, 2015: 506).

In these circumstances, Cameron's reaction was to emphasize an ideally minimalist view of the EU, claiming that Brussels has 'got too big, too bossy, too interfering' and that it should be a case of 'nation states wherever possible, and Europe only where necessary' (*The Guardian*, 28 May 2014). In September 2014 he indicated that he would be prepared to recommend a vote to leave the EU if he failed to secure major changes to Britain's membership terms, while maintaining that he personally hoped to retain membership.

The eclipse of the Europhiles

By Autumn 2014, there was a seemingly unstoppable body of Eurosceptic opinion within the parliamentary Conservative Party. If temporarily appeased on one front, it simply opened up another front. It was increasingly unclear as to how far the Conservative leadership could go in claiming to believe in the benefits of EU membership while offering concessions and pledges to opponents of membership.

By this time, Ken Clarke, the veteran government minister and one of the few leading and vocal pro-EU spokespersons left in the Conservative Party, warned that appeasing the Eurosceptics was like 'feeding crocodiles'. He nevertheless conceded that the pro-EU case in the party no longer attracted support: 'it's a dead argument, we've lost' (*The Guardian*, 29–30 September 2014). The committed pro-EU advocate seemed to have become an endangered species largely confined to long-standing campaigners like Clarke himself and Michael Heseltine. Clarke's pessimistic view was shared by Charles Clarke, director of the pro-EU Centre for European Reform, who reckoned that the chances of Britain leaving the EU before 2020 were at least 50–50: 'I will fight to keep us in, but I think it's a losing battle' (Vail, 2015).

This view was all the more evident as the financial crisis of 2007–2008 greatly undermined the EU's reputation for delivering economic growth, prosperity and stability during a period (2009–2014) when the average annual growth in the euro area plunged to –0.2 per cent. Besides, a proactive European policy increasingly met strong headwinds in the form of popular Euroscepticism in the Conservative Party, in UKIP and in large sections of the media. Furthermore, a deathly silence rather than outspoken support for the EU descended on the traditionally pro-European Liberal Democrats.

Meanwhile, the Labour Party leadership opposed the Conservative-inspired push for a referendum. The issue of EU membership, however, remained so problematic that Ed Miliband, who succeeded Gordon Brown as Labour Party leader (September 2010), avoided mentioning it as much as he could in his first three years as leader. Like Brown he distanced himself from Blair's trumpeted euroenthusiasm. On finally delivering a speech on Europe (November 2012), he stressed the 'failures' of the EU and thereby blurred his message in favour of membership (Schnapper, 2014). At the same time he resisted calls from the media and from other quarters to support the Conservative programme for a renegotiation of EU membership and a referendum by the end of 2017. Under the leadership of Brown and Miliband, therefore, the handling of EU membership had much in common with that of Wilson and Callaghan in its ambivalent, pocket calculator approach to the matter. In addition, there was an alertness to the views of Labour's traditional constituency of support in areas under threat of an advance by UKIP.

The European Arrest Warrant and 'the debate that never was'

By late 2014, Eurosceptic opinion especially in the parliamentary Conservative Party was further outraged at the government's handling of the issue of the European Arrest Warrant. While this item attracted limited public interest, it greatly exercised Eurosceptic opinion in the Conservative Party so much so that Cameron promised a Commons debate and vote on the matter.

This particular controversy originated in two EU treaties: Maastricht (1992) and Lisbon (2007). Through the Maastricht Treaty, the EU acquired competence in the field of Justice and Home Affairs (JHA), originally one of the three pillars of the treaty and subsequently known as Police and Judicial Cooperation (PCJ) in criminal matters. The Lisbon Treaty extended full European Court of Justice (ECJ) jurisdiction and Commission enforcement powers to all pre-Lisbon legislation on police and judicial co-operation in criminal matters.

The British government, however, negotiated a specific Protocol to the Treaties on the grounds that the measures had not been negotiated with the ECJ in mind. The substance of this Protocol was that Britain was required to decide by 31 May 2014 whether or not it should continue to be bound by all PCJ measures which were adopted before the Lisbon Treaty entered into force. Furthermore, the government could exercise its right to opt out of all the measures or apply to rejoin individual measures. In July 2013, Cameron informed the EU Council of Ministers that the government intended to opt out of all pre-Lisbon measures, but that it wanted to rejoin a smaller number of measures to give British police and law enforcement agencies vital and practical help in the fight against crime and in view of earlier terrorist attacks in the United States (September 2001), Madrid (March 2004) and London (July 2005) (HM Government, 'Review of the Balance of Competences between the United Kingdom and the European Union Police and Criminal Justice', December 2014: 11).

Government plans to opt back into some of the measures, including and especially the European Arrest Warrant, were viewed by Eurosceptic opinion as transferring more powers to Brussels. More worryingly, they put at risk Conservative parliamentary seats in the face of the upsurge of support for UKIP. The promised debate and vote on the European Arrest Warrant as such did not materialize. It was thus dubbed 'the debate that never was', because when the Commons motion was published it mentioned only some of the minor EU justice and home affairs measures, and not the whole package including the European Arrest Warrant. The government held that those were the only measures that required legislation and that the Commons vote would be indicative of the views of MPs on the whole package.

In an extraordinary attack on the government's handling of the matter, however, John Bercow, Speaker of the House of Commons, spoke for many across the political spectrum when he suggested that the government's attempts to avoid a vote on the issue – and therefore a backbench rebellion – would be regarded by the public as contemptuous, that 'a commitment should be honoured', and that 'things should not be slipped through via some sort of artifice' (*The Guardian*, 10 November 2014). In the end, the government won the vote with only 36 MPs rebelling.

The Balance of Competences Review

The European Arrest Warrant episode seemed to mark a disagreeable epilogue to the Coalition government's management of EU policy. On the eve of the May 2015 general election campaign, however, the EU membership question sparked off further controversy, this time centring on the Balance of Competences Review. In July 2012 the Coalition government had launched this two-year Balance of Competences Review under the supervision of the FCO and envisaging some 32 reports examining all areas where the treaties gave the EU competence to act. The exercise was hailed by Foreign Secretary Hague as the most extensive analysis of the impact of the costs and benefits of British membership of the EU ever undertaken. Other EU states were invited to participate but snubbed the invitation. The general conclusion of the first such report was on foreign policy and emphasized among other things that the balance of competence lay squarely with the member states. This conclusion was viewed as a 'Whitehall whitewash' by some strands of Eurosceptic opinion in the Conservative Party, understandably so as the exercise was largely supervised by senior Whitehall officials.

Nothing more was heard about the matter until March 2015 when a cross-party group of peers accused government ministers of trying to 'bury' the results of this review after it found no evidence that the EU was interfering excessively in any aspect of British life. In fact, the FCO had put the reports on its website as and when they appeared, the final batch appearing in December 2014 (see Bibliography). The more damaging aspect of this revelation to Cameron and the Conservative government ministers was twofold in terms of their management of policy towards the EU.

First, the review flatly contradicted the main thrust of their criticism of the EU and in particular the constant claims that the EU was becoming a superstate, that it had accrued excessive powers, and that therefore there should be a repatriation of powers from Brussels. On the contrary, the review found no area with a case for transferring powers back from Brussels: 'The single, clear message from the review' commented David Hannay, former British ambassador to the EU, 'is that in none of its 32 chapters is there a compelling case for the repatriation of powers from Brussels to Westminster and Whitehall' (*The Guardian*, 29 March 2015). This conclusion demonstrated the extent to which British governance and policy had become transnational and Europeanized (Gifford, 2014: 173).

Second, the job of renegotiating the country's terms of membership could be made far more difficult for Cameron in the event of returning to power as prime minister following the general election. In particular, governments elsewhere in the EU would have noted that Whitehall officials believed that there was no real case for repatriating powers, making it all the more difficult to obtain either significant EU reform or substantial concessions from the other EU states to impress Eurosceptic opinion and the public at large.

By the spring of 2015, Cameron was virtually sidelined in EU circles in much the same way as Thatcher and Major in the closing stages of their premiership. Certainly, Britain still had allies, but none at this juncture seemed to want to associate with British ministers. A notable exception was Viktor Orbán, the Hungarian prime minister, who preferred the company of Russia's President Putin to that of his EU peers and whose xenophobic impulses were on full display in his handling of the refugee crisis in 2015–2016.

Chancellor Merkel seemingly had less and less patience with the British: 'If they want to go, they'll have to go'. Nevertheless, there was a fair amount of ideological affinity between Cameron and Merkel and at this time, as later, Cameron set great store by cultivating relations with the German chancellor by periodic charm offensives, while she recognized and made allowances for the pressure he was under from Eurosceptics in his own party (Ashcroft and Oakeshott, 2015: 497–9). Among other things, they had a shared view about the importance of austerity measures in balancing public accounts (at least until 2012 when the Coalition government abandoned its original target to clear the deficit by the end of the 2010–2015 parliament).

Furthermore, it seemed possible that Germany, still lacking in self-confidence and fearful of being corralled in a Britain-less EU with France and Italy, might see some advantage in meeting British demands for EU reform in order to keep Britain in the club. Other states like Italy and Poland viewed continuing British membership as a necessary counterweight to a Franco-German partnership. Meanwhile, Cameron and Chancellor of the Exchequer Osborne scarcely endeared themselves to French President Hollande when they unfavourably likened France to the kind of country that Britain might become if Ed Miliband, the leader of the Labour Party, became prime minister (*The Guardian*, 30 March 2015). They regarded Hollande as presiding over a failed economic model, and at one G20 summit Cameron caused considerable offence by openly mocking French tax policies, seemingly unaware that one day French support on the already swelling camp of migrants in Calais might be required to assist him in winning a referendum on British membership of the EU. A common criticism of Cameron's stint at the head of the Coalition government in the conduct of EU policy was his failure to do more to build coalitions of support.

The Franco-German relationship at the centre of the EU was still very much in evidence in February 2015 when Merkel and Hollande went to Moscow to secure a ceasefire in the Ukraine. It was a matter of pointed comment that Cameron did not join them, while one British diplomat scornfully dismissed this Franco-German move as 'vanity diplomacy'. A month later, Cameron attended his last European Council as prime minister of the 2010–2015 Coalition government, by which time he seemed to be an increasingly isolated and mistrusted figure in the EU (Seldon and Snowdon, 2015: 369). He reportedly quipped that the other leaders 'will be glad to see the back of me', and he raised issues – a VAT problem for small firms and a purely British fund for building democracy in post-Soviet states – that were not on the agenda, were of no interest to the rest of the company, and were scarcely comparable in importance to the matters of the day including the future of Greece in the euro area. In time, this also proved to be similar to the Conservative government's strategy and tactics in dealing with the renegotiation exercise, with the same disconnection between what some viewed as minutiae compared with the major issues confronting the EU. At the time the workings of the euro area, the immigration crisis, the limitations of austerity economic policy and Russian policy towards the Ukraine loomed far larger in the minds of other EU leaders.

Neither believing nor belonging

If the possibility of not belonging to the EU was now being aired in some Conservative Party circles, the idea of believing was now a non-starter. Two developments spoke volumes in this respect, besides the limited inspiration of Cameron's Bloomberg speech.

First, there was the scornful reception given to the news (October 2012) that the EU had received the Nobel Peace Prize. The prize was for advancing the causes of peace, reconciliation, democracy and human rights in Europe. Neither the prize nor the reasons for the award were welcomed by the British public at large and least of all by the Eurosceptic press. Cameron was one of six EU leaders who did not attend the prize-giving ceremony. There was no official acknowledgement at the highest level of government of what Chancellor Merkel called 'a wonderful decision'.

Sections of the British press left little doubt about their derision: 'Nobel Peace Prize? EU Have Got To Be Joking!' screamed a headline in *The Sun* (12 October 2012), 'Don't honour a Brussels office block' declared Boris Johnson (*The Daily Telegraph*, 15 October 2012), 'A little late for an April fool's joke' chortled Conservative MEPs (*Daily Mail*, 12 October 2012). The blank refusal to acknowledge that the EU had any achievements to its credit suggested that in such company a valedictory event to mark Britain's exit from the EU was already in preparation. Belief in the value of the EU had never figured in such company and now any sense of belonging had also vanished.

Second, in May 2014 Cameron indicated that the most important change he wanted to see in renegotiating Britain's relationship with the EU was to obtain an opt-out from the EU's founding aim of 'ever closer union'. The Cameron view effectively demolished any emotional, open-ended commitment to the idea of European integration. As Cameron put it in a speech on the same day as he submitted his letter to the president of the European Council specifying the areas for renegotiation: 'Like most British people, I come to this question with a frame of mind that is practical not emotional. Head, not heart' (Speech at the Royal Institute of International Affairs, 10 November 2015). This view signalled to some continental circles a strange British addiction to looking at Europe mainly on the basis of an economic calculus and through the prism of a book-keeping mentality.

Any other precise objectives of the renegotiation exercise, however, still remained a mystery. Predictably, the issue of EU membership was scarcely raised in the 2015 general election campaign nor for that matter, at least overtly, at the Conservative Party conference following the unexpected election of a Conservative government.

The Conservative government and renegotiation

As a result of the general election of May 2015, a Conservative government under Cameron came to power with a parliamentary majority of 12, the slimmest such majority since 1974, and with a vote share of 36.9 per cent. The idiosyncratic character of the electoral system meant that while UKIP amassed 3.881 million votes (the third largest vote share of any party) but won only one seat, the SNP won 56 seats with 1.454 million votes.

In the months following the election, Cameron refused to be pinned down on his renegotiation demands, fearful that anything in writing would quickly leak and leave him hostage to Eurosceptic critics attacking his demands as inadequate. There was no let-up in criticism from this quarter. Predictably the new government's first parliamentary defeat (September 2015) occurred when 37 Eurosceptic Conservative MPs joined with the Labour and SNP opposition to oppose government attempts to seek changes to purdah, the month-long period before a poll when government announcements and spending are restricted. The opposition argued that the government was trying to influence the referendum result in favour of continuing EU membership.

Technical discussions about renegotiation commenced in July 2015. Nothing of substance happened until, under increasing pressure from the other EU states, Cameron had perforce to agree to submit a paper detailing the areas where he was seeking reforms ahead of a European Council meeting in December 2015. The paper was submitted to Donald Tusk, president of the European Council, and identified four main areas where the government was seeking reforms.

The first area – economic governance – focused on relations between the euro area and non-euro area members of the EU (19 and 9 respectively). The substance of the British case was that there should be legally binding principles that safeguard the operation of the EU for all 28 members states and a safeguard mechanism to ensure these principles were respected and enforced.

The second area – competitiveness – consisted of two main proposals, these being that the EU should fix a target to cut the total burden of regulations on business and should also do more to fulfil its commitment to the free flow of capital, goods and services.

The third area – sovereignty – basically consisted of three main proposals:

1   to end Britain's obligation to work towards an 'ever closer union' as set out in EU treaties, and to do so in a formal, legally-binding and irreversible way;
2   to enhance the role of national parliaments by allowing groups of national parliaments, acting together, to stop unwanted legislative proposals;
3   to see EU commitments to subsidiarity fully implemented with clear proposals to achieve that.

The fourth area – immigration – aimed to ensure that:

1   when new countries are admitted to the EU in future free movement will not apply to those new members until their economies have converged much more closely with the existing member states;
2   people coming to Britain from the EU 'must live here and contribute for four years before they qualify for in-work benefits or social housing. And we should end the practice of sending child benefit overseas'.

(Cameron to Tusk, 10 November 2015)

The deal

At their meeting of 18–19 February 2016, EU leaders agreed on a new settlement for Britain in the EU. On the basis of this settlement, Cameron announced that the referendum would be held on 23 June 2016 when voters would cast their response to the following question:

> Should the United Kingdom remain a member of the European or leave the European Union?

[Hereafter in this chapter the words 'Remainers' and 'Leavers' are used in the text to distinguish between supporters and opponents of British membership of the EU.] Legally the referendum is advisory but in practice its result will be binding. If Britain formally declared that it wanted to leave the EU, it would have to negotiate with the 27 other members for up to two years about the terms of departure under Article 50 of the Treaty of Lisbon. Parliament would also still have to pass the laws extricating Britain from the EU, starting with the repeal of the 1972 European Communities Act.

The main features of this agreement were as follows and in accordance with the four areas noted above:

Economic governance

Recognition of and protection for the pound in the EU. Under new rules to be inserted in a future treaty, Britain would be able unilaterally to delay Eurozone legislation if it believes it discriminates against non-euro area countries. If disagreement persists, or a council of ministers threatens to override the objection with a vote, Britain can demand that the issue is discussed at a summit of EU leaders. Ultimately, however, Britain will not have a veto, as was originally hoped.

Competitiveness

This section comprised a number of general statements but little of substance or specific to add to the many EU declarations on the matter since the Lisbon Agenda of 2000. New trade agreements with non-EU countries, and any repeals or simplifications of EU laws, will be subject to approval of the other member states and the EU Parliament on a case-by-case basis.

Sovereignty

Britain secured exemption from the idea of 'ever closer union'. This exemption will officially take effect on the next amendment to the EU treaties for which there is no date. It was also agreed that EU member states would stop discussing a proposal for a new EU law if just over a majority of parliamentary chambers (55 per cent) objected to it (the so-called 'red card') – unless the points raised by those national parliaments were satisfactorily addressed.

Immigration

Britain can impose limits on in-work benefits for EU workers for a period of up to four years after they start working in Britain. The mechanism can only remain in place for seven years (the so-called emergency brake that the British government had wanted to keep for 13 years). Seven years matches the time period other EU states had to keep eastern Europeans out of their labour markets following the EU enlargement of 2004. Britain was one of the few countries to allow eastern European workers into its labour market immediately after the 2004 enlargement.

On child benefits, Cameron originally wanted to stop all payments of child benefit going to children living outside the UK, whose parents were working in the UK. In the event, it was agreed that child benefit payments would be indexed to the cost of living for children living outside the UK, under new EU legislation. This will apply to new arrivals to the UK once legislation has been passed, and to all workers from 1 January 2020.

It was also agreed to deny automatic free movement rights to nationals of a country outside the EU who marry an EU national, as part of measures to tackle 'sham' marriages.

'Special status'?

Cameron's original negotiating aims and the final settlement predictably received a very mixed reception. Among the Leavers there was widespread criticism that the original negotiating brief fell far short of the fundamental far-reaching changes Cameron had promised in his Bloomberg speech; 'Is that it?' expostulated Bernard Jenkin, the veteran Eurosceptic Conservative MP on hearing the areas where Cameron was seeking reforms. The final settlement in these quarters was variously dismissed as cosmetic, window-dressing, a charade, a theatrical sideshow, trivial and amounting to nothing – at best 'thin gruel' according to a leading editorial in *The Times* (20 February 2016). Cameron himself hailed the deal as 'substantive not superficial' and indicated that Britain had now been accorded 'special status' in the EU. Somewhere between these two positions and perhaps closer to the truth was the view that the deal was neither trivial nor transformative, as the Open Europe think tank declared, and that the deal 'achieves things that can make a difference' (*The Guardian*, 19 February 2016).

Continental opinion tended to confirm the Cameron view and feared for the future of the EU in that the deal 'enshrined a multi-speed Europe' (Romano Prodi, former president of the European Commission), 'amplified the movement towards Europe à la carte' (*Le Monde*) and involved paying a 'high and unjustifiable price to secure the continued membership of a wayward partner' (Spain's *El País*, *Financial Times*, 22 February 2016). Predictably on the British side, however, some voices subjected the rest of the EU states to a British-devised test. One of Cameron's ministers, a Remainer, declared that the EU was 'in the last-chance saloon. We owe them one chance to show us that they genuinely are not going to force us into stuff that we don't want to do and that they will respect our position as half-in, half-out of the EU. If they don't, then all bets are off' (*The Sunday Times*, 21 February 2016).

What 'special status' meant was not entirely clear. In some respects, at least, the agreement simply formalized the realities of Britain's position in the EU since the Maastricht Treaty. According to that view there was no major breakthrough, or as Jean-Marc Ayrault, the French foreign minister, declared, 'there had been no treaty change, no veto for the UK on strengthening the Eurozone and no questioning of the principle of free movement' (*Financial Times*, 22 February 2016). Some degree of special status was indicated by the fact that Britain was the only EU member state to have had one referendum on EU membership in 1975 and was scheduled to hold another in June 2016. No other member state has held such a referendum, though Greenland (not an independent member state as part of Denmark) voted to leave the EC in 1985 after a referendum.

Even prior to the February 2016 deal, however, Britain had a distinctive if not special status in the EU (see Chapter 4) that limited Cameron's room for manoeuvre and meant the other member states were reluctant to grant further concessions. That position was summarized in the official record of the European Council proceedings of 18–19 February, recalling that Britain was entitled under the EU treaties:

- not to adopt the euro and therefore to keep the British pound sterling as its currency (Protocol No 19);
- not to participate in the Schengen acquis (Protocol No 19);

- to exercise border controls on persons, and therefore not to participate in the Schengen area as regards internal and external borders (Protocol No 20);
- to choose whether or not to participate in measures in the area of freedom, security and justice (Protocol No 21);
- to cease to apply as from 1 December 2014 a large majority of Union acts and provisions in the field of police co-operation and judicial co-operation in criminal matters adopted before the entry into force of the Lisbon Treaty while choosing to continue to participate in 35 of them (Articles 10 (4) and (5) of Protocol No 36).

Finally, it was recalled that:

> the Charter of Fundamental Rights of the European Union has not extended the ability of the Court of Justice of the European Union or any court or tribunal of the United Kingdom to rule on the consistency of the laws and practices of the United Kingdom with the fundamental rights that it reaffirms (Protocol No 30).
> (data.consilium.europa.eu – EUCO 1/16 Annex 1)

The idea of 'special status' appeared to arise out of Cameron's claim that the deal was 'already legally binding and irreversible' and could only be overturned by all EU states including Britain, a view publicly supported by Tusk, the president of the European Council. In addition, the particular exemption from the 'ever closer union' goal was judged to belong to this category. It was precisely at this point that the particular implications of the renegotiation deal were contested. The opponents of the deal challenged the package, none more so and more authoritatively than the government's justice minister, Michael Gove. The gist of Gove's case was that the EU's Court of Justice was not bound by the European Council's agreement until treaties were changed at some unspecified time in the future. Besides, it was the case that only two years earlier the European Council had acknowledged that the concept of ever closer union allowed for different paths of integration for different countries and respected the wish of member states that did not want to deepen integration any further. Charles Michel, the Belgian prime minister who reportedly played a key role in the renegotiation and who praised Cameron for negotiating a deal that clarified Britain's 'situation of ambiguity' regarding the EC, was adamant that any treaty changes were not irreversible and would require approval by national parliaments and possible referendums.

The immigration issue attracted the most headlines, but these were largely unaccompanied by any estimates as to how far these rules would affect, if at all, the number of migrants coming from other EU states. Handling of the issue was susceptible to impression and expectations management and of being seen to tackle the inflow of migrants from elsewhere in the EU, though migration from outside the EU was larger than from the rest of the EU. According to the Migration Observatory at the University of Oxford, the size and character of the migrant population from elsewhere in the EU was as follows:

- the population of EU-born in the UK stood at just three million in the first quarter of 2015;
- as of the first quarter of 2015, approximately 1.9 million EU-born were employed in the UK;
- EU citizens accounted for an estimated 48 per cent of total non-British inflows in 2014;

- half of all EU nationals coming to the UK for 12 months or more in 2014 were nationals of countries that joined the EU in 2004 or later;
- about two in three EU nationals migrating to the UK come for work related reasons. The next common reason was formal study.

(The Migration Observatory at the University of Oxford, 5 October 2015)

According to the most recent statistics for the year ending September 2015, net migration of EU citizens to Britain was estimated to be 172,000, still lower than the figure for net migration from non-EU sources (191,000). Some 165,000 EU citizens came to Britain to work, 59 per cent of whom had a definite job to go to (Office of National Statistics, February 2016).

The Conservative election manifesto of 2015 pledged to reduce the total net figure to 100,000. The impact of the rules in terms of reducing the net migration from the EU figure has given rise to divided opinions. According to Theresa May, Home Secretary, the Cameron deal would clamp down on the abuse of free movement and reduce the pull factor of the British welfare system and make it easier to deport people abusing the generosity of the British system (*The Guardian*, 26 February 2016). No independent assessment, however, has substantiated this view.

A more widely held view was that the availability of jobs and the disparity in income rather than welfare benefits was the main factor responsible for the inflow of migrants from elsewhere since the EU's enlargement in 2004. In 2004, average per capita income in the A8 countries that joined the EU in that year was around a quarter of that in the richest EU states (HM Government, 'Review of the Balance of Competences ... Social and Employment Policy', Summer 2014). Moreover, the government's national minimum wage was likely to have a far larger effect on the number of EU migrants than the rules in the renegotiation agreement. Iain Duncan Smith, whose department was closely involved in the matter of migrants' benefits, claimed that Cameron's deal would do nothing to reduce net migration to Britain and might also lead to a sharp increase in arrivals as people try to beat an emergency welfare brake.

Information on the subject of 'benefit tourism' is limited. In October 2013, the Home Office stated that it did not have data on the number of non-British EU nationals compared to British nationals claiming benefits over a given period, nor on the number of EU migrants making fraudulent claims. Besides, according to David Laws, a Cabinet Office minister (2012–2015) in the Coalition government, immigration was never really a priority for the Home Office but rather a secondary concern (*The Guardian*, 13 March 2016). The European Commission published a report claiming to show that in 2011, out of 1.4 million jobless benefit claims in the UK, fewer than 38,000 were made by non-UK EU citizens, less than 3 per cent of the total (Bootle, 2014: 205).

A Balance of Competences Review on the free movement of persons acknowledged that only limited data 'is currently available concerning the numbers of EU migrants claiming benefits in the UK'. It further declared that none of the evidence received in the course of the review was able to point to specific research or analysis on the importance of access to social security benefits in the decision to migrate. The review also noted that there was a broad consensus that highly skilled migrants from the EU were beneficial to the UK, but that there was less agreement from submissions to the Review regarding low skilled migration and a recognition of declining levels of support for the free movement of persons ('Review of the Balance of Competences', Summer 2014). It is also a fairly widespread view that the influx of migrant labour in the past ten years has figured as one of the reasons for Britain's relatively better economic performance than that of many other EU states.

There was general agreement that the settlement secured by Cameron would not affect voting intentions, though the way it was presented might do so. Claiming that the outcome was a 'reformed EU' was but one example of how the result could be framed and needed to be so framed to attempt to win support among Eurosceptic Conservatives for whom a reform package was one that required treaty changes. A 'reformed Europe' largely arose out of the required changes to treaties to accommodate the renegotiation agreement.

In some respects, parts of the agreement were as obscure and as unlikely to capture the interest of the public at large as the agreement negotiated by the Wilson government in 1975, when it won agreement to a formula for Britain's contribution to the EC budget. Again, similar to the Wilson deal and referendum, there was no indication as to what Cameron's agreement with the rest of the EU states had cost in terms of leverage and political capital in securing the support of the other EU states. In the case of the 1975 agreement, Wilson secured French support for an agreement but had to pay the price of agreeing to a French proposal for direct elections to the European Parliament. It remains to be seen what costs or IOUs, if any, were involved in the case of the Cameron agreement. Possibly the other EU leaders, preoccupied by other important matters, were simply ready 'to pay ransome money' to prevent Brexit (*Financial Times*, 22 February 2016).

A further similarity between the two episodes was that both Wilson and Cameron espoused the idea of major treaty change beforehand but in both cases pulled back from insisting on such a possibility. Wilson returned to power in 1974 with a manifesto pledge of 'fundamental renegotiation' of the terms of entry to the EC. His key decision on the issue in government, however, was to renegotiate membership only within the existing EC treaties. This acceptance of the *acquis communautaire* effectively limited the character of the exercise. Similarly, at an early stage in his preparations to renegotiate Britain's terms of EU membership when he sought to reopen the EU Treaty of Lisbon, Cameron was told in no uncertain terms by the president of the European Council that this was virtually 'mission impossible' (*The Guardian*, 15 March 2015), and that in turn nullified earlier predictions (mentioned above) of a lengthy, drawn-out affair.

In some EU circles, 'special case' Britain held out the prospect of other EU states pursuing the same strategy. Guy Verhofstadt, the former Belgian prime minister and one of the negotiators of the EU agreement with Britain, supported the deal and contested the view that the settlement amounted to a few 'minor tweaks' of Britain's EU membership. On the contrary, he argued that Britain had obtained 'a bespoke form of EU membership, which no one else has', and furthermore that it had secured a special mechanism to address its immigration concerns, even though there was little or no evidence of 'benefits tourism' within the EU, as noted above. And yet, Verhofstadt conceded that if every EU member state copied Cameron's strategy and acted as Britain had done 'it will be the end of the European Union'. As if to substantiate that view at the very same time Viktor Orban, the Hungarian prime minister, called an anti-immigration referendum aimed at stopping Brussels and Germany forcing Hungary to take in refugees under any EU quota schemes. This move confirmed fears in Brussels that Cameron's resort to a referendum to obtain policy changes in the EU would prove contagious (*The Guardian*, 25 February 2016). It would be highly ironic if Britain, the least committed and most detached EU member state, precipitated the collapse of the organization by leaving it.

Exemption from 'ever closer union', hailed by Cameron as a major change, was viewed by others as simply release from a meaningless mission statement. In the original negotiations for the Rome Treaty in 1955–1957, the aim deliberately covered a multitude of different views about the future of Europe, and it has done so ever since. Nor does it have much, if any significance in terms of EU law; 'ever closer union' refers to a union of peoples and *not* of states. Its legal significance in the framing of EU law and the rulings of the EU Court of Justice is a matter of dispute. A very small percentage (0.2 per cent) of the Court's Opinions and Judgments actually refer to this aim, but the 'spirit' of closer union is often referred to in Court of Justice rulings (House of Commons Library, 16 November 2015).

A possibly significant foretaste of the referendum campaign was the immediate marked contrast between how Cameron presented the agreement in his case for remaining within the EU and what the leading lights of the Leavers chose to emphasize in the first instance. In the process, the civil war within the Conservative Party that had become a standard feature of British politics for almost 25 years became decidedly incivil, as had been the case with the Labour Party at the time of the 1975 referendum. Five Cabinet ministers came out in support of the Leave campaign: Michael Gove (Justice Secretary), Chris Grayling (Leader of the Commons), Iain Duncan Smith (Work and Pensions Secretary), Theresa Villiers (Northern Ireland Secretary) and John Whittingdale (Culture Secretary). They were joined by Priti Patel (Minister for Employment who attends Cabinet) and Boris Johnson (Mayor of London who attends Conservative political Cabinet meetings). The latter's very public vacillations before joining the Leavers were described in his own words as 'veering all over the place like a shopping trolley'; he had first advocated and then rejected the idea of two referendums, and then subsequently described himself as like James Bond on a mission 'to rescue Britain from the Brussels baddies' (*The Times*, 27 February 2016). By late February 2016 the scale and depth of the division within the Conservative Party was on display; some 41 per cent of Conservative MPs supported the Remain side, 36 per cent supported the Leave side and 77 were undeclared (*The Independent*, 25 February 2016). Unsurprisingly, Conservative headquarters had earlier indicated that the party would remain neutral in the referendum campaign.

Preparing for the referendum campaign

Cameron declared that one word summed up his concerns – 'flexibility'. By the time of the European Council in February 2016, he had adopted the motto 'live and let live' as the best way for the rest of the EU to approach the question of Britain's turbulent relationship with the EU. Cameron thus changed from the reluctant European of earlier years to the supporter 'with all my heart and soul' of remaining within the EU. This change of tone and emphasis at the top of the Conservative government, if not in the local Conservative associations, was comparable to the shifting attitudes of Macmillan's Conservative government of the late 1950s as it pointed the party in the direction of the EC. At times, indeed, the Cameron case for remaining in the EU as protection against Russian aggression and against a rogue nation like North Korea sounded suspiciously like Macmillan arguing that the western alliance system would be dangerously divided if the EC states did not admit Britain as a member. Meanwhile, William Hague, the former foreign secretary and an intrepid critic of the EU and of its institutions, did not doubt that for all his past criticism of the EU the country should nonetheless vote to remain in the EU.

In the meantime, some of the key words for use in the domestic propaganda battle ahead to win the referendum vote for continued membership were given an airing with some familiar, well-polished phrases. Linking EU membership to 'prosperity' and 'security' were early favourites, forming a marked contrast to some long-standing descriptions of the EU in Conservative Party circles that clearly prioritized the western alliance and NATO and were dismissive of the EU in security matters. There was also a hint of 'Project Fear' in the background, meaning the fear that an unknown future (outside the EU) could prove worse than a familiar present – a feature of the referendum campaign on an independent Scotland in 2014 and of the referendum campaign of 1975 – 'It's cold outside'. While the risk of leaving the EU emerged as a key argument, however, it did not always sit easily with a government that had after all introduced risk in the first place by calling a referendum.

The Leavers' riposte and their version of 'Project Fear' was an adaptation of William Hague's line about euro area membership – 'a burning building with no exits'. Voters' volatility, widespread distrust of political elites, hostility to big business and banking, and the effects of tabloid-fuelled anti-'Brussels' coverage arguably underlined the need to reinforce the Remainers' case by playing on fear of the unknown. At the same time, acrimonious feuds within the Leavers' campaign with at least three organizations vying for recognition as the officially recognized referendum organization – Grassroots Out, Leave.EU and Vote Leave – did not augur well for their referendum campaign.

In many respects, Cameron's initial approach was an updated version of the 'bread and butter' pro-EC arguments in the 1975 referendum campaign, deliberately downplaying or ignoring as much as possible issues of sovereignty, national independence and parliamentary government that had for years preoccupied his hardline Eurosceptic backbenchers. The aim was to make EU membership appear normal. 'Securing the best of both worlds', and remaining 'in the parts of Europe that work for us, out of the parts of Europe that don't' were Cameron's catchphrases at the time of the agreement, or as one detached American observer commented: 'The UK wants to be in the EU when it suits them and out when it does not and to be the final arbiter of both' (*Financial Times*, 20/21 February 2016). There was little evidence here to suggest that the government wished to open the kind of debate often found in the editorial columns of the broadsheets: Who are we? What sort of country do we want to be? Where do we belong in the world? What's the future for our long-term prospects? Where is the audit of the country's strategic interests?

At the same time, Downing Street swung into action in marshalling support for the agreement. It orchestrated a letter from former British military chiefs defending EU membership, though one of the figures named in the letter was later found to have been named in error. It was also unclear from the letter how exactly the EU as an organization had a role to play in the international arena of defence and security (*Financial Times*, 24 February 2016). A letter to *The Times* from the top executives of 36 FTSE 100 companies was equally supportive and similarly organized by Downing Street, while international heavyweight organizations like the IMF and the Group of 20 warned of the dangers of exiting from the EU.

In their initial reactions to the agreement, leading figures in the Leavers' campaign, Gove as mentioned and Boris Johnson, highlighted the legal and sovereignty dimensions of the question. These were precisely the arguments unsuccessfully deployed by the anti-EC campaigners like Benn and Powell in 1975. However, Gove also offered a more substantive critique of the EU as an old-fashioned body designed to keep power and control with the elites rather than with the people – 'an analogue union in a digital age' (*The Spectator*, 21 February 2016), this being a response to the argument that the Leavers belonged to a past age. As in the 1975 referendum, there was a significant contrast between the arguments for and against EU membership, the former emphasizing second order or 'everyday life' advantages while the latter focused on issues of national independence and sovereignty (see Boxes 12.1 and 12.2).

Box 12.1 What's the EU ever done for us?

- The Single Market guarantees free movement of people, goods, services and capital, and in particular the freedom to travel, live, work, study and retire anywhere in the EU.
- Deregulation of air travel has increased the number of airline routes and low cost carriers making for safer and cheaper flights.
- British shoppers can shop in any EU state without being charged customs or excise duties on goods.
- Consumers have the same rights when shopping as they do at home.
- Improved consumer protection and labelling.
- Cheaper mobile charges as a result of EU legislation.
- Travelling and working in the EU has been facilitated by the introduction of the European driving licence.
- EU citizens receive emergency health care on the same terms as the citizens of the EU country they are visiting.
- The EU provides social protection for workers in three areas: working time, temporary work and parental leave.
- Pensioners can receive their UK state pension wherever they live in the EU.
- The EU's ERASMUS programme enables students and staff to study or work at another higher education institution in the EU.
- Students can study at a university anywhere in the EU on the same terms and fees as a local student (except in the case of English, Welsh and Northern Irish students in Scotland).
- Working elsewhere in the EU has been facilitated through the mutual recognition of qualifications.
- EU citizens have a vote in local and European Parliament elections wherever they live in the EU.
- Businesses only have to deal with one set of rules rather than 27 different sets of rules when exporting to or operating in more than one EU member state.
- EU competition law has enabled market monopolies to be tackled in a way not seen before in Europe.
- EU measures have made for cleaner beaches and rivers, and also cleaner air.
- The EU pet passport allows pets to travel more easily between EU member states without undergoing quarantine.
- Strongest wildlife protection in the world.
- Price transparency and removal of commission on currency exchanges across the euro area.
- Cross border policing to combat human trafficking, arms and drug smuggling.
- Lead free petrol.
- Restrictions on landfill dumping.

Sources: Official website of the European Union; The European Movement.

Box 12.2 Arguments for Britain leaving the EU

- Each British household could be better off by £1,000 more to spend each year, through cheaper food bills, no membership fees, with the cost of regulations lifted, too.
- Our laws would not be dictated to us by Brussels.
- MPs would become accountable to the public and we would once again be able to make and decide our own laws.
- We could regain control of important issues such as our borders, and we could stop an immigration system that means an open door to the EU while blocking people who could contribute to the UK coming from non-EU countries.
- We would have greater influence over our global trade, so that we can do our own deals with fast-growing Commonwealth countries and North America (without 27 other EU countries all arguing for their own special interests).
- We would get a great sense of pride from negotiating our own global trade deals.
- It's time to be part of the world rather than a smaller part of Europe, and to win back our country.
- We regain legal control of things like trade, tax, economic regulation, energy and food bills, migration, crime and civil liberties.
- We regain an independent voice in world trade negotiations with independent voting rights at the World Trade Organisation (unlike now).
- We regain seats on other international rule-setting bodies that we have given away to the EU.
- We use our stronger international influence to work for closer international co-operation.
- A vote to remain in the EU means being constantly outvoted as we now only have 8 per cent of the votes on vital EU decisions, and the 19 Eurozone countries now constitute a majority in the EU that can routinely outvote Britain. Since 1996, Britain has strongly opposed over fifty measures in the Council of Ministers, has been outvoted on every occasion and every one of those measures became UK law.
- The British public and courts and not the EU will control human rights.
- A vote to leave is the safer option.

Sources: Leave.EU; Vote Leave.

It remained to be seen how the referendum debate would proceed. Meanwhile, public opinion polls regularly suggested that some 15–20 per cent of voters were undecided about the matter and could greatly influence the result. In view of support for EU membership in the devolved nations, as noted in Chapter 6, the famous line of G. K. Chesterton seemed apposite on several counts: 'For we are the people of England; and we have not spoken yet'. And it is fair to say that the pollsters had no idea what the undecided would say on 23 June 2016.

Conclusion

This chapter on the period since 2010 has indicated the extent to which the country's relationship with the European Union has often involved an unpredictable trajectory full of policy twists and turns. At the beginning of this period, there was no suggestion in mainstream political circles that Britain's relationship with the EU should be renegotiated and that a referendum should be held on the outcome.

We have traced the emergence of this idea with particular regard to divisions within the Conservative Party and to the influence of electoral politics. Cameron's attempts during the first half of the Coalition government to appease the rising tide of Euroscepticism in his party increasingly proved unavailing. At the same time, he was sidelined by choice or of necessity in EU circles, often presenting British policy as defensive and obstructionist in key episodes such as the making of the Fiscal Pact. There was throughout a deliberate attempt to insulate Britain in the public mind from the problems of the euro area and of the Schengen area.

We have noted that the Bloomberg speech, in particular, marked a decisive moment in Conservative Party politics about the EU with the decision to renegotiate Britain's relationship with the EU and to hold a referendum on the outcome. Immediate assessments of the renegotiation deal were mixed but seemed unlikely to change minds or to play a significant part in the result of the referendum. Yet much remained unknown at the time of the announcement of the date of the referendum which is why our conclusion is entitled journey to an unknown destination.

Conclusion

Journey to an unknown destination

> In politics we always have to consider 'what is the alternative'. The European Community or what?
>
> (Margaret Thatcher, *The Daily Telegraph*, 4 June 1975)

Introduction

This conclusion comprises three main sections. First, it highlights some of the key themes and aspects of the multidimensional subject matter of this book. It does so in the form of a brief assessment of the degree of continuity and change in British policy and attitudes towards the EU. Second, it considers the question of alternatives to EU membership. Finally, it discusses the course and outcome of the referendum campaign on EU membership that culminated in the vote of 23 June 2016.

Journey to an unknown destination

The February 2016 agreement was the latest example of the long-standing British quest for special conditions, opt-outs, assurances and exclusion clauses in its EU membership. In this lengthy process, British governments have sometimes given the impression of attempting to control traffic in the fast lane to European integration while continuing to occupy the slow lane. All the while they have sought to avoid mishaps and accidents in an atmosphere encouraging a persistent sense of crisis and road rage. The controversy over Britain's EU membership often appears to be a case of a conflict without resolution or of a matter that is too indeterminate for reasoned argument to prevail. The wide variety of descriptions over time of EU membership reflect the extraordinary effects relating to EU membership: the end of a thousand years of history, a thorn in the side of British politics, a subject triggering the most visceral reactions in the British psyche, the cause of a nervous breakdown in the political class, and an issue guaranteed to reduce politicians and press to a pantomime routine of foot-stamping, finger-wagging and name-calling.

Few commentators at the time of Britain's entry to the EC in 1973 could have predicted the course of events over the next 40 or so years. Yet the often unpredictable trajectory of British policy towards the EC/EU was evident long before membership. In the late 1950s, when the Conservative government wrestled with a number of options in coming to terms with the nascent EC, the continental European press often portrayed the British government as following an unsteady and unplanned course. To such mainland European observers it seemed that the British ship of state was zig-zagging from one destination to another. Occasionally, it appeared to dock at mainland Europe, only to reverse direction and make its way back across the English Channel. The 'journey', so to speak, was seemingly to an unknown destination.

In the early 1970s on the eve of Britain's admission to the EC, the BBC Reith lectures for 1972 were given by Andrew Shonfield, Director of the Royal Institute of International Affairs under the title *Europe: Journey to an Unknown Destination*. Shonfield expressed the view that if the EC seriously addressed itself to the essential purposes of the European construction – as set out in the lectures – 'the British people, after some direct experience of what is involved, will not want to desert it'. Over the next 40 years Shonfield's view proved to be the case even if EU membership invariably involved controversy, political drama, complicated diplomatic manoeuvres and often sullen acceptance of the status quo. His view was put to the test in the referendum vote of 23 June 2016 (see below), while the hope expressed in the concluding sentence of his book – 'to create a mood and set of habits which will make it feasible in a crisis situation to engage in joint European action on a scale that we have never approached before' – is proving to be a daily challenge in the contemporary EU (Shonfield, 1972: 8, 96).

Continuity and change

Continuity rather than change has often sounded as the dominant note struck in the evolution of British policy and attitudes towards the EC/EU. On the first day of EC membership (1 January 1973), an editorial on the event in *The Guardian* feared that 'If the trumpet gave an uncertain sound, who shall prepare himself for the battle?', and it further warned about the need to avoid a new, semi-permanent rift in British society between pro- and anti-Europeans. In the event and less than three years after joining the EC, a war of words between pro- and anti-common marketeers broke out in the referendum campaign of 1975. To a greater or lesser extent the conflict has endured as a more or less permanent feature of British politics ever since.

At various points in this book we have noted long-standing, powerful narratives about British policy towards the politics and international relations of mainland Europe, whether in the tensions between limited liability and continental commitment (as noted in Chapter 2) or in the different perspectives of exceptionalist and declinist accounts (as discussed in Chapter 11). One persistent feature is to the effect that any form of engagement should be strictly limited. The strategy of restricted involvement and fear of costly continental entanglements has proved deeply rooted, frequently finding expression in defensive-minded strategy and tactics. At the time of the origins of the EC in 1959, as we noted earlier, Macmillan expressed the view that 'The question is how to live with the Common Market economically and turn its political effects into channels harmless to us' (NA., PREM 11/2985). Substitute euro area for Common Market in that statement and the result is another example across the decades of continuity in the challenge facing Britain's EU policy and the problems of EU membership outside the euro area.

Limited involvement has also found expression in a set of ambiguous attitudes towards the EU/EC. Such attitudes are often rooted in a curious combination of arrogance or superiority and an acute sense of weakness and insecurity. They assume particular forms whether in anxiety about the preservation of national independence and sovereignty or suspicions about proposals originating in other EU capitals and fears about being hoodwinked by smarter operators there. They also find expression in the view that the EU is at one and the same time both a threat to British power and independence but too weak an institution to protect or advance British interests.

These contrasting attitudes express a wide variety of unresolved contradictions and tensions in British attitudes towards the EU. They arise out of markedly different assessments of the impact of EU membership on the country. For the anti-marketeers of the 1970s as for current opponents of EU membership, Britain is often viewed as the helpless subject of a club largely shaped by its other members. In short, the EU is something that happens to Britain.The opposing or Remainer view maintains that, far from suffering from delusions of weakness, British policy within the EU has a number of achievements to its credit since joining the EC/EU. Moreover, it is sometimes argued from the same vantage point that as often as not the EU debate in Britain is at least ten to 15 years behind the times in failing to recognize that the EU has been moulded as much by Britain as by any other member state since the turn of the century, most notably in terms of:

* pressing for the completion of the Single Market, especially in the financial services sector;
* playing a key role in supporting the case for the enlargement of the EU;
* figuring as a leading advocate of market liberalization and deregulation;
* perfecting the art of opt-outs in terms of the euro area and the Schengen Agreement;
* occupying a leading role in the making of the Treaty of Lisbon;
* shaping the EU's Common Foreign and Security Policy.

This book has studied in detail the interminable haggling about terms of entry to the EC, about the signing of EU treaties, and about the opt-outs, opt-ins and 'red lines' accompanying the evolution of Britain's EU membership. All such activities demonstrate the extent to which Britain's alignment with, rather than outright resistance to, the EC/EU has proved a disagreeable necessity, or as a former British ambassador to the EC put it 'our line is mistrusted because it is seen as proceeding from congenital lack of enthusiasm' (Trewin, 2008: 397). A semi-detached, associate or country membership mentality has often been in evidence, frequently perpetuating the view that British strength is defined by standing apart and by resorting to the language of boycotts, showdowns and referendums. At the same time, such arrangements have signified the very flexibility that British policymakers have emphasized and sought in their EU dealings. As we noted in the last chapter, Cameron singled out flexibility as a key principle in his Bloomberg speech, and immediately after the renegotiation agreement of February 2016 he claimed that flexibility summed up his concerns.

Some of the pronounced themes of Britain's European policymaking in the years immediately after the Second World War have had a lasting influence. In terms of external relations and particularly Britain's European policy, Churchill's three circles model of Britain's role and standing in the wider world has figured as possibly the most obvious example of continuity in the country's foreign policy. True, its survival has long since attracted criticism on the various grounds that it is outdated, broken-backed and imprisoning in terms of discouraging creative thinking about foreign and defence policy.

Nevertheless, some of the particular aspects of Britain's EC/EU policy are directly or indirectly related to views of this model in policymaking circles, most notably:

- the importance and uniqueness of Britain's self-styled role as a global power with global reach, acting as a 'global hub';
- an emphasis on an Atlantic rather than a European community with Britain acting as a transatlantic bridge (though less evident since 2010), involving among other things close alignment with the United States in its defence commitment to Europe through NATO and its management of the capitalist system;
- suspicion of any exclusively EU defence, security and financial apparatus;
- a pronounced preference for intergovernmental co-operation rather than any supra-national construction, the former being based on the legitimacy, power and veto capacity of national government;
- a determination to strike a desirable balance between European and extra-European interests and commitments, prioritizing the idea of a global, multilateral free trade system over any exclusively regional European arrangement;
- an aversion to making an irrevocable choice in favour of one sphere of interest/influence in the world at the expense of another.

This study has also noted how, why and when British policy has followed a broadly consistent line in terms of precise aspects and preferences in the EC/EU, with different degrees of support, interest, resistance and opposition across a range of policy areas. Some of the particular features overlap with or illustrate the strategic themes noted above. In particular, the following are among some of the long-standing hallmarks of British engagement with the EC/EU:

- an emphasis on minimal goals and on 'negative' integration (i.e. the removal of existing restrictions on economic, commercial and financial transactions between EC/EU states);
- scepticism about 'positive' integration (i.e. the introduction of new common policies), but with some exceptions notably the Single Market in which Britain has played and continues to play a leading role;
- the quest for unconditional and ideally freerider access to the economic benefits of EC/EU membership;
- the prioritizing of the enlargement of the EC/EU over further integration, with Britain as a leading advocate of expanding the membership of the EU;
- government projections of the EC/EU as primarily an economic rather than a political phenomenon;
- antipathy towards the idea of a federal European superstate, and a strong inclination to view EU membership as a fall-back or defensive position rather than as a base camp for an advance towards further integration;
- the domestic functions and use of EC/EU membership for a wide variety of purposes unrelated to membership;
- EC/EU membership as an aspect of competition between political parties and, more importantly, as a source of rancorous discord and division within parties;
- considerable distaste for the open-ended commitment to the EC/EU treaty goal of 'ever closer union among the peoples of Europe', and a corresponding attitude of

'so far and no further' most marked in the disengagement from EU affairs of post-2010 governments;

- deep suspicion of rhetoric suggesting an irreversible journey to an unknown destination combined with a palpable lack of ideological and emotional commitment to the cause of European integration;
- an aversion to a tight, inward-looking Europe, and support for global trade liberalization in which Britain has played a leading role in the EU;
- a strong emphasis on parliamentary sovereignty and national independence accompanied by distaste for 'foreign' notions of the divisibility of sovereignty and of multilayered political authority (though qualified in later years by the process of devolution in the latter case);
- a distinction between the view of political elites about the importance of EU membership in terms of international status and leadership aspirations, and the public's opinion of the EU as primarily a trade organization with occasional single issues, e.g. immigration, assuming political importance;
- the important role of myth and history in shaping the public debate about the EC/EU;
- the gulf between the winner-takes-all or zero-sum British political system (in which a gain for one party entails a corresponding loss for the other party/ies) and the conduct of EU negotiations with the emphasis on compromise, consensus, alliance building and variable sum politics (in which all parties may be winners);
- the striking contrast between the profusion of statistical claims and counter-claims about EU membership and the absence of an independent, authoritative body constantly and exclusively analysing the economic, commercial and financial impact of the EU on the country.

Another enduring feature of British membership of the EC/EU has concerned the perception of membership as representing a threat and an opportunity. Opponents of membership have long focused their attention on the threat that membership represents to national sovereignty and independence, and the threat that globalization and Europeanization pose to the living standards of British citizens. Supporters of membership, however, have viewed the EU as an opportunity to embark upon much-needed modernization and as a means of responding to and coping with globalization.

It is also the case that the presentation of EC/EU membership as a threat or as an opportunity has proved to be an endemic feature of domestic politics, most evident in the priorities of, and the conflict between, the political parties. In the early decades after the Second World War, a large body of Labour Party opinion viewed the EC as a capitalist club and as endangering the party's stand on national economic planning and controls. Similarly, Thatcher in her Bruges speech of 1988 completely rejected the prospect of a European superstate as a threat to her declared domestic programme of rolling back the frontiers of the state. Both major parties, most notably when in opposition, have seized the opportunity to capitalize on the government's perceived failings in the handling of EC/EU affairs. Shortly after becoming Chancellor of the Exchequer in 1997, Gordon Brown reportedly commented that the key was to change the nature of British perception and to make the British think of Europe 'as an opportunity, as a way of finding a new role for Britain in the world' (Trewin, 2008: 538). In fact, for much of the period since 1997, the sense of threat has overshadowed the idea of opportunity; one well-informed commentator observed that even in Whitehall it was quite hard to find any real sense that Europe is an opportunity rather than a threat (Stephens, 2005). As a general rule over the period since the 1960s, government and public have viewed the EC/EU more favourably as domestic economic conditions have worsened and less favourably as the British economy has performed relatively well.

EU membership has also represented both a threat and an opportunity to the devolved nations. Prior to EC membership, each of the devolved nations had its own Secretary of State in the UK Cabinet who could potentially exercise influence at the heart of government. After Britain joined the EC, however, they had to rely on other government departments to represent their interests in the EC's decision-making system. Their access to decision-makers was less direct in a formal sense, and there was the accompanying threat that their interests might be ignored or inadequately represented. However, the EU platform since the emergence of the original devolution settlement has opened up a political space for projecting the distinctive emphases of the devolved nations, though formally policymaking towards the EU still remains a Westminster reserved power. Discussion of the devolved nations and the EU in Chapter 6 also noted a key change of attitude towards EU membership in the devolved nations (most markedly so in the case of Scotland) at least according to opinion polls. The results of the 1975 referendum indicated that support for EC membership diminished in the northerly and westerly parts of the British Isles. In recent years, however, such a trend would probably be reversed as support for EU membership has dropped in parts of eastern and southern England excluding London (see below for the outcome of the referendum).

Conflicts over Europe have exacted a heavy cost in British politics, whether in contributing to the downfall of political leaders like Thatcher and Major or in causing upheavals and divisions within governments. A basic change has involved a reversal of policy as between the two major parties over the past 40 years. In the 1960s and 1970s the Conservatives were regarded as the pro-European party, while the Labour Party treated EC membership as anathema and eventually supported withdrawal from the EC in the early 1980s. By the 1990s these roles had reversed, after each party had moved in opposite directions in the intervening period for a variety of reasons, some of which had little to do with EC/EU affairs.

In these circumstances, the absence of any long-term national consensus concerning the value and purposes of European integration has figured as a more or less permanent feature of the British political landscape for the past 50 years. The Single Market project, however, has come closest to attracting support across the political spectrum. Furthermore, the EC/EU policy of the government of the day has been saved at critical junctures by the support of opposition parties and votes. The parliamentary vote on the principle of EC membership (28 October 1971) under the Heath Conservative government would have been lost but for the support of 69 Labour MPs who defied a three-line whip and voted with the government. It was also the case that the outcome of the referendum vote of 1975 was assured of a majority in the face of a deeply divided Labour Party and government by virtue of the support of the opposition parties for EC membership. Prior to the referendum vote of June 2016, moreover, it was widely believed that the official Remain recommendation of the divided Conservative government and party would succeed as the support of pro-Remain Labour, Liberal Democrat and SNP supporters outnumbered Conservative opponents of EU membership. In short, a Conservative-generated renegotiation and referendum exercise, largely devised to address the problems and divisions within the party, would command a national majority in favour of continued EU membership.

No government has been so assured of its domestic position without looking over its shoulder at its parliamentary and countrywide support when conducting EU affairs. That has proved particularly evident at times when parliamentary majorities were small or non-existent, notably in the periods 1974–1979, 1992–1997 and since May 2015, or in the case of the Coalition government between 2010 and 2015 which brought together the still relatively pro-EU Liberal Democrats and the increasingly Eurosceptic Conservatives. Such conditions have had a paralysing or disengaging effect on British policy towards the EU.

In these and other circumstances, government has often addressed two audiences, European and domestic. It has done so with such contrasting language and tone as to cloud the national debate about the pros and cons of various EU decisions. As noted in the discussion of the press coverage of the EU there is little by way of a nuanced assessment of EU affairs in such quarters. Press and particularly tabloid coverage over the past 40 years has undergone a significant change in attitude from being positively supportive of EU membership in the 1960s and 1970s to a heavily critical view in the past 25 years, largely drowning out any positive views about EU membership. The fear of press and public reactions in the course of EU deliberations has often meant that British government ministers travelling to EU meetings 'dragged a heavy ball and chain behind them', and that the role which domestic politics has played in defining Britain's stance on EU issues 'has been almost invariably negative' (Hannay, 2013: 283, 295).

Among the major changes that have occurred since Britain first attempted to join the EC in the 1960s, two in particular stand out and have a bearing on the country's long-term relationship with the EU. First, the sense of relative decline in the 1960s and 1970s, that impelled British governments to seek EC membership and to shake off the label of 'the sick man of Europe', disappeared in later years. At that time a key determinant in the case for EC membership focused on the need to galvanize and regenerate a still sizable British manufacturing industry. EC membership, however, coincided with the beginnings of a decline in the importance of manufacturing industry in the British economy that has continued to the present day. Since 1973, in fact, there has been a substantial decline in the share of manufacturing in total British output at current prices from 31.9 per cent in 1973 to 12.4 per cent in 2007 and down to 11 per cent by 2015 and still falling (Broadberry and Leunig, 2013; *The Guardian*, 31 March 2016).

During this period other alternatives to EC membership emerged as possible responses to the endemic problems of the British economy and especially of manufacturing industry, most notably the impact of economic recession and the application of domestic solutions to economic problems. Some 20 per cent of the country's industrial manufacturing capacity was lost in the economic recession of 1979–1981 resulting in rising unemployment but also higher productivity – a rare phenomenon as British productivity has often lagged behind that of other western economies. In the aftermath of the Falklands War, Thatcher declared that 'We have ceased to be a nation in retreat' (July 1982). On the economic front, however, 1982 was also the last year to date in which the country ran a trade surplus, while the annual economic growth rate during the Thatcher governments in the period 1979–1990 – 2.3 per cent – was actually below the trend rate of growth of the British economy in the period 1945–1979 (2.5 per cent). More importantly, by the 1980s, the British economy increasingly looked healthier in *relative* terms because of the marked slowdown in the economic growth of the other major EC/EU states.

Foreign prescriptions or panaceas for the country's economic problems, as advocated in the 1960s and 1970s and especially linked to EC membership, gave way to a resurgence of domestic solutions and of a free market capitalist model under the Thatcher governments of the 1980s. This development formed a sharp contrast to what was portrayed as the social democratic, managed capitalist model elsewhere in the EC. According to Thatcherite apologists, it also represented a marked change to what they routinely described as the demoralized condition of Britain in the 1960s and 1970s.

The record of the EU represents a major change that has in turn influenced British attitudes towards the organization. At the time when Britain joined the EC, the organization was widely regarded as a highly prized model of a modernizing, dynamic, economic growth-based, and trade expanding venture. It represented modernity and also suggested the emergence of a significant European political bloc. It was, moreover, a single integrating body with no special provisions or arrangements for individual members.

The EC/EU brand, however, proved less appealing in later years. In particular, the pound's exit from the ERM and the emergence of the euro area resulted in a distancing between Britain and the euro area, the latter being one of the key changes in the EU (like the Schengen Agreement) that have not applied to Britain. The gulf between Britain and the rest of the EU became all the greater following the financial crisis of 2007–2008. An increasingly troubled EU was immersed in a series of major problems, most notably huge public and private debts and an economic slump, large-scale immigration, the rise of right-wing populist parties, the growing appeal of nationalist and authoritarian politics in central and eastern Europe, the headlong retreat of mainstream national parties, and increasing doubts about the EU's governance structure, fitness for purpose and future direction.

The EU has also changed beyond recognition since 1973 not only in terms of size and institutional development but also as a body reflecting a more multi-tier, multi-speed and multi-directional character. At the very least, recent events have clouded the identity and future development of the EU as an undifferentiated entity. In that respect, the terms of the British renegotiation agreement of February 2016 highlighted the degree of diversity. Given these conditions and the relatively better performance of the British economy as compared with the EU average, EU membership became a less attractive proposition as compared with semi-detached status.

We have also traced and examined the following significant changes over the past 43 years of British membership of the EC/EU:

- the emergence of the euro area and of the division between the 'euro ins' and 'euro outs', and the impact of this development on Britain's EU interests, especially with reference to financial services;
- the extensive degree of what might be termed 'quiet Europeanization' that has penetrated the British political and economic system at primary and secondary levels;
- the growth of Euroscepticism and of a party – UKIP – committed to seeking Britain's withdrawal from the EU, and more widely still elsewhere in the EU the rise of a plethora of anti-EU and anti-regime political parties.

It was noted in the early sections of this book that 60 years ago mainland Europe was widely perceived in British circles as belonging to the foreign policy sphere. Europe was not regarded as a source of institutions and measures penetrating domestic affairs. EC/

EU membership, however, has profoundly transformed this relationship. What were previously classed as 'domestic' or 'internal' affairs wholly determined by national bodies have become Europeanized. Consequently, the dividing line between domestic and EU policy matters has become increasingly blurred. EU legislation or forms of co-operation between member states have gradually impinged upon many areas of British life including foreign, defence and security policy, fiscal and economic policy, judicial and home affairs, environmental policy, international crime, terrorism and human rights issues. EU business now engages the interest of all government departments, as there is an EU dimension to a diverse range of issues as well as inputs from the devolved nations.

Continuity and change are also intimately interrelated in certain aspects of govern-ment management of EC/EU membership. This aspect has a bearing on the extent to which the country never came to terms with the idea of major or radical change involved in joining the EC. From an early stage of EC membership, politicians and public alike tended to treat membership grudgingly, equivocally, defensively and subse-quently selectively, never quite embracing wholeheartedly and persistently the idea of membership as serving some long-term goal or mission.

In the early years of EC membership, the widespread use of the expression 'common market' spoke volumes for what was viewed as an organization of limited application, appeal and significance. From the outset, membership was presented to the public as a case of change but not such a drastic change as to upset the dominant narrative of con-tinuity in British history. So framed, EC/EU membership could continue to be regarded as a subsidiary, bolted-on extra belonging to the external environment rather than a widely acknowledged integral feature of public life. Membership was neither an end in itself nor a matter of great principle; 'It all depends on the terms' has featured as a constant, reassuring refrain of prime ministers from Harold Wilson to David Cameron. Public bewilderment about the meaning and significance of the EC/EU partly stems from this presentation of the subject as a case of change but within a deeply laid conti-nuity. It also derives from the impression that the entire business of EU membership is a matter of judgement for the political elite rather than for the electorate, except when the latter is called upon in a referendum in the event of party divisions to settle major, complex affairs of state.

Finally, one aspect of the Cameron government's renegotiation settlement of February 2016 represents both continuity and change: the decision to exempt Britain from the 'ever closer union of peoples' goal in the EU treaties. This measure marks a change, however symbolic, in the identity and projection of the EU in Britain. It may be unclear how a state can stop the ever closer union of *peoples*, and how the govern-ment of such a state can press a referendum case for EU membership on strategic and defence grounds while ruling out ever closer union *in all circumstances*. Exemption from the 'ever closer union' goal also finally and formally undermines the conventional EU view that all member states are committed to further European integration, but are sim-ply doing so at different speeds. At the same time, this exemption signifies a measure of continuity in British attitudes towards the EU.

What is the alternative?

One element of the continuity and change theme lies in the question – what is the alternative to EU membership? It is a question that has attracted enduring interest ever since the first unsuccessful attempt to secure EC membership in the early 1960s. It also loomed large in the referendum campaign preceding the vote on 23 June 2016.

In Chapter 2 we briefly noted a Foreign Office paper of 1969 that offered a classic exposition of the view that there was no alternative to EC membership. This paper concluded that the arguments for EC membership were 'overwhelming', while acknowledging that the prospect of membership and potentially of a unified Europe did not enjoy substantial public support.

The paper identified four options as compared with EC membership, even the best of which was judged to be not 'merely second but fourth or fifth best' (NA., PREM 15/369). For comparative purposes and in the light of current options, it is worth noting the conclusions concerning the four alternatives to EC membership if the third application for membership had failed:

- 'Go-it-Alone' policies;
- co-operation with European countries outside the EC;
- new forms of association with non-European countries;
- policies involving coooperation with the EC states.

A key argument against 'Go-it-Alone' policies was that these would do lasting damage to Britain's relations with the EC and with the United States without deflecting the EC from its course. The second option was rejected on the grounds that there was no realistic prospect of the European Free Trade Assocation (EFTA) with its seven member states including Britain becoming either a stronger, more cohesive body or a unit in international relations. Meanwhile, close ties with eastern Europe, besides offering only limited commercial gains, ran the risk of adversely affecting relations with the United States. In the context of a divided, Cold War Europe, any British move to draw nearer to eastern Europe would be regarded as a major defection from the western camp.

The third option of new forms of association with non-European countries was ruled out on several counts. The Commonwealth and especially the old white self-governing Commonwealth states were adjusting to new centres of power in the world, and Britain lacked the leverage to arrest or reverse this trend. The other set of ties under this option concerned transatlantic relations and in particular the idea of a North Atlantic Free Trade Area (comprising Britain, Canada, the United States and possibly other EFTA states). This idea was dismissed on the grounds that the United States showed no interest in such a scheme and that British industry would be overwhelmed by US competition. Furthermore, it would offer Britain no political base in the world but would rather mean that the country would be increasingly overshadowed by the United States.

The final option of co-operation with the EC held out some advantages but these were far outweighed by disadvantages. Most notably, such co-operation might meet public opposition following a third failure to secure EC membership and that some form of association was not available for a developed country like Britain. Furthermore, any possibility of a trading arrangement between the EC and the EFTA would fall foul of the same obstacles encountered by the Macmillan government in 1959–1960.

One or two of these options have been overtaken by events in the intervening period but others are still in play and raise questions about alternatives to EU membership. Opponents of EU membership – the Leavers – have often incurred criticism for failing to map out and collectively agree on an alternative to EU membership. Supporters of EU membership – the Remainers – are often hard-pressed to provide agreed data on the precise economic and commercial impact of the EU. They do, however, cite government figures that indicate the magnitude of the EU market and that offer something of a template against which to view possible alternatives:

- The Single Market gives UK businesses access to the world's largest trading bloc with 500 million people and 21 million companies generating £11 trillion in economic activity.
- Since 1992, the UK's bilateral trade with the rest of the EU has more than trebled and trade with the rest of the EU accounts for roughly 3.5 million jobs, around 11 per cent of the workforce.
- The UK is Europe's largest economy for services, and better implementation of the EU's Services Directive could result in a 2.6 per cent increase in GDP.
- In December 2015, 38 per cent of Britain's total exports went to the rest of the EU, while over the previous 18 months that figure ranged from 38 per cent to 49 per cent, and again in December 2015, 55 per cent of Britain's total imports came from the rest of the EU, while over the previous 18 months that figure ranged from 49 per cent to 55 per cent.

(UK Government, Department for Business Innovation and Skills, Policy Paper '2010 to 2015 Government Policy: European Single Market', 8 May 2015; HM Revenue and Customs, 6 February 2016)

We have already noted some of the problems involved in handling such statistical data. Several recent detailed studies offer a corrective view to headline statistics that do not stand up to critical scrutiny (see, for example, Burage, 2016).

That said, however, what alternatives to EU membership have featured in the referendum campaign? The current equivalent of a 'Go-it-Alone' policy is for Britain to rely on membership of the World Trade Organisation (WTO) and its most favoured nation treatment to ensure access to global markets including that of the EU. Other possibilities envisage British participation in some kind of trade bloc whether one in existence such as the European Economic Area (EEA) and the North American Free Trade Agreement (NAFTA) or possible formations like a Commonwealth free trade area or a Britain–EU deal comparable to that between the EU and Switzerland.

The features of some of the alternatives to EU membership are briefly identified below (see also Table C.1 for the Treasury's assessment of three main alternatives).

The World Trade Organisation is:

- not a standard-setting body like the EU;
- not a customs union and consequently British exporters would pay the EU's common external tariff;
- an organization that requires no negotiations to join.

The European Economic Area (comprising Iceland, Norway and Liechtenstein plus the 28 EU member states) means the three non-EU countries:

- have access to the Single Market in return for accepting the four freedoms of the EU Single Market;
- have to make a substantial budgetary contribution to the EU;
- have to apply all Single Market rules, but have merely a consultative role in the EU legislative process.

The idea of a bilateral free trade agreement between Britain and the EU is another alternative under this heading, with the proviso that the deeper the trade agreement the more EU regulation Britain would have to accept.

The North American Free Trade Agreement, comprising Canada, Mexico and the United States, was formed in 1994 and has eliminated trade barriers. A comparable scheme was cited as a possible option in the 1969 paper, and British membership of such an organization has figured as an evergreen favourite of opponents of EC/EU membership. While the United States is a major trading partner of Britain, buying 12 per cent of total British exports, British trade with the EU accounts for far more at 46 per cent of exports (2013). Besides, the EU is currently negotiating a trade agreement with the United States (the controversial Transatlantic Trade and Investment Partnership, TTIP) and recently agreed one with Canada (the Comprehensive Economic and Trade Agreement, CETA).

A Commonwealth free trade area suggests an organization comprising 54 widely scattered countries at various stages of economic development. The case for such a possibility is that the Commonwealth comprises some two billion people, accounts for some 20 per cent of the world's trade, and has potentially better growth prospects than the EU. Some of the arguments counting against such a possibility, however, were used when Britain opted to join the EC, not least of these being that Britain has far more in common with the advanced economies of the rest of the EU than with many Commonwealth countries.

These alternatives left much room for speculation and divided opinion as to the availability of alternatives to EU membership and their likely impact. The Leave argument was a claim about the future, based on trading relations that did not yet exist, rather than an analysis of the past. Meanwhile, the Remain case had to contend with the problems of producing a precise, persuasive account of exactly how much EU membership had directly benefited the country.

A debate about what was inherently unknown also extended to disagreement between the Remainers and the Leavers over the negotiating power and leverage that the country possessed in the event of exiting from the EU. The Leavers argued that the British market was so important to the EU that Britain could negotiate favourable trading terms. The Remainers, however, maintained that Britain would not be in a strong position when negotiating with the EU. At the very least, neither side seriously disputed the view that a British withdrawal from the EU would have important implications for the rest of the EU, representing a loss to the EU of about 15 per cent of its economy, nearly 12.5 per cent of its population and almost 20 per cent of its exports (excluding intra-EU trade). In the final section of this Conclusion we consider these and other matters in the context of the referendum campaign and its outcome in June 2016.

Table C.1 Overview of economic aspects of alternative relationships

	Access to the Single Market in goods and services		
	Tariff-free trade	Customs union and external trade	Level playing field/non-tariff barriers
EU membership	Full	Full. No customs costs. Access to EU FTAs	Full
The UK's special status	Full	As above	Full
EEA (Norway)	Some tariffs remain on agriculture and fisheries	None. Customs costs apply. No access to EU FTAs	Agriculture and fisheries not substantively covered by the EEA agreement
Bilateral agreements:			
Switzerland	Some tariffs remain on agriculture	None. Customs costs apply. No access to EU FTAs	Minimizes non-tariff barriers in sectors covered. Limited coverage for services. No financial services passport
Turkey	Only applies to manufactured goods and processed agricultural goods	No customs costs for manufactured goods. Obligation to align external trade policy with EU	Removes most other barriers to trade in goods. No special access for services. No financial services passport
Canada	Some tariffs remain on agriculture. Some tariffs on manufactured goods remain for a transitional period	None. Customs costs apply. No access to EU FTAs	Partial liberalization of services. No financial services passport
WTO membership	EU external tariffs apply	None. Customs costs apply. No access to EU FTAs	International agreements and standards apply. No financial services passport

Table C.1 (cont.)

	Obligations		Influence
	Other policy and regulations	Financial contributions	Votes on EU rules
EU membership	Full	Full EU budget contributions	Full
The UK's special status	UK is not a member of the single currency	UK receives a rebate on EU budget contribution	Full
EEA (Norway)	Accepts most EU rules, including market/product standards, free movement of people, environment, energy, climate and social policy	Pays for EEA Grants, Norway Grants, admin costs and programme costs	None
Bilateral agreements:			
Switzerland	Adopts EU rules in sectors covered. Participation in free movement of people and EU rules on e.g. environment, energy, climate and social policy	Gives grants to new EU member states. Pays admin and programme costs	None
Turkey	Adopts EU product standards, committed to equivalent rules on competition, state aid etc. and complies with environmental standards linked to goods trade	Turkey is in receipt of some EU funding	None
Canada	Firms trading into EU conform to EU standards. International agreements and standards apply	None	None
WTO membership	Firms trading into EU conform to EU standards. International agreements and standards apply	None	None

Notes: EEA (European Economic Area) comprises the EU member states together with three non-EU states (Iceland, Liechtenstein and Norway).

FTAs – Free Trade Agreements.

WTO – World Trade Organization.

Financial services passport refers to the process whereby a firm in a European Economic Area (EEA) state is entitled to carry on permitted activities in any other EEA state either by exercising the right of establishment (of a branch and/or agents) or providing cross-border services. This is referred to as an EEA right and the exercise of this right is known as 'passporting'.

Source: HM Treasury Analysis, 'The Long-Term Economic Impact of EU Membership and the Alternatives', 18 April 2016.

Table C.2 Annual impact of leaving the EU on the UK after 15 years (difference from being in the EU)

	European Economic Area	Negotiated bilateral agreement	World Trade Organization
GDP level (%) – central	−3.8	−6.2	−7.5
GDP level (%)	−3.4 to −4.3	−4.6 to −7.8	−5.4 to −9.5
GDP per capita – central *	−£1,100	−£1,800	−£2,100
GDP per capita*	−£1,000 to −£1,200	−£1,300 to −£2,200	−£1,500 to −£2,700
GDP per household – central*	−£2600	−£4,300	−£5,200
GDP per household*	−£2,400 to −£2,900	−£3,200 to −£5,400	−£3,700 to −£6,600
Net impact on receipts	−£20 billion	−£36 billion	−£45 billion

Notes: GDP – gross domestic product.

* Expressed in terms of 2015 GDP in 2015 prices, rounded to the nearest £100.

The reference to 'central' in the Table means central estimates defined as the middle point between both ends of the range.

The table is based on three existing alternatives to EU membership:

* membership of the European Economic Area (EEA), like Norway;
* a negotiated bilateral agreement, such as that between the EU and Switzerland, Turkey or Canada;
* World Trade Organization (WTO) membership without any form of specific agreement with the EU, like Russia or Brazil.

The most quoted figure in the media was the annual loss of −£4,300 per household under the 'Negotiated bilateral agreement column'.

Source: HM Treasury Analysis, 'The Long-Term Economic Impact of EU Membership and the Alternatives', 18 April 2016.

Endgame? The course and outcome of the referendum campaign

> Things fall apart; the centre cannot hold;
> Mere anarchy is loosed upon the world …
> The best lack all conviction, while the worst
> Are full of passionate intensity.
>
> (W. B. Yeats, 'The Second Coming', 1919)

This final section examines a few of the main features, issues and implications of the course and outcome of the referendum campaign. It thus covers some of the immediate, multidimensional aspects of an episode that by any measure ranks among the most important in British national life for several generations. What follows is inevitably a highly provisional, incomplete assessment that was written, unlike the rest of the book, during the turbulent weeks in British national life and politics immediately after the referendum. The sheer scale, rapidity and significance of events in this period await numerous historical studies, and call to mind Lenin's observation: 'There are decades where nothing happens; and there are weeks where decades happen.'

The ten-week referendum campaign officially opened on 15 April 2016 and culminated in the referendum on 23 June, posing the question:

> Should the United Kingdom remain a member of the European Union or leave the European Union?

Legally, the referendum verdict was advisory rather than mandatory but was always understood to produce a binding result whatever the consequences (see Chapter 5 for the uses, dangers and limitations of a referendum as a simple solution to a complex problem). At the time of the 1975 referendum, Margaret Thatcher, who regarded referendums as a device for dictators and demagogues, highlighted the difficulties that could arise if the referendum vote went against the government's recommendation, thus addressing precisely the situation that obtained following the 23 June result (*H.C. Deb.*, vol. 888, cols. 310–14).

Two organizations were designated to represent each side of the debate. The Remain campaign was organized under the banner Britain Stronger in Europe (with the unfortunate acronym of BSE). Stuart Rose, its chairman, was a businessman who cut a lackluster figure in the political world. BSE did not include all pro-EU membership elements, the SNP earlier excluding itself. Hereafter, therefore, the expressions Remain or Remainers will be used to indicate all support for EU membership from whatever source.

Vote Leave was the official leavers' campaign organization, though as in the Remain case some campaigners chose to operate independently, notably UKIP under the Leave. EU title. Hereafter, the expressions Brexit and Brexiter will be used to denote all elements opposed to EU membership. Gisela Stuart, a Labour MP and chairman of Vote Leave, was more knowledgeable than most parliamentarians about EU affairs and stood out among the largely male, middle-aged leading campaigners on both sides of the debate. Unlike the anti-marketeers in 1975, the Brexiters could call on some large financial backers such as Peter Hargreaves and Arron (also known as Aaron) Banks who bankrolled the Leave.EU campaign.

It is a truism that Britain's European question is about a lot more than EU membership. How much more became apparent during the course of the campaign. What then were some of the key features and issues of this landmark event?

A divided Conservative government and party

First and foremost, the referendum campaign was a contest fought in, for and by the Conservative government and party. It dramatized the deep divisions in the party that, as we have seen, stretched back at least 25 years to when the issue of EU membership was sometimes referred to as the party's 'San Andreas Fault'. The campaign was regularly portrayed as a battle for the soul of the Conservative Party and featured a largely right-wing element in the parliamentary party that had long opposed EU membership and Cameron's leadership. More particularly, the contest was a struggle over the succession to Cameron who had announced (March 2015) that he would not serve a third term as prime minister in the event of a Conservative government emerging from the general election of May 2015.

There were several candidates for Cameron's position, notably George Osborne (reportedly Cameron's favoured successor), Boris Johnson and Theresa May. The intense rivalry and conflict between Cameron and Brexiter Johnson, however, dominated the scene. Reports of an earlier meeting between the two men, which had ended up with them wrestling over a set of papers, reflected several aspects of the referendum battle, or what Angela Eagle, then a member of the Labour Shadow Cabinet, described as 'the unmistakably masculine and noisy playground spat ... between Tory blokes who are fighting a proxy leadership election' (*The Sunday Times*, 15 May 2016; *The*

Guardian, 24 May 2016). At times, indeed, the referendum campaign and its aftermath suggested that the issue of EU membership had become a plaything of the struggle for Conservative Party leadership.

In these circumstances, the other political parties were often viewed as performing a largely marginal role. A Loughborough University report (23 May 2016) on media coverage concluded that Labour voices were 'sidelined' while the Liberal Democrats and SNP were 'virtually invisible'. The Labour Party was widely believed to be pro-Remain, though one poll suggested that 45 per cent of Labour voters did not know the party's position on the EU. Corbyn, the party leader, had voted against EC membership in the 1975 referendum and had also rejected the Maastricht and Lisbon treaties. He supported Remain in a major speech (13 April), but otherwise damned the EU with faint praise and asserted that his support for the EU was not unconditional; evidence later emerged to suggest that Corbyn and his aides engaged in 'deliberate sabotage' of the Remain campaign (*The Guardian*, 27 June 2016). Unsurprisingly, he was regarded in Brexit quarters as a Remainer of convenience, not conviction.

The SNP as the third major party at Westminster prided itself on its European credentials. However, criticism of the Conservative government for its overblown warnings about Brexit together with speculation about a second Scottish independence referendum in the event of a majority for Brexit, figured as prominently as any strong, positive support for Remain in party circles. Sturgeon, the SNP leader, rounded on the Conservatives for scaremongering but did not hesitate to warn that Brexit would mean 'the most rightwing Tory government ever' (*The Telegraph*, 15 June 2016). The issue did not seem to interest the party overmuch, lending some substance to the view that the EU was 'largely a propaganda prop for the SNP' (Gallagher, 2015: 292). Besides, for much of the campaign the party was adjusting to its reduced standing as a minority government as a result of the Holyrood elections (May 2016). It was also distracted by other matters such as revelations about a 'love triangle' sex scandal involving two SNP MPs, Stewart Hosie, the party's deputy leader, and Angus MacNeil.

Trading statistics

At an early stage in the campaign the public was subjected to a heavy statistical bombardment from both sides. A major Treasury report (18 April 2016), on the long-term economic impact of EU membership and the alternatives, emphasized the degree of economic uncertainty and geo-political instability in the event of Brexit. The 200-page report included complex algebraic equations running to four lines, all of which served the purpose of yielding a single headline figure arising out of one scenario; each household would be £4,300 a year worse off by 2030 following Brexit (see Table C.2). This degree of forecasting precision over such a lengthy period of time met with a mixture of suspicion and derision in Brexit quarters. Similar forecasting by Brexit was no less questionable, as when it warned that Britain would need seven new prisons by 2030 (evidently a favoured year for such futurology) if immigration was not controlled.

The Treasury report, however, was more or less in line with other assessments. Few if any of the latter envisaged a higher GDP resulting from Brexit, and the large majority predicted both a short-term economic shock and long-term economic damage from leaving the EU. A survey by the pro-Remain *Financial Times* (22 February 2016) concluded that 'With clear and easily specified risks in the short and medium-term, Brexit does not easily pass any cost–benefit analysis'. Such top-down perspectives on the likely performance of the national economy, however, carried little or no weight among large sections of the population (see below). Their standard of living had not improved since the financial crash of 2007–2008; according to some data in fact net national disposable income per head of population in early 2016 was still 3.1 per cent below its pre-crisis peak in 2008 (*The Times*, 16 July 2016).

A further Treasury report (23 May) was unveiled by Cameron and Osborne at the headquarters of B&Q. The venue was chosen to emphasize that Brexit would result in an instant 'DIY economic recession'. In case the TV audience failed to get the message Cameron appeared with hammer and drill in order to communicate the meaning of DIY. At the same time, the government took the precaution of ensuring that parts of its legislative programme were so tailored to ensure that it did not alienate support for the Remain cause. Further afield, moreover, another Greek bailout package, unlike earlier ones, was quietly agreed by the Eurozone leaders, thereby removing a potential reminder for the British electorate of the EU's dysfunctional state.

In the absence of a supportive State apparatus, the Vote Leave economic case lacked the impact of Treasury papers. It also revealed divisions of opinion about alternatives to EU membership and about the relative importance of economic and non-economic issues in pressing their case (see below). One of the more developed presentations of the Vote Leave case appeared in a report: *The Economy after Brexit*. This 45-page document was drawn up by eight economists led by Patrick Minford, the former economics adviser to Thatcher and long-standing opponent of EU membership.

The gist of this report was that post-Brexit output would be higher, the City of London would thrive, unemployment would fall and the trade deficit would narrow as Britain would no longer be tied into the protectionist trade agreement accompanying EU membership. In addition, Vote Leave made much of the dangers of being shackled to a floundering EU at a time when Britain was enjoying faster economic growth than the other major EU economies.

There was limited support for Brexit in business and finance circles. On the eve of the referendum, more than 1,280 executives, including directors from 51 FTSE 100 companies, signed a letter backing the Remain campaign, while Vote Leave could point to only a few leading businessmen like James Dyson, the vacuum cleaner manufacturer, to support its case. Vote Leave leaders also proved vulnerable when they tried to counter the Remainers' economic arguments; Gove's claim that the EU was a 'job destroying machine' was supported only by the collapse of his father's fishing business and no other evidence. A more telling piece of Vote Leave propaganda was the factually incorrect statement that EU membership cost the country £350 million every week, this being a gross figure that took no account of the rebate (£74 million a week) and additional deductions (£115 million per week). The Brexit economic case was also strongly challenged on the international stage.

International reactions

The Remain campaign boasted a galaxy of supportive international political and economic elites. The most highly prized endorsement was that of US President Obama on a visit to London (21–23 April). He offered effusive support together with a key headline warning that Britain out of the EU and seeking trade agreements with the

United States would be 'at the back of the queue'. This statement represented a horrifying prospect for a British political establishment accustomed to its much cherished view of the country as the privileged partner of the United States with preferential treatment at the head of the queue whether in the distribution of Marshall aid after the Second World War or subsequently exclusive access to US nuclear missiles and intelligence sharing. Whether Obama's intervention had the desired effect on the British electorate is debatable. Brexiters could tap into public resentment at outside interference. Few, however, rushed to defend the comments of some of their number like Boris Johnson who had a long record of undiplomatic sayings such as referring to black people as 'flag-waving piccaninnies', likening Hilary Clinton to 'a sadistic nurse in a mental hospital', and writing an obscene limerick about the Turkish president. In this instance Johnson claimed that Obama's attitude to Britain was influenced by his 'part-Kenyan' heritage. Farage simply advised Obama to 'butt out' of the EU referendum.

An arguably more immediate concern to the Brexit cause was that international economic institutions like the IMF and the OECD uniformly presented doom-laden forecasts in the event of Brexit including a stock market crash, plunging house prices and tax increases. The Brexit response was to dismiss such forecasts as emanating from institutions that had failed to predict the financial crisis of 2007–2008 and that exhibited a high degree of groupthink, political collusion and highly questionable assumptions.

More serious still in terms of Brexit alternatives to EU membership were the views of organizations that directly figured in Brexit plans. The possibility of an agreement with the EU to secure full access to the Single Market, an early favourite, seemed to recede into the distance, especially when Juncker, President of the European Commission, warned that Britain would not receive a friendly reception from EU countries if it left the EU: 'deserters will not be welcomed with open arms' (*The Times*, 21 May 2016); A. A. Gill, the columnist, commented that the Brexit idea of continued access to the Single Market after leaving the EU was akin to wanting 'a divorce where you can still have sex with your ex' (*The Guardian*, 16 June 2016), an arresting, one-line image that seemed to elude Remain scriptwriters.

The attractions of the WTO, favoured by the Minford group of economists, were made to appear uninviting by its head, Roberto Azevedo. He insisted that Britain would be forced to renegotiate trade deals with 161 WTO member states that would be akin to joining from scratch – and this at a time when Britain's trade deficit stood at 7.2 per cent of GDP in the fourth quarter of 2015 according to the Office of National Statistics, the country's largest such deficit since 1948.

With so much international support for Britain's EU membership, the Remainers were able to sneer that Brexit was likely to attract only some undesirable allies such as Albania, Islamic State (Daesh) and Russia, while actual declared support was limited to a few unwanted supporters, notably the National Front in France and Donald Trump, the US Republican presidential nominee.

Risk and fear

Risk and fear were central elements in this drama on both sides, giving rise to much alarmist rhetoric about what was often inherently unknown. Scaremongering featured on both sides – on the economy in the case of Remain and on immigration in Brexit quarters. Competing fears jostled for attention. The Remainers' support for the status quo (qualified by the idea of a reformed EU) was accompanied by the fear that Brexit would weaken Britain's international position and leave the country on the sidelines seeking an agreement with the EU but having rules imposed by the EU in return. All in all, Brexit was simply not a risk worth taking, least of all in view of alleged consequences in terms of costs and dangers across the board: the loss of thousands of jobs (Osborne), the NHS in ruins (Jeremy Hunt), a decade of uncertainty (Bank of England), an economic downturn (Institute for Fiscal Studies), and a threat to pensions and to the unity of the United Kingdom (Cameron). While these claims were debatable, less disputable was the view that there would be 'no going back' after a Brexit vote and that a government seeking to re-enter the EU would have to join the euro and Schengen areas, and also surrender the British budget rebate.

For their own part, Brexiters feared that continued EU membership meant being sucked into an emerging European superstate and the further loss of democratic control, sovereignty and identity. In particular, they drew on fears of a future consisting of huge waves of Brussels regulations, of immigrants and of rampant terrorism resulting from EU membership. The Brexit tabloid press was also on hand to press any argument that portrayed German dominance in the EU in an unfavourable light. *The Sun* reported that Cameron's EU renegotiation was 'secretly controlled' by German chancellor Angela Merkel, highlighting the allegation under a front page headline 'Cam's in her Hans' (*The Sun*, 10 May 2016).

As in the case of the Remain campaign, all kinds of topics were drawn into the Brexiters' scattergun arguments. They touched on multifarious reasons for leaving the EU, except possibly the view that the EU would be better off without Britain. While scaremongering, exaggeration for effect and apocalyptic rhetoric coloured the Remain campaign, unreasoned argument, bogus simplicity and falsehoods were sometimes perceived as features of the Brexit case. The EU was routinely dismissed as an undemocratic and unreformable institution in Brexit circles, though occasionally it was unclear where exactly the EU's polity fell short of the British system of democratic government with its hereditary monarchy, an unelected House of Lords, and a Conservative government elected by 37 per cent of the popular vote.

What characterized the debate on both sides was the often insular, self-absorbed perspectives with limited interest in the future of the EU at large. This condition was reinforced by the narrowness of the media's coverage, obsessively focused on the conduct of the campaign and personal rivalries at the heart of government. Cameron's references to a future, reformed EU scarcely advanced beyond a rhetorical flourish to a detailed programme. His reference to the risks and dangers of Brexit frequently met with the awkward question posed by Brexit campaigners and press alike: 'If he [Cameron] believes the dangers are so great, why did he call the referendum in the first place?' Nor did some of Cameron's general arguments elicit much support. One TV studio audience guffawed when he observed that the EU was a way for countries that had fought against each other to talk to each other (*The Sunday Times*, 5 June 2016); evidently the Battle of the Somme or the Nazi death camps were viewed as tedious, irrelevant details in such quarters. More generally, Cameron's difficulty in advancing the Remain case was compounded by the extent to which none of his prime ministerial predecessors had uncompromisingly and systematically responded to criticism and myths about EU membership. Time and again, they had presented Europe as 'them' rather than 'us'. A day of reckoning in that regard seemed to draw closer. Meanwhile, the Brexit campaign was so England-only in outlook that it rarely, if at all, considered the possibly serious constitutional consequences of the Brexit slogan 'taking back control' for Scotland and Northern Ireland.

In the circumstances, the public was occasionally baffled as to who should be trusted in the midst of claims and counter-claims and statistical overload, especially in the contest between Cameron and Johnson. Cameron's circuitous route to the referendum and long-standing doubts about his EU views and policy ('a natural supporter of Brexit' according to Steve Hilton, his former adviser and confidant who supported Brexit) did little to enhance his trustworthy image in the public view. In public opinion polls, in fact, he lagged well behind Johnson in this respect. A ComRes poll for *The Independent* (14 May 2016) reported that Johnson was trusted to tell the truth on Europe by twice as many voters as Cameron: 45 per cent against 21 per cent. A YouGov poll (27 May 2016) reported that 18 per cent of people trusted Cameron on the EU as against a figure of 31 per cent for Johnson.

Such poll ratings for Johnson were a mystery to his critics who were familiar with his long-standing record of false statements and fabrication of myths about the EU combined with his pronounced reputation as a self-publicist. In such quarters, moreover, it was commonly believed that his Brexit stance was largely unprincipled and designed to advance his case for leadership of the post-Cameron Conservative Party. His jokey, cavalier preference for evidence-free, blustery assertions meant that his critics viewed him as an exponent of post-truth politics with a cultivated bumbling personality. Johnson undoubtedly had an eye for the applause-seeking, meaningless statement ('We do not need to be in the EU to guarantee our humanity'). It was nevertheless the case that he was perceived in some quarters as bringing to the Brexit cause a vitality and rabble-rousing that were less evident in the Remain camp.

The prose and the passion

The Brexit campaign often exhibited a greater degree of passion than its opponents. It was a matter of widespread comment that the Remain case was based on the head rather than the heart and that as a defence of continuing EU membership it lacked the powerful emotional pull and appeal of the Brexiters. As in the case of the Scotland independence referendum of 2014, there were difficulties in defending the status quo without entering the territory of unappealing, negative arguments. The Brexit camp showed a marked lead in terms of headline-grabbing slogans and soundbites. Meanwhile, Boris Johnson highlighted what he viewed as key weaknesses in the Remain position, notably that it had 'not a shred of idealism' and 'no underlying loyalty to the idea of Europe' (*The Guardian*, 15 April 2016; *The Times*, 21 May 2016).

It was relatively easy to portray the Remain side as bland, boring and lacking in enthusiasm. David Cameron reflected some of the difficulties in this respect, not least in his major speech of 9 April in which he set out what he called 'the big, bold patriotic case' for the Remain side. He projected a purely instrumental view of EU membership. This stance was indicated in his repeated references to the EU as a 'tool', an expression that scarcely generated interest in or excitement about EU membership. But then this was a speech that conveyed conflicting messages, as did the Brexiters' diverse opinions.

Mixed messages

We have noted elsewhere that EU membership was not a matter of lively interest and commitment for Cameron, that he did not 'love Brussels', that he had declared himself willing to campaign for Brexit if his demands had been rebuffed by the rest of the EU in the renegotiation process, and that he believed Britain's 'brilliant economy' was strong enough to survive whatever the referendum result.

Such views did not sit easily with his subsequent warnings about European defence and security and the risk of Europe entering an age of competing nationalisms in the event of Britain leaving the EU. Some Remain supporters were driven to despair by Cameron's transition from the whingeing club bore to his new-found support for EU membership; Polly Toynbee, the *Guardian* columnist, maintained that because Cameron had spent his entire decade as party leader undermining support for the EU – 'He deserves to lose [the referendum], but we hope to God he doesn't' (*The Guardian*, 18 February 2016). Cameron took the view that a majority of the British public did not share the certitude of the campaigners on both sides and that ultimately its innate conservatism together with the background noise of doubts and fears about the effects of Brexit would be sufficient to produce a majority result for Remain. A senior figure on the Remain side spoke of the Remain cause as representing the pluralist, liberal, centrist force in British politics, and in that respect Cameron gambled on the EU referendum because he thought the centre was secure (*The Guardian*, 5 July 2016).

From the outset, the Brexit campaign was fractured by personality differences and, more importantly, divisions of opinion over what exactly a post-Brexit Britain would look like. Prior to Vote Leave's designation as the official organization, there were rancorous disputes with the other organizations in the field, Grassroots Out and Leave. EU, so much so that the Remain side portrayed the Brexiters as an unholy alliance of disparate elements.

Among the Brexiters, there were several fundamental differences of opinion and a series of mixed messages. Deregulation or escaping from government controls at the EU and national levels was a popular theme among right-wing, Conservative Brexiters, especially in regard to employment law, job security, and health and safety laws. However, there was a major split over the relative importance of reclaiming lost sovereignty regardless of long-term economic disruption, as compared with the value of greater independence chiefly as a route to greater prosperity and developing Britain as a free market, capitalist offshore hub.

Trading alternatives to EU membership attracted a wide variety of views, often revealing a simple or cynical belief that, after voting for Brexit, the EU would continue to trade with Britain on British terms. Each of the possibilities indicated in Table C.1 had its supporters. Such differences and the lack of a clear economic plan were exploited by Remain to indicate core weaknesses of the Brexit case. Besides considerable shades of opinion over immigration (see below), there was also much confusion over such matters as globalization. Some elements opposed globalization because of its impact on employment and immigration, and they veered towards a protectionist point of view. Others argued that EU membership blunted the opportunities for globalization and for turning Britain into an offshore free market. It looked entirely possible, therefore, that the British electorate could agree to exit the EU without any alternative, agreed plan covering the strategic, political, economic and commercial consequences.

Sovereignty

The issue of sovereignty loomed far larger in the Brexit campaign than it did in the case of Remain. At an early stage, Gove lent intellectual weight to the Brexit cause with a piece on sovereignty that elicited no comparable response on the Remain side.

Brexit sloganizing in this regard emphasized the need 'to take back control' or, in UKIP language, 'We want our country back'. These were the catchphrases that ultimately lodged in the public memory rather than the often dull, complicated rejoinders of the Remain campaigners

The Remain campaign studiously avoided references to sovereignty as much as possible. Significantly, there was no sovereignty bill in the Queen's speech of May 2016 which Cameron had promised following the completion of his renegotiation with the EU in February 2016. There was nonetheless a defence of the case for pooling sovereignty to achieve national objectives that the country could not achieve on its own. Moreover, apart from EU immigration, the British government still determined the vast majority of policy over matters of the greatest concern to the electorate, including defence and border security, education, health, monetary policy, pensions and welfare. Furthermore, in the welter of Brexit rhetoric about taking back control, it was easy to lose sight of the fact that the British government controlled more than 98 per cent of its public expenditure and that, as we have traced in this study, it had vetoes in all the important areas including defence, transfers of power, enlargement, taxation, non-EU immigration, asylum and criminal law, the single currency and the EU budget rebate. Finally, there was one aspect of the sovereignty issue that Brexit chose to ignore or overlook, namely that parliament could repeal the European Communities Act of 1972 and the country would be out of the EU in one fell swoop – such is the power of a sovereign state in a parliamentary democracy.

Immigration

Immigration was the most difficult issue for the Remain side, putting it on the defensive against increasingly sharp Brexit criticism. This issue was the Brexiters' 'trump card' in the view of John Major, the former prime minister and Remain supporter. Cameron's record on the subject was attacked on several counts, most notably that his past promises (dating back to January 2010) of cutting net immigration to 'tens of thousands' were not achievable as long as Britain remained in the EU and had to preserve the principle of free movement of economic migrants. During the course of the campaign, the latest official statistics were released demonstrating that net migration from the EU was 184,000 in 2015, 10,000 higher than in 2014.

Brexit leaders insisted that the government lacked democratic consent for its immigration policy. The most damaging attack on Cameron came in a joint statement (29 May) by Gove and Johnson that branded Cameron's failed pledge to curb immigration 'corrosive of public trust'. At the same time, however, there were doubts about the trustworthiness of some of Vote Leave's claims. Their target figures for net immigration in the EU context ranged widely from 30,000 to 100,000 per annum. In addition, there was criticism of Vote Leave's misleading poster with the inscription 'Turkey (population 76 million) is joining the EU. Vote Leave, take back control'. Penny Mordaunt, a Brexiter and government defence minister, maintained that she did not think Britain could stop Turkey joining the EU, seemingly unaware of EU admissions procedures for prospective member states. There were also accompanying claims that an additional million people would be added to the UK population from Turkey alone within eight years and would threaten national security as well as public services. Meanwhile, a UKIP poster entitled 'Breaking Point', disowned by the other Brexiters who were nonetheless viewed as being in the Farage slipstream on immigration, was widely regarded as playing to the dark side of xenophobia and anti-migrant opinion. Farage himself claimed that the Vote Leave campaign had openly used UKIP slogans, policies and language, including the UKIP slogan 'Believe in Britain', the Australian-style points system, and the branding of 23 June as the UK's independence day. A high degree of rage shot through the Brexit campaign, most especially in its UKIP form with its pronounced emphasis on fear, conspiracy, unthinking jingoism, nostalgia and suspicion of non-white people, the latter evident in the 'Breaking Point' poster with its snaking queue of dark persons suggesting that these were EU migrants descending on Britain rather than what they were: Syrian refugees arriving in Slovenia with no chance of getting anywhere near Britain.

In the blizzard of figures surrounding the subject, some of the myths and benefits of immigration struggled to attract attention, most notably that according to HM Revenue and Customs data recently arrived migrants paid £2.5 billion more in taxes in 2013–2014 than they received in tax credits and benefits. Furthermore, and according to the OECD, immigration accounted for half of UK GDP growth since 2005. Evidence of immigrants taking jobs away from British nationals, however, was more disputable, though a Home Office review of the evidence concluded that immigration did not adversely affect native employment during normal times (Devlin *et al.*, 2014). The impact of recent immigration on underfunded public services in particular areas was more demonstrable.

The Brexit campaign exploited broader concerns as the immigration issue became a prism through which several grievances were viewed, ranging from stagnating living standards to underfunded public services. The erosion of cultural and economic identities was encapsulated in the message 'to get back control of our borders'. There was little attention to such matters as to how this was inconsistent with any trade agreement with the EU that would entail freedom of movement, nor with the fact that net immigration from the non-EU world was larger than that from the rest of the EU. It was also the case that Norway and Switzerland, both of which were cited as non-EU states with the sort of agreements with the EU that could apply to Brexit Britain, actually had higher levels of migration from within the EU and as a proportion of their population than Britain.

The Brexit anti-elite theme

The Brexit campaign capitalized on a widespread anti-elite tide of opinion that suggested a populist view of a major gulf between elites and the public. A host of discontents came to the fore: anti-elites, anti-big business, anti-globalization, anti-Brussels, anti-immigration. In the political field alone, Steve Hilton argued that the 'professionalisation of politics' had left 'too many people feeling as if politics is a game played by an insular ruling elite of politicians, advisers, pollsters, donors, journalists and assorted hangers-on' (*The Times*, 21 May 2016; *The Guardian*, 26 May 2016). Non-political elites were also to the fore in pledging support for Remain; some 600 economists and 300 historians rallied to the cause, as did a large number of scientists greatly concerned about EU-generated research grants and projects.

Tapping into the reservoir of generalized discontent was made all the easier with Cameron and Osborne as the chief spokesmen of the Remain campaign whose opponents caricatured them as out-of-touch 'posh boys'. Osborne's threat to introduce fiscal tightening measures in the event of an emergency Brexit budget (dubbed a 'punishment budget') virtually eliminated him as a possible successor to Cameron. He was immediately subjected to the type of criticism that flourished after the referendum result, more or less to the effect that he possessed a negative mindset in disputing the Panglossian views of the Brexiters.

In the anti-elite climate of opinion fostered by the Brexiters, establishment endorsements were made to appear as carrying little or no weight and were for the most part counter-productive. Brexiters maintained that there was an institutional ganging up on 'the poor British voter', as one Brexit government minister put it (*The Guardian*, 15 May 2016).

There was a marked contrast between Brexit leaders like Gove and Johnson claiming to be on the side of the people against arrogant elites while they themselves had impeccable elitist credentials at the very heart of the British political establishment. Gove himself declared that the 'people in this country have had enough of experts' – presumably including himself in that number. He later made a bizarre comparison between Brexit-warning economic experts and Nazis who smeared Albert Einstein's findings during the 1930s. John Major, the former Conservative prime minister, made a withering assessment of this type of Brexit leadership. In response to Brexit claims that leaving the EU would provide more funding for the NHS, Major recalled that Gove had wanted to privatize the NHS, that Johnson wished to charge people for health services, and that Iain Duncan Smith advocated moving to a social insurance system. Major concluded that the NHS would be as safe with Gove and company 'as a pet hamster would be with a hungry python' (*The Guardian*, 5 June 2016).

Knockabout politics and incendiary rhetoric

At the midway stage in the referendum campaign, *The Sunday Times* (22 May 2016) headed its editorial 'A Referendum Campaign of Yah Boo Sucks', describing the event as an unedifying spectacle. This view was shared by some other sections of the media, notably the broadsheets and also veteran TV news presenters like Jon Snow who could not recall a worse-tempered campaign characterized by negativity, bickering, foul-mouthing and wholesale abuse of facts by both sides (*The Guardian*, 31 May 2016). Certainly, the electorate had never before been subjected to such a concentrated barrage of (mis)information and (mis)interpretation about the EU. Without nuance and as a simple binary choice between in and out, the referendum proved to be a 'conflict maximizing mechanism'.

Incendiary language in the early stages of the campaign, such as David Miliband's description of Brexit as 'an act of political arson', soon gave way to much more colourful, venomous name-calling as Conservative figures clashed with each other. Meanwhile, to keep himself in the public eye, UKIP leader Farage claimed that the possibility of sex attacks by migrants on women would be the 'nuclear bomb' of the referendum campaign. Boris Johnson, who had earlier described UKIP members as the sort of people 'who have sex with vacuum cleaners', helped to set the tone by dismissing Cameron and the Remainers as 'the Gerald Ratners of modern politics' who admitted that the EU is 'crap but insist there is no alternative' (a reference to the jewellery chain owner, Gerald Ratner, who described one of his own products as 'total crap'). Language in parliament was equally unedifying; David Lidington, the Europe minister, was accused of 'polishing poo' by Steve Baker, chair of the Eurosceptic Conservatives for Britain, as he set out details of the February EU agreement. Osborne described the Brexiters as 'economic illiterates' – two former Conservative Chancellors of the Exchequers being among this number (Nigel Lawson and Norman Lamont), while Iain Duncan Smith compared Osborne to 'Pinocchio'. Unsurprisingly, the cross-party parliamentary Treasury committee called for an end to the arms race of ever more lurid claims, bogus assertions and mountains of exaggeration.

In the closing stages of the campaign, Farage declared that the voters were beginning 'to put two fingers' up to the political class. Out on the streets, some of the gestures were equally tasteless; a gang of English supporters in Marseille for the Euro 2016 football championship rampaged through the town chanting 'Fuck off Europe, we're all voting out' (*The Guardian*, 12–13 June 2016). Two days later (14 June), *The Sun* shared this view when it officially came out for Brexit in its front page headline 'BeLeave'.

There seemed to be no end to the vicious exchanges, the ugly mood and abusive language as the campaign entered its final week. At this point, however, one event brought a temporary halt to the acrimony: the murder of Jo Cox, the Labour MP for the Batley and Spen constituency (16 June). Cox was one of the brightest and best of the 2015 intake of MPs. Her exemplary public service and humanitarian work put to shame the cheap gibes against MPs in the media and especially among social media commentators. Campaigning was suspended for two days and parliament was recalled (20 June) to pay tribute to the MP. Hostilities resumed, however, as Brexit campaigners accused the Remain camp of emphasizing the pro-Remain views of Cox, while the Remain campaign strongly criticized the Brexit campaign for whipping up anti-immigrant feeling.

The polls: the decided and the undecided

The pollsters were on the defensive in their conclusions about voting intentions, not least because of their failure to predict that the Conservatives would gain an absolute majority in the 2015 general election. Consequently, there was much discussion about the relative merits of telephone polling and online polls. Some patterns began to emerge during the course of the campaign. In the authoritative Poll of Polls undertaken by NatCen Social Research, Remain was usually ahead and was more able to keep a lead than Brexit, but that lead vanished by early June so that on the basis of six polls on voting intentions (9–13 June) 48 per cent favoured Remain and 52 per cent favoured Brexit, which proved to be the outcome (but see below for a post-referendum verdict).

There was invariably a large undecided contingent (as high as 15–20 per cent in some cases) that complicated matters for the pollsters. There was also considerable room for speculation about turnout and about the extent to which the core support for Brexit was more likely to vote than its Remain counterpart. Then, too, it was difficult to factor in some oddities, such as the 9 per cent of UKIP voters who did not back Brexit in one poll. In the event, the polls got it wrong as they had done in the 2015 general election; John Curtice, the polling expert, noted that in the latest polls before the referendum on average eight polling companies between them anticipated that Remain would win with 52 per cent of the vote and Leave would end up with 48 per cent.

As compared with the 1975 referendum, the political parties were no longer mass membership organizations whose members could be relied upon to follow the advice of the leadership. Whereas in 1983 some 3.8 per cent of the electorate belonged to one of the three major parties – Conservative, Labour, Liberal Democrat – the comparable figure for 2015 was 1.0 per cent. The explanation of Roy Jenkins for the result of the 1975 referendum result – that the public took the advice of political leaders they were used to following – scarcely applied to the much more fragmented, volatile and less deferential electorate of 2016.

The role of the media in influencing public opinion is a matter for later study. During the course of the campaign, one review of articles in the press (undertaken by the Reuters Institute for the Study of Journalism) concluded that the national press was biased in favour of Brexit by a margin of 45 per cent to 27 per cent. The Press Gazette reported that during the last month of the referendum campaign 90 million newspapers were published with front pages favouring Brexit, but only 30 million were published with front pages favouring Remain (*Financial Times*, 25 June 2016). Predictably, the *Daily Mail* included the most pro-Brexit articles followed by the *Daily Express*, the *Daily Star*, *The Sun* and *The Daily Telegraph*. The newspapers with the most pro-Remain articles were in order the *Daily Mirror*, *The Guardian* and the *Financial Times*. *The Times* was evenly balanced between the two positions with a slight preponderance of pro-Brexit articles, but eventually it declared for Remain, while *The Sunday Times* supported Brexit. The Murdoch press thus supported both campaigns, as did the Rothermere press in the contrast between the *Daily Mail* and the pro-Remain *Mail on Sunday*. Across the board, newspapers were far more likely to quote Conservative rather than Labour politicians by some 69 per cent to 14 per cent.

The most cited arguments in either Remain or Brexit news stories were: the economy/business (33 per cent), sovereignty (29 per cent), migration (18 per cent – a surprisingly low score in view of its blanket coverage by Brexit and the media), regulations (14 per cent) and terrorism/security (6 per cent) (*The Independent*, 23 May 2016). There was also a marked contrast between the context of the 1975 referendum when total newspaper circulation was 15 million copies as against a total figure of just under seven million (2015). The influence of the newspapers was correspondingly smaller, except to say that newspapers still often set the agenda for broadcasters (see Chapter 7).

The result

At 7 a.m. on Friday 24 June 2016, it was formally announced that the referendum had resulted in a victory for the Brexit campaign. 51.9 per cent of votes (17,410,742) were cast in favour of leave, and 48.1 per cent of votes (16,141,241) were cast in favour of remain, and this on a turnout of 72.2 per cent – the highest UK-wide turnout since the general election of 1992. By chance, midsummer's day fell on the date of this momentous announcement. The timing could not have been more appropriate. Jubilation mingled with despair in immediate reactions. For the majority the declaration represented a 'midsummer night's dream' allegedly in the form of liberation and national independence. For the losers it amounted to a 'midsummer night's nightmare' with a deep-seated sense of loss of identity, country and familiar landmarks.

Nobody emerged more triumphantly from this verdict than UKIP leader Nigel Farage. He rightly claimed credit for the calling of the referendum, and he hailed the result as a 'victory for ordinary, decent people', raising questions about the character of the Remain voters. He also boasted that victory had been secured without a single bullet being fired, a characteristically insensitive remark when only a week earlier the MP Jo Cox had been murdered by a gunman who reportedly shouted 'Britain First' as he shot her. Farage then proceeded to Strasbourg where he crassly insulted members of the European Parliament; the little Union Jack perched on his desk for effect was reportedly upside down, and that fairly reflected the chaotic state of British politics, which included, a week later, his resignation for the third time from leadership of UKIP.

By contrast, gloomy expressions on the Remain side were all too evident, ranging from shock to black humour. Martin Wolfe, chief economics commentator at the *Financial Times*, claimed that the result was probably the most disastrous single event in British history since the Second World War (*Financial Times*, 24 June 2016). Frankie Boyle, the comedian, wryly commented that 'It's important to just accept the result and move on, possibly to another country', adding that 'at least we have put a stop to economic migration, by making the pound worthless', the pound having immediately sunk to its lowest level on the currency markets for 30 years after the result (*The Courier and Advertiser*, 25 June 2016).

In between these positions there were varying degrees of concern and interest. For some people Brexit was regarded as casually as not renewing the annual gym club membership or, more seriously, house insurance. For others it was a matter of discovering what exactly they had voted for *after the event*. Google reported that in the hours immediately after the result 'What is the EU?' was its second most popular EU-related question, an interesting reflection on the effectiveness of the referendum campaign. Then, too, others voted to leave the EU but quickly regretted doing so, not least of whom was Kelvin MacKenzie, former editor of the *The Sun* – long-standing opponent of Britain's EU membership – who suffered from 'buyer's remorse' days after the vote. The result demonstrated all too clearly that there was not a sufficiently large reservoir of ideological interest and emotional commitment to carry the day for Remain. At the same time, in the population at large, beyond the columns of the Europhobic press, there was little evidence of large-scale celebrations as the country entered a period of profound political, economic and constitutional crisis.

Resignation and recriminations

Shortly after the declaration of the referendum result, Cameron announced his resignation. On realizing he had lost the referendum, his reported comment echoed the view of Enoch Powell, 'All political lives end in failure' (*The Independent*, 2 July 2016). His failure, however, was more spectacular and self-inflicted than some, for he was likely to be remembered as the man who took the country out of the EU. He was clearly most to blame for calling a referendum and for a series of miscalculations and failed expectations about holding and winning it. The outcome of his attempt to deal with divisions in his party had instead divided the whole country. The Conservative Party was immediately plunged into a leadership contest in which earlier favourites – Osborne and Johnson – were overtaken by an unexpected contest between Theresa May, the Home Secretary, and Andrea Leadsom, a junior energy minister, that was cut short when the latter withdrew from the contest leaving May to succeed Cameron (13 July).

Meanwhile, the Brexit victory risked shattering the fragile balance and stability of the UK by threatening the peace settlement in Northern Ireland (with Sinn Féin demanding a vote to reunite the province with the Irish Republic) and the possibility of a second independence referendum in Scotland. In addition, the prospect of major political and constitutional struggles issues attending withdrawal from the EU was immediately raised on all sides, whether in terms of relations between government and parliament or between a parliament with a pro-remain majority and a pro-leave majority among the public.

In these circumstances, there was little or no appreciation of the complex, protracted process that lay ahead in withdrawing the country from EU membership. The Remain campaign was unwilling to concede such a possibility in advance and the civil service was told not to plan for Brexit, while the Brexiters were less concerned about process than about outcome and, as noted above, did not agree among themselves about a Brexit plan. In the days immediately after the referendum, therefore, there was a political vacuum. Mark Carney, the governor of the Bank of England, sought to reassure the markets, if not the British public, that the Bank was prepared to deal with what he called 'An economic post-traumatic stress disorder'.

In the meantime, cries of betrayal rang through the air. Some Brexit voters regretted their decision and felt betrayed as with almost indecent haste several Brexit leaders either rowed back on what they had said during the campaign or maintained that others and not themselves had made certain claims. Boris Johnson was a principal target of criticism in this regard especially when his *Daily Telegraph* column a few days after the result was not only stripped of all the one-liners on which he had campaigned but presented a vision of Britain little changed as a result of the verdict.

More importantly, the referendum outcome also took its toll on what passed for Labour Party unity. Indeed, what was regarded in some party circles as a half-hearted referendum campaign by Corbyn precipitated a challenge to his leadership; a large majority of his Shadow Cabinet (at least 20 in number) resigned and an equally substantial number of the parliamentary party (some 80 per cent) passed a vote of no confidence in his leadership. A contest for the party leadership was arranged to take place over the summer culminating in the announcement of the result on 24 September, thus allowing for a lengthy, internecine conflict and also forming a marked contrast to the Conservatives' change of leadership within three weeks of the referendum result.

The failure of the Remain campaign to achieve a majority also caused recriminations between political parties. This was markedly so in the case of relations between the Labour Party and the SNP. Each blamed the other for failing to mobilize the Remain vote in order to cancel out what, according to one post-referendum survey, was a substantial Conservative majority for Brexit (see Table C.3). Corbyn's allies blamed the SNP for failing to bring out the Remain vote as a result of a lackluster campaign with minimal ground activity; the turnout in Scotland (67 per cent) was substantially lower than in England and Wales and considerably down on the turnout for the 2014 Scotland independence referendum (84.59 per cent). The SNP for its part shared the criticism of some of Corbyn's opponents in the Labour Party which was to the effect that his

Table C.3 How party voters divided in the EU referendum of 23 June 2016 (%)

Party	Remain	Leave
Conservative	42	58
Labour	63	37
Liberal Democrats	70	30
UKIP	4	96
Greens	75	25
SNP	64	36

Source: Survey of 12,369 people after they had voted in the Britain and EU referendum,23 June 2016.
Lord Ashcroft Polls (http://lordashcroftpolls.com/).

handling of the Remain case was at best qualified and lukewarm. In fact according to survey evidence Labour and SNP voters split in more or less equal proportions between Remain and Leave (see Table C.3).

A disunited kingdom

Across the country, the referendum campaign and result revealed contrasting voting patterns, most notably in terms of geography, age and class. There was a majority for Brexit in England and Wales, and a majority for Remain in Northern Ireland and Scotland (see Table C.4), suggesting that the country was not a united nation-state, but a divided state of nations involved in a chilling culture war according to some commentators. There were also considerable regional variations, most markedly so in England where there was a majority for Remain in London but large majorities for Leave in Eastern England, the Midlands, and Yorkshire and Humber (see Table C.5).

In terms of age and voter turnout, the most recent polling survey at the time of writing was carried out by Opinium in association with the London School of Economics. It surveyed 2,002 people and reported the following voter turnout according to age:

18–24 age group – 64 per cent (much higher than was originally reported)
25–39 age group – 65 per cent
40–54 age group – 66 per cent
55–64 age group – 74 per cent
65 and over – 90 per cent

(*The Guardian*, 10 July 2016)

Table C.4 Britain and the EU referendum of 23 June 2016: final result and results by country (%)

Results by country	
UK-wide results	
Remain	48.1 (16,141,241 votes)
Leave	51.9 (17,410,742 votes)
Turnout	72.2
England	
Remain	46.8
Leave	53.2
Turnout	73
Northern Ireland	
Remain	55.7
Leave	44.3
Turnout	62.7
Scotland	
Remain	62
Leave	38
Turnout	67
Wales	
Remain	48.3
Leave	51.7
Turnout	72

Source: *The Telegraph*, 25 June 2016.

Table C.5 How the regions voted in the Britain and EU referendum of 23 June 2016 (millions)

Region	Remain	Leave
SE England	2.39	2.57
London	2.26	1.51
NW England	1.70	1.97
Scotland	1.66	1.02
SW England	1.50	1.67
Eastern England	1.45	1.88
West Midlands	1.21	1.76
Yorkshire and Humber	1.16	1.58
East Midlands	1.03	1.48
Wales	0.77	0.85
NE England	0.56	0.78
N Ireland	0.44	0.35

Source: PA Regional results.

Survey evidence (see Table C.6) together with media reports indicate that younger voters tended to support Remain, while a large number of older voters and most markedly so over the age of 65 voted for Leave.

Social class differences were also in evidence in terms of voting patterns, again at least according to survey data and media reports. These were more or less to the effect that the appeal of Leave was particularly strong among the skilled, semi-skilled and unskilled manual occupations, the unemployed and the lowest grade occupations (see Table C.6).

A detailed explanation for such differences awaits further study, suffice it to say that at the time explanations for this voting behaviour ranged from the impact of immigration to a deep-seated sense of alienation from the political and economic system, a whole-sale rejection of the government's austerity policies, and the assertion of a pronounced sense of English identity and nationalism. The issue of immigration was a matter of considerable concern in regions like Eastern England where there had been large-scale immigration for some years from the new EU member states of eastern Europe and where concerns about strained public services and the lack of affordable housing were frequently expressed (the failed pledge on immigration was joined by Cameron's failed pledge on housing). Support for Remain was far greater in areas like Northern Ireland and Scotland where immigration had occurred on a much smaller scale.

The Leave vote, however, was only partly related to EU membership and then almost entirely with respect to immigration. The Brexit campaign also drew on and reflected a large number of other sources of discontent that had not so far found a platform for full expression. Blaming the EU for the country's problems was a form of displacement activity, using it as so often in the past as a convenient whipping boy. In many respects the referendum registered the largest and most consequential protest vote in modern British history.

In so far as the Leave vote was often greatest in areas hardest hit by low pay, job insecurity with agency work and zero-hours contracts, and deprivation, it registered the views of 'left-behind Britain' in working-class areas. In this social milieu, the political establishment was viewed as arrogant and remote in much the same way as metropolitan, liberal, global-oriented London was regarded as an alien world. The vote was expressive

Table C.6 Survey of 12,369 people by gender, age and socio-economic classification after they had voted in the Britain and EU referendum 23 June 2016 (%)

	Remain	Leave
Total	48	52
Male	48	52
Female	48	52
18–24	73	27
25–34	62	38
35–44	52	48
45–54	44	56
55–64	43	57
65+	40	60
AB	57	43
C1	49	51
C2	36	64
DE	36	64

Notes:

AB: higher and intermediate managerial, administrative, professional occupations.

C1: supervisory, clerical and junior managerial, administrative, professional occupations.

C2: skilled manual occupations.

DE: semi-skilled and unskilled manual occupations, unemployed and lowest grade occupations.

Source: Lord Ashcroft Polls (http://lordashcroftpolls.com/). Socio-economic classification produced by the UK Office for National Statistics.

of a 'nothing to lose mentality' among people for whom, as one senior Remain campaigner put it, 'Emotional fear wasn't credible because they felt their lives were already shit' (*The Guardian*, 5 July 2016). The fact that such people decamped to UKIP had parallels with the way in which disenchanted Labour voters in urban Scotland, especially in Glasgow and Dundee, had abandoned their traditional Labour Party loyalties and supported the SNP in the 2014 independence referendum. In some respects the referendum result was not unlike one description of the Suez crisis of 1956: a flash of lightning on a dark night that illuminated a political landscape that had long been changing.

Any fear-based message appeared to command little or no support among economically disaffected voters, even in places with large-scale foreign investment like Sunderland (Nissan), Swindon (Honda) and Flintshire (Airbus) where Remain's warnings about the threat to foreign direct investment in the event of Brexit fell on stony ground.

Support for the Brexit campaign, especially via UKIP, was also indicative of the extent to which the Leave vote represented, however inchoate and undeveloped, an expression of English identity and nationalism with a marked degree of xenophobia at the extremes. In Chapter 5 we discussed the view that Euroscepticism was deployed as a proxy for English nationalism and that the key to understanding English nationalism was to focus on sovereignty. The slogan 'taking back control' encapsulated that sentiment in a powerful way among sections of society that had little or no control over stagnating living standards and were susceptible to anti-immigrant populism and opposition to globalization.

The prospect of a long goodbye or breaking up is hard to do

The process of negotiating withdrawal from the EU is unlikely to be anything other than protracted, painful, messy and costly, rendered all the more complex by the fact that while the country voted to leave the EU on 23 June it did so without a plan or any agreement on a way forward. At the time of writing (July 2016), the path ahead appears strewn with formidable problems, obstacles and possibilities. Some of the procedures concerning withdrawal are clear-cut while a number of the accompanying issues are disputable or clouded in uncertainty and dependent on political conditions.

On the first day of her premiership, Theresa May declared that 'Brexit means Brexit'. This declaration, however, begged a host of questions about what exactly Brexit meant; 'No two people know what Brexit means' observed the veteran pro-European Ken Clarke. Significantly, May appointed a trio of Brexit campaigners to come up with answers: Boris Johnson as Foreign Secretary, David Davis as Secretary of State for Exiting the European Union, and Liam Fox as Secretary of State for International Trade. In terms of domestic politics, these appointments suggested an astute move in managing the Conservative Party, especially the right wing and its anti-EU press allies. The appointments placed three of the leading Brexiters in the firing line of the consequences of their action. They were saddled with responsibility for negotiating the sort of trade-offs and compromises that could give rise to charges of Brexit betrayal if Remain government ministers had been assigned the task. May, however, took charge of the new ministerial committee on Brexit. Furthermore, as one Conservative commentator noted, May's Brexit was not the Brexit of the Europhobe ultras in the parliamentary Conservative Party, and as such Johnson and company could soon find themselves as either shameless collaborators, broken reeds, busted flushes or helpless hostages to May's plan for Brexit-lite (Matthew Parris in *The Times*, 16 July 2016).

In the wider international system, Johnson's appointment was greeted with a mixture of horror and amusement. Unsurprisingly, he commanded little or no respect in the other EU states, least of all in view of the way in which he had just won the referendum by denigrating the whole EU project and likening it to Hitler's aims for Europe. His counterparts in France and Germany – Jean-Marc Ayrault and Frank-Walter Steinmeier – recalled his referendum lies about the EU while Tusk, President of the European Council, denounced Johnson's 'absurd arguments', and some at home and abroad appreciated the comment of Kevin Brennan, the Labour MP, who called Johnson's appointment the most remarkable since Caligula appointed his horse as senator.

Immediate reactions to the Brexit victory elsewhere in the EU were mixed. They were marked less by disappointment than by astonishment at the turn of events, often giving rise to a rapid revision of stereotypical views of the English as imbued with common sense and belonging to a stable political order capable of contingency planning and not given to emotional spasms; 'England has collapsed, politically, constitutionally and economically' exclaimed Mark Rutte, the Dutch prime minister, as if every stereotypical picture of the country had been overturned (*Financial Times*, 29 June 2016). Angela Merkel described the event as 'a turning point for Europe', but she urged caution and perhaps unwittingly turned on its head the Second World War British song 'Don't let's be beastly to the Germans' by advising other EU states 'Don't be nasty to the British'. In a 'letter to Europe', *The Guardian*'s elegiac plea to the rest of the EU was 'Please, bid goodbye in sorrow, not anger; and for all our sakes, do not bolt the door' (*The Guardian*, 4 July 2016). Meanwhile, France seized the opportunity to attract the substantial euro clearing business carried out in the City of London, though Frankfurt seemed more likely than Paris to be a major beneficiary of any post-Brexit fallout in the British financial sector.

There was widespread agreement among the EU states that negotiations about Britain's withdrawal should be undertaken quickly in order to keep uncertainty to a minimum. There was an evident desire to limit economic instability. What also had to be avoided was the spread of exit contagion in a beleaguered EU under assault from a resurgence of right-wing nationalism and populism (though some early evidence indicated that in a number of EU states the Brexit aftermath had fostered a more pro-European climate, *The Guardian*, 8 July 2016). There was also a consensus among EU leaders that a particular sticking point in any negotiations would concern the relationship between British access to the Single Market and the principle of free movement of EU workers. In addition, there was opposition to the idea of a Single Market *à la carte* arrangement for Britain; 'Married or divorced, but not something in between' declared Xavier Bettel, the Luxembourg prime minister, adding that 'We are not on Facebook, with "it's complicated" as a status' (*Financial Times*, 29 June 2016).

In taking up such a stance, EU leaders evidently commanded popular support for the view that Britain should be given 'no favours' in negotiating a post-Brexit trade deal, possibly giving another dimension to the German federal elections and French presidential elections in 2017. A YouGov post-Brexit poll of voters in six EU countries found that voters wanted their governments to take a hard line on free trade and immigration. Only a majority of British and Danish voters expected a 'generous deal', while respondents in the other four countries – France, Finland, Germany and Sweden – registered majorities against the idea of such a deal, particularly in France and Germany.

Article 50 of the EU Treaty of Lisbon sets out how a member state might voluntarily leave the EU, specifying that a leaver should notify the European Council of its intention, negotiate a deal on its withdrawal and establish legal grounds for a future relationship with the EU. On the EU side, the agreement needs a qualified majority (QMV) of member states and consent of the European Parliament. Negotiators are given two years from the date of triggering Article 50 by the British government (via royal prerogative powers and not parliament, though this is currently – July 2016 – being contested in the courts) to conclude new arrangements. Failure to do so results in the exiting state falling out of the EU with no provisions in place, unless all of the remaining states agree to extend the negotiations.

One (pre-referendum result) representation of the mechanisms, process and possible problems of withdrawal usefully identifies the following aspects:

- Article 50 skews the balance of power in the negotiations in favour of the continuing EU states because of the two-year rule and the unanimity requirement for extensions to that period;
- there is no requirement for the British Prime Minister to trigger Article 50 immediately after the Brexit vote;
- there is general agreement in the referendum campaign that the whole process would take several years;
- the process of withdrawal will involve three sets of negotiations – (a) the negotiation of the withdrawal terms themselves, (b) the negotiation of a trade deal with the EU, (c) the negotiation of the terms of British membership of the WTO (it remains unclear whether some of these negotiations can take place simultaneously);
- parliament would be able to vote on the withdrawal deal as that would be a treaty, and would also have a great deal of legislating to do, including the repeal of the European Communities Act of 1972;
- Scotland's position within the UK would probably become even more contested;

- there are concerns in Northern Ireland that Brexit would undermine the peace process;
- there is no easy route to a second referendum, as the idea of a second referendum or a vote on the terms of a Brexit deal are both legally perilous options, though in practice some way round these difficulties might well be found.

(UCL Constitution Unit, http://constitution-unit.com/2016/06/20/
the-road-to-brexit-16-things-you-need-to-know-about-
what-will-happen-if-we-vote-to-leave-the-eu/)

It would serve no practical purpose at this stage to speculate on likely outcomes when many narratives or scenarios are possible. Potential problems and pitfalls abound on all sides, including the following:

- EU states striking a very hard bargain, as Britain would have more to lose from the absence of a deal than the rest of the EU;
- a parliament with a 'Remain' majority rejecting a deal (there is reckoned to be a 3-to-1 cross-party majority in the 2016 parliament for Remain with the minority largely comprising right-wing Conservatives);
- the relationship between particular forms and degrees of access to the Single Market (with or without access for financial services) and immigration from the EU;
- the accommodation of Scottish and Northern Irish support for continuing EU membership including the problematical consent of the devolved legislatures to repealing EU law.

There is certainly a widespread recognition of the mammoth size of the withdrawal exercise. Estimates vary about the length of this process from five to ten years according to some. The only precedent for such a situation is Greenland whose exit from the EU (1985) took two years of negotiation and this for a population of 55,000 with only one product: fish. There are also accompanying doubts about whether Whitehall and the civil service can cope with such tasks as reviewing 43 years of EU and domestic legislation, undertaking trade negotiations hitherto wholly conducted at the EU level, and giving some semblance of strategic order and settlement to the re-definition of the country's global role, profile and identity. According to some estimates, the British government will have to renegotiate 80,000 pages of EU agreements, deciding those to be kept in UK law and those to be jettisoned; the entire process could clog up parliament for years.

Finally, there is only a limited amount of mutual understanding and sense of empathy between Britain and the rest of the EU with regard to substantive issues. In EU circles, for example, Cameron's decision to hold a referendum together with the Johnson-led Brexit campaign were perceived as representing a betrayal of trust; Britain had after all pressed for the enlargement of the EU to the post-communist countries of eastern Europe and had voluntarily accepted an uncontrolled flow of immigrants from this source only to abandon the EU when facing the consequences of this policy. In British circles, and again to take but one example, there was resentment that EU leaders continually emphasized the importance of the free movement of workers but had done much less to open up the market for services in which Britain was most competitive; some 60 per cent of services were still not tradeable across the borders between EU states.

Full circle

In the immediate post-referendum circumstances the one certainty about the future is that the UK, however constituted, will have a relationship with the EU. What sort of relationship is unclear, as the country even more so than over the past 43 years is on a journey to an unknown destination. In some respects, the 23 June referendum result means that we have come full circle in this study. In the early 1950s Britain refused full involvement in the beginnings of the European Community. Throughout the remainder of the 1950s, however, as we noted in Chapter 2, British governments increasingly wrestled with the problem of coming to terms with the EC and of seeking, as now, a new relationship with the EC. They fruitlessly pursued several different types of relationship with the EC – association in the first instance, then close association followed by closest association and, finally, near identification before eventually gravitating towards the idea of EC membership.

Many of these expressions about different kinds of relationship will no doubt find their way into the process of unravelling the country's EU membership and negotiating new terms of engagement, most obviously with reference to the Single Market. What remains to be seen is whether eventually the process of withdrawal proves so fruitless, costly, complicated or subject to changing political conditions as to result in either the reversal of the referendum result or the adoption of one of a wide range of possibilities from a minimalist to a maximalist Brexit. The eventual settlement is unlikely to reflect the black and white or yes and no clarity of the referendum result, and may instead reveal the extent to which, to amend a common saying, 'you can take Britain out of the EU but you can't take the EU out of Britain'. In short, a referendum cannot by itself resolve the complex issues facing a country where both Euroscepticism and the EU are deeply embedded parts of national life and 'where a vote to stay in the EU can't kill off Euroscepticism and Britain's awkwardness in the EU, but a vote to leave can't kick the EU out of Britain' (Oliver, 2015).

In conclusion, the views of two former Conservative Party prime ministers have a bearing on the current state of Britain's relationship with the EU. At the time of the 1975 referendum, Margaret Thatcher registered her support for EC membership by posing a question: 'In politics we always have to consider "what is the alternative". The European Community or what?' (*The Daily Telegraph*, 4 June 1975). That question will hang over the negotiation of Britain's new relationship with the EU. The contemporary response to that question may result in new departures in British domestic and foreign policy. It is also possible, however, that the question may eventually come back to haunt Brexit policymakers and voters alike.

In terms of the Remain cause, it should be recalled that the outcome of the referendum vote was not without parallel in the turbulent history of Britain's relations with the EC/EU. At the time of de Gaulle's veto of the first British application to join the EC in January 1963, Edward Heath, leader of the British delegation to the entry negotiations whose pro-European views arose out of a 'Never again' response to the European bloodbaths of the twentieth century, had every reason to be depressed. In taking leave of a tearful company of negotiators (except the French), he made one of the most passionate speeches of his life:

> The end of the negotiations is a blow to the cause of the wider European unity
> for which we have been striving. We are a part of Europe, by geography, history,

culture, tradition and civilization ... We in Britain are not going to turn our backs on the mainland of Europe or the countries of the Community.

(Heath, 1998: 235)

The veto of 1963, however, was not the end of the story. Subsequent developments indicated that Britain's relationship with the EU, whether in the domestic or European context, rarely lost the capacity to surprise. That is likely to remain the case in the years ahead. The referendum result itself was not the endpoint in this saga. Rather it marked a new stage in the inescapable, complex and interminable debate about the country's contested role and place in Europe.

Appendix

How the European Union works

The European Union in brief

At the core of the EU are the member states – the 28 states that belong to the Union – and their citizens. The unique feature of the EU is that, although these are all sovereign, independent states, they have pooled some of their 'sovereignty' in order to gain strength and the benefits of size. Pooling sovereignty means, in practice, that the member states delegate some of their decision-making powers to the shared institutions they have created, so that decisions on specific matters of joint interest can be made democratically at European level. The EU thus sits between the fully federal system found in the United States and the loose intergovernmental co-operation system seen in the United Nations.

The EU treaties

The EU is based on the rule of law. This means that every action taken by the EU is founded on treaties that have been approved voluntarily and democratically by all EU countries. The treaties are negotiated and agreed by all the EU member states and then ratified by their parliaments or by referendum.

The treaties lay down the objectives of the EU, the rules for EU institutions, how decisions are made and the relationship between the EU and its member states. They have been amended each time new member states have joined. From time to time, they have also been amended to reform the EU's institutions and to give it new areas of responsibility.

The last amending treaty – the Lisbon Treaty – was signed in Lisbon on 13 December 2007, and came into force on 1 December 2009. Earlier treaties (see introduction) are now incorporated into the current consolidated version, which comprises the Treaty on European Union (TEU) and the Treaty on the Functioning of the European Union (TFEU).

The Treaty on Stability, Coordination and Governance (TSCG) in the Economic and Monetary Union was signed by all EU member states except the Czech Republic and the United Kingdom in 2012 and entered into force on 1 January 2013. It is not an EU treaty but an intergovernmental treaty, and the intention is to bring it into EU law. It obliges the countries to have firm rules to guarantee balanced budgets and it strengthens the governance of the euro area.

The main institutions of the EU

The European Parliament

The European Parliament was officially called the Common Assembly until the Single European Act of 1986, although its members called it the European Parliament from 1962.

Members of the European Parliament (MEPs) are directly elected by EU citizens to represent their interests. Originally, British MEPs were elected on the first-past-the-post-system. Since the EP elections of 1999, however, British voters have elected MEPs under a proportional representation system. Elections are held every five years and all EU citizens over 18 years old (16 in Austria) – some 380 million – are entitled to vote. The Parliament has 751 MEPs from all 28 member states.

The official seat of the European Parliament is in Strasbourg (France), although the institution has three places of work: Strasbourg, Brussels and Luxembourg. The main meetings of the whole Parliament, known as 'plenary sessions', take place in Strasbourg 12 times per year.

The seats in the Parliament are allocated among the member states on the basis of their share of the EU population. Most MEPs are associated with a national political party in their home country. In the European Parliament the national parties group into EU-wide political groupings and most MEPs belong to one of these.

The political groupings following the European parliamentary election of May 2014 (with the number of seats in brackets) are as follows:

Alliance of Liberals and Democrats for Europe – ALDE (67)
European Conservatives and Reformists – ECR (70)
Europe of Freedom and Direct Democracy – EFDD (48)
European People's Party (Christian Democrats) – EPP (221)
European United Left – Nordic Green Left – EUL/NGL (52)
The Greens/European Free Alliance – Greens/EFA (50)
Non-attached MEPs – Members not belonging to any political group (52)
Progressive Alliance of Socialists and Democrats – PASD (191)

The Parliament has three main roles:

1   It shares with the Council (see below) the power to legislate – to pass laws. The fact that it is a directly elected body helps guarantee the democratic legitimacy of EU law.
2   It exercises democratic supervision over all EU institutions, and in particular the Commission (see below). It has the power to approve or reject the nomination of the president of the Commission and Commissioners, and the right to censure the Commission as a whole.
3   It shares authority with the Council over the EU budget and can therefore influence EU spending. At the end of the budget procedure, it adopts or rejects the budget in its entirety.

The European Council

The European Council brings together the EU's top political leaders, i.e. prime ministers and presidents along with its president and the president of the Commission. They meet at least four times a year in Brussels to give the EU as a whole general political direction and priorities. The High Representative of the Union for Foreign Affairs and Security Policy also takes part in the work of the European Council.

As a summit meeting of the heads of state or government of all the EU member states, the European Council represents the highest level of political co-operation between the member states. At their meetings, the leaders decide by consensus on the overall direction and priorities of the Union, and provide the necessary impetus for its development. In a number of cases, however, qualified majority voting applies (see below), such as the election of its president, and the appointment of the Commission and of the High Representative of the Union for Foreign Affairs and Security.

The European Council does not adopt legislation. At the end of each meeting it issues 'conclusions', which reflect the main messages resulting from the discussions and take stock of the decisions taken, also as regards their follow-up.

The work of the European Council is coordinated by its president who is responsible for convening and chairing European Council meetings and driving forward its work. The European Council president also represents the Union to the outside world. Together with the High Representative of the Union for Foreign Affairs and Security Policy, he or she represents Union interests in foreign affairs and security matters.

The president is elected by the European Council for a once-renewable term of two-and-a-half years. The presidency of the Council is a full-time job; the president may not simultaneously hold a national office.

Outside of the European Council, the heads of state or government of those states whose currency is the euro also meet at least twice a year, together with the president of the European Commission. The president of the European Central Bank is also invited to these euro summit meetings. The meetings are an opportunity to discuss the governance of the euro as well as major economic policy reforms. The euro summit was formally established by the Treaty on Stability, Coordination and Governance (TSCG) in the Economic and Monetary Union.

The Council

The Council, also known as the Council of Ministers, is an essential EU decision-maker. Its work is carried out in Council meetings that are attended by one minister from each of the EU's national governments. Which ministers attend which Council meeting depends on the subjects on the agenda. Meetings are held in Brussels and Luxembourg.

The Council has five key responsibilities:

1 to pass EU laws – in most fields, it legislates jointly with the European Parliament;
2 to coordinate the member states' policies, for example, in the economic field;
3 to develop the EU's common foreign and security policy, based on guidelines set by the European Council;
4 to conclude international agreements between the EU and one or more states or international organizations;
5 to adopt the EU's budget, jointly with the European Parliament.

Decisions in the Council are taken by vote. In most cases a decision requires a qualified majority. In some cases the treaties require a different procedure, for example a unanimous vote in the field of taxation. In order for a proposal to be decided by qualified majority, it must obtain a double majority of both member states and population. The votes in favour must be at least:

* 55 per cent of the member states, i.e. 16 of the 28 countries;
* member states that represent 65 per cent of the EU's population. This means roughly 329 million out of the population of 506 million.

In addition, to block a decision from being taken there must be at least four countries voting against, representing more than 35 per cent of the population.

These rules mean that all decisions taken by the Council have broad support across Europe, but also that small minorities cannot block decisions from being taken.

Before November 2014, a different system was used whereby each country had a certain number of votes.

The European Commission

The Commission is the politically independent institution that represents and upholds the interests of the EU as a whole. In many areas it is the driving force within the EU's institutional system. It is headed by the president of the Commission and members of the Commission are known as Commissioners. There are 28 Commissioners, one from each EU country. The Commission is appointed every five years. The day-to-day work of the Commission is done by some 33,000 people working in the Commission – fewer than the number of staff employed by most medium-sized city councils in Europe. The Commission is located in Brussels.

The Commission remains answerable to the European Parliament, which has the power to dismiss it by adopting a motion of censure.

The Commission has four main roles:

1   to propose legislation to the Parliament and the Council;
2   to manage and implement EU policies and the budget;
3   to enforce EU law (jointly with the Court of Justice);
4   to represent the Union around the world.

The Court of Justice

The Court of Justice of the EU ensures that EU legislation is interpreted and applied in the same way in each member state – in other words, that it is always identical for all parties and in all circumstances. To this end, the Court checks the legality of the actions of the EU institutions, ensures the member states comply with their obligations and interprets EU law at the request of national courts.

The Court is located in Luxembourg. It is composed of 28 judges, one from each member state, so that all the EU national legal systems are represented. The Court has the power to settle legal disputes between member states, EU institutions, businesses and individuals.

The European Central Bank

The purpose of the European Central Bank (ECB) is to maintain monetary stability in the euro area by ensuring low and stable consumer price inflation. The bank is located in Frankfurt am Main and is headed by a president appointed by the European Council.

The ECB was set up in 1998, when the euro was introduced, to manage monetary policy in the euro area. It is an institution of economic and monetary union (EMU) to which all member states belong. Joining the euro area and adopting the single currency – the euro – is the final phase of EMU. Not all EU member states belong to the euro area: some are still preparing for their economies to join, and others like Britain have opt-outs.

The ECB stands at the core of the European System of Central Banks, which brings together the ECB and the national central banks of all EU member states.

The ECB sets the interest rates for lending to commercial banks which influences the price and the amount of money in the economy. It holds and manages the official foreign reserves of the euro area members. Its other tasks include conducting foreign exchange operations, promoting efficient payment systems in support of the Single Market, and approving the production of euro banknotes by the euro area members.

Decision-making at EU level

Every EU law is based on a specific treaty article, referred to as the 'legal basis' of the legislation. This determines which legislative procedure must be followed. The treaty sets out the decision-making process, including European Commission proposals, successive readings by the Council and Parliament, and the opinions of the advisory bodies. It also lays down when unanimity is required, and when a qualified majority is sufficient for the Council to adopt legislation.

Generally, it is the European Commission that proposes new laws, and it is the European Parliament and Council that adopt them. The member states and the Commission then implement them.

There are several types of legal acts which are applied in different ways:

A **regulation** is a law that is applicable and binding in all member states directly. It does not need to be passed into national law by the member states although national laws may need to be changed to avoid conflicting with the regulation.

A **directive** is a law that binds the member states, or a group of member states, to achieve a particular objective. A directive specifies the result to be achieved. It is up to the member states individually to decide how this is done.

A **decision** can be addressed to member states, groups of people, or even individuals. It is binding in its entirety. Decisions are used, for example, to rule on proposed mergers between companies.

Recommendations and **opinions** have no binding force.

(Source: adapted from European Commission (2014)
'How the European Union Works')

Chronological table

1945	May	End of the Second World War in Europe (May 8).
	July	Labour Party under Clement Attlee won the general election.
	July/August	Potsdam conference of American, British and Soviet leaders.
1947	January	Merging of American and British occupation zones in Germany (Bizonia).
	March	France and UK signed a 50-year friendship treaty: Treaty of Dunkirk. Announcement of the Truman doctrine, prompted by a British warning that it could no longer offer aid to the Greek government.
	June/July	First steps taken in the creation of the Marshall Plan.
	September	Churchill's Zurich speech calling for a United States of Europe.
	October	General Agreement on Tariffs and Trade (GATT) signed.
1948	March	Brussels Treaty signed by Benelux states, France and UK.
	April	Organisation for European Economic Co-operation (OEEC) established to administer the European Recovery Programme (Marshall Plan).
	May	Congress of Europe at The Hague called for the political and economic union of European nations.
	June	Berlin blockade started.
1949	April	North Atlantic Treaty signed by Belgium, Canada, Denmark, France, Iceland, Italy, Luxembourg, Netherlands, Norway, Portugal, UK and United States.
	May	Statute of the Council of Europe signed by ten states including the UK.
1950	May	Announcement of the Schuman Plan.
	June	Outbreak of the Korean War.
	October	Announcement of the Pleven Plan for a European army.
1951	April	European Coal and Steel Community (ECSC) Treaty signed by Belgium, France, Italy, Luxembourg, the Netherlands and West Germany.
	July	ECSC began to function.
	October	Conservative Party under Winston Churchill won the general election.
1952	May	European Defence Community (EDC) Treaty signed by the six ECSC states.
1954	August	French National Assembly rejected the EDC Treaty.
	October	Signature of the Paris Agreements and the formation of the Western European Union allowing for the restoration of full sovereignty to a rearmed West Germany and NATO membership.
	December	Treaty of Association between the ECSC and the UK.
1955	April	Anthony Eden succeeded Churchill as prime minister.

	June	Messina conference of the six ECSC states.
	July	Spaak committee convened to consider plans for further European integration.
1956	March	Spaak report on the creation of a common market.
	October/ November	Suez crisis.
	November	Announcement of a British plan for a free trade area (FTA).
1957	January	Harold Macmillan succeeded Eden as prime minister.
	March	Treaties of Rome signed establishing the European Economic Community (EEC) and the European Atomic Energy Community (EAEC).
	October	Formation of the Maudling Committee under the aegis of the OEEC to consider the plan for an FTA.
1958	January	Treaties of Rome came into operation.
	December	France blocked further discussion of the FTA plan.
1959	January	First EEC tariff reductions and increases in import quotas.
1960	January	European Free Trade Association (EFTA) Convention signed in Stockholm by Austria, Denmark, Norway, Portugal, Sweden, Switzerland and the UK.
	May	Failure of Four-Power summit in Paris.
	December	OEEC reorganized into the Organisation for Economic Co-operation and Development (OECD).
1961	August	First UK application to join the EC.
1962	January	Agreement on the main features of the EC's Common Agricultural Policy (CAP).
	December	Kennedy/Macmillan meeting at Nassau and the Polaris agreement.
1963	January	De Gaulle vetoed UK membership of the EEC. Treaty of Friendship and Cooperation signed by France and West Germany.
	October	Alec Douglas-Home succeeded Macmillan as prime minister.
1964	October	Labour Party under Harold Wilson won the general election.
1965	April	Merger Treaty of the European Communities (EC) signed. It entered into force on 1 July 1967.
	July	France began a boycott of EC institutions.
1966	January	Luxembourg Agreement ended French boycott of EC institutions.
	March	Labour Party won the general election. De Gaulle announced the withdrawal of France from NATO.
	May/July	EC negotiated an agreement on the CAP.
1967	May	Second UK application for EC membership.
	November	De Gaulle vetoed UK membership of EC.
1968	July	Completion of the EC customs union.
1969	April	De Gaulle resigned as president of the Fifth French Republic.
	December	The Hague summit of EC leaders agreed in principle to enlarge the EC and to devise a plan for economic and monetary union.
1970	April	EC agreement on new arrangements for financing the budget through automatic revenue ('own resources').
	June	Conservative Party won the general election under Edward Heath. EC opened membership negotiations with Denmark, Ireland, Norway and the UK.
	October	Publication of the Werner Report on Economic and Monetary Union and the Davignon Report on European Political Co-operation.
1971	March	EC Council of Ministers agreed to embark on the first of the three stages towards economic and monetary union by 1980.
	October	UK parliament approved EC membership. Labour Party conference voted in favour of 'No entry on Tory terms'.
1972	January	Conclusion of EC membership negotiations and signature of Treaties of Accession by Denmark, Ireland, Norway and the UK.

	July	European Communities Act passed. Roy Jenkins resigned from the Labour Party Shadow Cabinet.
	October	UK parliament voted in favour of the principle of UK membership of the EC. Paris summit of EC leaders reaffirmed the goal of achieving economic and monetary union by 1980.
1973	January	Accession of Denmark, Ireland and the UK to the EC.
1974	February	Election of a minority Labour government under Harold Wilson with a commitment to renegotiate the terms of entry to the EC.
	April	Labour government opened renegotiation of EC entry terms.
	October	Labour government under Wilson returned to power after general election.
	December	EC leaders agreed to meet regularly as European Council.
1975	February	Lomé Convention brought former British colonies into aid and trade relationship with the EC.
	March	Conclusion of the UK's renegotiation of the terms of entry to the EC.
	June	UK referendum resulted in a majority for the renegotiated terms of entry and continued membership of the EC.
	December	Rome European Council meeting agreed to hold direct elections to the European Parliament.
1976	April	James Callaghan succeeded Wilson as prime minister.
	September	Sterling crisis: IMF loan terms imposed.
1977	November	Direct elections to the European Parliament postponed until 1979 due to UK failure to meet the original deadline.
1978	July	Franco-German proposal for a European Monetary System (EMS) announced at the Bremen European Council meeting.
	December	Formal announcement of UK decision not to participate in the Exchange Rate Mechanism (ERM) of the EMS.
1979	March	Exchange Rate Mechanism of the EMS began to function.
	May	Conservative Party under Margaret Thatcher won the general election.
	June	First direct elections to the European Parliament.
1980	May	EC Council of Ministers agreed to reduce UK contribution to EC budget for two years.
	October	Labour Party conference voted to withdraw from the EC.
1981	January	Accession of Greece to the EC.
	March	Launch of the Social Democratic Party.
1982	January	Common Fisheries Policy agreement.
	April	Britain tried unsuccessfully to invoke the Luxembourg Compromise in order to veto agricultural price package in the Agricultural Council.
1983	June	Conservative Party under Thatcher won the general election.
1984	January	Free trade area established between the EC and the EFTA.
	June	Fontainebleau European Council meeting agreed a formula for reducing the UK contribution to the EC budget. British paper entitled 'Europe – the Future'.
1985	January	Jacques Delors appointed president of the Commission.
	June	Milan European Council meeting agreed in principle to establish a Single Market by the end of December 1992 and to convene an intergovernmental conference (IGC) on EC reform. Schengen Agreement signed by five of the ten EU states, establishing the principles of an area in which there would be no internal border controls (Schengen – a small town in Luxembourg).
	December	Luxembourg European Council meeting agreed on the principles of the Single European Act.
1986	January	Accession of Portugal and Spain to the EC.
	February	Single European Act signed in Luxembourg.

1987	June	Conservative Party under Thatcher won the general election.
	July	Single European Act came into force.
1988	April	Labour Party recommitted to EC membership.
	June	Hanover European Council meeting instructed a committee chaired by Jacques Delors to consider plans for the achievement of Economic and Monetary Union (EMU).
	September	Thatcher's speech at the College of Europe in Bruges. Delors' speech to the TUC.
	October	Labour Party conference formally abandoned withdrawal from the EC policy.
1989	January	Delors reappointed president of the Commission.
	April	Delors Report on a three-stage progression towards the achievement of EMU.
	June	Madrid European Council meeting agreed to begin first stage of EMU on 1 July 1990.
	October	Nigel Lawson resigned as Chancellor of the Exchequer.
	November	Fall of the Berlin Wall.
	December	At the Strasbourg European Council meeting all EC states except UK approved the Charter of Basic Social Rights for Workers (Social Charter) and also agreed to establish an IGC on EMU at the end of 1990.
1990	June	Dublin European Council meeting agreed to convene an IGC on Political Union.
	July	First stage of EMU came into effect.
	October	UK entered the ERM of the EMS. Rome European Council meeting agreed to implement the second stage of the Delors Plan for EMU by 1994.
	November	John Major succeeded Thatcher as Conservative Party leader and prime minister.
	December	The two IGCs on EMU and Political Union opened in Rome.
1991	December	Maastricht European Council meeting agreed the Treaty on European Union (Maastricht Treaty). UK government secured opt-outs covering the Social Chapter and the third and final stage of EMU.
1992	February	Treaty on European Union signed in Maastricht.
	May	Conservative Party under Major won the general election. EC and EFTA signed a treaty establishing the European Economic Area (EEA).
	June	Danish voters rejected the Treaty on European Union in a referendum.
	September	UK withdrew from the ERM.
1993	January	Single Market came into effect.
	February	EC opened negotiations with Austria, Finland and Sweden (and Norway – April 1993) on their application for membership.
	May	Danish voters approved the Treaty on European Union after Denmark obtained opt-outs from the Treaty.
	June	Copenhagen European Council endorsed the process leading to eastern enlargement of the EC.
	July	UK ratified the Treaty on European Union.
	November	Treaty on European Union formally came into effect.
1994	January	Second stage of EMU came into effect with the establishment in Frankfurt of the European Monetary Institute as a precursor of the European Central Bank.
	June	Britain vetoed choice of Jean-Luc Dehaene as next president of the Commission.
	July	Tony Blair elected leader of the Labour Party.

1995	January	Austria, Finland and Sweden joined the EU.
	March	Seven EU states adopted Schengen Agreement on open borders.
	June	Cannes European Council meeting recognized that the introduction of a single currency by 1997 was unrealistic. Madrid European Council meeting confirmed introduction of the single currency for 1 January 1999.
1996	March	IGC convened to review the Treaty on European Union.
	December	Dublin European Council meeting agreed a single currency stability pact.
1997	May	Labour Party under Blair won the general election and announced its intention to end Britain's opt-out from the EU Social Chapter.
	June	Amsterdam European Council meeting agreed the Treaty of Amsterdam following the IGC review of the Treaty on European Union. Britain accepted the Social Chapter.
	October	Gordon Brown, Chancellor of the Exchequer, specified five economic tests for UK entry into the euro and indicated that the UK would not be ready for entry before the end of the current parliament.
	December	Luxembourg European Council meeting invited Cyprus, the Czech Republic, Estonia, Hungary, Poland and Slovenia to start membership talks in March 1998 with a view to entry to the EU early in the next century.
1998	May	11 of the 15 EU states agreed to proceed to the third and final stage of EMU (scheduled for 1 January 1999) with provision for the establishment of a European Central Bank (ECB), the fixing of exchange rates and the introduction of a single currency – the euro. Denmark, Sweden and the UK had previously obtained opt-outs from this timetable, while Greece was deemed to have failed to qualify.
	December	British and French governments agreed principles of a defence and security policy for the EU through the St Malo Declaration.
1999	January	The euro was launched as an accounting currency and adopted by Austria, Belgium, Finland, France, Germany, Ireland, Italy, Luxembourg, Portugal, Spain and the Netherlands.
	February	Blair announced a 'national changeover plan' for the possible replacement of the pound sterling by the euro.
	March	Resignation of Santer Commission in response to claims of wasteful expenditure and fraud.
	May	The WEU member states agreed in principle to incorporate the WEU into the EU.
	November	A joint meeting of EU foreign and defence ministers, the first of its kind in the history of the EU, considered how to increase the military powers of the EU in the aftermath of the conflicts in Bosnia and Kosovo.
	December	Helsinki European Council further endorsed EU enlargement and set headline goal of developing European Rapid Reaction Force.
2000	March	Greece formally applied to join the EMU. EU leaders at a meeting in Lisbon launched a ten-year programme to make the EU the world's most competitive economic area by 2010.
	November	14 states agreed to provide armed forces for European Rapid Reaction Force.
	December	EU states agreed the Nice Treaty and proclaimed the Charter of Fundamental Rights of the European Union.
2001	January	Greece adopted the euro.

	February	Treaty of Nice signed. EU justice and home affairs ministers agreed to accelerate harmonization of the immigration and political asylum policies of the EU member states. EU ban on exports of UK livestock, meat and dairy products imposed as a result of a foot and mouth epidemic in the UK.
	March	Switzerland rejected EU membership at a referendum.
	June	Ireland rejected the Treaty of Nice in a referendum. Labour Party under Blair won the general election.
	September	Terrorists hijacked four passenger aircraft in the United States. Two of the planes smashed into the twin towers of the World Trade Center in New York. A third plane demolished part of the Pentagon, and the fourth plane crashed in a field in Pennsylvania.
	October	NATO-led intervention in Afghanistan with contributions from every EU member state except Cyprus and Malta.
	December	European Convention established.
2002	January	Euro notes and coins came into circulation. Convention on the Future of Europe began work on a draft constitution for the EU.
	June	EU heads of government meeting in Seville agreed on a new plan to tackle illegal immigration. The 50-year treaty establishing the ECSC expired and the functions of the ECSC were absorbed by the EC.
	October	Ireland voted in favour of the Treaty of Nice in a second referendum.
2003	February	Treaty of Nice came into effect. In the biggest backbench revolt since Tony Blair came to power in 1997, 122 Labour MPs supported an anti-war amendment to a government motion on the Iraq crisis.
	March	The EU was involved in peace-making operations in the Balkans as a result of its Common Foreign and Security Policy. The EU agreed to create an area of Freedom, Security and Justice for all of its citizens by 2010. Invasion of Iraq led by United States and Britain with support from other European countries but strong opposition from France and Germany.
	May	Gordon Brown, Chancellor of the Exchequer, announced that four of the five economic tests for taking Britain into the euro had not yet been met.
2004	April	In a major policy reversal, Tony Blair announced that a national referendum would be held on the proposed EU Constitutional Treaty following agreement on a text.
	May	Eight Central and Eastern European countries joined the EU (Czech Republic, Estonia, Hungary, Latvia, Lithuania, Poland, Slovakia and Slovenia). Cyprus and Malta also joined.
	October	25 countries signed a Treaty establishing a European Constitution.
2005	May	France rejected the Constitutional Treaty in a referendum. Labour Party under Blair won the general election.
	June	The Netherlands voted against the Constitutional Treaty.
2007	January	Bulgaria and Romania joined the EU.
	June	Gordon Brown succeeded Blair as prime minister and Labour Party leader. European Council abandoned Constitution for Europe.
	July	ECOFIN Council approved the adoption of the euro by Cyprus and Malta from 1 January 2008. Formal opening of the IGC on the Draft Reform Treaty for the EU.
	August/ September	Beginnings of financial crisis in UK with the first run on a British bank (Northern Rock) for 150 years and subsequent nationalization of Northern Rock (February 2008).
	September	David Cameron, leader of the Conservative Party, gave a guarantee to hold a referendum on the Lisbon Treaty following the election of a Conservative government.
	December	Treaty of Lisbon signed.

2008	January	Cyprus and Malta adopted the euro.
	June	Ireland rejected the Lisbon Treaty in a referendum.
	July	British parliament ratified Treaty of Lisbon.
	September	Collapse of the Lehman Brothers bank in the United States.
	October	UK government bailed out several banks including HBOS, Lloyds TSB and the Royal Bank of Scotland.
2009	January	Slovakia adopted the euro.
	October	Greece announced 2009 budget deficit estimated at 12.7 per cent of GDP. Second referendum in Ireland accepted Treaty of Lisbon.
2010	May	Greece bailed out for the first time as euro area finance ministers agreed loans worth 110 bn. euros. General election resulted in the formation of a Conservative and Liberal Democrat Coalition government under David Cameron.
	June	European Financial Stability Facility created by euro area states to provide financial assistance – a temporary measure subsequently replaced by the ESM (see February 2012 entry).
	November	Ireland bail out of 85 bn. euros agreed. Lancaster House Treaties between Britain and France on security and defence.
2011	January	The European Banking Authority was established as a regulatory agency of the EU based in London to conduct stress tests on European banks. Estonia adopted the euro.
	March	NATO military intervention in Libya largely led by Britain and France and eventually resulting in the death of Gadaffi, the Libyan leader, in October 2011.
	May	Portugal bailout of 78 bn. euros agreed.
	July	British Parliament passed the European Union Act.
	September	EU agreed a collection of six new laws, known as the 'six pack'.
	October	81 Conservative MPs defied a three-line party whip and supported a referendum on British membership of the EU. The motion calling for a referendum was defeated in the House of Commons by 483 votes to 111.
	December	Cameron vetoed the proposal for an EU treaty-based Fiscal Compact. 'Six pack' economic governance legislation entered into force.
2012	January	25 EU states signed the Fiscal Compact (formally Treaty on Stability, Coordination and Governance).
	February	Euro area states signed the treaty establishing the European Stability Mechanism (ESM) – the area's permanent financial assistance mechanism.
	March	Greece bailed out for a second time in a deal worth 130 bn. euros.
	July	EU financial assistance given to Spain. Mario Draghi, president of the European Central Bank (ECB), said that the ECB would do 'whatever it takes to preserve the euro'. Balance of Competences Review launched to examine the balance of competences between the UK and the EU.
	October	Nobel Peace Prize awarded to the EU.
	December	Spain bailout of 39.5 bn. euros.
2013	January	In his Bloomberg speech, Cameron announced that if the Conservatives won the next election they would seek to renegotiate the UK's relationship with the EU and hold a referendum by the end of 2017. The Treaty on Stability, Coordination and Governance entered into force.
	March	International Monetary Fund (IMF) and euro area agreed financial assistance package to Cyprus.
	July	Croatia joined the EU.
	December	Ireland and Spain exited their financial assistance programmes.

2014	January	Latvia adopted the euro as its currency, becoming the eighteenth member of the euro area.
	March	EU sanctions imposed against persons in Russia responsible for undermining the territorial integrity of Ukraine. Ed Miliband, Labour Party leader, indicated that the Labour Party would not hold a referendum on the UK's membership of the EU unless there were proposals to transfer further powers from London to Brussels.
	May	European Parliament elections – in Britain UKIP emerged as the largest party with 24 seats.
	June	Portugal exited its financial assistance programme.
	September	Residents in Scotland voted 'No' in a referendum on Scottish independence.
	November	New rules entered into force for voting in the EU Council of Ministers.
2015	January	Lithuania adopted the euro.
	May	Conservative Party under Cameron's leadership won the general election with a majority of 12 seats and immediately pledged to make good on their election manifesto promise to hold a referendum on the UK's membership of the EU by the end of 2017. Labour Party dropped its opposition to a referendum on the UK's membership of the EU.
	August	Third bailout agreed for Greece worth 86 bn. euros.
	September	Cameron's Conservative government suffered its first defeat in the House of Commons after Eurosceptic Conservatives joined forces with opposition MPs over the government's proposed changes to the rules covering government activity during the final phase of the EU referendum campaign. German government adopted an open-door policy as response to the influx of refugees and asylum seekers from the Middle East and North Africa. Hungarian government closed its border with Serbia and built a razor wire fence to stop the flow of migrants.
	November	Cameron set out a new settlement for the UK in a reformed EU.
2016	February	Brussels meeting of the European Council. UK referendum on EU membership set for 23 June 2016.
	June	Referendum on UK membership of EU resulted in a majority (52 per cent) voting in favour of leaving the EU. David Cameron resigned as Prime Minister.
	July	Theresa May became Conservative Party leader and Prime Minister.

Bibliography

Aldous, R. and Lee, S. (eds) (1996) *Harold Macmillan and Britain's World Role*, London: Macmillan.

Alexander, P. (2000) 'The Commonwealth and European Integration: Competing Commitments for Britain, 1956–1967', unpublished thesis, Cambridge University.

Alexander, P. (2003) 'From Imperial Power to Regional Power: Commonwealth Crises and the Second Application', in Daddow, O. J. (ed.) *Harold Wilson and European Integration: Britain's Second Application to Join the EEC*, London: Frank Cass Publishers.

Anderson, B. (1992) *John Major*, London: Headline.

Anderson, P. J. and Weymouth, A. (1999) *Insulting the Public? The British Press and the European Union*, Harlow: Longman.

Aron, R. (1954) *The Century of Total War*, Garden City: Doubleday.

Ash, T. G. (2001) 'Is Britain European', *International Affairs*, January, Vol. 77, No. 1, 1–13.

Ash, T. G. (2009) *Facts are Subversive: Political Writing from a Decade Without a Name*, London: Atlantic Books.

Ashcroft, M. and Oakeshott, I. (2015) *Call me Dave*, London: Biteback.

Ashton, S. R. (2007) 'British Government Perspectives on the Commonwealth, 1964–71: An Asset or a Liability?', *The Journal of Imperial and Commonwealth History*, Vol. 35, No. 1, 73–94.

Auden, W. H. (1963) 'Going into Europe', *Encounter*, Vol. 112, No. 53, 53–64.

Avery, G. and Cameron, F. (1998) *The Enlargement of the European Union*, Sheffield: Sheffield Academic Press.

Baker, D. and Seawright, D. (eds) (1998) *Britain For and Against Europe: British Politics and the Question of European Integration*, Oxford: Clarendon Press.

Baker, D., Gamble, A. and Ludlam, S. (1994) 'The Parliamentary Siege of Maastricht 1993: Conservative Divisions and British Ratification', *Parliamentary Affairs*, Vol. 47, No. 1, 35–59.

Ball, G. W. (1982) *The Past has Another Pattern: Memoirs*, New York: Norton.

Ball, S. and Seldon, A. (eds) (1996) *The Heath Government 1970–74: A Reappraisal*, London: Longman.

Banks, I. (2002) *Dead Air*, London: Little, Brown.

Bartlett, C. J. (1992) *'The Special Relationship': A Political History of Anglo-American Relations since 1945*, London: Longman.

BBC TV (1999) *The Major Years*, 2nd programme.

Beetham, R. (ed.) (2001) *The Euro Debate: Persuading the People*, London: Federal Trust.

Bell, D. (November 2015) 'Immigration to Scotland and Brexit', Centre on Constitutional Change.

Bell, P. (1996) 'A Historical Cast of Mind: Some Eminent English Historians and Attitudes to Continental Europe in the Middle of the Twentieth Century', *Journal of European Integration History*, Vol. 2, No. 2, 5–20.

Bell, P. (2004) *The Labour Party in Opposition, 1970–74*, Abingdon: Taylor & Francis.

Bell, P. M. H. (1997) *France and Britain 1940–1994: The Long Separation*, London and New York: Longman.

Beloff, N. (1963) *The General Says No: Britain's Exclusion from Europe*, London: Penguin.

Beloff, N. (1973) *Transit of Britain*, London: Collins.

Benn, T. (1988) *Out of the Wilderness: Diaries 1963–67*, London: Arrow Books.

Benn, T. (1989) *Against the Tide: Diaries, 1973–77*, London: Arrow Books.

Benn, T. (1996) *The Benn Diaries: Selected, Abridged and Introduced by Ruth Winstone*, London: Arrow Books.

Bennett, G. (2013) *Six Moments of Crisis: Inside British Foreign Policy*, Oxford: Oxford University Press.

Bennett, J. C. (2004) *The Anglosphere: Why the English-Speaking Nations will Lead the Way in the Twenty-First Century*, Lanham: Rowman & Littlefield.

Benvenuti, A. (2005) 'Dealing with an Expanding European Community: Australia's Attitude towards the EC's 1st Enlargement', *Journal of European Integration History*, Vol. II, No. 2, 75–96.

Bevir, M., Daddow, O. and Hall, I. (2013) 'Introduction: Interpreting British Foreign Policy', *The British Journal of Politics and International Relations*, Vol. 15, 163–74.

Bevir, M., Daddow, O. and Schnapper, P. (2015) 'Introduction: Interpreting British European Policy', *Journal of Common Market Studies*, Vol. 53, No. 1, 1–17.

Bill, J. A. (1997) *George Ball: Behind the Scenes in US Foreign Policy*, London: Yale University Press.

Biscop, S. (2012) 'The UK and European Defence: Leading or Leaving?', *International Affairs*, Vol. 88, No. 6, 1297–313.

Blackwell, M. (1993) *Clinging to Grandeur: British Attitudes and Foreign Policy in the Aftermath of the Second World War*, Westport: Greenwood Press.

Blair, A. (2002) *Saving the Pound? Britain's Road to Monetary Union*, Harlow: Pearson.

Blair, T. (2010) *Tony Blair: A Journey*, London: Random House.

Bloemen, E. (1995) 'A Problem to Every Solution: The Six and the Free Trade Area', in Olsen, T. B. (ed.) *Interdependence versus Integration: Denmark, Scandinavia and Western Europe 1945–1960*, Odense: Odense University Press.

Blunkett, D. (2006) *The Blunkett Tapes*, London: Bloomsbury.

Boehme, L. M. (2004) 'Our Man in Paris: The British Embassy in Paris and the Second UK Application to Join the EEC, 1966–67', *Journal of European Integration History*, Vol. 10, No. 2, 43–58.

Bogdanor, V. (1994) 'Britain and the European Community' in Jowell, J. and Oliver, D. (eds) *The Changing Constitution*, 3rd edition, Oxford: Clarendon Press.

Bootle, R. (2014) *The Trouble with Europe*, London: Nicholas Brealey Publishing.

Bower, T. (2007) *Gordon Brown Prime Minister*, London: Harper Perennial.

Brandt, W. (1978) *People and Politics: The Years 1960–1975*, London: Collins.

BDOHP (British Diplomatic Oral History Programme), Interview with Michael Butler, 1 October 1997, Churchill College, Cambridge.

BDOHP, Interview with Roy Denman, 4 May 1999.

BDOHP, Interview with John Killick, 14 February 2002.

BDOHP, Interview with Donald Maitland, 11 December 1997.

BDOHP, Interview with Michael Palliser, 28 April 1999.

BDOHP, Interview with Charles Powell, 18 July 2000.

BDOHP, Interview with Frank Roberts, 3 July 1996.

Brivati, B. (1996) *Hugh Gaitskell*, London: Richard Cohen Books.

Brivati, B. and Jones, H. (eds) (1993) *What Difference did the War Make?*, Leicester: Leicester University Press.

Broad, M. and Daddow, O. (2010) 'Half-Remembered Quotations from Mostly Forgotten Speeches: The Limits of Labour's European Policy Discourse', *British Journal of Politics & International Relations*, Vol. 12, No. 2, 205–22.

Broad, R. and Preston, V. (eds) (2001) *Moored to the Continent: Britain and European Integration*, London: Institute of Historical Research.

Broadberry, S. and Leunig, T. (2013) 'The Impact of Government Policies on UK Manufacturing since 1945', London: Government Office for Science.

Brocklehurst, H. (2015) 'Educating Britain? Political Literacy and the Construction of National History', *Journal of Common Market Studies*, Vol. 53, No. 1, 52–70.

Broussard, J. H. (2014) *Ronald Reagan: Champion of Conservative America*, London: Routledge.

Brown, G. (1972) *In My Way*, London: Gollancz.

Brown, G. (2005) *Global Europe: Full Employment Europe*, London: HM Treasury.

Buller, J. (2000) *National Statecraft and European Integration: The Conservative Government and the European Union, 1979–1997*, London and New York: Pinter.

Bullock, A. (1983) *Ernest Bevin: Foreign Secretary 1945–1951*, Oxford: Oxford University Press.

Bulmer, S. and Paterson, W. (1987) *The Federal Republic of Germany and the European Community*, London: Unwin Hyman.

Bulmer, S., George, S. and Scott, A. (eds) (1992) *The United Kingdom and EC Membership Evaluated*, London: Pinter.

Bulmer, S., Burch, M., Carter, C., Hogwood, P. and Scott, A. (2002) *British Devolution and European Policy-Making: Transforming Britain into Multi-Level Governance*, Basingstoke: Palgrave.

Bulpitt, J. (1983) *Territory and Power in the United Kingdom*, Manchester: Manchester University Press.

Burage, M. (2016) *Myth and Paradox of the Single Market: How the Trade Benefits of EU Membership Have Been Mis-sold*, London: Civitas.

Burk, K. and Cairncross, A. (1992) *'Goodbye Great Britain': The 1976 IMF Crisis*, New Haven and London: Yale University Press.

Butler, D. and King, A. (1965) *The British General Election of 1964*, London: Macmillan.

Butler, D. and Kitzinger, U. (1976) *The 1975 Referendum*, London: Macmillan.

Butt, P. (1992) 'British Pressure Groups and the European Community', in George, S. (ed.) *Britain and the European Community*, Oxford: Clarendon Press.

Byrd, P. (ed.) (1988) *British Foreign Policy under Thatcher*, Oxford: Philip Allan.

Cairncross, A. (ed.) (1982) *Anglo-American Economic Collaboration in War and Peace 1942–1949 by Sir Richard Clarke*, Oxford: Clarendon Press.

Callaghan, J. (1987) *Time and Chance*, London: Collins.

Campbell, A. (2011) *The Alastair Campbell Diaries Volume Three: 1999 to 2011*, London: Hutchinson.

Campbell, A. (2012) *The Alastair Campbell Diaries: The Burden of Power: Countdown to Iraq*, London: Hutchinson.

Campbell, J. (1993) *Edward Heath: A Biography*, London: Jonathan Cape.

Campbell, J. (2003) *Margaret Thatcher: The Iron Lady*, London: Jonathan Cape.

Camps, M. (1964) *Britain and the European Community 1955–1963*, London: Oxford University Press.

Castle, B. (1990) *The Castle Diaries, 1964–1976*, London: Macmillan.

Castle, B. (1993) *Fighting All the Way*, London: Macmillan.

Cecil, G. (1921) *Life of the Marquis of Salisbury*, Vol. II, London: Hodder & Stoughton.

Centre for European Reform (2014) 'The Economic Consequences of Leaving the EU', London: Centre for European Reform.

Charlton, M. (1983) *The Price of Victory*, London: BBC.

Charmley, J. (1995) *Churchill's Grand Alliance: The Anglo-American Relationship 1940–57*, London: Hodder & Stoughton.

Charmley, J. (2004) 'Splendid Isolation to Finest Hour: Britain as a Global Power, 1900–1950', *Contemporary British History*, Vol. 18, No. 3, 130–46.

Charter, D. (2012) *Au Revoir, Europe What if Britain left the EU?*, London: Biteback Publishing.

Chatham House (2012) *'Hard Choices Ahead'*, YouGov Survey, London.

Chryssogelos, A. (25 November 2015) 'Refugees: The EU's Crisis Within a Crisis', https://euobserver.com/opinion/132233.

Churchill, R. S. (ed.) (1950) *Europe Unite – Speeches: 1947 and 1948 by Winston S. Churchill*, London: Cassell.

Cini, M. (ed.) (2007) *European Union Politics*, Oxford: Oxford University Press.

Clemens, G. (2004) 'A History of Failures and Miscalculations? Britain's Relationship to the European Communities in the Postwar Era (1945–73)', *Contemporary European History*, Vol. 13, No. 2, 223–32.

Clifford, D. (2004) 'How Devolution Changed European Policy', *Agenda*, Spring 2004, Cardiff: Institute of Welsh Affairs.

Coles, J. (2000) *Making Foreign Policy*, London: John Murray.

Colley, L. (2014) *Acts of Union and Disunion: What Has Held the UK Together – and What is Dividing it?*, London: Profile Books.

Colman, J. (2004) 'The London Ambassadorship of David K. E. Bruce during the Wilson-Johnson Years, 1964–68', *Diplomacy and Statecraft*, Vol. 15, 327–52.

Connolly, B. (1995) *The Rotten Heart of Europe: The Dirty War for Europe's Money*, London: Faber & Faber.

Conservative Party Central Office Publication (1962) *Common Market Commonsense No. 9: Religious Freedom*, London.

Conservative Party Conference (1994) Conservative Party Archive, Oxford: Oxford University.

Cook, R. (2003) *The Point of Departure*, London: Simon & Schuster.

Cooper, R. (2012) 'Britain and Europe', *International Affairs*, Vol. 88, 1191–203.

Coopey, R., Fielding, S. and Tiratsoo, N. (eds) (1993) *The Wilson Governments, 1964–70*, London: UCL Press.

Cornish, P. (1995) *British Military Planning for the Defence of Germany 1945–50*, London: Springer.

Croft, S. (1994) *The End of Superpower: British Foreign Office Conceptions of a Changing World, 1945–51*, Aldershot: Dartmouth.

Crossman, R. (1976) *The Diaries of a Cabinet Minister, Vol. 2: Lord President of the Council and Leader of the House Commons 1966–68*, London: Hamilton Cape.

Curtice, J. (2015) 'Divided Britain? Who Supports and Who Opposes EU Membership', NatCen, October.

Curtice, J. and Evans, G. (2015) 'Britain and Europe: Are we all Eurosceptics now?', NatCen Social Research.

Cyr, A. I. (2012) 'Britain, Europe and the United States: Change and Continuity', *International Affairs*, Vol. 88, No. 6, 1315–30.

Daddow, O. J. (ed.) (2003) *Harold Wilson and European Integration: Britain's Second Application to Join the EEC*, London: Frank Cass Publishers.

Daddow, O. J. (2004) *Britain and Europe since 1945: Historiographical Perspectives on Integration*, Manchester: Manchester University Press.

Daddow, O. J. (2007a) 'New Labour and the Reinvention of British and European History', Queen's University, Belfast.

Daddow, O. J. (2007b) 'Playing Games with History: Tony Blair's European Policy in the Press', *British Journal of Politics and International Relations*, Vol. 9, 582–98.

Daddow, O. J. (2011) *New Labour and the European Union: Blair and Brown's Logic of History*, Manchester: Manchester University Press.

Daddow, O. J. (2012) 'The UK Media and "Europe": From Permissive Consensus to Destructive Dissent', *International Affairs*, Vol. 88, No. 6, 1219–36.

Daddow, O. J. (2013) 'Margaret Thatcher, Tony Blair and the Eurosceptic Tradition in Britain', *The British Journal of Politics and International Relations*, Vol. 15, 210–27.

Daddow, O. J. (2015) 'Interpreting the Outsider Tradition in British European Policy Speeches from Thatcher to Cameron', *Journal of Common Market Studies*, Vol. 53, No. 1, 71–88.

Darwin, J. (1988) *Britain and Decolonisation: The Retreat from Empire in the Postwar World*, London: Macmillan.

Day, R. (1989) *Grand Inquisitor: Memoirs*, London: Weidenfeld & Nicolson.

Deighton, A. (2002) 'The Past in the Present: British Imperial Memories and the European Question', in Muller, J.-W. (ed.) *Memory and Power in Post-War Europe*, Cambridge: Cambridge University Press.

Dell, E. (1995) *The Schuman Plan and the British Abdication of Leadership in Europe*, Oxford: Oxford University Press.

Devlin, C. *et al.* (2014) 'Impacts of Migration on UK Native Employment: An Analytical Review of the Evidence', Home Office, March.

Denman, R. (1996) *Missed Chances: Britain and Europe in the Twentieth Century*, London: Cassell.

Dewey, R. F. (2009) *British National Identity and Opposition to Membership of Europe 1961–63*, Oxford: Oxford University Press.

Dicey, A. V. (1885) *Lectures Introductory to the Study of the Law of the Constitution*, London: Macmillan.

Dinan, D. (2004) *Europe Recast: A History of European Union*, London: Palgrave Macmillan.

Dockrill, S. (1991) *Britain's Policy for West German Rearmament, 1950–1955*, Cambridge: Cambridge University Press.

Documents on British Policy Overseas, Series II (1986) Vol. 1, London: HMSO.

Donoghue, D. and Jones, G. W. (1973) *Herbert Morrison: Portrait of a Politician*, London: Phoenix Press.

Dorey, P. (ed.) (2006) *The Labour Governments 1964–1970*, London: Routledge.

Dorey, P. (2011) *British Conservatism: The Politics and Philosophy of Inequality*, London: I. B. Tauris.

Douglas-Scott, S. (13 October 2014) 'British Withdrawal from the EU: An Existential Threat to the United Kingdom?', www.centreonconstitutionalchange.ac.uk/blog/british-withdrawal-eu-existential-threat-united-kingdom.

Duff, A., Pinder, J. and Pryce, R. (eds) (1994) *Maastricht and Beyond: Building European Union*, London: Routledge.

Dutton, D. (ed.) (1995) *Statecraft and Diplomacy in the Twentieth Century*, Liverpool: Liverpool University Press.

Dyson, K. and Featherstone, K. (1999) *The Road to Maastricht: Negotiating Economic and Monetary Union*, Oxford: Oxford University Press.

Eichhorn, J. and Kenealy, D. (2015) '(Mis)understanding the Public? An Independent Scotland and the EU', December.

Eichhorn, J., Kenealy, D., Parry, R., Paterson, L. and Remond, A. (2015) 'Elite and Mass Attitudes on How the UK and its Parts are Governed – Public Preferences and the Process of Constitutional Change', March, www.aog.ed.ac.uk.

El-Agraa, A. M. (1983) *Britain within the European Community*, London: Macmillan.

Elias, A. (2008) 'Introduction: Whatever Happened to the Europe of the Regions? Revisiting the Regional Dimension of European Politics', *Regional and Federal Studies*, Vol. 18, No. 5, 483–92.

Élie, J. B. (2005) 'Many Times Doomed but still Alive: An Attempt to Understand the Continuity of the Special Relationship', *Journal of Transatlantic Studies*, Vol. 3, No. 15, 63–83.

Ellison, J. R. V. (2000) *Threatening Europe: Britain and the Creation of the European Community 1955–58*, Basingstoke: Macmillan.

EurActiv newsletters, www.EurActiv.com.

Eurobarometer, http://Europa.eu/public opinion/archives/eb.

European Commission (2014) *How the European Union Works*, http://europa.eu/en/how-the-european-union-works.

European Commission, *The EU: What's in it for me*, http://ec.europa.eu/united kingdom.

European Council (2000) http://eur-lex.europa.eu.

European Union website, http://ec.europa.eu.

European Unity, a statement published by the NEC of the British Labour Party, May 1950.

Eurostat, www.europa.eu.int/comm./eurostat/.

Evans, E. J. (1997) *Thatcher and Thatcherism*, London: Routledge.

Evans, H. (1981) *Downing Street Diary: The Macmillan Years 1957–1963*, London: Hodder & Stoughton.

Federal Trust Report (2013) '*Over the Edge? Britain on the European Sidelines*', London.

Fella, S. (2002) *New Labour and the European Union: Political Strategy, Policy Transition and the Amsterdam Treaty Negotiation*, Aldershot: Ashgate.

Fisher, H. A. L. (1935) *A History of Europe*, London: Eyre and Spottiswoode.

Fontana, C. and Parsons, C. (2014) '"One Woman's Prejudice": Did Margaret Thatcher Cause Britain's Anti-Europeanism?', *Journal of Common Market Studies*, Vol. 53, No. 1, 89–105.

Ford, R. and Goodwin, M. (2014) *Revolt on the Right: Explaining Support for the Radical Right in Britain*, London: Routledge.

Foreign and Commonwealth Office (2007) *The Reform Treaty: The British Approach to the EU Intergovernmental Conference*, July.

Foreign Relations of the United States, Washington: U.S. Department of Defense.

Forster, A. (2002) *Euroscepticism in Contemporary British Politics: Opposition to Europe in the British Conservative and Labour Parties since 1945*, London: Routledge.

Forster, A. and Blair, A. (2002) *The Making of Britain's European Foreign Policy*, Harlow: Longman.

Franklin, M. (2013) 'Could and Should Britain have Joined the European Exchange Rate Mechanism in 1979? A Personal Memoir', *Journal of Contemporary European Research*, Vol. 9, No. 5, 760–6.

Fraser, I. (2014) *Shredded: Inside RBS, the Bank that Broke Britain*, Edinburgh: Barlinn.

Full Fact, https://fullfact.org/.

Gallagher, T. (2015) *Scotland Now: A Warning to the World*, Edinburgh: Scotview Publications.

Gamble, A. (2003) *Between Europe and America: The Future of British Politics*, Basingstoke: Palgrave Macmillan.

Geddes, A. (2013) *Britain and the European Union*, Basingstoke: Palgrave Macmillan.

George, S. (1990) *An Awkward Partner: Britain in the European Community*, 1st edition, Oxford: Oxford University Press.

George, S. (ed.) (1992) *Britain and the European Community*, Oxford: Clarendon Press.

George, S. (1998) *An Awkward Partner: Britain in the European Community*, 3rd edition, Oxford: Oxford University Press.

Giddings, P. and Drewry, G. (eds) (2004) *Britain in the European Union: Law, Policy and Parliament*, Basingstoke: Palgrave Macmillan.

Gifford, C. (2014) *The Making of Eurosceptic Britain*, 2nd edition, Farnham: Ashgate.

Gilmour, I. (1992) *Dancing with Dogma*, London: Simon & Schuster.

Glencross, A. (2015) 'British Euroscepticism as British Exceptionalism: The Forty-Year "Neverendum" on the Relationship with Europe', https://dspace.stir.ac.uk/bitstream/1893.

Goodhart, P. (1976) *Full-Hearted Consent: The Story of the Referendum Campaign*, London: Davis-Poynter.

Goodwin, M. and Milazzo, C. (2015) 'Britain, the European Union and the Referendum: What Drives Euroscepticism?', Chatham House Briefing, December 2015.

Gould, B. (1995) *Goodbye to All That*, London: Macmillan.

Gowland, D. and Roebuck, S. (1990) *Never Call Retreat: A Biography of Bill Gowland*, London: Chester House.

Gowland, D. and Turner, A. (eds) (2000a) *Britain and European Integration 1945–1998: A Documentary History*, London: Routledge.

Gowland, D. and Turner, A. (2000b) *Reluctant Europeans: Britain and European Integration, 1945–1998*, Harlow: Longman.

Gowland, D., Dunphy, R. and Lythe, C. (3rd edition, 2006) *The European Mosaic: Contemporary Politics, Economics and Culture*, Harlow: Pearson Education.

Gowland, D., O'Neill, B. and Dunphy, R. (2nd edition, 2000) *The European Mosaic: Contemporary Politics, Economics and Culture*, Harlow: Longman.

Gowland, D., O'Neill, B. and Reid, A. (1st edition, 1995) *The European Mosaic: Contemporary Politics, Economics and Culture*, Harlow: Longman.

Gowland, D., Turner, A. and Wright, A. (2010) *Britain and European Integration since 1945: On the Sidelines*, London: Routledge.

Grant, C. (1994) *Delors: Inside the House that Jacques Built*, London: Nicholas Brealey.

Gregory, F. E. C. (1983) *Britain and the EEC*, Oxford: M. Robertson.

Grieve, D. (2015) 'Britain's International Obligations: Fetters or Keys', Palliser Lecture.

Griffiths, R. T. (1995) 'The United Kingdom and the Free Trade Area: A Post Mortem', in Olsen, T. B. (ed.) *Interdependence versus Integration: Denmark, Scandinavia and Western Europe 1945–1960*, Odense: Odense University Press.

Griffiths, R. T. and Ward, S. (1996) *Courting the Common Market: The First Attempt to Enlarge the European Community, 1961–1963*, London: Lothian Foundation Press.

Haas, E. B. (1958) *The Uniting of Europe*, Stanford: Stanford University Press.

Hannay, D. (2013) *Britain's Quest For a Role: A Diplomatic Memoir from Europe to the UN*, London: I. B. Tauris.

Harvey, M. (December 2011) '*Perspectives on the UK's Place in the World*', London: Chatham House Paper.

Hattersley, R. (1995) *Who Goes Home? Scenes from a Political Life*, London: Warner Books.

Hawkins, B. (2012) 'Nation, Separation and Threat: An Analysis of British Media Discourses on the European Union Treaty Reform Process', *Journal of Common Market Studies*, Vol. 50, No. 4, 561–77.

Healey, D. (1990) *The Time of My Life*, London: Penguin Books.

Heath, E. (1998) *The Course of My Life: My Autobiography*, London: Hodder & Stoughton.

Heggie, G. (2006) 'The Scottish Parliament and the EU Constitution: Moving Beyond the Principle of Partnership?' in Kiiver, P. (ed.) *National and Regional Parliaments in the European Constitutional Order*, Groningen: Europa Law.

Henderson, A. and Mitchell, J. (27 March 2015) '*The Scottish Question, Six Months On*', University of Edinburgh.

Hennessy, P. (1990) *The Hidden Wiring*, London: Phoenix.

Hennessy, P. (1992) *Never Again: Britain 1945–51*, London: Jonathan Cape.

Hennessy, P. (2001) *The Secret State: Whitehall and the Cold War*, London: Penguin Global.

Hepburn, E. (2014) 'Immigration, Nationalism and Political Parties in Scotland', in Hepburn, E. and Zapata-Barrero, R. (eds) *The Politics of Immigration in Multilevel States: Governance and Political Parties*, Basingstoke: Palgrave Macmillan.

HM Government, 'Review of the Balance of Competences between the United Kingdom and the European Union Foreign Policy', July 2013.

HM Government, 'Review of the Balance of Competences between the United Kingdom and the European Union Trade and Investment', February 2014.

HM Government, 'Review of the Balance of Competences between the United Kingdom and the European Union Research and Development', February 2014.

HM Government, 'Review of the Balance of Competences between the United Kingdom and the European Union Single Market: Free Movement of Goods', February 2013.

HM Government, 'Review of the Balance of Competences between the United Kingdom and the European Union Fisheries Report', Summer 2014.

HM Government, 'Review of the Balance of Competences between the United Kingdom and the European Union The Single Market: Financial Services and the Free Movement of Capital', Summer 2014.

HM Government, 'Review of the Balance of Competences between the United Kingdom and the European Union Agriculture', Summer 2014.

HM Government, 'Review of the Balance of Competences between the United Kingdom and the European Union Single Market: Free Movement of Persons', Summer 2014.

HM Government, 'Review of the Balance of Competences between the United Kingdom and the European Union EU Budget', Summer 2014.

HM Government, 'Review of the Balance of Competences between the United Kingdom and the European Union Social and Employment Policy', Summer 2014.

HM Government, 'Review of the Balance of Competences between the United Kingdom and the European Union The Single Market: Free Movement of Services', Summer 2014.

HM Government, 'Review of the Balance of Competences between the United Kingdom and the European Union Economic and Monetary Policy', December 2014.

HM Government, 'Review of the Balance of Competences between the United Kingdom and the European Union Subsidiarity and Proportionality', December 2014.

HM Government, 'Review of the Balance of Competences between the United Kingdom and the European Union Police and Criminal Justice', December 2014.

HM Government, 'Review of the Balance of Competences between the United Kingdom and the European Union Voting, Consular and Statistics Report', December 2014.

HM Government, 'Review of the Balance of Competences between the United Kingdom and the European Union EU Enlargement', December 2014.

HM Treasury, 'European Union Finances', December 2015.

HM Treasury, HM Treasury Analysis 'The Long-Term Economic Impact of EU Membership and the Alternatives', 18 April 2016.

Hogg, S. and Hill, J. (1995) *Too Close to Call*, London: Warner Books.

Holt, A. (2005) 'Lord Home and Anglo-American Relations, 1961–63', *Diplomacy and Statecraft*, Vol. 16, 699–722.

Horne, A. (1988) *Macmillan, Volume 1 (1894–1956)*, London: Macmillan.

Horne, A. (1989) *Macmillan, Volume 2 (1957–1986)*, London: Macmillan.

House of Commons European Scrutiny Committee (2001–2002), 'Democracy and Accountability in the EU and the Role of National Parliaments', 33rd Report.

House of Commons European Scrutiny Committee 'The Application of the EU Charter of Fundamental Rights in the UK: A State of Confusion', 43rd Report of Session 2013–14.

House of Commons Library 'How Much Legislation Comes From Europe?' Research Paper, 10/62, 13 October 2010.

House of Commons Library 'Leaving the EU' Research Paper, 13/42, 1 July 2013.

House of Commons Library 'The European Union: A Democratic Institution?' Research Papers, 29 April 2014.

House of Commons Library 'EU Exit: Impact in Key UK Policy Areas' Research Briefings, 9 June 2015.

House of Commons Library ' "Ever Closer Union" in the EU treaties and Court of Justice Case Law', 16 November 2015.

House of Lords, European Union Committee, 14th Report of Session 2004–5, 'Strengthening National Parliamentary Scrutiny of the EU – the Constitution's Subsidiarity Warning Mechanism', HL Paper 101, 14 April 2005.

House of Lords, European Union Committee, 3rd Report of Session 2015–16, 'The Referendum on UK Membership of the EU: Assessing the Reform Process', HL Paper 30.

House of Lords, Select Committee on the European Union (Sub-committee B), 'Inquiry into Re-launching the Single Market', 7 October 2010.

Howard, A. (1987) *RAB: The Life of R. A. Butler*, London: Jonathan Cape.

Howe, G. (1994) *Conflict of Loyalty*, London: Macmillan.

Howe, S. (1993) *Anticolonialism in British Politics: The Left and the End of Empire 1918–1964*, Oxford: Clarendon Press.

Hughes, K. (27 October 2015) 'Scotland Might Keep the UK in Europe', UCL European Institute.

Hurd, D. and Young, E. (2010) *Choose Your Weapons*, London: Weidenfeld & Nicolson.

Huth, S. (1995) 'Anglo-German Relations 1958–59: The Postwar Turning Point', *Diplomacy and Statecraft*, Vol. 6, No. 3, 787–808.

Hyman, R. (2008) 'The state in industrial relations' in Blyton, P. et al. (eds) *The Sage Handbook of Industrial Relations*, London: Sage.

Janis, I. L. (1982) *Groupthink: Psychological Studies of Policy Decisions and Fiascoes*, Boston: Houghton Mifflin College Div.

Jeffery, C. (ed.) (1997) *The Regional Dimension of the European Union: Towards a Third Level in Europe?*, London: Cass.

Jenkins, R. (1989) *European Diary, 1977–81*, London: Collins.

Jenkins, R. (1992) *A Life at the Centre*, London: Pan Books.

Johnson, E. (17 May 2013) *The European Dream: 'We Must Go Deeper'*, Church of God, A Worldwide Association, Inc.

Johnson, G. (2004) 'Introduction: The Foreign Office and British Diplomacy in the Twentieth Century', in Johnson, G. (ed.) 'The Foreign Office and British Diplomacy in the Twentieth Century', *Contemporary British History* (special issue), Vol. 18, No. 3, Autumn, 1–12.

Johnson, K. (1983) 'The National Interest and the Foreign Policy Process: The British Decision on EEC Membership, 1955–61', unpublished thesis, Cambridge University.

Johnson, N. (2004) *Reshaping the British Constitution*, Basingstoke: Palgrave Macmillan.

Jones, B. and Keating, M. (eds) (1995) *The European Union and the Regions*, Oxford: Clarendon Press.

Jones, K. (1994) *An Economist among Mandarins: A Biography of Robert Hall (1901–1988)*, Cambridge: Cambridge University Press.

Jones, M. (2003) 'Anglo-American Relations after Suez, the Rise and Decline of the Working Group Experiment and the French Challenge to NATO, 1957–59', *Diplomacy and Statecraft*, Vol. 1, 49–79.

Jones, R. W. and Rumbul, R. (2012) 'Wales: 40 Years of EU Membership', *Journal of Contemporary European Research*, Vol. 8, No. 4, 555–62.

Jowell, R. and Hoinville, G. (1976) *Britain into Europe: Public Opinion and the EEC, 1961–1975*, London: Croom Helm.

Kaiser, W. (1996) *Using Europe, Abusing the Europeans: Britain and European Integration, 1945–1963*, Basingstoke: Palgrave Macmillan.

Kaiser, W. and Staerck, G. (eds) (2000) *British Foreign Policy, 1955–64: Contracting Options*, Basingstoke: Macmillan.

Kaiser, W. and Staerck, G. (2002) 'A Never-Ending Story: Britain in Europe', *British Journal of Politics and International Relations*, Vol. 4, No. 1, 152–65.

Kane, E. (1996) 'Tilting to Europe? British Policy towards Developments in European Integration 1955–58', unpublished thesis, Oxford University.

Keating, M. (2001) *Plurinational Democracy: Stateless Nations in a Post-Sovereignty Era*, Oxford: Oxford University Press.

Keating, M. (2014) 'Scotland, Devolution and the European Union', Edinburgh: Centre on Constitutional Change.

Keating, M. and Jones, B. J. (eds) (1985) *Regions in the European Community*, Oxford: Clarendon Press.

Keesing's Contemporary Archives, London: Chadwyck-Healey.

Kellner, P. (2012) 'Key Survey Insights', The Chatham House/YouGov Survey 2012.

Kennedy, D., Gorecki, P., Nuttall, G., Sweeney, B. and Wilson, R. (1998) *Post-Agreement Northern Ireland and the European Union*, European Liaison – Institute of European Studies, Belfast: Queen's University of Belfast.

Kenny, M. (2015) 'The Return of "Englishness" in British Political Culture – The End of the Unions?', *Journal of Common Market Studies*, Vol. 53, No. 1, 35–51.

Kent, J. (1993) *British Imperial Strategy and the Origins of the Cold War*, Leicester: Leicester University Press.

Keynes, J. M. (1920) *The Economic Consequences of the Peace*, New York: Harcourt, Brace and Howe.

King, A. and Crewe, I. (2013) *The Blunders of our Governments*, London: Oneworld Publications.

Kitzinger, U. (1968) *The Second Try*, Oxford: Pergamon.

Kitzinger, U. (1972) *Diplomacy and Persuasion: How Britain Joined the Common Market*, London: Thames & Hudson.

Kitzinger, U. (1976) *1975 Referendum*, London: Macmillan.

Knudsen, A.-C. L. (2005) 'The Politics of Financing the Community and the Fate of the First British Membership Application', *Journal of European Integration History*, Vol. II, No. 2, 11–30.

Koestler, A. (ed.) (1963) *Suicide of a Nation? An Enquiry into the State of Britain*, London: Vintage.

Kohl, H. (2005) *Erinnerungen 1982–1990*, Munich: Droemer Knaur.

Kynaston, D. (2011) *City of London: The History*, London: Vintage.

Kynaston, D. (2014) *Modernity Britain: A Shake of the Dice, 1959–62*, London: Bloomsbury.

Lamb, R. (1987) *The Failure of the Eden Government*, London: Sidgwick & Jackson.

Lamb, R. (1995) *The Macmillan Years 1957–1963: The Emerging Truth*, London: John Murray.

Lamont, N. (1999) *In Office*, London: Little, Brown.

Langford, P. (2000) *Englishness Identified: Manners and Character 1650–1850*, Oxford: Oxford University Press.

Laughland, J. (2008) 'Why the "Anglosphere" is No Alternative for the EU', *Brussels Journal*, www.brusselsjournal.com/node/2821.

Lawson, N. (1992) *The View From No. 11*, London: Bantam Press.

Lee, S. (2007) *Best for Britain: The Politics and Legacy of Gordon Brown*, Oxford: Oneworld Publications.

Leonard, M. (1998) *Rediscovering Europe*, London: Demos.

Leveson Report (November 2012) www.official-documents.gov.uk/document/hc1213/hc07/0780/0780.asp.

Levitt, S. D. (2012) *Freakonomics*, New York: HarperCollins.

Liddle, R. (2014) *The Europe Dilemma: Britain and the Drama of EU Integration*, London: I. B. Tauris.

Lidington, D. (2012) 'EU Common Security and Defence Policy: The UK Perspective', Speech by the Minister of State for Europe, 27 June.

Lieber, R. J. (1970) *British Politics and European Unity: Parties, Elites and Pressure Groups*, Berkeley: University of California Press.

Lizieri, C., Reinert, J. and Baum, A. (2011) '*Who Owns the City 2011: Change and Global Ownership of City of London Offices*', Department of Land Economy, University of Cambridge.

Lord, C. (1993) *British Entry to the European Community under the Heath Government of 1970–4*, Aldershot: Dartmouth.

Lord, C. (1998) ' "With but not of": Britain and the Schuman Plan, a Reinterpretation', *Journal of European Integration History*, Vol. 4, No. 2, 23–46.

Louis, W. M. R. and Bull, H. (eds) (1986) *The 'Special Relationship': Anglo-American Relations since 1945*, Oxford: Clarendon Press.

LSE IDEAS (2015) 'Investing for Influence: Report of the LSE Diplomacy Commission'.

Ludlow, N. Piers (2002) 'Us or Them? The Meaning of Europe in British Political Discourse' in Malmborg, M. and Stråth, B. (eds) *The Meaning of Europe: Variety and Contention Within and Among Nations*, Oxford and New York: Berg.

Ludlow, N. Piers (2003) 'A Waning Force: The Treasury and British European Policy, 1955–63', *Contemporary British History*, Vol. 17, No. 4, 87–104.

Ludlow, N. Piers (2005) 'A Welcome Change: The European Commission and the Challenge of Enlargement, 1958–73', *Journal of European Integration History*, Vol. II, No. 2, 31–46.

Ludlow, N. Piers (2015) 'Safeguarding British Identity or Betraying It? The Role of British "Tradition" in the Parliamentary Great Debate on EC Membership, October 1971', *Journal of Common Market Studies*, Vol. 53, No. 1, 18–34.

McCormick, J. (2014) 'Voting on Europe: The Potential Pitfalls of a British Referendum', *The Political Quarterly*, Vol. 85, No. 2.

MacCormick, N. (1999) *Questioning Sovereignty*, Oxford: Oxford University Press.

Macmillan, H. (1972) *Pointing the Way, 1959–1961*, London: Macmillan.

Macmillan, H. (1973) *At the End of the Day, 1961–1963*, London: Macmillan.

MacShane, D. (2005) *Britain's Voice in Europe*, London: The Foreign Policy Centre.

Major, J. (1999) *The Autobiography*, London: HarperCollins.

Mangold, P. (2006) *The Almost Impossible Ally: Harold Macmillan and Charles de Gaulle*, London: I. B. Tauris.

Marjolin, R. (1989) *Architect of European Unity: Memoirs 1911–1986*, London: Weidenfeld & Nicolson.

Marquand, D. (2008) 'England and Europe: The Two E's that Lie in Wait for Brown's Britishness', 1 February, www.opendemocracy.net/ourkingdom/articles/browns_britishness.

Marsh, S. and Baylis, J. (2006) 'The Anglo-American "Special Relationship": The Lazarus of International Relations', *Diplomacy and Statecraft*, Vol. 17, 173–211.

Marshall, H. E. (1905) *Our Island Story*, London: T. C & E. C. Jack.

Mazey, S. and Mitchell, J. (eds) (1993) *Lobbying in the European Community*, Oxford: Oxford University Press.

Melissen, J. and Zeeman, B. (1987) 'Britain and Western Europe 1945–51: Opportunities Lost?', *International Affairs*, Vol. 63, 81–95.

Menon, A. (ed.) (2004a) *Britain and European Integration: Views from Within*, Oxford: Blackwell.

Menon, A. (2004b) 'Leading from Behind: Britain and the European Constitutional Treaty', *Groupement D'Études et de Recherche*, Notre Europe.

Mény, Y. (2012) 'Conclusion: A Voyage to the Unknown', *Journal of Common Market Studies*, Vol. 50, 154–64.

Miller, V. (2012) *How the UK Government Deals with EU Business*, London: House of Commons Library.

Milton, J. (1644) *The Doctrine and Discipline of Divorce*.

Milward, A. S. (1984) *The Reconstruction of Western Europe 1945–51*, London: Methuen.

Milward, A. S. (1992) *The European Rescue of the Nation-State*, London: Routledge.

Milward, A. S. (2003) *The Rise and Fall of a National Strategy 1945–1963: The United Kingdom and the European Community*, Vol. 1, London: Frank Cass.

Mitchell, J. (2014) *The Scottish Question*, Oxford: Oxford University Press.

Monnet, J. (1978) *Memoirs*, London: Collins.

Moore, C. (2014) *Margaret Thatcher The Authorized Biography Volume One: Not For Turning*, London: Penguin Books.

Moore, C. (2015) *Margaret Thatcher The Authorized Biography Volume Two: Everything She Wants*, London: Penguin Books.

Moravcsik, A. (1998) *The Choice for Europe: Social Purpose and State Power from Messina to Maastricht*, London: University College London Press.

Morgan, A. (1992) *Harold Wilson: A Life*, London: Pluto Press.

Morgan, K. (1997) *Callaghan: A Life*, Oxford: Oxford University Press.

Mullen, A. and Burkitt, B. (2005) 'Spinning Europe: Pro-European Propaganda Campaigns in Britain, 1962–75', *The Political Quarterly*, Vol. 76, No. 1, 110–13.

Muller, J.-W. (ed.) (2002) *Memory and Power in Post-War Europe: Studies in the Presence of the Past*, Cambridge: Cambridge University Press.

Murakami, H. (2012) *IQ84*, London: Vintage Books.

Murkens, J. E. (2001) *Scotland's Place in Europe*, London: The Constitution Unit.

National Archives, HM Government Papers in the PREM 11 and FO 371 series.

Naughtie, J. (2002) *Rivals: The Intimate Story of Political Marriage*, London: Fourth Estate.

Nelsen, B. F. and Guth, J. L. (2015) *Religion and the Struggle for European Union: Confessional Culture and the Limits of Integration*, Washington, DC: Georgetown University Press.

New Dictionary of National Biography (2004–2005) Oxford: Oxford University Press.

Newman, M. (1983) *Socialism and European Unity*, London: Junction Books.

Niblett, R. (2015) *'Britain's Place in the World'*, London: Chatham House Paper.

Nutting, A. (1960) *Europe Will Not Wait*, London: Doubleday.

O'Farrell, J. (1998) *Things Can Only Get Better: Eighteen Miserable Years in the Life of a Labour Supporter, 1979–1997*, London: Doubleday.

Office for Official Publications of the European Communities, *Annual Abstract of Statistics*, https://publications.europa.eu.

Oliver, T. (2015) 'To Be or Not to Be in Europe: Is That the Question? Britain's European Question and an In/Out Referendum', *International Affairs*, Vol. 91, No. 1, 77–91.

O'Neill, C. (2000) *Britain's Entry into the European Community: Report by Sir Con O'Neill on the Negotiations of 1970–1972*, edited by Hannay, D., London: Whitehall History Publishing in association with Frank Cass.

Open Europe and Ciuriak Consulting (March 2015) 'What If? The Consequences, Challenges and Opportunities Facing Britain Outside the EU', London: Open Europe.

Open Europe Today, openeurope.org.uk/.

Ormston, R. (October 2015) 'European? Not us Brits', http://whatukthinks.org.eu.

Orwell, G. (1941) *The Lion and the Unicorn*, London: Secker & Warburg.

Orwell, G. (1946) *Politics and the English Language*, London: Horizon.

Ottaviano, G., Pessoa, J., Sampson, T. and Van Reenen, J. (2014) 'Brexit or Fixit? The Trade and Welfare Effects of Leaving the European Union', London: LSE Research Online Documents on Economics.

Ovendale, R. (1998) *Anglo-American Relations in the Twentieth Century*, London: Macmillan.

Owen, D. (1991) *Time to Declare*, London: Michael Joseph.

Palmer, J. (11 April 2013) 'The British Press and Euroscepticism: Mirror or Magnifying Glass?', www.ecfr.eu/blog/entry.

Park, J. (1997) 'Wasted Opportunities? The 1950s Rearmament Programme and the Failure of British Economic Policy', *Journal of Contemporary History*, Vol. 32, No. 3, 357–79.

Parliamentary Debates (Hansard), *House of Commons Official Report*, London: Chadwyck-Healey.

Parr, H. (2005) 'A Question of Leadership: July 1966 and Harold Wilson's European Decision', *Contemporary British History*, Vol. 19, No. 4, 437–58.

Parris, M. (2002) *Chance Witness: An Outsider's Life in Politics*, London: Penguin.

Parris, M. and Bryson, A. (2010) *Parting Shots*, London: Viking.

Patten, C. (1998) *East and West*, London: Pan Books.

Patten, C. (2005) *Not Quite the Diplomat*, London: Allen Lane.

Peden, G. (2012) 'Suez and Britain's Decline as a World Power', *Historical Journal*, Vol. 55, 1073–96.

Peston, R. (2005) *Brown's Britain*, London: Short Books.

Phinnemore, D., McGowan, L., McCall, C. and McLoughlin, P. (2012) 'Northern Ireland – 40 Years of EU Membership', *Journal of Contemporary European Research*, Vol. 8, No. 4, 564–70.

Pickering, J. (2002) 'Politics and Black Tuesday: Shifting Power in the Cabinet and the Decision to Withdraw from East of Suez, November 1967–January 1968', *Twentieth Century British History*, Vol. 13, No. 2, 144–70.

Pimlott, B. (1992) *Harold Wilson*, London: HarperCollins.

Pine, M. (2004) 'British Personal Diplomacy and Public Policy: The Soames Affair', *Journal of European Integration History*, Vol. 4, No. 2, 59–76.

Ponting, C. (1989) *Breach of Promise: Labour in Power, 1964–70*, London: Hamish Hamilton.

Prescott, J. (2008) *Prezza My Story: Pulling No Punches*, London: Headline Review.

Price, L. (2006) *The Spin Doctor's Diary: Inside Number 10 with New Labour*, London: Hodder & Stoughton Books.

Price, L. (2010) *Where Power Lies: Prime Ministers v the Media*, London: Simon & Schuster.

Radice, G. (1992) *Offshore*, London: I. B. Tauris.

Rawnsley, A. (2001) *Servants of the People: The Inside Story of New Labour*, London: Penguin Books.

Redwood, J. (2001) 'Sovereignty and Democracy', in Rosenbaum, M. (ed.) *Britain and Europe: The Choices we Face*, Oxford: Oxford University Press.

Redwood, J. (2005) *Superpower Struggles: Mighty America, Faltering Europe, Rising Asia*, London: Palgrave Macmillan.

Reynolds, D. (1986) 'A "Special Relationship"? America, Britain and the International Order since the Second World War', *International Affairs*, Vol. 62, 1–20.

Reynolds, D. (1991) *Britannia Overruled: British Policy and World Power in the 20th Century*, Harlow: Longman.

Riddell, P. (1991) *The Thatcher Era and its Legacy*, Oxford: Blackwell.

Riddell, P. (2003) *Hug Them Close: Blair, Clinton, Bush and the 'Special Relationship'*, London: Politico's

Riddell, P. (2005) *The Unfulfilled Prime Minister: Tony Blair's Quest for a Legacy*, London: Politico's.

Roberts, A. (1999) *Salisbury: Victorian Titan*, London: Weidenfeld & Nicolson.

Roberts, A. (2006) *A History of the English-Speaking Peoples since 1900*, London: Weidenfeld & Nicolson.

Robins, L. J. (1979) *The Reluctant Party: Labour and the EEC, 1961–1975*, Ormskirk: G. W. and A. Hesketh.

Rollings, N. (2007) *British Business in the Formative Years of European Integration, 1945–1973*, Cambridge: Cambridge University Press.

Rosamond, B. (2000) *Theories of European Integration*, Houndsmill: Palgrave.

Routledge, P. (1998) *Gordon Brown: The Biography*, London: Pocket Books.

Roy, R. (2000) 'The Battle for the Pound: The Political Economy of Anglo-American Relations 1964–68', unpublished thesis, London School of Economics.

Ruane, K. and Ellison, J. (2004) 'Managing the Americans: Anthony Eden, Harold Macmillan and the Pursuit of "Power-by-Proxy" in the 1950s', *Contemporary British History*, Vol. 18, No. 3, 147–67.

Rumsfeld, D. (2011) *Known and Unknown: A Memoir*, New York: Sentinel.

Salamone, A. (2014) 'Britain's Representation in the European Parliament', *Britain's Europe (Ideas on Europe)*, 11 July 2014, britainseurope.uk/20140711.

Sampson, A. (1968) *The New Europeans*, London: Hodder & Stoughton.

Sampson, A. (2004) *Who Runs This Place? The Anatomy of Britain in the 21st Century*, London: John Murray.

Sandbrook, D. (2005) *Never Had It So Good: A History of Britain from Suez to the Beatles*, London: Little, Brown.

Sandbrook, D. (2006) *White Heat: A History of Britain in the Swinging Sixties*, London: Little, Brown.

Sandbrook, D. (2015) *The Great British Dream Factory: The Strange History of Our National Imagination*, London: Allen Lane.

Sanders, D. (1990) *Losing an Empire, Finding a Role: British Foreign Policy since 1945*, Basingstoke: Macmillan.

Schaad, M. (1998) 'Plan G – A "Counterblast"? British Policy towards the Messina Countries, 1956', *Contemporary European History*, Vol. 7, 39–60.

Schenk, C. R. (1994) *Britain and the Sterling Area: From Devaluation to Convertibility*, London: Routledge.

Schieren, S. (2000) 'Independence in Europe: Scotland's Choice?', *Scottish Affairs*, No. 31, 111–27.

Schnapper, P. (2014) 'The Labour Party from Brown to Miliband: Back to the Future?', *Journal of Common Market Studies*, Vol. 53, 157–73.

Schoenbaum, T. J. (1988) *Waging Peace and War: Dean Rusk in the Truman, Kennedy and Johnson Years*, New York: Simon & Schuster.

Scott, A., Peterson, J. and Millar, D. (1994) 'Subsidiarity: A Europe of the Regions v. the British Constitution', *Journal of Common Market Studies*, Vol. 32, No. 1, 47–67.

Scott, D. (2004) *Off Whitehall: A View from Downing Street by Tony Blair's Adviser*, London: I. B. Tauris.

Scottish Executive External Relations (2005) 'The Scottish Executive's European Strategy'.

Scottish Global Connections Survey 2013, www.gov.scot.

Scottish Government (November 2013) 'Scotland in the European Union', www.scotland.gov.uk.

Scottish Government (November 2013) 'Scotland's Future: Your Guide to an Independent Scotland', www.scotland.gov.uk.

Scottish Government (February 2014) 'Scotland's Priorities for EU Reform', www.scotland.gov.uk.

Scully, R. (27 February 2015a) 'Welsh Attitudes towards EU Membership Revealed', www.cardiff.ac.uk/cy/news/view/82643-welsh-attitudes-towards-eu-membership-revealed.

Scully, R. (19 October 2015b) 'Attitudes to the EU in Wales – an Update and Comparison', http://blogs.cardiff.ac.uk/electionsinwales/2015.

Seeley, J. R. (2009) *The Expansion of England*, London: BiblioLife.

Seldon, A. (1997) *Major: A Political Life*, London: Weidenfeld & Nicolson.

Seldon, A. (ed.) (2007) *Blair's Britain 1997–2007*, Cambridge: Cambridge University Press.

Seldon, A. and Lodge, G. (2010) *Brown at 10*, London: Biteback Publishing.

Seldon, A. and Snowdon, P. (2015) *Cameron at 10: The Inside Story 2010–2015*, London: William Collins.

Seldon, A., Snowdon, P. and Collings, D. (2008) *Blair Unbound*, London: Pocket Books.

Seldon, A., Ballinger, C., Collings, D. and Snowdon, P. (2005) *Blair*, London: The Free Press.

Shanks, M. (1961) *The Stagnant Society*, London: Penguin.

Shaw, J. (2012) 'Scotland: 40 Years of EU Membership', *Journal of Contemporary European Research*, Vol. 8, No. 4, 547–54.

Shonfield, A. (1972) *Europe: Journey to an Unknown Destination*, London: Penguin Books.

Short, C. (2004) *An Honourable Deception?*, New York: Free Press.

Shuckburgh, E. (1986) *Descent to Suez: Diaries 1951–56*, London: Weidenfeld & Nicolson.

Siedentop, L. (2001) *Democracy in Europe*, London: Penguin Books.

Sillars, J. (1989) 'Independence in Europe', in Paterson, L. (ed.) *A Diverse Assembly*, Edinburgh: Edinburgh University Press.

Simms, B. (2007) *Three Victories and a Defeat*, London: Allen Lane.

Smith, J. (2005) 'A Missed Opportunity? New Labour's European Policy 1997–2005', *International Affairs*, Vol. 81, No. 4, 703–21.

Smith, J. (2012) 'The European Dividing Line in Party Politics', *International Affairs*, Vol. 88, No. 6, 1277–95.

Smith, L. (1964) *Harold Wilson: Authentic Portrait*, London: Fontana.

Spaak, P.-H. (1971) *The Continuing Battle: Memoirs of a European, 1936–1966*, London: Weidenfeld & Nicolson.

Spence, J. (2012) 'A High Price to Pay? Britain and the EU Budget', *International Affairs*, Vol. 88, No. 6, 1237–60.

SPICe The Information Centre, 'Proposals to the Smith Commission on Further Powers in EU and International Affairs', 30 October 2014, www.scottish.parliament.uk.

SPICe The Information Centre, 'The Smith Commission Report – Overview', 8 January 2015, www.scottish.parliament.uk.

Spiegel, P. (11 May 2014) 'How the euro was Saved', *FT Series*.

Spiering, M. (1997) 'Why the British are not Europeans', *Europa*, Vol. 2, No. 1, 127–49.

Springford, J. (2014) 'Will the Eurozone Gang Up on Britain?', London: Centre for European Reform.

Springford, J. and Tilford, S. (January 2014) '*The Great British Trade-Off: The Impact of Leaving the EU on the UK's Trade and Investment*', London: Centre for European Reform.

Springford, J. and Whyte, P. (2014) 'The Consequences of Brexit for the City of London', London: Centre for European Reform.

Standard Eurobarometer 83, Spring 2015, July 2015, http://ec.europa.eu/public_opinion/index_en.htm.

Steel, D. (1989) *Against Goliath: The David Steel Story*, London: Weidenfeld & Nicolson.

Stephens, P. (1996) *Politics and the Pound: The Conservatives' Struggle with Sterling*, Basingstoke: Macmillan.

Stephens, P. (2005) 'Britain and Europe: An Unforgettable Past and an Unavoidable Future', *The Political Quarterly*, Vol. 7, No. 1, 12–21.

Stirk, P. M. R. and Willis, D. (eds) (1991) *Shaping Post-War Europe, 1945–57*, London: Pinter.

Tarditi, V. (2010) 'The Scottish National Party's Changing Attitude towards the European Union', Working Paper No. 112, Sussex European Institute.

Tebbitt, N. (1989) *Upwardly Mobile*, London: Weidenfeld & Nicolson.

Thatcher, M. (1993) *The Downing Street Years*, London: HarperCollins.

Thatcher, M. (1995) *The Path to Power*, London: HarperCollins

Thillaye, R. (March 2014) 'British Political Parties in Europe: Reliable, Ambiguous, Reluctant and Dismissive', *Policy Network Paper*, www.policy-network.net.

Tombs, R. (2014) *The English and Their History*, London: Allen Lane.

Tournier-Sol, K. (2015), 'Reworking the Eurosceptic and Conservative Traditions into a Populist Narrative: UKIP's Winning Formula?', *Journal of Common Market Studies*, Vol. 53, No. 1, 140–56.

Tratt, J. (1996) *The Macmillan Government and Europe: A Study in the Process of Policy Development*, Basingstoke: Macmillan.

Treaty Establishing a Constitution for Europe, 2005, European Communities, Luxembourg.

Treaty of Lisbon, amending the Treaty on European Union and the Treaty Establishing the European Community, 2007, Official Journal of the European Union, C 306, Vol. 50.

Trench, A. (2003) 'Intergovernmental Relations', in Hazell, R. (ed.) *The State of the Nations 2003*, Thorverton: Imprint Academic.

Trevelyan, G. M. (1946) *English Social History*, London: Longman.

Trewin, I. (ed.) (2008) *The Hugo Young Papers: Thirty Years of British Politics – Off the Record*, London: Allen Lane.

Trollope, F. (1836) *Paris and the Parisians in 1835*, New York: Harper & Brothers.

Tugendhat, C. (1986) *Making Sense of Europe*, London: Viking.

Turner, J. (1994) *Macmillan*, London: Longman.

Turpin, C. (2001) 'The Constitutional Impact of British Membership of the European Union', in Broad, R. and Preston, V. (eds) *Moored to the Continent? Britain and European Integration*, London: Institute of Historical Research.

Urban, G. (1996) *Diplomacy and Disillusion at the Court of Margaret Thatcher: An Insider's View*, London: I. B. Tauris.

Usherwood, S. (2013) 'The Shifting Focus of Opposition to the European Union', *Journal of Contemporary European Research*, Vol. 9, No. 2, 279–96.

Usherwood, S. (17 March 2014) 'Euroscepticism as a Problem, Euroscepticism as a Proxy', http://policy-network.net/pno_detail.aspx?ID.

Vail, M. I. (2015) 'Between One-Nation Toryism and Neoliberalism: The Dilemmas of British Conservatism and Britain's Evolving Place in Europe', *Journal of Common Market Studies*, Vol. 53, No. 1, 89–105.

Vital, D. (1968) *The Making of British Foreign Policy*, London: Allen & Unwin.

Wall, S. (2008) *A Stranger in Europe: Britain and the EU from Thatcher to Blair*, Oxford: Oxford University Press.

Wall, S. (2013) *The Official History of Britain and the European Community, Volume II: From Rejection to Referendum, 1963–1975*, London and New York: Routledge.

Wallace, H. (2012) 'The UK: 40 Years of EU Membership', *Journal of Contemporary European Research*, Vol. 8, No. 4, 531–46.

Wallace, W. (1980) *Britain in Europe*, London: Heinemann.

Wallace, W. (2005) 'The Collapse of British Foreign Policy', *International Affairs*, Vol. 81, No. 1, 53–68.

Walters, A. A. (1990) *Sterling in Danger: The Economic Consequences of Pegged Exchange Rates*, London: Fontana Paperbacks.

Ward, S. (ed.) (2001) *British Culture and the End of Empire*, Manchester: Manchester University Press.

Warner, G. (2002) 'Review Article on Why the General Said No', *International Affairs*, Vol. 78, No. 4, 869–82.

Warner, G. (ed.) (2005) *In the Midst of Events: The Foreign Office Diaries and Papers of Kenneth Younger February 1950–October 1951*, London: Routledge.

Weight, R. (2002) *Patriots: National Identity in Britain 1940–2000*, Basingstoke: Macmillan.

Wellings, B. (2011) 'Political Resistance to European Integration and the Foundations of Contemporary English Nationalism', 61st Annual Political Studies Association Conference, London, 19–21 April.

Wellings, B. and Baxendale, H. (2014), 'Euroscepticism and the Anglosphere: Traditions and Dilemmas in Contemporary English Nationalism', *Journal of Common Market Studies*, Vol. 53, 123–39.

Werth, A. (1965) *De Gaulle: A Political Biography*, London: Penguin Books.

Western European Assembly (1963, 1964) Florence: Historical Archives of the European Union.

White, R. (1995) '"Through a glass darkly": The Foreign Office Investigation of French Federalism, January–May 1930', in Dutton, D. (ed.) *Statecraft and Diplomacy in the Twentieth Century*, Liverpool: Liverpool University Press.

Willans, G. and Searle, R. (1973) *Down with Skool!*, London: Lions.

Williams, P. (1979) *Hugh Gaitskell: A Political Biography*, London: Jonathan Cape.

Williams, S. (2003) *God and Caesar: Personal Reflections on Politics and Religion*, London: Continuum.

Wilson, G. (2009) *SNP: The Turbulent Years 1960–1990*, Stirling: Scots Independent (Newspapers) Ltd.

Wilson, G. (2014) *Scotland: The Battle for Independence – A History of the Scottish National Party 1990–2014*, Stirling: Scots Independent (Newspapers) Ltd.

Wilson, H. (1970) *Final Term: The Labour Government 1974–76*, London: Weidenfeld & Nicolson and Michael Joseph.

Wilson, H. (1971) *The Labour Government, 1964–1970*, London: Weidenfeld & Nicolson.

Wolf, M. (2014) *The Shifts and the Shocks: What We've Learned – and Have Still to Learn – From the Financial Crisis*, London: Allen Lane.

Wright, A. (ed.) (2000) *Scotland: The Challenge of Devolution*, Aldershot: Ashgate.

Wright, A. (2005) *Who Governs Scotland?*, London: Routledge.

YouGov, https://yougov.co.uk.

Young, H. (1990) *One of Us: A Biography of Margaret Thatcher*, London: Pan Books.

Young, H. (1998) *This Blessed Plot: Britain and Europe from Churchill to Blair*, London: Papermac.

Young, H. (2008) *The Hugo Young Papers*, London: Allen Lane.

Young, J. W. (1996) 'The Heath Government and British Entry into the European Community', in Ball, S. and Seldon, A. (eds) *The Heath Government 1970–74: A Reappraisal*, London: Longman.

Young, J. W. (2000) *Britain and European Unity*, 2nd edition, Basingstoke: Macmillan.

Ziegler, P. (1993) *Harold Wilson: The Authorised Life*, London: Weidenfeld & Nicolson.

Ziegler, P. (1995) *Wilson: The Authorised Life*, New York: HarperCollins.

Ziegler, P. (2010) *Edward Heath: The Authorised Biography*, London: Harper Press.

Index

Acheson, Dean 273, 278, 289, 302
acts, agreements, regulations and treaties
153, 180, 196, 319; Anglo-Irish Agreement
1985 182; Ankara Agreement 32; Atlantic
Pact 275; The Charter of the Fundamental
Rights of the EU 10, 136–7, 140, 277, 305,
319; Copenhagen Report 292; Declaration
of Arbroath 1320 14; Dublin Regulation
43; EEC Treaty of Rome 78, 112, 223, 321;
European Communities Act 1972 14, 196,
304, 317, 349, 360; European Union Act
2011 165, 307; Fontainebleau Agreement
1984 82, 219, 227–9; Franco-German
Treaty of Friendship and Cooperation 1963
119; Good Friday Agreement 180, 182,
185–6, 195; The Government of Ireland
Act 1920 180; The Government of Wales
Act 1998 180; The Government of Wales
Act 2006 180; Lisbon Treaty 2007 37, 110,
115, 132, 135–6, 149, 157, 171, 179, 209,
215–16, 259, 269, 289, 293, 308, 311–12,
319; Luxembourg Agreement 1966 35,
226–7; Maastricht Treaty 1992 28, 30, 33–
5, 38–9, 105, 107–8, 112–13, 132–5, 137,
157–8, 178–9, 189, 202–3, 210–11, 248, 293,
295–6, 312; MacSharry Reform 1992 230;
Nassau Agreement 71, 85; Peace I (1995–
1999) 182; Peace II (2000-2006) 182; Peace
III (2007–2013) 182; Schengen Agreement
43–4, 114, 130, 134, 190, 294, 318–19, 326,
329, 334; Schuman Plan 37, 57–9, 112, 118;
Scotland Act 1998 180, 196; The Single
European Act 1986 30, 34, 95, 98, 102,
128, 147, 157–8, 178, 211, 228, 245, 292; St
Malo Declaration 1999 106, 297–8; Treaty
of Accession 77, 146; Treaty of Amsterdam
134; Treaty of Nice 2001 212; Treaty on
European Union 1992 also known as the
Maastricht Treaty 28, 30, 33–5, 38–9, 105,
107–8, 112–13, 132–5, 137, 157–8, 178–9,
189, 191, 202–3, 210–11, 248, 293, 295–6,
312; Treaty on Stability, Coordination
and Governance 41, 306; Treaty on the
Functioning of the European Union 34;
Werner Plan 237–8
Adenauer, Konrad 81
The Advertiser 87, 204
Afghanistan 43, 287, 289, 298
Africa 49–50, 275, 297
African colonies 49
agreements 35, 38, 95–6, 99, 113, 116, 130,
134, 138, 180, 182, 220, 224, 226–9, 232–3,
237, 317–18, 320–3; binding 181, 230; final
96; financial 234; international 192, 339–40;
permanent 96
agriculture 11, 145, 181–2, 220, 223, 225, 227,
229–31, 339
Airbus 358
Albania 32–3, 43, 345
Alliance Party of Northern Ireland 181
allies 4, 51, 69, 120, 132, 161, 167, 247, 267,
282–3, 286, 314, 345; anti-EU press 359;
European 284, 296; Germany 44; of Jeremy
Corbyn 355; potential 125
Alternative für Deutschland 305
alternatives to EC membership 75, 79, 138, 336
America (*see also* USA) 4, 23, 27, 41, 49,
52–4, 58, 62–4, 71, 73–4, 125, 131, 239–
41, 266–7, 283–5, 287–8, 298, 308; bids
for the British helicopter firm over a
European consortium 64; and Britain's
European leadership credentials 53; failure
to maintain the value of the dollar since
the collapse of the Bretton Woods fixed
exchange rate system 239; intelligence
agencies 285; and a matching commitment
to the European continent with Britain
54; nuclear weapons delivery systems from
Polaris 284; and the pressure to export
more British coal to assist the European
recovery 58; and the 'special relationship'
with Britain 283
Anderson, B. 205, 208
Andrew, Herbert 68

Anglo-American relations 62, 284
Anglo-Irish Agreement 1985 182
Anglosphere concept 27, 281–3
Ankara Agreement 32
anti-Brussels 350
anti-EU 21, 305, 334; opinion 91, 113, 208;
    parties 39; positions 106; press 126
Anti-Federalist League 155; *see also* UKIP
anti-globalization 350
anti-immigration 15, 156, 305, 350; *see also*
    immigration
anti-integrationists 281
anti-marketeers 64, 78, 86–90, 92, 120, 139,
    148–9, 161, 163–4, 204, 329; early 71; and
    Eurosceptics 204; factions 85, 149; and Lord
    Beaverbrook 210; opinions of 163; slogans 27
Armstrong, Robert 226
Aron, Raymond 203
Ash, T.G. 8, 23, 27, 38, 43
Ashcroft, M. 142, 234, 259, 304–7, 311, 314
Ashton, Catherine 141
Asia 264, 275, 281, 283, 299
Assad regime 286
Athens European Council 227
Atlantic Alliance 52, 55, 71, 275, 283
Atlantic Pact 275
Attlee, Clement 24, 29, 46–8, 50, 52–4, 56, 59,
    210, 274–5, 288
Attlee government 47–8, 52–4, 56, 274–5
Auden, W.H. 22, 78
Australia 275, 278, 281
Australian-style points system 350
Austria 31, 40, 43–4, 64, 114, 123, 160, 191,
    235, 293
Ayrault, Jean-Marc 318, 359
Azevedo, Roberto 345
Aznar, Jose Maria 132, 168

bailouts 41–2, 264; improvised 41; largest bank
    266; made to indebted euro area states 41
Baker, Steve 351
Baldwin, Stanley 214
Balkans 33, 44
Balls, Ed 108, 256, 261
Bank of England 51, 246–7, 249, 252, 257,
    259, 265, 268, 346, 355
banking 8, 266, 323; crisis 265; culture 266–7;
    industry 268; regulations 269; sector 259,
    264; systems 251, 259
banking union 39, 42, 169, 262, 269
banks 41, 51, 246–7, 252, 257–60, 262, 264–70;
    domestic 260; failed 42, 262; and insurers
    267; integrated global trading 263; and
    lenders 268
Banks, Arron (also known as Aaron) 342
Baricevic, Branko 47
Barroso, Jose Manuel 140, 142, 182, 233, 236,
    291, 308

Bartlett, Chris 62
Baxendale, H. 28, 48, 281–2
BBC News 200, 213
BBC Reith lectures 19, 328
BBQ 93, 219
BDOHP 102, 119, 123, 146, 157, 171
Beaverbrook, William Maxwell Aitken (Lord
    Beaverbrook) 204, 210
Beaverbrook press 57, 145, 210
Belarus 33
Belfast 180, 182
Belgian Sub-national Entities 178
Belgium 6, 11, 30–1, 39–40, 43, 53, 56, 58, 63,
    72, 81, 92–3, 183, 192, 242, 262, 296–7
'Believe in Britain' (UKIP slogan) 350
Bell, D. 90, 189
Benelux bloc 119
Benghazi 290
Benn, Tony 37, 71, 86–8, 148, 158, 162–4,
    243–4, 323
Bennett, G. 29, 65, 67, 73, 279, 281
Bercow, John 313
Berlin 43, 119–21, 124, 231, 290, 300
Bettel, Xavier 360
Better Off Out (Conservative organization)
    159
Bevan, Aneurin 5, 284
Bevin, Ernest 29, 48, 52–3, 55, 58, 134, 275
Biffen, John 84
bilateral relations and trade 59, 185, 273, 283,
    285, 299, 337
Biscop, S. 295–6, 298
'Black Wednesday' 120–1, 139, 211, 249, 252
Blair, Tony 103, 106–9, 114–15, 117, 119,
    121, 131–2, 136–7, 146–7, 151–3, 165,
    206, 212–16, 219, 229–33, 252–9, 285–6,
    288–9; administrations of 215, 287; attitude
    towards EU affairs 106–7, 151, 256; attitude
    towards EU affairs and the British position
    106; enthusiasm for the Euro 121, 258;
    government of 106–8, 126, 131–2, 135–7,
    141, 151, 153, 155, 168, 184, 203, 213–14,
    232, 248, 252–5, 259, 288, 297; and the
    government's Atlanticist outlook 125;
    leadership 108, 230; media advisers 107;
    premiership of 108, 119, 124, 132, 147, 168,
    215, 218, 251, 285; preoccupation with the
    Third Way 132, 253; trilateralist aspirations
    119
bloc 269, 305, 308; centre-left 168; European
    monetary 240; largest trading 50, 275, 337;
    monolithic 263; political 308; western 52
'Bloomberg speech' 147, 149, 309, 315, 318,
    326, 329
Blunkett, David 258
Boehme, L.M. 118
Bonn 59, 119, 238–9
Bootle, R. 3, 9, 66, 69, 320

borders 21, 23, 32–3, 44, 129, 175, 185, 262, 325; external 44, 134, 195, 294, 319; internal 134; land 195; national 8; sealing of 44
Bosnia-Herzegovina 32–3, 294, 296
Bovine Spongiform Encephalopathy *see* BSE
Bower, T. 255
Boyle, Frankie 354
BP 83
Brandt, W. 73
Brennan, Kevin 359
Bretherton, Russell 61, 240
Bretton Woods system 76, 82, 238–9
Brexit 9, 263–5, 271, 303, 321, 343, 345, 351, 358; and the alternatives to EU membership 345; and the anti-elite theme 350; and the assertion by Roberto Azevedo that Britain would be forced to renegotiate trade deals with 161 WTO member states 345; becomes a badge of honour among some Conservative ministers and backbenchers 303; campaigners 86, 88, 192, 342, 346, 348–9, 352, 358–9; campaigns 271, 346–8, 350, 352–3, 357–8, 361; and claims that leaving the EU would provide more funding for the NHS 351; and concern expressed by the IMF and the OECD 345; dismisses the EU as undemocratic 346; and divisions of opinion over what a post-Brexit Britain would look like 348; economic case is strongly challenged on the international stage 344; fears that continued EU membership means being 'sucked into an emerging European superstate and the further loss of democratic control, sovereignty and identity' 346; forecasts that Britain would need seven new prisons by 2030 if immigration was not controlled 343; and immigration 125–6, 155, 158, 167, 175, 189, 201, 216, 305, 316–17, 320–1, 331, 343, 345, 348–50, 357, 361; leaves Britain seeking an agreement with the EU, but having rules imposed by the EU in return 346; 'likely to attract only some undesirable allies such as Albania, Islamic State (Daesh) and Russia' 345; limited support for Brexit in business and finance circles 344; 'offers freedom from EU regulations and red tape' 271; and the possibility of an agreement with the EU to secure full access to the Single Market 345; regarded by 81% as detrimental to Britain's competitiveness as a financial centre 263; and the resultant 'DIY economic recession' 344; and the role of Boris Johnson 347; and the second referendum 343; sees Cameron lagging behind Johnson in the polls 347; and the slogan 'taking back control' for Scotland and Northern Ireland 346; and

Theresa May's statement that 'Brexit means Brexit' 359; a welcome prospect to some City interests such as hedge funds that are contributing to various Brexit campaigns and UKIP 271
Bristow, Keith 268
Britain 1–4, 6–10, 12–15, 19–31, 45–56, 60–5, 67–73, 75–9, 85–93, 104–38, 140–4, 201–11, 221–44, 252–61, 263–7, 269–303, 316–22, 327–38; and the 60 percent of services tradeable across the borders between EU states 361; absence from the origins of the EC 15; advocates enlargement of the EU 125; application for EC membership 71, 223; and the budget rebate 126, 231, 236; claims to great power status in the post-war world 274–5, 277; and continental Europe 26, 28–9; contribution to the EC budget 82, 88, 93–4, 140, 223, 229, 235, 301, 321; and the cynical belief that, after voting for Brexit, the EU would continue to trade with 348; and the debate about withdrawal from the EU 12; EC application blocked by France 124; EC/EU budget 235; EC/EU policy 330; EC membership 44, 82, 103, 167, 202; entry into the EC 8, 17, 19, 78, 80, 82, 92, 115, 121, 146, 180, 256, 289, 327; EU research and technological funding programme 235; and Europe 4, 21, 27, 55, 87, 89, 147; and the European policy 15–16, 329; exit from the EU 186, 265, 303; exports 6, 57, 240–1, 264, 276, 338; and the insistence by Roberto Azevedo that all trade deals would have to be renegotiated with the 161 WTO member states 345; maritime traditions 282; membership terms 1, 13, 19, 80, 148, 175, 199, 218, 237, 311; and misconceptions on the net contribution of 201; net contribution to the EU 201, 226–7, 232, 234; policy towards Europe and the Commonwealth 275; and preserving the principle of free movement of economic migrants 349; and reconciling European and extra-European interests and commitments 122; and the regret felt by those who voted to leave the EU but are re-thinking their position 354; relationship with the EU xiii, 1–2, 21, 74, 92, 106, 111, 130, 174, 271, 309, 315, 326; renegotiating EU membership 196, 308; retention of border controls 134; 'special case' 321; tardiness in seeking and securing EC membership 115; terms of EU membership 14; and the Vote Leave claim that Britain was enjoying faster economic growth than the other major EU economies 344; and the warning by Jean Claude Juncker that Britain would not receive a friendly

reception from EU countries if it leaves
the EU 345; and the warning from US
President Obama on a visit to London
(21–23 April) 344

*Britain and the European Community
1955–1963* 15

British Budgetary Question *see* BBQ

British Commonwealth *see* Commonwealth

British Diplomatic Oral History Programme
see BDOHP

British foreign policy 19, 21, 49, 71, 116–17,
125, 136, 273–4, 277–9, 281, 283–4, 287, 302

British government 12, 15, 59–61, 96–7, 99,
106–7, 111–13, 117–18, 124, 140, 181,
243, 247, 251–2, 265–7, 283–9, 309, 327;
antipathy of 208; in CAP negotiations 191;
marginalized in EC/EU policy areas 117;
ministers 157, 163, 212, 333; policy towards
the EC/EU 116–17, 143; and Tony Blair's
lack of progress towards a referendum on
euro area membership 107

British-Irish Council 182

British-Irish Intergovernmental Conference
182

British leadership 68, 281, 292, 297; awaited
by advocates of EC membership 291; of the
Commonwealth 276; in Europe 297; of the
OEEC 70, 123

British membership 2–3, 6, 8, 17–19, 21,
89–90, 104–5, 107–8, 118–19, 148–9, 191–3,
195, 201–2, 214, 262–3, 301, 306–7, 313–14;
history of 19, 163; referendum on 1, 154,
175, 191, 193, 195, 202, 307, 309, 314;
supported by a majority of respondents 173

British ministers 60, 120, 128, 174, 185, 314;
see also ministers

British National Party (BNP) 156

British officials 62, 140, 142, 211

British Petroleum *see* BP

British policy 2–4, 10, 12, 16–18, 20, 44,
46–7, 49–50, 52, 59, 61, 110–11, 136–7,
261, 263, 275, 283, 326–30; in the EC/
EU context 115, 122, 143; in Europe 16,
156; and the goodwill towards the British
Commonwealth 49; towards post-war
European organizations 49

British policymakers 11, 15, 54, 58–60, 107,
110, 114–15, 121, 123, 230, 235, 261, 276,
279, 283, 288, 302, 306; dominant historical
narrative guiding 52

British politics 1–3, 5, 124, 126, 141, 143–4,
148, 150, 154, 156, 159, 165, 177, 183,
275, 322, 327–8, 332; domestic 175;
eighteenth-century 26; and the impact of
EC membership on 90; and the influence
of the press and public opinion on 18; and
the transition by which the Conservatives
ceased to be 'the party of Europe' in 103

British pound sterling *see* pound

British press 6, 15, 19, 21, 86, 114, 147,
199–200, 202, 207, 210, 308–9, 315; attitudes
of 204; changes in attitudes 204; coverage
of 205; and the Eurosceptics 110, 137, 207;
overwhelmingly supports membership of
the EC 204; *see also* newspapers

British Prime Ministers 12, 29, 49, 51, 84,
141, 240, 259; Alec Douglas-Home 74, 76,
279; Anthony Eden 56, 59–62, 66, 275, 277,
283; David Cameron 121, 127–8, 146–9,
165–6, 169, 216–17, 234, 286, 290–1, 304–23;
Edward Heath 75–8, 84, 87, 90, 93, 146–8,
150–1, 210, 223, 226; Gordon Brown 25,
73–4, 107–10, 114–15, 118, 137, 141, 146–7,
209, 212, 214–15, 231–2, 252–60, 278, 280,
285, 290, 312; Harold Macmillan 29, 56,
61–2, 64–71, 74, 76–7, 117–18, 131, 145–6,
161, 210, 276, 280, 283, 285, 287, 322, 328;
Harold Wilson 67, 72–4, 76–7, 82–7, 89–90,
92–3, 113, 118, 120, 131, 145–6, 148–51,
161–4, 187–90, 224, 276, 278, 321; James
Callaghan 83, 90–3, 113, 119, 139, 145–6,
149, 151, 154, 240, 242–4, 247, 285, 287,
312; John Major 24, 100, 104, 112, 125,
146–7, 165, 211–12, 247, 249, 262, 267, 308;
Margaret Thatcher 28–9, 73, 75, 78, 93–104,
112–13, 118, 120–1, 146–7, 151–2, 155,
162–3, 224–30, 243–8, 286–7, 289, 292,
331–3; Theresa May (July 2016) 290, 320,
342, 354, 359; Tony Blair 103, 106–9, 114–15,
117, 119, 121, 131–2, 136–7, 146–7, 151–3,
165, 206, 212–16, 219, 229–33, 252–9, 285–6,
288–9; Winston Churchill 4–5, 19, 29, 47–9,
51, 59, 61, 65, 71–2, 209, 274–5, 281–2, 286,
288, 290, 329

British rebate 168, 219, 224, 229, 231–6

British sovereignty 104, 157, 166, 185, 204, 213

British tabloid press *see* British press

British trade unions 48, 188

Brivati, B. 90, 161

Brooks, Mel 3

Brooks, Rebekah 216

Brown, George 73, 118, 138–9

Brown, Gordon 25, 73–4, 107–10, 114–15,
118, 137, 141, 146–7, 209, 212, 214–15,
231–2, 252–60, 278, 280, 285, 290, 312;
convinced that taking Britain into the euro
would be an unjustified gamble 108; and
David Miliband 312; government of 115,
136–7, 141, 154, 280, 288; and Robin Cook
255; succeeds Tony Blair 258

Bruges 102, 104, 147, 245

The Bruges Group (Conservative
organization) 159

Brussels 10, 12–13, 37, 102, 140–4, 146, 156–7,
162–4, 177, 180, 185–6, 188, 191, 197, 206–7,
245, 311–13, 321; British delegations in 140,

144; bureaucrats 88, 160; and Germany 321; government negotiators in 118

Brussels Council of Ministers 226, 232

Brussels European Council 228, 232

Brussels Treaty Organization *see* BTO

BSE 174, 211, 342

BTO 53, 116, 275

budgets 6, 17, 19, 83, 162, 201, 215, 219–21, 223, 225–6, 228–36, 252, 295; British rebate 126, 231, 236; of federal states 220

Bulgaria 31–2, 40, 43, 124, 126, 134, 260

Bundesbank 41, 238–9, 247, 249

Burgess, Guy 53

Burke, Edmund 152

Burns, Terence 252

Busby, Matt 59

Bush, President George W. 286, 288

business-based organizations 10, 159, 192; Better Off Out (Conservative organization) 159; The Bruges Group (Conservative organization) 159; Business for Britain 26, 159; The Fresh Start Project 159; OpenEurope 9, 13, 159, 207–8, 318

Business for Britain 26, 159

Business Taskforce on EU Red Tape 129

Butler, Michael 88, 90, 99, 172, 229

Butler, R.A. ('Rab') 81, 144–5

Cabinet and Cabinet Office 5, 24, 67, 70, 86, 90, 104–5, 149, 164–5, 180, 212–13, 226, 243–5, 247–8, 258, 305, 320, 322

Cabinet ministers 5, 47, 49, 66, 78, 83, 89, 141, 146, 149, 162, 167, 255, 322

Cairncross, A. 46

Callaghan, James 83, 90–3, 113, 119, 139, 145–6, 149, 151, 154, 240, 242–4, 247, 285, 287, 312

Callaghan government 83, 90, 151, 239, 243

Cameron, David 1, 3, 112, 121, 127–8, 146–9, 165–6, 169, 185–6, 216–17, 234, 286, 290–1, 303–23, 342, 344, 346–8, 350–1; and the 1922 Committee 306; announces his resignation shortly after the declaration of the referendum result 354; and the battle for the soul of the Conservative Party 342; and the 'Bloomberg speech' 147, 149, 309, 315, 318, 326, 329; and the candidates for the leadership 342; and the Coalition government 19, 125, 129, 149, 163, 165, 233–4, 261, 265, 280, 282, 286, 290, 295–6, 303, 306, 308; and the Conservative government 19, 271, 290, 303; espouses the idea of a major treaty change 321; 'gambles on the EU referendum because he thinks the centre is secure' 348; government of 7, 14, 28, 124, 138, 141, 153, 234, 282, 335; and his circuitous route to the referendum and long-standing doubts about his EU views 347; and his reference to the risks and

dangers of Brexit 346; and his relationship with Chancellor Merkel 314; and his renegotiation with the EU in February 2016 349; and his repeated references to the EU as a 'tool' 347; and the joint statement by Gove and Johnson that brands Cameron's failed pledge to curb immigration, 'corrosive of public trust' 349; leadership of 216, 311; renegotiation stance on the EU 121; strategy and tactics 310; and the *Sun* report that his EU renegotiation was 'secretly controlled' by German chancellor Angela Merkel 346; and the Treasury Report emphasizing that Brexit would result in an instant 'DIY economic recession' 344; and the vetoing of the Fiscal Compact 263, 265

campaigners 86, 88, 192, 342, 348–9, 358; anti-EC 323; Brexit 86, 88, 192, 342, 346, 348–9, 352, 358–9; long-standing 311

campaigns 25, 27, 74, 87–9, 129, 147, 163, 177, 190, 195, 202–3, 211, 322, 342–4, 346–7, 349–53, 355; and the anti-Europeans 203; Brexit 271, 346–8, 350, 352–3, 357–8, 361; corporate-finance fact-based 203; lackluster 355; organization of 342; and the slogan 'Vote Leave' 323, 325, 342, 344, 348–50; sustained 231; and the UKIP slogan 'Believe in Britain' 350; 'Vote Leave' 323, 325, 342, 344, 348–50; well-financed pro-European 214; worse-tempered 351

Campbell, Alastair 24, 129, 206–7, 213–15, 223, 255

Camps, Miriam 15

Camus, Albert 55

Canada 31, 50, 275, 281, 336, 338–41

CAP 86, 89, 105, 115–16, 127, 168, 181, 183–4, 191, 208, 221, 223, 226–32, 234, 236–7, 295; and Common Fisheries Policy 191; negotiations 191; payments 223, 234; reform 169, 230; and social regulation 168; and the unpopularity of the regime in Britain before joining the EC 223

Cardiff European Council 213, 231

Carr, Robert 85

Carrington, Peter 94–5, 100, 226–7, 284

Carswell, Douglas 156

Cash, Bill 28, 158, 307

Castle, Barbara 78, 86, 89, 167

CBI 88, 128, 253, 255

Ceylon 49, 275

CFP 116, 144, 190–1

CFSP 122, 133, 273, 291, 293–4, 296–8, 302, 329

Chancellors of the Exchequer 67, 152; Alistair Darling 260; Denis Healey 83, 85, 92, 120, 139, 145, 241–2, 248; George Osborne 146, 163, 165, 268, 290, 314, 342, 344, 346, 350, 352, 354; Gordon Brown 25, 73–4, 107–10,

114–15, 118, 137, 141, 146–7, 209, 212, 214–15, 231–2, 252–60, 278, 280, 285, 290, 312; Harold Macmillan 29, 61–2, 64–71, 74, 76–7, 117–18, 145–6, 283, 285, 287; Jim Callaghan 83, 90–3, 113, 139, 145–6, 149, 151, 240, 242–4, 247, 285, 287, 312; John Major 24, 100, 104, 112, 125, 146–7, 165, 211–12, 247, 249, 262, 267, 308; Kenneth Clarke 48, 128, 146, 212, 251, 262, 311; Nigel Lawson 100, 104, 139, 163, 244, 246–7; Norman Lamont 120, 237, 249, 282, 304, 352; R.A. ('Rab') Butler 81, 144–5; Roy Jenkins 84, 88–9, 92, 94, 138, 141, 145–6, 152, 154, 161, 163–4, 219, 225–6, 239, 352; Winston Churchill 4–5, 19, 29, 47–9, 51, 59, 61, 65, 71–2, 209, 274–5, 281–2, 286, 288, 290, 329
Charles V 28
Charlton, M. 58, 60–1, 70, 81, 275
Charmley, J. 288
The Charter of the Fundamental Rights of the EU 10, 136–7, 140, 277, 305, 319
Chatham House/YouGov Survey 193, 202–3
Chirac, Jacques 72, 119, 125, 231–3, 297–8
CHOGM 276
Christian Democratic Group 167
Christian Democrats 167–8
Churchill, Winston 4–5, 19, 29, 47–9, 51, 59, 61, 65, 71–2, 209, 274–5, 281–2, 286, 288, 290, 329
City of London 19, 51, 114, 209, 251, 260–1
Clappier-Schulmann paper 240
Clarke, Charles 311
Clarke, Kenneth 48, 128, 146, 212, 251, 262, 311
Clegg, Nick 7, 156
climate change 155
coal 57–8
Coalition government 7, 27, 118, 124, 137, 149, 152, 156, 189, 260–1, 269, 290, 303, 310, 313–14, 320, 326, 333; continental 156; and euro area reforms 269; failure of 136; management of 313
Cohen, Richard 209
Cold War 33, 52, 336
Coles, J. 117, 139
College of Europe, Bruges 102, 142, 147, 245
Colley, L. 23, 25, 49
Committee of the Regions *see* CoR
committees 306
Common Agricultural Policy *see* CAP
Common Fisheries Policy *see* CFP
Common Foreign and Security Policy *see* CFSP
Common Security and Defence Policy *see* CSDP
Commonwealth 49–50, 57, 62, 64, 68, 70, 75–6, 115, 145, 161, 187, 241, 274–7, 281, 287, 289, 336–8; appeal and Eurosceptic

identification 282; citizens 302; countries 276–7, 282–3, 325, 338; and Europe 50, 68, 275; immigrants 302; legacy of connections and trade 68; preference system 223; trade 57, 68, 73, 274
Commonwealth Heads of Government Meeting *see* CHOGM
Commonwealth Office 74, 277
communist states 33, 47, 64, 87, 106, 204
Concordats 181, 193
Concordats between central government and the devolved administrations 181
Concordats on Coordination of European Union Policy Issues 192
Concorde airliner 71
Concours (entrance test) 143
Confederation of British Industries *see* CBI
Conference on Security and Cooperation in Europe *see* CSCE
Congress of Europe 55
Congress of the New Right 170
Connolly, Bernard 3
Conquest, Robert 282–3
Conservative government 1, 25, 61, 63, 66, 75, 97, 103–4, 130, 133, 244, 249, 310, 315, 322, 327, 342–3, 346; and the budget question confronting Thatcher's 224; and the Remain recommendation 332; strategy and tactics dealing with the renegotiation exercise 314; sympathetic to the concerns of the bankers 266
Conservative MPs 71, 84, 144, 149, 159, 234, 307, 322; anonymous 302; backbench 306; veteran Eurosceptic 318
Conservative Party 68, 84–5, 87, 97, 103–6, 145, 147–51, 155–8, 166–71, 212, 215–16, 244, 247–8, 252, 255–6, 303–5, 307–8, 311–13; and David Cameron's leadership 165, 169, 212; divisions 146; election manifesto 137; funding 307; leadership post-Cameron 342, 354, 359; in Scotland 188
Conservatives *see* Conservative Party
continental Europe *see* Europe
Cook, Robin 136, 138, 203, 213, 253–5
Cooper, R. 116, 276, 294–5, 299
Copenhagen European Council meetings 240
Copenhagen Report 292
CoR 179, 189
Corbyn, Jeremy 150, 343, 355
Coulson, Andy 216
Council of Europe 21, 53, 140, 275
The Courier and Advertiser 354
Couzens, Kenneth 139, 240
Cox, Jo 352–3
Crafts, Nick 256–7
Craxi, Bettino 98
Creutzfeldt-Jakob disease *see* CJD
Croatia 31–3, 40, 44, 48, 124, 134, 260

Crosland, Tony 83, 85
Crossman, Richard 162, 279
CSCE 292
CSDP 293–9
Cudlipp, Hugh 217
culture 20, 281, 287; banking 266–7; British
    civil service 140; common European 78,
    203; political 5, 18, 48, 143–4, 152, 210, 281;
    popular 72, 277, 287; technocratic 37
currencies 50, 133, 190, 237–8, 249, 257, 260–1,
    318; benchmark 239; common 68; euro
    23, 30–1, 33, 39, 41–2, 107–8, 113–14, 165,
    182–4, 189–90, 203, 213–15, 231–4, 237,
    251–72, 290, 299–300, 307–8; global 274;
    international 241; national 238; pound 19,
    50, 68, 83, 109, 120, 139, 147, 212, 236–44,
    246–72, 317–18; reserve 50, 241; single
    European 30, 107, 134, 238, 244, 246, 252–5,
    340; weak 239
Curtice, John 173–5, 190, 194, 352
customs union 8, 34, 54, 57, 138, 337
Cyprus 22, 31–3, 40, 43, 124, 134, 191, 293
Cyr, A.I. 283
Czech Republic 31–2, 40, 43–4, 123, 125, 172,
    260, 306

Daddow, O.J. 16, 21, 103, 108, 137, 151, 161–2,
    199, 209–11, 214, 218, 286
Daily Express 57, 202, 204–6, 211, 217, 353
Daily Mail 155, 204–6, 212, 214–18, 315, 353
Daily Mirror 23, 204, 217, 353
Daily Star 206, 217, 353
The Daily Telegraph 10, 23, 27, 137, 204–7, 213,
    217, 234, 249, 278, 283, 315, 327, 353, 355, 362
Daily Worker 64
Danish voters 360
Darling, Alistair 260
Davis, David 359
Davis, Howard 266
de Gasperi, Alcide 81
de Gaulle, Charles 35, 59, 70–4, 84, 86, 115,
    223, 282, 284; and Harold Macmillan 223;
    launches a plan for political union of the
    Six 70; and the letter from Paul Reynaud
    registering regret at the veto 72; and the
    motives underlying the veto 71; patronizing
    tone and Macmillan's allusive style 71
de Ziegler, Philip 150, 164
de Zulueta, Philip 71
Declaration of Arbroath 1320 14
deficits 42, 50, 231, 314; budgetary 39–40;
    'communication' 208; democratic 37,
    152, 171; excessive 260; large trading 290;
    mounting government budget 261
Dehaene, Jean-Luc 308
Dell, Edmund 243
Delors, Jacques 98, 100–2, 104, 108, 152, 189,
    203, 205, 226, 245, 248, 308; and the feud

with Margaret Thatcher 101, 245; speech at
    the TUC 101–2
democracy 33, 315; entrenching 33; and
    human rights in Europe 315; liberal 1;
    parliamentary 23, 73, 349; participatory 152
Democrats for Europe 167
Denman, Roy 115, 157
Denmark 30–3, 38, 40, 43, 63–4, 91–4, 98, 114,
    116, 133, 183, 235, 241–2, 249, 260, 297, 318
Denning, Lord 10
Der Spiegel 307, 309
d'Estaing, Valéry Giscard 86, 94–6, 119–20,
    135, 205–6, 224–7, 229, 239–40
Devine, Tom 190
devolution 36, 132, 166, 177, 179–80, 188,
    190, 192, 196, 331; administrative 180;
    and European Union membership 177–98;
    executive 180; legislative 180, 196; predated
    186; processes 14; for Scotland and Wales
    180; settlement 18, 178–9, 186, 192, 332
Diego Garcia (base) 284
DIY economic recession 344
Donoghue, Bernard 57, 164
Douglas-Home, Alec 74, 76, 279
Douglas-Scott, S. 197
Draghi, Mario 41
Dublin 95, 182, 225–6
Dublin European Council 86–7, 94–5, 226
Dublin governments 182, 185, 195
Dublin Regulation 43
Duncan Smith, Iain 320, 322, 351–2
Dyson, James 344

EAGF 183
Eagle, Angela 342
Eastern England 356–7
Eastern Europe 12–13, 29, 33, 38, 43–4, 52,
    106, 123–7, 172, 231, 297, 317, 334, 336;
    communist states 32; and the Eastern
    Partnership countries 33; and the EU
    initiative in extending membership to the
    former communist bloc countries of 33; and
    the former East Germany 32, 124
Eastleigh byelection 217
EBA 269
EC 8–10, 15–20, 29–30, 32–5, 54–8, 61–98,
    100–6, 115–19, 144–8, 150–2, 161–4, 187–9,
    218–25, 227–9, 241–5, 280–1, 327–9, 331–6;
    affairs 93, 96–7, 101, 225, 243; businesses
    83, 178; councils 245; and the creation of
    an economic and monetary union (EMU)
    82; currency countries 242; defence and
    security 296; history of 97; institutions
    82; party 243; policies 90, 115; politics 96;
    renegotiations 146; Single Market initiative
    8; symbols become a familiar part of the
    Scottish landscape 188; and the terms of
    entry 224, 241; treaties 37, 77, 239, 321

EC/EU 14–16, 29–30, 61, 112–18, 121–2, 127, 137, 139–40, 148, 160, 173, 185, 187–8, 203–4, 280–1, 283–4, 327–32, 334–5; affairs 150; and the British contribution to the budget of the 139; expenditure 96, 220–1, 228; farm prices 227; with France the largest agricultural producer in the 223; governments 118; institutions 35, 77, 104, 188–9; institutions boycotted by France 35; membership 9–10, 122, 138–9, 145, 148, 150, 160, 163, 167, 182–3, 188, 202–3, 330–1, 335, 338; membership considered anathema by the Labour Party 150; membership proves a major political battleground between the UK parties 150; negotiations 119; policies 18, 117, 120, 140, 178, 332; projects 61, 138; prospect of a two-tier 113; relationships 284; treaty goal of 'ever closer union among the peoples of Europe' 330

EC/EU legislation 8, 10, 34, 91, 98, 130, 134, 140, 181, 192, 259, 291, 310, 317, 324, 335; agriculture 11, 145, 181–2, 220, 223, 225, 227, 229–31, 339; employment 128; environment 34, 129, 141, 181, 208, 230, 293, 340; financial services 267; fisheries 11, 181–2, 339; labour 136; Single Market 181, 271; social policy 133, 245

EC membership 27, 73–5, 77–9, 81–5, 90–3, 116, 131, 145–7, 149–52, 154, 172, 180, 182, 186–7, 210, 221, 223, 332–6; alternatives to 75, 79, 138, 336; application for 138, 145–6, 161; bid vetoed by de Gaulle 84; favoured 68; and Heath's approach to the 1970–1972 negotiations securing 77; link to economic reconstruction and industrial revival 63; opposed by an 'ill-assorted and highly marginalized group of papers' 204; positive arguments favouring 67; press consensus favouring 210; supported by Hoyer-Millar 68, 150; treated as anathema by the Labour Party 150; and the welfare effects of British membership 8

ECB 30, 34, 36–7, 41–2, 100, 109, 238, 246, 256, 269–70

Eccles, David 24, 65

ECJ 36, 67, 106, 123, 267, 270–1, 312

economic 2–5, 7–9, 53–4, 62–6, 72–8, 81–3, 88–93, 124–7, 131–3, 160–5, 235–47, 249–62, 289–92, 330–5, 337–8, 343–6, 348–52, 354–60; activity 290, 337; advisers 108, 246, 256, 344; affairs 241, 278; arguments 76, 139, 272, 344; assistance 185; change 96, 158; depression 29; governance 316–17; grievance 158; growth 8–9, 38, 42, 63, 73, 112, 235, 258, 311, 333, 344; migrants 349; post-traumatic stress disorder 355; recession 90, 131, 140, 162–3,

202, 205, 251, 260–1, 290, 333; structures 132, 257; success 184, 239

Economic and Monetary Union *see* EMU

The Economist 92, 100, 108, 138, 205, 240, 256, 258

EDC 56, 59–60, 291

Eden, Anthony 56, 59–62, 66, 275, 277, 283

Eden government 61

EEA 337, 339–41

EEAS 169, 293–4

EEC *see* EC, EC/EU

EEC Treaty of Rome 78, 112, 223, 321

EFSF 265

EFTA 33, 64–5, 72, 105, 123, 161, 336

Egypt 61–2

Eichhorn, J. 194, 196

EMS 139, 151, 224, 236–41, 243, 270; membership 241, 243; negotiations 243; and party politics 243; projects 238–9

EMU 33–4, 82, 99–101, 114, 133–4, 138–9, 237–8, 244–6, 252–3, 256–7; final stage of 113–14, 249; joining 257

England 22–5, 27, 49, 51, 68, 70–1, 89, 153, 155–6, 166, 172, 176–7, 184, 193–8, 246–7, 252, 257, 355–7; Eastern 356–7; 'in effect is insular' (De Gaulle) 70; and Europe 71; and nationalism 101, 166, 358; NW 357; and Scotland 24; SE 193; SW 357

English identity 25, 357–8

English nationalism 25, 101, 166

environment 34, 129, 141, 181, 208, 230, 293, 340; natural resources 11; operating within a discursive 214; policy making 118, 335; stable monetary 238

EP 36–7, 86, 91, 101, 106, 109, 135, 140, 142, 153, 166–72, 185, 200, 208, 304, 308, 354, 360; election campaigns 163; elections 112, 127, 132, 169, 171, 305, 308–11; party 170

EPC 273, 291–2, 295

ERC 236

ERDF 182, 221

ERM 100, 103–5, 113–14, 120–1, 138–9, 147, 151, 237–40, 242–51, 253; band 249; currencies 239, 249; debacle 257; entry 246–8, 253, 256; framework 100; II (successor to ERM) 261; membership 245–6, 250, 256; straitjacket 250

ESDP 273, 293, 298

ESM 265

Estonia 31–3, 40, 123

EU 8–10, 12, 15–47, 77–80, 82–98, 100–6, 115–19, 129–34, 146–8, 172–3, 178–80, 186–9, 191–4, 199–225, 227–9, 243–5, 291–3, 334–6

EU Commission 12, 37, 41, 94, 96, 101, 136–7, 140–2, 192, 201, 207–8, 224, 226, 230–3, 236, 245, 254, 308; and Council delegations 293; enforcement powers 312

EU Commissioners 37, 230
euro area 6, 19–20, 33–4, 38–42, 107–9, 112–14,
138–9, 237, 239, 251–2, 256–8, 260–3, 265–71,
289–91, 306–7, 314, 328–9, 334; banking
union 114, 270; bloc 269; collapsing of 262;
crisis 3, 38–9, 260–1, 290, 307; integration
271, 306; integration of 270; leaders 258, 290;
member states 39, 41–2, 113–14, 252, 260,
262, 265–6, 268–9, 271, 290, 307; membership
42, 107, 251, 257–8, 269, 271, 323; project
261–2; reforms 269; states 41, 107
Eurobarometer opinion polls 38, 92, 109, 171,
200–1, 217
Eurocurrency market 263
Europe 3–4, 12, 15–18, 20–56, 64–6, 68–9,
71–3, 89–90, 139–42, 146–51, 205–7,
213–17, 275–7, 279–89, 294–300, 303–9,
322–5, 330–2; independence in 187–8;
integrated 58; inward-looking 122, 331; non-
communist 51; risk of entering an age of
competing nationalisms 348
Europe – The Future 96
Europe of Freedom and Direct Democracy
167, 169
Europe Will Not Wait 15
European immigration 216
European Union Act (2011) 165, 307
European Agricultural Guarantee Fund *see*
EAGF
European Arrest Warrant 312–13
European Assembly 37, 53
European Atomic Energy Community 1957
30, 56
European Banking Authority *see* EBA
European Central Bank *see* ECB
European Coal and Steel Community 1951
30, 35, 56–7
European Commission 31, 36–8, 98–9, 101,
106, 109, 123, 132, 135, 140, 142, 152, 182,
189, 201, 205, 318, 320
European Commissioners 24, 226, 245
European Communities (Amendment) Bill 211
European Communities Act 1972 14, 196,
304, 317, 349, 360
European Community/European Union *see*
EC/EU
European Conservatives and Reformists 167,
169–70, 304
European Convention 108, 135, 196, 205–6
European Council 32–3, 36–8, 135, 220, 293,
306, 308–9, 314–16, 319, 321–2; decisions
135; meetings 1, 38, 94, 98, 110, 136, 224–5,
290, 316; proceedings 318
European Court of Justice *see* ECJ
European defence 52, 298, 330; co-operation
117; identity 106, 296, 298; industry 130
European Defence Community *see* EDC
European Democratic Group 168

European Economic Area *see* EEA
European Economic Community *see* EC/EU
European External Action Service *see* EEAS
European Financial Stability Facility *see* EFSF
European Free Trade Association, *see* EFTA
European integration 1–2, 11–12, 15, 17–20, 26,
34–6, 46–7, 55–6, 111–12, 116–18, 122,
138–9, 144–5, 157, 166–7, 185, 187–90,
331–2; and nationalist demands 180;
overshadowed by globalization 280
European Monetary System *see* EMS
European Parliament *see* EP
European People's Party 167–9, 304–5, 308
European Political Cooperation *see* EPC
European Regional Development Fund *see*
ERDF
European Research Council *see* ERC
European Security and Defence Policy *see*
ESDP
European Stability Mechanism *see* ESM
European Union *see* EU
European Union Act 2011 165, 307
European Union membership 18, 177–98
Europhobic press 354
euros 30–1, 33, 39, 41–2, 107–8, 113–14, 165,
182–4, 189–90, 203, 213–15, 231–4, 237,
239, 251–72, 290, 299–300, 307–8
Euroscepticism 18–19, 30, 103, 120, 125, 156–9,
166, 174, 199, 253, 326, 334, 358, 362; and
English nationalism 166; entrenched 307;
evolution of 125; instinctive 101; mounting
Conservative 188; parliamentary-based 171;
popular 311; public 171
Eurosceptics 23, 204, 211, 282; and anti-
marketeers 204; attitudes of 173; as
backbenchers 127, 323; and Conservative
MPs 103, 135, 150, 316, 321, 333, 351;
Conservative parliamentary 165; and
discourse about the EU 204–5, 214; and
Europhile opinion 47; and Europhiles 159;
opinions of 3, 27, 97, 105, 136, 149, 176,
202, 209–10, 217, 236, 249, 261, 271, 282,
305, 307–8, 311–14; and the press 204, 206,
208, 215–16, 233, 254–5, 306, 315; and Sinn
Féin 185; slogans and solutions 204; and
the tabloid press 208
Eurozone 41, 271, 318; countries 325; leaders
344, legislation 317
Evans, E.J. 65, 67, 173–5
Ewing, Winnie 188
exchange rate 100, 237; floating 244; fixed 238;
fluctuating 237
Exchange Rate Mechanism *see* ERM
Express Newspapers 211
external borders 44, 134, 195, 294, 319

Falconer, Charlie 255
Falklands War 96, 227, 287, 333

Fannie Mae 258

Farage, Nigel 13, 155–6, 167, 169–70, 217, 345, 350, 352–3

FCO 6, 74, 277, 313; ministers responsible for 200, 278; position undergoes a greater degree of change than Treasury 138

FDI 9, 183, 241

finance ministers 42, 109, 114, 245, 289

Financial Conduct Authority 266, 268

Financial Times 3–4, 14, 108, 114, 204–5, 215, 217, 233, 235, 253, 256–8, 264–8, 270, 318, 321, 323, 353–4, 359–60

financial transactions tax (called the 'Robin Hood' tax) 113, 267

Finland 31, 40, 110, 123, 293

First Minister of Northern Ireland 185

First Minister of Wales 183

First World War 22, 29, 67, 121, 134

Fiscal Compact 41, 263, 265, 306

Fisher, H.A.L. 16

fisheries 11, 181–2, 339

Flint, Douglas 268

Fontainebleau Agreement 1984 82, 219, 227–9

Fontainebleau European Council 1984 95, 139, 228

Fontana, C. 98, 103

Foot, Michael 86–7, 154

Ford, R. 155, 159

Foreign and Commonwealth Office *see* FCO

Foreign Direct Investment *see* FDI

Foreign Office 12, 16, 48, 54–5, 59, 65, 67–9, 94, 99, 104, 118, 138, 141, 144, 226, 229, 241, 275–6; approach to business was to proceed by patient diplomacy and accommodation 94; and the Economic Relations Department 66; opinion in favour of British involvement in a west European customs union 138; senior officials' role in foreign policy 69

foreign policy 2, 29, 58, 69, 115, 129, 134, 161, 178–9, 274, 277, 279, 286, 291–3, 299–301, 313, 329, 362; advisers 96, 99, 120; assets 280, 286; coherence of 274; Commonwealth element in British 281; influenced by decisions made 'in response to unexpected events and to actions by players over whom we had no, or little, influence or control' 16; making 117; priorities 12, 125; problems 162; questions 292; speeches 309; traditional attitudes 58

Foreign Secretaries: David Miliband 168, 261, 285, 288, 311–12, 314; David Owen 138, 154; Douglas Hurd 105, 138, 146, 247, 274, 278; Ernest Bevin 29, 48, 52–3, 55, 58, 134, 275; Geoffrey Howe 94, 104, 138, 146, 227–8, 230, 244, 246–8; George Brown 73, 118, 138–9; Jack Straw 138, 232; Peter Carrington 162; Philip Hammond 138, 284, 291; Robin Cook 136, 138, 203, 213, 253–5;

Selwyn Lloyd 16, 65, 138; William Hague 55, 82, 138, 142, 147, 151–2, 165, 196, 282, 292, 313, 322–3

Forsyth, Bruce 74

Fouchet negotiations (1960–1962) 70, 291

Fox, Liam 47, 282, 359

France 28–35, 38–40, 51–4, 58–60, 63–4, 70–1, 92–3, 119–21, 124–5, 142, 223, 227–8, 231–4, 240–2, 285–6, 290–1, 296–301, 359–60; dismissed by Donald Rumsfeld as 'old Europe' 297; in a dominant position in western Europe 66; isolationist danger and the weakening of west European unity 12; persuaded to sign the EC Rome Treaty 223; support for British membership of the EC 118; support for the idea of a united Germany 39, 118, 314; unpreparedness for further integration 60; withdrawal from military participation in NATO 74

Franco-German 56, 119, 238; axis 125, 225; co-operation 119; conflicts 12; core alliance 119; disagreements 207; partnership 125, 314; rapprochement 59, 121; reconciliation 121; relationship 118–19, 239, 314

Franco-German Treaty of Friendship and Cooperation 1963 119

Franklin, M. 139, 240–1

Franks, Oliver 49, 62

Fraser, I 259, 268

Freddie Mac 258

free trade 104, 281, 360; multilateral 57; negotiations 65

Free Trade Area *see* FTA

French presidential elections (2017) 360

Fresh Start Project (Conservative organization) 159

Front National (France) 39

FTA 64, 129, 145, 310, 337–8

Gadaffi, General 290, 298

Gaitskell, Hugh 22, 161–2

Gale, George 75

Gamble, A. 287

GATT 230

GCHQ 285

General Agreement on Tariffs and Trade *see* GATT

general election 342

General Election (May 2015) 342, 352

George, Eddy 265

German federal election 360

German Länder 178

German Social Democratic Party 168

Germany 31–2, 38–44, 47–9, 51–2, 58–60, 63, 66, 119, 121, 123, 231, 234–5, 238–9, 242, 247, 249, 296–301, 359–60; absorbing into a new united Europe 56; budget contributions 231; defeated and occupied 48; government

42, 120–1, 124, 290; intake of migrants 290; unification 32, 39, 120, 124, 238

Gifford, Chris 73, 105, 115, 163, 212, 240, 260, 283, 300, 313

Gilmour, Ian 94–5, 162, 226

Global Europe 280

globalization 132, 158, 192, 230, 241, 279–80, 331, 348, 358; economic 240; and Europe 290; and Europeanization 331

GNI 220, 233

Goldsmith, James 154

Goldsmith, Zac 159

Goldwyn, Sam 303

Good Friday Agreement 180

Goodwin, Fred 155, 159, 174, 259

Gove, Michael 27, 319, 322–3, 348–9, 351

The Governance of Britain (Green Paper) 154

Government Communications Headquarters *see* GCHQ

The Government of Ireland Act 1920 180

The Government of Wales Act 1998 180

The Government of Wales Act 2006 180

Grayling, Chris 322

Great Britain *see* Britain

Greece 22, 31, 33, 39–40, 42–4, 47, 92, 114, 123–4, 241, 262, 291, 296–7, 307, 314

Green Party 168, 170

greenhouse gas emissions 183

Greenland 32, 318

'Grexit' threat 42, 262

Grieve, Dominic 308, 310

gross national income *see* GNI

The Guardian 313, 343, 345, 347–8, 350–3, 356, 358–60

Gummer, John 224

Hague, William 55, 82, 138, 142, 147, 151–2, 165, 196, 282, 292, 313, 322–3

Hailsham, Viscount 152

Hall-Patch, Edmund 53–4

Hammond, Philip 138, 284, 291

Hannay, David 16–17, 94, 141, 164, 211, 221, 245, 277, 283, 287, 292, 313, 333

Hargreaves, Peter 342

Harvey, Oliver 53, 274, 279–80, 285–6

Hattersley, Roy 101, 200

Healey, Denis 83, 85, 92, 120, 139, 145, 241–2, 248

Heath, Edward 56, 67, 75–8, 84, 87, 90, 93, 97, 106, 120, 131, 146–8, 150–1, 210, 223, 226, 238, 244; application for EC membership 77, 138–9, 187, 223; committed to membership of the EU 78; and European policy 77; Godkin lectures 147; government 75, 77–8, 83–5, 115, 150, 163, 221, 237, 244, 279, 283, 285

Heffer, Simon 23

Helsinki European Council 293–4

Hennessy, P. 59, 62

Hepburn, E. 189–90

Heseltine, Michael 64, 146, 255–6, 311

Hill, Jonathan 141

Hilton, Steve 10

Hirsch, Étienne 81

HM the Queen's speech to Parliament (May 2016) 349

HM Treasury 222, 234; *see also* Treasury

Hollande, François 291, 306, 311, 314

Holmes, John 290

Holyrood election 184

Home Office 320

Hongkong and Shanghai Banking Corporation *see* HSBC

Horne, A. 70, 72

Hosie, Stewart 343

House of Commons 84–6, 137, 204, 313

House of Lords 77, 153, 196, 302

Howard, Michael 145, 165, 215, 258

Howe, Geoffrey 94, 104, 138, 146, 227–8, 230, 244, 246–8

HSBC 263, 268

Hume, John 185

Hungary 31–2, 40, 44, 124–5, 260, 309, 321

Hunt, Jeremy 346

Hurd, Douglas 105, 138, 146, 247, 274, 278

Iceland 32–3, 134, 337, 340

IGC 98, 100, 136, 157, 182, 206

immigration 125–6, 155, 158, 167, 175, 189, 201, 216, 305, 316–17, 320–1, 331, 343, 345, 348–50, 357, 361; and the Australian-style points system 350; crisis of 43, 315; and free trade 349, 360; and the impact on underfunded public services 350; issues 126; large-scale 334; non-EU 349; policies of 11, 43, 349; reducing and restricting 155–6

independence referendum 190, 196–7, 354, 358; campaign 190; in Scotland 197

The Independent 100, 205, 211, 214, 217, 253, 255, 286, 322, 347, 353–4

The Independent on Sunday 286–7

India 49–50, 125, 275, 278, 282

Intergovernmental Conference *see* IGC

International Outlook: Educating Young Scots about the World 186

investment 8, 17, 39, 76, 82, 127, 208, 285; banking 266; foreign 9, 183, 241; misguided sentimental 288; policies 127

Iran 243, 286, 297, 299

Iraq 108, 121, 285, 288–9, 296–9

Ireland 21, 25, 28, 31, 40, 42–3, 63, 92–4, 116, 124, 126, 129, 134, 180, 182–5, 195, 293, 297

Irish Free State 275

Irish government 182

Irish nationalism 185

Irish parliament 186, 195

Italy 11, 29–32, 39–40, 42–3, 56, 59, 63, 81, 92–3, 124, 167–8, 241–2, 247, 256, 262, 297, 307, 314

Jenkin, Bernard 158, 307
Jenkins, Roy 84, 88–9, 92, 94, 138, 141, 145–6, 152, 154, 161, 163–4, 219, 225–6, 239, 352
JHA 11, 43, 130, 133, 136, 293, 312
Johnson, Boris 153–4, 206–7, 270, 283, 309, 315, 322–3, 342, 345, 347, 349, 351, 354–5, 359; appointment as Foreign Secretary 359; as candidate to succeed David Cameron as leader 342; denounced by Donald Tusk, Jean-Marc Ayrault and Frank-Walter Steinmeier 359; highlights weaknesses in the Remain position 347; and his long record of undiplomatic sayings 345; presents a vision of Britain in his newspaper (*The Daily Telegraph*) column 355
Jospin, Lionel 114
Juncker, Jean-Claude 141, 205, 305, 308–9, 345
Justice and Home Affairs *see* JHA

Kaufman, Gerald 101
Kavanagh, Trevor 217
Keating, M. 179
Kenealy, D. 194
Kennedy, Charles 71, 178, 255
Kennedy, Paul 279
Kennedy, President John F. 64
Keynes, John Maynard 22, 46, 51, 272
Killick, John 123
Kilmuir, Lord (Lord Chancellor) 67
Kinnock, Neil 101
Kissinger, Henry 292
Kitzinger, U. 88, 90, 172, 204
Klein, Joe 131
Knott, John 244
Kohl, Helmut 24, 86, 94–6, 107, 117, 119–21, 212, 224–8, 238–41, 243
Kohnstamm, Max 56
Kosovo 32–3, 293–4, 297
Kynaston D. 51, 64, 66, 249, 263, 265, 271, 276

Labour Force Survey 2015 189
Labour governments 46, 57, 72–3, 85, 106, 118, 139, 151–2, 210, 212, 214, 251, 281; incoming 72, 107, 121; minority 83; re-elected 256
Labour Party 84–7, 89–90, 92, 101, 103, 131, 133, 148, 150–2, 154, 161, 163–4, 166–8, 183–4, 243, 257, 275, 355; divided 83, 332; divisions and internecine quarrels 85, 91, 149; long-standing 289; modernization of 132; opinions influenced by the growing strength of the Left 84; policies 154; pro- and anti-marketeers 149; renegotiation agenda 85; representation in the PASD 168; retreats into Europe 72; swings to the left 163
Labour Shadow Cabinet 342
labour voters 155, 343, 358

Lagarde, Christine 267
Lamont, Norman 120, 237, 249, 282, 304, 352
Latvia 31–3, 40, 124
Laws, David 320
Lawson, Nigel 100, 104, 139, 163, 244, 246–7, 352
Le Monde 227, 309, 318
leadership 15, 42, 46, 51, 53, 108, 112, 145, 149–50, 243, 248, 274–5, 277, 298, 303–5, 347, 352, 354–5; ambitions 67–8, 145, 254, 331; Conservative Party 165, 169, 212; contests 354; financial 241; intellectual 189; international 279; Labour Party 67, 168, 183, 255, 311; moral 289; party 150, 160, 165, 355
Leadsom, Andrea 354
Leavers 317–18, 322–3, 336, 338, 342, 360
Lee, Frank 65, 68
Lellouche, Pierre 169
Leveson, Lord Justice 199, 207
Liberal Democrats 148, 154, 156, 168, 170, 178, 255, 261, 332
Liberal Party 83, 87, 91, 154, 168
Libor 268–9
Libya 286, 290, 297–8, 300
Liddle, Roger 102, 106–7, 132, 141, 154, 166, 206, 212–14, 232, 236, 253–4, 256–7, 265
Lidington, David 141, 296–7, 308, 351
Liechtenstein 33, 134, 337
Lilley, Peter 165
Lisbon 34, 38, 110, 135–7, 157, 209, 293, 296, 312, 317, 321, 329; goals 132; strategies 38; text of the Treaty 293
Lisbon Agenda 2000 117, 132, 317
Lisbon Treaty 2007 37, 110, 115, 132, 135–6, 149, 157, 171, 179, 209, 215–16, 259, 269, 289, 293, 308, 311–12, 319
Lithuania 31–3, 40, 124, 237
Lloyd, Selwyn 16, 65, 138
Lloyd George, David 210
Lodge, G. 109, 141, 258–60, 289
London 132, 153, 159, 206, 283; donors bankroll the Conservative Party and UKIP 209; media 190; policymakers 53; residents 189; and the success of the British-inspired WEU scheme 60
London Evening Standard 205, 268
London Interbank Offered Rate *see* Libor
London School of Economics 356
Ludlow, N. 78
Luxembourg 11, 30, 37, 40, 53, 56, 134, 191, 237, 242, 296–7, 308
Luxembourg Agreement 1966 35, 226–7
Luxembourg European Council 1980 226

Maastricht Treaty 1992 28, 30, 33–5, 38–9, 105, 107–8, 112–13, 132–5, 137, 157–8, 178–9, 189, 202–3, 210–11, 248, 293, 295–6, 312

Macedonia 32–3
MacKenzie, Kelvin 354
Maclean, Donald 52
Macmillan, Harold 29, 56, 61–2, 64–71, 74,
    76–7, 117–18, 131, 145–6, 161, 210, 276,
    280, 283, 285, 287, 322, 328; application for
    EC membership 161; government 62, 64–6,
    77, 210, 310, 336; seeks terms of entry to
    the EC 77, 145, 276
MacNeil, Angus 343
MacSharry Reform 1992 230
The Mail on Sunday 278, 353
Major, John 24, 100, 104, 112, 125, 146–7,
    165, 211–12, 247, 249, 262, 267, 308
Malta 31–3, 40, 43, 124, 293
Mandelson, Peter 12, 141, 213, 255
Marjolin, Robert 61, 81
Marquand, David 154, 178
May, Theresa 290, 320, 342, 354, 359
media 140, 164, 200, 208, 210, 213–14, 311–12,
    341, 351–3; biased 25; coverage 343; and the
    Murdoch empire 205–6, 209, 211–13, 215–16,
    218, 253, 353; and the Murdoch media empire
    205–6, 209, 211–13, 215–16, 218, 253, 353;
    sensationalism of 15
Member of the Scottish Parliament *see* MSP
Members of the European Parliament *see*
    MEPs
Menon, A. 108, 135–7, 140, 211
Menzies, Robert 70
MEPs 13, 37, 166, 168–70, 185, 188, 304
Merkel, Angela 41–3, 121, 169, 235, 260, 290–1,
    305–8, 314–15, 346, 359
Messina Conference 59, 61, 81
MFF 169, 220, 231–5; agreement 220;
    negotiations 234–6
Michael, Alun 184
Michel, Charles 319
Middle East 32, 43, 49, 52, 73, 134, 291–2, 294
migrants 3, 7, 43–4, 126–7, 175, 290–1, 294,
    314, 319–20; claiming benefits 7, 320;
    economic 349; illegal 44; and refugees 43;
    skilled 320
migration 43, 189, 319, 325, 350, 353; crises
    44; economic 354; low skilled 320; net 320,
    349; open-door 156
Milan European Council 98
Miliband, David 168, 261, 285, 288, 311–12, 314
Milton, John 288
Milward, A.S. 81
Minford, Patrick 344–5
ministers 35–7, 61–2, 67–8, 70–2, 75–6, 97–9,
    103–6, 109–10, 116–19, 137–8, 141–2,
    145–8, 210, 213, 225–7, 254–6, 312–14,
    321–2; devolved administration 193;
    economics 164; finance 42, 109, 114, 245,
    289; foreign 56, 73, 81, 127, 285, 292; junior
    48, 65, 148, 162, 200; referendum campaign

86; Scottish and Welsh 186; senior 145, 246,
    255; treasury 244
Mitchell, J. 25, 187–8
Mitterand, François 95–6, 98, 121, 164, 227–9
Mitty, Walter 249
Modell Deutschland 238
Modernization and Re-equipment Plan
    (France) 56
Monnet, Jean 35, 41, 56, 58, 64, 77, 81, 118
Montenegro 32–3
Moore, Charles 24, 28, 73, 75, 78, 94, 96–8,
    100, 102, 120–1, 207, 211, 224, 226, 229,
    234, 244–8, 284
Mordaunt, Penny 349
Morgan, A. 83, 243
Morning Star 87, 204
MSP 192
Multiannual Financial Framework *see* MFF
Murdoch, Rupert 210–15, 217
Murdoch media empire 205–6, 209, 211–13,
    215–16, 218, 253, 353

NAFTA 337–8
Nassau Agreement 71, 85
Nasser, President 61
NatCen Social Research 194, 352
National Executive Committee *see* NEC
National Referendum Campaign (1975) 87
National Security Agency *see* NSA
national sovereignty 14, 78, 204; formal 288; and
    independence 139, 331; loss of 57–8, 60, 78
nationalism 55, 166, 184, 198, 282, 357–8;
    cultural 184; and England 25, 101, 166;
    and European Union membership 184;
    Eurosceptic 212; Irish 185; political 184;
    populist 43, 104, 106
NATO 52, 74, 106, 187, 275, 284–5, 293–8,
    323, 330; commitments 296; history of 299;
    member states 284, 286, 296
Nazi Germany 29
NEC 90–1, 163, 276
negotiations 16–17, 56, 67–9, 71–3, 77, 108,
    112, 115, 133–6, 144–5, 181–2, 219, 221,
    228–9, 233, 292, 299, 359–62; for Britain's
    withdrawal 12, 27, 154, 185, 195–6, 281,
    334, 338, 359; critical 254; initial 221; policy
    and legislative 181; tortuous 230; trade 230,
    361; treaty 122, 133
Netherlands 6, 11, 30–1, 34, 40, 43, 53, 56, 58,
    63, 92–4, 129, 135, 183, 231, 235, 242, 297
Neuberger, David 10
New Labour 106, 131–2, 151, 206, 212
The New Statesman 282
The New York Times 209
The New Yorker 132
New Zealand 50, 69, 72, 77, 86, 275, 278, 281
news magazines: *Der Spiegel* 307, 309; *The
    Economist* 92, 100, 108, 138, 205, 240, 256,

258; *The New Statesman* 282; *The New Yorker* 132; *The Spectator* 4, 75, 87, 204, 213, 247, 305, 323
newspapers 110, 200, 202, 204, 206–8, 210–11, 213–14, 216–17, 253; *The Courier and Advertiser* 354; *Daily Express* 57, 202, 204–6, 211, 217, 353; *Daily Mail* 155, 204–6, 212, 214–18, 315, 353; *Daily Mirror* 23, 204, 217, 353; *Daily Record* 217; *Daily Star* 206, 217, 353; *The Daily Telegraph* 10, 23, 27, 137, 204–7, 213, 217, 234, 249, 278, 283, 315, 327, 353, 355, 362; *Daily Worker* 64; *Financial Times* 3–4, 14, 108, 114, 204–5, 215, 217, 233, 235, 253, 256–8, 264–8, 270, 318, 321, 323, 353–4, 359–60; *The Guardian* 12–13, 27–8, 42–4, 110, 150–3, 189–91, 195–6, 203–5, 207, 215–17, 232–3, 267–8, 310–11, 313–14, 320–1, 347–8, 350–3, 358–60; *The Independent* 100, 205, 211, 214, 217, 253, 255, 286, 322, 347, 353–4; *The Independent on Sunday* 286–7; *Le Monde* 227, 309, 318; *London Evening Standard* 205, 268; *The Mail on Sunday* 278, 353; *Morning Star* 87, 204; *The New York Times* 209; *Scottish Daily News* 87, 204; *The Sun* 102, 173, 204–6, 209, 212–13, 215–17, 253, 315, 346, 352–4; *The Sun on Sunday* 205, 211, 278, 287; *Sunday Express* 50, 204–6; *The Sunday Telegraph* 205, 309; *The Sunday Times* 3, 95, 205, 211, 228, 266, 271, 278, 290, 318, 342, 346, 351, 353; *The Times* 205, 211, 214, 217, 223, 227, 307, 350, 353, 359; *Tribune* 87, 204; *The Wall Street Journal* 83
NHS 346, 351
Niblett, R. 279, 284, 286
Nobel Peace Prize 2012 315
non-EU states 6, 43, 134, 241–2, 317, 325, 337
North American Free Trade Agreement *see* NAFTA
North Atlantic Treaty Organization *see* NATO
Northern Ireland xiii, 10, 18, 89, 153, 166, 172, 177, 180–6, 193–7, 346, 354, 356–7, 361; degree of Europeanization in 185; European politics and interests of 177; party system in 195; Peace and Reconciliation programmes 182; peace settlement in 197; and the perceived benefits of EU membership 182; political leaders in 183; power-sharing arrangements in 182; public opinion in 172; and Scotland xiii, 172, 183–4
The Northern Ireland Act 1998 180
Northern Ireland Assembly 153
Northern Rock (bank) 259
Norway 32–3, 64, 89, 112, 116, 134, 337, 339–41

Nott, Ken 177
NSA 285
nuclear power 284
Nutting, Anthony 15

Oakeshott, I. 142, 234, 259, 304–7, 311, 314
Obama, Hussein Onyango (President Obama's grandfather) 286
Obama, President Barack 41, 286, 344–5
observers 65–6, 81, 102, 109, 115, 156, 170, 207, 226, 248–9, 262, 268, 290, 303, 306; American 323; British 226; close 292; European 328; expert 252; informed eighteenth-century 26; non-British 295
OECD 63, 70, 129, 240, 274
OEEC 53, 70, 123, 127, 274–5, 285
O'Neill, Con 12, 77
OPEC 292
OpenEurope 9, 13, 159, 207–8, 318
Orbán, Viktor 314
Organisation for Security and Cooperation *see* OSCE
Organization for Economic Cooperation and Development *see* OECD
Organization for European Economic Cooperation *see* OEEC
Organization of Petroleum Exporting Countries *see* OPEC
Orwell, George 13, 22
Osborne, George 146, 163, 165, 268, 290, 314, 342, 344, 352; considered a candidate for the leadership 354; considers Brexit would lead to the loss of thousands of jobs 346; threatens to introduce fiscal tightening measures 350–1
OSCE 292

Paisley, Ian 167, 185
Pakenham, Frank 48
Palliser, Michael 105, 157, 226
Paris 30, 56, 59, 63–4, 72, 118–20, 124, 157, 223, 229, 258, 263, 265, 269; meeting attended by Gordon Brown 259–60; warning of de Gaulle's scepticism about the possibility of British membership of the EC 118
parliament 37, 66–7, 78, 149, 167, 169–72, 249, 254, 261, 291, 293, 304, 314, 317, 349, 351–2, 354, 360–1
parliamentary democracy 23, 73, 349
parliamentary sovereignty 13–14, 26, 87, 123, 152, 158, 166, 197, 331
Parris, Matthew 3, 48, 83, 359
party leadership 150, 160, 165, 355
Patten, Chris 137, 141, 288
Peace and Reconciliation programmes 182
Peace I (1995–1999) 182
Peace II (2000-2006) 182

Peace III (2007–2013) 182
Peel, Robert 145
Peston, Robert 108, 117, 200, 215, 252, 254, 256
Phinnemore, D. 182, 185, 195
Pimlott, Ben 74, 89, 162
Pitt, William 68
Poland 31–2, 40, 43–4, 124–5, 142, 172, 231, 233, 297, 314
Polaris 71, 85, 284
Polish Law and Justice Party 170
political leadership 4, 10, 96, 185, 271
political parties: Alliance of Liberals and Democrats for Europe 167–8; Alliance Party of Northern Ireland 181; Alternative für Deutschland 305; British National Party (BNP) 156; Christian Democrats 167–8; Conservative Party 68, 84–5, 87, 97, 103–5, 145, 147, 149–51, 155–8, 166, 216, 230, 247–8, 282, 303–5, 307–8, 311–13, 326; Democratic Unionist Party 167, 170, 181, 185; Europe of Freedom and Democracy 169; Europe of Freedom and Direct Democracy 167, 169; European Conservatives and Reformists 167, 169–70, 304; European Democratic Group 168; European People's Party 167–9, 304–5, 308; Front National 39; German Social Democratic Party 168; Green Party 168, 170; Labour Party 84–7, 89–90, 92, 101, 103, 131, 133, 148, 150–2, 154, 161, 163–4, 166–8, 170, 183–4, 243, 257, 275; Liberal Democrats 148, 154, 156, 168, 170, 178, 255, 261, 332; Liberal Party 83, 87, 91, 154, 168; Polish Law and Justice Party 170; Progressive Alliance of Socialists and Democrats 167–9; Referendum Party 154–5; Scottish National Party 170, 180–1, 184, 187–93, 195, 197, 315; Sinn Féin 170, 181, 184–5; Social Democratic Labour Party 181, 185; Social Democratic Party 89; UK Independence Party (UKIP) 13, 126–7, 135, 149, 154–6, 158–9, 165, 168–70, 173, 176, 201, 209, 217, 271, 310–12, 315, 334; Ulster Unionist Party 181; Welsh Nationalist Party – Plaid Cymru 184
Poll of Polls 352
poll tax 104, 188, 245
polling 93, 158–9, 172, 190, 193–4, 201, 352, 356; companies 159, 172, 201, 352; data 194; experts 352; surveys 356; telephone 352
pollsters 325, 350, 352
Pompidou, President Georges 77, 90, 116, 210, 223
Portillo, Michael 165
Portugal 31, 33, 39–40, 42, 47, 64, 74, 123, 262, 296–7
post-Brexit 344, 348, 359–60; Britain 348; fallout 359; output 344
post-war Germany 48, 55, 59

pound 19, 50, 68, 83, 109, 120, 139, 147, 212, 236–44, 246–72, 317–18; and Europe 237; exit from the ERM 103, 105, 138–9, 173, 238, 248, 251, 334
Powell, Charles 28, 78, 88, 96, 99, 120, 146, 277, 323
Powell, Enoch 78, 87, 116, 150, 277, 354
Powell, Jonathan 213–14
pre-referendum results 360
Prescott, John 256
Press Gazette 353
Price, Lance 212
Private Eye 73, 84, 155
privatization 188
pro-Brexit articles 353; *The Courier and Advertiser* 354; *Daily Express* 57, 202, 204–6, 211, 217, 353; *Daily Mail* 155, 204–6, 212, 214–18, 315; *Daily Star* 206, 217, 353; *The Daily Telegraph* 10, 23, 27, 137, 204–7, 213, 217, 234, 249, 278, 283, 315, 327, 353, 355, 362; *Financial Times* 3–4, 14, 108, 114, 204–5, 215, 217, 233, 235, 253, 256–8, 264–8, 270, 318, 321, 323, 353–4, 359–60; *The Sun* 102, 173, 204–6, 209, 212–13, 215–17, 253, 315, 346, 352–4; *The Sunday Times* 3, 95, 205, 211, 228, 266, 271, 278, 290, 318, 342, 346, 351, 353; *The Times* 205, 211, 214, 217, 223, 227, 307, 350, 353, 359
pro-Remain articles 343, 353; *Daily Mirror* 23, 204, 217, 353; *Financial Times* 3–4, 14, 108, 114, 204–5, 215, 217, 233, 235, 253, 256–8, 264–8, 270, 318, 321, 323, 353–4, 359–60; *The Guardian* 12–13, 27–8, 42–4, 110, 150–3, 189–91, 195–6, 203–5, 207, 215–17, 232–3, 267–8, 310–11, 313–14, 320–1, 347–8, 350–3, 358–60; *The Mail on Sunday* 278, 353
process 79, 82, 111, 124, 157, 221; democratic 164; peace 182, 361; protracted 5, 355; renegotiation 348; of withdrawal 12, 27, 154, 185, 195–6, 281, 334, 338, 359
processes, devolution 14
protest vote 156, 171, 188, 357
protocols 133–4, 136, 312, 318–19
PSBR 83
public opinion polls 13, 68, 87–8, 91, 128, 159, 171–3, 175, 193–5, 197, 201–3, 208, 216–17, 253, 316, 325, 332; Eurobarometer 91; in Scotland 193
Public Sector Borrowing Requirement *see* PSBR
publications: *Britain and the European Community 1955–1963* 15; *Europe Will Not Wait* 15; *International Outlook: Educating Young Scots about the World* 186
Putin, President 314
Pym, Francis 227

QE (quantitative easing) 41–2, 257
QMV 34, 36, 98, 123, 135–6, 269, 301, 360
Qualified Majority Voting *see* QMV
Queen Elizabeth the Queen Mother 24

Rapid Reaction Force (deployment of EU
    forces) 293, 297
Ratner, Gerald 351
RBS (Royal Bank of Scotland) 259–60, 266
Reagan, President Ronald 287, 292
rebates 162, 215, 219, 222, 224, 228–9, 231–5;
    annual 95, 225–6, 228; Britain's budget
    126, 231, 236; lump sum 235; for net
    contributors 224; and receipts 222
recriminations 354–5
Redwood, John 28, 47, 165
referendum 1, 24–5, 84–5, 87, 89–90, 145–50,
    152, 163–8, 190–2, 195–7, 202–4, 215–16,
    253–4, 303–7, 309–12, 316–19, 321–3,
    326; anti-immigration 321; on Britain's
    membership of the EU 1, 175, 305;
    Cameron government's 85; campaign xiii,
    3, 17, 19, 87, 89, 146, 149, 154, 163–4, 173,
    186–7, 195, 200, 282, 322–3, 327–8, 336–8;
    commitment 310; consultative 85; on EC
    membership 145; on euro area membership
    107; government by 202; independence
    (2014) 190, 196–7, 354, 358; independent
    Scotland 190, 196–7; outcome 355; pledge
    149, 165, 253, 307; politics 195, 224; on
    renegotiated terms of entry 121; results
    90, 172, 191, 197, 316, 342; on Scotland's
    independence 191; on sovereignty 195;
    verdict 90, 108, 154, 235, 253, 353, 355; vote
    25, 56, 196, 305, 322, 328, 332
Referendum Movement 155
Referendum Party 154–5
Reilly, Patrick 118
Remainers (or Remain) 317–18, 323, 329,
    337–8; argue that Brexit is likely to
    attract only some undesirable allies such
    as Albania, Islamic State (Daesh) and
    Russia 345; majority in London for 356;
    in Northern Ireland and Scotland 356;
    support for the status quo (qualified by the
    idea of a reformed EU) 345
Renwick, Robin 229
Reuters Institute for the Study of Journalism
    353
Reynaud, Paul 72
Reynolds, Emma 51, 308
Ridley, Nicholas 247
Rippon, Geoffrey 74, 144, 152
Robinson, Peter 75, 116, 185
Rocard, Michel 309
Rodgers, Bill 154
Romania 31–2, 40, 124, 126, 134, 269

Rome 1, 8, 10, 22, 30, 35, 56, 67, 98, 187, 227,
    247
Roosevelt, President 5, 51, 71, 286
Rose, Stuart 342
Rothermere's Associated Newspapers 211, 353
Rothschild, Robert 61
royal prerogative powers 360
Rumsfeld, Donald 17, 125, 297
Russia 29, 31, 33, 49, 279, 299, 341
Rutte, Mark 359

Salmond, Alex 147, 190
Sampson, T. 135, 209, 279
Sandbrook, D. 50, 67, 72, 74
Santer, Jacques 254, 308
Sarkozy, Nicolas 41, 258, 266, 290
scaremongering 343, 345–6
Schengen Agreement 43–4, 114, 130, 134, 190,
    294, 318–19, 326, 329, 334
Schmidt, Helmut 86, 94–6, 119–21, 224–7,
    238–41, 243
Schnapper, P. 23, 103–4, 106, 165, 204, 280,
    312
Schulz, Martin 168
Schuman, Robert 55–6, 58, 81
Schuman Plan 37, 57–9, 112, 118
Scotland xiii, 5, 10, 14, 17–18, 24–5, 28, 71,
    89, 153, 166, 170, 172, 177, 180, 183–97,
    354, 356–7; in the European Union 191;
    independence of 17, 187, 191; independence
    referendum campaign 6, 177, 191–2, 196, 347,
    355; and Jim Sillas architect of 'independence
    in Scotland' 191; and the possibility of
    a second independence referendum 196;
    relationship with the EU 186; as a sub-state
    subordinated within the UK 189; turnout in
    the referendum 355; and Wales xiii, 18, 28,
    153, 172, 177, 180, 185–6, 197
Scotland Act 1998 180, 196
Scott, A. 254
Scottish Daily News 87, 204
Scottish government 181, 183–4, 190–1;
    figures 183; independent 191; ministers
    192–3; and parliament 192
Scottish National Party *see* SNP
Scottish Parliament 153, 180, 186, 190–2
Scottish sovereignty 191
Scully, R. 194, 197
SDI 292
Serbia 32–3, 44
Shanks, Michael 69, 131
Shonfield, Andrew 19, 44, 81, 328
Shore, Peter 78, 158
Short, Clare 255
Sillars, Jim 188, 191
The Single European Act 1986 30, 34, 95, 98,
    102, 128, 147, 157–8, 178, 211, 228, 245, 292

Single Market 8, 11, 96–7, 99–101, 127–30, 132–3, 203, 261, 263–5, 269–70, 291, 300, 302, 306, 324, 329–30, 332, 337–9; initiative 19; legislation 181, 271; member constituencies 91; programme 34; rights 271; rules 338
Single Transferable Vote (STV) 153
Sinn Féin 170, 181, 184–5, 354
SIS 134
Sked, Alan 155
slogans 74, 164, 188; anti-marketeer 27; 'Believe in Britain' 350; headline-grabbing 347; UKIP 350, 358
Slovakia 31–3, 40, 44, 124, 172, 191
Slovenia 31–3, 40, 124, 172
Smith, John 28, 84, 107, 120, 133, 135, 148, 167, 169, 249
SNP 187–8, 193, 343; attitudes against the EC 187; conference insists that all negotiations should recognize Scotland as an independent country 187, 196; First Minister Alex Salmond 190; government 186, 190, 192–3; handling of EU matters 190; leader Nicola Sturgeon rounds on the Conservatives for scaremongering 343; members 187; supported by traditional Labour Party voters in urban Scotland, especially in Glasgow and Dundee 358; the third major party at Westminster 343; victory in the Holyrood election 2011 184
Soames, Christopher 88
Solomon, Ezra 4
South Africa 50, 70, 275–6, 278
sovereignty 5, 13–15, 23, 48, 67, 78, 88, 166, 192, 195–6, 316–17, 323, 329, 331, 346, 348–9, 353, 358; losing of 180, 192, 348; pooling of 42, 192, 262; and primacy of EC law 78; Scottish 191; surrender of 67, 150
Spaak, Paul-Henri 60–1, 81
Spain 28–9, 31, 33, 40, 42–3, 47, 123–4, 178, 183, 191–2, 296–7, 318
The Spectator 4, 75, 87, 204, 213, 247, 305, 323
Spinelli, Altiero 96
St Malo Declaration 1999 106, 297–8
steel industry 57–8
Steinmeier, Frank-Walter 359
Stephens, Philip 3, 138, 140, 148, 246–7, 332
Stettinius, Edward 51
Stewart, Michael 73, 278
Strategic Defence Initiative *see* SDI
Straw, Jack 138, 232
Stuart, Gisela 135
Sturgeon, Nicola 193, 195–6
STV 153
Suez crisis 61–2, 66, 72–3, 161, 277, 283

The Sun 102, 173, 204–6, 209, 21–13, 215–17, 253, 315, 346, 352–4
The Sun on Sunday 205, 211, 278, 287
Sunday Express 50, 204–6
The Sunday Telegraph 205, 309
The Sunday Times 3, 95, 205, 211, 228, 266, 271, 278, 290, 318, 342, 346, 351, 353
survey, post-referendum 355
surveys 22, 87, 144, 183, 193, 195, 200–1, 263, 343, 355, 358; NatCen Social Research unit 194; Poll of Polls 352; show evidence Labour and SNP voters split in more or less equal proportions between Remain and Leave 356
Sweden 31, 33, 40, 44, 64, 114, 123, 126–7, 172, 231, 235, 293
Syrian refugees 43, 290
Syriza Party 42

tabloid press 23, 211, 217, 223
Tapsell, Peter 99
Tavern, Dick 310
Taylor, Alan 5
Tebbit, Norman 28
Telegraph group 211
telephone polling 352
television 277
TFEU 34
TGWU 102
Thatcher, Margaret 28–9, 73, 75, 78, 93–104, 112–13, 118, 120–1, 146–7, 151–2, 155, 162–3, 224–30, 243–8, 286–7, 289, 292, 331–3; and biographer Hugo Young 162; and the 'Bruges speech' 98, 100, 102–4, 331; and Chancellor Helmut Kohl 120; and Giscard 95; and Jacques Chirac 233; refers to Brussels and the EU bureaucracy as the 'Belgian empire' 29
Third Way 131–2
Thomson, George 151
Thorneycroft, Peter 11–12, 65
Thorpe, Jeremy 87
The Times 205, 211, 214, 217, 223, 227, 307, 350, 353, 359
Tobin, James 267
Todd, Ron 102
Tory government 259, 342–3
Toynbee, Polly 348
trade 7–8, 11, 54, 57, 61, 64–5, 68, 88, 127, 129–30, 156–7, 161, 203, 243, 247, 334, 337, 339; bilateral 59, 185, 273, 283, 285, 299, 337; in Brussels 156; expansion 8–9, 112; flows 9, 299; intra-EC 32, 130, 238, 241, 338; intra-European Community 242; liberalization 53, 257, 331; surplus 264, 333; threatened West Germany's buoyant export 242; wool 26

trade agreements 317, 338, 344, 350; bilateral free 338; protectionist 344
trade deals 33, 78, 325, 345, 360
trade negotiations 230, 361
Transatlantic Trade and Investment Partnership (TTIP) 14, 299, 338
Transport and General Workers' Union *see* TGWU
Treasury 51, 54, 66, 68, 83, 107, 109, 138–9, 163, 227, 232, 236, 238, 241–2, 247–9, 252–4, 256, 304; assessment team 257–8; estimates 242; figures 91; morale 139, 252; officials 54, 77, 139; opinions 256; parliamentary 7; teams 254; thinking 253
treaties 1, 14, 30, 34, 36–8, 41, 105, 110, 133–7, 157, 179, 215–16, 293, 295–6, 306–8, 312–13, 316–19, 321
treaty negotiations 122, 133
Treaty of Accession 77, 146
Treaty of Amsterdam 134
Treaty of Nice 2001 212
Treaty of Rome 78, 112, 223, 321
Treaty on European Union 1992 also known as the Maastricht Treaty 28, 30, 33–5, 38–9, 105, 107–8, 112–13, 132–5, 137, 157–8, 178–9, 189, 191, 202–3, 210–11, 248, 293, 295–6, 312;
Tribune 87, 204
Trident 284
Trump, Donald 345
Tsipiras, Alexis 42
Tugendhat, Christopher 225–6
Turkey 32, 44, 124, 339–41, 349
Tusk, Donald 44, 216, 316, 319
Tyrie, Andrew 7

UK 6–8, 11, 14, 30–2, 109, 124–30, 173, 177, 183–4, 189–98, 242, 257, 263–4, 269–70, 298–301, 316–20, 337, 339–40; based students 142; businesses 337; delegation in EU negotiations 193; exit from the EU 195; and the future (post-Brexit) relationship with the EU 362; Government 118, 141, 153, 181, 186–7, 189, 192–3, 196, 337; and the intense rivalry and conflict between Cameron and Brexiter Johnson 341; law 11, 325; opinion polls 195; parliament 11, 196; policy positions 188, 192; and the risk of a Brexit victory shattering the balance and stability of the 354; where both Euroscepticism and the EU are deeply embedded parts of national life 362
UK Independence Party (UKIP) 13, 126–7, 135, 149, 154–6, 158–9, 165, 168–70, 173, 176, 201, 209, 217, 271, 310–12, 315, 334
UK Statistics Authority *see* UKSA

UKIP 13, 126–7, 135, 149, 154–6, 158–9, 165, 168–70, 173, 176, 201, 209, 217, 310–12, 315, 334, 354–5, 358; and anti-EU support grows in the polls 202; bankrolled by the millionaire Paul Sykes 155; with its pronounced emphasis on fear, conspiracy, unthinking jingoism, nostalgia and suspicion of non-white people 350; leader Nigel Farage 13, 155–6, 167, 169–70, 217, 345, 350–3; originally named the Anti-Federalist League 155; poster entitled 'Breaking Point' 349–50; slogans 350, 358; voters 155, 159, 201; won votes in traditional Labour heartlands 155
Ukraine 33, 142, 291, 314–15
UKSA 7
undecided voters 174, 352
United Kingdom *see* UK
United Kingdom Independence Party *see* UKIP
United Nations Organization 125
United Nations Security Council 274
United States *see* USA
Uruguay Round of trade negotiations 230
USA: government 258, 285; leadership 70; Presidents 71, 95, 286, 288; pressure on Britain to join the EC 64; pressure on the EU states to make a greater contribution to Europe's defence and security 298
Usherwood, S. 158
USSR 49, 52, 70

Value Added Tax *see* VAT
VAT 85, 96, 115, 220, 233; contributions applying only to member states 228; problems for small firms 314; revenues 228; revenues allocated to the EC 228
Verhofstadt, Guy 321
vetoes 34, 36, 70–4, 98–9, 136, 232–3, 243, 246, 306–9, 317–18; capacity of national governments 330; national 34–5, 37, 96, 105, 115, 227; permanent 254; potential 178; and the speech by De Gaulle 70, 72; surrendering Britain's 98; 'velvet' (exercised by De Gaulle) 74; and 'the veto that never was' 306
Villiers, Theresa 322
von Dohnanyi, Karl 226
'Vote Leave' 323, 325, 342, 344, 348–50
voters 25, 85, 88, 164, 171–3, 180, 195–6, 201, 316, 325; disaffected 358; ill-informed 173; mobilizing of 147; non-UKIP 173; protest 156, 171, 188, 357; in Scotland 196; undecided 174, 352; uninformed 164; volatility of 323; younger 357

voting 34, 98, 105, 196, 269, 348, 352; for Brexit 348; intentions 175, 321, 352; numbers 197; patterns 172

Wales xiii, 10, 18, 24, 28, 89, 153, 155, 166, 172, 177, 180, 183–6, 188, 193–4, 196–7, 355–7; public opinion polls in 194, 197; and the result of the referendum in 180; rural 184; and support for staying in the EU 194
Wales European Centre 186
Walker, Peter 227
Walker-Smith, Derek 71, 78
Wall, S. 12, 16, 71–2, 95, 98, 100, 103, 113, 117, 140, 156, 203, 219, 224, 227, 229–30, 245, 258
The Wall Street Journal 83
Wallace, William 128, 281, 285, 289, 302
Walters, Alan 246
Washington 12, 52, 76, 121, 239, 283–8, 292, 298–9; administration's handling of international trade and monetary policy 76; and Heath's lack of interest in the maintenance of a 'special relationship' with 76; and the St Malo Declaration 297
Wellings, B. 28, 41, 48, 166, 281–2
Welsh government 181, 184, 186
Welsh National Assembly elections 184
Welsh Nationalist Party – Plaid Cymru 184
Welsh Office 180
Werner Plan 237–8
West Germany 11, 30, 33, 47–8, 56, 59, 63, 81, 93, 96, 119, 156, 168, 221–2, 224, 227, 238–41, 256; and Chancellor Angela Merkel 41–3, 121, 169, 235, 260, 290–1, 305–8, 314–15, 346, 359; and Chancellor Helmut Kohl 24, 86, 94–6, 107, 117, 119–21, 212, 224–8, 238–41, 243; and Chancellor Helmut Schmidt 86, 94–6, 119–21, 224–7, 238–41, 243; coal and steel production 56; and incorporating a rearmed 60; rearmed and fully sovereign 59; and the role of John Killick in devising the constitution of 123
Western Europe 28–9, 43, 48, 53–5, 57, 60–1, 64–6, 70, 79, 83, 116, 238, 292; and the changing political landscape in 79; and the foundations of a British-led 53; gas pipeline project 287; revisionist power in 55
Western European Assembly 70
Western European Union *see* WEU
Westland affair 64, 146
Westminster Parliament 102, 121, 140, 153, 156, 180–1, 186, 188, 190–1, 196–7, 259, 307, 313, 332; and the conflict with the coalition building and variable sum politics in Brussels 156; and the Scottish National Party 190; and system of single-member constituencies 91

WEU 59–60, 116, 296
Weymouth, A. 205, 208
White House 51, 286
Whitehall 49, 53–5, 62, 68, 74, 98, 121, 136, 138, 140, 155, 241, 248, 276, 313, 331; assesses that France is unfit to join a common market 60; culture and norms of policymaking 62, 81, 118; Eurosceptic departments in 138; officials 80, 99, 157, 160, 313
Whitelaw, Willie 246
Whittingdale, John 322
Williams, Shirley 22, 136, 154, 162, 278
Williamson, David 99
Wilson, Gordon (SNP leader 1979–1990) 187–90
Wilson, Harold 67, 72–4, 76–7, 82–7, 89–90, 92–3, 113, 118, 120, 131, 145–6, 148–51, 161–4, 187–90, 224, 276, 278, 321; biographer Ben Pimlott 162; Cabinet members 84, 148; complaint on the issue of EU membership 145; favourite expressions 85; government of 72, 118, 161, 163, 321; handling of the referendum on EC membership issue 145; membership bids 77; premiership of 157; refusal to send British troops to support the Americans in Vietnam 287
Wilson, Richard 78, 108
withdrawal 9, 12, 62, 76, 101, 106, 112, 150, 166, 195–6, 202, 204, 298, 304, 332, 354, 359–60, 362; from the EC seen as disastrous for British industry 88; and the impact on cross-border institutions introduced under the Good Friday Agreement 195; in January 2016 two-thirds of Conservative MPs supported 159; meaning an external border of the EU would run through the island of Ireland 195; negotiations for Britain's 12, 27, 154, 185, 195–6, 281, 334, 338, 359; and the political consequences 169
Wolf, Martin 41–2, 268
Wolfe, Martin (commentator for the *Financial Times*) 354
Wood, Leanne 195
World Trade Organisation *see* WTO
Wright, A. 186
WTO 325, 337, 339–41, 345, 360

YouGov post-Brexit poll of voters 175, 194, 215, 347, 360
YouGov surveys 175, 194, 215
Young, Hugo 27, 162, 229, 288
Yugoslavia 294